ESSAYS
FOR COLLEGE & COMPETITIVE EXAMS

By

A. KUMAR
BE (Electrical), MBA
Software Diploma

Engineering and Management Connoisseur

Revised by

A.K. CHATURVEDI
Retd. Head of the Department of English
and Principal, M.L.K. (Postgraduate) College
Balrampur (U.P.)

GOODWILL PUBLISHING HOUSE
B-9, RATTAN JYOTI, 18, RAJENDRA PLACE
NEW DELHI-110008 (INDIA)

Published by
Rajneesh Chowdhry
for
Goodwill Publishing House
B-9, Rattan Jyoti
18, Rajendra Place
New Delhi-110008
Tel. : 25750801, 25755519
Fax : 91-11-25763428

© Publisher

All rights reserved. No part of this publication may be reproduced, stored in a retrieval system or transmitted in any form or by any means – electronic, mechanical, photocopying, recording or otherwise – without the prior permission of the publisher.

Price : **Rs. 125/-**

Typeset at
Radha Laserkraft
R-814, New Rajinder Nagar
New Delhi-110060 • Tel. : 25730031

Printed at
Star Offset Printers
New Delhi

AUTHOR'S NOTE ON THE REVISED EDITION

This is the revised edition of the book of Essays — 125 Essays, being presented to our readers. The revision has been done keeping in view that some outdated topics be deleted while some such new and significant topics be added which the readers preparing for the different examinations would find important and more relevant. Thus this is an attempt at updating this book.

Eleven essays have been added and all the eleven topics chosen are of contemporary interest and importance. Candidates preparing for the different competitive examinations would find the new topics of great significance.

It is hoped that this revised edition would find favour with the reading public — not only students.

A.K. CHATURVEDI
Author of the Revised Edition

PREFACE TO THE SECOND EDITION

We welcome our worthy readers in the new millennium and pray for their success in all of their endeavours.

The second edition of the favourite volume *125 Essays for Competitions and Excellence* is in the hands of our readers. We have added three major features in this volume : (a) detailed information and facts; (b) provocative thoughts; and (c) solutions of every topic or problem discussed. We hope that these essays would upgrade the mental faculties of our readers.

The publisher, the editorial staff and the processing staff deserve all the praise for bringing out such a fine volume. The author is deeply indebted to all of them. This is a team effort and has proved to be effective and synergistic.

The author, the publisher and the supporting staff have done their best to make the presented volume a fine piece of published work. However, some mistakes might have crept in due to human or machine errors. The worthy reader is requested to point them out for the sake of better volumes in future.

Wishing you a happy new millennium......

(A KUMAR)
Engineering and Management Connoisseur

PREFACE TO THE SECOND EDITION

We welcome our worthy readers to the new millennium and pray for their success in all of their endeavors.

The second edition of the Requisite volume (7D, Essay for Competition and Interview) is in the hands of our readers. We have added three major features in the volume: (a) detailed information and facts, (b) provocative thoughts, and (c) solutions of every topic or problem discussed. We hope that these essays would improve the mental faculties of our readers.

The publisher, the editorial staff and the processing staff deserve all the praise for bringing out such a fine volume. The author is deeply indebted to all of them. This is a team effort and has proved to be effective and synergistic.

The author, the publisher and the supporting staff have done their best to make the presented volume a fine piece of published work. However, some mistakes might have crept in due to oneness or machine errors. The worthy readers are pleased to point them out for the sake of better volumes in future.

Wishing you a happy, new millennium.

(A. KUMAR)
Eminences and Management Consultant

CONTENTS

Author's Note on Revised Edition (vi)
Preface to the Second Edition (vii)

CURRENT ESSAYS 1 – 47

1. The New Afghanistan — How India Sees It ... 1
2. The Import and Purpose of Terrorism. How to Tackle It ? ... 3
3. The Role of Army in Pakistan's Politics ... 7
4. Indo-Pak Relations — Seen in Retrospect and Prospect ... 12
5. Has Democracy Worked Successfully in India ? ... 17
6. Science and Religion — Are They on the Crossroads ? ... 21
7. Election Reforms — A Must for Our Country ... 25
8. Indian Constitution Needs A Review ... 29
9. Rewriting History ... 34
10. India China Relations — A Need for A Closer Tie ... 39
11. Iraq War — The American Onslaught — How and Why ? ... 43

INDIAN ECONOMY 48 – 101

12. Public Sector Undertakings : Should They Continue ? ... 48
13. Have Five Years Plans Failed ? ... 52
14. Economy and Political Flow ... 55
15. The Securities Scam ... 61
16. Indian Economy : The Challenges Ahead ... 65
17. EXIM Policy ... 69
18. How Can We Raise Indian Productivity ? ... 73
19. Small Scale Industries ... 76
20. India's External Debts ... 81
21. The Rich Get Richer ... 84
22. Black Money ... 88
23. Economic Liberalisation ... 96

TECHNOLOGY   102 – 133

24. India and Internet   102
25. Is Computerisation Necessary ?   105
26. ERP   108
27. What to Import : Technologies or Products ?   112
28. Is India a Software King ?   117
29. The Information Technology Revolution   121
30. Non-Conventional Energy Sources   125
31. The Latest Microsoft Star   130

INDIAN SOCIETY AND CULTURE   134 – 220

32. Fifty Years of Independence   134
33. Moral Values in Indian Society   139
34. Youth and Drugs   144
35. Western Culture : What to Adopt ?   147
36. Status of Women in India   150
37. AIDS   153
38. Population Threat : Indian Experiences   156
39. Beauty Sells   160
40. Western Culture : Indian Viewpoint   164
41. Social Problems in Indian Milieu   166
42. The Crime Scenario   171
43. Reservation Re-defined   175
44. Unemployment in India   178
45. The Corruption Menace   182
46. The Strangled Media   185
47. Religious Conversions   189
48. Indian Festivals   195
49. Private Coaching for Academic Excellence   198
50. Mental Prostitutes   204
51. India in the New Millennium   208
52. Role of Women in Child Development   212
53. God's Verdict   215

THE WORLD-POLITICAL 221 – 265
54. The Seattle Fiasco — 221
55. The Fallout of Glasnost — 225
56. The Commonwealth — 229
57. Fifty Years of UN — 233
58. Pakistan After the Kargil War — 239
59. The Global Government Concept — 243
60. The Kashmir Imbroglio — 247
61. How India is Viewed by the West ? — 250
62. The American Defence Policy — 253
63. Give Me My Land — 258
64. The Magnificent Indians — 261

THE NUCLEAR DEBATE 266 – 286
65. India is a Nuclear Power — 266
66. CTBT—Should India Budge ? — 270
67. Could India and Pakistan Have a Nuclear Conflict ? — 273
68. Nuclear Energy : Boon or Bane ? — 276
69. Nuclear Conflict in South Asia — 282

INDIAN EDUCATIONAL SCENARIO 287 – 327
70. School and Society — 287
71. Indian Education at the Crossroads — 290
72. Private Coaching Institutes — 298
73. Higher Education in India — 302
74. Education in Our Schools — 307
75. Vocation Oriented Educational System — 310
76. Educational System of the Future — 313
77. Studying Abroad — 318
78. Career Options For the New Millennium — 325

INDIAN DEFENCE 328 – 341
79. IAF — 328
80. Indian Space Research Feats — 333
81. India's Defence Preparations — 338

DISTINGUISHED PERSONALITIES   342 – 351
   82. Mother Teresa—An Angel of Love   342
   83. The Saint Warrior   344

THE GLOBAL ECONOMY   352 – 367
   84. An Overview of the Global Economy   352
   85. The American Economy   358
   86. Is WTO Biased Towards the West ?   362

OUR ENVIRONMENT   368 – 391
   87. Environmental Challenges   368
   88. Ill-effects of Urban Pollution   372
   89. Indian Environment   376
   90. India's Environmental Strategy   381
   91. Air Pollution   386

INDIA-POLITICAL   392 – 443
   92. Physical Features of India   392
   93. The Unfit to Rule Always Rule Us   398
   94. The Fourth Front   402
   95. Is Democracy a Game of Numbers ?   406
   96. The Decay of Indian Institutions   410
   97. Coalition Politics : A Critical Review   414
   98. USSA   417
   99. Politicians of the New Century   420
   100. Students and Politics   425
   101. Politics and Religion   428
   102. Need for Electoral Reforms in India   431
   103. Women's Reservation Bill   435
   104. Centre-State Relationships   439

THE SPORTS SCENARIO   444 – 456
   105. Can We Produce Olympic Gold Medallists?   444
   106. India in Cricket   447
   107. India in Hockey   449
   108. World Soccer   452

MANAGEMENT 457 – 507

109. Management : The New Religion 457
110. JIT 463
111. Giga Marketing 468
112. Specialists *Versus* Generalists 472
113. Management of Morals 476
114. Communication 482
115. Leadership 497
116. The U-matic Technique 502

POPULAR QUOTES 508 – 537

117. Peace Hath Her Victories No Less Renowned Than War 508
118. Sweet Are the Uses of Adversity 511
119. Knowledge is Power 514
120. Six Feet of Earth Make All Men Equal 516
121. Failures Are the Pillars of Success 522
122. Everything That Glitters is Not Gold 525
123. Time is a Tyrant 529
124. Power Corrupts 531
125. Where There is a Will, There is a Way 534

MANAGERIC

- 108. Management – The New Religion ... 437
- 109. IT ... 463
- 110. Quo-Vax-Camp ... 465
- 111. Executive Upward Immobility ... 470
- 112. Management of Men ... 476
- 113. Communication ... 482
- 114. Leadership ... 491
- 115. The Corporate Delusion ... 502

POPULAR DOUBTS

- 116. Peace Until His Virtuous Mask are Removed and Their Veil ... 508
- 117. Sweetening the Inedible Sugarcoat ... 511
- 118. Knowledge Is Power ... 514
- 119. The Fear of Dr. A. Marc Albert Aggres Board ... 516
- 120. The World, the Flesh of Mine ...
- 121. Shopkeeping: That collection not stock
- 122. Jumping of Dust
- 123. The Good Crisis
- 124. When Their Real World Stops ... when

CURRENT ESSAYS

1. THE NEW AFGHANISTAN — HOW INDIA SEES IT

> The new face of Afghanistan looks fresh and radiant, having been freed from Taliban. It is breathing fresh air — political, social and cultural. India can well appreciated. The Loya Jigra was held after a long gap of 38 years which elected its own President. A healthy sign is the active participation of women who had been kept in bondage by the Taliban. India wanted Afghans to take their own decisions, which they are taking. It is just a coincidence that all the top men there have old links with India. India has been the first to land an all out support in the reconstruction of Afghanistan. What the Taliban had been doing and pressing men and women to do had been most be Islamic. The most welcome feature is that the democratic process has taken roots in Afghanistan.

The new face of Afghanistan, after having been redeemed from the Taliban bears a fresh and radiant look, that is what the Indian special envoy to Afghanistan, Satinder K. Lambah reports. This is a welcome sign indeed. After having suffered intolerable sufferings of all kinds — political, social, cultural — Afghanistan is breathing a fresh air, U.S. fought its battle against Taliban which it treated as a terrorist regime and India lent its full support in that fight. India, itself has been suffering terrorism for the last fifty years from across the border from the Pakistan side, so India knows what sufferings there are in store when there is terrorism. India does hope that the U.S. which has been proclaiming from house-tops that it would fight terrorism wherever it would be, India rightly expects the U.S. to render at least its moral support to fight this terrorism against India.

But that is not the context in the present scenerio. Here is what India sees happening in the new Afghanistan and how it is emerging as a nation now.

The Loya Jigra was held after a long gap of period. It was an impressive meeting of Afghan leaders of all shades of opinion, that is what is being reported. The most important aspect of the Loya Jigra was electing a President.

What appeared to be a very healthy and promising a start was the active participation of women in the whole process — women under the Taliban regime were forced to remain confined inside their homes — inside their four walls — but it was after 38 long years that they breathed fresh air. The last Loya Jigra was held as far back as in 1964.

India had always appreciated freedom for all sections so from the Indian point of view this new face of Afghanistan was a very welcome feature.

Afghans, had temperamentally been a fighting race so India wanted Afghanistan to take its own decisions by themselves without any external forces working upon them. So what was happening with the convening of the Loya Jigra was temperamentally suited to Afghans and Afghanistan and India always wanted that to happen. Even when consultations were going on Bonn amongst at the international level India always opined that Afghanistan should decide its own future.

That Ex-King Zahirshah, relinquished his claim for any top job was a very well-meaning gesture on his part, for which he needed a little persuasion, but that was all so done that it did not at all hurt the Afghan ego. So, U.S. and India remained passive but really interested spectators, though, aloof and apart from the whole process, Loya Jigra decided everything. It was primarily the Afghan show.

It was just a coincidence that all the top men who have taken over the new regime in Afghanistan, have had old relations with India. Ex-king Zahirkhan's father and brother were born in Dehradun, former President Mojadidi's anscestors are buried in Sirhind, in Punjab, former President Najibullah's widow lives in Delhi while the newly elected President — Karzai was educated in Simla. Even Buddhism reached Afghanistan — the Bamiyan Statue of the Buddha which the Taliban regime tried to blast and demolish, bears testimony how Buddhism had flourished in Afghanistan.

India was the first to reach out to Afghanistan in Afghanistan's efforts at its reconstruction. India has promised a total $ 100 million aid to Afghanistan and India has already started the process. India has welcomed the new regime of Afghanistan and is all-out to see it succeed. Taliban proclaimed that it was strictly following the tenents of Islam and the mandates of the Koran.

Asghar Ali Engineer — a great scholar of the Islamic religion says, "Religion provides certain ideals and values for people to adopt and set right their lives. But people adopt them selectively to suit their whims and fancies. Hence there has always been a tension between theologists and sociologists." He further explains how Islam is a religion based on equality, human dignity and equality. As about the status of women Engineer further elaborates how it has often been said that Islam does not mete out justice to women. But, he says, no tenet of the Koran pronounces any discrimination between men and women. The Koran, as he explains, recognises full rights to women. The Taliban, thus restricting women's freedom, flagrantly violated the tenents of the Koran.

India has welcomed this sea-change in the general perspective towards women in the New Afghanistan.

The most welcome feature for India has been that the democratic process has begun to take roots in Afghanistan. This would give India a greater confidence to establish relations with the New Afghanistan, particularly because India has the largest number of Muslim population in the country, to whom Indian democracy has given equal rights as citizens.

So the New Afghanistan would emerge out as a welcome friend of India — this is India's perception of the New Afghanistan.

●

2. THE IMPORT AND PURPOSE OF TERRORISM. HOW TO TACKLE IT ?

Terrorism means 'an organised system of intimidation especially for political ends'. The purpose is, somehow, to gain a ground where it does not exist and make people and nation to give in.

It can only be tackled by being tough and alert. Conventional methods would not work. Conditions which allow terrorism to prosper should be corrected and people of the area worst affected should be made to feel safe and their life made more secure — economically and physically and their morale boosted up.

Terrorism has been a malaise with which India has been suffering now for the last fifty years. Infiltration from across the border, from beyond the LOC line, has been constantly plaguing India and India, even after having fought four wars with Pakistan — the neighbour sponsoring and supporting terrorism and Pakistan having lost all the four times, feels all the more frustrated and if nothing more, it wants to keep pricking our sides and to send on terrorists is the only way to do it. It has training camps for terrorists, they are provided with the most sophisticated weapons, bombs, and grenades and worst of all their minds are filled with so much of venom that they even turn into 'fidayeen', ready to sacrifice their own lives. And for what is all this being done — Kashmir is the core issue which Pakistan wants to grab by any means. Kashmir, for all intent and purpose, has become an integral part of India and India can never allow any of its body-part to be truncated. That is the bone of contention. And to achieve that end Pakistan has done all that it could but has every time failed.

Talks and talks — the Simla agreement; the Lahore agreement and the Agra Summit — all have met with the same result — failure at any solution as the bone of contention has been Kashmir.

Thus far only India was plagued with the problem of terrorism and unaffected as it was the international community was not that concerned about India's problem in this regard. Ever since the attack on the World Trade Centre and Pentagon in U.S., the whole world seems to have suddenly woken up to this problem. The Al-Qaida outfit of Taliban has been suspected of this gravest of the dare-devil attempt in which it succeeded. The master mind behind it has been Osama Bin Laden, and Afghanistan as the centre of his activities. Ever after this attack on U.S., terrorism has become the talk all the world over. It was with the end in view to get Osama Bin Laden and to finish his centre of activity and the Taliban regime that the U.S. launched its attack on Afghanistan. It has succeeded, of course, in bringing the Taliban regime there to an end but Osama Bin Laden remains elusive inspite of all hunt for him.

And now it is that the U.S. and Britain have begun to take interest in the Pakistan sponsored terrorism in India and the matter is being taken up seriously.

General Musharraf's position, as an otherwise stooge of the U.S., has become precarious and he is being pressed hard by the U.S. to end cross-border terrorism against India and to get the terrorist training camps dismantled. And the latest is that General Musharraf has promised to do the needful in both these matters. This in itself, so clearly indicates, how terrorism from across the LOC had ever been Pakistan sponsored.

The clearest examples of these blatant activities have been the December, 13, 2001, attack on the Indian Parliament. Prior to that was the attack on the Red Fort on December 24, 2000, the attack on Srinagar Army HQ on December 25, 2000, the attack on South Block of Central Secretariat, on May 9, 2001, then the grenade blast over the BSF HQ CGO complex on May 20, 2001; the attempt on the North Block through a 4 kg bomb placed in a tiffin box; on January 15, 2001 a three-hour cross firing on the Srinagar airport; the exchange of fire at the Jammu Railway station; the explosive laden Tata Sumo blowing up in the J&K Assembly complex.

All the above mentioned attempts had been partly successful, partly unsuccessful in their final objective but terrorism on such a large scale has been with which India has been suffering.

L.K. Advani, India's Deputy Prime Minister as well as the Home Minister did admit, "It is not our policy at fault, it is the nature of our policy ... Our policy is not wrong but our society has become soft. Its response to the grave challenge, we are faced with, is inadequate. When the Indian Airlines plane was hijacked from Kathmandu day after day we witnessed demonstration at the Prime Minister's residence demanding the release of the terrorists in prison. In such situations the government cannot be totally unmindful of popular sentiments. But, that, unfortunately is the weakness to fight against terrorism".

Moreover, the opposition parties, instead of standing up all united with the government in this fight, finds occasions to prick holes in the pockets. That gives a leaverage to the terrorist groups.

In the U.S. after the 9/11 attack on the twin Trade Towers, the whole nation stood up as a solid block to raise their voice to fight terrorism wherever it be and at whatever cost. That solidarity gives strength to the national will and that is the way to fight terrorism.

So now India has to set its own house in order to fight terrorism. Terrorism is like cancer, as a columnist Jug Suraiya has rightly described. It has to be fought with a will not by legislations like TADA or POTA. If not caught at the initial stages, it would spread as it has done in all parts of the world. Europe's Red Brigade was known to have links with Japanese terrorist organisations, the LTTE with the extremists People's War Group in India. Smuggling of arms and narcotics to provide big money for arms are the activities of all such terrorist organisations.

India has one more problem. After the 9/11 attack in the U.S. none was treated as a VIP or VVIP in the matter of intelligence checking. In India the MPs, the MLAs or the ministers — State or Central — consider it infradig to be put to a check by the intelligence agencies. That was the season why the terrorist took a white Ambassador car, the red flashing light is available in the market and so is the military uniform and they took advantage of the VVIP status to sneak upto the Parliament building unchecked. So in the matter of intelligence check up none needs to grudge, rather all must cooperate. The intelligence agencies even stopped the Home Minister's car for a checkup. The Home Minister should have appreciated it and that is what has to be.

Moreover, India should know that it has to fight its war against terrorism itself. The U.S. or Britain can be 'facilitators' because their own shoe pricks, otherwise prior to 9/11 why was the U.S. sitting quiet watching and ignoring what was happening to India. It is for the first time that the U.S. has actively involved itself to pressurise Pakistan to stop terrorism from its side and respond positively to India's gesture for peace-talks without any pre-condition. Jawali, the Pakistan Prime Minister has said it that Pakistan was prepared to discuss all issues, Kashmir could be one of these while earlier the Agra Summit failed as Musharraf was insistent on discussing Kashmir first.

Terrorism has to be fought with a will, with a determination and it has to be fought as a Nation, irrespective of party differences, there is now a wave to fight against this menance on the international level which is a great plus point.

H.G. wells, the great political philosopher had said about War, "War is a horrible thing, constantly more horrible and dreadful, unless it ends, it will end the human society". What he said about war is equally true of terrorism. Terrorism is a horrible thing unless it ends, it will end the human society, the Social peace.

3. THE ROLE OF ARMY IN PAKISTAN'S POLITICS

Army has ever played the major role in governing Pakistan for the last fifty two years on its very inception. General Musharraf has taken over, at present, the complete Control of the administration while remaining the Army chief, by ousting Nawaz Sharif, not a voice was raised against this coup. Actually the public psyche in Pakistan is more amenable to the army rule rather than a democratic one. The popularly elected leaders got deeply involved in corruption and nepotism and the people disgusted by them welcomed a military rule. That had happened with Z.A. Bhuttooo, and then with Nawaz Sharif. The real perception has grown that none can rule Pakistan without the support of three 'As' — America, Army and Allah'.

Gen. Zia, Gen. Ziaul Haq, Field Marshal Ayub Khan; Gen. Iskamder Mirza, Gen. Yahyakhan and at present Gen. Musharraf — all has been Presidents after coups by them. Kashmir has been the main issue rakedup to win people's support.

Army has ever played a very major role in the politics of Pakistan ever since Pakistan's formation. Otherwise the role of Army normally in every country remains to guard and protect its frontiers, to stand for a cause and to fight for that cause and in an hour of emergency — floods, earthquakes or any such natural calamity to come to the help of the civilian population. The men in the army are tough people and they, during the course of their training are trained in many such feats in which the civilian population hardly and normally has no training. Therefore also, army is generally called in even when there are large scale riots or a major fire. That is what the role of the army remains.

But in Pakistan, army had been playing a fourth role — normally unknown in any other country and that has been to control the politics of the country. The other roles have remained secondary while the last one has been the primary for the army in Pakistan. Virtually the army in Pakistan had been playing the role of a political party. In Pakistan's political scene on more occasions has the civilian government failed to deliver and had to get out or be ousted or over thrown and this game has been played by the army. Just as at the present moment the army has played the role of the player as well as the umpire and has 'whistled' a goal and led to a decisive role of a victory. Incidentally the so-called mass-leaders during their respective regimes bungled matters to such an extent that when the army worked out a coup, the people in general felt a riddance, hence no voice of protest had ever been raised. Such has been the 'usurper' army's role that even the judges of the highest court took the oath of allegiance to the coup commander who assumed to himself the role of the emancipator and a protector. In the scenerio as at present in Pakistan, General Musharraf assumed the authority of the President, kept to him the designation of the Chief of the army and also the Chief of the administration. Even the highest court upheld the coup. And not a voice was raised against all this, particularly because the background for all this was such. Nawaz Sharif, under the U.S. pressure ordered the withdrawal of the armed forces from Kargil, which misadventure was master-minded by General Musharraf and the perception of the general public was that by ordering withdrawal of the armed forces the Prime Minister — Nawaz Sharif completely lowered the prestige of Pakistan as a Nation — Kashmir ever has remained a prestige issue for Pakistan and even for its populace. This meant that General Musharraf who had launched the offensive against India was the prestige-keeper while Nawaz Sharif proved to be a betrayer. Hence his being ousted was welcomed rather than having been protested against.

Benazir Bhuttooo had once rightly commented that none can rule Pakistan without the aid of three As — Allah, Army and America. At least in the present context this observation seems totally apt.

As earlier observed it has been the misfortune of Pakistan that the popularly elected leaders had ever been found to be corrupt; dead deep in nepotism and all that goes by the name of mal-administration. Hence the people in general found their ouster so welcome for the nation. The people, having once elected a government, even being thoroughly dissatisfied with its performance could not get rid of them till the completion of the term, army was the only means to oust them through a coup and people breathed a sigh of relief. All the coups — there is a history of these in Pakistan's fifty years history — had, therefore been 'bloodless'.

It seems that the popular psyche of the people of Pakistan had been more prone and more amenable to the army rule. This is what stands proved during these last fifty two years. Democracy does not suit the people as democracy has failed to deliver.

Nawaz Sharif was a creation of the army. He sprang out from nowhere as an arch-rival of Benazir Bhuttoo. The former ISI chief, Lt. General Ghulam Geelani Khan was the governor of Punjab. Gen Zia, the then army chief deputed him to approach the father of Nawaz Sharif — Mian Mohammad Sharif — who was a known opponent of Benazir Bhuttoo's People's Party, and was a man of riches and influence. The Governor of Punjab — the Lt. General, approached the Mian to spare one of his sons to join the Muslim League which Gen. Zia had patronised and got formed. The father had a flourishing business and that was looked after by him and by his younger son, whom, for that reason he could not spare. Nawaz Sharif — the elder son was neither interested in business nor had any other achievement to his credit. He was only interested in cricket. So the Mian spared this son of his and allowed him to play the game of politics. A coalition called the Islami Jamhoon Ittehad — was formed which arranged the finances and Nawaz Sharif was propped up as rival to Benazir Bhuttoo. Naturally, a complete novice in the game of politics, Nawaz Sharif became entirely dependent on the army, commanded and controlled by Gen. Zia who had never seen eye to eye with Benazir. General Zia began playing the game of politics and first propped up Jammat-e-Islami and its youth wing Jammat-e-Tuleba to confront Bhuttoo's PPP. The Jammat was Gen. Zia's 'A' team and the Muslim League its 'B' team. Muslim League itself was a creation of the army, General Ayub Khan, the first military dictator of Pakistan had created it in 1986.

Gen. Zia first propped up an entirely non-entity, Mohammad Khan Junejo as the Prime minister but when Junejo began to show signs of assertion he was pushed away and Nawaz Sharif then got the chance to be the Prime Minister, Benazir Bhuttoo had earlier lost the election. Nawaz Sharif, an entre novice in politics found the position cosy for his comforts and for the comforts of his near and dear ones as the son of a businessman, he made the Prime Minister's post also a business and got neck deep in corruption. In the meantime there was Atal Behari Vajpayee's Lahore Bus Journey and in the background Gen. Musharraf's Kargil misadventure which miserably failed. To add to his woes, Nawaz Sharif was directed by America to withdraw forces from Kargil which he had to order to be done. To the people of Pakistan to whom Kashmir is an issue so dear to their heart — they have been so attuned to consider it so that Nawaz Sharif's order of withdrawal of forces was taken by the people of Pakistan as a complete loss of face and Nawaz Sharif the main culprit while General Musharraf the hero. Hence the coup by Gen. Musharraf suited the present psyche of the people and Gen. Musharraf had sensed it. So no tear was shed for Nawaz Sharif. So much so that Gen. Musharraf even planned to get him hanged in the same manner as Zulfikar Ali Bhuttoo had been executed. He was given the option to leave the country if wanted to escape the gallows and Nawaz Sharif is since then in exile. Benazir Bhuttoo already stands self-exiled as there have been framed serious charges against her that if she comes to Pakistan, she would be put in jail. This is, thus the fate of the popularly elected leaders in Pakistan and the army pleasantly rules.

Former Army Chief, General Mirza Aslam Beg was the army chief when Nawaz Sharif first came in power. He rightly observes that no political dispension in Pakistan can succeed without the aid of the army. The army can never be pushed back to the barracks. His observation stands proved by what has ever been happening in Pakistan over these last fifty two years. There is nothing new in this in Pakistan's history.

Z.A. Bhuttoo began his career as a lawyer, then entered politics, won elections and held several cabinet posts under Mohammad Ayub Khan. Then he formed his Pakistan People's Party (PPP) in 1967 and won the majority in West Pakistan in 1970 but not a legislative majority. East Pakistan revolted against Bhuttoo's voiding the elections and a civil war erupted and East Pakistan gained independence and became Bangladesh. Bhuttoo became President in 1971 and then the Prime Minister under a new constitution in 1973. Gen. Zia ul Haq led a military coup against him in July 1977 on the formation of Bangladesh and then Bhuttoo was tried and hanged, on the charge of getting his political opponent murdered.

His daughter, Benazir assumed the leadership of the PPP but was put in house arrest from 1981 to 1984 and sent in exile from 1984 to 1986. Gen. Zia accidently died in a plane crash and she came back from exile, won the election and became the Prime Minister. She was later dismissed by the President on August 6, 1990 and was charged with power abuse and corruption. PPP decisively lost in the elections held in October 1990 when Nawaz Sharif rose to power with the support of the army.

Trace back Pakistan's history, Field Marshal Ayub Khan assumed the presidentship of Pakistan on the formation of Pakistan in 1947. He was the first Commander-in-chief of the Pakistan Army (1951-58), then also served as Defence Minister (1954-55).

An army General, Iskander Mirza became the President. Ayub Khan was appointed as administrator of martial law in October 1958. Ayub Khan ousted Iskander Mirza and himself became the President by a referendum in 1965. But then he had to resign on March 26, 1967 on charges of corruption and riots also broke out on the formation of Bangladesh. Ayub Khan, instead of transferring power to any civilian preferred to transfer it to General Yahya Khan but after the Bangladesh formation the army revolted against him and he had to go.

Army has ever projected itself as the only saviour of the country's honour — the political powers have ever been subservient to the army. It is the 'tail wagging of the dog' situation which had ever existed in Pakistan.

"In National Interest" is the only saleable slogan ever raised inspite of the fact that Pakistan's economy has ever been in the doldrums. Confrontation with India, raising the Kashmir issue — these have been the ever convenient factors which over-shadow everything and the people of Pakistan have got accustomed to be ruled by the army and have resigned themselves to this as a fact in their fate.

4. INDO-PAK RELATIONS — SEEN IN RETROSPECT AND PROSPECT

The attack of Indian Parliament on December 13, 2001 took the Indo-Pak relations to the lowest-level. Even Kargil was not treated with that concern as this attack. India withdrew its High Commission. U.S. still did not show any concern as U.S. needed Pakistan's help in nabbing Osama Bin Laden.

India way have to carry on its fight against terrorism alone. A no-war pact not possible.

Efforts are on to resume talks to resolve issues.

Seen in retrospect, Indo-Pak relations have ever remained strained. The history of the last fifty two years has proved it. Initially Pakistan was created by bifurcating the Indian country only with the hope that this would resolve for all times the tension that had ever existed between the two communities — Hindus and Muslims. It was the demand of Jinnah to form an Islamic state and with much reluctance, the demand was accepted by the Indian leaders — Gandhi never favoured it, though that was done.

The result was mass migration of population from one part of the other part and mass genocide too. So the two countries were created over the corpses of thousands. That augured badly at the very outset.

Then emerged another issue — Kashmir. Though predominantly with Muslim population, the Maharaja of Kashmir, when plagued by the insurgency from the Pakistan side ran to Delhi and signed the Instrument of Accession in favour of India. Thus constitutionally and legally Kashmir — the whole of it — became an integral part of India. Still this action of the Maharja irked Pakistan and ever since then Pakistan had been making efforts after efforts — all proving abortive — to grab Kashmir. Kashmir with India is a thorn pricking the side of Pakistan and has thus been the cause of not one — but four wars—- in 1947, in 1965, in 1971 and finally in 1999, just for Kashmir but Pakistan failed on all the four occasions and had to bite the dust. Still the effort goes on and infiltration of terrorists trained in the terrorist camps have been causing unrest. Negotiations after negotiations have been arranged and held but Kashmir remained the point of no-compromise and the talks failed.

Incidentally the peace moves have always been from the Indian side, never from the Pakistan side. That itself is quite an indication how India has been desirous of having peace, Pakistan has never been. Militancy and fundamentalism is writ large in the Pakistan's psyche and its entire politics hinges on one issue — Kashmir.

The attack on the Indian Parliament on December 13, 2001, was the culmination of the evil designs of Pakistan against India. The militant outfits — Lashkar-e-Toiba and Jaish-e-Mohammad were the two well-trained terrorist outfits which were responsible for this attack. All the attackers were Pakistanis which got amply proved by what was discovered on their person.

The Indian government made it clear to the Pakistan administration — general Musharraf being the sole and single one administering the country — to take immediate steps against these militant outfits but there was no response from his side. India had to lodge its protest in the diplomatic manner and called back its High Commissioner from Pakistan, cancelled the Samjhauta Express running between Delhi and Lahore and the Bus service between India and Pakistan. The Indian Prime Minister declared that India had 'many other options' but did not spell out those options. The Indian Government, the MEA, also called the Pakistan Deputy High Commissioner to tell him that India was prepared to hand over the dead bodies of the five militants who were killed by the Indian security forces but the bodies were never claimed.

Washington had, only a few hours before this Parliament attack incident, given a clean chit to Pakistan. And, therefore, the action taken by India against Pakistan had a message for Washington too.

Instead of expressing any concern at this incident, the Pakistan reaction was of 'surprise' in the recalling of the High Commissioner of India. After this incident, which drew international attention and concern President Bush, to show his face to the world had to phone up General Musharraf to rein in the militant outfit. India acted with great restraint otherwise that was a very pertinent a cause and occasion to launch a full scale offensive on the military level against Pakistan. Of course, the U.S. never would like a full scale conflict to aggravate between India and Pakistan as that would have hindered the U.S. search for Osama Bin Laden and Mulla Omar. U.S. was not prepared even to condemn Pakistan as a 'rogue state' as in Pakistan the U.S. seeks a favourable ally. Therefore was it that the Indian Deputy Prime Minister and Home Minister had to go on record to say that India need not depend upon any one but would fight its battle against terrorism alone.

It is in this background that the Indo-Pakistan relations need to be seen. Pakistan has already fought four wars with India on previous occasions — all without success but that only reveals the evil intentions of Pakistan.

To go back in history, on November 22, 1981 Pakistan had made an offer of a 'no war' treaty to India. Indira Gandhi, the then Prime Minister had reservations on Pakistan's offer. She did issue a statement, the last paragraph of which noted, "On our part we are prepared to enter into immediate consultations for the purpose of exchanging mutual guarantees of non-aggression and non-use of force in the spirit of Simla agreement". Atal Behari Vajpayee, then in opposition cautioned the government to study the 'offer' thoroughly. Thirty years ago India had made such an offer which Pakistan had outright rejected. This time the November 22 offer was rejected by India. On July 4, 2000 Parvez Musharraf, the all-in-all of Pakistan, once again revived the non-war move in one of his interviews to an Indian T.V. Channel, but the matter remained only there.

There have been a history of Summit meets and their ultimate violations and failures due to Pak actions — the Tashkant, the Simla, the Lahore, and lastly the Agra. The bone of contention had been Kashmir. Pakistan's diplomacy and its politics survives only by raking up Kashmir, which India will never negotiate upon. Actually India lost golden chances due to its 'softness' otherwise in the Simla Summit Z.A. Bhuttoo was brought to his knees and a little more pressure would have decided the matter in India's favour but Indira Gandhi got 'soft' on the verbal promises of Bhuttoo and did not insist on those promises to be put in black and white and Bhuttoo, after the Summit, and on returning to Pakistan began sprouting venom and brimstone declaring of a 'hundred years of war' on the Kashmir issue.

There were great expectation and a great hype raised for the Agra Summit but Musharraf had come only with one point agenda — Kashmir — to be discussed first — India rejected the point and he had to leave in a huff.

Pakistan survives on anti-India and all its politics revolves round Kashmir, which for India is not 'negotiable'. Hence it continues and shall continue — that is all about Indo-Pak relations seen in their retrospect.

Presently some prospects have again revived, again the initiative has been taken by the Indian Prime Minister. But this time the move has all the caution and restraint. It is not like the Lahore Bus Journey like move. This time India has laid down its condition — no peace talks till the cross-border terrorism does not stop. Advani, the Deputy Prime Minister has done some tough talking even to U.S. The U.S. Deputy Secretary of State, Richard Armitage made attempts to spell out the steps that India would take to initiate dialogue. Advani is believed to have 'ignored' the questions. In fact, adamant on Pakistan stopping 'cross-border terror' before dialogue, Advani told Armitage that the U.S. clout with Pakistan would work in ending the latter's sponsorship of terrorism in India.

The double standards of the U.S. in dealing with India and Pakistan has its own ways. While on one hand the U.S. wanted, through Armitage, India to initiate the dialogue process the U.S. told Pakistan that it may consider its request to write off a $8 billion debt in addition to $1 billion it had recently written off. This clearly demonstrates the soft corner of the U.S. towards Pakistan. But this time India is not going to be roped in. Vajpayee had told the Parliament as well as has been assertive in announcing to the media that this was going to be his third and the ever time last effort to arrive at a solution of the Indo-Pak conflict and no steps would be taken in any hurry, and all depended on Pakistan to take steps to end cross-border terrorism and to dismantle the terrorist training camps of which full details of their locations and positions have been provided to the U.S.

"Even while there is manifest eagerness for peace and friendship, it is for Pakistan to respond suitably for a dialogue to take place" — said a tough L.K. Advani. Advani also pointed out that Pakistan has so far done nothing about handing over the 20 criminals and terrorists wanted by New Delhi.

At last the U.S. says that India to decide if Musharraf has fulfilled his pledge and the U.S. gives India carte blanche on how to respond if it is unhappy. Further the U.S. also says that it would not arm twist Pakistan on Parvez Musharraf's pledge to dismantle the terrorist camps if they exist.

So the situation is that of a thaw and the prospects of a dialogue or a solution, seem remote as things stand at present. The U.S. has its own double standards in dealing with the issue, it pats Pakistan on the back by writing off debts while asking India to spell out the points on which the dialogue could begin. India fully understands the U.S. game in the matter. 'Negotiator' the U.S. cannot be as that is not acceptable to India, 'facilitator' it could be, which role it hardly seem to play effectively.

India has to take its own decisions and this time they have to be tough and thorough. ●

5. HAS DEMOCRACY WORKED SUCCESSFULLY IN INDIA ?

The question has been raised time and again if Democracy has successfully worked in India. The recently held J&K assembly elections successfully conducted have amply proved that Democracy has succeeded in India.

The Preamble to the Indian Constitution lays down 'Democracy and Secularism' as the base.

Elections have been held time and again and have shown results. The percentage of voter's turn out may be not very high; there may be charges of rigging; conflicts and law and order problems, but the voter has shown his preference on the lines as predicted. Lack of education is a deficiency and a handicap but the Indian rural voter has a lot of commonsense — that stands proved. India and the Indian Psyche has demonstrated its preference for Democracy and successfully too.

The recently held J&K assembly elections have amply and justifiably proved how democracy has been successful in India. There were large scale apprehensions about the law and order problems, about the Pakistani terrorist outfits intimidating the voters, but the Kashmiri voter braved all these challenges; came out in a reasonably larger numbers and the voting pattern and the election results were on the predicted lives. The National Conference lost; the BJP lost very badly and Mufti Mohammad Sayeed's party gained and has formed a coalition government. This amply proves the voter's resentment against the previous regime and a desire for a change. Illiterate the voter might be but he has a lot of commonsense — that gets amply proved.

So was it in Gujarat. The results were on the predicted lines. There also, inspite of the mass massacres and the intense communal frenzy, the elections were held fairly and the results come out on expected lives.

The credit for the successful conducting of elections in J&K and in Gujarat does go to a great extent, to the Election Commission of India, which even mastered the local administration to act on the right lives. Nothing was left to chance.

For the last half a century, elections are being held in the country at all levels and though at several places and in some of the states large scale rigging and the use of other corrupt means get reported, but then elections have been held in a democratic manner. India and its people have accepted democracy as the right form of government.

Lack of education among the masses has been the major drawback in the Indian system. Voters vote not so much for principles or policies — which they do not or cannot lay much stress upon in taking a decision — local problems, local issues, caste, community and such narrow considerations do influence their choice, but then that is a large scale problem which has not been solved during this more than half a century of independence. People in general get led away by cheap and popular slogans. Indira Gandhi, at one stage, raised the slogan of 'Garibi Hatao'; she and her party did win taking advantage of this slogan, though even during such a long tenure of her Prime Ministership, 'Garibi' could not be removed rather the richer grew richer and still more richer. A bigger line was drawn to shorten the existing line.

Another, not very healthy a situation has ever been there and is growing more and more is, the caste and communal factor being used and exploited in the elections. Even parties, while giving tickets see to the caste equation in a particular constituency which determines the credentials of a candidate. The new phenomena that has appeared on the scene — may V.P. Singh live long to have created that scene with his Mandal Commission commitment — the upsurge of the 'Dalit' factor. The BSP has emerged as a strong contender and the SC and ST have a large population to tilt the balance of any election anywhere at any level. This factor, though this population there ever was, but had not risen up in that militant manner as it has done during the last decade or a little more. Now while electing even the speaker to the assemblies or to the Lok Sabha or even to the high office of the President and the Vice-President of the country — the 'Dalit' or the 'minority' factor has begun to weigh heavily.

It is not so much the general capability but the caste that plays quite an important part at all levels and at all stages.

This is really the most unfortunate and unhealthy a development in the working of democracy in India, but now this factor has not only come to stay but is gaining more ground. A political decision — even though in the best interests of the country — has to be taken keeping in view how it would affect the 'Dalit' or the minority vote bank, which vote-bank, all parties remain keen to win over.

The reservation for the Scheduled Castes and the Scheduled Tribes was kept in the Indian Constitution the main framer of which was Dr. Ambedkar himself, only for ten years during which period the constitution — makers envisaged that these classes would come up to the regular level and be on equal footing with all others. But because this comprises a large population and constitutes a big vote-bank no party and no government has dared to stick to the date-line set up by the Constitution but remain eager to extent their quota and now their reservation has to go on *ad-infinitum*.

So is the case with the minorities, particularly the Muslims. Their interests have to safe-guarded now that their population has gone up to more than 14 crores in the one billion Indian population — more than even the total population of Pakistan — an Islamic state. But India is committed to Secularism and, therefore there can be no discrimination on the basis of religion. No matter one is a Muslim or a Christian one has equal right as any other to exercise his right of franchise and chose the representative of his choice. That is the beauty of the Indian Constitution.

The preamble of the constitution states — "We, the people of India, having solemnly resolved to constitute India into a sovereign, socialist, secular, democratic, republic and to secure to its citizens. Justice, Social, Economic and Political liberty of thought, Expression, Belief, Faith and Worship : Equality of status and opportunity and to promote among them all fraternity, assuring the dignity of the individual and the unity and integrity of the nation in our Constituent Assembly do hereby adopt, enact and give to ourselves this constitution".

Thus the Constitution guarantees, democracy and secularism side by side. Now it is for the representatives who get elected or want to get elected to choose whether they uphold the dignity of our constitution or besmear it with narrow, parochial, casteist bias. Unfortunately for our country, they have been doing it. Such and such is a leader of the Dalits, such and such is the leader of the Yadavs, of Kurmis, of Bhumihars, of tribals, of this caste or of that caste, this constituency has predominantly a Brahmin population, therefore, parties would search for a Brahmin candidate. The Thakur dominated constituency should have a thakur and a backward one, backward. There is so much of the Backward, the other Backward (OBC) classification that it goes baffling. That has been the worst and the most deplorable aspect of the otherwise successful democratic process in our country.

Then the rigging of votes the intimidation by the dominant community; the money, the Mafia that has also ruled over the election process. Even the official class stands influenced by the caste or communal factor; the Election commission has discovered grave discrepancies in the electoral roles and have even asked the state government to transfer, even suspend the erring officers, whose erring is deliberate to please their bosses at the helm of affairs in the state. Such grave discrepancies have been found in Madhya Pradesh, in Rajasthan, in Bihar and the EC has ordered action. Such orders were issued even during Gujarat elections.

The other canker which is eating into the vitals of our political system is corruption. Now this corruption, of late, has percolated even in the judiciary. Supreme Court judges, High Court judges, least to say of the District judges or the judicial officers — all seem to have become purchasable. Glaring examples of this have been discovered. The constitution — makers, perhaps, never dreamt of such a sordid scenerio as provision for a quick process of punishment for such ignoble 'protectors of justice', should have been made. The government has been rattled by such cases and is seriously considering enacting laws in this regard. This is a baneful aspect of Democracy that things have to be done very cautiously and judiciously and the judicial process is a very prolonged one.

These are some of the black spots of our Democracy which need to be erased at the earliest. While in the U.S. even the President had been impeached, in Japan the Prime Minister had to resign on charges of corruption, but in India nothing of that sort has ever happened while charges of corruption have been framed against Supreme Court judges, against Prime Ministers, against Chief Ministers, but none has ever thus for been punished. Cases have lingered on and on for years and years. Even if there had been one conviction, that might have set things right or at least would have alerted and alarmed others. Rajiv Gandhi and his party lost the election on the Bofor's Scandal; Narsimha Rao faces charges but nothing thus far could finally happen. And so goes on the game of corruption.

So, the above noted two major counts bring a slur on our Democracy, otherwise, the illiterate electorate has become very enlightened in casting his vote, even women still in 'purdah' exercise their right of franchise and decide the fate of their constituency and vicariously the fate of the country.

Something needs to be urgently done to root out the rot and our Democracy would stand out as a glowing example to the international world — we a one billion plus a nation now. ●

6. SCIENCE AND RELIGION — ARE THEY ON THE CROSSROADS ?

We live today in the age of Science and cannot do without it even for a moment. Science is based on observation and experiment and its basis is rationalism.

Religion — any one of the many — has its base on conviction and faith. But that does not mean that it negates 'reason'. Even faith has a 'reason' behind it which the originators, propagators and protagonists of that religion have identified in laying down its tenants. But 'Religion' should not be taken in a parochial sense as it is generally taken or understood to be taken.

It should only show the path for an honest and desirable living. It is not rituals that form or constitute 'Religion' — Religion means a way of life — and if that is how Religion is interpreted then there are no crossroad with Science as Science also aims at a better way of life if science is rightly issued and not misused.

There has ever been a controversy about the concept that define Science and Religion and it has very generally and commonly been said that "Where Science advances Religion declines". But this is a great misconception treating Science and Religion as on crossroads. This 'crossroad' concept mainly grew in England after the Industrial Revolution when there was a sudden upsurge of the advancement of Science resulting in the large scale industrialisation. The abject faith and self-surrender of Wordsworth to nature as the manifestation of the Divine where every thing was great and good, pious and pure and the Industrial Revolution poet Lord Tennyson Seeing "Nature red in tooth and claw", created an impression that Tennyson was negating all that Wordsworth had believed and said : there were other writers and thinkers too of the Victorian age who professed a Scientific thought. But that does not mean that whether it was Teunyson or Herbert Spenser who completely negated the faith and the almightiness of the Almighty. It was Tennyson who wrote —

"more things are wrought by prayer".

which clearly reflects that there is 'some power' beyond the worldly power who listens to the prayers and prayers work. This does not and should not mean or be inferred that the belief in a 'heavenly power' is all that Religion stands for. Religion, as would be explained later has a much wider ramification and rationale.

Science has shown how the mind of man has evolved gradually to probe into the mysteries of nature. Much earlier had Shakespeare wrote in his "Hamlet", "there are many things in heaven and earth which are beyond our philosophies". That was written in the 16th. Century. Now we are living in the 21st Century and those 'mysteries' which were beyond our philosophies are getting unravelled and discovered. Moon had been a 'God' and so had been the 'Sun'. They are celestial bodies no doubt. But man — the modern Scientists — has succeeded in reaching the Moon — otherwise the much believed saying had been when somebody wanted an impossible thing to be done that it was as if 'crying for the moon'. Now there need not be any 'crying for the moon' — there can now be a 'cry for reaching the moon' when our astronauts have already been there and have safely come back. Similarly Science has opened up so many fresh avenues of life — the impossible seems possible now. The smallest particle of matter 'atom', could be blasted to produce tremendous energy — unheard of and unthought of. Man had been believed to be the creation of God, now babies in test tubes are a reality. Germination of multi-crops from the same plant has been made possible. The mysteries of the universe are mysteries no longer; going into space has become a reality. Unmanned planes, missiles, the remarkable revolution in the I.T. technology — all these are remarkable feats achieved by Science. What still more would be achieved, one only can watch and wait for. Our every moment, our every activity stands governed by Science.

Still there is one mystery which Science has yet not been able to unravel is 'What after Life?'. Is there anything like a 'Soul?'. If there is what happens to it after the body dies?

Religion has a very wide field, and one should not misunderstand that it lies in certain rituals or certain ceremonies. Religion embodies within the concept of what life is meant for, what is the meaning of a man's existence?, how life has been created and what its purpose is. Why are there men, animals and birds, who has created this Earth, who created the law of gravitation which keeps the Earth, the sun, the moon, the stars at their places? — there must be some power Supreme and Super than human. Otherwise why should a man die, if he can control his existence. This does not mean that Religion has an answer to all these questions but it does make one set thinking of some 'Supreme' power beyond human power and Religions has been endeavouring to reveal that mystery. There is a no laboratory to observe and experiment and discover. The human mind, the human spirit makes its own efforts and Religion helps in that effort.

One should not mistake Religion as Hinduism, Islam or Christianity — these are confinements of thoughts in a particular form and should not be mistaken as Religion. Religion is a very wide term with very wide ramifications. The human life has three parts — the physical the mental and the moral. Science takes care of the physical and partly of the mental. Religion takes upon itself the moral aspect of life entuning the mind to act in a manner which reveal an enlightenment towards goodness of thinking and goodness of action. Without a good thought a good action is not possible and the purpose of religion is the righteous. This is the training which it can impart even to the Scientist. How best to use his invention in the best interests of human life is the path that religion has taken upon itself to show.

'Man does not live by bread alone' — the physical needs have to be satisfied to make the mind rest in peace and when that peace comes then comes the role of the purpose for which human life has been granted. That purpose of life is what Religion gives; Science only produces, Religion shows the way how best to use it. If the moral side is not there what Science would do is what the U.S. did in II World war with Hiroshima and Nagasaki. If the U.S. had been governed by the true principles of Christianity, they would have followed the precept 'Love thy neighbour as thy own-self' as preached by Jesus Christ, but the Scientists in the U.S. mindset made them think themselves all powerful — an animal instinct not a moral one. The lion devours the fox — that is how the animal instinct works. Religion teaches, tolerance, benevolence, charity and welfare of all as the prime concern and duty of mankind. It is here only that Science and Religion appear to be on crossroads. Religion teaches that you may have all power but there is a Power above all powers and that path Religion shows. 'The one remains, the many change and pass' — Shelley, the English poet said it. It has been said in the Hindu scriptures — "धार्यतीत धर्म:" (Dharayateet Dharma) — that which upholds is Dharma — Religion — upholds what? — the moral values. Even Einstein, the great Scientist surrendered himself to the 'Will of God'. Bertrand Russell rightly said, "We are in the middle of a race between human skill as to means and human folly as to ends, resulting in strife, insecurity and sorrow. Unless men increase in wisdom as much as in knowledge, increase of knowledge will be increase of sorrow. 'Do the right Duty perform the Right Act' — this is the basic of Religion and if this call is listened to 'increase of sorrow' as pointed out by Bertrand Russell shall end.

7. ELECTION REFORMS — A MUST FOR OUR COUNTRY

India has opted for Democracy and for adult franchise.
After independence the only party which held the sway was Congress.
Gradually more and more political parties, mostly regional, have come into existence and have been winning.
Coalition Governments have become a general trend.
But independents also win who fix their price for supporting a particular party.
Defections have been found very common.
Some major reforms are needed and have become necessary. They are —
No independents be allowed to contest.
A defector should seek re-election.
Expenditure be limited. Identity cards for voters be made compulsory,
Some minimum educational qualifications be laid down for candidates.
Candidates should declare their asserts.
Criminals be debarred from contesting elections.
No confidence motion rules be made more stringent.
Voting on the pattern of proportional representation be made a rule.
A high power commission of constitutional and legal experts along with representatives of the recognised parties be formed to draft the amendments. ¾ majority of this Commission should pass the amendments, which may not be challengeable in any law court.

India, in its constitution accepted the democratic system for the country and the country is being governed for the last more than half a century under this system.

The constitution framers, framed the constitution in all good faith, still so many amendments have been made in its original form over the years.

In the formative years of an independent India, Congress was the only and the single party which formed governments at the centre and the states.

But gradually other parties began to be formed on different bases — some on purely religional lines; some on communal lines and some on certain other considerations. For example BJP had its earlier form — Jan Sangh — which was a Hindu dominated Party though with an agenda for the country as a whole, the only party formed on a national basis.

The Socialist Party had a concentrated base in U.P. and Bihar.

The Samata Party slowly and gradually remained just confined to Bihar in particular.

Then emerged the regional parties like the Trimool Congress — an off-shoot of the original Congress — only concentrated in West Bengal.

The CPM(M) had West Bengal and Kerala as its strong holds with smattering of its cadres here and there.

The Shiv Sena — a Hindu dominated party got formed in Maharasthra and tried to spread its tentacles in northern India but not with much success — still it became a party with a power to be reckoned with.

The Akali Dal — a Sikh dominated party — remained confined to Punjab.

The National Conference headed by Farooq Abdullah and the party headed now by the daughter of Mufti Mohammed Sayeed, the present Chief Minister of J&K, are parties confined only to J&K.

The Rashtriya Janata Dal — an off shoot of the original Janata Dal is just limited to Bihar. So is the DMK and AIADMK confined to Tamil Nadu, the Biju Janta Dal confined to Orissa and there are parties just confined to the North Eastern States.

So India has become a multiparty country and every party has its own base and its own vote-bank.

Committed to the Dalit agenda is the Bahujan Samaj Party which has held its sway in Northern India and is at present heading the government in Uttar Pradesh with its coalition with the BJP.

Then there are independents who align themselves to no party but get elected with their local clout and then they remain open to join any party for a price.

So the political scenerio of the country with so many parties, showing up their presence and making their presence felt by electing MLAs and MPs, has become rather blurred and looks bleak.

It seems, therefore, necessary to amend the election laws and make them more practical and more permanent.

The present central government — the NDA — itself a coalition of 24 parties — has started a serious thinking exercise to reform the election laws. The present Election Commission has also come in the picture by suggesting how candidates should declare their assets and their education qualifications as also if any criminal cases stand lodged against them in which if convicted they could be sent to jail. These suggestions and requirements have in a way, put the cat among the pigeons and have created a great flutter.

But there is indeed the need to give a serious consideration to a change in the election laws.

Just it so happened that a duly elected government headed by Atal Behari Vajpayee had to quite having lost the majority in the house just by one vote, the AIADMK's one vote played the trick and now same Jayalalitha is supporting the NDA Government. So all these gimmicks and games should be put to a stop and a government duly elected and installed must be allowed to run its full term and a no-confidence motion could only be allowed to be moved when the mover presents to the speaker the name of the leader of the alternative government and the actual number supporting the motion.

Defections have become a very regular scene in the present political system. Inspite of the anti-defection law passed by the Rajiv Gandhi government there still exist many loopholes and the defectors take advantage of these. The law should lay down that one who got elected on the symbol of a particular party shall have to seek re-election in the event of his defecting from the party on which he or she got the public mandate. Defection from one party to another means belying the confidence of the electorate who elected the candidate on the basis of the agenda of that particular party. This amounts to a breach of trust on the part of the defector and the electorate stands befooled.

Independents should not be allowed to contest an election. It is money and muscle power which generally makes an independent candidate win. May be his local clout with the electorate may also have proved helpful but one easily knows how much money gets involved in contesting an election and in the event of a hung verdict, the independents would like to have their price to support a particular party, and so much as to make up for the expenditure incurred by him. This is so unhealthy and so unethical but this is what has been going on. This rot needs to be put a stop to. One could contest only on a party-symbol — that should be law.

Expenditure of the elections should be state controlled. That would avoid the use of illegal money power on the part of candidates with which they purchase votes. Even though the election commission has fixed limits but that is more violated in practice than adhered to and the candidate argues that the expenditure was incurred by the supporters. All this manipulation of accounts goes on, has been going on and shall go on. The figures of election expenses have gone up whoppingly high and all that is national money, after all.

Seshan, as Election commissioner tried his best to make the use of identity card as a must for all electorate but the proposal could not work and has gone into oblivion. Of course, the electronic voting system has begun working but that does not stop impersonation, it only expedites the vote-counting process.

In the eventuality of one of the candidates dying after filing the nomination paper, the election should not be countermanded, rather the party be given time to nominate another candidate and the election schedule be readjusted according to the time given.

Parties should form a pre-coalition prior to the elections and such coalition partners should contest election on a common manifesto. Such coalition partners, wishing to withdraw from the coalition should be required to seek re-election on the manifest of the party that they propose joining. This measure would, to a great extent eliminate the instability of governments.

Rigging at the polling booths, or impersonation should be treated as a criminal offence and stern and stringent action to be taken in such cases. M.S. Gill had rightly suggested that those found guilty of these offences must be given a minimum five-years imprisonment.

Criminalisation in politics has become something of a rule and this has to be curbed at all levels.

It is, therefore, necessary to set up a high-powered Commission comprising retired Supreme Court judges, a few constitutional and legal luminaries, representatives of recognised political parties and a decision taken by the ¾th majority should become mandatory and binding and should not be challengeable in any court of law.

Reforms have become necessary in the election laws. That alone would establish the credentials of real democracy — a political system which India has adopted and religiously adheres to.

8. INDIAN CONSTITUTION NEEDS A REVIEW

The Vajpayee Government at the centre has set up a Constitution Review high power commission to review the Indian Constitution. But the rider to its powers is that the basic structure of the parliamentary system shall remain unchanged.

There has been a long controversy whether there be a parliamentary form of government or a presidential one.

Even Pandit Nehru and Indira Gandhi favoured a review of the constitution.

The recommendation of the Commission remain challangeable in the Supreme Court which would be the final arbiter to decide whether the basic structure has been kept intact.

The nation and the people of the country have a full right to review the Constitution. Already several amendments to the Constitution have been made during the regime of Indira Gandhi

and Rajiv Gandhi which means that there has been found something wrong somewhere in the constitution.
Therefore a full scale review is the need.

There was furor, as ever it is, when the present NDA government takes any major step. 'Saffaronisation' is the key word that is raised up at each and every point. But then the Central government, unmindful of such whimsical allegations has to go ahead with whatever is considered necessary. And it is this concern and sense of necessity which led the present Central government to set up a high power Constitution Review Commission by an ordinance dated February 23, 2000. The Commission is headed by Justice M.H. Venketchallaya, members of which are Justice B.P. Jeevan Reddy, Justice R.S. Sarkaria, Justice Kondapalli Punnayya, Attorney General Soli. J. Sorabjee Ex. Attorney General K. Parasaram, Ex-Lok Sabha General Secretary — Subhas Kashyap, Journalist and Constitutional Expert C.R. Irani, Ex-diplomat Abid Hussain, Ex-Lok Sabha Speaker and present member of the Lok Sabha P.A. Sangama and social activist — grand daughter of Mahatma Gandhi; Sumitra Kulkarni.

The Commission shall have the full authority to regulate its functioning and methodology of working.

No detailed terms of reference have been given to the Commission but two very significant riders have been laid down — first the Commission shall not propose any amendment to the present system — that is the parliamentary form of government and second, it has not to tamper with the basic structure of the present constitution. The opposition would have raised up its voice that the NDA government has some 'hidden agenda' behind the setting up this Commission but these two riders have taken away the teeth from the opposition's opposition of the proposal. Of course, a hue and cry was raised at P.A. Sangma having been made a member of the Commission as at one point of time he did raise up the issue of Sonia Gandhi's foreign origin. But the Commission has on it such leading luminaries that one voice of P.A. Sangma has hardly much relevance. The deterrents imposed by the Government have also granted confidence to the people of the country that the Government's intentions are well-meaning.

But seen objectively, such restrictions imposed on the Commission do not appear to be fully justified as, when a Review of the total structure of the Constitution was to be made, the Commission should have been left free to take decisions and frame its recommendations on the basis of the long fifty years of experience of the working of the present constitution which has from time to time been required to amend some of its provisions over the years. Why at all was there any apprehension in the mind of the government that the Commission may even recommend a change in the basic structure of the present Constitution. And if really the present Constitution in its present form has not worked well, where was the fault in proposing to change it fundamentally. And it is no secret that in many ways the present system has failed. However, now the dictat his been issued the Commission has to work under their restrictions. But it must work otherwise it would all mean an exercise in futility. Three years have passed and thus far nothing tangible has been reported. That does not augur well. This much too slow a pace for the Commission's working makes one pessimistic about not result.

The discussions on the form and structure of the Constitution have been a point of debate many a times during these fifty years — what is more suitable for our country — the Parliamentary form or the Presidential form. This point was thoroughly discussed and debated upon even in the Constituent Assembly. But finally the Constituent Assembly adopted this present form of government. Somehow, a prominent member of the Constituent Assembly — Sri K.M. Munshi who had vehemently pleaded in favour of the Parliamentary form in the Constituent assembly changed his stance by 1967 when he pleaded for a review and showed his preference for the American form of Presidential system. Strange though it may look that K.M. Munshi, an eminent one of the framers of the Constitution began pleading for a review. This amply proves the point that there was found something wrong 'with the state of Denmark' to quote Shakespeare's 'Hamlet', which set even the framers of the Constitution think about reviewing it. So the demand of 'a review' is not any NDA agenda; it has a history and a precedence.

In the eighties Vasant Sathe raised up the issue that the parliamentary system be changed to a Presidential system. Then it was thought that he was making this suggestion with an ulterior motive that Indira Gandhi wanted to assume the powers of the President. What was at the back of Vasant Sathe's mind no one can say but then it again means that there was some thinking at some level which had gone on regarding the reviewing of the Constitution. At least the riders imposed upon the present Commission can allay apprehensions that Atal Behari Vajpayee aspires to become the President. None should feel disturbed at the setting up this Commission at least on this count,

Even if the apprehensions of Indira Gandhi trying to became the President may vaguely be correct still one should deeply study the American system and then comment. Even in the American system, the President has to seek the sanction of the Senate. The President does not turn autocratic. He is also answerable to a bigger and a larger authority. America cannot become Pakistan where the President has assumed all authority centred in himself. India is also a country where people's voice has held its authority and none can turn autocratic — not even a President in the Presidential form of government. There will have to be some body bigger in authority to rein the President. But for the present discussion on this point in the present context is out of question — as the question of changing the basic structure shall not be on the agenda of the Review Commission. It is only during 'Emergency' that the Prime Minister becomes all powerful as Indira Gandhi did become but that also needed a Fakruddin Ali Ahmad as President, pliable and pitiable to sign the order of imposing Emergency. The Review Commission can, of course, look into this provision and give its recommendation whether 'Emergency' can ever be imposed. But Indira Gandhi had to pay the price for imposing Emergency when she and her party lost at the general elections.

The Constitution Review Commission has also been directed not to change the basic structure of the present constituion. This brings us directly to the question as to what is the basic structure of the Indian Constitution. The Supreme Court has partially tried to define some salient features of the basic structure of the constitution in cases like 'Keshavanand Bharti (1973), Minerva Mills (1980), Kehoro Holohan (1992). But a comprehensive defining has not been done and needs to be exhaustively and finally done. We cannot wait for the Supreme Court to decide them. The Commission has on it judges who have been on the Supreme Court bench and they can as well define and elaborate upon the point. Still inspite of everything, if challenged at the level of the Supreme Court, it is the present Supreme Court which will be the final arbiter. The Review Commission will have to decide upon the respective powers of the Parliament, the Executive and the Judiciary.

The general populace will also have its voice on the provisions proposed by the Review Commission and if the nation by a consensus favours the amendments, the judiciary shall also have to honour it. That would be in the interest of justice — natural justice. Though, of course, the majority of the population, illiterate as they are shall remain unconcerned what the Review Commission recommends and what the Government accepts, but at least the elite class shall remain concerned about what ultimately comes out of the whole exercise.

The Congress as the major opposition party should support the government on the Review. It, as a party, is bound by history to do so, and if it does not it would be negating its own leadership. The party needs to be reminded how Jawahar Lal Nehru got the Congress Working Committee on April 4, 1954, under his own Chairmanship set up a ten member Committee 'to study the question of changes in the Constitution and in the People's Representation Act and to suggest amendments! Indira Gandhi set up a Congress panel headed by Swaran Singh in 1976 to take a good fresh look at the Constitution and make whatever recommendations it considered necessary ... It was even permitted to go into the question whether India should continue with the Westminister model or switch over to the presidential form of government. This has been the history of the Congress and the present Congress leadership is morally bound to support the government. Not only that Sonia Gandhi is on record to have said on October 27, 1976 rubbishing the idea of 'no change in the basic structure' restriction on the Commission by saying that "those who want to fix it in a rigid and inalterable frame do not know the spirit of our Constitution and are out of time with the spirit of the new media. We have always maintained that the Parliament has an unfettered, unqualified and unbridgeable right to amend the constitution. We do not accept the dogma of basic structure."

The Congress must oppose what the government at present in power does. If the government had allowed full freedom to the Commission even to change the 'basic structure', Congressmen would have cried hoarse that the government wants to strike at the root of democracy. If the government has directed the Commission not to change the basic structure, the Congress leader has to oppose this restriction.

Let the Congress move the matter in the Lok Sabha and have the directive cancelled — let it face the music in the Lok Sabha if it dare to. That the Congress would not do as it would fail to muster support. It should, as a party, play the honourable role of cooperating with the government. The nation stands committed to democracy and Congress cannot change this Commitment. That is the basic structure of the Constitution as at present — the people's voice is supreme, — which is supreme only in a democratic set up. Let Congress see reason and be not blinded with only the opposing vision.

All these are premature matters — the stage has not yet been reached. What is necessary is that the Commission expedites its process. The nation eagerly awaits it.

9. REWRITING HISTORY

History of India, as thus far had been written and had been taught and read does need a recasting. There are some very glaring misrepresentations and certain major omissions which thus far were never looked into and the pattern continued. Nobody bothered perhaps. But the nation's history needs to be an impartial unbiased statements of facts and events — that only would present to the students and to the public in general a correct perspective of events and personalities which really mattered and who have played an important part in framing the history of the nation. It has been with this point in the vision which led the NCERT to have the history of India to be rewritten and facts and personalities which and who have thus far remained ignored should be placed and presented in the right perspective. But those who thus far had been dominating the history — writing scene have begun to raise a hue and cry and the only charge that they have raised and that they could raise is the set charge — the HRD ministry headed by Dr. Murli Manohar Joshi is making an attempt at 'saffronisation' of history.

Actually the trouble is that so far the writing of history scene has remained dominated by the historians with a leftist leaning. This group of historians are those whom Dr. Nurul Hasan, the Minister of Education under Indira Gandhi's regime — himself a historian of repute had unfortunately the leftist leanings: He formed the Indian History Congress and manned it with such historians who also were dominated and still remain dominated with the leftist leanings. These historians had their own predilections and prejudices and when history is written with such a mental background, it cannot present an unbiased view of events and personalities. Most of this group of historians have written history after the World War II in which war U.S.S.R. was an ally of the British. These historians derived their mental inspiration from the U.S.S.R. ideologies and naturally the British historians who hardly could highlight the Indian patriots who fought against the British rule and prior to that with the Muslim rules, did not receive any recognition. The History of India written by Vincent Smith remained the text book in Indian schools and colleges. To this group of Indian historians whom Dr. Nurul Hasan patronised and gave prominence were — Dr. Romilla Thapar, Satish Chandra, Dr. R.S. Sharma and such others. They, in their histories did not think it proper even to mention the prominent Indian patriots like Rana Pratap, Shivaji, Tatia Tope, Rani Lakshmi Bai, Guru Tegh Bahadur Singh, Guru Gobind Singh, the revolutionaries like Bhagat Singh, Chandra Shekhar Azad, Savarkar or even Subhas Chandra Bose. They rather denigrated and deried them.

Even the ancient Indian history was belittled and nothing much was mentioned about the Mauryan period or the Gupta period or Harsh Vardhan or Ashok. Rather R.S. Sharma has described the period prior to the Muslim Rule as the 'Dark Ages'. R.S. Sharma even wrote about Lord Mahavir, the Jain Tirthankar with such a derision. He writes, "Mahavir kept wandering for 12 years from place to place ... During the course of the long journey, it is said, he never changed his clothes for 12 years". Another historian of the same group writes about Shivaji, "Although Shivaji had assumed the title of "Hindava-Dharmodharak (protector of Hindus), he plundered mercilessly the Hindu population". No credit has been given to Shivaji for fighting against the Muslim rulers and his encounter with Shaiyasta Khan and Afzal Beg.

About Aurangzeb, who was known to be the greatest bigot among the Mughal rulers, Satish Chandra in his 'Medieval India' writes, "Aurangzeb took a number of measures which have been called puritanical but many of which were really of an economic and social character and against superstitious beliefs. Thus he forbade singing in the court and official musicians were pensioned off".

This is what the Taliban did in Afghanistan so let us eulogise them too.

No credit has been given to Rana Pratap for his valiant fight for independence single handedly — he could not succeed though but sacrificed everything to save his territories. His valiant struggle needs to be presented in golden letters. So was the role of Rani Lakshmi Bai, or Tatia Tope, or Tipu Sultan. Aurangzeb needed to have been condemned for beheading Guru Tegh Bahadur. Guru Gobind Singh sacrificed his sons but did not surrender.

The sacrifice of Rani Padmavati to save her honour against the evil designs of Alauddin Khilji needed to have been highlighted.

So were the sacrifices of the revolutionaries — Bhagat Singh, Chandra Shekhar Azad and Savarkar, who fought the British for the sake of their country. They kept the flame of patriotism lighted and blazing.

It is now that Veer Savarkar's portrait having found a place in the Central Hall of the Parliament — a recognition, though so belated but has rightly been given.

Akbar has been described as 'Akbar the Great'. His policies were liberal and more adjusting. Hindus got a place of honour in his court — Todarmal, Birbal and many others. Man Singh, the cousin of Rana Pratap got the honoured place but had to pay a very heavy price — marrying his sister Jodha Bai to Akbar. Akbar's "Deen Ilahi" — whether it was a policy or a faith — is a controversial issue. Has it been a faith to which many during his life time began subscribing — perhaps to win his favour — gave it up after Akbar's death. Deen Ilahi died a natural death after Akbar — that, in itself means, that those who adhered to it had no real faith in it otherwise they should have continued with it. A policy dies with the policy maker.

The leftist historians never could digest the idea that Aryans were the native inhabitants of India. If, as the historians hold, came from outside, there must have been some who would have been living in the northern part of the country. To create a wedge in the national integrity of India, these historians put up the theory that the Dravidians were driven South by the Aryans; hence they are the inferior race dark-complexioned. Complexion has hardly anything to do with greatness. South has produced the greatest scholars, philosopher and religions leaders. They have produced the greatest intellectual giants — no less inferior in any way to the northerners — rather superior to them. If Aryans came from outside and occupied the northern part, there must have been some people who would have been living in the north. Who were they and where did they go ? This question remaining un-answered established that Aryans were the original inhabitants of India.

Last but not the least is the leftists prejudice shown towards Subhas Chandra Bose, the great and honoured freedom fighter and recognised thus, in that capacity.

As Subhas Chandra Bose fought against the British — an ally of U.S.S.R. during World War II — he has been condemned in the worst terms by the leftists. The leftists say, "The group which make up the forward Bloc (the party formed by Bose), the party of traitor Bose. This was said by the CPI in its first Congress in 1943. Bose and his forward bloc was declared as 'the worst enemy of the nation and driven out of political life and exterminated". In the party paper 'People's War', Bose was portrayed as a "blood thirsty devil riding on the back of the Japanese militarists" (July 19, 1942 — People's War).

There have been the blatant misrepresentations of Indian history which need to be corrected. The Indian youth has the right to know the true nature of Indian culture, philosophy and history, which thus far has never been presented in the true light or ignored totally. Hence the right and urgent necessity to rewrite history.

Historians, while writing the history of modern India, after independence shall have to research and record as who was responsible for referring the Kashmir matter to the UNO ?, who was responsible for the division of the country on the linguistic basis thus creating an all time picture of the country as a diversified entity and what good did this division result in ?, who was responsible to have lost the war against China in 1962 and what were the reasons for it ?, who did not allow one lingua franca — Hindi as that — to be accepted by the country when in the flush of enthusiasm after independence anything and every thing could have been accepted if sponsored and proposed in the name of national honour and national integrity ?, who accepted the partition of India into two nations — Pakistan and India ? All these are problems which have kept pricking the sides of India as a nation. Those responsible for creating all these problems need to be highlighted. The nation has the right to know it and historians have a duty to research and present the real facts. It is the present generation which is suffering for the follies of the previous generation and the real culprits behind the problems must be exposed. This only historians can do and should do.

Let history of the country be written on a clean state — these has to be no red, no green, no saffron but a pure white slate on which the true, correct and unprejudiced history be written.

That is a great duty of the scholars and the great need of the hour.

10. INDIA CHINA RELATIONS — A NEED FOR A CLOSER TIE

India and China are the two countries in Asia with the largest population and with the greatest potential for growth. But the relations between the two countries have never been very cordial. China has grown economically and has also controlled its population but treats India as its most potent rival in the continent. That is, perhaps, the reason why China does not want India to gain a political mileage in the international politics. While if the two countries are able to cooperate, they can emerge out as a great power bloc.

Efforts are being made. The Indian foreign minister had visited China recently and the Indian Prime minister is also visiting China in June 2003. The outcome of these visits have to be watched.

Tourism is a field in which both the countries can find a common meeting ground. That would mean a man to man interaction which can be conducive to cordial relations.

Let us hope for the best.

Ever since Chou-en-lai, the then Prime minister of China visited India in the 60s and Pandit Nehru coined the slogan of 'Hindi China Bhai Bhai', there have been attempts at forging a cordial relationship between the two countries.

But then the 1962, Chinese attack on India which took Pandit Nehru with a shock and a surprise spoilt the game. Ever since then there has always remained a sense of suspicion and doubt in the minds of the two countries though, there have been, even thereafter exchange of visits of the Prime Ministers of the two countries, off and on. But the fact that China has never supported India in India's Kashmir imbroglio and Pakistan has ever sought China's support means that Pakistan finds the Chinese leadership amendable to it. That is why whenever in trouble the Pakistan Prime Minister or President runs to China for support — it is because there should be an expectation of support from China. During the Kargil misadventure, faced with a pressure from the U.S. Nawaz Sharif ran to China though did not get the desired support. General Musharraf has also gone to China to seek China's support on the Kashmir issue and the Chinese foreign office did issue a statement stating that Kashmir was the 'core issue'. India had to lodge its protest over this statement. That is how a peculiar tension and suspicion keeps hovering over the horizon of the mutual relationship of the two countries. Pakistan gave away to China a large chunk of land which was in Pakistan's unauthorised occupation. A friend of a foe is a natural foe — that is what the situation between China and India is. Any world power supporting Pakistan cannot be a friend to India while China has been showing up an ever sympathetic gesture towards Pakistan. Even after the terrorist attack on the Indian Parliament, the entire international community expressed dismay and concern but there was not a word from the side of China. There sprang a lot of hope after China's National People's Congress Chairman Liping's last visit to India and a warm welcome extended to him by the Indian government, and all show of courtesy and exchange of pleasantries, the situation overall remains unchanged. China does not want India to rise up as a superpower in Asia and to rival China on that level. The basic advantage with China, of course, is that it has a single party rule and what it does or wants to do is done while India, a democracy has to face so many pulls and pressures and its political leadership has to strike a compromise at so many levels. The present NDA government at the centre is a 24 party coalition where every coalition partner has his own position and his own pressure. It is only Atal Behari Vajpayee, as an astute politician, who is keeping the flock together. Such a situation has its own compulsions and China very well knows it. Still India is trying at its own level to forge a workable and available relationship. The impending visit of the Indian Prime minister due in June 2003, may clear some position. Let there be a hope for the best.

How treacherous it was on the part of China to have launched an attack on India in 1962 only a short time after Chon-en-lai's visit and Nehru's great faith in China's friendliness. That attack was such a shock to Nehru that it became one major cause of his death — as it is believed.

So faith and frustration both go side by side for India dealing with China.

Otherwise China and India have a very ancient history of cordial relationship. Huang-Sang and Fahei-e-yan were travellers who visited India, stayed here for long and have made detailed recording of their experiences which are a part of Indian history. Buddhism travelled from India to China and was welcomed there.

Economic relations between the two countries are going on at full swing. Indian market are in good demand in China, also equally responsive to Indian goods — that is not fully known. But just possible the Indian Prime Minister's visit may provide an opportunity for some joint declarations even on economic front.

There is one field yet not fully explored, which can bring the peoples of the two countries closer. The coming closer of the people, the general population, men, women and children of the two countries is bound of create one atmosphere of cordiality. People's voice is God's voice, as is said, therefore, for forging closer relations between these two giant nations of the continent 'tourism' is a field which needs to be fully explored. China, thus far, has remained a 'walled country', not every part of it has been accessible to the outsider. If at all a tourist goes there, he is required or allowed to visit only the marked destinations — these tours are conditioned ones — that defeats the purpose of the real spirit of tourism. One who goes to a country as a tourist wants to be left free to move wherever one pleases or desires to. But that is not so in China.

That way India has an open field — go anywhere and everywhere — no restrictions unless, of course, you are a suspect of having come with some surreptitious evil plan. Still the Chinese visiting India and Indians visiting China, as tourists has not been presenting a very encouraging picture though, politics apart, this is the most non-controversial field. From figures available in 1999 only about 8000 tourist from India visited China and mere 6500 Chinese visited India. With such a vast population as the two countries have this number is a negligible number. The two countries have a 4000 km common border and unparalleled cultural and civilisation offerings. That is what stands amply revealed by the traveller Huang Sang visiting India in the 7th century A.D. and records his accounts of 14 years of sojourn

Fahieyan travelled throughout India. And travel on the southern branch of silk route arching down over the Kara-Korum through Kashmir Rajasthan and Gujarat took place well before Marco Polo and others popularised the west-east road across central Asia from Samarkand to Xian.

Both the countries stand to benefit from this activity. It would create a heart-warning atmosphere between the peoples and boost up the development of the tourist centres. The hitherto neglected spots — tourist friendly would be developed and spruced up. There is such an economic advantage too to the two countries. Again to go back to the figures of 1999, three years backward, China's inbound tourist figure is 9.2 million people, second only to Japan (16 million) and is growing at 20% annually. India has nearly five million inbound tourists. Countries all over the world are keen to visit these two countries and Australia, Japan, Korea and Switzerland have opened tourists, centres in China. Australia, Switzewland, U.S., Malaysia, Thailand, Singapore are looking forward to India as a tourist attraction. By the year 2001, Chinese tourist number went up to 50 million while of India to 25 million. By 2010 the figures are going to be up tremendously. Each tourist spending something upto $1000 on an average. What a great economical benefit accrues to the countries ! India, for that matter, has such a variety to offer. From the glaciers of the northern mountainous regions for skiing and other ice-spots to Kerala's lustrous beauty, the Goa beach in the West and the Puri beach in the East; the heritage hotels of Rajasthan, the Ellora and Ajanta caves, the Khujraho temples, the shrines Amarnath, Badrinath, Gangotri, Yamunotri, to down south Kanyakumari and the beautiful temples — there is such a variety for the tourists to choose from.

Much is not known about China due to its closed door policy but then and ancient country with an ancient civilisation there must naturally be may regions and many places which should be of interest for tourists.

What is more than anything important is that tourism, will bring the two countries, India and China closer, people to people contact is very important to forge closer ties.

Look at the geographical closeness of the two countries. The distance between Kolkatta and Kumning is just 1500 km. and between Delhi and Kashgar the distance is just 1000 km. Thus travel costs for a tourist from one country to another would be so much less. And, therefore, if tourist agencies of the two countries work in unison, tourist packages can be planned and the process can become so attractive and lucerative too.

Economically also the two countries stand to benefit a lot. A tourist, when he would set out for a tour would be ready to spend at least a $500. If the number of tourists can touch 25 million, the earning would be $ one billion — what an income it would be. India and China can open up the ancient road routes linking India with China through Ladakh, the North East and the historic Hindustan Tibet road. But all this needs mutual trust and cordial relations. To cover a 1000 km one step forward is necessary which political will and the political atmosphere must permit.

India and China as friendly nations can become a big international power.

11. IRAQ WAR — THE AMERICAN ONSLAUGHT — HOW AND WHY ?

The occupation of Iraq has been the American agenda ever since 1991. But it seems more an obsession with the George Bush family — first the father, the elder Bush as President wished it and now the son, George Bush, the present President of U.S. has fulfiiled it.

It is more like the 'Lamb and the Wolf' story — making the water of the stream dirty — as a pretext to make the Lamb its prey. Though Iraq has been no lamb, that way, but the U.S. needed some pretext to attack it — Iraq has chemical weapons which are a danger to the world. The U.S. got the UN to send international inspectors Iraq under Saddam first resisted but then gave in. The inspectors did not find any such weapons, still the ghost of suspicion was kept lingering that Saddam Hussain has managed to delude the inspectors. The world must get rid of Saddam Hussain to be a safer place to live — that became the U.S. agenda. Saddam Hussain was defiant and he relied on the strength and potentiality of his Republical guards and his people — their spirit of patriotism to resist the U.S. But the U.S. had a much superior military power and a greater sophistication of their armament and just by sacrificing 168 soldiers, the U.S. force have occupied Baghdad — the capital of Iraq. Very much like not being able to find Osama Bin Laden — dead or alive, Saddam Hussain has also not been found dead or alive by the U.S. but Iraq has been taken control of with the civilian population suffering a lot and several ancient and historical monuments destroyed — libraries with rare literature razed to the ground.

How step by step this war has been won and what is the ulterior aim of the U.S. in taking Iraq under its control has to be understood. Strategically Iraq has such a geographical position that by occupying it the U.S. can control the entire Arab world around and the oil-field of Iraq would be great assets for the U.S. for all times.

The U.S. has launched this offensive for the first time, the European powers — France, Germany, Russia vehemently opposing it. Only the U.K. has been an active supporter.

So the U.S. has occupied Iraq but on great risks of its international alienation but the U.S. is proud of its power and defies opposition.

The U.S. has at last succeeded in occupying Iraq, which had been on its agenda ever since 1991. One of the pleas taken for launching this offensive had been that Saddam Hussain had tried to assassinate the elder Bush, the then President of the U.S. But that has been just a plea with no tangible evidence available. Then the other plea taken by the U.S. has been that Iraq under Saddam Hussain has an arsenal of chemical and biological weapons which are a potential threat to the world at large. It is, as if, the U.S. has taken upon itself the sole responsibility of being the saviour of mankind. The U.S. made the U.N. send inspectors to inspect Iraq's arsenals — they could even inspect Saddam Hussain's personal palaces. At the outset Saddam Hussain resisted this inspection but then finally gave in. The U.N. inspectors were accompanied by the CIA/MI6 teams to quietly locate and pin point targets which, in the event of a U.S. attack they would target first.

Saddam gave up resistance to this inspection as any resistance would have created a world wide suspicion that there really was something which Saddam wanted to hide and the resistance would have invoked the U.N. resolution passed in 1991 directing Iraq to allow such an inspection or incur punishment. The U.S. also expected that as Saddam's regime had ever been most autocratic, the people never a free lot, the U.S. attack would have the impact that the local population would join the U.S. forces to dethrone Saddam as it happened in Afghanistan. Of course, the U.S. knew that as Saddam would be fighting for his life, it would be a bloody battle. So the U.S. built up forces to over, 2,50,000 to launch their attack in January. The U.S. had developed much better, weaponary since 1991. The US's apprehensions were that Saddam would use his tested small, pilotless planes to spray bio-chemical germs and gas. Therefore, the U.S. preferred a winter war when protective uniforms could be put on and be bearable. At the same time the U.S. wanted a quick action which may prove decisive. The U.S. only expected a tough resistance from the Republican Guards. The U.S. had a hope that Saddam's generals would switch sides to avoid reprisals.

Iraq was militarily much weaker. It had 6,50,000 troops but only 1,00,000 strong Republican Guards and only 40 long range Scud missiles. Its one third aircraft could not fly and it has no navy.

But the question that poses itself glaringly is why at all did the U.S. attack Iraq. Was it really to destroy its bio-chemical weapon's stock? The U.N. inspectors during the course of its inspection did not find any such weapons. Then why an action?

Of course, the people of Iraq were fed up with the Saddam regime. They had hardly ever seen or met their ruler; they, if ever, had only seen his 'doubles' or have had the looks of Saddam's statutes of all shapes and forms all over. That is all that they knew of Saddam. The economy of Iraq has been in shatters. Except for the smugglers who have gained riches and all benefits, there is no other class which felt comfortable. Hence it was that there was little sympathy over the overthrow of Saddam among the people in general; rather, there had been jubilation too that was witnessed. Thus losing just about 168 soldiers the U.S. has occupied a country which strategically is very significant for the U.S. power in the Middle-East, particularly in the Arab World.

How it all happened — it is a step by step story.

The U.S. along with U.K. had used the U.N. resolution since 1991 to cripple Iraq's fighting potential. Since last year, the year 2001 a diplomatic campaign to isolate Iraq was also launched. Using a wide range of precision weapons JDAM and CBU — 105 bombs — the U.S. struck at Saddam's power bases and neutralised much of Iraq's resistance. Then to create a psychological impact to win popular Iraqi people's support ship loads of food and medicines arrived once the port of Umm Qasr fell. To capture the cities and oil wells at Rumiala the British fought in Basra. The U.S. sped northward to Nasiriyah, Najaf and Karbala. Aided by massive air-support the U.S. Army rapidly moved tens of thousands of troops over 500 km of Iraqi territory. The capture of the bridge on the Euphrates brought the U.S. artillery within striking distance South West of the city of Baghdad. The Iraqi forces were unable to counter the U.S. forces and Baghdad came close to falling soon. Then began the final assault on Baghdad. The defiance disappeared and the report spread of Saddam's possible death. Thus Baghdad fell and Iraq stood conquered.

So why was this attack on Iraq necessary — this is all important a question which has got to be answered. The U.S. and the U.K. used the plea that they wanted Iraq's chemical and biological weaponry to be destroyed. Secondly, they wanted to end the autocratic regime of the cruel and heartless dictator to end and bring democracy. But these are apparently appear to be just pretentious pleas.

The major and the all important reason behind dethroning Saddam was to capture Iraq's oil resources.

It has all been a politics of oil. The U.S. desires to control potentially the biggest oil reserves and play a larger role in the Gulf. This has been the underlying U.S. policy in dismantling the ruling regime of Iraq. Thus for U.S. has been patronising Saudi Arabia which have the biggest oil reserves and has been controlling the international market. Moreover U.S. has been uneasy about Saudi Arabia ever after 9/11 as the U.S. knows that a larger part of funding of Al-Qaida is done by Saudi Arabia. By controlling Iraq, the U.S. shall have a greater potential to fight fundamentalism and its off-shoot, terrorism.

Iraq's oil reserves are estimated at 115 billion barrels, second only to Saudi Arabia with estimated 261 billion barrels. The Iraq officials claim that the Iraqi reserves would grow to 300 billion barrels outgrowing those of Saudi Arabia in the near future. For the U.S., Iraq would prove to be gold mine. It was only for oil that the U.S. supported Iraq in the Iraq-Iran conflict.

So oil has been the major incentive for the U.S. to control Iraq.

Then Iraq stands in the centre of the Arab world — Jordan, Iran, Saudi Arabia, Syria, Lebanon all bordering Iraq. Thus the U.S. would become the centre of power and would dominate the entire Arab world and from already a super-power, the U.S. would become a super-super power — a role that the U.S. would like to play. Hence it has been that it has ignored opposition for its Iraq adventure by the European powers like France, Germany and Russia. India has been lukewarm in its condemnation of the U.S. action in Iraq while Pakistan has been quiet. India did it for its political compulsions of keeping the minority community satisfied. While Pakistan is already deeply indebted to the U.S.

So the Iraq war has seen the fall of a dictator and the emergence of a democratic dictator — the U.S. The U.K. shall play only the second fiddle.

INDIAN ECONOMY

12. PUBLIC SECTOR UNDERTAKINGS : SHOULD THEY CONTINUE ?

PSUs major vehicles of our economy—PSU figures for 1995-96—Negative points of PSUs—Inefficiency, low productivity, losses, red-tapism—All objectives could not be achieved—Economic growth slow due to PSUs—Railways and Electricity —Total PSUs are 236—134 PSUs making profits—Boards are inefficient—BHEL and SAIL are star performers—Disinvestments being ordered by central government for many PSUs—Should not scrap PSUs as they build infrastructure and are helpful in the upliftment of weaker sections.

The Public Sector Undertakings (PSUs) are the prime growth vehicles of Indian economy. Some of the leading PSUs of India (like BHEL) are also in the list of Fortune 500 companies. On May 5, 1997, Public Enterprises Survey for 1995-96 was tabled in the Parliament which stated that the profits of the PSUs had increased by Rs 9,788 crore in 1995-96. This was an increase of 20.4 per cent over the figure of the previous year. The investments in the PSUs had gone up by Rs 5,336 crore-an increase of 3.08 per cent over the precious year. There are 134 PSUs, which made a profit to the tune of Rs 14,704 crore (during 1995-96). The gross margin to the capital employed was 23.31 per cent in 1995-96 as against 20.55 per cent in 1994-95. The total investments in the PSUs stood at Rs 1,78,628 crore as compared with the figures of 1994-95 of Rs 1,73,292 crore. While ONGC topped the list of profit making PSUs with gross profit of Rs 2354.32 crore, Hindustan Fertiliser Corporation Ltd posted a net loss of Rs 474.41 crore.

During 1995-96 period, export earnings of Rs 13,216 crore showed a rise of 15.1 percent over the figures of previous year. This has set a good trend and is a harbinger of our good export performances in the future. During 1997-98, nett profit of the PSUs increased at the rate of 37.36 per cent. During the fiscal year 1997-

98, nett profits of Rs 13,725 crore was generated; in 1996-97, this figure was 9,992 crore.

The PSUs, however, have always been under attack by the opposition, the private sector and the public at large. Delayed decisions, inefficiency, red tapism and widespread corruption at all the levels have spoiled the applecart of the PSUs. Even the good performers have been given negative marks by the critics. The "mixed economy concept" of our policy makers essentially promoted the PSUs for the developing the infrastructure across the country, building of a better society through a favourable fair industrial climate and improving the economic standards of the poorer and the weaker sections by assuring them of stable careers in these firms. All the objectives could not be achieved. We have built sound industrial, economic and technical infrastructures. The weaker sections of the society have also got a helping hand. But the economic growth has been at a painfully slow pace and the limitations of the PSUs have contributed a lot in this direction.

The most inefficient PSUs are Railways, Air India (estimated losses for 1998-99 were nearly Rs 165 crore) and Electricity Boards. Further, 100 PSUs are in the red and there are very little hopes for their revival. Trade unionism and strikes are the order of the day. Moreover, the current debt to equity ratio is 1 : 1 in PSUs whereas it is only 0.5 : 1 in the private sector. The debts on the PSUs carry interest and the poor performance of these enterprises aggravates the debt problem. No doubt, therefore, a World Bank Report wonders whether Indian economy could ever be released from the burden of PSUs. This opinion and the grudge of the public towards the PSUs motivate us to take a decision to scrap them forever.

Improvement in the operations and productivity of the PSUs could be effected through the following measures :—

    (A) A clear focus on the nett margin of each product.
    (B) Sale of those products that generate better profits.
    (C) Reduction of inventories and adoption of procedures related to JIT.
    (D) Strict control over defective products, work-in-process goods and wastages.
    (E) Concrete improvements in techno-economic parameters.

(F) Adoption of value addition measures so that products and services could fetch higher contributions.

However, there is also a positive side of this coin. The PSUs have employed millions of Indians who are happy due to job security, such job content and their contribution towards the development of this vast nation. The profits of profit-making PSUs are up. BHEL is the global leader in steam turbines and electrical machinery. It employs 61,000 employees worldwide. SAIL is also doing very well. Multinational culture has brought productivity concepts in the PSUs as well. As the engines of growth, PSUs can do a lot for our economy. Therefore, we should not do away with them. However, we should scrap the loss-making or inefficient PSUs even if we have to lay off some personnel. So far, 54 PSUs have been referred to Board for Industrial and Financial Reconstruction (BIFR) for rehabilitation. NTC is a glaring exmaple of loss-making PSU, which must be scrapped and its assets must be sold off to the private sector. The carefully picked up PSUs should be made the prime vehicles of economic development and social upliftment. Giving a death blow to the concept of PUs could disturb our planning process and hence, our economic growth.

The government has announced that it would grant functional autonomy to 97 PSUs. At least 98 profit-making PSUs (excluding the *Navratnas*) would be allowed to make investments of up to Rs 300 crore without any clearance from the government. Another 49 PSUs (which are making profits) would be allowed to go ahead with the investments of Rs 150 crores. These companies would be treated as *Mini Ratnas*.

Let us study the major areas of operation of the PSUs. The planning process is aimed at developing the infrastructure and the core sectors in our country. The private sector, always looking for quick money, would not be interested in long gestation projects. The PSUs were promoted in the areas of electricals (BHEL), shipping (Bharat Heavy Plate and Vessels Ltd and Garden Reach Workshop Ltd), railway engineering (Rail India Technical and Economic Services), cables (Hindustan Cables Ltd), chemicals (Hindustan Organic Chemicals Ltd), railway coaches (Rail Coach Factories at Kapurthala and Perambur), coal (Coal India Ltd and Neyveli Lignite

Ltd), insecticides (Hindustan Insecticides Ltd), hotel industry (Ashoka Hotels Ltd), railway engines (Diesel Locomotive Works and Chittranjan Locomotive Works), instruments (Instrumentation Ltd), machine tools (Hindustan Machine Tools Ltd), latex products (Hindustan Latex Ltd) etc. Further, Atomic Energy Commission was set up in August, 1948, for the development of atomic energy in the country. Nuclear Power Corporation started its operations in 1969 with Tarapur Atomic Power Station (with a power generation capacity of 420 MW) in Maharashtra. Indian Space Research Organisation has designed and implemented successful launch programmes. Defence Research and Development Organisation (DRDO) has developed missiles like Trishul, Nag, Prithvi and Agni. Agni II was successfully test-fired in April, 1999. Our defence research efforts must continue at a fast pace in the wake of the recently of Kargil war. PSUs could make must significant contributions for developing conventional and nonconventional arsenal, tanks, fighter aircraft and other defence equipment. These examples prove that our development over the past four decades has been the result of the performance of these PSUs only. These sectors were exclusively under the State control. The PSUs were supposed to bring the nation to a respectable level of progress in these sectors and some of them have been successful in meeting their targets.

The *Navratna* companies are likely to face the wrath of Disinvestment Commission. The government has referred 40 PSUs to the Disinvestment Commission; 20 PSUs are from the core sectior and 15 PSUs are from the non-core sector. The commission recommended the off-loading of 51 percent of equity in the core sector and upto 74 percent in the non-core sector. These steps would certainly justify the operations of PSUs; only healthy PSUs would be allowed to thrive due to scarcity of financial resources.

We can conclude that the loss-making and inefficient PSUs should be scrapped. The profit-making PSUs should be promoted and developed with the help of corporate sector, foreign institutional investors and funding through the Five Year Plans. The conversion of PSUs into joint venture firms could be a valid step towards free market economy. However, the star performers could be retained as PSUs forever.

13. HAVE FIVE YEAR PLANS FAILED ?

Five years plans have developed Indian economy—Brief figures and targets of all Five Year Plans given—Plan outlays and major objectives—Planning should be retained as infrastructure development, upliftment of weaker sections and international trading can be done successfully with their help—Our planning system effective but implementation needs scrutiny.

Five Year Plans have developed India as an independent nation. We have completed fifty years of independence with these mega-plans, which are the essential building blocks of our national economy. We need Five Year Plans as they are the vital engines of our economic growth.

The First Five Year Plan (1951-56) had a public sector outlay of Rs 2,356 crore in the public sector whereas the actual expenditure was Rs 1,960 crore. The investments were made by the private sector was Rs 1,800 crore. The spread of community development projects and an effort for raising the living standards of the people through agricultural productivity were the chief features of this plan. The rise in the natural income was also faster. The Second Five Year Plan (1956-61) had major objective of industrialization. There was also an attempt for building rural India and for increasing employment opportunities. The public sector outlay was Rs 4,800 crore while the actual expenditure was Rs 4,672 crore. The investments made by private sector were Rs 3,110 crore. During this plan, the national income increased by 19.5 per cent.

The Third Five Year Plan (1961-66) had a target to achieve— to increase the national income at the rate of over 5 per cent per annum. Self-sufficiency in food grains and development of core sectors (like steel, fuel, machinery and power) were the other objectives. The public sector outlay was Rs 7,500 crore while the actual expenditure was Rs 8,577 crore. The private sector investment was Rs 4,190 crore. The plan failed due to price rise (20 per cent), Chinese aggression, in 1962, Indo-Pak conflict in 1965 and poor monsoons in 1964-65 period. This period was declared a "Plan Holiday" period.

The Fourth Five Year Plan (1969-74) had two objectives— growth with stability and self-reliance. Another objective was to attain social justice and upliftment of the weaker sections of the society.

The total outlay stood at Rs 24,882 crore while public sector outlay was Rs 15,902 crore. Private sector investments were to the tune of Rs 8,980 crore. The realised growth rate was always lower (*eg*, 4.7 per cent in 1969-70 and 3.41 per cent in 1973-74). The target rate of growth of 5.7 per cent was never achieved.

The Fifth Five Year Plan (1974-79) aimed at the removal of poverty and achievement of self-reliance. The plan also started Minimum Needs Programme and stated measures for checking inflation. The target growth rate was 5.5 per cent. The total plan outlay was of Rs 66,353 crore. Public sector outlay was Rs 39,304 crore and expected private investment was to the tune of Rs 27,049 crore. The plan was terminated in its fourth year (*ie*, on March 31, 1978). The performance was reasonable in foodgrains and cotton cloths whereas in the areas of sugarcane, coal, petroleum, fertilisers, steel and electricity, the performance was below targets. The national income increased at the rate of 5.2 per cent.

The Sixth Five Year Plan (1980-85) had manifold objectives—improvement of growth rate of economy, reduction in poverty and unemployment, improvement in quality of life, control of population growth and protection and improvement of ecological and environmental assets of the nation. The total plan outlay was Rs 1,72,210 crore. Public sector outlay stood at Rs 97,500 crore whereas private sector outlay was Rs 75,710 crore. The national income grew at the rate of 5.4 per cent per annum against the target of 5.2 per cent. The actual saving rate was 23.3 per cent (In 1984-85). The plan was dominated by power shortages and poor performance of the core industries.

The Seventh Five Year Plan (1985-90) aimed at accelerating growth in foodgrain production, increasing employment opportunities and finally, raising productivity in all the sectors of the economy. The aggregate plan outlay was Rs 3,48,148 crore — Rs 1,80,000 crore for the public sector and Rs 1,68,148 crore for the private sector. Many targets were exceeded. The annual growth rate of GDP was 5.8 per cent as against the plan target of 5 per cent. The annual growth rate of industrial sector was 8.5 per cent that was only marginally lower than the plan target of 8.7 per cent. The production of foodgrains was raised to 171 million tonnes (in 1989-90) as against

148.5 million tonnes (in 1984-85). Public sector savings, however, fell short of the target. The gap between the income and expenditure of the government increased. The fiscal deficits of the government spilled over into current account deficits. These deficits had to be financed at the cost of low foreign exchange reserves through fresh external borrowings.

The Eighth Five Year Plan (1992-97) was delayed by two years. It envisaged an aggregate investment of Rs 7,98,000 crore—Rs 3,61,000 crore for the public sector and Rs 1,49,000 crore for the private sector. An investment of Rs 2,88,000 crore was allocated for the household sector. The plan had many objectives—generation of employment, control of population growth, spread of elementary education, eradication of illiteracy and finally, growth of the economy,.

The Ninth Five Year Plan (1997-2002) has envisaged public sector investments of Rs 8,59,000 crore. Private sector investments would be Rs 6,83,000 crore. The export growth rate has been fixed at 11.8 per cent and import growth rate would be 10.8 per cent. Average fiscal deficit would be 5.1 per cent of GDP.

Keeping the aforementioned facts and figures in view, we can conclude that Five Year Plans have proved to be the agents of economic change for our growing economy. We should continue to rely upon Five Year Plans because we have been able to meet many of the short term and long term objectives envisaged in them. It is true that every planning process has some limitations and there are negative fallouts as well. However, the Five Year Plans have been able to build industrial and economic infrastructure of the country. The poor and the deprived have also got benefits from these plans. Therefore, for protection of the interests of weaker sections, development of basic industrial infrastructure and handling major issues like unemployment, energy, industrial harmony, international trade *etc*, we must continue to rely upon Five Year Plans. In fact, Five Year Plans are the pride of Indian economy.

Every coin has two facets. So, Five Year Plans are also not free from limitations. The major bottlenecks include red tape, bureaucratic delays, fall of governments (and hence, the associated delays in plan implementation process), allocation of the resources to the non-priority areas *etc*. During 1999-2000, the GDP growth rate was 5.9 per cent, which was a good figure. Nuclear tests carried out by India had brought economic sanctions against India and that would affect our economic growth. Planning would have to be tuned to the renewed situation arising from the changed international economic scenario. Further, unemployment, development of SSI industries and worsening "balance of payment" position would also have an adverse effect on our Five Year Plans. Finally, the consumer-oriented economy is generating demand for computers, entertainment products and consumer non-durables. However, the core sectors are being sidelined by the planners in the interest of short-term gains through consumer markets, which yield high turnovers. Planning must be done in a balanced manner so that infrastructure development and upliftment of the standards of living of masses go on simultaneously. We can conclude by stating that careful economic planning must continue but the implementation of the plans must be made more efficient.

14. ECONOMY AND POLITICAL FLOW

Coalition governments could not perform well during the past—India has a long record of coalition governments—BJP led government was the first practical coalition government—BJP-led coaliation lost by 1 vote during April, 1999—But trends now changing—The parties with differing ideologies must unite under a coalition government so that the nation does not break up—Regionalism represents a victory for democracy—But coalition must succeed so that the progress of a nation is not hampered—We must live and govern together for the sake of national interests—In Europe, some coalition governments are successful now—We should also make coalition politics a success—The impact of political changes on economy could be severe and far reaching—Political chaos have always led to economic strain—Stability in centre and in the states is a must for economic growth.

The fall of coalition government led by BJP at the centre has of created political choas in our country. We witnessed coalition coarse governments earlier also (under the premiership of Mr Charan Singh, Mr Chandrashekhar, Mr AB Bajpayee, Mr HD Deve Gowda and Mr IK Gujral; the latter two were the prime ministers of the governments led by United Front that was supported by Congress). Some of the governments were formed through coalitions while others were supported by a major political party from outside. Many political pundits had foretold that Indian politics would not be fit for coalition governance. They went on to add that coalition governments could not do well in France, Italy and Japan. However, we disagree on this account and support a coalition government culture in the centre well as in the states. In our view, it is the true mirror of democracy in our national political fabric.

Coalition government is not the result of opportunistic alliances as some political analysts might think. True, during the past, the partners of the coalition government tried to reach the highest offices of power in the absence of a single dominant political entity. But in a democratic system, this is quite natural. The past was a dark chapter but the future of these alliances would be bright.

The voters of India have always given prudent ballot decisions in the favour of genuine political performers. Hence, the regional and local political groups have surfaced everywhere. As a result, the Parliament as well as the state assemblies have been witnessing a wide range of political players from all the corners of the nation. This proves that the single-party rule (or the rule of a limited number of parties) has been replaced by multi-party rule where in which all the new entrants represent their regions fully well. A reversal in this trend could thwart the attempts of Indian masses for electing the representatives of their own choice. These trends are healthy.

A note of caution is important here. Too many regional parties would naturally lead to chaos. Hence, we support the power of the people and respect their decisions. At the same time, we would also expect some electoral understandings before elections so that small regional parties could unite to form a powerful national alternative to the existing set of ruling parties.

A large number of political parties would protect our national interests. Further, if these small players have been sent by the masses to the Parliament or state assemblies, they should support the national and regional political and economic causes. For achieving that objective, they must unite behind a solid political leadership (that could emanate from any party). This would not only take adequate care of the interests of the masses, but also would ensure better Parliament-level and state-level outputs. Hence, coalitions would be made and accepted in Indian polity in future as well. The elections for the thirteenth *Lok Sabha* have resulted in victories for the regional parties. The major parties would have to share power with them.

However, the stock markets have never seen a bearish trend since the commencement of the coalition party governance. Their concern is natural as business always seeks stability. Industrial production is also low and economic growth rate has been little over 5 per cent during the past years. In 1997, the Finance Bill was a victim of the political crisis which was a result of the coalition governance at the centre. The leg-pulling exercise was at its ugly maxima as sanctimonious politicians were busy shouting at each other. The nation was sidelined and the base interests were the top priority. Such ego wars, personal conflicts and party issues occupied the centre stage during the rules of the three coalition government.

Ms J Jayalatha was able to pull down the BJP-led coalition government in New Delhi by 1 vote. Her alliance with Congress sealed the fate of the government led by Mr AB Vajpayee. She also plans to fight the ensuing elections of *Lok Sabha* along with Congress. The quick change-over was not unexpected. But the nation had suffered on account of her wily tactics; a poor nation like India could hardly afford elections after 13 months.

The limitations of coalition party rule described earlier are not enough. The national economy must grow at the rate of 7 per cent per annum or higher. But in order to grow at this rate, we need political stability, which would be difficult ti achieve through a coalition governance system. The stock markets must stabilise so that foreign direct investments are increased. The sluggish industrial production rate must pick up. All this requires political will and this could be achieved only with great efforts in a coalition government system. The previous alliances based on coalition governance were opportunistic and opportunistic alliances always spell doom for a country. The number of days, for which a coalition government is able to maintain its PM in office, decides our political, social and economic stability. Moreover, India is viewed by the world with respect. If our democracy faces tantrums, it is certainly going to raise many an eyebrow in the international diplomatic and economic circles. We are a part of the world and cannot isolate ourselves on any account.

Table I shows the tenures the Prime Ministers of India from Independence till date. The trend is not healthy as the Prime Minister of a coalition government has stayed for only a few days in office.

Further, Table II describes how economic flow of the nation is decided by our political flow.

We can conclude from Table II that political instability is partially related to economic progress. We must note that during the times of political chaos, especially during the periods of coalition governance, the GDP growth rate was excellent. Thus we cannot always correlate political flow and economic growth rate. Sometimes, the industry performs well but could give a dismal performance due to circumstances beyond its control. Some external factors—like global economic trends—do not auger well for industrial development. Some factors may not always be political.

Further, the people and the politicians feel that the political parties with highly polarised ideologies must think and act in a

TABLE-I : The Profiles of Indian Premiers

Prime Minister	Tenure (Dates)	Tenure (Days)
Jawahar Lal Nehru	(15-08-1947 to 27-05-1964)	6131 Days
Gulzari Lal Nanda	(27-05-1964 to 09-06-1964)	14 Days (Caretaker PM)
Lal Bahadur Shastri	(09-06-1964 to 11-01-1966)	582 Days
Gulzari Lal Nanda	(11-01-1966 to 24-01-1966)	14 Days (Caretaker PM)
Indira Gandhi	(24-01-1966 to 24-03-1977)	4078 Days
Morarji Desai	(24-03-1977 to 28-07-1979)	857 Days
Charan Singh	(28-07-1979 to 14-01-1980)	171 Days
Indira Gandhi	(14-01-1980 to 31-10-1984)	1753 Days
Rajiv Gandhi	(31-10-1984 to 01-12-1989)	1858 Days
V P Singh	(01-12-1989 to 07-11-1990)	341 Days
Chandrashekhar	(07-011-1990 to 21-06-1991)	224 Days
P V Narasimha Rao	(21-06-1991 to 16-05-1996)	1790 Days
Atal Behari Bajpayee	(16-05-1996 to 28-05-1996)	13 Days
H D Deve Gowda	01-06-1996 to 21-04-1997)	325 Days
I K Gujral	(21-04-1997 to 27-03-1998)	341 Days
Atal Behari Vajpayee	(27-03-1998 to 17-04-1999)	387 Days
Atal Behari Vajpayee	(18-04-1999 to 12-10-1999)	178 Days (Caretaker PM)
Atal Behari Vajpayee	(13-10-1999 onwards)	Till date

TABLE-II : How Indian Economy Behaves with Political Upheavals ?

S No	Period	Political Flow	Annual GDP Growth Rate (%)
1.	1960-69	—	3.7
2.	1969-71	Congress splits. Indira forms Congress-I. Heads a minority government till May, 1971 with support of left. GDP growth rate jumps to a new peak.	5.8
3.	1971-75	India wins Indo-Pak war in December, 1971. Indira returns to power with thumping majority. Political stability but without growth. This paradox cannot be explained by the economic and political analysts.	1.6
4.	1975-80	Indira imposes emergency in June, 1975. Hundreds are tortured or massacred by black laws. Indira ends emergency. Morarji Desai becomes new Prime Minister of India in 1977 and heads first non-Congress government. Morarji Desai in power for 27 months. Janata party does well on economic front. Charan Singh takes over as Prime Minister in 1979, with support of Congress-I. GDP rises but monsoons are poor in 1979-80.	3.6
4.	1980-89	Indira returns to power. The nation supports a stable political arrangement at the centre. Terror in Punjab, Jammu and Kashmir and Assam. Economy grows at an average rate of 5 per cent. Indira is shot dead in 1984. Rajiv Gandhi becomes Prime Minister. Congress-I wins with a majority and crushes all political opposition. Rajiv is viewed as young and liberal Prime Minister. Economic reforms are carried out by Manmohan Singh. Free market forces start playing in Indian markets. Bombay Sensex crosses 4000 mark. FDIs improve. New investors keen to invest in India. Economic reforms continue.	5.3
5.	1989-91	Rajiv loses power. VP Singh takes over. Gets BJP support for 11 months. 11 November, 1990, Chandrashekhar takes over with support from Congress-I, but forced to bow out after four months. Remains caretaker for another four months. Fresh polls announced by the President. Rajiv is assassinated. A mighty paradoxical economic boom is witnessed that results in high GDP growth rate of 6.2 per cent.	6.2

S. No.	Period	Political Flow	Annual GDP Growth Rate (%)
6.	1991-96	Congress returns to power. Rao continues economic reforms. But GDP growth is low.	5.3
7.	1996-97	Congress is voted out of power. AB Vajpayee is Prime Minister for a brief period of 13 days. United Front musters support of 14 parties. Congress (I) decides to support from outside. Deve Gowda is Prime Minister of UF Led coalition. GDP growth rate high. Economy looks up.	7.0
8.	1997-98	Sitaram Kesri fires his salvo against Deve Gowda and forces him to quit. IK Gujral is the choice of UF. Coalition government loses confidence motion, due to manipulations by Congress. Fresh elections are announced. AB Vajpayee heads BJP-led coalition government at the centre but finds it difficult to please his coalition partners, especially Ms. Jayalalitha. Economic slump continues.	5.0
9.	1998-99	A B Vajpayee takes over as Prime Minister on 27.03.98. The coalition of 13 parties is unable to pull along due to greed of Ms J Jayalalitha. On 17.04.1999. the coalition loses the confidence motion in the Lok Sabha by 1 vote. President dissolves the Lok Sabha and election dates are announced. Bitter war follows in Kargil, Drass and Batalik.	6.0-7.0
10.	1999-00	Kargil war ends. Vajpayee not allowed to take vital decisions regarding transfer of bureaucrats. Elections held. Stock markets crash. NDA-led government assumes power in the centre.	5.9-6.0

responsible manner and in the interest of the nation. The UF coalition government had an alliance that had no roots as the UF candidates fought their elections on the plea of keeping Congress out. Then, why UF got the support of Congress once it had categorically stated that Congress ought to be kept at an arm's length ? Similarly, the BJP-led gogernment relied upon Ms J Jayalalitha who pulled the carpet off its feet. Time teaches all the lessons. Our politicians would also learn to behave in a mature manner in the times to come. Petty politics would take a backseat. Nation and her economy are the top priorities today. A coalition government must be allowed to function.

It is a nascent concept in Indian polity. It should be nurtured by the political parties as well as by the masses.

There were some coalition disasters in Europe. But know that erstwhile USSR and the NATO alliance eliminated their differences and ended a bitter cold war. Had the two superpowers not shared an a common platform, our planet would have witnessed the nuclear doomsday much earlier. There is no problem that cannot be solved by across-the-table negotiations and empathy. A political rival could also be correct in his opinion. We should respect his opinion in the interest of the nation. We should learn to sit under one roof of Parliament and should sort out the problems of our country. A majority of our population is living below the poverty level. We face threats from China and Pakistan more frequently in terms of their defence preparations. Our industrial slow-down is costing us dearly. Unemployment is taking its own toll. Infrastructural development has also slowed down. Economic reforms have to be continued. India is seeking a permanent membership in the UN Security Council. There are so many vital issues before us. Why cannot we organise politics of consensus and take decisions jointly ? India needs unity in political diversity and not chaos through regional and local mandates. Political upheavals would certainly harm our economy and our image. We must learn to live and govern together. The mandate of the masses must be respected and coalition governments would certainly be the best *modus operandi* for shouldering this noble and vital responsibility.

15. THE SECURITIES SCAM

Total amount of Securities Scam exceeded Rs 3,000 crore—Mr Harshad Mehta and five others sentenced to imprisonment for 5 years in connection with illegal transfer of Rs 38.97 crore from MUL into the account of Mr Mehta—If Mr Mehta would have been allowed to operate for more time period, the losses to the investors could have been much higher—Thousands of families lost their assets, cash reserves and dignity—India is a land of scams—Most of the funds in the securities scam remain untraced.

The judgement day finally arrived. The "Big Bull" was sentenced to a term of rigorous imprisonment for five years by the Mumbai High

Court on September 28, 1999. The three associates of Mr Harshad Mehta were Mr PK Manocha (former Deputy Finance Manager of Maruti Udyog Ltd) Mr VB Deosthali (former Manager of UCO Bank) and Mr RN Popli (former Executive of ANG Griendlays Bank) and they were also awarded the same punishment. This judgement, which came after seven years from the date of declaration of the securities scam, was delivered in respect of the illegal transfer of Rs 38.97 crore into the personal account of Mr Harshad Mehta from Maruti Udyog Ltd (MUL). A stock broker commented, "Finally, justice has caught up with Harshad."

Justice delayed is justice denied. However, the central investigating agencies as well as the judicial machinery of our nation were able to deliver concrete results. Harshad Mehta had been facing 23 other cases of fraud and conspiracy. He was the mastermind behind the securities scam, which had a total amount of Rs 9,130.75 crore attached to its evil jaws. The case related to MUL involved such a meagre amount that it would not be able to satisfy the common investors who lost all their investments. Mehta was the kingpin behind the securities scam, the total value of the same being more than Rs 3,000 crore.

The notorious saga of securities scam began in April, 1992, when the scam was brought to light. On May 14, 1992, the bank accounts of Harshad Mehta and his firm, M/s Growmore Financial Services, were frozen. On June 22, 1992, a special court was set up and in the month of September in the same year, the hearings began. In 1993, Mehta claimed that he had paid bribe to the tune of Rs 1 crore to the erstwhile PM, Mr P V Narasimha Rao. In December, 1994, Mr Mehta and 21 others were charge-sheeted by CBI under the Prevention of Corruption Act. In March, the 1997, a special court attached the *benami* shares of Mr Mehta, which were valued at Rs 430 crore. In July, 1998, the trial began and on September 28, 1999, Mr Mehta was sentenced to a rigorous imprisonment for 5 years.

Mr Mehta had many sympathisers as well. They contended that if the scam had operated for some more time, he could have paid all his dues. However, judicial views and opinions of the brokers were different. If Mr Mehta were to be allowed to operate for more period, the share prices would have climbed to new peaks. The prices had to crash and after the crash, the losses to small investors would have been much higher.

A sentence of five years would not be able to unearth the funds that were invested by the small and medium investors. During the previous seven years, most of these investors lost their properties, cash assets, jewellery and other valuables as a result of the scam. Several hundred thousand families lost their basic earning mechanisms, assets and dignity. Their hopes of receiving back at least a part of that investments could not been enlivened by the judgement declared by the special court. The reason is that most of the funds involved in the scam remain untraced till date. Mr Mehta has lost his Limousines and Cadillacs but the poor investors have lost everything they had. The plight of these investors should be taken into consideration so that their agonies could be mitigated to some extent. The State should play a role for restoring a part of their investments.

The Western nations also recognise India as a nation of scams. Other prominent scams are : (*a*) Bofors Scam (1987)—Rs 64 crore; (*b*) Hawala Scam (1996)—Rs 65 crore; (*c*) CRB Scam (1996)—Rs 1,200 crore, (*d*) Urea Scam (1996)—Rs 133 crore; (*e*) Fodder Scam (1996)—Rs 960 crore; (*f*) Telecommunications Scam (1996)—Rs 34.68 crore (*g*) Ayurveda Scam (1995)—Rs 26 crore; (*h*) Jharkhand Mukti Morcha Scam—(1994-95) Rs 4.5 crore; and (*i*) Tarcoal Scam (1996)—Rs 500 crore. If we add up the Rupee values of all these scams, we would find that this amount would have been able to meet the short-term and long-term needs of the nation for making her an economic superpower; we, therefore, missed the opportunity for becoming financially strong and prosperous country. We cannot put the blame on others because our great nation has not given us businessmen who would think beyond their base interests. Whosoever comes to power, exercises it for filling his own coffers and Mr Mehta took the same step. Stock markets are so volatile that within a period of a few hours, an investor could become either a billionaire or a man on the street. This spurt of stock exchange business would be used by dishonest share brokers like Mr Mehta in future as well.

Agatha Christie once wrote, "Where large sums of money are concerned, it is advisable to trust nobody." In order to curb the irregularities in the capital market, Securities and Exchange Board of India (SEBI) was formed. SEBI has been able to control the activities of notorious stock traders. This is a good sign for our stock trading activities but the government has to realise that it has to promote a free market mechanism in stock trading but at the same time, it has to keep the spurious and opportunist middlemen at bay. This is not an easy task because our stock exchange activities do have serious loopholes.

Many experts contend that these scams are a part of the natural economic growth process of our nation. In other words, they have a premonition that these scams were likely to occur. However, we do not agree with those who try to toe this idea in order to justify their alignment with the limitations of our banking system and stock trading activities. The operational mechanisms at the bourses could have been designed in advance before leaping for the free market mechanism in the stock trading activities. We have moved cautiously in every area of industry and business before finally embracing a free market mechanism. Controls are lifted with a chary finesse and the government remains vigilant about the economic transactions in those areas, which become a part of the free economy. But in the case of stock trading activities, no such controls were designed or implemented. The government rose to the occasion and pressed CBI into the service only after the securities scam was unearthed. Today, all efforts are being made to keep the trading activities (at the bourses) completely clean and sans any 'shaded' transactions. Why did this not happen earlier ? Why, for example, SEBI was not formed in the early seventies (or even earlier) so that the stock trading mechanism could not be misused by shrewd manipulators like Mr Harshad Mehta.

The roles of the banks in the securities scam are also questionable. The employees of public sector undertakings (in this case, the employee of MUL was also involved) have also tried to reap rich benefits. This has proved beyond doubt that PSUs are the nurseries of corruption and illegal transactions with evil-minded businessmen.

The securities scam has not ended; only a chapter related to the transactions with MUL has been closed. There are many more chapters, each one more shocking than the other. The new century is likely to witness some startling revelations that would be made by the investigating agencies and judiciary in the context of the 23 cases, which are pending against Mr Mehta. However, we would feel more pleased if the untraced finds are somehow recovered and some parts of the investments are given back to the small and medium investors. As on date, this seems to be a mere Utopian dream. ●

16. INDIAN ECONOMY : THE CHALLENGES AHEAD

Economic Editors' Conference held in New Delhi—Indian economy to grow at the rate of 6.5 per cent (expected growth rate predicted by Mr Yashwant Sinha then finance minister)—Many challenges for Indian economy—Rising population—Excessive borrowings by the government—Slow growth of industrial sector—Negative growth in agriculture—Subsidies on food and petroleum (which are likely to be reduced)—Threat from unstable Pakistan—No political instability in the centre—Markets of Europe, Asia and America have come out of recession—Common man continues to suffer—Our poverty is our only enemy—Be more productive, efficient and growth oriented.

On November 17, 1999, the Economic Editors' Conference was organised in New Delhi. The then Finance Minister, Mr Yashwant Sinha expressed the hope that the economy would grow at the rate of 7-8 percent per annum. He also stated that the overall economic situation was favourable and the macro-economic indicators had indicated a progressive economy in the years to come. Other ministers, Mr Ram Naik (Petroleum and Natural Gas) and Ms Mamta Banerjee then (Railways), also addressed the Conference. Despite a rosy picture presented by the Government, the sailing would not be smooth for Indian economy in the times to come. We have come out of some crises but there are many more, which are hidden in the dark ravines of time. We discussed some important challenges that ought to be met in order for the Indian nation to tread a stable economic path.

The first major issue in the context of our economy is that of the growing population. On January 13, 1999, the population of India stood at 98,98,44,092. It grew to 100 crore in the second half of year 1999. Every year, 17 million people are added to Indian population.

By 2050 AD, our population would touch an all-time high of 162 crore and we would be the most populous nation of the world. The economic prosperity generated by our industrial enterprises, trading houses, exporters and government undertakings has to be divided among a large number of individuals. Naturally, everybody would not be able to get his due as there are more people to feed but productivity levels in all the sectors of the economy are unable to sustain them. Economic instability could also lead to political and social chaos by the year 2010. The government is not making any extra effort to curb the population. Unemployment has risen to record levels during the last ten years and this has created frustration among the youth. The Draft Ninth Five Year Plan proposed the creation of 44.36 crore jobs. If this plan got implemented, Indian youth could be given gainful employment and they would be able to serve various sectors of economy, generating income and prosperity for their families in return.

Further, excessive borrowings by the government have led to a crisis in the fiscal scenario of our economy. In fact, we have been forced to bite more than we could chew. The expenditures of the government have also reached unreasonable limits and the Finance Minister has admitted it during the Economic Editor's Conference. Higher expenditures have to be incurred on food, fertilisers and defence, the former two heads drawing large subsidies. The fiscal deficit in the first six months of the fiscal year 1999-2000 was 6.6 per cent of the annual target. It was 2 per cent more than the fiscal deficit during the corresponding period of 1998-99 fiscal year. The minister declared that non-plan expenditure would be slashed. An amount of Rs 90,000 crore was to be paid as interest during the fiscal year 1999-2000.

Mr Sinha had, however, assured that if austerity measures were taken, the infrastructural development would not suffer. For example, the Surface Transport Ministry has been assured that its funds requirements would be met.

Another vital area of Indian economy is the industrial sector. Industrial growth rate was a meagre 6.2 per cent during 1999-2000. We have been investing a lot in this sector since independence but the output has not been able justify the inputs. Industrial growth is the backbone of our economic prosperity. And it is sad to observe that our industry, despite many achievements, has not delivered concrete results during the past three years. Industrial infrastructure demands huge investments but the expenditures on defence, telecommunications and IT, fertilisers and service-based sectors have forced the government to cut down the allocations in the industrial sector. This, along with dismal export performances during the past three years, has led to poor productivity in all the industries.

The next issue is that of agriculture. India has an agrarian economy. Our agriculture sector ought to grow at the rate of 4.5-5.0 per cent per annum but its growth rate is −2.2 per cent as on date. Kharif crop during 1999 was likely to be 102-103 million tonnes and is not a matter of solace for our agricultural scientists, farmers and the government due to severe draught in Gujarat and Maharashtra and the supercyclone, which recently hit Orissa. If the Rabi crop was not up to the mark, our foodgrain reserves would have to be utilised for meeting the ever-growing demands of the PDS. In that event, the export of some agricultural commodities may have to be restricted or even banned. Foodgrain production during the fiscal year 1999-2000 was expected to be 199.1 million tonnes.

The government has also to give subsidies to petroleum-based industries and fertiliser industries. These subsidies might be reduced in the near future. This would lead to a hike in the prices of LPG, petroleum, diesel, petroleum-based products and foodgrains.

Indian economy also faces threats from our militant neighbour—Pakistan. We have already spent Rs 1,984 crore on the Kargil war and after the hijack of the plane of Indian Airlines, it could be predicted that within three years, we might have to go to the battle front once again. This would cost us dearly in terms of men, ammunition and money. The defence outlay of the budget (1999-2000) had provisions for this factor but if the war escalates (or, if Afghanistan and the militants supported by Mr Osama Bin Laden also enter the fray), then we might have to spend more on the war. This would mean more taxes and the economic prosperity, which is being witnessed since October, 1999, might fade away into oblivion. But fortunatelynow Afghanistan is out of the hands of Taliban and that has changed the situation vastly.

It is pleasing to note that the NDA-led government, under the able leadership of Mr AB Vajpayee, is doing extremely well. We have started the new millennium on a positive and stable note. The stock markets are also showing bullish trends in the wake of formation of a stable government in the centre. Foreign Institutional Investors are now keen to invest in India, which is the need of the hour. A war with Pakistan is not likely to spoil our plans for economic growth.

Further, the markets in Europe, Asia and America have also come out of recession. The Seattle Conference of WTO was a failure but the next conference is likely to take far-reaching decisions in the context of International trade. India has to take pragmatic decisions regarding international trading policies and her stand with respect to labour, environment and agricultural trading. This task is not easy and our representatives have not been able to impress at Seattle. Perhaps, we would be better prepared during the next round of WTO talks.

The process of economic liberalisation continue unabated but a lot more needs to be done. The fruits yielded by embracing a free market system must be enjoyed by the common man as well. Only the MNCs and the corporate sector are the beneficiaries of the free market system. Indian economy is no longer a mixed economy. It is a free market economy with some debris left from the mixed economy, which still rule the roost in many vital economic sector. Disvestments in PSUs are continuing. However, disinvestments could garner Rs. 1,479 crore instead of the target value of Rs. 10,000 crore. Further, National Hydroelectric Power Corporation is being sold off to National Thermal Power Corporation for Rs 4,500 crore.

The woes of a common man are still beyond the gamut of the economic system. And this is a weak point of our economic mechanism; we tried to create the sources for sustenance and prosperity but the same could not be created. Even if they were created, the *hoi polloi* could not make use of them. We remain largely illiterate, backward and poor nation. Nearly 29.9 per cent of Indian people lived below poverty line during 1997-98 and this figure could be 40 per cent after the assessment of fiscal year 1999-2000. UNDP has released the latest World Development Report (1999) and according to the same, India has been ranked 132 among 174 countries according to Human Development Index (HDI) calculations. Indian economy, therefore, faces the formidable task of providing food, clothing, shelter, education, health care and economic security to millions of individuals. Ironically, Indian economy was supposed to be people-oriented but it is not. Now, it has already embraced a free market system and the interests of the common masses might be totally overlooked by the economic planners or politicians. This fear of masses has to be allayed by the policy makers and leaders of the nation.

We have already entered the new century. The era for economic take-off has arrived. Earlier, we planned for a sustainable economy. But now we would have to plan for an ambitious or growth oriented economy. This would mean that we would have to follow the examples of economies of Japan, Taiwan, Singapore and other Oriental nations. Our poverty is our only enemy. If our economic system delivers concrete results, our masses would become strong enough to meet any challenge at home or abroad. For this purpose, we would have to boost exports, generate maximum revenues through direct taxes and cut down unnecessary expenditures on the government enterprises. This era of change requires us to be efficient, productive and growth oriented. Our economic planners, industrial enterprises and business firms would have to take some harsh steps in order to surge ahead on the path to prosperity. And above all, if we remain united as a nation, our economic prosperity is ensured. These challenges would evaporate, provided we are united, committed and meticulous on the national economic front.

17. EXIM POLICY

EXIM policy was declared in May, 1998 for a period up to March 31, 2002—Salient features of the policy discussed—SIL list trimmed—More incentives for trading houses—Flexible licencing—Value limit of free gifts was raised to Rs 25,000—On April 13, 1999, Mr Hegde then minister commerce announced slight changes in EXIM policy declared earlier—Import of some other items liberalised—Export and import figures given—India is eighth in the list of global debtors—Our contribution in world trade could be raised to 2-3 per cent of global trade transactions.

There is a good news for the importers and exporters of India. The recently announced the EXIM Policy declared by the government at the centre, had given a new hope to the international traders of India—

a hope for growth, liberal procedures and a thrust on the export activities.

It is worth mentioning here that the coalition government led by Mr Vajpayee has already declared a comprehensive EXIM Policy till March 31, 2002. The former Commerce Minister, Mr Ramakrishna Hegde, declared this policy in May, 1998. Before we discuss the EXIM Policy for year 1999-2000, let us study the chief characteristics of the policy declared in May, 1998. The chief characteristics of this policy, which would remain valid till March 31, 2002, are as follows :—

(A) The number of items in Restricted and Special Import License (SIL) Lists was cut down to 340; these items were put under the Open General License (OGL) List.

(B) An anti-dumping directorate, termed as "Directorate General of Anti-dumping and Allied Duties" was proposed to be established. The honourable minister had stated that its duty would be to investigate anti-dumping case and subsidy case as well as to recommend anti-dumping duties in those cases, in which, imports were likely to affect the domestic industrial entrepreneurs. This directorate was supposed to have quasi-judicial powers. It would have initiated its investigations only if dumping threatened to inflict serious injury upon the domestic industrial firms.

(C) All the licenses for the Negative List of Imports, the advance licenses approved by the Advance Licensing Committee (ALC) under the aegis of DGFT, the licenses for Export Promotion Capital Goods (EPCGs) and finally, the licenses under the Zero Duty Scheme (approved by the EPCG Committee) were required to be issued by the Licensing Authority.

(D) Flexible licensing was allowed, for allowing changes in the description of the products to be exported, in the case of electronics industries and garments industries.

(E) Provisions were made for setting up Private Bonded Warehouses (PBWs). These would supply and import of items (including those under the Negative List) upon the payment of duties against specific licenses and without payment of duty against Advance Licence. Further, the government had also proposed that private PWBs would be allowed to operate.

(F) The threshold limit for imports under the EPCG Scheme for electronics, textiles, leather, gems and jewellery, sports goods and food processing sectors was brought down from Rs 200 million to Rs 10 million.

(G) The policy aimed at neutralising the basic customs duty on the import contents of the exported products through Duty Entitlement Pass Book (DEPB).

(H) Advance licenses with actual usage condition were permitted and were supposed to be based on Positive Value Addition only. The requirement of Minimum Value Addition of 33 per cent for this category of Advance License was scrapped.

(I) The time limit for filling post export DEPB claim was raised from 90 days to 180 days. The limit of shipping bills that could be filed per application for a post-export DEPB claim had been raised from 10 to 25.

(J) In electronics sector, the threshold limit under the EPCG scheme for software was brought down from Rs 200 million to Rs 1 million.

(K) The depreciation limit for EOUs and EPZs was increased from 70 per cent to 90 per cent over a period of 5 years for electronics goods and over a period of 8 years in respect of other goods.

(L) The Export House, Trading Houses, State Trading Houses and Superstar Trading Houses were given new threshold limits; for export houses, this limit was Rs 125 million on an average FoB value of exports made during the three preceding licencing years.

(M) additional Special Import Licences were granted and were based on incremental export values.

(N) The export of oilseeds such as HPS groundnut, seasame seeds, sunflower seeds and mustard seeds was allowed to be without any quantitative restrictions or licencing requirements. However, these items were supposed to be exported for consumption purposes only. Further, export of oils such as coconut oil, cottonseed oil, coin oil, kardi oil, linseed oil, mustard oil, niger-seed oil, palm oil, palm kernel oil, rape seed oil, rice bean oil, salad oil, sunflower oil, seasame seed oil and soyabean oil have been made free. But export of containers of 5 kgs was made free. The export of oil in bulk containers was restricted.

(O) The value limit of free gift was raised Rs 25,000. Exporters of medicines and pharmaceutical formulations were allowed to import free samples and physician's samples up to a value of 1 per cent of their exports of similar items in the previous licencing year.

On April 13, 1999, Mr RK Hegde, the then Union Commerce Minister, announced a modified EXIM Policy (1999-2000). The policy set an export target of 20 per cent (US$ 75 billion). The government planned an anti-dumping cell, proposed for relaxing bank guarantee norms and decided to simplify licencing procedures. It also assured speedier issue of advance licences as well as liberal import of capital goods, software, garments and electronic goods. The government declared an agro-export policy. Restrictions on the import of 340 items (including fruits, vegetables, CD-ROMs, camcorders, monitors, furniture, paints, toys, wrist watches and toys) were lifted completely. Further, import of some times (including shrimps, onions, medicated soaps, fax paper, safety razors, files and fabrics) was liberalised.

The exports of India in during April December, 1999 was US$ 34.5 billion whereas import figure was US$ 27.4 billion. The rising trade deficit shows a dangerous trend; our exports are not rising at a higher pace but imports are increasing. The exporters utilise the provisions of the EXIM policy in order to import goods, technologies and services but do not make efforts to boost exports.

Further, growth in exports was 12.93 per cent during 1999-2000. As balance of payments position is not in favour of India, she has assumed the status of a major debtor nation of the world. In the list of 15 top debtors, our position is eighth. A big portion of our national budget is spent on the payments of interests on loans. If we wish to be independent, we would have to :

(a) cut down the dependence on loans from financial bodies of the world;
(b) increase exports; and
(c) generate revenues in-house through taxation measures.

During 1998-99 EOUs and EPZz exported goods orth Rs. 16,120 crore. EPZs are located at Kandla, Santa Cruz, Cochin, Chennai, NOIDA, Falta and Vishakapatnam. Private EPZs would be located at Mumbai, Surat, Tirunelveli, Kancheepuram, and Greater NOIDA.

India's stand at WTO is dubious. Mr Murosoli Maran led the Indian delegation at Seattle. The issues discussed at WTO included agriculture, labour and environment. As the Seattle meeting had ended in a stalemate, India has been able to steal time for taking decisions in respect of international trade agreements. But vital decisions cannot be deferred in the next meeting of WTO.

EXIM policy would reflect our commitments to the new international trading norms. This policy needs implementation in letter and spirit. The new government is stable and is required to boost exports of our country in all the vital sectors. Today, the thrust should be on exports, which are on a low ebb. The contribution of India in the global trade is less than 1 per cent. This figure would have to be increased to 2-3 per cent. This is an ambitious target but it could be achieved if our leaders followed the right policies in international trading arena.

18. HOW CAN WE RAISE INDIAN PRODUCTIVITY ?

Indian economy growing at slow rate—Poor productivity levels and inefficiency—PSUs are least productive—Government banks close early—Increase productivity at village, state and national levels—Files must be moved quickly—Eliminate bureaucratic bottlenecks—Search for new markets abroad—Software products, agricultural products, engineering goods, textiles, handicrafts etc could be exported—Train managers and workers in the basic concepts of management, TQM and productivity—Adopt ISO-9000 norms—Accept MBO, JIT—National level efforts needed.

Indian economy is growing at a snail's pace. Our economic growth rate was 5-6 per cent during 1999-2000. Industrial production had increased at the rate of 9.8 per cent during the first seven months of 1996-97. The same figure for the first seven months of 1995-96 was 11.7 per cent, thus indicating a reduction of 1.9 percentage points. The slowdown in industrial production could be attributed to a fall in growth of electricity production, a 10 per cent decline in crude oil production and a slowdown in the growth rate of the mining sector. Add to this, the overall international recession, the depreciated value of Rupee against US Dollar and general industrial slump. The overall economic and industrial scenarious are fraught with uncertainties. There was no government in the centre and the political leaders had been busy in chalking out election strategies during 1999.

The international and national indicators apart, the Indian economic slowdown has been attributed to low levels of productivity in the PSUs, bureaucracy, judicial delays and the complete failure of the institutions. Political chaos, red tapism, corruption and delays lead to lack of productivity or low productivity in the Indian industrial, business and trading sectors. The State and the private sector units must be motivated to work for extra hours (and overtime wages must be paid) so that the productivity levels are raised. The banks are closed at 3.30 PM. Why should the banks not work till 5 PM ? We have examples of foreign banks operating in India and providing services for twenty-four hours. Why Indian banks cannot follow the similar norms ?

Further, most of the government offices are closed for the weekends. Their output during a five-day week is known to everybody. Why should the public sector enterprises not resort to six-day office norm for raising production levels ? The State must consider the long term impacts on economy, which are likely to be positive if such measures were taken.

Productivity is reduced due to men, machine or money. If the man behind the machine is underpaid and insecure, he would work half-heartedly. He would tend to produce lesser than the norm. Similarly, a machine, if overworked and regularly overburdened, would produce lesser output. Finally, money is needed for powering the engines of economy. It is our duty to take care of the vital needs of men, repair the machines regularly or replace them with new ones if they are absolete. We must also give enough of financial inputs into the economic machanisms. These steps would certainly raise productivity.

In order to raise productivity at village, industry, regional and national levels, we must eliminate corruption from the PSUs, municipal corporations, national and regional financial institutions and the government offices. Files must be moved quickly so that projects are cleared for launch and modernisation.

Further, we must locate new markets around the world that could absorb our products and services. We have sound industrial infrastructure, highly skilled technical and managerial manpower, fastest growing core sector industries and above all, excellent relationships with all the nations of the world. We can excel in those products and services for which, we have comparative advantage over other nations. We must also produce and export those products that could be produced indegenously. However, there is no harm in importing good technologies as well provided we are able to export with the help of these technologies. We must concentrate on software exports, heavy engineering, farm outputs, processed food, rice, jute, textiles and apparels, furniture, handicrafts, handlooms, steel products, iron ore, horticulture products, electrical engineering projects, sea-food, railway projects, engineering consultancy and management consultancy. It must be noted that our capabilities should be utilised in a prudent manner so that we are able to have economical production, management and export in only those strong areas. We must not try to export everything under the Sun.

Indian productivity can be enhanced if our workers and managers are trained about latest concepts in management, productivity techniques (engineering) and Total Quality Management (TQM). Currently, ISO 9000 and ISO 14000 systems of certification are in vogue for effecting quality control in all the vital areas of engineering and business. ISO is a new philosophy and is quite effective. It is heartening to note that many Indian firms have been awarded ISO certifications due to strict adherence to the quality control norms.

Education about quality control should be imparted during the educational and training periods. This knowledge would be consolidated when these students of today would be joining industry and business. In Japan, perfection is the only norm to be followed.

And we have seen the Japanese firms ruling the worlds of technology and business due to their strict conformance to quality control norms.

Finally, our students, workers, executives and trainers must be exposed to latest techniques in management leadership, communication, participative management, Management By Objections (MBO) etc are some of the techniques to be adopted. For example, the Japanese have achieved almost 100 per cent efficiency in their operations by adopting Just In Time (JIT) inventory techniques. The soul of this technique is simple—get raw materials, components and spares only at the time of receipt of the order. Make the product and despatch immediately. Keep almost nil or a minimum levels of inventory. Do not stock too much or too low. The JIT technique as well as other Japanese management techniques have helped raise the productivity levels of industries around the world.

We can conclude that Indian productivity could be raised. Our human resource requires extensive training in the areas of quality control, engineering, exports, production norms and above all, human relationships. The nation needs efficient output at all the levels and from all the citizens. Let us start with a dream of a prosperous India and try to raise our efficiency levels. We could realise this coveted dream of economic and industrial prosperity through toil and commitment towards maximum productivity.

19. SMALL SCALE INDUSTRIES

SSIs promoted since Independence—Vital backbone of Indian economy—Total 23.52 lakh SSIs in 1997-98—Total 6.62 unregistered units in 1997-98. Total number of items manufactured was 1,076 but only 60 items contributed towards the 80 per cent production of SSIs—Shortages of power, raw materials, technical staff and managerial staff—Facing many problems on the home front and on the export front. Some solutions suggested—NSIC promoted by the government—It ought to look after the interests of SSIs.

When India attained independence, the industrial scenario was fraught with uncertainties; low productivity, lack of power and fuels and above all, a confusion about the real markets of the products manufactured. Industrial management systems were in the doldrums. The evil shadow of partition had its impact on industry as well.

We struggled during the period from 1947 to 1951. Industrial development was not at the requisite pace. Initially, small industries were established. Later, some medium and large enterprises were also set up. Another problem faced by the industrialists was the shortage of capital. India was a very poor nation during those times. She had attained independence and her economic and industrial policies had to be given concrete shape. There was no assistance of foreign investors. This was a precarious situation for Indian masses.

However, the government showed the path of prosperity to the nation by declaring that Five Year Plans would be the major growth engines of Indian economy. Consequently, the First Five Year Plan was initiated in 1951. The economic mechanisms of the country funnel some objectives to achieve and therefore, there was an euphoria in the industrial sector due to the declaration of the First Five Year Plan. New enterprises were established and industrial development was witnessed by the masses and the leaders of the nation, albeit at a painfully slow pace. The industrial enterprises were established with limited capital. Hence, these were termed as Small Scale Industries (SSIs). After a period of 5-10 years, the SSIs grew to become Medium Scale Industries (MSIs). Some of the MSIs became Large Scale Industries (LSIs). These LSIs did not come into existence in one single year or decade; behind their present forms, is the toil of several hundred thousand people who worked from the time of inception of those enterprises. And we should remember that the LSI of today was a SSI during the post-independence era.

From the aforementioned discussion, we conclude that SSIs could be expanded to make them MSIs or LSIs. The concept of conceiving a LSI and operating it as one was not logical in the context of the economic scenario that prevailed immediately after independence. The entrepreneurs preferred to grow in a steady manner, adding up to the production capacities, capital, market niches and assets slowly but surely. Perhaps, this is an ideal strategy for developing ndustrial infrastructure in a nation like ours.

However, the government did develop MSIs and LSIs from the inception stages. But that had to be done in order to develop a sound industrial infrastructure in the country. Coal, steel, power generation, nuclear energy, railways and defence manufacture could not be handed over to SSIs. Hence, SSIs were allowed to concentrate on those products that were :

(a) required by MSIs;
(b) required by LSIs or their subsidiaries;
(c) required by other SSIs; or
(d) required by the masses or the ultimate customers.

When the government decided, through the Five Year Plans, to concentrate on the core sectors and steady development of infrastructure, the focus areas of SSIs were clearly demarcated. Therefore, SSIs were opened and operated to manufacture textile products, toys, plastic items, bicycle parts, automobile parts, packaged foods, garments, small engineering products (like pumps, motors, valves, seals etc), printing inks, dyes, various types of chemicals, rubber and neoprene parts *etc*. It could be a sole proprietorship, partnership or a private limited firm. Many SSIs are also operated by Hindu Undivided Families (HUFs) under the supervision of the owner (*karta*) of the HUF. To begin with, a SSI could also be a sole proprietorship business. The turnover of the firm and its investments in plant and machinery would decide whether it is to remain as a SSI, in case it decides to grow. If the turnover and the investments in plant and machinery exceed the norms laid down for SSIs, it would become either a MSI or a LSI, depending upon these two factors.

According to the report of SIDBI for SSI (for the fiscal year 1999-2000), the SSIs may grow at the rate of 7.5-8.5 per cent in real terms. The SSI sector has shown higher levels of growth *viz-a-viz* the performances of other industrial sectors. Growth in terms of exports of SSIs is likely to be 4.5-5.0 per cent during the fiscal year 1999-2000. SSIs give employment to lakhs of technical and non-technical personnel. Hence, they contribute effectively towards the solution of the grave crisis of unemployment. The growth in employment would be nearly 4.5 per cent during 1999-2000.

The SSIs are also involved in exports. In value terms, the exports of the SSIs, in 1999-2000, could touch the value of US$ 13.41-13.47 billion. Therefore, SSIs contribute effectively towards the generation of valuable foreign exchange reserves of the country. During 1999-2000, the overall rate of growth of SSIs could be 8.3-8.8 per cent.

The government has extended credit facilities, capital, fuel, power and technologies to the SSI sector during the past 25 years and the results of these efforts have yielded good results.

In 1990-1991, there were 13.78 lakh registered SSI units. The number of registered SSI units rose to 23.52 lakh units in 1997-98 whereas the number of unregistered units rose to 6.62 lakh. Out of 1,076 items, which are dealt with SSIs, only 60 items contributed towards 80 per cent of total production of reserved items in the SSI sector. Many SSIs have developed themselves to become MSIs and some are even LSIs. The credit goes to the hard work of the owners, labour and the technical staff of the SSIs. The growth rate of SSI is more prominent and healthy as compared to the growth rates of MSIs or LSIs. The reason is that the governments in the centre and at the state levels promote these industries so that all the industrial pockets of the nation are developed. The policy-makers of the nation have succeeded in achieving many coveted objectives in the context of the operations of the SSIs.

However, SSIs also face many problems. Some of the problems are as follows :—

(A) SSIs face chronic funds shortage. The government does not extend easy credits in terms of working capital loans or long term loans. The applications of the entrepreneurs are processed after long time periods. This retards the growth rates of the SSIs.

(B) The major financial institutions like IDBI and ICICI are not allowed to invest in SSIs. They enjoy strong financial clout that is a dire need of the SSIs.

(C) Employee turnover is a major problem in the operations of the SSIs.

(D) Many entrepreneurs start SSIs but they lack the technologies, managerial skills and human resources, which are required to operate a successful enterprise. As a result, the SSIs becomes sick. The investments of the government as well as those of the entrepreneurs are wasted as a result.

(E) SSIs also face power shortage, red tape and problems due to strikes, labour unrest and *force majeuré*. These factors do not allow them to generate profits.

(F) The operations of the SSIs are labour intensive. The entrepreneurs do not buy (or are unable to buy) semi-automatic or automatic plants and machinery. This factor reduces their productivity levels.

Some solutions for the improvement of the performance of the SSIs are as follows :—

(A) The government should extend soft loans to the SSIs. The "holiday period," ie, the period during which, the SSI is not required to pay the interest to the financial institution, has to be increased. The working capital limits should also be increased.

(B) The entrepreneurs should operate the SSIs on professional lines.

(C) SSIs would have to be allocated higher quotas of power, coal, fuels and other vital raw materials.

(D) SSIs would have to concentrate more on exports rather than on the domestic markets, if they wish to grow at a faster pace. Import of technologies and machinery would have to be resorted to in order to be competitive and productive.

(E) The sick units must not be allowed to operate as they would consume more capital but would generate low outputs.

(F) The issues of red tape, bureaucratic delays and corruption would have to be handled with a stern hand by the government so that SSIs are able to overcome their functional problems.

For guiding the entrepreneurs of the Small Scale Industries, National Small Industries Corporation (NSIC) has been promoted by the central government. Its objective is to facilitate the growth of SSIs. Its headquarter is located in New Delhi.

We would conclude by stating that SSIs would witness high rates of growth in the new century. These would be a part of the economic backbone of the nation in this century. Industrial development and economic prosperity are closely linked to the formation, sustenance and growth of SSIs in our country.

20. INDIA'S EXTERNAL DEBTS

During early nineties, India's external debts were high—During 1992-1994 period, the debt problem was simplified—We have debt taken loans from IMF, NRI, short term and through long term deposits—Finance Ministry monitoring the debt situation closely—Indian economy also growing—Multilateral borrowings on the rise—Instead of heavy debts, encourage foreign direct investments.

India is a growing economy. She is rich in terms of resources but lacks funds. In order to import new technologies and products, India has to depend upon huge external borrowings. The oil pool is responsible for foreign exchange outflows. Moreover, financial commitments in international trading circles call for funds that cannot be generated within the country. Therefore borrowings from IMF, IDA and other UN organisations as well as rich nations are rightly justified.

During the early nineties, India had to ask for an loan from IMF in order to discharge her foreign debt obligations. Earlier also, there was a serious debt problem in 1991. By the end of September, 1999, India's external debts stood at US$ 98.87 billion or, Rs 4,31,264 crore. The Debt-to-GDP ratio (during 1998-99) was 23.5 per cent.

Table I gives the external debt figures for three fiscal years.

Table-I : India's External Debts
(As at the end of March)

S No	Debt Category	Debts (US$ million)		
		1992	1995	1996
1.	Multi-lateral	23,000	28,542	28,375
2.	Bilateral	15,466	17,444	16,154
3.	External borrowings and Trade Credit	15,705	22,440	19,601
4.	IMF	3,451	4,300	2,374
5.	NRI Deposits	10,083	14,695	14,351
6.	Rupee Debt	10,420	9,624	8,155
7.	Short Term Trade Related Debt (beyond six months and less than one year)	7,070	1,991	2,151
	Total	8,585	99,042	91,161
	Debt stock—GDP Ratio (Percentage)	41.1	33.0	28.9
	Debt Service Ratio (Percentage for fiscal year)	30.2	27.6	26.3

Table I clearly shows that there was a reasonable growth in NRI deposits. Rupee-debt has come down as compared to 1992 figures. Our dependance upon IMF borrowings has reduced. However, multilateral borrowings are on the rise.

These indicators of our debt position reflect considerable improvements over the trends last the few years. Therefore, the ratio of external debt to GDP fell from 41.1 per cent at the end of March 1992 to 36.9 per cent at the end of March, 1996. The Debt Service Ratio declined from 30.2 per cent by end of March, 1992, to 27.5 per cent by the end of March, 1995, and further, to 26.4 per cent by end of March, 1996.

Improvement in debt position can be attributed to two factors. Firstly, the Finance Ministry has been monitoring the debt position closely and has substituted the short term high interest bearing loans with long term or medium term loans, which carry lower rates of interest. The concession of debt obligations in terms of loans in those currencies, which have stable exchange rates, has also tilted the balance in our favour. Secondly, the Indian economy has grown in all its sectors. The GDP growth rate was 5.9 per cent per annum during the beginning of 1999. Further, inflation rate was 4.2 per cent. Despite the economic sanctions, World Bank had made a commitment of US$ 2 billion, including US$ 900 million as IDA concessional lending. The disbursement ratio for India, as calculated by World Bank officials, was 18 per cent; this average for the developing nations was 15 per cent. Further, the absolute value of disbursement rose to US$ 1,395 million during the beginning of 1999, as compared to the figure of previous year that touched US$ 1,440 million.

On April 28, 1999, the governor or RBI, Mr Bimal Jalan, had separate meetings with the President of World Bank the Managing Director of IMF. It was observed by Mr Jalan that Indian economy had done well despite the tantrums faced by it. India was ready with projects worth US$ 3 billion. However, due to economic sanctions (in the wake of Pokhran II), projects worth US$ 1.2 billion were held back on the plea that these did not represent basic human needs. During the fiscal year 2000, India planed for projects worth US$ 3 billion. Out of this outlay, IDA would provide loans worth US$ 900 million. In October, 1999, the USA withdrew most of the economic sanctions. Steady flow of Dollars was expected in the fiscal year 2000-2001.

Table I further specifies that while the aggregate debt stock had increased from US$ 85.3 billion during 1992 to US$ 91.2 billion in 1996, in relative terms, the debt burden was reduced. Therefore, we can conclude that under the impact of economic reforms, considerable progress has been made by the country for bringing external debt problem under control.

The present trend is of Foreign Direct Investments (FDI) in public sector enterprises and private sector firms. Therefore, public and private borrowings have been reduced, which is a good sign. We should get more financial partners for industrial and trade growth and should not ask for debts for developing our economy. The South Korean example is before us. This tiny nation has overcome her external debt problems and now, she has a surging economy. India has also adopted similar approach—Foreign Direct Investments (FDI) with export-led growth and a check on the short term borrowings. However, the Indian industry and international export sectors must perform well in order to eliminate the debt burden completely. Then only, we can build a strong and an independent economy.

We must note the following features of the debt situation in Indian context :—

(A) Economic sanctions have hurt projects of core sectors. Some of the G-7 nations have agreed that loans for investments in power sector should be considered as a basic human need. However, sanctions on power sector did hurt our growth plans.

(B) The current rate of economic growth was not satisfactory. The debt repayment situation could be affected adversely if we spend too much of precious foreign exchange during the fiscal year 1999-2000.

(C) The stock market crashes (in India and worldwide) did have an adverse impact on our economy. This would, in turn, affect our debt repayments.

(D) The rising import of petroleum products would necessitate more external borrowings. Higher export levels would offset this factor in the long run.

21. THE RICH GET RICHER

All men born equal—But rich-poor divide expanding—Exploitation of poor by the rich going on—The rich getting richer—The urban and rural poor suffer equally—Capitalistic system exploits to the maximum extent—Other systems are also harsh on common man—The budgetary allocations of Ninth Plan of Rs 18,59,000 crore was but no benefit for the common man—According to international economic observers poor nations exploited by the rich nations—Resist exploitation—Some solutions suggested.

All men are born equal. But riches and prosperity are still regarded as the exclusive rights of the few. And in the context of our vast nation, this fact is more glaring and disturbing. Although we have developed in all the fields during the last five decades, yet the fruits of progress have not percolated down to the mass level. It seems that something is missing somewhere and our masses are being deprived of their rights due to some national malpractices, which are not easily identifiable.

More than 29.9 per cent of Indian population lives below poverty line. The standards of living have deteriorated despite media hype about our national economic growth. We are now a nation of 1,000 million people. The rural areas are still regarded by the West as the backwaters of human civilisation. The absence of civic amenities in the urban areas, burgeoning population, rising pollution levels and high level of congestion of the urban centres point to the fact that even the urban areas of India have not been able to support a good quality of life. Ason date 28 per cent of India population is living in urban areas. By 2020 AD, this figure would jump up to 40 per cent.

However, troubles for survival bother lower, middle, lower-middle and lowest income strata only. The problems and agonies are glaring for these classes only. The lines in a ration shop are meant for the plebian. The rich man has no problem due to the rising inflation or due to the acute shortages of vital commodities in the markets. The rich men gets richer but the poor man has nothing to do accept to cry over his woes. And ironically, the disparity between the rich and the poor is increasing. The number of cars and the number of diseases in the slum areas of Delhi (or the resultant casualties due to those diseases) are increasing in equal proportions. Karishma Kapoor has clothes but would never wear and the common man longs for basic minimum garments for his growing children but he shall never get the same during his lifetime.

Our political and economic systems are purely capitalistic. The rich man has most of the opportunities for growth and prosperity. But the poor man would be thankful to the Almighty if he is able to arrange square meals for his family at the end of the day. The world is awestruck by our poverty; many Westerners visit India only to find out how we live as the poorest nation on the earth ! Amartya Sen was awarded Nobel Prize for Economics and did India proud. But his theories and revelations emanated from the poverty of India. In other words, we are also respected because of our poverty. What a phenomenon !

The State has tried to bridge the gap between the rich and the poor. We are witnessing the progress of Five Year Plans. The basic objective of planning process has been the alleviation of poverty. But every administration has severe limitations. The chief limitation is the lack of resources. The Ninth Five Year Plan had a budget allocation of Rs 8,59,000 crore for the public sector andRs. 6,83,000 crore have been earmarked for the private sector. However, it is difficult to visualise why this huge sum of money was not able to improve the ever-deteriorating standards of living of sweepers, bus drivers, autorickshaw drivers, mechanics, labourers, farmers and other operative staff employed in industry and business. On the other hand, the people, who employ these workers, are able to earn more every year and their profits keep on soaring. India is a fine example of exploitation of man by man. The masses cannot come out of the vicious circle of poverty and it is a pleasure for the rich to milk them and consolidate their own empires.

The poor and economically weaker nations like India, Bangladesh, Pakistan, Nepal, African nations and other East, European nations have to ask for humanitarian or financial assistances from the rich Western countries or from the UNO. Poor nations have no options; if they are not helped by the rich few, they would be doomed. And it is a fact that economic dependance brings political conformance (mostly negative). Pakistan was a trusted ally of the USA. The recent attacks of the Tomahawk missiles on the Afghan territories accidentally led to one strike in the Pakistani territory as well. So, Pakistans are up in arms against the USA and do not like to align themselves with the west, so is the policy of the Pakistani military Junta.

We have to seek solutions for these problems. Our family, society, nation, environment and the international community are being deeply affected because of the widening gap between the rich and the poor. The communist ideologies were partially successful in bringing parity between the rich and the poor. But eventually, these ideologies were replaced by free market forces. In a free market economy, the chances of exploitation of a poor man by the rich few are very high. We do not state that the free market system should not be allowed to take over. We would like to provide some unique solutions to the growing menace of the rich-poor divide, which are as follows :—

(A) The executives and workers are not paid according to their abilities. Once the abilities have been developed (through a free market system and through educational curricula), the candidates must be assisted by the state governments and the centre so that they could be absorbed by the corporate sector firms as well as the PSUs. If the corporate sector does not pay well to the deserving candidates, it should be punished.

(B) The opportunities in the fields of education as well as avenues for education in the foreign universities should be provided by the State for the lower income groups of the society. If the requisite number of candidates is not available from the lower income levels, then the next higher income group should be selected and the candidates should be selected from that group strictly on the basis of merit.

(C) The issue of poverty is easy to address if Indian youth were not migrating to the cities. They should start their own enterprises in their villages or towns and the state goverments and the central government should extend loans, technical, training, consultancy and infrastructure for the unemployed youth so that they could achieve their goals and economic independence in their home states.

(D) The rich classes should not be allowed to avail of the facilities extended to the poor classes. For example, the rich man can afford to purchase sugar from the free market at the rate of Rs 18 per kg whereas the poor man is able to afford the sugar only from the ration shop in his locality. He cannot purchase sugar at higher price but the rich man would also have a share in the sugar quota distributed by the government through Public Distribution System (PDS). The government has stopped the sale of sugar through PDS after the declaration of budget of 2000-2001 and only those persons, who belong to economically weak strata, would be allowed to buy through PDS shops. In our view, this would hurt the budget of middle income groups. This decision of the government ought to be reviewed.

(E) Vocational training institutes should be set up in the rural areas so that the students are able to become independent immediately after they get vocational training for a period of three years. This would eliminate unemployment and millions of families would be able to improve their standards of living.

(F) The government organisations, which support self-entrepreneurship for the poor masses, should give priority and facilities to the poor classes first. Their standards of production and marketing must be monitored and enhanced. They should persuade these classes to adopt TQM and ISO in all the areas of their operations. It is not expected that these masses or classes would yield outputs of high quality in one day. However, they should be given a period of three years (from the date of placement of order by the agency) to improve their production norms and product quality. If these entrepreneurs or individuals are not able to come up to the mark of the concerned agency (or financial institution), then all the technical, financial and assistance cooperation should be withdrawn by the concerned agency.

In sum, we can state that the widening hiatus between the rich and the poor could be filled by the efforts of the State. It must extend a helping hand to the poor masses and should provide them with ample opportunities, training and finances. The poor masses must utilise such opportunities and should make the best usage of the offers in hand. Nothing is impossible for the Indian nation. ●

22. BLACK MONEY

Black money is unaccounted for wealth—18-20 per cent of our national income—Generated due to the greed of man—The Indian psyche is to follow the Western Standards—In India also, the lower Income group tries to emulate the next higher income group—Businessmen resort to black marketing and tax evasion—Bureaucrats and politicians generate black money—Political uncertainties generate black money—PSUs are major sources of black money—VDIS is a good scheme—Channelise black money into national economic stream—Pass strict laws, implement laws but be liberal.

The term "Black Money" refers to various types of unaccounted for money, which could be gained due to tax evasion, graft, smuggling, *Hawala Dealing,* non-payment of taxes and carrying out a business without proper documentation. The black money menace has been dominating the Indian social and economic systems for the three decades. The growth in business operations and an orientation towards the free market system have brought this issue at the top priority in the agenda of our policy makers. It has been estimated that black money, circulated without any scrutiny by the State and without any accountability on the part of the culprit person or firm, could wipe out the debt burdens of the Indian economy and India could emerge as one of the most prosperous nations of the world. The policies of the State do not allow the black money to surface and it gets mingled with the national economic transactions.

The Direct Taxation Enquiry Committee (1970) describes the term "Black Money" as unaccounted for money or concealed income or wealth as well as the money involved in those transactions, which are wholly or partly suppressed. An economy triggered off by black money is mightier than the national budgets of many small nations. The black money economy is also referred to as parallel economy and it works very secretively under the white economy of a nation. India is a major victim of the black money economy because of the strict regulations of the State for generating and distributing wealth.

According to a study sponsored by the National Institute of Public Finance and Policy in 1985, the amount of black money in India would be 18-21 per cent of the national income. Mr AM Khusro, a former member of the Planning Commission, explains three sources of black money :—

(A) Illegal income earnings from the sale of commodities at the prices beyond the government-controlled prices.

(B) Gains from the sale of goods in a volume that exceeds the government quotas and regulations with respect to those goods.

(C) Tax evasion measures resorted to by individuals and firms.

Further, the Direct Taxes Enquiry Committee (1977) attributed the generation and proliferation of black money in Indian economy to corrupt business practices and to the complete deterioration in moral standards. Man wants to earn more; this is the centuries-old tendency of all the human beings. Black money is the result of man's greed. This is the age of fast food, fast money and materialism. Everybody wants to be rich and prosperous. In the Western countries, there is no hankering for money as the individuals have ample opportunities for earning the same. In India, the opportunities are quite fewer in number. Moreover, the available opportunities are not very remunerative. The taxation structure does not favour the businessman and the corporate sector. Hence, the businessman tries to earn the extra money without informing the State about it. It is easy to satisfy human needs but there is no method of satisfying human greed. It is an irony that black money is generated and circulated by those people and firms, which are much more prosperous than the masses. A poor man cannot generate black money as his activities and financial standing are transparent to the State.

The standards of living in the Western countries are very high. The rich Indian classes as well as the middle income niches try to emulate the Western materialistic patterns. These include fast cars, cosmetics, air travel, costly and gaudy celebrations, expensive weekends, discotheque luxurious travels, liquour and costly foods. The only route for acquiring these luxuries is black money. Further, in Indian context also, the individuals try to emulate the living standards of the people who are in an economic bracket, which is immediately above their own economic bracket. They sincerely feel that jumping up and moving up the economic ladder would bring solace and prosperity. Similarly, the lower income groups chase wild dreams of prosperity and buy colour televisions, cable connections, electronic gadgets and second-hand cars. Every class of people is therefore, trying to jump on to the economic and materialistic standards of the class immediately above it. The routine jobs and business efforts are not able to fetch enough of money in order to realise these dreams. Hence, unaccounted for wealth is sought to be earned. Every human being nurtures a lust for getting rich through 'extraordinary' means. Hence, it would be appropriate to state that the basic tenets of black money have become deeply embedded in all the strata of Indian society. The individuals from all the income groups try to evade taxes, earn extra money without proper accounting norms and generate extra income by adopting artificial pricing policies.

It is very easy for the businessman to make illegal money. He also knows the *modus-operandi* for protecting his illegal wealth from the Income Tax sleuths and Vigilance Department officials. He chalks out very foolproof methods for obtaining funds from legal or illegal sources. He wants to acquire the maximum amount of money in the shortest possible time frame. Morals and societal aspects of business take a backseat. Therefore, the raids of Income Tax department and other government agencies normally do not unearth unaccounted for income. Add to it, the corruption prevalent at all the levels of bureaucratic system. The culprits go scot-free and continue to earn "Extra Incomes" as usual.

Black money is a universal phenomenon now. It exists in all the strata of society in all the nations. Tax evasion is the most common method of acquiring black money. One should not evade tax liability and must pay his or her taxes in time. Wrong reporting of income, exaggeration of expenses and deductions and payment of a tax amount, which is lower than the amount one is liable to pay, are some of the prevalent malpractices. There are only a few tax deductions under the income tax laws and the individual and the firm must consult a counsel in this connection. During 1978-79, the approximate evasion of income (which evaded income tax) was nearly 12-14 per cent of national income. The tax-evaded income is growing at a faster pace than the growth rate of the national income. The culprits are getting richer at much faster rate than we could imagine. Under the Economic Recovery Act (1981), while the personal income tax was reduced by 25 per cent, the magnitude of tax evasion has not been reduced in any manner. It should be noted that the personal income tax was reduced by 5 per cent in 1981 and by 10 per cent each in 1982 and 1985. Therefore, reduction of income tax is a welcome move but the citizens of the nation must come forward voluntarily for filing income tax returns and for paying their taxes. Voluntary Disclosure of Income Scheme (VDIS) was successful in generating Rs 10,500 crore. The one-out-of-six scheme, promoted by Mr Yashwant Sinha the then Finance Minister, does not seem to be logical. *Kar Vivad* scheme is good and must be implemented with full force. In sum, some of the measures taken by the State are effective whereas others do not motivate the tax payers to pay taxes.

Variation in the payment of amount of income tax is another issue, which leads to the generation of black money. The tax burden involved in running the nation must be borne by the tax payers in proportion to their incomes or wealth levels. There are many loopholes in our taxation system. Some tax payers pay small amount of tax while others pay in relatively higher proportions. Honest tax payers suffer on account of lack of knowledge. The rich and shrewd tax payers are able to learn the loopholes from the income tax specialists who are paid well by them. The ordinary man is not aware of income tax laws and the procedures for saving income tax. These tax inequities would have to be removed in order to collect taxes regularly and according to the actual earnings of the people.

Further, political uncertainties, elections, leniency in dealing with the offenders and corrupt government officials perpetuate the causes which lead to the generation of black money. Further, the government officials, accountants, CAs, businessmen and anti-social elements join hands and devise efficient procedures and prepare "window-dressed" documents for evading taxes. Politicians spend huge amounts of money during election campaigns. According to the rules of the Election Commission, a candidate, for a berth in the Parliament, cannot spend more than Rs 4.5 lakh. However, it is well known that the election expenses are to the tune of Rs 50-75 lakh per candidate. And this is a mere estimate. The actual figures are never disclosed by the political parties. This money is contributed by the parallel economy. The businessmen invest their black money in the elections of the political parties. They spend for their promotion, election campaigns, wining and dining, transportation and even for the horse-trading activities during the process of formation of government in the centre or in the states. When the political party supported by them comes to power, these businessmen encash their investments. The politician, who is now a minister, helps these businessmen get quotas of coal, LPG and petroleum products, jobs for the senior party cadres in the PSUs, orders for contracts and major tenders of the PSUs as well as other non-monetary favours. A businessmen invests money in a political party and is able to reap rich dividends when that party comes to power. The businessmen cannot make donations, which should exceed 5 per cent of their net profits earned over the three preceding financial years. The rules have been drafted to this effect under the revised rules of the Companies Act, Section 293A (1985). The business firms are also required to declare the political party who would receive these donations. But most of the companies fear that if the rival political party would ascend to power, they could face reprisals. Hence, the donations are secret. This business has been going on for the past thirty years in our country. The State, the police and the judiciary are aware of the facts but there are no solutions for this growing menace. The evil nexus between the politician, the bureaucrat and the businessman has broken the confidence of the common man in the rotten system of national governance.

The public sector is also a major source of generation of black money. The government officials are hand-in-gloves with the corporate firms. *Hawala* is the widely known as the name of parallel market for foreign exchange and its turnover is unimaginable. The politicians and ministers award the contracts to those firms who contribute towards their election campaigns, transportation expenses and asset-building. These companies have to look after the interests of the politicians and in return, the politicians award the contracts. Therefore, politics is the biggest business and is next only to business itself.

It is interesting to note that in the prestigious projects (which include huge amounts of money), cost escalation, usage of cheaper or inferior materials and inputs, payment of wages to the labour at the rates, which are lower than the contracted rates and preparation of false accounts are the common practices followed. All these practices benefit the politician who is the legal promoter of the project and the businessman who is the developer and the financier of the project.

The Indian masses are ashamed of scams. There are many examples which are a part of our everyday discussions — *Hawala* scam, Fodder scam, Sugar scam, Urea scam etc. The transactions of Jain brothers with the bureaucrats of the PSUs, for the purpose of securing lucrative contracts for the favoured parties, took place during 1988-91. *Hawala* emerged in the 1950s and 1960s as a consequence of strict control of the foreign exchange markets of the nation. The *Hawala* route has been utilised by the firms for making payments abroad and for paying for the travel expenses of their executives. The investors used this method for paying the money in foreign banks or for purchasing assets in foreign countries.

The free market winds have been blowing in the country since 1991. However, the parallel economy could not be curtailed even after the introduction of economic reforms. *Hawala* transfers are used by the countries for avoiding direct and indirect financial transactions. Indian businessmen also resort to under-invoicing or over-invoicing in the import and export transactions and this is done in a very organised fashion through illegal foreign operators.

The Sugar scam has cost the nation approximately Rs 133 crore. Some private firms have been able to mint money on account of the scam but the nation is the real loser. Further, telecommunication sector has also witnessed a scam and the residential premises of a former telecommunications minister were raided in this context. A huge sum of money was recovered from the residence of the minister. The new industrial policy is oriented towards free market reforms but it has also benefited those who are capable of generating black money in a short span of time. Therefore, we can state that economic liberalisation has taken its own toll.

Black money is a stumbling block in the process of economic reforms. It affects the social, economic, cultural and political systems of the nation. It is big barrier on the road to healthy and quick development of the country. The core sectors are ignored and the luxury goods are traded and produced to the largest extent. The rich get richer but the poor people are unable to afford the products and services for the survival of their families. Tax evasion results in the shrinkage of the tax base. It erodes the progression of tax rates and also undermines equity aspects of taxation. The masses from lower income brackets are God-fearing people and hence, they pay their taxes regularly. However, rich classes avoid taxation. Tax evasion also reduces the income elasticity of income tax. This means that a rise in the national income does not result in the corresponding increase in the tax revenues. This vicious cycle ultimately reflects in terms of the poor economic progress and lower national income for the central and the state governments. It should be noted that economy, business and industry are healthy in our country but their outputs are not generating enough of revenues for the state governments and for the central government because of the circulation of black money. The government is starving due to the lack of funds and the national growth is anything but satisfactory.

The published figures on public expenditure are higher than the actual outlays. The balance of funds is diverted to the bureaucracy and the intermediaries in the form of black money. The welfare programmes lack effectiveness because they lack support of funds. Education and other vital heads of economy are allowed to suffer whereas luxury thrives in those circles, which operate because of black money. The plans are always ambitious but the funds are consumed by the corrupt politicians and bureaucrats. The black money hoarders wield financial and political powers. They remain unscathed and enjoy the luxuries of life. The poor nation suffers. The major national development projects also suffer on account of lack of funds. Economic growth is not up to the mark and poverty amongst the masses increases. An economy, with a parallel operation of black money, is prone to inflation. So, the prices of the essential commodities increase and the poor man suffers as his purchasing power is limited. Rising prices encourage the traders and businessmen to hoard some commodities. They earn a lot in the wake of the rising prices.

The Government of India has adopted measuress for curbing black money. These include :

- (a) appointment of special commissions for seeking ideas on the nature, causes, magnitude and solution of the problem of black money;

(b) steps taken for unearthing black money; and
(c) efforts for the control of black money in future.

The simplification of direct and indirect tax laws, strengthening of tax administration and regulations for curbing illegal economic activities are some of the measures adopted by the government for controlling black money. The State has also resorted to demonetisation, issue of special bearer bonds, income tax raids and acquisition of immovable property. Voluntary Disclosure of Income Scheme (VDIS) has been promoted by the government and it has proved to be highly effective. Under this scheme, the individual can declare 100 per cent of his income (generated as black money) and can retain 70 per cent of it after paying 30 per cent to the government. The government has also reduced the marginal tax rates and tightened the tax administration in the areas of investigation and enforcement. The State is allowing the market forces to operate. This would lead to lower amount of black money, the government officials point out.

The menace of black money has already assumed dangerous proportions. It is surprising to note that even the efforts for liberalisation of the economy (and its subsequent tuning with the major economies of the world) were not able to eliminate the black money generation process. Obviously, the mentalities of the businessman, trader and the individual need drastic transformation. Indian masses must think about the nation and the societal aspects of business in this mad race involving commercialism and materialism.

The State must pass laws and must enforce these laws through Enforcement Directorate, Customs Department, Excise Department, Income Tax Department, VDIS Scheme, Vigilance Department and the Police.

The media campaigns should adopt a moderate and soft attitude towards the tax payers. They should not be forced to pay income taxes but should be morally motivated so that they could realise their responsibilities towards their motherland. The fear of oppression by the State always leads to tax evasion. The free market world calls for tension-free business norms and strict regulations must go. This policy would help the government and it would be able to collect the maximum tax revenues. Further, the income tax slabs for the lower and middle income classes should be liberalised. During 1998-99 fiscal year, the slab for non-taxable income has been put at Rs 50,000. We feel that the same should be Rs 1,00,000. Other slabs should be upgraded proportionately.

Finally, the black money generation process is a result of the starvation, which is spread throughout the length and breadth of the nation in all the strata of the society. The only difference is that of the level. A policemen earns less and tries to earn one hundred Rupees from his 'client.' A corrupt government official earns more but he wants to earn much more and hence, asks for Rupees one thousand from his 'client.' These officials are not at fault. They must be paid good salaries (or opportunities to earn money) so that they do not resort to unfair means for earning money. The basic needs of Indian families are not being met through routine income generation methods. Hence, the Indian psyche gets tilted towards unfair means for earning money. After a few years, the black money becomes a part of their lives. This affects them morally but they cannot get out of this sinful cycle. The State, the society and the free market economy have to be oriented towards a fair, prosperous and liberal economic system (as has been prevalent in the West). We hope that black money menace would be controlled as our economy would embrace the free market system gradually within a period of ten years. The black money menace cannot be completely eliminated but it can be controlled to a great extent. It requires strict legislations, time and moral training of the Indian masses. Above all, the citizens of this nation must understand that the national progress suffers on account of black money. It is the duty of the individual, the State, the income tax authorities and the corporate sector to control this menace for the sake of more pious national objectives.

23. ECONOMIC LIBERALISATION

Indian economy started opening up during the eighties—Other developing economies doing very well—Rajiv Gandhi introduced reforms—Narasimha Rao also continued the reforms—OGL category broadened—Economy looked up—Exports and Imports would rise due to liberalisation—It would also upgrade living standards of Indian masses—Our economy would be blended with global economy—Private Investors, manufacturers and MNCs allowed to play freely but within some broad regulatory norms—

Foreign players could cut deeply into our economy—Our domestic production could be affected—Free market system favours only the rich—Poor could suffer—We could not depend upon foreign aids any longer—Economic liberalization is slow and painful—Now Indian economy growing again after Kargil war and slump.

During the early eighties, a need was felt for giving a respite to the ailing Indian economy. Although our performance in all the industrial and agricultural sectors was good, yet the economy had not developed a thrust for going beyond the take-off stage. Further, the benefits of development had not seeped down to the level of common masses. India was, by and large, a poor nation. Economic progress had been made but that was not sufficient for propelling the engines of growth.

On the other hand, the economics of China, Taiwan, Malaysia, Indonesia and Singapore performed very well. Their exports, per capita production and per capita income rose sharply and now, these nations have already become developed enough for imparting good living standards to their masses. The industrial development is also impressive in the case of these nations.

Therefore, India saw a change in the course of events for good. Rajiv Gandhi came to power in 1989 and decided that India should move towards a free market economy in a phased manner. The economists, industry doyens and international economic fora welcomed the move. The idea was to eliminate the inefficient and non-productive economic system and bring in a new transparent and globally oriented economic system.

Rajiv Gandhi did well on his part. Imports were liberalised. Exports increased on account of a better EXIM policy. Gold imports were liberalised in the nineties and the government decided to open Indian markets for foreign products and technologies. During the prime-ministership of Mr Narasimha Rao, the then Finance Minister, Dr Manmohan Singh, gave further impetus to economic reforms. His budgets were public-oriented and led to increased industrial production as well as healthy agricultural growth.

There were changes in the political scenario at the centre and the states. However, these reforms continued. The GDP showed a growth trend during this period of liberalisation. However, due to political uncertainties and also due to a poor budget from the United Front Government, the slowdown in economic growth was witnessed from 1995 to 1997. The new government, led by Mr Atal Behari Bajpayee, undertook the crucial responsibility of continuing the economic reforms.

The pace of economic liberalisation would also manifest itself in terms of layoffs of inefficient staff of the PSUs. This step would be harsh for an Indian families but it is inevitable. The government has been paying salaries to the redundant staff of the mills of National Textile Corporation for decades. A vast variety of sick mills of NTC would have to be sold off to the corporate sector. Similarly, other inefficient PSUs would either be sold off or would need serious corporate and financial restructuring. Air India, NTC, Power Grid Corporation of India, Shipping Corporation of India and Hotel Corporation of India must be sold off to private sector at the earliest date. Many consumer goods are being produced in India. But due to the rapid pace of economic liberalisation, more firms from abroad would flood the markets with of high quality cheap goods. Indian manufacturers have been feeling the heat in computers, textiles, light machinery, apparels, consumer electronics and other vital consumer goods sectors.

Due to liberalisation of the economy, exports and imports would increase. Hence, the economic growth would be faster. As an example, the USA, Canada, the UK are the leading importers of the world. They are also the leading exporters of the world and also enjoy highest economic and social living standards in the world. Imports should not be a reason for worry. They are necessary for our economic growth and for our social development on a mass scale.

Economic liberalisation would upgrade our living standards. It has done so during the past as well. Indian consumer has a wide ranging choices in televisions, music systems, cars, clothes and textiles, state-of-the-art home appliances, cellular phones and accessories and many more products. This has been made possible due to competition from the foreign players in India. The business operations are being computerised at a very fast face and Internet has already arrived in India We are producing the best machinery, products and services with foreign collaborations. Paperwork in exports is being cut down. Red tape is being reduced. Bureaucracy is assisting in the process of economic development. Indians have always welcomed new technologies and products. Latest techniques in management have been adopted by us. Education in the rural areas has been given a big boost. The emphasis is on vocational education rather than an theoretical and directionless cramming of the books and notes.

The private sector has been allowed to have a free hand in domestic as well in foreign trade. The businessman can plan his operations and markets freely. Licensing system has been liberalised. District Industrial Centres (DICs) are helping the regional industrial enterprises in their efforts for survival and growth. The rural economy is looking up. The rural masses are also enjoying the benefits of liberal telecommunications policy of the government. We can see colour televisions, cable networks and telephones, STDs and ISDs in all the rural areas of the country. Many villages still need electrification. This task would be completed within a decade. Further, the rural masses are enjoying better living standards with the advent of new and cheaper technologies in the Indian economic scene; refrigerators, televisions, CD players, computers, water pumps, cellular phones, cable TV networks, better farm seeds, fertilisers, latest health facilities, medicines, transportation networks *etc* are some of the few blessings bestowed by the liberalised economy upon the rural masses. Urban Indians are also working hard and are enjoying every bit of it. The economic standards have improved. There has been a steep rise in the material assets, property and cash inflows.

We must remain optimistic but should not ignore the dismal features of our economy. Firstly, the multinationals have penetrated deeply into our urban and rural markets. These corporations have good financial muscles and are competent on managerial and technical fronts. These firms have thrown many local companies out of competition. Our masses are hungry for imported technologies in music systems, televisions, cellular phones, telecommunications, fast food, medicines *etc*. The local manufacturers have suffered on this account very heavily as they have lost their own local and regional market niches due to the advent of the MNCs.

Secondly, economic liberalisation has ushered us into a free market system. In such a system, the powerful and rich would be able to compete in the modern times. However, nearly 40 per cent of the population of this nation is below poverty line. They are unable to think in terms of "free market norms." For example, a rickshaw puller would find it very difficult to establish a retail business as we would no longer be able to get a government loan or a grant. He would not get any help from the rich businessman whom he serves. He does not have money and it is needed for earning more money. It is true that he would earn more money as the prices have gone up. But he has to spend more money on food, clothing, shelter, education of children and health of the family. So, he would be drawn into a vicious circle of poverty and would be exploited by the rich. Economic liberalisation may have helped the rich and the neo-rich classes. However, poor people are becoming poorer.

Thirdly, the educational system has become practice oriented or job oriented. This is good for the masses. However, new researches would be avoided by our young students. They would be more keen to develop those skills, which help them make money. Everybody wants to become a part of some money-making mechanism at the earliest. The basic set of knowledge is ignored by most of the students, which is required for technical, economic and cultural upliftment of the nation.

Fourthly, economic liberalisation has forced our national economy to depend more upon ourselves. That would mean that we can borrow to a lesser extent from the financial institutions of the world. That would amount to increasing our GDP and GNP. That would require high economic growth rate. However, our economic growth rate has been 5.9 per cent and that is not sufficient to sustain economic reforms and fuel the engines of our economy. Almost all the fronts of our economy have shown a dismal trend of growth or flat growth rates during 1998-99. These signs are not good for a developing nation like India. We can have foreign aids but these are available at high costs. Our internal production and exports must be improved drastically if we want to match the global economic superpowers.

During July, 1999, some healthy trends were observed in Indian economy. Industrial production was up and stock trading activities staged a comeback. Kargil war came to an end. Elections were round the corner and the economic mood of the corporate world was upbeat. In sum, economic liberalisation is a slow and painful process. Our economy is doing well but it ought to do better in order to sustain itself in the competitive times of tomorrow. Indian citizen can contribute in this pious national effort by working hard, generating worthwhile technical, industrial, managerial or professional outputs, wasting less and producing more. The State and the individual must join hands so that the nation grows as an entity. Free market winds would ultimately be good for our economy. The teething troubles should never deter us from taking a full-fledged course towards a free market system. ●

TECHNOLOGY

24. INDIA AND INTERNET

Total Internet connections in India more than 1.5 million till 2000 AD—More opportunities for Internet users for expanding trade and for sharing global information—VSNL and DoT are sole service agencies—Now private ISPs being given licenses for providing Internet services—This would reduce fees—MTNL entered the fray and offered cheaper Internet connections in Delhi—5,00,000 Internet connections possible for international traders, exporters, software professionals—Operating costs likely to come down—Bright future.

The year 1999 saw the entry of private sector Internet Service Providers (ISPs) in India. Private ISPs, have been allowed to set up Internet gateways. They would be issued licenses for 15 years. No license fee would be charged for first 5 years and Re 1 would be charged per annum for subsequent years. Private ISPs would be allowed to define their own tariffs. This is a healthy step for the development of sound infrastructures in the fields of telecommunications and Information Technology (IT) in particular and for the national economy in general.

This bold step (and many more steps likely to taken in future) would open new vistas for the latest information technologies during the next millennium in this country. Inernet is an intricate web of satellites and optical cable networks. These networks connect millions of computers worldwide. Information is shared in the form of text), data, pictures, graphics and voice between the computer systems through this latest technology. Internet is an information super-highway, which would be used by people from all walks of life. Its applications would include Internet surfing, database access, information about cities and their vital services, education, business communication and entertainment.

In India, the number of Internet connections was 0.8 million by the end of 1999. This figure crossed the value of 1.5 million by the end of 2000 AD. This includes dial-ups and leased connections.

Furhter, there are 21.59 million telephone lines operating in India. At present, there are three types of Internet accounts for which, prices vary from Rs 2,250 per annum to Rs 10,000 per annum.

Videsh Sanchar Nigam Ltd (VSNL) was the sole provider of Internet services in India. However, the government has done well by ending its monopoly. DoT would also be sidelined in favour of the private ISPs. The revenue structure has been modified for Indian businessmen, students and scholars. Internet Services Providers (ISPs) would be able to further rationalise the fee structure. It is worth noting that the rate for Internet connection in the West is only US $15-20 per month. E-mail, voice mail, Internet telephony and E-com are very popular in Canada, the USA and the UK.

Most of the hardware vendors are modifying their computer configurations for making them more Internet-friendly. In 1996 alone, the market was flooded with many web servers. Most popular applications of Internet in India include web browsing, E-mail and File Transmission Protocol (FTP). The credit for this would be attributed to a growth in the number of PCs, networking (LAN and WAN) and Electronic Commerce (E-com). Table I shows the trends of Internet connections in India.

TABLE I: Projected Internet Connections in India

S. No.	Year	Internet Connections (million)
1.	1997	0.2
2.	1998	0.45
3.	1999	0.8
4.	2000	1.5
5.	2001	3.5
6.	2002	8.0

Internet revolution has taken the Indian businesses and industries by storm. Internet browsing and its constituent World Wide Web have been beneficial for Indian Industries for marketing their products and services. Electronic mail is the single biggest advantage of such a facility.

Further, Indian businessmen have been able to generate brand awareness of their products and are able to seek partners (financial and technical) in a shorter time span.

With the liberalisation of the economy and with the emerging business and economic opportunities, the government has been considering the creation of a national information backbone, which would be used for national information infrastructure and for the promotion of Internet services. DoT and VSNL have given away the business of Internet operations to the ISP on a platter.

India must get out of the agricultural age and must jump on to information technology bandwagon. The possibilities on Internet are endless. For example, it would be possible to have voice transmission via Internet in near future. All the major national streams—defence, industry, software development and exports, international trading, bilateral agreements, information exchange and information needs for daily usage—would benefit from this latest technological marvel.

Today, there is a lack of a good data transmission networks in India. DoT would have to increase the capacity in intra-state transmission networks. Private operators are likely to provide good quality networks as quality would decide their competence and hence, their market niches. VSNL has provided local dial-up services to the Internet surfers within a radius of 100 km. The telephone lines would be made local for this radial distance in each district of the country. This would cut down the operational costs of Internet.

According to a survey, there is likely to be a demand of 5,00,000 Internet connections in the four metropolises. The problem is of the supply and not of the demand. High operating cost could be another factor, which is dissuading some of the prospective customers from hooking on to Internet. It is just possible that they might be waiting for reduced Internet costs. They need not wait for a longer period of time.

By 2003, number of Internet users in Asia would rise to 64 million. We have potential in software exports as we have the second largest English-speaking manpower in the world. However, Internet users are very few. On the other hand, there are 40 million Internet connections worldwide and eighty per cent of the business is being carried out through Internet.

Our software exporters would also witness growth trends and they would demand full-blown Internet services. International trading and E-com would also depend upon Internet connectivities. The prices of micro-computers are falling everyday thanks to the latest budget (2000-2001). India must cash on this opportunity and use this new gift of information technology for the benefit of her citizens.

Currently, the most serious application of Internet is in the area of E-mail. E-mail services are very cheap and are used by businessmen and individuals worldwide for information transfer. The next major usage is in the area of sale of Electronic Commerce (E-Com) which would generate a business of US $32 billion in Asia by 2004. This service involves the speedy transfer of business and accounting information worldwide. Other services provided by Internet include cinema, web page design, latest happenings around the world, city guides, education, database browsing and entertainment.

Unfortunately, there are some thorns attached to this technology. Operating costs are still high as modem connection is required (which would transfer information through a telephone connection). Further, information available on most of the websites is garbage. Finally, children or youngsters use Internet for access to obscene information and cheap entertainment. The usage of Internet for business and data transfer is not being done in India. However, it is being hoped that India would be able to utilise Internet to the maximum extent within three years and utilise its potential for making her mark in this age of information technology.

25. IS COMPUTERISATION NECESSARY ?

Computers are technological marvels—India is a growing country—Growth not satisfactory—Other countries growing at much faster rates due to computerization—Computers make us efficient—We can do more productive work—Computerisation in all sectors of economy—It does not make people redundant—just for growing countries like India—Would raise living standards—Internet would be common in the times to come—Computers playing vital roles in telecommunications, education, Internet, technology and information exchange—India must computerise Her economy and technology so that she remains connected to the world.

Computers have been dominating the technology scenario since the seventies. This wonderful machine has not only won over the hearts of billions, but also it has entered all walks of our lives. The latest trends in computerisation include Internet, Pentium-based systems and Artificial Intelligence. A computer could not be defeated by man in a game of chess. And the irony is that the computer is a product of human brain itself.

Indian economy has grown at a sluggish pace for the past five decades. However, the second half of the fiscal year 1999-2000 has witnessed economic boom and improved industrial performance. The GNP and exports figures are not very rosy *viz-a-viz* our Asian neighbours during the recent past. For example, Taiwan, Indonesia, Malaysia and Singapore are known as "Swift Economies," which have catapulted them on to international business platforms. And let us not forget "the land of rising Sun," which has risen from the ashes of the Third World War to become the number one economic superpower of the globe.

And precisely, how was that made possible ? The plain answer is—computers are a part of these economies and control the productivity and commercial functions in close unison with the international economic powers. And therefore, they prosper at very fast rates.

At present, a computer system with a CPU speed of 500 MHz, a CD-ROM Drive (48X), a hard disk drive of 10.3 GB, multimedia (with speakers), large-size colour monitor, colour printer, Internet connectivity and an array of useful software packages would be available for a price of Rs 30,000-45,000. The programmes (software) could be loaded in the computer depending upon the requirements of the user. Computer are the most essential building blocks of Information Technology (IT). IT would be the growing field of the world during the next decade. Obviously, computers would play a vital role for its sustenance and growth.

We cannot imagine any area in which computerisation has not been done; business, banking, electronic publishing, engineering design, international communication through E-mail, creative designing, fashion designing, Internet surfing, web page designing, electronic commerce*etc* are some vital fields, which have witnessed the extensive usage of computers.

One must raise a valid question—would computerisation make people redundent ? The answer is no. And the reason is simple—a man, who was doing the job of a clerk, would now execute more productive assignments. So, he would contribute more towards his firm, society or nation. And in this effort, he would always be accompanied by his friend—the computer. Computerisation is creating more jobs for DTP specialists, programmers and hardware professionals. It is a sound business proposal for new entrepreneurs, a sea of knowledge for the ever inquisitive student and a child's delight as he can play all types of games on it. In sum, it is a necessity and would improve knowledge levels, productivity, earnings and living standards of all the classes of our society.

Japan, the USA, the UK, Malaysia, Indonesia, Singapore, Taiwan, Germany and France have used computers extensively in the fields of automobiles, automation, business transactions, health management, education and communication. These are the economic superpowers of the world. If India wants to emulate them on economic, technological and social fronts, complete computerisation and linking of Indian economy and industries with international information superhighway is a must. This is possible only with the help of computers and Internet networks.

Computers save our time. They make us more efficient and complete repetitive tasks in small time intervals. Computer programmers from India are the best known programmers in the world. Computer programming has vital applications in Internet website design, telecommunications, engineering design and Computer Integrated Manufacturing (CIM). If routine jobs are handled by computers, executives and operatives are able to concentrate on more productive and result-oriented tasks. Creativity and thinking are beyond the limits of computers, though major breakthrough has already been achieved in the field of Artificial Intelligence (AI).

Computerisation is essential in Indian context as telecommunication and satellite imagery are based on computers. Life in urban cities cannot be imagined without telephone, E-mail, fax, Internet connectivity and cellular phones. Most of these services demand the usage of computer for operation and maintenance. Therefore, computerisation is necessary in urban areas.

In rural areas as well, computerisation can play a vital role in crop development, seed research, crop disease management, rural employment, software development for rural sector industries and rural education. Rural telecommunication scanario has been revolutionised by computers. Now, we can make an ISD or a STD call from all the remote corners of India, thanks to telecommunications revolution, which is essentially coupled with computer operations.

Education is a vital sector in which, computers could play a vital role. National Literacy Mission and Vidya Vahini Scheme (involving India's latest satellite—INSAT-3B) are examples from the educational field. The state governments and the central government are giving special emphasis on computerised education and Internet. Internet operations have been opened for the private Internet Services Providers (ISPs). Further, all types of accounting, commercial, technical and classified information have been stored in the computers. Hence, computers have become indispensable tools during the present century.

In sum, we can state that India must computerise her economic, meteorological, educational and technological operations for succeeding in the new millennium. The world is a global village now and India can keep pace with the world through computerisation only. This technology would benefit her on economic, technological and social fronts. The present millennium truly belongs to computers ! ●

26. ERP

Successful organisations manage resources efficiently—Types of resources described—ERP is the short form of Enterprise Resource Planning—A managerial concept has been integrated in the software and implemented—ERP is effective but new—Functional areas include Production, Works, HRD, Finance, Sales and Marketing—SAP AG Baan and IBM have developed ERP software—Indian firms also in the fray—Costs are high but benefits are tangible—ERP likely to dominate corporate operations in future.

Information technology and computers have entered the modern business organisation for making it more effective, result oriented and productive. One of the techniques, which use computers for improving the functions of business organisations, is Enterprise Resource Planning (ERP). This technique has been adopted by many a firm around the world and is likely to be adopted by many more business firms in the present millennium.

The successful operation of an organisation depends upon its resources and the manner in which, these resources are managed. The resources of an organisation are as follows :—

(A) Human Resource.
(B) Fixed Assets (land, building, tools etc).
(C) Liquid Assets (Money).
(D) Investments (in the form of loans granted and interests earned).
(E) Methods (the techniques for running the plants and guiding the personnel).
(F) Organisational Structure.
(G) Materials (raw materials, work-in-process goods, semi-finished goods and finished products).
(H) Machinery (the technology-dominated plants and equipment that produce goods or services).
(I) Goodwill of the firm in the domestic, regional and national markets; for the MNCs, the goodwill in international markets is the most vital resource.

These resources have to be managed by the organisation in order to generate profits. However, it is easier said than done. If a commercial enterprise has to succeed, it has to consider three vital factors—the Enterprise (E), the Resources (R) and the Planning of these resources (P). If we combine these three separate components to generate a synergistic effect, we arrive at ERP. The basic gist of ERP is the concept of efficient management of the resources of a firm so that overall costs are minimised while the output is enhanced and is of high quality.

It must be noted that efficient management techniques for resource planning do exist in modern organisations, belonging to the business strata or to non-business strata. ERP as a concept has been integrated with Information Technology (IT) and the managers have been given a "complete software package" so that all the figures and data are available under one roof. For this purpose, software has been developed on computers by experts and the firms have been given efficient computers to manage their operations through ERP software. It must be noted that ERP software is machine-specific, which means that special computer systems are required to operate this specialised set of computer programs. Ordinary PCs are not able to operate this software.

The history of ERP is quite interesting. Like all other components of IT, ERP was also developed in North America. A university in that part of the world had an operating budget of US$ 562 million. It was supporting 52,000 students and had 11,000 faculty members. It wanted to operate efficiently and therefore, needed an integrated software that could help it achieve its coveted goals. To start with, a financial accounting module (which included accounts payable, purchase, assets and funds management) and a human resource module were developed for the university. For achieving maximum operational efficiency in these two key areas, RS 6000 SP solution, developed by IBM Corporation was selected. The computer, on which, the solution (software) was loaded, had multiple-CPU architecture. The university ordered five nodes cooperating terminals) but planned for buying eight more nodes at a later stage. Thus the ERP system merged with IT techniques and methodologies (in the form of a computer software). This ripple became a wave and more firms in the USA adopted ERP system for more productivity, efficiency and control.

ERP is quite new in India. It began to make a foothold in India during the early nineties. Naturally, a new concept takes some time before it is given the level of recognition it deserves. ERP has now come of age in India and large multinationals and Indian corporate houses have adopted ERP, albeit with some variations. It has a bright future in India due to the power of exhaustive control that it could have over the entire gamut of organisational evolution, sustenance and growth.

The key functional areas of ERP are as follows :—

(A) **Production**—The manufacturing operations of a firm could be planned and controlled through comprehensive ERP packages. Production targets, sales forecasting and quality control have been integrated in ERP solutions. Most of the production units use semi-automatic techniques or fully automatic processes. CAD and CAM packages are used for designing and modifying the products, processes and components. Further, testing, fault location, maintenance schedules and breakdown maintenance are also automatic and highly efficient in ERP parlance.

(B) **Works**—In the production units, PPC at the shop-floor, product design, component design, machinery design, plant layout, purchase, inventory control, vendor development, preventive maintenance routine maintenance, life cycle support to equipment and above all, ISO and other TQM systems are of vital significance. ERP takes due care of these components. Works are a part of the production system and hence, both must be viewed, analysed and managed as a dynamic but integrated entity.

(C) **HRD**—The requirements of recruitment training, welfare, placement, fixation of salaries and perks, firing, bonus payments, salary deductions, labour unions and industrial disputes are taken care of in the ERP packages. It goes without saying that human resource is the key resource for managing a firm and ERP plays a significant role in the management of the same.

(D) **Finance**—Financial management involves the arrangement of finances, payroll management, dealings with financial institutions, income tax issues, sales tax matters and the problems related to excise duty. Already, many small packages are available in the market that make the job of the Finance Manager quite easy. ERP also incorporates these functions.

(E) **Sales and Marketing**—This vital area comprises market research, business promotion strategies, customer databases, market plans, sales strategies, management of distribution networks (retailers and wholesalers) customer support and after-sales service. ERP gives due consideration to the vital parameters of the markets and also judges how the marketing function is performing *viz-a-viz* its targets.

The firms that develop the ERP packages are quite sensitive towards the needs of their clients. Hence, they develop only those modules that might be needed initially by their clients. The basic set of modules is developed first and some more modules, depending upon the requirements of the client, are added a few months later. It is better for the ERP vendor to carry out a "technical and business audit" of the client firm. That is because many firms (clients) may be interested only in a package that need not be altered time and again. If the facts and figures about the firm are clear to the ERP programmers, an exhaustive package could be developed within a shorter time frame (and with good efficiency).

The minimum prerequisites of an ERP solution are : architecture of the computer system; selling ability; performance; integration; data warehousing facilities; operating system alternatives; and systems management. This information would help the user and the ERP firm to select suitable hardware, software as well as interaction platforms of the operator and the computer system.

It is interesting to note that ERP is no longer the apple of the eye of the big and multinational firms; small and medium budget firms can also use ERP solutions for integrated business management. According to Price Waterhouse Associates, the small-budget and medium-budget firms of the Indian ERP market account for a share of 35 per cent. Their share was worth Rs 2,250 million in 1997-98. And this figure is likely to touch a new peak in 1999-2000. Any firm can now afford to be efficient, productive, cost-effective and growth oriented, thanks to the variety of ERP solutions.

The leading ERP developers of the world are SAP AG (Germany), Baan (the Netherlands) and IBM (the USA). There are many new software vendors that are entering this vast market every year. For example, Eastern Software Systems has developed an ERP solution, which is being sold under the brand name of *Makess*.

As the proud residents of new millennium, the corporate players and small firms welcome ERP. It is a logical combination of the modern management techniques (related to planning, budgeting and control) and the high-technology tools related to computer software. This is a great combination for the manager, the entrepreneur, the vendor, the customer, the engineer, the buyer and the society. If ERP is implemented in 50 per cent of Indian business and non-business organisations, our productivity could jump to unimaginable heights. As on date, our commercial and industrial enterprises long for ERP solutions.

27. WHAT TO IMPORT : TECHNOLOGIES OR PRODUCTS ?

India is a growing nation—Indian economy at nascent stage of development—We import technology as well as products—Products raise living standards—Technology is vital for infrastructural development—Imports of products would lead to a decline in imports of services—We need imports of services also as future is services-oriented—If technologies are imported, our infrastructure would be sound—But living standards would not improve immediately—New technologies would lead to more production—Pay-offs are received after 10-15 years in technology imports—Guidelines for imports—Import 40 per cent products and 60 per cent technologies.

India is a growing nation of more than 1 billion million people. Her requirements for survival and growth are typical. We followed a very selective and conservative economic policy during the formative years of Indian economy. However, since the beginning of the nineties, free market forces have been allowed to play for ensuring balanced development on the industrial and economic fronts.

Indian economy is in a nascent stage. It is not as mature as Japanese, European or American economies are. Hence, we need imports of technologies more often than other developed nations do. We also import products, which are basically raw materials, finished and semi-finished components, spare parts, chemicals, accessories and electronic goods in Complete Knocked Down (CKD) or Semi Knocked Down (SKD) conditions.

For growth on a long term basis, imports of technologies are essential. For growth on a short term basis, products have to be imported. Products raise the living standards as well. As Indian economy and industry are growing, new products and technologies need to be imported. For example, India is a major importer of petroleum products, electronic goods and parts, gold, vital chemicals, fertilisers capital equipment, computer parts, processing machinery and medical equipment. Similarly, India has also been importing technologies for power generation, rail and road construction, civil aviation, mining, nuclear power generation and utilisation and other infrastructure related projects. The question now arises—what should we import ? Whether we should import technologies or we should import products in finished and semi-finished stages ? Let us explore.

If we import only the products, we would be the biggest consumers of foreign goods on account of our burgeoning population. We would produce more (in terms of agricultural, industrial and service related outputs) in order to import these products. Our living standards would improve. Imports would increase, Gross Domestic Product (GDP) would also increase as imports would necessitate the generation of additional resources. So, economy would certainly grow. For example, petroleum products are imported by us and we import them only after we generate enough of resources so that we could pay in terms of US Dollars. That would automatically mean that our exports would also grow.

However, there would be no investment in infrastructure development. Construction, roads, communications, railways, steel, coal, power and fertilisers would be ignored. New technologies for generation of better products or services in these core areas would not be developed. There would be no generation of additional jobs, which should be an essential ingredient of our economy. People must be absorbed in productive operations. There must be jobs for our masses—from workers to managers. But if we import products only, we would not be able to achieve the low or nil unemployment levels, which would harm our economic growth. This could lead to large scale industrial unrest. The consumers of products would work hard to earn extra money (so that they could buy those products). However, the basic engines of economy would not generate opportunities for jobs, business or entrepreneurship. Hence, in the long run, they would not be able to buy imported goods.

Imports of product import would lead to a decline in imports of services. The import of services includes industrial consultancy and management consultancy. As this is not related to imports of products, nobody would buy these vital services from abroad. As a result, we would be deprived of the latest developments in computers, Internet, electronics, management consultancy, human re-engineering, telecommunications, farming, plant breeding, seed technologies, factory automation, heavy electricals, mining and other vital fields. India would lag behind other developing nations in these areas. Our services sectors would also suffer because services are always supported by latest technologies, which are generally imported.

Now, let us take a look at the other side of the coin as well. If we import only the technologies, we would develop the basic infrastructure to arrive at the self-reliance stage. We would be able to develop new and indigenous technologies on our own after we have imported latest technologies for power generation, defence, mining, shipping, metal extraction, chemical plants, fertilisers and telecommunications. Indians can tune themselves and their plant operations according to all the types of imported technologies for their local needs. The example can be cited of PARAM, the first fully operational supercomputer built by Centre for Development of Advance Computing (CDAC). We can create records in economic development, industrial production, software development and exports, manufacturing and allied areas provided that we are fully conversant with the latest technologies from the West. Another example could be cited in the context of Indian software programmers. The computer was developed in the USA and was adopted by Indians. Now, Indians comprise the largest technical manpower pool in the USA for on-shore and off-shore software development projects. This proves our versatile abilities to excel in new technologies.

Import of new techniques would lead to more production. This would, in turn, lead to more jobs and a rise in the GDP. Hence, there would be a rise in the productivity of core sectors, secondary industrial sectors and services sectors. There would be a boom in Indian economy. Exports would grow, which would make up for the expenses being incurred by increased imports (for import of technologies).

But there are some strings attached to the import of technologies. We have to spend first and the payoffs would come later. In case of imports of products, a single act of import would automatically trigger off a chain reaction in the economy. But industrial infrastructure would take years to develop. The import of technologies would not have a visible impact on the economy. True, it would pay us later. But the Indian populace needs products as well. Living standards would have to be raised. Vital life-saving drugs must be imported. Computers and other electronic components must be purchased within specific time frames. Imports of products cannot be stopped as Indian economy would not start producing these products within a short time span. Our indigenous manufacturing facilities would lead to the development of industry and economy. But our industry would not be able to produce good quality products (which are at par with imported ones) in just one go.

The solution has to be sought in terms of a balance between the two imports. The two basic guidelines in this context are as follows :—

(A) We have to import those products, which cannot be produced at home (for example, petroleum, vital electronic components *etc* cannot be manufactured for sustaining the nation of more than billion people). The national exchequer has to bear the burden of these imports. These products do not require imports but adoption of technologies is free of cost or cheap by all standards.

(B) We must try to indigenise the production of all other products, which could be manufactured at home (for example, steel, vital medicines, computers, telecommunications equipment, agricultural equipment *etc* are being manufactured successfully and latest norms for their production—like ISO and TQM—are being followed in the manufacture of these items). These products could be manufactured in India. In order to produce the products of best quality, we can import latest technologies from abroad. The basic infrastructures would either have to be built or upgraded. Import of technologies would also be a burden on our national exchequer. However, we would learn the art of making good products with gradual exposure to latest technologies.

Therefore, the action plan could be summarised as follows :—

(1) Import those products, which cannot be produced or manufactured economically in India.

(2) Manufacture those products and technologies, which are vital for :

(*a*) infrastructure development; and

(*b*) for raising the standards of living of the masses.

Both these categories have to be given a certain ratio. Let us give it a ratio of 40 : 60 (products : technologies). We should import lower quantities of products because products do not improve our productivity and are unable to impart latest technologies to our masses and industrial entrepreneurs. They do raise our living standards. The imports of technologies are investments for the future. They build our nation so that she becomes more independent and self-reliant. Our main objective should be a growing and self-sustaining economy without foreign aid and assistance from the international financial institutions. This ratio would be ideal for the achievement of our national objectives and for the attainment of a healthy rate of economic development.

The main issue of economic development must never be ignored at any cost while importing products and technologies. The State as well as the importers must ensure that the imports being made by them are for the benefit of their respective industries. The foreign cash reserves are limited and the worldwide recession has triggered off industrial slowdown and a reduction in exports. Hence, imports of technologies or products must be resorted to after careful discussions and predictions about the future of international trading in the times to come. India cannot remain aloof from the global economy. All the major economies are importing products as well as technologies. The importers of some products are the exporters of others; the same is true for technologies as well. India must tune her process of economic development according to global trends.

28. IS INDIA A SOFTWARE KING ?

Indian software programmers rated as the best in the world—Information technology revolution began during the eighties—Our software development capabilities would depend upon the trade sanctions, introduction of Euro-currency by European Union, slowdown in the major economies of the European Union and withdrawal of GSP by the European Union—Exports of software, hardware and electronic goods registered a growth of 38 per cent during 1997-98. Healthy growth expected in the current fiscal year\—Offshore software development in vogue—But on-shore software development would also continue—WTO would play key role in future—Export target for 1999-2000 (April-October) is Rs 23,615 crore.

Indian manpower is rated as the best in the world. We have achieved many landmarks in the fields of sciences, engineering, management, medicine, nursing, architecture, petrochemicals, textiles, chemicals and international trading. In all the fields of human endeavour, we have set new standards and have also achieved them. With the advent of the era of information technology, we have arrived in a new world, which is a global village in the true sense of the word. For meeting the strict requirements of this technology, computer software is an essential tool. And Indians are proud of their achievements in this vital field of the next millennium. This is another feather in our cap and the world admits it.

The information technology revolution began in India during the early eighties. The government liberalised the economy and tried to tune it with the global economy. This required current information and the absolute necessity of latest telecommunication equipment. Management of information, operation of telecommunication equipment and the total management of business, engineering and trading activities required software. Indians had already showed their technical expertise in other vital areas of engineering, sciences and technology. Our able software programmers took no time in learning the intricacies of software development. And during the current decade, software development and exports reached new pinnacles.

However, since the beginning of this decade, conditions were not very conducive for the growth of software development and export business. The ability of the software industry to develop its targets would depend upon the following factors :—

(A) The American economy has come out of the lean phase. Software imports by the USA would depend upon the behaviour of her economy in 2000-2001.

(B) Introduction of Euro-currency by the European Union.

(C) Growth of industries in India and abroad.

(D) Growth in activities related to E-com.

These factors are likely to affect the export of electronics hardware, computer software and related services. We can assume that computer software is a major foreign exchange earning activity out of these three major export heads. Hence, these factors would affect software exports with far-reaching implications.

If we analyse the technical expertise of our programmers, system analysts and information technology managers, we can proudly state that India is the software king of the world. Recently, the US administration has allowed the maximum number of work visas to be granted to the Indian programmers—a matter of pride for Indians. Our programmers and systems analysts who go to the USA and other Western nations at initial pay packages ranging from US$ 9,000–20,000. But there is another side of the coin as well. We are not exporting according to the talent, resources and the market demands of the software markets. And competition is already cutting into out market niches. Let us analyse this aspect.

Firstly, computer software is required for the telecommunications sector as well. The information technology revolution is currently sweeping the world. We are not developing much of software for this vital sector. The union budget 2002-2003 has provided much relief to the telecommunications industry. This would affect software development and exports in a healthy manner.

Secondly, for major application areas, software development has taken a new course. There is a trend towards off-shore software development *(ie,* the programmer need not go to a foreign country that needs his or her services) and on-shore software development is taking a backseat. This would mean that the programmer would earn in Indian Rupees and not in terms of US Dollars. This is a loss for the programmer and for the country. However, the market trends have changed and we have to accept the new norms.

Thirdly, WTO is likely to become more powerful in the world trade scenario. Its decisions could affect software exports.

Fourthly, Internet operations could enhance the software exports as this new and thrilling invasion from the skies would certainly give competitive advantage to Indian programmers. Internet is a global information technology link, which could send software files to the customer in a matter of minutes. E-mail and E-commerce are most popular tools of Internet. Indian programmers could communicate with their clients and collect vital information regarding software, hardware and information technology through Internet.

Finally, the costs of computer hardware in India must be reduced as individual programmers are still unable to purchase their own computers. As prices of computers have been brought down in the union budget (2000-2001), software programmers can get an access to the latest hardware and software tools. This would boost exports.

The major application areas in software development include the following :—

    (A) Computer Aided Design (CAD) and Computer Integrated Manufacturing (CIM).

(B) Artificial Intelligence (AI) and robotics for factory automation.

(C) 3-D Graphics for multimedia, animation and cinematical effects.

(D) Database Management and Relational Database Management Systems.

(E) Computer Aided Engineering (CAE).

(D) Desk Top Publishing (DTP) and manufacture of CD-ROMs.

(G) Packaged Software development for databases, financial accounting, inventory control and other business applications.

(H) Programming in Visual Basic (VB 6.0) and C++ for specialised applications of the customers.

(I) Programming in HTML, SGML and Java for web page designing and Internet operations.

(J) Programming for operations of Mainframe computers.

(K) Programming for engineering applications and project management.

(M) Software development for telecommunications projects and equipment.

Table I describes the trend of export of computer software.

TABLE I : Computer Software Exports

S.No.	Year	Export (In crore Rs.)	Growth (%)
1	1995-96	2,650	80
2.	1996-97	4,113	55
3.	1997-98	6,800	65
4.	1998-99	17,775	106

If we analyse Table I, the growth trends would give us solace and would also boost the morale of our programmers. However, a lot more needs to be done. These figures are not very rosy *viz-a-viz* the trends in the manufacture and export of software around the world. India has not been able to get the major share of the global software markets.

During April-September, 1999-2000, the government had set a target of exporting software worth Rs 23,615 crore. Computers and beripherals have been made cheaper. Further, India-based employees of software companies would be able to get Stock Dollar option. This scheme would encourage off-shore software development and brain-drain would be curtailed. If these decisions are implemented, then the current budget could prove to be software-friendly. Therefore, India could become a software king by the international trading norms as well. The trends are healthy and our technical manpower would certainty make our nation proud in the times to come. ●

29. THE INFORMATION TECHNOLOGY REVOLUTION

Information technology has changed the lives of the citizens of this planet—Fastest growing field—Indian software exports showing healthy trends—First major growth area is E-mail—Second vital growth area is E-com—Third key growth area is consumer electronics—Fourth vital growth sector includes Internet shops and cafes—Fifth feature involves easy and cheap communication during the next millennium—Mutlimedia, AI, CAD, CIM and CAM would dominate the industrial and commercial sectors—Resource shortages, Industrial recession and the policies of governments could have a negative impact.

The new millennium is witnessing a complete revolution in the history of mankind—the information technology revolution. Although Information Technology (CIT) has already entered the homes, offices and hearts of our global citizens, yet some new feats are likely to be performed by our information technology experts within a period of five years from now.

We know that information technology is the fastest growing field in the world. India has a major stake in this field and our software experts, hardware firms and information technology specialists have been contributing a great deal towards this ever-growing field. For example, the annual revenues of Indian software industry touched the US$ 6 billion mark by the year 2000. During 1995-96, Indian software exports were 16.2 per cent in the global customised software market, which is a great achievement keeping in mind that there was an overall recession in most of the major economies of the world. Therefore, our interest in information technology is natural as Indians have already made their presence felt in this vital field.

Let us now discuss what lies ahead. We are already aware of cellular phones, pagers, LAN/WAN networks, thrilling games, Internet and finally, high-quality software for applications related to engineering, sciences and business. However, information technology experts are aiming even further. Let us have a look at the future.

The first major area of IT in the next few years to come would be Electronic Mail (briefly termed as E-mail). This is a high speed communication mode of Internet. An E-mail costs less than 0.50 Rupee per page and can be sent to or received from any corner of the world. This unique facility is already operational in the West. In India, it is catching up fast. It is cheap, economical and efficient. All we need is a computer (a Pentium computer with 32 MB RAM and a CPU of speed of MHz 300 would be good enough), E-mail account, a telephone with local dial-up facilities and a modem card. E-mail would be the medium of communication for the future. It would eliminate the need of postage, courier and telephonic conversations. Data, text, picture, tables and all types of special information can be transferred via E-mail.

Second most vital area of development would be Electronic Commerce (also called E-com). E-com has already been initiated in Europe and the USA. The concept is simple; we would send an E-mail to the nearest grocery shop for our daily grocery needs. The information would be sent to the grocery shop through Internet and the grocery would be delivered at our doorsteps. The concept of E-com goes even beyond this. Corporate firms would float their tenders and projects through Internet. The vendors, management consultants, engineering consultants and other business associates would discuss the project on-line through Internet. Information related to costing, calculations, engineering details and prices would also be shared on-line. The orders would be placed on-line and the executions would also be through Internet. The process of information transfer would involve engineering information and all types of text, graphics, tables and figures. The concept of E-com is picking up in Indian industry as well.

Information technology would make its presence felt in consumer electronics as well. In fact, it has already created new concepts at home and in the office. Examples could be cited of cellular phone trunking systems, computer monitors with facilities of television, digital monitors, Magneto Optic Drives (MO drives), Digital Video Disks (DVDs) for video applications, STD calls at the rate of Rs 3 per minute, high definition stereo systems and a host of facilities for the telephone users. These services have not been provided in India with complete efficiency or in all the parts of the country. How-ever, it is hoped that within two years, these new gadgets of information technology would storm the markets of urban and rural India.

Another significant development envisaged in the field of information technology is the advent of Internet shops in all the parts of urban India. Internet surfers would be delighted to send an E-mail, receive an E-mail, surf through various sites of Internet and collect information required by them. Internet is also full of fun. All the magazines, newspapers, city guides, fashion news, movies and other entertainment shows are available on-line on Internet. So, we should not be surprised if the STD booth in our area would soon have Internet connectivity. In the years to come, people would surf through Internet for education, information, business and leisure.

Further, the new millennium would find people communicating with great ease. The cellular communication modes would become very cheap. The price of the cellular phone has already come down, thanks to Union Budget (200-2001). MTNL had offered cellular phone services at extremely low rates. A new technology has also been developed, which would enable our telephone to be used as a cellular phone. A base set would be connected to the telephone line at our home or in our office. We would carry an instrument like the cellular phone with us. We can communicate with our office or home in which, the base set would be installed and there would be no charges payable. The base set would also be able to communicate with the mobile set. Further, if we want to make a call (while we are on the move), we would be able to do so through our telephone (or base set). But the range of this phone would be limited to 25-30 kms. Now there are global mobile.

Further, another extension of the technology of mobile communication described earlier would be quite thrilling. This is a combination of radio mobile trunking system and a cellular phone. A base set installed at the office or our residence where the consumer has been allotted the telephone connection. The consumer can have any number of mobile sets which would always be linked to the base set. The mobile sets, would be able to communicate with the base set at nil cost. Further, the base set would also be able to communicate with them. And what is more, the mobile sets would also be able to communicate each other. They would be able to use a single phone connection (connected to their base set) for making mobile phone calls. The entire system would be efficient but would remain limited to a distance of 15-25 kms only. Their range is likely to be increased after the researches in the field yield more concrete results.

Satellite phones would be another feather in the cap of IT professionals during this millennium. We would have satellite phones for talking to any person across the globe or sending a fax or E-mail to him. Satellite phones are not popular in India. But going by the current trends in IT, we could soon witness major growth of IT in India. Cost is the basic inhibiting factor; when the costs would come down, the satellite phones would also be sold like hot cakes.

Information technology would usher the modern man in the era of a paperless office. All the offices and homes would be connected through LAN/WAN networks and Internet. Internet connectivity would also be common by the beginning of new century. Information would be collected, analysed, tabulated, presented and transferred electronically and through cordless modes. The real emphasis would then, be on performance and not on paperwork.

Other vital growth areas of IT would include multimedia, animation, Internet, website development, Computer Aided Engineering, Computer Aided Design, Computer Integrated Manufacturing, Artificial Intelligence, Factory Automation and new and efficient facilities in telecommunications. The trends are healthy and are likely to consolidate in the Indian subcontinent. However, resource shortage, industrial recession, policies of the government and above all, global IT trends could adversely affect the growth of the IT products and services in India. Let us hope that only healthy trends spill over into this millennium.

30. NON-CONVENTIONAL ENERGY SOURCES

In the new millennium, dependence upon the conventional energy sources would have to be reduced—Coal reserves in India would last for 200 years—Fossil fuels would last for 150 years—Seven atomic power plants generating more than 2,000 MW of power—Solar energy potential in India is 20 MW per square km—Wind energy can be tapped in wind farms—India has the largest wind farm in Asia with power generation capacity of 28 MW—Gasohid could be prepared from sugarcane juice—Cars could be run on gasohal—CNG is also useful, though it is a part of fossil fuels—Potential of biomass energy in India is 17,000 MW—OTEC process used to thermal energy from the oceans—Small hydroelectric tap power plants could also generate the much needed power.

In the new millennium, dependence upon conventional energy sources has to be reduced. And in the context of Indian economy, this fact is more subtle. During the second half of 1999, the global population touched a new peak of 6 billion. The population of India touched the 100-crore mark. The energy needs of a nation like ours cannot be met from the conventional energy sources—petroleum, diesel, to coal, kerosine and other fossil fuel reserves. The emphasis would have to be shifted to the non-conventional energy sources as the fossil fuel reserves would not be able to last for more than 200 years.

In India, the coal reserves would last for 150-200 years. Fossil fuels would last for 100-150 years. The hydro-electric projects have long gestation periods, though they would continue to supply power to the nation on a long term basis. Most of the power generation stations of India use coal as the basic fuel. Electricity is required in every field of human endeavour. This precious energy source could be generated through the non-conventional methods. There is a need to generate electric power through the non-conventional methods but unfortunately, Indian planners have not laid much emphasis on this aspect.

The non-conventional energy sources include, nuclear power solar energy, gasohol, CNG, tidal energy, naphtha, biomass energy wind energy and thermal energy from the oceans. Let us discuss them in brief.

In India, nuclear energy is generated by splitting the atoms of the radioactive elements, chiefly Uranium-235 and Plutonium. Thorium is used to produced Uranium-235, which is used directly in a nuclear reactor. By the end of year 2020, India has planned to generate 20,000 MW of nuclear power—7,000 MW through LWR, 2,500 MW through FBR and 10,500 MW through HWR. At present, only 2 per cent of the nuclear power generated in the country comes from the nuclear power plants. We have 78,000 tonnes of natural Uranium and 4,00,000 tonnes of Thorium. A three-stage programme links the fuel cycles of one stage with those of another. We use Pressurised Heavy Water Rectors (PHWRs) for the first stage so that Uranium could be utilised as a fuel. The second stage utilises Fast Breeder Reactors (FBRs) that consume Plutonium. The final stage utilises Heavy Water Reactors (HWRs) that consume Thorium. It must be noted that we have enough of reserves of Thorium that could generate 3,50,000 MW of nuclear power for 300 years. The logical choice, in the nuclear energy parlance, would be to use HWRs that consume Thorium.

India has seven fully operational nuclear power plants. These are : (a) Tarapur Atomic Power station (2×160 MW-BWR); (b) Rajasthan Atomic Power Station (100 MW and 200 MW-PWR); (c) Rawatbhata Atomic Power Station (220 MW-under construction and nearly complete); (d) Narora Atomic Power Station (2×235 MW-PHWR); (e) Madras Atomic Power Station (2×220 MW-PHWR); (f) Kakrapara Atomic Power Station (2×220 MW-PHWR); and (g) Kaiga Atomic Power Station (2×220 MW-PHWR).

In September, 1999, the second unit of Kaiga atomic power plant was made critical and it started generating electric power. Heavy water, an essential ingredient used in nuclear power plants, is being manufactured at Vadodara, Nangal, Thal, Hazira, Managuru, Trombay, Talcher and Tuticorin. Thorium is abundantly available in Kerala, Bihar, Tamil Nadu and Karnataka. Barium rods are used to absorb the extra neutrons in a nuclear reactor; this element is available in the mines of Bihar, Maharashtra, Madhya Pradesh and Rajasthan. The total quantity of energy generated through nuclear fuels in India is slightly more than 2,000 MW; some of the power generating stations are still under construction and would achieve criticality in the near future. It should be noted, however, that the nuclear energy generation potential in India is nearly 20,000 MW on an annual basis. We are utilising only 10 per cent of the total nuclear energy available.

Solar energy is available in India from March to October, every year. These are known as the sunshine months. In the Southern states, solar energy is available even during the months of December to February. The potential of solar energy in India is 20 MW per square km. We have not been able to utilise this source simply because of lack of infrastructure. Solar energy can be for heating water, making stream, heating space, desalination, power generation and water distillation. The most exciting application of solar energy is the photovoltaic cell. These cells absorb the solar rays and yield a DC output. This output could be used for small scale heating purposes, street lights, electronic equipment, TVs, emergency lights *etc*. Solar energy can be tapped only after investing heavily in terms of infrastructure and technological inputs.

Wind energy can be tapped by setting up wind farms. These farms are large blades of metal, which move due to the flow of the wind at high speeds, thus generating mechanical energy as output. In India, wind energy potential is 20,000 MW. Wind energy could be used for pumping water, milling, grinding, power generation and for small cottage industries. The costs of setting up wind farms are high and the source is environment-friendly and sustainable. India has already set up her first wind farm in Gujarat. Its power generation capacity is 28 MW and it is the largest wind farm in Asia.

Gasohol is obtained from the by-product of the sugarcane juice. Sugarcane is processed in a sugar factory and the leftover material is called molasses. Molasses is treated with suitable chemicals to produce alcohol. This alcohol is mixed with other organic compounds to produce power alcohol or gasohol. Gasohol could be used in the modern-day automobiles, albeit with some modifications in their carburettors. In Brazil, almost all the cars are powered by this wonderful fuel. India produces record quantities of sugarcane and there are several hundred sugar mills across the length and breadth of our nation. Gasohol could be used in automobiles, as a heat source, as a fuel for generating electrical energy and as a chemical in the industry. As on date, no new action plans are being designed and implemented in respect of commercial production of this fuel, which promises a lot in terms of its applications as a clean fuel.

Compressed Natural Gas (CNG) is a byproduct of the fossil fuels, which are extracted from the earth. CNG is also a clean fuel, though we ought to treat it as a conventional fuel only. It could be used in buses and cars and for heat generation, power generation and lighting. The potential of CNG as a fuel is unlimited and it is an environment friendly fuel. The government and the state agencies are concentrating on it and our worthy readers must have seen many a vehicle plying on the roads with CNG fuel.

Tidal energy is the energy generated by the movements of tides. There are two types of tides—rising (waxing) and falling (waning). In the waxing tides, the water level of the oceans in the coastal areas rises whereas the same falls when the tides are in the waning period. This difference of the head of water could be utilised for generation of energy. The chief application of tidal power is in the field of electricity generation. The high capital costs deter the private firms from entering this arena. The total tidal power potential in India is 9,000 MW. India has a coastline of 6,100 kms and the tidal power plants could be set up at all those places where the difference between the heads of waxing tides and waning tides is quite high.

Naphtha, like CNG, is also a conventional fuel. However, it was not used till the late eighties of the previous century as a dependable fuel. Now a days, it is being used as a fuel and chemical in industries of India. It has bright prospects as a fuel and the world has large reserves of the same. Indian industry should also concentrate on its effective utilisation as an energy source during the present century.

Biomass energy is the latest energy source for the mankind that is environment friendly, cheap and sustainable. There is a potential of generation of 17,000 MW per annum through this source in India. Biogas comprises an organic compound, Methane, which is a gaseous compound. It has a high calorific value and does not generate toxic byproducts upon combustion. Biogas could be used for cooking in villages, power generation in the city suburbs, power generation in the small and medium factories and lighting in the remote rural areas. Capital investments are moderate and the basic fuel component—the excreta of the livestock—is available in abundance in all the parts of our country. The enormous potential of this clean source of energy has already been realised. Several hundred thousand biogas plants are working successfully across the length and breadth of India. Biogas plants could be installed and maintained either in the community or by a single household. The biogas plants are more successful in rural areas. The costs of setting up these plants are very low if community biogas plants are installed and maintained in the villages of India. Biogas does not generate any pollution, though it is a toxic gas. Being an odourless gas, Methane could cause harm to the users or operators of the biogas plants and so, effective measures would have to be taken for its early detection in the event of a leakage. India has the largest number of livestock in the world and hence, biogas could become her chief energy source in this century.

Thermal energy from oceans has assumed prominence since the eighties of the century goneby. When the solar rays hit the surface of the oceans, the solar energy gets trapped in the upper layers of water of the oceans. The lower layers remain cool. This temperature difference could be used to heat water and to generate steam. This steam could be used to run a steam turbine and the steam turbine, in turn, could be coupled to a generator. Therefore, ocean energy could be coverted into electrical energy. The entire concept or the technology is termed as Ocean Thermal Energy Conversion (OTEC). The potential of OTEC energy is nearly 50,000 MW per annum in India. The projects of OTEC have high capital cost tags. However, research and projects are being carried on in this vital area, which has a bright future.

Among other sources, small hydroelectric power generation systems could be mentioned. In India, there is a potential of generation of 10,000 MW of energy on an annual basis through small hydropower stations; however, the total hydel power potential is 85,000 MW and we are utilising only 25 per cent of it. These stations could produce electricity, assist in irrigation, produce power for lighting or help the farmers carry out simple machine tasks. The cost of setting up a project for (small) hydro-electric power generator is quite high. However, this source has an unlimited potential and it is environment-friendly as well.

The total energy demand of India for 2001-2002 was 1,31,726 MW. The non-conventional energy sources would reduce (and eventually, eliminate) our dependence upon the fossil fuels as energy sources. In India, the non-conventional energy sources would have to be exploited in a professional manner. Technologies, machinery and manpower could be imported to utilise these sources in an effective manner.

31. THE LATEST MICROSOFT STAR

> Bill Gates was a school dropout—Worked hard to become the richest man on the earth—Earlier, he promoted MSDOS—Several versions of MSDOS—MS Windows 95 promoted and launched—MS Windows 95 is popular in India—Internet activities are on the rise—MS Windows 95 is not an Internet browser—So MS Windows 98 launched—Competition of Microsoft is Netscape Navigator—Navigator could be installed alongwith MS Windows 98—Communication, data crunching, entertainment, computing and 3-D images possible with MS Windows 98—Indian markets have accepted MS Windows 98—Windows 2000 launched in February, 2000.

Nearly twenty years ago, a school dropout was told to write an operating system code for a PC. The boy had no resources or moral support but he had a will to succeed. He continued to struggle in the mad world of systems software and eventually, he succeeded. The world knows him as the richest man on earth and his name is—Henry William Gates.

Microsoft was the brainchild of Henry William Gates (he is better known as Bill Gates). With passage of time, Bill Gates and his team developed state-of-the-art software under the brand name of MSDOS. The company released many versions of MSDOS. But the innovative mind of Bill was not complacent. He wanted to do something more for his clients who were spread throughout the world. He proposed a simple "pull-down menu version" of MSDOS and termed it as Microsoft Windows. He released some versions of MS windows but was not satisfied with any one of them. His keen analysis of the markets and the problems of the users kept him thinking for a better Operating System (OS) for the micro-computer.

After years of hard work and agony, Bill and his team members developed MS Windows 3.1. It was a window-based, menu driven and efficient operating system. It incorporated networking as well. It was an instant success in all the parts of the world. The minimum requirement for MS Windows 3.1 was a computer with 80386 CPU and a Random Access Memory (RAM) of at least 4 MB. MS Windows 95 version, the next version of windows 3.2, required a 80486 CPU and a minimum of RAM of 16 MB. The lower versions of computers, however, could not accept MS Windows 95. This operating system faced competition from OS2 and other popular operating systems of main-frame computers and minicomputers. But MS Windows 95 was clearly the leader in all the information centres of the world.

And then, arrived the technology of the new millennium. Internet operations multiplied worldwide. This new development necessitated the need for 'navigation' or "surfing on the Net." For this purpose, MS Windows 95 was not a suitable operating system. Hence, Bill Gates and his team worked harder to incorporate Internet surfing, E-mail, E-com and interactive Internet operations in their new operating system. The new operating system has been rightly termed Microsoft Windows 98. This is the latest product from Microsoft and was released in Aug 1998.

MS Windows 98 is also known as Microsoft Internet Explorer. It is an operating system as well as an Internet browser. It is in direct competition with Netscape Navigator, a browser software developed by another company-Netscape. In fact, the concept of Internet browsing was developed by Netscape and Bill Gates had to recreate his entire company around Internet in order to meet stiff competition from Netscape. Netscape Navigator arrived in the markets earlier than MS Windows 98. Bill Gates has envisaged a new lifestyle with the help of his software packages. All the vital activities—TV, entertainment, games, Internet surfing, education, Internet telephony, voice mail services, E-com, E-main *etc.*—would be carried out through computers only.

All the browsers have been working on the windows platform; Netscape Navigator so far can also be operated under MS Windows 98. But the threat to Microsoft was that the browser could have displaced MS Windows 95 as the standard man-machine interface. MS Windows 98 has eliminated that heat as a cool browser. But there would not be a need for two browsers in one computer system or network.

Further, MS Windows 98 needs 120–295 MB of hard disk space. The most significant feature of MS Windows 98 is that it has laid the foundations for efficient, cost-effective and quick communication, data crunching, education, computing and entertainment. For example, when MS Windows 98 would be combined with a tuner card, it would allow the PC to receive television broadcasts (even in a little window, if the user asks for the same). Further, the user would be able to combine multiple modems and telephone lines for faster access to Internet.

In addition, joysticks, video-conferences, cameras, scanners and other peripheral devices can be connected to the PC without rebooting it. This facility would enable MS Windows 98 to support 3-D images in future. Windows 98 is also prepared for Digital Versatile Disks (DVDs) which would replace CD-ROMs in near future. It also supports multimedia tools for creation of all types of images and graphics.

MS Windows 98 also incorporates a utility, which ensures that all the Windows files are of current version (by replacing those that are not). It also provides a facility under which, the newly installed software does not overwrite the crucial system files without making back-up files first. Further, it also supports a more efficient storage mechanism for the hard disk. This ensures a lot of free space on the hard disk. It is also easier to install the driver files for the peripheral devices. The MS Windows 98 Update Feature, which is found in the Start Menu, takes the users to the central website. There is a Wizard, which scans the hard disk drive and replaces all the outdated drivers. Then, it downloads the latest versions of the drivers.

Another new facility is that of Print Troubleshooter. If a user wants to go back to Print Troubleshooter, then he would be asked whether the printer is printing anything. If the user replies in the negative, then MS Windows 95 would prompt the user to click an option, sending a test page to print.

MS Windows 98 also includes Front Pad, which is a stripped-down version of the popular Web-page Maker of Microsoft, known as Front Page. Front Page allows the user to go through the entire page creation process, in steps. It also incorporates the Personal Web Server and Web Publishing Wizard. Therefore, the PC itself would be deemed to be a Web Server.

MS Windows 98 has been criticised for media hype and for having too many operational features (some of which, could be discarded, according to them). In India, MS Windows 95 is more popular as Indians have not hooked fully on to Internet. Therefore, Indian markets are good for standalone PCs and hence, for MS Windows 95. However, Windows 98 could make quick inroads into the corporate sector where Internet browsing is next only to profits. The new PCs would essentially be loaded with MS Windows 98. As on date, a PC with a Pentium CPU (having a speed of 300 MHz) and with a RAM of 32 MB would be good enough for MS Windows 98. However, a Pentium-500 with better configuration would be an ideal system for the modern PC user of this century.

Microsoft also launched MS Office-2000 which is, likely to revolutionise computer operations in the modern offices. This new package was introduced during the early months of 1999 and offers many useful facilities to the modern office executives.

During the month of Octcber, 1998, the US Justice Department filed an anti-trust suit against Microsoft Corporation. It alleged that Microsoft was undercutting competition by giving away its Internet Browser along with Window 98 package. This controversy would hurt the sales of the package but the fact remains that the utility of the package has been enhanced due to the presence of Internet Browser.

Bill Gates has already resigned as Chairman of Microsoft but he would continue to pull the strings of the IT world from the backstage. Microsoft has already planned to launch Windows-2000. In the meantime, Windows 2000 was also launched by Microsoft in February, 2000. However, Windows 98 would continue to rule Indian software markets till the fag end of 2000 AD.   ●

INDIAN SOCIETY AND CULTURE

32. FIFTY YEARS OF INDEPENDENCE

India freedom is more than fifty years old—We have not grown at a fast pace—Education not imparted at primary levels—Higher level education also not imparted to many deserving candidates — Population pressures are high—Family Planning not emphasised upon by the State after emergency In 1975— Economy growing at a slow pace—Industrial production is low and imports are more—Some economic indicators mentioned— No improvement in condition of common man—Basic quality of life of ordinary citizen is very poor—Our manpower proved its mettle in software, heavy engineering, space, missile development and nuclear technology—India was respected earlier on international fora due to NAM—Kargil war, controversies at NAM Summit and economic sanctions have put us in a critical situation.

India has completed fifty years of her independence which was indeed won in unique and distinguished manner when the nation freed herself from the chains of foreign rule and exploitation. She dreamed of a future full of prosperity, equality and justice for all. We have achieved a lot during the past five decades but our progress has not been satisfactory in many vital fields. It is an irony that India, which is one of the richest in natural resources, has been rated as one of the poorest countries of the world. We must celebrate our Golden Jubilee for introspection and for pragmatic planning in the future.

Education

Our greatest mistake has been the neglect of primary education. It has been specifically laid down in our Constitution (which the nation gave to herself soon after Independence) that free and compulsory primary education would be provided to all the children and this goal was to be achieved within ten years from the inception of the Constitution, (by the year 1961). Our first Prime Minister— Jawaharlal Nehru—was not only a prominent member of the Constituent Assembly, but also commanded more power than the President in a

Presidential form of Government. Hence, our dismal record in the field of primary education—as required by the Constitution—speaks volumes about the failure of our leadership.

Today, our population is more than 1 billion and it is increasing at the rate of about 1.9 per cent every year. So, even if we assume that the country has adequate schooling facilities for the existing population, we need to open about one lakh new primary schools per year to meet with the primary educational requirements of about 50,000 additional children that are arriving everyday. Obviously, a nation must provide school education to the children right in their childhood itself. Let us not allow our children to grow into illiterate adults for want of proper schooling facilities and then, launch ineffective adult literacy programmes, which do not yield concrete results.

Population Growth

The second major drawback of our policies manifested itself in terms of high population growth. The urban centres became the backwaters of human civilisation. Growth in rural population was also tremendous. The rising population levels have put severe pressures on our economy and society. The result is a slowdown in all the spheres of our economy and society.

In 1951, when JRD Tata explained his concern to Pandit Nehru about India's population, he snubbed JRD and said that a large population was the greatest source of power for any nation. Nehru, therefore, believed that population was an asset for the nation. However, Nehru, unlike Gandhi, had nothing against the usage of contraceptives. The population increased from 36 crore in 1951 to 55 crore in 1971 and was still growing at a staggering rate of 2.24 per cent per annum.

By the time Indira Gandhi could consolidate her position politically and became powerful enough, our population had reached ominous proportions. However, Indira Gandhi thought that all that was needed to control the population growth was to promote literacy and reduce the infant mortality rate. So, despite the fact that she did not consider population as a national asset, she could not make any significant headway for controlling the population growth rate. And then, came the Emergency of 1975 and she pressed the panic button. The over-enthusiasm to promote birth control proved counter-productive. Emergency and family planning became almost synonymous. The fallout of that coercive measure is that population control is a taboo for the politicians.

The credit for creating such an apathy and fear against family planning in the minds of the public and politicians goes to the elite and opinion makers. Due to their zeal for condemning the emergency, they highlighted the excesses (committed during that period by family planning authorities) to such an extent that emergency and family planning are still feared by the masses of India.

Economy

Indian economy had witnessed Green Revolution (during the seventies), White Revolution (during late seventies and early eighties), economic *Glasnost* during the mid-eighties, information revolution during the late eighties and finally, complete imformation technology miracle (in the form of Internet) during the late-nineties. India was a nuclear novice in 1974. However, the successive five nuclear blasts on May 11 and May 13, 1998, proved that India had unmatched nuclear finesse as well. In fact, the nuclear tests conducted by India might affect her economy; at least, that is what the critics opine as the economic growth process is not able to sustain the nation.

It must be noted that industrial growth was 12.8 per cent per annum during 1995-96 period and the same figure had come down to 6.9 per cent per annum 1996-97 period. Industrial growth rates for 1998-99 and 1999-2000 were 3.7 per cent and 6.2 per cent, respectively. Manufacturing sector did not perform well. Agricultural sector was also at its lowest ebb. Draughts, famines and floods could not be controlled in any part of the country.

Indian economy is coming out of recession. The stock markets are heading towards bullish trends. Industrial production is up and trading is brisk in major commercial centres. However, the economic growth rate, which our nation deserved from August 15, 1947 onwards, was not observed in to various sectors of our industrial, economic and trading activities. On the other hand, economies like those of Taiwan, Malaysia, Singapore and those of other Oriental countries have performed very well. Japan was liberated from the clutches of fanatic nationalism in 1945. Japanese started their economic marathon (after rising from the ashes of the Second World War) and now, they rule this planet. We got freedom only two years later-in 1947, and we are no match for the Japanese technological and economic competence. Our progress has been painfully slow. There is no doubt that we have developed a sound industrial infrastructure and a resilient economy over the last fifty years. However, our progress could have been more rapid. The scams, the politician-criminal-bureaucrat nexus, the four wars and above all, the Indian psyche played a havoc for our economic growth process.

Common Man

After independence, the common man in the street was a free bird. But he was caught in the chains of poverty, illiteracy, unemployment and backwardness. The growth in all the sectors of economy did not percolate down to the lowest levels of our society. The poor became poorer. The rich became richer. Let us not be impressed by colour televisions, satellite televisions, amazing electronic gadgets and gaudy dresses, which are adorned by people in the name of fashion. The quality of life is determined in terms of qualities of food, clothing, shelter, sanitation, education, habitat, environment, health and employment. Indian citizens have been deprived of good standards of living on all these fronts. The urban centers have shown progress but the slums in all the major cities indicate that all the people have not been able to reap the benefits of freedom, industrialisation and free market system. The politicians had a major share in the loot. The bureaucrats came next. The common man waited for the realisation of his dreams but he was deprived even of the rights to live with dignity. Police tortures, exploitation in the office and in the industry, famines, poor foodgrain supplies at the outlets of Public Distribution System (PDS), shortages of electric power, food and medicines, bureaucratic delays, corruption at all the levels of the state governments and those of the central government administrations *etc* are some of the woes of the deprived masses of India. And the irony is that he goes to the polls after every five years (even earlier than this) in order to vote for the elected representatives so that his fortunes might be changed. The common man has suffered on all accounts and freedom from the British was the only solace for him.

Science And Technology

Indians can be proud of their achievements during the past fifty years. We are a nuclear power, thanks to the tests conducted at Pokharan on May 11 and May 13, 1998. Indian Scientists have made the nation proud of them. We are also an agricultural power due to the hard work and dedication of our scientists and farmers. Our engineers and technologists are working in all the parts of the world. They are contributing effectively towards the economies of the world. Our software programmers comprise the most coveted manpower resource from India because of their technical abilities. India has successfully launched remote sensing satellite IRS-P4 (also known as Ocean Sat-1) through the latest satellite launch vehicle PSLV-C2 on May 26, 1999. We are now able to launch payloads of 1,200 kg in space. Further, India is a military superpower, thanks to development of Nag, Prithvi, Agni and Agni-II missile systems. These missiles are totally indigenous and speak volumes of our achievements in the fields of science and technology. India has state-of-the-art nuclear power plants, thermal power stations, steel plants, processing units and other vital industries, which are essential for putting us on the industrial map of the world.

International Relations

India is a non-aligned country and a member of SAARC. We have no differences with any other nation except some serious boundary disputes with China and Pakistan. We have fought three major wars and a minor war (during May-July, 1999) with Pakistan. We also had a major conflict with China in September, 1962. However, our foreign policy is of defence and not of offence. We believe in "I am OK, you are OK" situation in which, both the parties are satisfied with the outcome of the negotiation. We were an ally of the erstwhile USSR but now, that friendship has been modified in the favour of broad international brotherhood and co-operation. Now, everybody is a friend. The leaders of the former government (led by BJP) had issued 'hot' statements for reclaiming the territory occupied by Pakistan and China. This should not happen as international relationships call for careful diplomatic protocols even for the purpose of issuing statements on international disputes. The Pakistani side has also been equally vocal after they have carried out nuclear tests. Pakistani side is immature. But we should also maintain restraint while negotiating or issuing statements related to sensitive boundary disputes. The raising of Kashmir issue in the UNO (which was a bilateral issue according to India) proves that our politicians were not able to handle this sensitive issue with poise and determination. Indian leaders recently asked Mr Bill Clinton, the American President, to declare Pakistan a terrorist State. This statement came in the wake of Kargil war. But would this (branding Pakistan a culprit in the issue) solve the problems?

Conclusion

India has come a long way after independence. Our achievements are worth mentioning. However, we could have achieved more in the past fifty years. We have to ensure a good standard of living for our masses. We must provide them with better food, water, health, education, employment and business opportunities. The institutional decay must be checked. The defence preparations must be done at war footing as the signals from across the border are not positive. Industrial growth must be improved. Agricultural and farming sectors must be given more priority and resources. International relations hips must be improved with visits to all the important nations. Anti-India lobbies must be defeated in the UNO through peaceful and carefully planned efforts. We must grow at a pace, which must be double than the present growth rate. Targets are difficult to achieve and the road to success is strewn with thorns. We must unite as a nation for overcoming all our problems.

33. MORAL VALUES IN INDIAN SOCIETY

Man must possess and support high moral values—In India, moral values were very high during the past—Significant changes due to Westernisation—Joint family replaced by nuclear families—Corruption—Scams—MNCs selectively take employees who are able to toe their line of action —Indian culture and values sidelined—No respect for elders—Common man corrupt out of necessity—Murders of Jessica Lal in the capital is the manifestation of the absolute decay of morality in the metropolises—Poor educational system does not consolidate ancient moral values in our children and youth—Sex before marriage—Risk of AIDS—Rich employer does not pay complete wages to staff and labour—Solutions.

Human beings enjoy the maximum freedom and power for governing their habitat and environment. This power enables them to misuse the resources or exploit the not-so-privileged at will. Materialism, advanced technologies and a lack of understanding of the basic cause of existence has led us to a degradation in our moral values.

Let us take the case of India. We are the most ancient civilisation. *Vedas* were written here. Buddha got divine knowledge here. We are proud of our rich cultural, historical and spiritual heritage for which, we are well known around the globe. But today, have we kept those ideals, values and principles close to our hearts, which were so dear to our ancestors ?

Take for example, the concept of joint family. Today, no young couple prefers a joint family. Nuclear families—on the pattern of division of the family in the USA and the West—create a sense of insecurity among young people. They are financially dependent upon their elders whom they have left. They do not want to be grateful to their parents. Rather, they want to disown them. True, rapid industrialisation and urbanisation forces young boys and girls to explore new and green pastures. However, old parents at home suffer due to the apathy of their children.

The next most prominent degradation in our moral values reflects itself in the form of corruption. In India, corruption is prevalent at all the levels; peon, officer, SDO, telephone lineman, engineer, doctor, general managers, directors, ministers, cabinet secretaries, prime ministers *etc* comprise the small cross-section of the long shocking list. And the irony is that even if we accuse that they are guilty, they remain supreme. Rather, they have an opportunity to regain their seats in the state assembly, *Lok Sabha* or *Rajya Sabha*. Examples could be cited of two recent scandle-prone VIPs—Sukh Ram and Narasimha Rao. Further, Hawala scam, Bofors gun deal, Fodder scam, Urea scam *etc* gobbled up the precious resources of the country in a slurp and nobody ever knew where the funds had gone. The politician-bureaucrat-criminal nexus has consolidated itself during the last two decades. These developments do not auger well for the national economy and the moral conditioning of our younger generations.

The common man has his own reasons to be corrupt. A head constable in Indian police force draws a meagre salary. He has to feed a family and support their basic needs. So, he forces his 'clients' to give them a 'decent' fee for his 'services.' The common man is caught up in the vicious cycle of created by poverty, illiteracy and ignorance. He has purposely lost his moral values to the new era of commercialism. The free market economics has added fuel to the fire. He finds that everybody is corrupt. So, he wastes no time in becoming the part of a corrupt system because that suits him as well as his fellow citizens.

The famous model, Jessica Lal, was murdered recently during a cocktail party in New Delhi. Whatever may have transpired between the victim and her killer, it surely should never have led to a murder. In a bid to dominate or prove ourselves to be righteous, we go to the wrong extremes.

Another steep decline in moral values manifests itself in the form of our poor educational system and teaching methodologies. In fact, the poor educational system in all the parts of the nation has led to poor moral values in the society. And the educational system has deteriorated beyond compare due to rise in commercialism, thanks to the ill-efects of the free market economy. The students do not respect their teachers. The teacher is forced to respect them (else he would either be transferred from the institution or he would be shot dead). Copying during the examinations is a compulsory exercise. Student unrest, politics at the campus and inter-group rivalries put education, career and academic excellence to a backseat. Best of the brains are drained to the West and we are left with nothing but chaff. If, instead of importing goods and technologies, we could somehow stop the export of our talented professionals to the Western nations, we would need almost nil imports after ten years from now. The reason is that we would be self-sufficient due to our human resources and would be able to produce everything at home. But this remains a dream as money and materialism beckon our professionals from across the seas. The offers are tempting and nobody misses the opportunity if offered one.

Another prominent characteristic of Indian society (especially, the youth) is over-indulgence in free sex prior to marriage. The cable TV boom, Internet operations, cinema and pornography have affected our young minds adversely. The teenagers are falling prey to the lust for the flesh and do not mind having multiple sexual affairs. The moral degradation apart, this over-indulgence is also spreading HIV among the youth. Ironically, the young minds are not aware of this tragic consequence of free and multi-partner sex. Even the individuals from older age groups are making full usage of the free market winds that blow in our social and cultural lives. We must find a quick solution to this menace; usage of condoms, avoiding multiple partners, medical testing of the partners prior to sex and above all, avoiding sex before marriage could be some of the concrete steps for curbing this menace.

Further, in Indian society, respect for elders is taking a backseat in the name of modernisation. Our cultural values have taught us to respect our parents and help them during the times of their helplessness. However, the growth of nuclear families has led to complete ignorance of parents and elders. The offsprings even offend them so that they remain away from their personal lives. What an irony of fate ! The parents are forced to seek shelter in old-age homes because their children or sons-in-law (or daughters-in-law) are rude and insulting. We never approve of such a deformed social and cultural chaos in our nation that was known for her warmth, empathy and family traditions for over several hundred centuries.

The decline in moral values in our social milieu has also manifested itself in large scale violence and riots on religious grounds. Caste conflicts have been used by the politicians for settling their scores with their rivals. The bureaucracy and government machinery at the state or the central levels manipulate the masses and exploit them for their base ends. The industrialist does not pay full wages to the toiling labour. The prosperous businessman or trader takes away more from his employees than he gives to them. The entry of the Multinational Corporations (MNCs) has brightened the human side of enterprise. However, the MNCs have their typical snobbish attitude towards Indian workers. A highly qualified Indian (who is affluent as well) is eligible for a cushy job in a MNC. But a poor candidate, who has only merit to his credit, may not be able to join the same because he is not well connected or because his profile is too simple for a highly acclaimed multinational. Materialism has put all the Indian traditions and values in the dumpyard. Every Indian is running for well-defined and cash-convertible goals. Nationalism, family, society and morality no longer matter for him.

The solutions for this dangerous moral decay do exist. We must follow the following action plan :—

(1) We must break the bureaucrat-politician-criminal nexus. Bureaucracy must be separated from political machinations. Criminals should be banned from politics and should be treated with an iron hand if they try to disturb the democratic norms laid down by our Constitution.. The Election Commission has done well by forbidding candidates with criminal records from fighting elections.

(2) In our schools, the traditional Indian values must be taught and reinforced. Schools can change the face of our society. Sadly, commercialism has started raising its ugly head even in the schools. This must be stopped immediately.

(3) Educational and cultural programmes must be organised in all the localities of Indian cities and townships. The virtuous deeds of our national leaders and freedom fighters should be narrated through poetry, prose and theatre. These programmes should also involve children in whom, the basic social, cultural and moral values have to be reinforced for building a morally sound nation.

(4) Corrupt politicians should be tried by Indian courts and should not be allowed to take part in any political activity.

(5) Foreign culture, especially the MNC culture, should not be allowed to overtake our traditional values. We believe in becoming modern and technology oriented but not at the cost of our national dignity and social norms.

(6) The concept of joint families must be promoted among the young couples. This concept would enable them to take fruitful guidance from their elders and would also ensure better future for their posterity.

(7) Indian cultural heritage should be promoted and protected through festivals, music concerts and conferences. Literary interests should be developed among the youth. They should be persuaded to take in more interest in Indian arts, music, crafts and historical monuments.

(8) Education should be imparted according to Western norms. However, Indian values must also be enforced so that our children remain in touch with their roots. The promotion of *gurukuls* is one such example in this context. ●

33. YOUTH AND DRUGS

Youth are the pride and builder of India—They are energetic—They are taking drugs and liquor, which are destroying their careers—Education, productivity, social interaction affected—Drugged young individual becomes a criminal—The young person himself should have will power—The State and society must also help him eliminate drug menace—Drugs change the behaviour of youth—Early detection is able to provide a cure—Support from parents and friends desirable.

The young citizens of this nation constitute the most vital human resource. Indian youth has made a mark in all the walks of life—education, sports, literature, software, Internet technology, social causes *etc*. The young mind is fresh and energetic and hence, can contribute towards the growth of a nation in the most effective manner. This energy can be channelised for building the nation and for sustaining her growth.

However, drugs and alcohol have taken the toll of our youth in an adverse manner. Young boys and girls take smack, brown sugar, heroin and other contraband drugs, which are spoiling their lives. Drugs affect the minds permanently. A person, who takes drugs even once, cannot escape from them for life. Further, some young boys and girls take medicines that contain drugs or alcohol. Their parents and teachers are unaware that their children or wards have committed themselves to complete annihilation under the disguise of medical treatment. Some popular drugs consumed by the students as drugs are Luminal, Mandrax, Cannabis, E, Heroin and other alcohol-based medicines.

Drugs affect mind and body equally. The young mind stops thinking positively. His body becomes lethargic and he tries to remain under the effect of the drug throughout day and night. His behaviour becomes abnormal and his psyche becomes sick. He resorts to fighting, stealing and his behaviour becomes highly volatile. He becomes a living caracass. The withdrawal symptoms, after the consumption of the drug, are even more dangerous and lead to irritating behaviour among the youth.

Education, productivity and social interaction are also deeply affected. There are economic fallouts as well. Some boys are the only wage earners for their families and they too, fall into the drug net. Some girls, who get caught in this web, lose their academic abilities and even chastity.

Drugs are available in big metropolitan cities. The drug sellers use the youth as peddlers. Once a young person is caught in this intricate and dangerous racket, he can never get out of the same. He becomes a criminal and is watched by the police with suspicious eyes.

The solution for the drug problem lies in the willpower of the young mind. The youth taking the drug should stop taking it and must allocate more time to studies, sports and career-building. After all, it is the mind, which is sick and not the body. The government agencies have initiated many anti-drug programmes. The rehabilitation of the youth after treatment is a must else they would be tempted to resort to their old lifestyles. The State and the youth can join hands for eradicating this menace for our young generation. The family should also adopt a positive attitude. A drugged youth means a drugged nation and sick nations have no future. We must control and eliminate this menace before it overcomes our youth.

Despite all the efforts by police and other law-enforcing agencies, drugs are being distributed around the world to the youth. The USA is a haven for drug peddlers despite all the efforts by the American administration for controlling this menace. In India, drugs are smuggled from across the border, through airports, coastal areas and seaports. The customs officials seize record quantities of herion and other drugs but many consignments escape their watchful eyes. Similarly, drug peddlers transport drugs through international border with Pakistan. It should be noted that opium production in Pakistan and in the border areas of India is a prominent cause of drug manufacture and peddling. When the young persons take drugs for the first time, they enjoy their influence and a sense of comfort. The usage for a single time leads to drug addiction. The desperate student or young scholar gets the drugs from drug peddlers and organised gangs in all the major and miner cities. The victim takes up odd jobs for earning money so that he could buy drugs. He also resorts to stealing from home or gets involved in minor or major crimes with the help of his classmates or other drug-addicted friends. So, he gets completely involved in the drug net and the ultimate result is either a police lock up (due to a crime) or death (due to excessive or long term consumption of drugs).

If the behaviour of the drug addicted boy or girl is carefully observed by a friend or family member, he or she would find that the victim is shaken, confused, fumbling in speech, lonely and gloomy. He loses his health and is not interested in sports or leisure. He remains confined to his bed and never participates in social activities. He tries to remain secluded in his limited world. If a friend or a family member is able to identify the change in the victim, he or she should immediately talk to the senior members of the family of the victim. If treated early, the drug addiction problem can be completely cured. The state and central governments have established "Drug Rehabilitation Centres" throughout the country. Medical treatments and psychological counselling facilities are also available. The willpower of the drug addict can pull him out of the darkness of drug addiction. He should admit to his parents or friends that he has starting taking drugs. He can also contact a doctor or a drug rehabilitation centre. The treatment is complicated and costly. The drug addicted boy or girl must be willing to come out of his shell. The family members and friends must extend all cooperation. The police force must also be sympathetic towards these drug victims and must not use coercive methods for extracting information about drug peddlers from the drug addicts. The social organisations and NGOs could play vital roles in this context.

Drug menace is assuming very dangerous proportions. It could spoil the future of nations. It must be eliminated so that the young minds would be saved from the scourge of drug addiction.

35. WESTERN CULTURE : WHAT TO ADOPT ?

> Great difference between Eastern and Western ideologies—Eastern culture supports simple living, morality, ethical conduct, prayer, family traditions—Being satisfied with whatever we have—Western culture is materialistic, growth oriented, logical advanced, fast—creates physical and mental imbalances—We must adopt efficiency, hard work and logic from Western culture—Very high speed also dangerous—Accept only the good and relevant influences for assimilation in our society.

Kipling once wrote, "*East is East and West is West and never shall twain meet.*" He was right. There are some fine points of difference between the Eastern and the Western cultures. These are two different styles of living. Both have their shortcomings and advantages. Let us analyse.

Eastern culture is prevalent in India, Pakistan, Bangladesh, China, Nepal, Indonesia, Burma, Japan, Sri Lanka, middle-East and most of the Asian nations. Western culture is accepted in the USA, the UK, entire Europe, Thailand, Singapore and some nations of the Orient. Eastern culture is family oriented. It believes in the societal norms. It is based on religion (Hinduism, Islam, Jainism and Buddhism). It calls for respecting and thanking the Almighty for all the blessings that He has showered on us. It believes in settling for less when less is available. Marriage, religious ceremonies, business and social interactions are guided by our culture and religions. The materialistic values take a backseat in Eastern culture.

Western culture is individual oriented. The needs, rights and privileges of the individual are of utmost significance. Man has learned to master the forces of nature under the Western cultural influence. Western culture is materialistic. It is not satisfied with whatever has been gained by an individual. There is always lust for more money and materialistic assets. The mind, therefore, remains unstable and shaken. Western influences make the person more logical, calculative and rational. He forgets his taboos and useless pre-conceived notions, which are normally associated with Eastern culture. Western culture also emphasises upon hard work and toil. It calls for incessant quest for knowledge. It is based on scientific and materialistic ideologies.

What should we adopt from Western culture ? Naturally, we should assimilate only those plus points from that culture that are suitable for us and those social norms that can be accepted by our masses easily.

Let us take an example. In the Eastern societies, dating would mean that a boy and a girl would meet each other and would try to understand each other. They would remain friends without any physical interaction. They would meet most probably to plan their life together but that may not always be necessary. However, in Western parlance, dating would mean that a boy and a girl share physical intimacy. They would remain man and wife without marriage. After some time, they could part company and could find a new partner for each other. This attitude towards love, sex and marriage is not acceptable in Eastern culture.

Let us take another example. Eastern culture proposes that whatever would be, would be. We should work hard. And here lies the point. We do not work hard at all because we know that whatever *Karma* we do, we are not going to gain much. Western philosophy concludes that we should work hard and hard work never goes wasted. So, we should accept this plus point from the Western culture and should not shirk work. We must pray to God; however, we must keep an pushing our boat towards the shore.

These two examples give ample evidence about the Western thoughts for our adoption. We must accept whatever is rational, logical and truthful in Western culture. Our *Upnishadas, Vedas* and other holy scriptures have also emphasised upon the values of *Satya* celebacy and *Karma*.

We should adopt meticulous behaviour, rational attitude and discipline from the Western culture. We should learn to carry out tasks efficiently. We should strive to change our society for good. We must eliminate poverty, bureaucratic procedures, corruption, religious influences in daily life and inefficiency from our culture. These anomalies are not present in their culture and that is why, they are ahead of us.

True, we should not accept the decline in moral values, a negation of family norms, evil manipulations in all walks of our lives and business and surrealism. Our culture has not been designed to accept these influences. As a result of the assimilation of wrong aspects of the Western culture, our society is becoming sick. If we do not check this degradation our society, we shall fall prey to mental sickness and moral decay due to the ill-effects of Western culture.

It is the opinion of the great philosophers that a simple life without much ambitions is worth living and enjoying. Eastern culture prohibits any ambitions (or, it does not support the ambitious behaviour). In Western culture, however, growth is the only sign of life. We should adopt a delicate balance between the two. We must have ambitions but these ambitions should always be within our physical, mental and financial limits. We must not push our abilities and capacities too far and suffer an account of our ambitions. Western culture promotes chaos and even violence for the sake of achieving one's ambitions.

Further, Western culture teaches us to be more pragmatic, meticulous and calculative. We must adopt these features as the technological growth around the world has made its global impact on the mankind. We cannot remain immune to the developments and researches in all the fields. We must keep in tune with tomorrow. Hence, being meticulous, calculative and business-like is not harmful. However, we should not forget the human values that are skilfully ignored by the Western culture for the sake of money, power or fame.

Finally, we must accept the efficient educational system of the West. It teaches us to be more knowledgeable and practical. It prepares us for life. We must utilise and accept new engineering skills, technologies and results of medical research as well as scientific discoveries for the development and prosperity of our masses. For example, a firm in the USA has developed an inhaler that releases a fixed amount of insulin in the lungs of a diabetic patient. The patient no longer needs painful injections of insulin. Such techniques must be adopted by our medical institutions with immediate effect as these are for the benefit of mankind.

Like a swan, we must pick all the pearls of the Western culture and should assimilate them in our social and cultural environments for the sake of a better society and nation.

36. STATUS OF WOMEN IN INDIA

Women respected in ancient India—Manu degraded the status—Pre-independence era gave great women personalities—After independence, women contributed towards national growth—Today's women is modern but her status is lower—Still tortured and degraded—Illiteracy and backwardness in rural India—Male psyche must change—State to play stellar role—Women must educate and liberate themselves.

In the ancient Indian scriptures, woman was given a glorified status. She was an embodiment of *Shakti*. No religious ceremony was complete without her. However, Manu made such statements about women as relegated her to a position of backwardness and timidity. Her status and respectful position in the society suffered a jolt during the times of *Manusmriti*.

During the Mughal period, the status of women was degraded further. *Purdah* system came into vogue. *Sati* system was very prominent, which put serious scars on the contemporary society. The *Sati* system was stopped by legal action when Raja Ram Mohan Roy took up the issue with the State during the British rule over India.

During the distant past, Savitri, Parvati, Seeta and Ahilya were the role models of Indian Society. During the freedom struggle, Aruna Asaf Ali, Sarojini Naidu, Kasturba Gandhi, Sucheta Kriplani and other women played steller roles for the liberation of their motherland from the clutches of the British. They struggled and fought against all odds along with their male counterparts. At no point of time, their energy or commitment could be derated *viz-a-viz* those of their male counterparts during those times.

At present, women have been playing major roles in politics, economy, household, society and nation-building. With the advent of the technology-dominated era and commercialism, women have also changed. The timid female form in the saree has been replaced by a youthful, fashion conscious and smart girl in jeans and T-shirts. Women are jostling shoulders with men and are competing with them in engineering, sciences, space research, medicine and business. They are more hardworking and sincere in all the walks of life and are more productive than their male counterparts.

The glory of modern Indian women continues to enlighten the world. Who can forget Indira Gandhi, Rani Laxmibai, Shabana Azmi, MS Subbulaxmi, Kiran Bedi, Mother Teresa, Medha Patkar, PT Usha, Madhuri Dixit, Meena Kumari, Arundhati Roy, Kalpana Chawla and Mohsina Kidwai. These great daughters of India have done us proud in the fields of politics, administration, sports, cinema, performing arts, medicine and science. Girls perform better than boys in board examinations and competitive examinations. Some women are successful business tycoons and have made a mark in the international arena as well. But alas ! Despite all the glory and sacrifice, the women in India are still treated as second class citizens. The stories of female tortune, rape, bride burning and *Sati* are heard even today. The primitive instincts of the modern society have taken their toll. Women represent 48.1 per cent of Indian population (1991 census). But they do not enjoy the prominence in this vast country at social, family, national and international levels, which they rightly deserve. The obvious reasons are—male dominated society, male ego, religious and social beliefs and above all, the illiteracy and backwardness of women. For the last elections of Lok Sabha in September-October, 1999, no political party had issued enough tickets to female candidates. Further, the issue of reservation and seats in *Lok Sabha* and in the state assemblies is in jeopardy. The new *Lok Sabha* might be able to get the Bill passed, according to some expert political analysts, albeit with some difficulties.

Dowry, sex determination during the time of maternity, prejudice against the female child, denial of ancestral property rights for the females, eveteasing, wife-beating and child marriages are still prevalent in Indian society and the villages are the most affected. If the woman is a housewife, she has a limited social and intellectual circle. Her capabilities are limited to the precints of the household. If she works in an office, she has to face the malicious insinuations of her male colleagues. She connot travel extensively, cannot make friends at will (as the males do) and is treated as weaker than males. He has no right to perform better than males in any walk of life.

The solution to this problem is deeply rooted in our psyche. The male ego must be made compatible with the female identity. A husband must respect his wife even if she is a housewife. He must cooperate with her if she is a working woman. She must treat her as a friend and not as a mere money-making tool.

Secondly, the State must pass and enforce legislations so that the status of women in society is brought to a respectable level through the long arms of the law. In 1985, a separate Department of Women and Child Development was set up. In the Sixth five year plan, a separate chapter, on "Women and Development" was included. The government had started and implemented major programmes like Support to Training-cum-Employment for Women (STEP), *Mahila Kosh*, Woman's Development Corporation etc. The female literacy figure is 164 males to 100 females (1991 figures), which is a good sign and has been made possible because of the efforts of the State agencies. However, legislations and efforts of the State have not made deeper inroads into the rural and urban areas. For example, sex determination of foetus still continues in all the rural regions of the country despite the enforcement of legislation on Pre-natal Diagnostic Technique (Regulation and Prevention of Misuse) Act, which was passed in 1994. Finally, the women of India, especially the rural women, must liberate themselves from the shackles of illiteracy and backwardness. They must oppose all types of tortures inflicted upon them — eve-teasing, bride burning, child marriages, exploitation in the offices, lower wages for labour *etc*. Several women's organisations have been working relentlessly towards this goal. Women from all walks of life must unite and must give priority to their education, growth and the prosperity of their families.

The discussion brings a major conclusion to light—the status of women could be improved by women themselves and nobody else. It is the modern era of satellites, achievements and technology-based gadgets. The primitive society of India is being replaced by liberal, optimistic and hard working society that would be guided by the free market forces. Why should women be left behind ?

The major thrust areas of education, growth and enlightenment of women should be the rural pockets. The urban women are quite modern and up-to-date with the realities of life. The rural women, however, need a close encounter with freedom, liberalisation and knowledge. The State is doing its best but a lot more needs to be done. Female infanticides, female torture, *Sati* and dowry must be banned in the country. Police should accept more female officers and constables so that they are able to empathise with the female victims of our society.

Finally, women must become literate as education is beneficial for them as well as their families. The family web is woven around the woman. She has to be up to the mark and educated so that she could fend for herself and her family during the hour of crisis. The status of women would improve only if they educate themselves and grab every opportunity to become stronger and more powerful than before.

The true colours of the *Shakti* would be evident only when she is educated, enlightened and aware of her rights in this male dominated society. ●

37. AIDS

AIDS is a deadly disease—HIV virus can be contracted by human body through sexual intercourse with HIV infected partner, usage of infected syringes and needles, from AIDS infected mother to her child during pregnancy and through the cuts of the HIV-infected knife—No medical treatment—Human immune system destroyed systematically—Three stages of development—2.5 million Indians are infected by AIDS Multiple partner sex must be avoided—Use sterilised injection syringes and needles—AIDS assuming alarming proportions—Treat AIDS patient with compassion. Some drugs (like AZT) developed for curing AIDS.

AIDS stands for Acquired Immuno Deficiency Syndrome. It is a deadly disease in which, the ability of a human being to fight diseases is lost. The basic cause is a virus called HIV (Hepatitis one V), which was discovered in the early eighties in the USA. It is the most tragic incident in the history of mankind (and of medicine) after the dropping of nuclear bombs at Hiroshima and Nagasaki. It has been estimated that if AIDS is not treated and eliminated, it could wipe out half of the population of our planet by the middle of next century.

How AIDS virus works ? Very carefully indeed. The HIV virus can be acquired by a human body through :

(*a*) sexual intercourse with a person who is infected with HIV;
(*b*) sharing of needles or syringes of the person who has AIDS or HIV;

(c) transfer of HIV from the AIDS-infected mother to her child during pregnancy; and

(d) transfer of HIV by a small or cut sharp edges (for example, the razor of a barber could pass on the HIV virus from one person to another).

The HIV virus enters the body of a healthy person and multiplies. It cannot be destroyed by antibiotics, drugs, innoculations or alcohol. It never dies but kills the infected person slowly and painfully. It kills the T-cells by attacking the special protein—CD4—surrounding these cells. T-cells are responsile for building immunity of the body against diseases and infections. When the T-cell count falls below 600, HIV is imminent. So it 'kills' the "Immunity System" of the human body. The symptoms of HIV Infection include pneumonia, headache, nausea, endless bleeding, non-recovery of wounds, throat troubles, fever, jaundice, weakness, lack of appetite, syphlis, and other sexually transmitted diseases.

The HIV virus enters the human body through the afore-mentioned routes. It could remain dormant for as long as twenty years. The infected person may never know that he has contracted the virus. Such a stage (called Stage-I) is termed as HIV interaction stage. This stage can be detected if the patient is tested. He has no symptoms of the disease as the virus remains dormant.

The second stage (Stage-II) is the HIV infection stage. The virus starts multiplying and starts distroying the vital immunity mechanisms of the body. But the patient is not affected much as this is only the beginning. He ignores these primary signals and takes them in his stride. The third stage (Stage-III) is of full-blown AIDS. The virus destroys the immunity system systematically and the patient is very serious. Death occurs within 10-20 years from the date of contracting the virus. Some patients could live longer. AIDS has no cure. It is a challenge for the medical science and remains an unsolved riddle despite, media hype and expenditures of millions of Dollars on the research for ending this evil terminator. The official figure of HIV infections in India was 3.5 million by the end of December, 1999. However, unofficial estimates put this figure at nearly 5 million. And the figures are increasing everyday.

The National AIDS Control Organisation (NACO) has prepared a project of Rs 1,425 crore for the next five years. It would get assistance from USAID and Department for International Development of the UK government. The objective of the project, according to the project director of NACO, Mr JVR Prasada Rao, was to restrict the spread of AIDS to less than 5 per cent in Maharashtra, less than 2-3 per cent in Andhra Pradesh, Manipur, Karnataka and Tamil Nadu and to less than 1 per cent in the rest of the country. In Maharashtra, AIDS is prevalent in 2-2.4 per cent of people in the age group of 15-49 years. In Andhra Pradesh, Manipur, Karnataka and Tamil Nadu, the prevalence rate is 1-2 per cent whereas in the rest of the country, the prevalence rate is less than 1 per cent.

The conference concluded the following :—

(1) Every country of Asia and the Pacific must collect data on its behavioural, socio-economic and epidemiological vulnerabilities to HIV and AIDS. It must devise a national plan for controlling AIDS.

(2) These nations should stop rejection of people infected with AIDS.

(3) Drug injections (usually called 'shots'). oral consumption of drugs (through 'puffs' and by mixing the drugs in tobacco of cigarettes), homosexual behaviour and unsafe surgeries must be stopped.

(4) The local districts or regions of every country must develop their own plans and must allocate more resources for this stupendous task.

(5) Safe sex must be practised through the usage of condoms. Multiple-partner sex must be avoided. Truck drivers must abstain from having casual sex on the highways as they are the most eligible candidates for contracting the virus. Prostitution centres must be closed. If at all they have to be run, the State must intervene and proper medical checkup of every sex worker and customer must be made mandatory.

AIDS is already taking its toll. The well-known pop singer Fredie Mercury, Rock Hudson and Olympic stars (Greg Louganis and Magic Johnson) have seen and tolerated all the agonies associated with AIDS. The patient is left alone, scolded and allowed to die an early death. That is more painful than his ultimate day. Therefore, the patient must be treated with compassion and care. AIDS is not spread from a cause other than those mentioned earlier. So, it is safe to handle the patient and give him a moral support and careful assistance. Almost 90 per cent of people are being infected due to the transmission of the HIV virus through sexual intercourse. The balance 10 per cent include cases of blood transfusion and drug abuse. Indian housewives are also falling prey to the deadly AIDS disaster primarily due to the lack of sex education.

Unfortunately, AIDS is spreading like a wild fire on the Indian subcontinent. The youth of today are getting addicted to drugs and premartial sex. Both these activities are contributing immensely towards the spread the killer disease. Despite the efforts by the State, no control can be devised to curtail this menace unless the youth and the responsible citizens of the nation accept the responsibility of fighting it. According to a recent estimate, there are 40,00,000 patients of AIDS in India, the highest number in the world. This ugly spread of the killer disease could overtake students, housewives, executives, sex workers, truck drivers and labourers with an alarming pace. The cost of testing and treating a patient is still very high; for an AIDS test, a patient used to spend Rs 1,000-1,500, which is very high amount for the lowest strata of our society. Now a days, some AIDS kits have been developed that test the disease at a nominal cost of Rs 300-400 only. But medical treatment for AIDS is costly. The most commonly used medicines for the treatment of AIDS include Zidoudine, Didanosine drugs and Dideoxycytidine. Keeping in mind the apathy of the family and the trauma of patient, we could conclude that prevention is always better than cure. The issue needs careful attention from the individual, the State and the medical community alike.

38. POPULATION THREAT : INDIAN EXPERIENCES

Indian Population was low during the fifties—Tremendous growth—Now more than1 billion people—Higher population pressures lead to unemployment, violence, unrest and lowering of living standards—Family planning efforts made by the government but not enough—Vasectomies and sterilisations on the rise—Urban people control population due to economic causes—Ninth Five Year Plan aims for checking the population growth—Social reform must—Solutions are available.

India is the second largest populous country in the world. A developing nation by economic status, India cannot afford to increase her population. China, the most populous country, has been able to achieve a population growth rate of almost zero. If the current trend of population rise continues, India could be the leading country in terms of population by the year 2020 AD.

Our population was 361 million in 1911, which rose to 252 million in 1951. The average growth rate was 1.33 per cent. During the 1911-921 period the death rate was 27.40 per thousand, which rose to 48.60 per thousand. The birth rate was 49.2 per thousand during 1901-1911 period. During the 1941-1951 period, birth rate was 39.90 per thousand. These trends indicated that the high death rate was due to famines, poverty, lack of medical facilities and other natural calamities, though the birth rate was also high. The rise in population of India was, therefore, off set by a high death rate..

The death rate dropped to 22.80 per thousand in 1961 census and to 15 per thousand during 1981. The birth rate was 41.20 per thousand in 1971 and came down to 37.20 per thousand in 1981. As per the 1991 census, the birth rate fell to 32.50 per thousand and death rate fell down to 11.40 per thousand. During 1981, the annual population growth rate was 2.22 per cent whereas the same figure was 2.14 per cent in the 1991 census. These results proved that the efforts made by the State proved to be fruitful.

On March 1, 1991, 846.30 million people resided in India. Indian population was 16 per cent of the world population (1991 estimates). In the latter half of the year 1999, Indian population touched a new peak of 1,000 million. The world is awestruck by the manner in which, we have grown in terms of numbers. Most of the population concentrations are in urban areas and small townships. Population pressures have perpetuated poverty, illiteracy and unemployment. Lack of water, land, power and other vital resources for survival and growth has been more discernible during the eighties and the nineties. The living standards of Indians have degraded whereas the Western countries have advanced on account of low or nil population growth rates.

Indian response to population growth came in terms of family planning programmes. During the First Five Year Plan, a sum of Rs 6.5 million was allocated for family planning. During the Eighth Five Year Plan (1992-97), funds for the family planning programmes were to the tune of Rs 65,000 million. The *Panchayat Samitis*, Village Development Committees and *Mahila Mandals* were involved for carrying out the herculean tasks of family planning and female education.

In 1965, Intra Uterine Devices, (IUDs) did not get a good response from the masses. During 1970s, the state and central governments laid more stress on vasectomies and sterilisation programmes. During the emergency period, the wrong policies and coercion by the State proved to be suicidal for the masses. Many sterilisation operations were performed on the young, unmarried and non-eligible individuals. During the 1977-1980 period, the family planning programme suffered many jolts. However, from 1980-81 onwards, the programme began to pick up gradually. During 1980-81 to 1988-89, 24.4 million people accepted various methods for population control. Gujarat, Haryana, Himachal Pradesh, Kerala, Maharashtra, Punjab and Tamil Nadu are the states, which adopted these methods.

During the Eighth Five Year Plan, the aim for birth rate was 27 per thousand and the death rate had been fixed at 8.20 per thousand by 1997. The annual average growth rate was expected to be 1.78 per cent. However, the targets (in terms of control of population,) were not achieved. The Ninth Five Year Plan (1997-2002) also aims at checking the growth of population. But the targets seem to be elusive.

By 2011 AD, the Indian population figure is likely to be 1164.25 million. Life expectancy would be above 67 years and birth rate would come down to 7-10 per thousand. Population growth rate would be 1.38 per cent per annum.

The rural areas remain untouched by the efforts of the Department of Family Welfare and other government agencies. The urban population accepts birth control measures due to economic reasons. The rural masses demand more off-springs as they need more people for labour jobs in the fields. Add to this, female illiteracy, backwardness in rural areas, early marriages and lack of proper devices for avoiding conception. Every family demands a son from the newcomer bride, which leads to abortions in favour of the male child. The girl child is also neglected in rural as well as in urban areas.

The solutions for this major problem would have to be devised quickly. Some of the solutions are as follows :—

(1) The State must support female literacy programmes in the rural areas so that women understand their rights and responsibilities.

(2) Intra Uterine Devices (IUDs), condoms and pills for birth control must be distributed free of cost in the country. This is being done but more supplies must be ensured so that the people do not find an excuse for increasing the population.

(3) The status of the girl child must be elevated to the one of respect in the rural areas as well as in the urban societies. The non-government organisations, social workers, state laws and central laws could deliver results.

(4) The economic compulsions of the urban middle income groups force them to have fewer children. However, the upper middle income groups do not find this as a reason for population control. These groups must be contacted personally and requested to control population growth.

(5) The laws, prescribing the minimum ages for boys and girls for marriage, should be enforced strictly. The State must deal with the wrong-doers with an iron hand. Registration of marriage must be made compulsory for making such laws effective.

(6) Social reforms must be effected in order to fight the banes of society like drinking, bride burning, preference for son in the family, unwanted pregnancies and exploitation of women.

(7) It would be very appropriate if the State agrees to take complete responsibility of the first child of every family. The education (upto classs X), mid-day meals for primary schools, books and career planning should be done by the government in consultation with the parents. The first child

should be given ample opportunities for graduation, post-graduation and vocational studies. He or she should be given grants for business or even a government job if he or she eligible for the same. The State should not take any responsibility of any other child of the family. This scheme, if implemented, could be very popular and would persuade families for adopting effective family planning measures.

(8) The contraception devices like condoms, IUDs *etc* are not easily available in rural areas and the lack of family planning devices leads to population pressures. The rural areas must be supplied with liberal quantitites of such devices. The doctors and nurses of Primary Health Centres must take additional responsibility of counselling the rural women on family planning issues.

A highly populous nation is a threat to her citizens and her social and economic growth. We must bring down this alarming growth rate in our population. China has already achieved almost nil population growth rate and the authorities are quite strict about family planning issues in that country. If India wants to avoid a social and economic disaster during the next millennium, then she must handle this sensitive issue with utmost seriousness.

39. BEAUTY SELLS

Ms Yukta Mukhey is the New Miss World—Colourful pageant at London on December 5, 1999—Earlier also, Indian beauties did us proud—Beauty pageants are money-making mechanisms—Why should beauty be commercialised ? Stages of the beauty contest appended—No rational criteria for judgement of the brains of presence of mind of the contestants—Artificial procedures and a veneer of formality present in the contests—Young boys and girls love to compete in these contests—These contests have been welcomed by the masses and the elites in a hesitant manner.

On December, 1999, twenty-year old Ms Yukta Mukhey, a beautiful damsel from India, was crowned "Miss World" in London. This exhilarating news was splashed in the print and electronic media of the world with unequalled enthusiasm and gloss. And Indians were proud once again. After the runaway success of Ms Sushmita Sen (Miss Universe-1994), Ms Aishwarya Rai (Miss World-1994) and Ms Diana Hayden (Miss World-1997), Ms Yukta Mukhey, the beautiful lady from Dubai and of Indian origin, won the laurels for her country in 1999. She was adjudged as the best contestant out of a total number of 94 candidates. Indian damsels have developed a consistent habit of winning such contests. However we would like to elaborate the ugly aspects of beauty contests that are, unfortunately, sponsored by the money-minded sponsors and entertainment-starved masses around the world.

Nevertheless, this pageant was a grand success. And we shall not raise any objection in connection with the morality and sanctity of using women as objects of exposure that feed upon the lascivious instincts of sex-hungry souls of the viewers. This issue is more or less connected to basic human psyche and human psyche chooses its moral standards, depending upon the situation encountered. Our subject of discussion is entirely different. We cannot stop these contests on the moral grounds. After all, where is morality left in the social, personal, business and religious segments of our lives ?

When a beauty pageant is organised, billions of Dollars are spent on the same. The entire exercise has a whopping cost and the sponsors foot the bill. There are seventy or eighty participants who are carefully hand-picked for the contest. For the sake of adding Indian tinge, some Indian models or students are selected. For the sake of representing South American States, a few girls are selected from those nations. Then, in order to represent the Negro race, a few black beauties are also selected. The considerations for selection have been defined. However, if the statistics match those of the pre-defined standards, the lady is short-listed for the beauty pageant. If the lady were of a weight of 55 kg, should she not apply ? If she is underweight, should she apply ? Let us suppose that ideal weight according to the norms of a beauty contest is 52 kg. Then, all those girls, whose weights do not match this figure, are ugly ? There is no logic for judging the proper health and physical fitness of a candidate. No one is interested to know that a woman confirming to a few specific health norms may not be the beauty queen of a nation, subcontinent or the entire world.

Let us move slightly further. The selected candidates are allowed to swim, play and chat. They are photographed in the bikinis, night gowns and party dresses. It is true that a woman expresses herself by getting ready for a particular occasion. But what about the judges? How do they realise that Miss X is the real beauty who walks perfectly, swims perfectly and talks gracefully? In fact, this is a very complex area of human psychology. A person may judge another person as malevolent, haughty and belligerent but this very person could be judged by another person as amicable, benevolent and empathetic human being. Further, how could we decide that ladies participating in the contest would always continue to behave in the same manner as they have done during the contest? In the pageant, their careers, the prestige of their respective countries and the funds of the sponsors are at stake. How could they possibly afford to be natural?

The final stage of the contest is organised in a big hall that is full of people and onlookers. The sponsors have already pumped in so much of money and the inputs of the media blitzkrieg that it is impossible to withdraw. The ladies are asked funny questions and they are supposed to give logical answers to all of them. A typical question could be, "If you get one million Dollars, what would you like to do?" The lady would reply like a parrot, "Sir. I would like to construct homes for the poor and the needy with a part of it. Rest would be donated to the Red Cross and other charity organisations." And she would be given a standing ovation by the audience. After a few more funny questions, the winner and the runner-up would be declared. And all this would happen in a period of three to four hours. The winner would take away the crown, a few tickets for travel around the world and a few hundred thousand Dollars. The grief-stricken runner-up would also be paid something. It would be stated that she had missed the crown by only one or two points.

Our readers would note the element of artificial procedures and a veneer of formality in these pageants. Beauty is a natural phenomenon. Then, why cover it under face-packs, costly and gaudy dresses, lipsticks and mascara? All these gimmicks are resorted to for generating money. The lady of the show and the organisers earn and so do the sponsors. Our readers must have observed that the "Law of Dollars" is applicable to the stage shows and fashion shows as well. The idea of enticing the audiences and TV viewers through the vulgar presentation of the fair sex has come of age now. And add to it the spice added by the male models and the formula for minting money is complete.

The artificial life of today cannot offer us more than this. We have, as already stated, not delved upon the thought of vulgarity in these shows and the degradation of the weaker sex, on-stage as well as off-stage. This is acceptable as no one would be able to oppose it in the wake of the rising opposition to all types of moral considerations. The basic thought is that the sponsors and organisers are able to "sell beauty" and earn millions. They have devised a wicked method for generating enormous volumes of profits and are not accountable for their deeds to anyone. If the government of the host city intervenes, it is paid a part of the loot as 'taxes' and the show goes on.

In the new millennium, our worthy readers are required to question every phenomenon that is beyond the purview of logic. If we do away with the logic of morality and misuse of the fair sex in these shows, what about the monetary aspect ? Is this method of making money (read "minting money") legal ? A worker works hard for days an nights and gets a salary that is not sufficient for him or his family to survive. But our beauty pageants make their organisers millionaires overnight. What a contrast !

Those young boys and girls, who watch these programmes on TV or live, yearn for the fortune or the fame that have been bestowed upon Yuktas, Aishwaryas, Dianas and Sushmitas. They do not know the artificial world that is behind these shows. That world is merciless, highly professional and mean in terms of its objectives. The concepts of beauty and modelling have been commercialised to such an extent as would put the business acumen of the corporate Mughals to shade. In this era of Dollars, the usage of a beautiful woman is only for bringing the audiences to the pageant hall. Nobody adores beauty in a beauty contest. The questions and answers, irrespective of their impact upon the plebian and the simple-minded rural folks, are structured. The selection process judges the contestants on the basis of on-the-spot assessment procedures. What the lady did during the past and what she is likely to do in future, is altogether a different affair.

We hesitatingly welcome our worthy readers to this new world of artificial beauty that does not lie in the eyes of the beholder but in the wallets of those who are avid viewers and admirers of these events, ultimately branded as a farce. There is no other option; we all have to stay in this artificial world ! ●

40. WESTERN CULTURE : INDIAN VIEWPOINT

Western culture money-minded and professional but Indian culture endured through ages—Fast life in the West—Now, the West affecting Indian culture—Our old values wearing off—Solutions lie in accepting only the positive aspects of their culture—Adopt technologies, productivity and global thinking from them—Do not let our value system be affected by Western culture—Western culture is pragmatic, affluent and technology oriented—Adopt these aspects—Tune the Western features to Indian needs—Do not take negative aspects of the Western culture.

Indian culture is supreme. It has withstood the test of time for 7,000 years. Our arts and crafts, dances, music, abilities in mathematics and sciences and the ancient scriptures have put us on the top of the cultural and scientific platforms of the world.

However, with the advent of television, satellites and cable TV networks, Internet and casual foreign culture, **we** Indians have forgotten our basic value system. Pornography, **drugs**, entertainment beyond limits and a casual approach to life are the products of the Western influence. Now, we do out buy a car for travel but to compete with our neighbour who had purchased one only last week. Western culture is materialistic, very fast and anxiety-prone.

Western culture teaches us to be professionals, thus forcing us to leave behind the values of our ancient culture. The respect for parents and teachers has evaporated as the young child thinks that he can do everything on his own. Joint family system has broken down to form nuclear family system. There is mad rush for making money. Religion, social values and simplicity have taken a backseat in the minds of the child, the young teenager and the household.

Let us discuss some of the solutions. Western attitude towards life is not that bad. There are some positive aspects as well. For example, Western countries have been able to control the forces of nature and are leading the world in terms of significant revolutions in all the spheres of business, industry and commerce. We must learn about new technologies from them and must adopt them for our development.

Secondly, Westerners work very hard. For example, Americans and Japanese work so hard for five days of the week that they are unable to go to their workplaces during the weekends. That is why, they have five-day weeks in their offices.

Thirdly, Westerners are more productive. Their attitude towards work is a religious one. They carry out all their assignments in a truly professional manner. The *Vedas* have stated—"*Yoga Karmasu Kaushalam,*" which means that *Yoga* means doing one's task in the most efficient manner. Our bureaucracy must learn a lesson or two from this ancient *Mantra*.

Fourthly, Western culture is efficient in many respects. Education, standards of living, business interactions and attitudes towards life are very practical. In India, the sick psyche of the individual affects his growth in all walks of life. Bureaucracy, red-tapism and corruption dominate our political, economic and social lives. The institutional decay takes the toll of the Indian masses everyday whereas the institutions are quite efficient and productive in the West. The agility, commitment towards goals and a pragmatic approach to life could be adopted by us for the sake of our national and societal growth.

Finally, Western culture is technology oriented. This is a good sign for the growth of mankind. We must adopt new technologies from the West. However, precaution is necessary here. Western society has become a slave of technology. For example, there is a new computer model after every six months and people rush to buy it. The speed with which, the computer technology changes, forces the executive, the household and children to join the mad rush for new technologies, hardware, software and supporting peripherals. Here, technology drives the man whereas the reverse should have been true. Similarly, there is a new model of every car in the West every year, which forces the consumers to buy new cars (even if the old cars are working properly). Indians must adopt new technologies but must not get into the mad rush for useless and unsafe technologies. Further, they should adopt Western technologies for Indian needs.

The negative impacts of the Western culture are hard to erase. Western culture supports free sex, independence after eighteen years of age, a free market system (in which individual is a mere cog in the machine) and the leisure-oriented lifestyle. It does not support marriage as an institution for social and family security etc. Indians should not adopt these values as these are the products of a confused Western mind. The Westerner lives for his own sake whereas an Indian lives for his children. Our social value system is respected by the world. It is an irony that many young boys and girls (especially, Indian youth staying in the Western countries) are adopting the negative social values of the West. The results are obvious—broken marriages, free sex, AIDS, family disturbances and suicides, mad rush for money and the eventual loss of health and money due to these influences.

Finally, the Western culture is global and intends to make this world a global village. Indian culture must be assimilated by the citizens of the world as its virtues would certainly get it accepted around the world. We are crazy about foreign goods, dances, music and personalities. Western people also value our arts and crafts, meditation, *yoga*, dance forms, music and cultural heritage.

We should emphasise here that nothing is bad; it is only the attitude that makes it so. We must adopt the positive influences of the Western culture and must weed out the negative influences. For example, we must never support indecent exposure on television but must support the spread of Internet, which is the new information superhighway. Indian individual has a discerning mind. He can make out what is good for him, his family and his society. Acceptance of positive Western norms is in our lands. And truly, the rejection of the adverse influences depends upon the fully aware Indian mind of today.

41. SOCIAL PROBLEMS IN INDIAN MILIEU

India a great nation—Many achievements—But social issues affect our national fabric—Dowry deaths—Religious violence—Deterioration in living standards despite good economic progress—Pollution in urban areas—Poor masses not given their dues—Female literacy—Lack of social interaction among friends, relatives and in neighbourhood—Ignorance about habitat and environment—Cheating of consumers by capitalistic system and free markets—Cultural threats from the West—Let Indian culture bind us.

India is great nation with rich cultural heritage and vast resources. Our tradition, arts, crafts and achievements in the fields of science and technology have put us on the top in the group of developing countries. India is a power to reckon with in NAM, is well heard in the UNO and leads the pack of SAARC nations. Our record of economic progress is laudable. Our political stability is a matter of pride for us. Our technical and managerial manpower has made the country proud in all the parts of the globe. Indeed, India is nation heading truly towards the new millennium.

However, all is not well at the home front. We are only fifty years old. We face a lot of social problems which are impinging upon our national fabric. Our elders wonder sometimes whether the youth of this country would be able to maintain the integrity of the country which was won after a long struggle. Many social issues face us and we are unable to find pragmatic and long lasting solutions primarily because of the lack of resources and to social backwardness.

Let us consider the growing problem of dowry deaths. Innocent girls are being sacrificed on the sinful alter of dowry due to the greed of money and materialistic assets. The society of today has matured with spread of education and development of technologies. However, the devil of dowry still haunts our young brides. Even educated bridegrooms demand dowry as a compensation for their education, foreign travel or for an upgradation in their living standards. Police, judiciary andorganisations supporting the cause of women are helpless on account of legal formalities or financial constraints. The real culprits always escape. The poor sufferers (bride and the parents of the bride) are unable to get justice even after years of court trial. Dowry deaths are on the rise. But the judicial system is so slow that most of the cases become too stale to be decided in favour of the suffering party. Voluntary organisations, NGOs and social organisations for women do take steps for justice, rehabilitation **and awareness**. However, our social milieu does not allow this evil tradition to be eliminated from the mind of an **average** Indian.

The other social issue is that of religious violence. Due to political reasons, religion has always been misused and thousands of innocent people are massacred every year in the Indian subcontinent. Almost all the major cities and townships of Indian subcontinent face communal tension. Curfews are imposed. *Lathi Charge*, tear gas and police firing are resorted for restoration of peace. However, anti-social elements always incite the innocent people and let them fight among themselves. This results in deaths, destruction and chaos.

The minority communities allege that they suffer the most. The majority community says that it has not got its due rights. The tensions always escalate on account of very minor issues. Even after fifty years of independence, the threat of communal hatred looms large over the Indian horizon. This is a great setback for our economic and social progress. The politician always plays the communal card to his advantage. The ordinary man on the street suffers on account of machinations of the political parties and a handful of extremist groups who spread nothing but hatred, discord and disagreement.

The third social issue that faces Indian masses is the deterioration in the standards of living. It is true that we have developed as a nation. We have many economic, technological and industrial achievements to our credit. We have the largest pool of technical manpower in the world. Our doctors, engineers, scientists and software programmers have done us proud in all the parts of the world. However, technological progress has been made at the cost of the society. The industries emit harmful pollutants. The toxic chemicals, gases and other substances have degraded our environment beyond compare. True, we have colour televisions, cable TV connections and Internet connectivities all around. However, we would not be able to get pure drinking water. This is especially true for metropolises like Delhi, Mumbai, Chennai, Bangalore and Ahmedabad. Traffic jams, noise pollution, degradation in foods and poor quality of air contribute towards the development of a physically and mentally sick individual. As a result, mothers are giving births to physically handicapped children. The decay in the quality of life has affected us adversely. Delhi is the fourth most polluted city in the world. Even in smaller cities and townships, the quality of life has not improved. Let us not be impressed by the media blitzkreig, satellite television, cable television networks, modern electronic gadgets and materialism in all the walks of rural and urban lives of Indian society.

The benefits of a free market economy and rapid industrialisation have not trickled down to the families at lower economic levels in our society. Rural poverty has increased over the last fifteen years. There is no change in the pitiable conditions of agricultural labourers, *Dalit* workers and scavengers. Even the Class-III employees are no better. Food, clothing and shelter standards enjoyed by them remain as low as ever.

We do not wish to state that a free market system is not fit for Indian Industry and economy. We do support free market economics. However, the poor masses do not get ample opportunities for earning despite the free market system. In order to survive in a free market world, one has to be either an expert in one field or he has to be highly connected or financially capable. Most of the Indian masses lack all these advantages and twenty per cent of the population (which enjoys at least two of these leverages) continues to grow at an amazing rate. Only a few can afford education for their children beyond ten-plus-two level. Proper education is a dream for most of the lower-middle income groups. As a result, they send their children for work after only twelve or sixteen years of schooling or college. Education makes us competent enough for earning and struggling amidst the jungle of hardships. Special attention must be given to female literacy campaigns as the hands that rock the cradle, rule the world.

Another striking feature of modern Indian social milieu is the lack of social interaction among friends, relatives and people in the immediate vicinity. This phenomenon is more prominent in urban centres. Modern age is the age of the professional. A professional has very little time for leisure or socialisation. He is unable to devote enough of time to his children, wife or friends. The urban centres are the commercial hubs of Indian economy. People work for days and nights for the sake of money and materialistic assets. They forget social norms and responsibilities and hence, get isolated. Isolation leads to frustration and rejection from family and neighbourhood. As a result, psychological problems arise, which are very difficult to cope with and solve.

Another problem that affects our social fabric adversely is the alarming illiteracy level. With the exception of Kerala (where literacy level is the highest in the country), the situation is grim in all other parts of the nation. An uneducated woman is unable to groom and train her off-springs for a better future. An uneducated man is not able to earn enough for the survival and growth of his family. Thus poverty perpetuates literacy and *vice versa*. Despite the media hype, the rural educational programmes have not been able to deliver adequate results. The parents refrain from sending the girl child to the school and this is the main hurdle in the development of our social, economic and industrial backbones. Although people are realising the value of education now, yet we have a long way to go before achieving complete literacy in our country.

Another social issue is of ignorance of individuals about their environs. India is a growing country. Rapid pace of Industrialisation, urbanisation and technological developments are visible across the length and breadth of the nature. This generates more pollution, garbage, industrial wastes and household wastes. The Indian mind is immune to dirt and garbage. Instead of clearing it, we tolerate it and try to generate more dirt and pollution. This affects quality of life in an adverse manner. Government certainly takes suitable measures. But these are not adequate, keeping in mind that India is a vast nation with limited resources. Our social responsibilities are always sidelined in favour of our lust for money. We lack time and resources but we have to protect our habitat and environment as well. Hence, a few steps, if taken judiciously, could save our environment and our habitat from dirt, garbage and pollution. This is for our benefit as our children would inherit all those complications tomorrow that we generate today.

Finally, the social issue that faces our society is the lack of support for the common man in his routine grievances. The consumers are cheated everyday on account of spurious or costly products. The employer turns out the labourers or workers from his establishment without giving their wages or salaries to them. Electricity, water, telephone, sewage, housing and transportation services are not adequate in any part of the country. Wherever these are adequate, the population pressures force the State to revise the costs of maintenance. The ultimate sufferer is the poor consumer. There are consumer protection fora in all the major and minor cities. But we are unaware of our rights and privileges as Indian citizens and hence, suffer on account of our own ignorance. There is a decay in the institutions;

police, judiciary, telecommunications, political mainstreams, primary health services are some of the glaring examples. And there is nobody to check their degradation. Everybody wants to grind his own axe out of the corrupt system and then, he sits quietly when he gets his share. Nobody speaks up against the system or its corrupt officials as he himself is either a part or a beneficiary of the same. So, we must admit that we are ourselves responsible for this decay.

We must conclude by stating that we are facing a very grim situation in our social context. However, India has withstood the test of time for seven thousand years. She would be able to overcome these problems as well. We must develop as a nation and not as individuals. We must understand our social, economic and human responsibilities. We must maintain our human values despite the onslaughts of Western culture and free market economics. We must remain Indians at heart. That is the only spirit which could bind all of us !

42. THE CRIME SCENARIO

Mumbai murders raised panic—Delhi also witnessing crime wae—Jessica Lal murder case—Media persons killed—Cinema, economic backwardness, greed for more money, unemployment etc contribute towards the rising crime graph—1984 riots in Delhi—Punjab problem solved after 10 years of strife—Kashmir problem still alive—Politician-bureaucrat-criminal axis maintained to perpetuate crime—Crimes against SCs and STs—Some solutions suggested.

Recently, the brutal assassinations of music magnate, Gulshan Kumar, film producer, Mukesh Duggal and trade union leader, Datta Samanta sent ripples of terror in Mumbai. Everybody asked one question, "Is Mumbai safe for living ?" Delhi is not far behind in the incidents of murder and arson. The colonies of South Delhi are the most vulnerable pockets. Children and senior citizens are falling prey to the killers and hooligans who operate at their will.

Deleterious depiction of violence by all the media, greed for money, economic backwardness, chronic unemployment and lack of effectiveness of the police force in many areas of the country have led us to believe that we are still living in the dark ages.

The riots organised in Delhi in 1984 have gone down the memory lane. Modern India has become a hotbed of hatred, violence and terrorism. We could barely overcome the terrorist threat in Punjab. And now, the Kashmiri militants are creating havoc in the entire Northern belt, thanks to support firm across the border. Despite a crushing defeat during the Kargil war, Pakistan continues to send armed foreign mercenaries to Jammu and Kashmir who attack soft targets and military personnel at will. The land of Lord Buddha, Lord Mahavira and Gandhiji is crying for peace and freedom from the machinations of a handful of people who they would go to any limits for their achieving their evil objectives.

Violence has entered all walks of life—business, industry, politics, social interactions, national and international fora and above all, interpersonal relationships. Some incidents have been recorded where violence was a mere result of ego clashes between the warring factions.

Political and economic factors lead to global terrorism. The AK-47 and AK-56 (automatic rifles) were developed during the Second World War. However, these have killed more people during peace than they did during the war. Nobel was the inventor of the dynamite and his invention served the world wars very well. However, the present, day compulsions of war and strike call for even more dependence upon dynamite and gunpowder. The concept was devised for a different purpose and its negative usage has been made in the present era for the most dangerous applications.

In India, after comparing the statistics of 1996 and 1997, it has been concluded that dacoites increased by 45 per cent, murders increased by 87 per cent, rape cases increased by 11 per cent and finally, dowry deaths increased by 15 per cent over the figures of 1996. The number of IPC cases is the same in 1997 as was during the previous year. However, most of the cases are not registered and the culprits manage a free life for themselves due to legal loopholes. During the last general elections, there were 123 candidates who had criminal records. Among them, 90 were accused of murder, 22 faced more than 3 murder charges and 28 others were history sheeters. The number of crimes against SCs and STs increased during the 1992-1994 period. Whereas the number of cases (in which, the underprivileged were victims) was 25,352 in 1992, the same figure was 38,926 in 1994.

Recently popular model, Jessica Lal, was murdered in a seemingly innocuous scuffle in a bar. Press reporters—Shivani and Irafaan—were murdered because they had tried to bring some antisocial elements into the light the day. The crime graph has been rising in all the major cities of the country. Life and dignity of woman are not safe in big cities after late evening hours. The nexus between the politician and the criminal has added a new thrust to the crime wave and ripples can be felt throughout the nation.

Cinema has played a subversive role in the crime scene of today. The movies of today reflect sex, violence and confusion on the screen, which are assimilated by the minds of the cinegoers. The violent state of the present era is depicted by the film makers on the celluloid and this, in turn, leads to more violence. This vicious circle continues and the youth as well as the tender minds of the children are occupied by destructive tendencies. For example, a child may not be able to recall any particular incident from his history textbook but is very well aware about the latest movie being shown in the cinema halls of the city. The world of cinema is directed by the market forces and the choice of the viewers. Some viewers, however, want peaceful, rational and constructive cinema whereas youth and children prefer suspenseful and violent movies. Some children attempted to carry out impossible feats by copying the lead character of soap opera-*Shaktimaan*-and lost their lives.

The society of the modern times is commercial, introvert and selfish. People are more interested in making money than in healthy activities like meditation, social gatherings, charity for the poor and the disabled and constructive leisure. True, money is important and must be earned to survive but hankering for money and for other materialistic assets is dangerous. Further, the individual of the modern era is egoistic and in order to prove himself to be supreme, he indulges in senseless violence, which proves to be fatal or injurious for him.

Solutions for the crime scenario are many. We have to adopt the right solution according to situation in a city, colony, state or region. Every criminal problem demands a unique solution. Some solutions are as follows :—

(1) We cannot uplift the standards of the poor and the underprivileged in one day. Removal of poverty would take time. However, the State must ensure a minimum survival **kit** for the citizens (especially for the rural populace). The

Common Minimum Programme promoted (CMP) by the government is a healthy step in this direction.

(2) The police personnel are bound to extort money from the public if their families remain starved. If the police force is trained effectively, paid well and is made an autonomous organisation, the crime rate would be reduced to one fourth of the present figures. Mr Shankar Sen, Member of the National Human Rights Commission, pointed out that police autonomy must be accompanied by accountability.

(3) Crimes against SCs and STs (which account for 25 per cent of the national population) should be checked with an iron hand.

(4) Technology should protect societal interests. The police force should be given modern communication tools, transportation facilities and advanced weapons for combat. How can a head constable, with a fifteen year old rifle, fight a terrorist with AK-56 rifle ? The State must equip the police and paramilitary forces with advanced equipment for checking terrorism and other subversive activities in the country.

(5) The central government should negotiate with terrorist groups like ULFA, Veerappan, Bodo extremists, LTTE and JKLF so that peaceful solutions could be devised. If, however, the solutions are far from sight, the paramilitary forces should control them through planned operations so that there is no harm to the public lives and property.

(6) The professionals, artists and promotors associated with media (Radio, TV, newspapers and magazines) should promote positive and healthy cultural values for which, India has been known for centuries. If we accept only the positive influences of the Western cultures, we would certainly overcome the crime wave, which is on the verge of breaking our national fabric.

Osama Bin Laden, Kashmiri militants, Irish Guerillas, Afghan terrorists, Sudanese mercenaries, LTTE commandoes, ULFA militants, terrorists of Algeria and other misguided sections of the global society would have to be moulded into healthy and human oriented shells through persuation and moderate levels of coercion. Terrirism must be put to an end around the world as it has already annihilated millons of humans and property worth billions of Dollars around the world. We cannot pay a higher price for survival. We want to live in peace. "Live and Let Live" should be our first motto. It it does not work, then we ought to follow—"Power flows from the barrel of a gun."

43. RESERVATION RE-DEFINED

Government expanded the reservation list by adding 126 subcastes from 17 states of India—This move is a political ploy to generate vote banks—All the governments resort to such measures—The creamy layers of the backward classes reap rich benefits—Others are left behind—Judicial opinions were against haphazard and high levels of reservation—Government did not pay head to the Judicial advice—Reservation to continue in the Lok Sabha till 2010 AD—Debar the creamy layers—Try to fix economic criteria as the building blocks of reservation in all the areas.

On November 19, 1999, the central government expanded the list of backward classes and added 126 more subcastes from 17 states of the Indian union. The decision was taken in the meeting of the union cabinet in which, it approved the recommendations of the National Backward Castes Commission. This was the second amendment in the list of backward castes in two months. Some subcastes, which were included in the list, are *Yadavas, Kasais, Telis Sahus, Teli Rathods, Ramgarhias, Julahas, Sainis, Swarnakars, Sukariars, Shersha Badis* etc. These subcastes belong to the states, of UP, Punjab, Bihar, Andhra Pradesh, Goa, Chandigarh, Kerala, Madhya Pradesh, Rajasthan, Karnataka, Gujarat, Orissa, Tripura, Tamil Nadu, West Bengal, Pondicherry and Sikkim. Most of the backward subcastes have been included from Uttar Pradesh. This step of the government has given a new fillip to the reservation issue. Clearly, the present government in the centre plans to extend its mass base that was always in favour of the governments and political ideologies promoted by the Congress party. This decision has a political tinge as the NDA-led coalition government would like to be "on its own" in the times to come and hence, it would like to make deep inroads into the vote banks of backward subcastes by pleasing them.

In the *Lok Sabha*, reservation of backward castes would continue for a period of 10 years, starting from the day of January 26, 2000.

It is our sanguine opinion that reservations would not cease even after January 26, 2000; a new legislation could be passed in the *Lok Sabha* in order to extend reservations in the *Lok Sabha* even after the stipulated date. It is an irony that the backwardness of a man is so vital for the survival of all the political groups. Hence, these groups try to extend 'favours' to them in order to keep their ships sailing. This honour is, perhaps, too much for the common man belonging to a scheduled subcaste, whose value is nothing more than the vote that he is required to cast at the hustings.

On the eve of the elections for the thirteenth *Lok Sabha*, the Jat Mahasabha had announced the withdrawal of its support to the Congress as it had failed to secure reservation for Jats. The BJP took the opportunity to secure reservation for Jats. Rajputs did not react kindly to this move. Muslims and Christians also demanded reservation. The Samajwadi Party, the BSP and Congress supported Muslims on the issue of reservation. BJP supported a wide array of subcastes for their inclusion in the coveted list and these were mainly Hindus and Sikhs. Therefore, all the parties have priorities in terms of reservation of castes as well. The BJP supported the "Jat Cause" and reaped rich benefits. Mr Sahib Singh Verma, the ousted CM or Delhi, was elected as a MP in the thirteenth *Lok Sabha*. The areas of Outer Delhi, as is well known, are Jat strongholds. The BJP outperformed all other parties in these areas and was way ahead of others.

Article 16 of the Constitution assures job reservation for any backward class, which has not been adequately represented in the services under the state in question. Clause (1) of this Article states, "There shall be equality of opportunity for all citizens in matters relating to employment or appointment to any office under the State." These two views were in contradiction with each other. Hence, the Supreme Court ruled in 1992 that the power of reservation under Article 16 ought to be exercised in a fair manner and within reasonable limits. The two provisions, stated above, are complimentary, provided that both are given equal importance without giving lower weightage to the other. The contradiction with each other and the issue of being complementary with each other were discussed by the apex court. The court had remarked, in the context of the Indira Sawhney versus the Union of India case that large segments of population (enjoying political advantages) could use their backward status. Therefore, these castes could gain in terms of economic benefits, issue of land and employment in the PSUs. The government was advised not to give reservation to these castes.

The apex court had also stated that backwardness under Clause (4) of Article 16 only meant "social backwardness" and that "backward classes of citizens" were those who had low social standing in the society and whose occupations as well as income levels were low.

The upper limit of reservation was also kept at 50 per cent through judicial rulings. The judiciary fears that excessive reservation is likely to lead to reduced number of opportunities for men of merit in those categories that are not reserved (the open merit list). The Supreme Court had advised the government that in the fields of medicine, engineering, nuclear research, aviation, research and development and other speciality areas, reservation of any type was not advisable; the highly technical nature of these jobs demanded only those candidates who possessed the skills to perform the specific tasks. The court had opined that there would always be those candidates who would be able to qualify in the open competitions due to their merits and toil, for admission to super-speciality courses. And this could be done without lowering the admission criteria for these candidates. In sum, if a candidate belonged to a backward caste, he could still become an engineer or a doctor, depending upon the hard work put in by him to achieve his goal. There is supposed to be a competition of the brains and not of the various castes and subcastes, as is being done at present.

But the rulings of the apex court have not been understood in the right perspective by any government; which has ruled in the centre. The Seventy-seventh Amendment of 1995 has restored reservation in the support of SC/ST employees; it was disallowed in the Indira Sawhney case. This was effected by inserting a new enabling provision [Clause 4(A)], in Article 16 of Indian Constitution. This Clause seems to promote the interests of those backward castes who enjoy political clout in the centre as well as in the states. The latest amendments increase the reservation to more than the level of fifty percent. Thus the concept of creamy layer has been eliminated, which debars the forward sections of the backward castes from the benefits of reservation. This move would hurt the candidates of the general category. The real objective of reservation was to help the backward castes come out of the darkness of social and economic backwardness. It was not meant to punish the meritorious candidates of the general category. If the thrust on reservation continues unabated, the problem of brain drain would assume serious proportions. The talented candidates of general category are already heading towards the West in search of greener pastures.

Further, within the same caste, there could be a dangerous formation of subgroups—backwards, more backwards and most backwards. The criterion for judgement would not be clear to any NGO, State-run institution or judiciary. This would lead to intra-caste conflicts. Inter-caste conflicts would also rise in terms of number and intensity as the members of every caste would like their caste to be included for reservations in the *Lok Sabha*, state assemblies, PSUs and educational institutions.

In order to curb the reservation menace, strict laws should be passed, which should be able to give reservation quotas to the candidates on the basis of economic backwardness. The criteria of social backwardness and religion ought to be done away with. As on date, the middle class people (the bourgouese)has been suffering on account of reservations. The middle class of Indian society has now become too powerful to be ignored. A reprisal from this group could be predicted in the year 2010 when the reservation issue in the *Lok Sabha* would be discussed again. Before that happens, the State must shift the criteria of reservation to "economically backward groups. All the lists for jobs, education and financial aid should be bifurcated according to the economic categories described earlier. This step could save India from a catastrophe that might lead to a grave crisis in the year 2010 AD.

44. UNEMPLOYMENT IN INDIA

India facing unemployment problem—Unemployment or underemployment perpetuates poverty—Youth get frustrated and adopt wrong courses—Rural unemployment is seasonal or disguised—Urban unemployment is industry based or education based—Government taking measures in during the Ninth Five Year Plan—Private Sector must also contribute towards employment generation.

India, with a vast population of over 1,000 million individuals, is facing the biggest problem of the century in the form of unemployment of worthy and productive citizens. This includes unemployment and under-employment of the young and the old. This results in low productivity and nil or very low incomes. This also leads to the further degradation of household standards and poverty is perpetuated. There is a net loss of national income and the economy suffers on account of low productivity. Add to this, the violent measures taken up by the youth, agitations and individual frustration, which reaches a new pinnacle every day. According to the latest estimates, there are 37.6 million people on the streets and seek employment in one form or the other. There is an addition of 7 million people to this figure every year.

A leisure oriented and unemployed person is a burden on his family and society. The unemployed man eschews all the morals and becomes a rebel. Some young persons take to drugs and illegal means of making money. Therefore, one menace leads to another and the unemployed person gets caught in a quagmire of crises.

Unemployment is more prominent in urban areas than it is in rural India. Unemployment or under-employment levels for women are higher than those for men. Further, the educated individuals tend to be more unemployed or underemployed than their illiterate counterparts. According to current estimates, 12 per cent of educated individuals are unemployed whereas overall unemployment percentage is 3.77 per cent. It has also been noticed that the unemployment rates rise with every successive higher level of education.

Unemployment has two aspects—rural unemployment and urban unemployment. Rural unemployment is either seasonal or disguised. Seasonal unemployment in rural area results due to crop rotation and disguised unemployment is the underemployment due to the lack of proper opportunities at the rural level. Urban unemployment is either industrial or educated unemployment. The industry refuses to accept engineers, chartered accountants, managemen graduates and other technically trained professionals who arive from rural or semi-rural backgrounds. The educated unemployed are the individuals who are either unemployed due to their high qualifications or are underemployed as a result of the wrong job profiles they are in. In either case, frustration forces them to shift to a new job, which could make them either underemployed or unemployed.

According to the Planning Commission and National Sample Survey, the number of unemployed is highest in the age group of 19 to 26 years. The total number of unemployed persons in India today is nearly 380 lakh.

Some of the measures taken by the State have been appended as follows :—

(1) The State is encouraging labour-intensive industry so that more individuals could be employed.

(2) The emphasis is being laid on agriculture, agro-based industries and cottage industries. The small scale industries also fall under this category.

(3) A number of employment programmes have been initiated— IRDP, JRY, HRY, SEPVP are some of the main programmes by the government.

(4) Vocational education is being stressed upon to eliminate the unemployment menace. A young graduate, who has studied Shakespeare, would do no good in an office, which expects him to know Microsoft Windows 98, wordprocessing and efficient file handling. That is why, the graduate immigrants can find jobs only as peons in the cities. Vocational education can make them adept at one particular skill so that they could start contributing from day one.

(5) Many of the unemployed individuals are from backward classes. State employs them through special recruitment drives. The newspapers and magazines advertise these vacancies regularly. "Employment News" reflects this effort of the government.

(6) State Governments have set up Employment Generation Councils, which look after the employment needs of their respective districts.

(7) The Ninth Five Year Plan lays adequate stress on the measures for reducing the already high unemployment levels in the country.

The measures taken during the Eighth Five Year Plan were supposed to result in GDP growth of 5.6 per cent during the plan period. The total number of employment opportunities created was nearly 9 million during the Eighth Five Year Plan. If the target for Ninth Five Year Plan is implemented properly, we could see 9.5 million employment opportunities during the next few years. Thus unemployment levels could reduce to negligible levels by theyear 2002.

Private sector jobs must be made open to the needy and not-so-deserving candidates on human grounds.Physically and mentally handicapped persons-already being looked after by the central and state employment agencies must be given adequate opportunities in the private sector as well.

Another aspect of unemployment is the lure of the good standards of life in the cities. A son of a farmer, who could work hard in his village and could even own a car, goes to the nearest city and finds himself a job of a clerk or a sales executive. This trend is not healthy. If the entire population migrates to the cities, who would manage our agriculture, which is the oldest and time-tested profession ?

The State must contribute by launching more infrastructure-based projects and core sector units. The wasted crop lands should be cultivated and should be issued only to the landless unemployed people. Private sector should launch more process industries, which employ large number of skilled and semi-skilled people in the rural areas. Going abroad is a profitable proposition only for the computer programmers, engineers, nurses, paramedical staff and skilled labourers. Others could find better opportunities in India as grass is no longer greener in the West and the middle East.

The present state of Indian economy does not offer good opportunities on the employment front. However, it is expected that the budget proposed by the Finance Minister—Mr Yashwant Sinha—would go a long way in removing the unemployment problems of the masses. The industrial growth rate was 6.2 per cent during 1999-2000. Our Finance Minister hopes that the economy would revive after a brief period of uncertainties. Unemployment would be eliminated only if the industry and business of the nation pick up. During April-December, 1999, Indian economy has shown signs of improvement.

Further, the Finance Minister has laid more thrust on the rural and agricultural sectors in his budget speech. These areas could generate a good number of the self-employment opportunities for the rural masses. Hence, migration to cities could be checked. The unemployed youth would try to remain at their villages or home towns.

Finally, the State must sponsor schemes for small scale entrepreneurship for the semi-illiterate and the illeterate people. Already, many schemes are in vogue but these need to be tuned to the needs of the unemployed. Red tape and curruption in government departments prevent the funds from being granted to the needy entrepreneurs. The youth should start small enterprises or manufacturing units of their own with the help of funds from the central and state funding agenicies as well as from Rural Regional Banks. They would also be able to give employment to a few more persons if they become entrepreneurs.

We must conclude by stating that unemployment issue must be tackled with utmost care and seriousness as it has already assumed alarming proportions in the social and economic scenarious of our nation.

45. THE CORRUPTION MENACE

Corruption pervades all the walks of society—People want to get rich quickly and therefore, adopt unfair means—Reasons are economic backwardness, inability of the individual in opposing corruption—Many scams faced by the nation—Police also corrupt—Make strict laws—Bureaucracy must assume greater responsibility—Raise the pay packages of police and government officials so that they are not tempted to be corrupt.

Indian democracy has many feathers in her cap. Our progress in all the fields of social, national and international context has been lauded by our elite thinkers as well as by the international community.

However, we have been facing the menace of corruption for a long and time period, has become a part of our national culture. Our nation has vested the power in the individual and he has left no stone unturned in order to get rich quickly. The politician, the bureaucrat, the government employee, the private sector businessman, who are the vital units of the national family, have contributed in the spread of the corruption menace. Corruption is now prevalent at all the levels of industry, business and administration and is an essential part of the national economic fabric. According to an estimate, if the funds earned due to corruption were to be circulated in the national economy, India would not have to look for a foreign aid for many years to come. Our growth would be tremendous in all the spheres and we would be an "independent economic entity" within a short time period. The black market economy, corrupt bureaucrat and industrial practices and dishonesty in administration have led to the generation of a parallel economy whose magnitude is much larger than our national budget.

Let us examine the case of funding issue of the ULFA militants by Tata Tea Company. We must realise that this episode could have taken birth due to the coercive power exercised by the militants. But the Tatas are equally guilty of supporting such terrorists for the sake of promoting their business interests. This proves that the corruption menace has been able to pierce the private industrial economy as well.

We walk into any office of the Municipal Corporation, Provident Fund, Electricity Board or any department run by the central or State governments. We know that the clerk must be "handled with utmost care", lest payments should be delayed. So, we grease the palms of the staff from top to bottom and get our work done. Police, courts, land development authorities and other government institutions are operating on the basis of "give and take."

Further, we have scams like Hawala, Bofors, JMM case, Fodder Scam and many small and big cases of misappropriation of the State funds. The politician-bureaucrat-criminal nexus has sucked the hard-earned money of the masses and has made a mockery of the national economic system. The fruits of labour, of over fifty years, have not reached our rural areas. We remain one of the poorest nations of the world due to corruption that prevails at all the levels of our society.

The Prevention of Corruption Act (1947) was supposed to include MPs and MLAs in its net so that they could also be held liable for their misdeeds. However, these "public servants" want to have any amendment to this effect because every powerful politician wants to avoid the legal net.

Solutions are many. We would list a vital few, which are as follows :—

(1) Corruption prevails in many parts of the world; even some Western nations are not spared by it. Therefore, some form of corruption would always remain in our social, economic and political systems. We must, however, assure that there is no corruption at the national and economic levels. Our image as a corruption-free nation must be built so that other nations view us with respect.

(2) An individual initiates corruption. He should stop giving 'tips' to the bureaucracy and public servants. He should warn the corrupt officials that if his objectives were not met (without paying bribes), he would take strict legal actions against them.

(3) The State must pass strict laws to this effort. Only honest and nationalist politicians should be allowed to contest elections. A politician with dubious record of scams and floor-crossing should be barred from taking part in the elections. The Election Commission has already issued guidelines to check the entry of corrupt and criminal-minded politicians into the echelons of power.

(4) The salaries of police, central and state government employees and bureaucracy must be raised to respectable levels so that their basic needs are satisfied. If the people are satisfied with what they are getting, they would not resort to unfair means for making money.

(5) The bureaucracy must shed five vowels—A (Apathy), E (Evasiveness), I (Incompetence), O (Obscurantism) and U (an Urge for power and money). Rather, it should adopt three Cs—Commitment, Consistency and Competence. Disclosure of wealth, administrative ethics and a positive attitude towards public at large must be their guiding gospels.

(6) The government has done well to launch Voluntary Disclosure of Income Scheme (VDIS-97) whereby an individual can pay 30 per cent of his illegal wealth and can keep a percentage of the same as white money. This scheme is likely to benefit the businessman and the country alike.

(7) The CBI, Vigilance Department and other agencies of the central and state government should monitor the corrupt

politicians and businessmen. At the same time, these agencies should not move according to the whims of the power hungry and manipulative politicians.

(8) The scars of red tape, black money and corruption on our tricolour flag can be wiped out only by our youth. Our young minds are fresh and can oppose all the anti-social and anti-national activities of the politicians, criminals and the business tycoons. They must form a movement or a forum to check the corrupt practices that have inflicted great economic and social losses upon our nation.

(9) The mass and media must expose the scams, scandles and corrupt politics so that the general public remains aware of the evil designs of the corrupt individuals.

(10) The policy of licensing in various fields—should be eliminated to check corruption in these areas.

Corruption is ubiquitous. Its detection is difficult and sentence for the wrong-doers is seldom decided due to loopholes in our legal framework. The urge of the people for a rags-to-riches tendency and earning money without hard work must be changed. Our social ethos must be modified in order to promote good moral values. India must do away with much of her past and corruption at all the levels must be eliminated as the very first initiative in this direction. ●

46. THE STRANGLED MEDIA

Shivani Jajodia, Shivani Bhatnagar and Irfaan Hussain murdered—Police clueless—This is an attack on the freedom of media—In a democratic nation, media must be allowed to speak, write and communicate freely—Corporate sector and criminal elements are hands-in-glove with each other—CBI, police and other investigations—Crime graph rising in the metropolises—Media themselves ought to exercise restraint while reporting—Their reportage should not be haughty or pointing directly.

The new century has heralded a new era, which is dominated by IT. Media include newspapers, magazines, TV, Cable TV, Internet, Computer networks and other modes for the dissemination of information. The role played by media can never be underscored as these are vital in all the spheres of human endeavour—social, economic, commercial and interpersonal. In order to a free and mentally healthy human race, the freedom of media is mandatory. However, some incidents shook the media world in India and forced the elite to think about the freedom and rights of media in a democracy. Let us analyse the grim situation in the context of operations of the media that form an inseparable part of our nation.

On November 19, 1997, Shivani Jajodia was murdered in her flat in Vasant Kunj, New Delhi. Shivani was a producer at NDTV. On November 22, 1999, she breathed her last as she succumbed to injuries in the hospital. On January 23, 1999 another upcoming journalist, Shivani Bhatnagar, was strangled and stabbed. She was with her four-month-old baby when she heard the knock at the door. There were two stab wounds and obvious marks of strangulation on her body. The police ruled out that this case was linked to robbery. Shivani Bhatnagar was an investigative journalist. On March 8, 1999, the famous young cartoonist, Irfaan Hussain, was known to be missing. His decomposed body was found later near Ghazipur in Uttar Pradesh. There were 28 stab wounds on his body. Irfaan had acquired fame due to his "knave and pinching cartoons" that could have irritated some unknown elements of the society. There is no need to predict that these elements must be having political linkages as well.

Police remains clueless regarding motives behind the three cases. The investigations are continuing but it is unlikely that these would be conclusive. An attack on people connected to media is a matter of serious concern in a democratic nation like India. Mediapersons are not given any police protection, like the politicians whom they try to expose, thus making themselves vulnerable to reprisals by the underworld. The true spirit of democracy lies not in supporting a State with free media operations but a State, in which media could thrive without any coercion or fear. The element of fear is used by politicians and the underworld dons in order to filter out that information, which could harm them (if it is disseminated). Hence, they force the mediapersons to withhold the negative information, facts and data. It could only be imagined how they do it. If the mediaperson does not conform to their dictates, the incidents of murder of Shivani Bhatnagar, Shivani Jajodia and Irfaan Hussain are repeated.

If media were to be handled mercilessly by the warlords, evil politicians and dons of the underworld, then honest and hardworking journalists would refrain from joining TV channels, newspaper conglomerates and the publishers of magazines. This would herald a new era that would ultimately lead to the deterioration in the quality of software that media produce. The strangulated media would print, show and expose only those news and views, which are approved by the mafias, warlords and the gun-totting politicians.

The police, the CBI and other investigating agencies move at a snail's pace while they try to "see through" these cases. The judicial process is sans efficiency; and the law of the land is callons, helpless and slow in delivering "poetic Justice" to the culprits because the killers are still at large. The senseless spate of violence, a typical characteristic of our urban lives, continues unabated. Who would bell the cat, then ?

A former CBI director commented, "They (the Delhi Police) don't have the attention span required for successful investigation. They slow down once the media pressure eases and move on to another case. Doggedness is missing." Further, the police is overburdened with cases, most of them involving road accidents, minor cases of theft, property disputes and general law and order situation in the metropolises. They do not have enough time to concentrate on the criminal cases that affect the national societal fabric.

And if mediapersons are also the targets of the wrath of criminal elements, the media themselves are to be blamed, some experts feel. They portray the criminals as demons, the politicians as wicked and the police as "Dirty Harrys" in the media blitzkrieg. This leads to senseless reprisals from those who are exposed. Therefore, if the Press and the electronic media are free to write and expose, the people on the other side of the fence are powerful enough to warn, settle scores through violence and ultimately, "dispose of."

The crime graph has soared to new peaks in the metropolises and the mediapersons are the prime targets. The State has to be alert and sensitive to such a dangerous course of events. Mr HK Dua, a former editor and a renouned mediaperson, was recently appointed as the Press Advisor to the PM, Mr AB Vajpayee. This shows that the government wishes to give due respect and place to the media. The State wants the media to investigate and expose. However, the security of the mediapersons must be given top priority by the governments in the centre and the states.

In a free nation like ours, the free and fair operations of media are vital for ensuring the tenacity and effectiveness of the democratic institutions. By the term 'free,' we mean that media should be allowed to investigate freely and expose at their well. However, by the term 'fair,' we mean that media must not cross all the limits of investigation of exposure so that some disgruntled elements might adopt coercive (and fatal) measures against the journalists and correspondents. For example, the correspondent of a newspaper might write, "Mr X has murdered Mr Y." Instead, he could write, "Mr X has been accused of the murder of Mr Y." When the investigations have been completed, the correspondent can point an accusing finger at Mr X but not before the completion of the investigations. The police is strong enough to protect itself as it is an armed organ of the State. But the security of media is questionable even if the police gives them adequate protection. The police would not be able to protect the Preps correspondents and other mediapersons for twenty-four hours whereas a criminal would dare not attack even a police constable who has only a small firearm. Unfortunately, the fear of a gun still dissuades the criminals from attacking the police force but there is no fear from the pen. As on date, the sword is still mightier than the pen. Mediapersons ought to understand this ironical fact and have to "tone down" their reports and revelations in such a manner as would not generate an ire from those who are the targets of their articles and reports.

In sum, if media do not wish to be strangulated, their investigations, reports and comments would have to be sans the venom against the targets whom they wish to expose. A pragmatic and soft approach towards news coverage and investigations is needed. If supercilious reportage continues against the targets, more mediapersons are likely to meet the fate that was bestowed open Irfaan Hussain, Shivani Jajodia and Shivani Bhatnagar. The law, as is always the case, is quite helpless and callous. It would take its own course. In the meantime, journalists and Press correspondents ought to move in a cautions manner while doing their duties. Fools rush in where angels fear to tread. Life is more important. If they live, they would be able to help the media thrive. If they do not survive, there would be no of media.

47. RELIGIOUS CONVERSIONS

Religious Conversions led to killings in Orissa—Graham Staines, Sheikh Rahman and Arul Doss killed mercilessly in Orissa—This is a reprisal of the majority against the forced or money-backed conversions of Hindus—The history of Conversions traced—There is no need for conversion into Christianity in order to learn and understand the Gospel of Jesus Christ—Article 25 (1) of Indian Constitution guarantees religious freedom—Visit of Pope could not create controversy or furore—Dissociate religion from society—Practise religion in the corner of the living room and sans distractions—Conversions are also not recommended but violent reprisals must be done away with.

The last year of the previous millennium made the flesh of many a noble citizen creep due to the dance of death in the Indian state—Orissa. On January 26, 1999, a Christian Missionary, Mr Graham Staines and his two sons were burnt alive in village Manoharpur in Keonjhar district. On August 26, 1999, Sheikh Rahman was burnt to death in Padiabeda in Mayurbhanj district. And finally, a Christian priest, Arul Doss, was killed by a mob on September 1, 1999, in Jamboboni in Keonjhar district. These incidents created a frenzy in the global media and the land of Buddha and Gandhi was portrayed as a soil that nurtured and propagated the seeds of violence against the minorities.

Indian subcontinent is the cradle of many a civilisation. However, despite the so-called furore created by our leaders regarding religious tolerance, some thorns always remained attached to the sweet-smelling Indian rose that was known for its communal harmony and love for the mankind. These thorns were attached to the rose by those who were not fond of our centuries-old gospel of accepting every human being as a messenger of the Almighty. The spate of killings in Orissa has pointed out that people in that backward state of India are more concerned about their religion than about the improvement of their living conditions and economy. It must be noted that Orissa remains one of the backwaters of India; poverty, illiteracy and social backwardness grow at an unprecedented pace in this Eastern Indian State. The Chief Minister was changed, the police force was sent to nab the culprits and elite minds were told to analyse why all this happened. However, the near and dear ones of the victims are still perplexed about the course of events and their final outcomes.

The crux of the issue remains unfathomable. Religious conversions have been going on in the country since the middle of the nineteenth century. These incidents could be a show of reprisal and protest against the religious conversions. Some members of the majority community are strictly against the operations and objectives of the minorities in the country, the minorities being Christians and Muslims. We would try to study the issue of religious conversions by giving the historical accounts of these conversions.

The history of religious conversions dates back to 1842 when 30 per cent of the population of Malabar was converted into Muslims. Then, there were conversions under the threat of the sword during the rules of Muslim emperors. Hindu masses were forced to get converted into Muslims through coercion and in the event of their non-conformance, they were beheaded. Mughal rulers perpetuated the trends of conversion and Emperor Aurangzeb was especially happy to be barbarous towards Hindu subjects of his State during his reign. Sikhs bravely fought the tyranny of the Mughal rulers and opposed this evil custom. Guru Gobind Singh, his father, his four sons, his mother and several hundred thousand Sikh warriors lay down their lives on the altar of religious democracy. The tortures inflicted upon the Hindu and Sikh masses cannot be described in a few words. And these citizens, who were parts of the minority communities, bore the brunt of religious conversions for nearly 1,000 years.

Then came the British, the Dutch and the Portuguese. The earliest churches were constructed in Kerala. The Christian missionaries set up missions in Kerala, Goa, Pondicherry and erstwhile Madras State for spreading the message of love and compassion given by Lord Jesus Christ. The British bureaucracy tried to convert the Hindu subjects into Christians through money power. Coercion was used by a few British officers and soldiers. Many Hindus were lured by money and they got converted into Christians in the hope of better lives and luxury.

In 1820, the government rejected a petition by a Christian missionary to 'Christianise' Indian State. After the revolt of 1857, the British officers were not very keen for pursuing religious conversions. In 1858, the British Queen proclaimed that the British nation did not wish to impose the convictions of the British administration on any of her subjects. In 1931, the undsay Commission on Christian Higher Education in India was of the view that Hindu religion was so much entrenched in Indian masses that Indian psyche that it could be touched only marginally.

But nevertheless, religious conversions did take place during the British rule as well. The poor Hindus and the affluent Hindu nobles were squarely responsible for slipping away from their own pack. In 1893, Swami Dayanand, under the aegis of *Arya Samaj* Movement, started *Shuddhi* Movement. It aimed at purifying the castes like Jats, Converted Rahtas, Oudhs and Meghs. After the split of 1893, the *Gurukul* faction of *Arya Samaj* encouraged prosletysation through paid teachers.

During the pre-independence years, Hindus and Muslims fought the British rule jointly. The issue of religious conversions was subdued as the chief objective was different and pious. There were minimal religious conversions during the period 1900-1947. The national pride and a longing for independence were the prime goals.

Immediately before independence, Mr MA Jinnah demanded a separate State for Muslims. This demand re-kindled the flames of communalism. In 1947, India was partitioned; she had to pay the price of independence. The riots of 1947 saw a gory saga of violence and barbarism. Lakhs of people were massacred, raped and looted. However, after independence, Indians settled down as a peace-loving nation in which, all the religious sects were allowed to prosper.

However, in independent India, religious conversions continued in Madhya Pradesh, Orissa, Bihar and Maharashtra. In 1952, *Vanvasi Kalyan Ashram* was set up in Jashpur (Madhya Pradesh) for opposing the efforts of those Christians who were trying to convert Oraon tribes. On February 19, 1981, Dalit families of Pallan subcaste converted into the Islamic fold. This decision of the Pallan community came in the wake of atrocities inflicted upon them by Thevars, another backward caste of Meenakshipuram. This town is now better known as Rehmat Nagar. Every Muslim in Rahmat Nagar has a *Dalit* relative and *vice versa*. Dalits as well as Muslims live in perfect harmony. Meenakshipuram was transformed into Rahmat Nagar due to economic compulsions, backwardness and the cruelty of the Thevars. The Pallan subcaste was the chief victim of the wrath of the Thevars. It was feared that mass-scale conversions could take place in other backward castes as well. During the same period, 3,00,000 *Dalits* also converted to Buddhism but no serious protests were raised against this conversion.

According to the 1981 Census, Hindu population of India was 549.7 million and the Christian population was 16.1 million. According to the 1991 census, Hindu population rose to 687.6 million whereas Christians were 19.6 million in number. Therefore, according to the 1981 census, Christians were 2.9 per cent of the Hindu population whereas in 1991 Christians were 2.8 per cent of the Hindu population. On January 13, 1999, the population of the country was 98,98,44,092 and this figure crossed the 1 billion mark in August, 1999. The Christian minority remains a meagre 2.9-3.0 per cent of the Hindu populace. This should not have caused furore in the majority community as the small number of Christians would never outnumber the majority of Hindus. Therefore, even the large scale conversions of Hindus into the Christian faith would not alter the balance in the favour of the Christian populace. At present, there are 1,168 Christian missionaries operating in India. Hindu leaders are annoyed by the conversions because they feel that this would "erode' the Hindu base but this notion is false and dumbfounded. Vishwa Hindu Parishad (VHP) and Hindu Jagran Manch (HJM) taken up the issue of conversions seriously but they forget to understand one basic fact— the reality facing the majority of the nationals or our nation is not religion; it is poverty. Hence, there are conversions and a deviation from the faith that one is practising. Life for a common man is very difficult. If a conversion helps him get better standards of living, he eagerly embraces another faith. Whereas the minority communities are also at fault for propagating the process of conversions, the majority community also should analyse why these conversions took place. The senseless reprisals against the minority communities should have been avoided, keeping in view the social and economic problems faced by converts.

The communal frenzy takes its toll in terms of lives and property worth millions every year. But despite these acts of communal carnage, people continue to give their respect and support to other faiths, beside their own. The Velankanni Church draws Hindus and Christians without any prejudice or bias. The Bheemapalli mosque is visited by Hindu and Muslim masses with equal fervour. The mosque at Ajmer Sharif is a holy shrine for Hindus and Muslims and Hindu masses might be equally attached to that pious *Sanctum Sanctorum*, as are Muslim followers. The Golden Temple at Amritsar draws devouts from all the parts of the world, their faiths not hindering their visits to that holy shrine of tranquillity and solace. Further, the Sabarimala temple is visited by Hindus, Christians and Muslims from all parts of India and the world. These examples prove that the mass base of human population is sans any religious hatred. A handful of religious preachers and politicians has created a resentment that has been imbibed by some disgruntled communal elements. This ultimately led to the reprisals on a violent scale. The masses live in perfect harmony. The religious machinations and the incessant spate of killings has not been able to defy our basic social and cultural norms.

A religious conversion is also deplorable on all grounds. A religious convert is not going to have a new life on this earth, except for the fact that he would be able to get some money, a new hut, some valuables and a job. One need not be a Christian in order to understand and imbibe the Gospel of Lord Jesus Christ. Lord Christ gave supreme sacrifice for the entire humanity and a particular faith cannot be singled out as the one supporting his teachings. Jesus Christ belongs to all the humans and He could not be viewed as a part of the Christian faith only. The same view could be stated regarding the saints and propagators of other faiths as well.

Article 25 of Indian Constitution guarantees the freedom of conscience to all the Indian masses. It also gives them the right to profess, practise and propagate any religion. This right is, however, subject to restrictions imposed by the State in the interest of public order, morality and benefit of the masses. In a ruling of 1977, the Supreme Court had stated that a person of one faith cannot be converted into another. Article 25(1) of the Constitution confirms this ruling. Therefore, the law of the land does not view conversions as legal, especially when they may have been done through money power or through coercive measures. Hence, we conclude that the issue of conversions should not be given publicity and a status of national crisis as the law, the moral code of conduct and our socio-cultural values do not allow these conversions to take place. Therefore, the demands of the majority community are also right in the sense that the conversions have been done illegally, taking monetary and coercive factors into account.

During November 5-8, 1999, Pope John Paul II visited India. The issue of religious conversions was again brought to light by media. The visit of the Pope was a quiet affair. Obviously, the Pope wanted to visit the country in which, Arul Doss and Graham Staines had been killed mercilessly. The global view of India was that of tolerant society. It is sad to note that this view is changing now.

As Christmas of 1999 approached, the Christian minority trembled with fear. The United Tribal Christian Council (UTCC) of Dangs district (Gujarat) expressed concern that its members might face reprisal by the members of Hindu Jagran Manch (HJM). The members of HJM had also proposed to lay the foundation of a Ram Temple in a village in Surat district (Gujarat). The president of HJM, Mr Janmbhai Pawar, was arrested for a brief period by Dangs police and later, released on bail. The police had alleged that the members of HJM were trying to incite communal sentiments and hurt the religious affiliations of the minorities. Incidents like these are quite common in Gujarat and Orissa.

It is quite distressing to note that religion continues to play a major role in the national society, polity and culture of India. Religion is supposed to give solace to the soul when the devout is praying before his deity. This act of worship or *Pooja* should not be made public. We should stick to our religion in the corners of our living rooms; there is no need to carry out communal processions and rallies because the relationship of man with the Almighty is on a one-to-one basis. Religion has to be dissociated from societal strings. It is a very personal affair of man and God; there cannot be a third party in this interaction because the deeds, conscience and character of a man make up his religious orientation and not his political party, the temple he visits or the militant group to which, he belongs.

The issue of religious conversions is a serious one but, as already stated, it should not be given importance by the political leaders and the media. At the same time, the minorities must be protected. Finally, religious conversions must be stopped as these could kindle the fire of a large-scale communal carnage across the nation.

48. INDIAN FESTIVALS

Indian festivals known for gaiety, fervour and joy—They mark the change of season or depict association with myths—Deepawali, Dussehra, Eid, Durga Pooja, Mahavir Jayanti, Buddha Jayanti, Guru Parav etc are major festivals—Basant, Holi, Onam, Pongal are seasonal festivals—Religious devotion, social harmony and festivities mark these festivals—Some people show off their riches—Strife and riots seen at many occasions—Wastage of resources and time—Should promote harmony and peace in society—They unite all the people of the nation.

A festival is a celebration of life. All nations have their religious and cultural festivals. However, Indian festivals have known to attract the world due to their harmony, variety, colourful appearances and excitement.

Our festivals are basically of two types—religious and seasonal. Most of the Indian festivals are based on religion or myths. They change the monotony of life, bring peace and joy to the masses and above all, promote social interaction and harmony. The insipid routine of life is broken for good and juvenile masses celebrate their faith or seasonal change with gaiety and enthusiasm. The festivals mark the healthy depiction of human life and depict religious associations of the masses.

Religious festivals include Eid-ul-Zuha, Eid-Ul-Fitr, Dussehra, Deepawali, Laxmi Pooja, Mahavir Jayanti, Shri Krishna Janamashtami, Ram Navami, Navratras, Christmas, Guru Parav and the festivals of Parsis and Jews. Hindus celebrate Dussehra and Deepawali in Northern India. The people of Bengal and Eastern Indian states celebrate Durga Pooja. However, Deepawali—the festival of light—is the most prominent of Hindu festivals. Hindu masses celebrate this day to commemorate the return of Lord Rama to Ayodhya after winning the decisive war against the evil forces of Ravana. Businessmen start their new accounts books. The households are cleaned and whitewashed. Children wear new clothes and sweets are distributed. On the Deepawali day, the people from all walks of life light up their homes and children enjoy crackers and sweets.

Muslim brothers and sisters celebrate Eid-Ul-Zuha and Eid-Ul-Fitr. Eid-Ul-Fitr is celebrated to mark the end of Ramzan. It was during the month of Ramzan that *Holy Quran* was revealed to Prophet Mohammed. Muslim brothers and sisters fast for the month of Ramzan. At the end of Ramzan, Eid is celebrated with feasts. They go to Eidgahs and offer prayers.

Christmas is the most important festival of Christians and is celebrated as the birthday of Holy Jesus Christ on December 25, every year. The Christmas tree is decorated and cakes and puddings are served. Santa Claus distributes sweets and cakes among children who are dressed in new clothes. Prayers are offered in the churches and cathedrals.

In a similar fashion, the Jews also celebrate their festival and go to the Synagogue to pray before the Almighty.

Sikhs celebrate the birthdays of their Gurus. Among these, the day of martyrdom of Shri Guru Arjun Dev is the most important. Guru Arjun Dev was martyred at Lahore after a painful torture by the Moghuls. Sikhs celebrate this day as a day of peace and harmony and distribute cold water, milk and food to the masses free of cost.

Similarly, Ram Navmi and Krishna Janamashtami are celebrated throughout India as the birthdays of Lord Rama and Lord Krishna respectively. In Bengal and the North-East, Durga Pooja is celebrated with pomp and show. Goddess Durga is worshipped for nine days and is then, immersed in water to mark the end of the festivities. In Maharashtra, Lord Ganesha is worshipped with religious fervour and devotion.

Parsees celebrate Naoroz during August-September every year. For them, it is the beginning of the new year. Similarly, Jains and Buddhists celebrate their religious festivals in the form of Mahavir Jayanti and Buddha Poornima respectively.

The other aspect of the festivals is the change of seasons and the healthy crops abound in the different regions of our country. Baisakhi is celebrated as a mark of harvesting of wheat crops in Punjab. Onam is celebrated in Kerala as a harvest festival. Pongal is celebrated in Tamil Nadu for similar seasons. Basant Panchami is celebrated throughout Northern India and marks the end of winter season. Children fly kites and enjoy themselves in the open grounds. Holi is the most colourful festival of all. It celebrates the victory of Prahlad over the evil forces. Seasonal changes mark the beginning of a new confidence and happiness prevails over the masses.

However, all is not well in India during festivals in the wake of rising commercialism and modern culture. Deepawali is not celebrated for paying respects to Lord Rama but for gambling and enjoying the pollution-generating crackers. The temples are decorated at a cost of millions of Rupees and people show off their riches at such occasions. The Holi festival brings many scars to the society in the form of indecency towards women and brawls of the drunkards on the streets. That is why, the police has to be alert all the time during such festivities. Riots, deaths, injuries and loss of property mar the spirit of the festivals. Therefore, festivals must be celebrated with humility, religious devotion and simplicity.

India is the only nation in which, the festivals are celebrated with pomp and show and with great devotion to the Almighty. Although it is a positive aspect of our culture, yet we are also forced to think about the negative influences of festivals on our society. For example, every festival comes with a holiday. The schools are closed. The government institutions (which already work for five days a week), are closed. Banks are also closed and this causes great inconvenience to business firms and industries. Payments are withheld. Children do not study properly during the Holi and Basant festivals and those are the crucial examination days in India. Further, communal tensions could take their toll of lives and property in any part of the nation.

Normally, during the days of festivals, the people are mercilessly massacred due to communal riots and stampedes. The recent incident in Haridwar, in which, several people died on account of clash between two groups of *Sadhus,* is an example worth mentioning in this context.

Our view is that the festivals should be celebrated with simplicity. They should be considered as the days of cleansing the souls and not the occasions for a dip in the Ganges. New promises should be made and should be kept as well. Colour is an essential part of Holi. But colours must not be sprayed on those people who do not want to play with colours. Crackers should not be burned as they increase pollution. Religious processions should be allowed only for a limited distance. Prayers could be offered at homes also. While celebrating the religous festivals, other communities should also be invited for promoting national integration and communal harmony. Our festivals must be celebrated keeping the national interests in view.

49. PRIVATE COACHING FOR ACADEMIC EXCELENCE

Private coaching institutes for giving training for competitive examinations—Branches throughout India—Some institutes are professionally managed—Some offer scholarships—Main objective is making money and not training the students for appearing in the examinations—No role of the State—Charge very high fees—Poor students cannot afford to pay—Nexus between these institutes and the professional institutes possible—Parents belonging to middle income brackets cannot afford training for their wards—Free market winds allow the free operations of such institutes—Parents must save money during their youth for this purpose—Students must also save money for training in such institutes—Some solutions suggested for streamlining the operations of these institutes

We are witnessing an era of academic excellence. When we wish to become professionals in any field, we study the basic concepts of that field and then, practise the profession. Gradually, we become adept at carrying out a few tasks that make us distinguished, respected and knowledgeable. No doubt, money also flows into our pockets. But a stage arrives when we do not bother about money but about the highest pinnacles of profession we are in. That stage is arrived at after an experience of twenty-five years (or may be more than that) in our chosen profession. A professional goes through tough training schedules prior to admission into a professional college. Then, he goes through testing procedures and examinations. These examinations could also include group discussions, interviews, psychological interviews, physical tests and other tests that could judge the inner facets of his personality and psyche.

It is quite natural that a government school, college or training institute would not be able to prepare students for professional courses. Something extra is required that could hone the skills of the candidates so that they could get admitted to professional courses of their choice. Our readers would be surprised to learn that there is not a single institute promoted by the government that is imparting training to the students in India so that they could get admission to various professional courses. Even if we are proved wrong and are able to point out some institutes, we would aware of the state of affairs in those centres of learning—a typical *Sarkari* atmosphere and nil dedication towards a result-oriented behaviour.

Enter the private coaching institutes and teachers spread across the length and breadth of Indian subcontinent and we have many problems solved. There are good training institutes that assist the students in preparation for competitive examinations like IIT-JEE, MBA, CAT *etc*. There are good teachers who help in the preparation of professionals courses like CA, ICWA and CS. Further, admissions to the courses of the defence streams like NDA, Indian Navy, IAF *etc* also require professional training. Therefore, many academies and training institutes have been started by professionals from armed forces and they help the students prepare for these examinations. These institutes have opened their branches in all the major and minor towns of India.

And some students definitely do very well, thanks to some of the professional training institutes. There are nearly 1,000 individual professionals for competitive examinations and nearly 500 professional training institutes in New Delhi alone, some of them very reputed. These institutes impart training to the students who are eligible for admission to graduate degree courses in engineering, architecture, chartered accountancy, management, secretarial practice, international finance, computer science, fashion design and technology, plastics technology, leather design, food science and technology, marine engineering, aeronautical engineering, space engineering, nuclear engineering etc. This list is not exhaustive. The students have to appear in the qualifying tests of these institutes and the selected candidates are required to pay hefty amounts of money as fees in order to get the requisite training. These training schedules (which include theory lectures, tutorials for practice exercises, group discussions, mock interviews, physical training and other relevant training sessions) are gruelling. Only a few students are able to prepare fully in terms of the syllabi of the entrance tests. The bright candidates clear the tests, interviews and other admission criteria. The training institutes then concentrate on the next batch of candidates.

The entire procedure seems to be very interesting, respectable and lucrative for the purpose of grooming professionals. It is not.

There are many negative aspects of this type of education and training. Let us discuss some of the aspects which are as follows :—

(A) The training institutes, especially the reputed ones, charge large sums of money as fees from the candidates. Most of the candidates cannot afford to invest these amounts but they certainly do for the sake of a better future. If they fail to achieve their targets, they lose the opportunity costs of these investments.

(B) These training institutes train the students according to the current trends of competitive examinations. But how could they have an access to the trends in examinations ? The syllabi and the modes of testing are quite confidential but it is quite strange that the training institutes train the candidates in such a manner as would insinuate towards a nexus between the professional institutions of learning and the training institutes that are the stepping stones towards these institutions. The State is silent whereas the common man is being exploited. The State must scrutinise the working of these training centres and must find out how they have an access to the vital information relating to tests or patterns of questions.

(C) The training institutes claim that they can polish even a mediocre student or a student with 45-50 per cent marks could also make it to a professional college of repute. How could that be possible ? It is true that the students with poor educational bases could also be trained to do better tasks. But how could they reach the top rung of the ladder by getting training for a few months (and more important, by paying a hefty amount of money) ? The marketing gimmicks of the training institutes motivate the students for joining them. If they are able to make it to the professional institute, then the students are able to recover the expenses incurred else they lose the hard-earned money of their parents.

(D) The students of Class X and Class XI are also motivated to take up coaching sessions so that they are also thoroughly prepared by the time they arrive at the age for competitive examinations. Although this trend for early preparation is good, yet it imposes a great burden on the students. They are already under pressures of vast syllabi in their schools. In addition, they have to work hard for the competitive examinations. This also puts a great burden on the financial resources of the parents who are forced by their wards to spend money on their coaching in such institutes.

We understand that the free market forces are blowing with full vigour in India. We do not oppose these trends either. However, nearly 50 per cent of Indian populace is deprived of basic facilities of food, clothing, shelter, basic education, health facilities and other vital inputs that are necessary for a decent living. How could a young boy or a girl from this segment could even dream of paying the colossal amounts of fees (according to their economic status) to these training institutes ? As a result, they stay back at their homes and slog it out themselves for the professional courses. Some of them do make to the top but others, who are not so resourceful, are left in the dark. They could have done much better, had their parents invested in their training. Therefore, even the talented and deserving candidates are not able to get admission to the professional colleges for want of resources, training and guidance. The vicious cycle of poverty is perpetuated. The students, belonging to the strongest economic niches of the society go abroad for studies. The middle income groups somehow spend the hard-earned incomes or savings and try to get their wards and children admitted into the professional courses. The poorest of the poor, as described earlier, are left out of the race for survival and prosperity.

We do not request the training institutes to show mercy on these candidates. Yes, they offer scholarship schemes and some of these institutes do offer scholarships as well. But how many scholarships could be awarded ? There is a resource constraint everywhere and all the educational and training institutes are no exceptions. The State is a neo-semi-corporate entity now. Closure of the loss-making the PSUs and the divestment ceremony for the star performers (*ie*, those firms in the public sector that are doing very well) are some of the steps being taken by the government in order to cut down its expenses. In this state of affairs, the State cannot be asked to support the aspirants of competitive examinations. In fact, the State is teaching us to be on our own so that we become independent without the crutches of government funding.

What else is left-the personal resources of the parents, pension and provident fund of father, property of ancestors or the personal earnings of the candidate ? Would that be sufficient to pay fees for this experiment ? We do not think that it would be. A candidate for a competitive examination has siblings as well and the resource allocations have to be done in such a manner as would ensure that all the children are settled in their lives and professions. Then, how could one brother or sister take away the major share of the cake for spending money in a costly course that may or may not lead him or her to a professional course ?

This is not a pleasant story but is the tragedy of every middle-income household of India. There are no solutions, though we would like to mention some for the benefit of the students and candidates for competitive examinations. Indian students are one of the best in the world and could achieve the unknown pinnacles in all the fields of knowledge. But resource constraints have forced them to lead academic and professional lives that could be anything but decent and honourable. India is the poorest country in the world simply because its most precious asset-the human resource-is not getting ample opportunities for excellence in the coveted fields. The stepping stones to success can be arrived at only with the help of toil, perseverance and money. But if money is missing, the other two components of the success formula take a backseat.

We have been doing well despite some financial constraints. However, our basic financial structure is such as to support the basic needs of the residents of this vast country; the higher order needs like good education, researches in various fields, training in professional institutions, arts and crafts, creativity *etc* do not draw investments. We have always been survival oriented; growth was never on the agenda of our students and youth. We are ourselves to be blamed for a chronic shortage of resources; we are not generating enough of them but have always been consuming them without keeping an eye on the future.

It is an oft repeated claim that training institutions offer "professional help" for admission to the professional courses. They assist students in developing the knowledge levels for tough and gruelling competitive examinations. What for ? Are they doing it for the sake of developing the human resource in India ? No. They are mere money-making shops. They are more interested in getting the maximum students enrolled in their short-term courses than in building the knowledge bases of the candidates who pour into their offices. If there were a better proposition for making money, they would quietly have a changeover. That is the ugly face of commercialism in education. Private tutors, who help the students clear the examinations of CA, ICWA and CS, also fall in this category.

Those students, who get admission into the professional colleges and universities, would be on the top of the world. But what about those who invested the hard-earned pennies of their parents and failed. For them, it proved to be a game of dice whose result turned out to be unfavourable for them. Shall we suggest some solutions so that the students, their parents and the training centres do not commit more mistakes during the times to come ? Some of them are as follows : —

(A) For the sake of developing the human resource of this nation, the government ought to spend money. If we could have the IITs or the IIMs, we could also have the State-sponsored institutions that trained the students for getting admission to these institutions. Why the private institutions should be given this responsibility ? A State-run institution (operating on all-India basis) could be an asset for the students. The only precaution to be taken is that this training centre must not be made a typical *Sarkari* enterprise else it would lose its charm and purpose.

(B) The private training institutes must be forced to give maximum number of scholarships to the deserving students. At present, these scholarships are very few in number. These institutes must be requested to bear their social responsibility as business enterprises; it would be wrong to state that they are educational institutions.

(C) The parents would have to plan the careers of their wards and children in advance. They have to keep some resources aside for the professional development of their children.

Planning for achieving this objective would have to be done in advance (when the parents are young and working). The state-funded policies and programmes like UTI, LIC, Mutual Funds and such schemes. The parents would have to start investing in these policies when they are young and earning.

(D) Finally, the students would also have to earn on their own. They can earn RS 1,500 -2,000 per month depending upon their abilities. They could also save the pocket money given to them by their parents. It would be appropriate to spend fewer amounts of funds on liquor, tobacco, discotheque and the opposite sex for the sake of a bright future. If the objective is pious, the students would be required to make some sacrifices for the same.

We hope that the State, the private coaching institutes and the students (who wish to make it big in professions of their choice) pay heed to these suggestions. We have to achieve the goals in academic streams in such a manner as would ensure the minimal wastage of precious financial resources and at the same time success rates are also satisfactory. The requisite efforts should start at the earliest possible date.

50. MENTAL PROSTITUTES

Great men suffered but continued to struggle for the goals—They achieved their goals—The modern man is not up to the mark and looses his dignity so often—He does so for the sake of money, materialistic assets and recognition—Total loss of dignity of the person—Servile, fearful and conforming—Due to this, rich exploit the poor—Poor becoming poorer—A learned man lacks resources—A wealthy man lacks knowledge—Both are exploited—Mental prostitutes increasing in number—Exploitation of man by man must be stopped.

More than one hundred years ago, MK Gandhi was thrown out of a train in South Africa. However, Gandhi did not give up and struggled to become one of the most influential agents of change in the modern times. Our history books are replete with sentences, which associate the Mahatma with Lord Jesus Christ and other figures whom ordinary mortals never dare to emulate. Similarly, Shivaji Maharaj opposed the evil forces of Aurangazeb with full vigour. Guru Gobind Singh Ji did the same and sacrificed his sons and followers for a noble cause—his motherland.

Thomas Alva Edison was punched on his ear and became deaf for life. But he did not give up. He continued to work hard and succeeded in delivering the best inventions for the benefit of the mankind. In fact, we owe a lot to Edison for the modern gadgets of today. Socrates was sentenced to death for speaking the truth but nevertheless, he drank his cup of poison for the sake of a noble cause.

More examples can be cited in this context to confirm that great men and women were opposed by the society and their enemies but they did not give up and created histories in their areas of endeavour. We have entered the new millennium with a high head because these great sons and daughters of mankind opposed all the tyrannies of their opponents and came out with flying colours.

Let us take a look at the modern man. He is not as brave as Guru Gobind Singh. He is not as tolerant as the Mahatma. He has an enormous appetite for new equipment, liquor, computers, disco, drugs, social parties, sex and smoking. He has only one objective—make tonnes of money and enjoy it. Whereas our forefathers struggled hard for the cause of humanity, nation and social values, the modern man is concerned only with his physical well being. He is trying to acquire money and other materialistic assets so that we could live comfortably (and may be, in luxury). He is so selfish that we could even ignore his family for the sake of his selfish interests. This truly manifests itself in terms of a large number of divorces in the Western nations. The couples in the West do not even marry. They simply live together. When they are bored with each other, they choose their new partners. There is no care for the societal norms, children or parents. What a life !

In an office, the manhood is lost immediately upon entry in the cabin of the superior. "Yes Sir" is the most common spoken phrase. Even if the boss is wrong, he is declared right. And why not ? He pays so well to his juniors. Even if the boss kicks, abuses and throws paper on the humiliated man's face, the man keeps on smiling. He has to understand the basics of life he is a mental prostitute. Had he been female, he would have certainly been a subjected to sexual harassment as is common in modern-day offices. However, he is a male and so is his boss. Hence, his body cannot be raped. Therefore, his mind is raped and that is done everyday.

The modern high-technology age has given us many blessings—car, bungalow, television, cellular phone, amazing varieties of food, jet aircraft, computers, entertainment etc. But it has also put our lives on the brink of social and economic disasters. The rich are getting richer and the poor masses are becoming poorer. The nuclear families are increasing in number in the urban context. The engines of social change are losing steam. The problems of unemployment, female exploitation, dowry, AIDS, caste conflicts, ethnic violences, environmental disasters, pollution *etc* have made a mockery of man and his ego.

It is true that in a free market world, man can scale any height, earn any amount of money, create anything he wishes and operate the MNCs with the flick of a button. However, he is too weak to do so if he is uneducated, poor, resourceless and without any references. If he is not well connected or rich, he cannot create enough of knowledge base and means for success for himself. If his educational background is poor, he would not be able to earn enough for himself and his family. If his poverty overtakes him, he is naturally caught in the vicious circle of shortages. Even if he starts a business, lack of knowledge, inadequate technology and money force and him to struggle for years.

Similarly, a learned man lacks resources. He has already spent his (or his father's) fortune on education. For getting a job or starting a business, he needs money. He lacks the financial prowess. His education is unable to help him earn enough for survival and growth.

Both the cases described above painfully represent the common man around the globe. His struggle does not pay rich dividends. Let us take a simple example. Every girl, who goes to Mumbai for becoming an actress, does not necessarily become an actress. Then, where does she go after spending a decade in Mumbai ? Naturally, in the flesh business at Falkland Road in Mumbai. She was also talented and beautiful. But she was given a boot by the film industry and finally, she landed in a brothel because going back to her parents was only a dream.

Every weak and poor individual around the world is exploited by the rich and the powerful. This tragedy has been repeated for the past several thousands years and would continue to be repeated in future as well.

We have developed on all the fronts. But we have not been able to give an individual his basic right-to live with dignity on this planet.

Ironically, the number of mental prostitutes is increasing everyday. That is because people from lower social and economic levels try to emulate the social and economic strata immediately above theirs. Thus they sell their bodies and minds to the capitalistic system that exploits them to the core. This exploitation continues and would continue.

This herculean problem of human race cannot be solved in one day. However, we must have solution oriented approach for all the issues that face us. We would propose that the resources should be shared equally among the poor and the rich. The exploitation of men as well as women in the corporate sectors should be stopped and must be made punishable by law. Exploitation of male employee should also be treated as an offence *(eg,* late sitting in offices, overwork, bonded labour, child labour, inadequate wages, poor working conditions *etc* are some of the atrocities inflicted upon the employees by private sector firms). Working hours should be made flexible. The government institutions for infrastructural development and finance allocation should be made more liberal, democratic and customer-oriented. They should not exploit their customers. Corrupt officials in government offices must be punished. They must not be allowed to exploit the public.

International Human Rights Commission should be made more powerful around the globe. Nomads, gypsies, unemployed persons and the disabled (who have the maximum chances of being exploited) should be sent to proper shelters or homes.

Exploitation of man by man is continuing. Man is the most intelligent animal on the planet. He has to devise far-reaching and pragmatic solutions for curbing this menace in the interests of a peaceful and morally upright lifestyle on this planet. That would also ensure a bright and agony-free future for the posterity. The sooner he rises to the occasion, the better. ●

51. INDIA IN THE NEW MILLENNIUM

New hopes for India in the new millennium—Development in all the sectors of economy, society and polity—Population pressures to rise to new limits—Many Issues faced by the State—WTO, CTBT, International trade, Indo-Pak relationships etc are some of the vital issues—Cultural and moral decay is imminent—The citizens would have to become more responsible. Regionalism has become more prominent—NGOs to continue—Free market forces would decede business, Economic and political directions.

The new millennium has brought new hopes for the masses of all the nations. The new century and the new millennium promise to solve many problems related to their survival, growth and well-being. Man has now become capable enough to sustain his life on this planet. Many problems remain but they would be solved by us to the utmost satisfaction of the residents of this planet.

Let us discuss the new millennium in the context of Indian culture, society, economy, polity and psyche. We have promised healthy standards of living and an identity with dignity to our nationals, as has been promised by our forefathers through various declarations and through the commitments declared in Indian Constitution. Let us analyse some key aspects and view the same in the perspective of the new era that has dawned upon the world.

Indian population crossed the 100-crore mark in 1999. This is the major issue that confronts our policy planners and leaders in the new century. Our economic development rate is 5-6 per cent. If the population soars to a new peak of 162 crore by 2050, as has been predicted, we could face serious problems on the economic and social fronts. This population level would have to be reduced to nearly 70 crore and this is a herculean task. It can sustain a population of 70-75 crore with case but not beyond this. The birth rate would have to be brought to zero if we plan to achieve this target. The economic benefits generated by Five Year Plans could be delivered to the masses only if we reduced our population to an innocuous level of 70 crore. In that event, better standards of life for every citizen would be ensured. It would be surprising to note that India needs a healthy population figure as well. That is because India is a vast country. Our agricultural backbone has to be made stronger and for that manpower is required as agriculture is a labour-oriented profession. The Western notion (that mechanised farming techniques would generate more revenues for farmers) is not applicable in Indian Context.

The next major issue is related to Indian polity. We have a stable government in the centre. It is likely to continue till the year 2004 AD. The crucial issues like WTO, CTBT, International trade norms, relationships with Pakistan and China, poverty, Ninth Five Year Plan, defence, infrastructure development and others would have to be addressed by Mr AB Vajpayee and his team. Coalition governments have come to stay in the centre. This trend is likely to be repeated in the states as well, thanks to the growing clout of the regional parties. After a political lull of about eight years, India has witnessed a stable political mechanism. This trend should continue. This political stability would lead to healthy economic development. We do not predict any major political upheavals because India would never go the Pakistani way. However, in order to sort out the crucial issues, Mr Vajpayee need not cut the Gordian knot. For example, the government has been facing opposition from many political parties, including those who are a part and parcel of the NDA-led government, with respect to the Women's Reservation Bill in the *Lok Sabha*. Mr Vajpayee ought to observe a chary policy of "wait and move." After all, we are a democratic nation and the views of all the political components, which make up the national organism of India, have a right to support or oppose the Bill. Today, the true victory of democracy would emanate from a consensus and not from a simple majority. The election of Mr G M C Balayogi as the Speaker of the *Lok Sabha* then the election of Manohar Joshi as well as the election of Mr Jaswant Singh as the leader of *Rajya Sabha* prove that despite political differences, all the factions do give reverence to a healthy political mechanism that has always prevailed in India.

Indian society has many components. The rich and the neo-rich components have completely aligned themselves with the Western social norms. The middle classes are in a dilemma; if they emulate the class that is immediate above them, they are also treated as Western individuals. If they try to retain their hackneyed moral values, they are branded as traditional, backward and socially deplorable individuals. However, Western influences would certainly take them out of their shells and ultimately, they would also copy the Western styles of living in a full-fledged manner. In that event, the typical Indian characteristics would be deleted from their social and moral codes of conduct. This is not a healthy sign but in the wake of the imminent decay in moral values, this trend cannot be reversed. It is an irony that we are pleased to attend the *Ghazal* concerts, Indian arts exhibitions and classical music festivals but we pay respect to our ancient culture and traditions only for a small time interval. Most of our time is consumed in aping the Western norms. This cultural and moral hypocracy would lead us to a new society that would be just like the American Society. In that society, the liberty of the individual is so prominent that it leads him to a state of confusion. He accepts one norm and renounces another. But when he encounters another new moral value, he quickly embraces that one and eschews the previous norm. In sum, the Indian messes, which make up the middle class, would continue to be harassed by "middle class hassles." A quick acceptance of the Western norms and a doubt about their righteousness has generated this confusion.

The lower middle income groups as well as the lowest income groups would continue their struggles for survival. They are the typical Indians who always plan to buy TVs, refrigerators, cellular phones and cars but are unable to buy the same. The vicious cycle of poverty would continue to divest them of their rights in the society.

On the international economic front, India would have to increase her share in the global trade transactions. At present, India's share in the global trade is only 0.5 per cent. This figure could be taken up to a healthy 2.5-3.0 per cent. Asian economies have always performed better than us. Although we have accepted the free market norms in terms of economic development at home and abroad, yet these radical policy shifts have not delivered any concrete benefits to our intonation trade. We hope that in the times to come, we would be able to reap rich benefits as a result of this shift.

Our economic growth should be given a big boost in the new century. The industrial infrastructure has been developed. We have the largest pool of technical manpower in the world. We also have a healthy banking system under the aegis of RBI. The economic growth factors, though not very strong, are capable of delivering concrete results on a long term basis. Further, if our economy is growing at a faster pace than those of the other Asian nations, it is not a matter of solace. Our economy is not an advanced system and acceptance of a growth rate of 5-6 per cent as a healthy one. We must grow at the respectable rate of 8-10 per cent and this is not possible at present. The advanced economies are already 'hot' and cannot grow at a rate of more than 3-4 per cent. But our economy ought to grow at a higher pace simply because it has not grown much during the past fifty years.

Cuts in subsidies and public sector disinvestments have come to stay. The results of these austerity measures would be manifested in terms of the increased prices of fuels, LPG, kerosine, foodgrains and other essential items. On the other hand, electronics goods, computers, software, cellular phones, consumer durables and other items of luxury are likely to become cheaper. Therefore, in the new century, we could envisage an easy access to TVs, mobile phones and cars for the common man but a shortage of fossil fuels or higher prices of foods, medicines and other basic commodities. This crisis could continue up to the year 2040.

Regional groups have a powerful clout in their respective areas. When they would be frustrated in their efforts to come to power, they are likely to form new political conglomerates so that they could have majority in the *Lok Sabha* or in the state assemblies. The dispersion of political ideologies is likely to be reduced in this century in the wake of reduced power bases of the small political groups.

NGOs are not likely to continue in the new century, except only those that would be supported by the State or by the UNO. The elements of 'profit' and 'productivity' would be deeply embedded in those organisations that operate across the length and breadth of India, whatever their areas of operation might be.

As has been predicted by the *Pundits* of technology, it would dominate the operations and lives of the Indian masses. Internet operations, communications and other forms of human interaction would cost less. Internet would host information, which would be useful as well as redundant. The avid surfer would have to pick up the pearls of data from the amazing variety of websites and he would have a difficult task in finding what is useful for him. By the year 2010, Internet and E-com would be totally commercialised and information would be available only at a cost.

A tired office-goer would not seek a recourse to spiritualism; he is too busy to indulge in these divine activities. The rich and neo-rich classes might use Internet and spiritual discourses in order to chop oft a part of their guilt. There would be an orientation towards spiritualism. People would continue to visit religious places but they are unlikely to get any spiritual comfort due to the simple fact that they would have become too commercial and materialistic to 'cleanse' themselves.

Indian people would face an uphill task in terms of social, moral and economic challenges. We have stood the test of time for more than 5,000 years. This century is slightly difficult to handle. Let us pray that we are able to sale through this century with hard work and strong moral values ! We are not in a position to comment upon the new millennium; its first century itself is a testing time period for all Indians.

52. ROLE OF WOMEN IN CHILD DEVELOPMENT

Woman is the most pious creation of God—Many roles for her to play —She shapes the future of her children—She develops the careers of her sons and daughters—These children are the foundations of our society—Role of mothers is child development very important—Due to poverty, illiteracy and backwardness, many mothers are unable to groom their children—Train mothers—Educate them—Nations have been built because of the effective and right training by the mothers to their children — Some solutions suggested—Allocate more resources to the rural areas—Train women in vocations and latest techniques—Remove illiteracy and provide facilities.

Woman is the most pious creation of God. She assumes the roles of a daughter, a mother, a wife and a nation-builder. She has saved mankind from many a disaster. Because of her contributions and scarifies, mankind is proudly surging ahead.

A great philosopher has stated, "the hands that rock the cradle, rule the world." How true he was ! Woman in the role of a mother has assumed the dignity and decorum equivalent to that of the Almighty. Elders state that her status is even more than that of the Almighty. Mother moulds the character and destiny of her child. She is responsible for his all-round development. Her training helps him achieve the unknown heights during his lifetime.

Take the example of Shivaji. His mother, Jijabai, trained him in studies, arts, military skills and above all, in politics. She trained him so that he could be groomed to become a great warrior and administration. The small but well-trained forces of Shivaji took a heavy toll of life and property of the army of emperor Aurangzeb. Shivaji proved to be an able administrator as well. All his training and perfection were due to his education at his mother's feet.

Napolean Bonaparte once said, "Give me good mothers and I will give you a good nation." History was not guided or made by men of courage but by the mothers of those men who taught them how to walk through difficult times. An educated mother would be able to teach and train in a much better manner than an illiterate mother could. This is a very important conclusion to be considered seriously by our policy makers. If our women folk are educated, trained and polished for a tough life, they would develop their own children for perfection. Therefore, an educated and trained mother would always develop her children so that they would be able to get whatever they desired.

The child learns his first lesson at the feet of his mother. He does not understand the ways of the world and his only world is his mother. He is a clean slate and anything could be written on it. So, if the woman is wise, she should teach him to become a perfectionist. If she is not educated and prudent, she would not be able to develop him. Therefore, the life and career of her children would be in jeopardy. Take an example of labourers working along the roadside. They are illiterate, poor, incompetent and belong to the lowest strata of society. How would we expect their children to grow in mental, social and economic terms when their mothers are unable to provide them adequate food, clothing and shelter ? The child of a labourer woman is likely to become a labourer. His mother could not teach him for a better career simply because she could not visualise that there was a different world beyond her own. Her handicap becomes the long-lasting limitation of her child. Her child cannot develop beyond his or her limited cocoon.

The solution to this problem lies in our societal texture. We must support female literacy in rural and urban areas. We must inculcate the knowledge about good health and hygiene, information about the environment, importance of quality education and awareness about our nation as well as information about the world in the female society of our country. The knowledge amassed by them would automatically be transferred to the next generation.

Mothers must be educated and trained. They must have a spirit of sacrifice for their children in particular and for entire humanity in general. A mother can make a child either an angel or a devil. Her courage, education and training would determine the future course of action of her children. And we are very well aware that today's children would be the essential components of tomorrow's society. Man plays a vital role in a family, society and a nation. But the role of mother is supreme. It is the real power responsible for the survival and growth of mankind.

Nations have been built and ruined on account of good or poor training and development of children by their mothers. This aspect of nation-building has been ignored by our leaders and policy-makers. We have always treated women as second class citizens. Instead of giving them the complete responsibilities and authority of home, we have tortured them beyond compare. Eastern societies are known for unforgettable and heinous crimes against women. How can woman develop her children in such grim situations ? And who suffers ultimately ?

It is true that now women have learned to stand up for themselves. They have entered all areas of human endeavour. They are working as hard as men are. They are training their children for better opportunities in life. But it is a pity to note that this feature is prominent in the urban context only. The rural women are illiterate, backward, resistant to change and above all, indifferent to the vital needs of their children. We would suggest the following measures to be taken so that women realise the importance of their contributions for shaping the careers of their children :—

 (A) The women of rural areas must be educated through part-time educational programmes. They should be trained in the vital areas of household, education, basic sciences, basic as well as advanced agriculture and health and hygiene.

 (B) The children should be sent to schools where trained teachers should shape their personalities and careers.

(C) Women should be allowed to travel (to big cities) once or twice a year so that they could know about the pace of progress of mankind.

(D) Exploitation of woman should be made severely punishable by law. A law has already been passed, which would combat the ugly menace of exploitation of women in offices.

(E) Women should be trained for the usage of new gadgets and tools for educating their children. For example, they should be trained in computers, technical trades, educational techniques, painting, fashion design, tailoring, clay modelling, handicrafts, textiles, handlooms, leather garments etc. They would be able to pass on their knowledge to their children. The children would become self-sufficient when they are trained by their mothers.

(F) Rural areas should be allocated more resources for additional health care facilities for the women folk.

(G) The women clubs and societies should organise seminars so that they could adopt latest training methods for their children.

(H) New and efficient techniques in education have been developed in the West. These techniques could be modified for Indian needs. Our women could be made experts in at least one educational stream. Once they have been trained, they should be persuaded to shape the careers of their children in that stream.

In sum, we can state that the role of women in shaping the future of a society and a country can never be underscored. Women must break the chains of economic, social and educational backwardness. They should be allowed to develop themselves and their posterity, which is supposed to take over the reigns of the nation.

53. GOD'S VERDICT

Whatever your sow, so shall you reap—Decay and death are inevitable—But do not oppress poor people—Do not torture else you would also be tortured—Alexander invaded India but finally died because of severe dysentery—The Philosophy of karma is very pertinent in today's context—Arson, communal violence, black marketing and commercialism pravelent in world—But we are paying the price—Satyuga likely to come after Kalyuga—World is growing but agonies are also growing—Have faith—Be religious—Do not torture your fellow brothers and sisters—Do one good act per day—Honesty, integrity and hard work must be accepted as norms.

It is an established fact that the deeds (*Karma*) of a person would fetch him befitting rewards or punishments depending upon their nature and intentions. The message of our great saints and visionaries was clear—whatever you sow, so shall you reap. And amazingly true ! The world is on the verge of the next millennium. But the basic tenants defined by the Almighty remain unchanged.

Decay and death are inevitable. Man knows this fact. But he uses his physical powers, financial whip and political goodwill for the destruction of his competitors. He forgets that there could be reprisals—not from the victims he decimated without any mercy but from the Almighty who owns and controls this world.

Let us take the example of Indian subcontinent. Many marauders, invaders and kings ruled over this nation. They looted the masses and deprived them of their lives, properties and dignity. And then they went to their native places. Did they leave in peace ? No ?

Alexander The Great invaded India and conquered it with the help of his men and the traitors of our nation. He looted the masses and butchered thousands of innocent people. The arrival of Alexander The Great in India can never be likened to be the smooth arrival of a saint or gentleman from a foreign land. He came for the gold, spices, valuables and the glimpse of the most prosperous nation of those times. He left the country and fell sick while he was going home in Macedonia. Even the best medicines could not cure him. He stated with a sigh, "I die by the help of too many physicians."

So intense was his dysentery that he could not survive for long time period due to the severity of the disease. His mother called the chief physician and asked why her son was not getting any relief. The learned physician took her to the sea beach and threw a dose of medicine in ocean water. The water froze within a few seconds. The physician told the queen that even this strong medicine was not affecting her son and that he did not have cure, which could be more powerful than this. The mother was fully convinced that her son was destined to die.

Indian mythology concentrates on the philosophy of *Karma*. The religious scriptures state that one should execute his duties efficiently. *The Geeta* also emphasises upon this universal fact. Our main objective is to perform the task for which, we have been sent to this world. And these tasks certainly could never include arson, communal violence, black marketing and hooliganism. After all, what is the difference between man and animals ? We are the finest creation of God Almighty. It is our duty to develop ourselves and protect our habitat and mother earth so that life could continue even after we are no more.

But man does not understand this fact and resorts to all types of immoral activities for making money and getting whatever he aspires to get. Since time immemorial, he has been ruling with the help of the sword and guns and has exploited his weak brothers and sisters. And God has given him a befitting reply by giving him an agony or a punishment in one form or another. And the irony is that we do not understand that diseases, losses in business, accidents, natural calamities and death are the natural sequels of our *Karmas*. After all, there is no *Swarga* or *Naraka* anywhere in the universe. Every misdeed or good deed would be judged in this mortal earth itself.

All the religions support this theory. We would have to pay for our sins before we leave this mortal earth. And remember, if at all we are spared, our posterity would have to pay the price. Let us cite a simple example. We are generating enough of pollution through automobiles, generators and industries. This alarmingly high level of pollution would lead to high levels of CO_2 in the atmospheric air. The heat from the surface of the earth would be trapped as CO_2 would reflect it back to the earth. The result would be global warming and greenhouse effect. The polar ice caps would melt. The countries like Bangladesh could be totally submerged as a result of the rising ocean levels. The temperature of the earth is higher by $0.25°C$ as compared to that of previous year. It has been predicted rise by 2 degrees temperatures over the Asian subcontinent. This is the impact of the Celsius by the middle of the century. endless pollution that is being spewed out by our vehicles and factories today. How can our posterity be spared from the deadly diseases like

TB, asthma, bronchitis, lung cancer, birth defects skin infections, eye problems and even serious psychological problems. Whatever we do today, would have an impact on our children and the generations to come in the future. If we are good to our friends, families, society, habitat and environment, our posterity would reap rich benefits else our children would face serious problems.

Life on the planet is becoming very difficult everyday. Moral values have eroded and commercialism has become the dominating force in all walks of life as well as in all the strata of society. We are misusing religion for our selfish ends. We should have used it for the peace of mind and as a guiding light in our lives. But we are decaying everyday through the misuse of religion and also are paying the price of this decay.

The black age of *Kalyuga* continues. But has been said that after *Kalyuga*, the next era would be of *Satyuga*. Men would not pounce upon men like animals. There would be no greed, hunger or communal strife in the world. The nations would work for a prosperous earth and mankind. There would be no pollution and we would enjoy the best standards of life due to the *avante garde'* technologies. There would be no agonies and humans would unite their abilities and powers for their growth of the earth and this universe. Is it a dream ? True ! It is a dream as no *Satyuga* would begin until we come out of the darkness of *Kalyuga*. We can reach the *Satyuga* age only if we overcome our wickedness and eliminate the poison that is in our minds. We would have to eliminate the evil forces that prevail upon us in *Kalyuga*.

This world continues to grow at a very fast pace. Physical and technological growth is visible from the developments in terms of computers, Internet, fast cars, jet aircraft, cellular phones, expanding international trade and above all, in terms of deadly nuclear bombs that continue to increase in number without control. But the mind suffers, the peace has evaporated and the internal confusion has reached its a more agonising situation. We are leading highly artificial and synthetic lives, which have everything in the of materialism. Our minds are hollow. We have ignored the meaning of good living. deeds are full of evil intentions and so, we are regularly punished by nature through various modes. God is silent but is the most powerful entity in this universe. No human activity could escape His attention or wrath.

Let us suggest some solutions so that our burdened souls could get some respite and we could bear the brunt of evil forces of *Kalyuga* :—

(A) Religion has been given a wrong shade due to commercialism, violence and political machinations. The masses must adopt religion for spiritual solace. However, religion is an personal issue and should be treated as very personal. It should not be allowed to spill into the societal fabric as normally, the ultimate colour of this fragile fabric becomes red with blood. We can profess any religion but should do so within the boundaries of our homes. We would not support any institutions that support or propound a particular religion or another. In fact, the practitioners of religion take us away from religion.

(B) We should do one good deed everyday. This should not be related to our family, business or children. It should be for the benefit of mankind.

(C) Honesty, integrity and hard work are the three major characteristics of a noble soul. Even if the prevalent environment around us has corrupted us, we could mend ourselves and could become good citizens of the world.

(D) The social interaction of people with their friends, relatives and those in their immediate vicinity has been lost. This should be revived. Social organisations and clubs (on non-commercial lines) should be set up for the benefit of people of all age groups. Social interactions should be encouraged.

(E) If a misdeed has been done, one has to admit it and he must be prepared for the consequences of that misdeed. The suffering party should be adequately compensated.

(F) The soul does not accept regulation of the State. Self-regulation is the only key to salvation. Therefore, we do not propose any legislations for spiritual growth and moral upliftment of the masses. Adherence to societal and moral values should be voluntary and not through coercion.

(G) Western influences have adversely affected our moral values. They have a good reason to live in a manner they like. But our society and culture would not be an ideal place for this experimentation. In fact, this mental instability in our social milieu has appeared since the onslought of Western influences. We do not negate the good effects of Western culture. Their good values must be adopted; efficiency, hard work and commitment are some of them. But violence, sex, liquor, drugs and materialism should not be adopted by our society as these have already caused immense damage to our culture and its social norms. Why should we suffer due to evil preferences of other societies whereas they are also fed up because of their ill-effects ?

We must conclude by stating that cleansing of our souls is in our hands. Let us take some constructive steps so that we could lead happy and peaceful lives.

THE WORLD POLITICAL

54. THE SEATTLE FIASCO

WTO meet at Seattle ended in a fiasco—Nearly 25,000 protestors stalled the proceedings—No concrete benefits to the developing nations or the third world—The USA and other Western nations went complete trade freedom and removal of trade barriers—European nations want agricultural subsidies to continue—Indian stand not clear—We have indirectly supported Western nations earlier—One to acceptance of Bretton woods Agreement, Indian agriculture suffered—Other issues include tariffs, environment, labour etc—The USA in a negative role but vehemently opposed at the Seattle meet—Some suggestions for Indian delegates to WTO appended.

In December, 1999, nearly 25,000 protesters marched in the streets of Seattle (USA) and Canada opposition was mainly from the USA and included young people, veterans. They belonged to labour organisations and non-governmental firms. Although they belonged to different groups, yet they had inter-group communication at the time of their protest rally, which did not allow the USA and other nations to go ahead with the agenda at the WTO. Therefore, democratic forces in North America stalled the proceedings at the conference and did not allow the economic superpower of the world to have their independent course of action. They did a favour to entire third world, the developing nations and the masses underpreviledged.

Why did the Seattle meet of WTO end in a fiasco ? Let us analyse. The USA and Canada have an agenda based on agriculture, investments and information technology. These nations want to impose their agenda on the WTO. The group belonging to the European Union (EU) has an agenda based on agriculture because these nations receive heavy subsidies in agriculture. The EU does not want these subsidies to be removed, lest the economies of the EU should be seriously affected. Further, there is a third group, called the Cairns Group, which has 15 members. The members of this group are Australia, Argentina, Brazil, Canada, Chile, Colombia, Fiji, Indonesia,

Malaysia, New Zealand, Paraguay, the Philippines, South Africa, Thailand and Uruguay. This group includes agricultural nations and exporters. The group wants that the subsidies on the agricultural commodities to go and the markets of the entire world to operate in a free manner. India, though not belonging to any one of the groups, represents the interests of the third world. As on date, there are 135 members of WTO and 20 more nations wish to join the same. China has already joined WTO and her entry would give concrete support to her economic reforms. Recently, China and India signed vital trade agreements; every member nation of WTO is supposed to sign these agreements with other member nation. She would also enjoy an honourable status in the international platforms, which are chiefly dominated by the Western nations. However, the entry of China into WTO would result in a loss of that country because Hong Kong would no longer be an intermediary between China and the West. China has also acquired its former province Macao, which was under Portuguese rule. The export growth had slowed down and consumer prices had fallen. Hence, China had to join the fray at WTO in order to facilitate the export growth trends. China has been able to visualise a bright future for her subjects through the Proceedings of WTO.

Indian stand at the WTO has been criticised. Our leaders have been accused of sidelining the vital interests of the developing nations and aligning the Indian trading norms with those of the West. This new development has a political tinge. India and the USA are very close to each other in terms of regional polity and international economic and strategic scenario. In 1989, India ignored the interests of the developing world. Mr Rajiv Gandhi told his representative during the Uruguay Round of talks that he should not oppose the proposals of the USA and other developed nations. Other nations of the developing world had opposed the Uruguay round of talks. India ignored these moves and as a result, agriculture, banking, services were also included in the agenda of the WTO. After Mr Gandhi, Mr PV Narasimha Rao continued the process of economic reforms. He did not take the Indian Parliament into confidence. He accepted those policies that were being promoted and supported by the West. It has been contended that these policies were against Indian economic interests.

The USA has always used clauses "Super 301" or "Special 301" against the developing nations. Because of these clauses, Indian leaders have been taking decisions, which are not in the interest of Indian masses. For example, the Patent Law of 1970 has been abolished and new Patent Law, as well as new Insurance Law, has been brought into effect. Critics feel that foreign investments in these areas would harm our interests in the long run. It is strange to note that on the issues of insurance and patents, the BJP and the Congress share the same platform, a fact, which is difficult to digest in the context of defeat of the BJP-led coalition Government by the parties supported by the Congress in 1999. The MNCs are entering Indian markets at will. They also bribe Indian bureaucrats and firms so that they could sail smoothly. Enron and Cogentrix are the two firms that have been identified as the firms, which proposed to pay bribes to Indian officials and politicians. It was alleged that Enron had earmarked Rs 60 crore for such payments.

The issues, which created a furore and earned the wrath of the protesters in Seattle, included labour and environment. The USA now knows that she would not be able to get the accords signed in her own favour. This opposition would grow and the protesters might form an anti-WTO forum within a few months from the date of protest. The critics of the WTO meet at Seattle opine that if Indian agriculture is declared as an industry, FICCI, CII and ASSOCHAM would reap the richest benefits. The critics of WTO are against the elimination of agricultural subsidies. European nations are not keen to let the subsidies evaporate into thin air because these subsidies are 50 per cent of their budgetary allocations. Other issues were related to trade protection norms and environmental control. The USA was supposed to the be the only beneficiary to proposals at the WTO.

India is an agricultural nation. WTO resolutions could affect our farmers in an adverse manner. After 1995, the trends of desperation were observed in our farmers, not withstanding the soothing effects of the "Green Revolution." Despite the fact that we have been receiving good monsoons, the agricultural output has plunged to low levels. Our population has increased over the past thirty years but our foodgrain production has not risen in that proportion. During the period of 1991-96, the foodgrain production grew at the rate of 1.7 per cent but population growth rate was 1.9 per cent during the same period. In 1995-96 period, the foodgrain production was reduced by

3.60 per cent. In 1997-98, it was reduced by 3.70 per cent. In 1997-98, it was reduced by 3.70 per cent. Foodgrain output has been reported to have fallen in Punjab, Haryana, Western UP and Tamil Nadu, Kerala is also not in a good command on the agricultural front. Famine was witnessed in Bundelkhand (UP), Kalahandi (Orissa), Bihar and Rajasthan. In Bundelkhand alone, 462 people died during the past three years. Due to debt burden, 500 farmers committed suicide in Andhra Pradesh, Karnataka, Punjab and Haryana. These circumstances were created, directly or indirectly, due to the economic policies promoted by Bretton woods Agreement. Further, due to excessive usage of chemical fertilisers, the soil lost its fertility. Nitrogenous fertilisers polluted the underground water reserves. As a result, our agricultural sector became sick and is heading towards a catastrophe. And if India gives in to the demands of the prosperous few at WTO, she would find her agricultural production (and quality levels) plummeting to new depths.

The trade liberalisation norms in respect of IT, biotechnology and industrial tariffs would also figure in the future negotiations at WTO. If trade across the national frontiers is liberalised, the USA and some Western nations would get the maximum benefits. The developing and the poor nations would have to remove subsidies and controls and the Western powers would find new market niches for their products and services. These nations have unlimited financial process whereas the poor and the developing nations lack the financial resources. And in the times to come, only the super-rich and technologically advanced firms and nations would survive in the global markets. As a developing nation, we are also in favour of liberalisation of trade and removal of trade barriers. However, an immediate acceptance and implementation of free trade norms would harm our interests, as has been described earlier in the context of agricultural scenario of India.

The solutions for this serious international crisis could be appended as follows :—

(A) India and the developing nations must clearly define their economic goals. They must also make pragmatic policies and procedures for achieving the same. These goals and procedures may not necessarily be in accordance with the norms laid down by WTO.

(B) India must support the developing world at WTO; however, India need not 'oppose' the West an any issue.

(C) There should be nation-wide discussion on the key issues of WTO.

(D) The negotiations at various platforms of WTO must be made transparent.

(E) The third world should plan the transactions of mutual trade without involving the provisions of WTO. We feel that barter system of trade would suit the nations of the third world as there would be no need of "Dollar transactions."

(F) In the subsequent negotiations at WTO, India should involve the NGOs as well.

(G) India is a member of the Green Room Group, which has 23 member nations. The Green Room concept dues not allow the poor nations to vote on the issues of WTO. India must ask for the inclusion of all the member nations of WTO in the Green Room. If this is not feasible, India must withdraw from the Green Room.

The fiasco at Seattle has proved that the ordinary citizens, NGOs, environmental activists and rational thinkers do not want the powerful nations to go berserk at the WTO. The new world would not belong to the rich few but to the poor many. India must align her policies with the poor many but at the same time, she must have a factful liaison with the rich few. Indian stand on WTO is still not clear. We have to be careful during the next meeting of WTO. We are supposed to look after not only the interests of Indian farmers, traders and industrialists, but also those of the developing nations. Our status in WTO is special and we must not forget this glaring fact. ●

55. THE FALLOUT OF GLASNOST

USSR a strong force in earth before Glasnost—During late eighties, Gorbachev brought Glasnost and freedom for Russia and her allies—Political wilderness—Economic problems—Afghanistan Problem—India suffered a setback—Poor supply of defence equipment and economic aid—Russian image of superpower eroded—Struggling to rise on her feet—India might suffer—China-USA-Pakistan axis could be dangerous for India—

US President visited China in June '98—Russian Premier Mr Primakov, also visited India and insinuated at India-China-Russia axis—Bipolar world must be acceptable for a balance among economic, political and strategic powers—World war in a bipolar world ruled out.

Prior to glasnost–the policy of openness–the USSR was a superpower. She commanded respect and awe in the minds of the Westerners. The value of the Rouble was strong in international markets and the Soviet block was a major political, economic and strategic player in the world.

Relationships of India with the USSR and the Eastern block nations were excellent. In fact, India was a major ally of the USSR from the third world.

During the late eighties, Michael Gorbachev took over the reins of the USSR after the sad demise of President Breznev. Breznev was a true friend of India and had helped her in many an economic and political crisis. Gorbachev launched the *Glasnost* drive that culminated in the complete removal of the communist curtain of the Eastern block. The USSR was divided into twenty independent states. The Rouble was devalued. Industrial production suffered and unemployment was on the rise. The mighty Russians had to struggle for decent wages. Vodka and bread were costlier in the markets. Free market mechanism had taken its own toll.

This had to happen. The free market system had inevitably to take over in the interest of efficiency and productivity and for the benefit of the communist masses. However, the Eastern block suffered some great blows on the international front. The allies of the USSR also became free markets that are now vulnerable to the West. The Russian influence decreased. India, which had a defence treaty with the USSR, had to look for a new defence partner. The Eastern block supplied economic aid and arms during the past forty years. Now, all the economic and monetary issues would be guided by the free market forces.

The most subversive fallout was for Russia who lost her position as a superpower. Ironically, Russians and the Eastern block had successfully countered the machinations of NATO for almost fifty years. The superpower game can be described in terms of a boxing match in which, one of the boxers has gone out of the boxing arena and has become a priest, leaving the other as the undisputed master of the game.

Whereas it is a positive sign that the cold war has ended, Indian interests have suffered. Russia is good friend but she too had her problems, mainly dominated by unemployment, poverty, internal uprisings, problems in Afghanistan and a free economic system to which, she has not been able to adopt so far.

In June, 1998, President Bill Clinton paid an official visit to China. Both the superpowers shared similar views on almost all the international economic, political and defence issues. The visit of the US President signalled to the world that the role of China as a watchdog of Asia is likely to continue. Instead of supporting a democracy like India, the USA is more than willing to support undemocratic nations like China and Pakistan.

Further, the two Koreas are again on a warpath. The Palestine issue was settled, though Israel had not agreed to give more land to Palestine in October, 1998. The nuclear tests carried out by Pakistan and India have caused serious concern in all the parts of the world. Euro has been introduced as the common currency of twelve European nations. Global economy is still in doldrums. The smaller nations of Asia and the Orient depend upon the Japanese economy. However, the Nikei Index disappoints investors. African nations are starving as a result of the drought and internal strife. Iraq and the USA are always willing to fight another battle in the gulf, thanks to the apathetic attitudes adopted by both Iraq and the USA. The world faces serious problems of poverty, illiteracy and hunger.

In the context of the situations faced by the world, it is imperative that another world power should arrive at the centre-stage. The USA-China-Pakistan axis would like to convert the globe into a unipolar entity. For the sake of stability, a bipolar world is of utmost necessity. There is no superpower in Africa as the nations of that continent are either pro-West or are struggling for economic or political survival.

During the first half of 1999, the former Russian PM, Mr Primakov, arrived in Indian Capital and favoured the formation of an axis comprising India, Russia and China. If Chinese leaders take these signals and return Indian land, a powerful trio could emerge in this part of the world that could make this world truly bipolar and stable. China and Pakistan are emotionally inclined towards each other. Pakistan has suffered a heavy defeat in the Kargil war and so, she may not join any axis of which, India is a crucial building block. We would also propose that the CIS nations should again join hands to emerge as the new power centre backed by India, NAM countries, Africa and the middle-East. That would mean that Russia would have to leave NATO and would have to regain her position as the second pole in the world. This would not lead to another cold war as it has already been decided by the USA and Russia that they would eliminate all the nuclear weapons systematically. Russians are fighting rebels in Chechnya. International opinion does not favour them but there is no interference from any nation or the UN.

So, it is obvious that Pakistan would not appreciate this new development. However, it is in the interests of Asia as well as the world to have a second superpower on the political platform of the globe. The unipolar world could see the single powerful entity going berserk and harming the interests of nations like India, Nepal, Bangladesh as well as the survival and growth of African and gulf nations. Russia is a democratic country now and she would not repeat any of the mistakes of the past. The CIS States could join hands on democratic and moral grounds. India could play a vital role in this context.

The post-*Glasnost* world is politically chaotic, economically bankrupt and strategically insecure. If *status quo* of the bipolar world is restored, India could be the major beneficiary of the new system. Free market system would govern the mechanism of the global markets. However, the bipolar defence and political initiatives would lead to a policy of military and political deterrence. In sum, a bipolar world could be a reality by the year 2040. The new power axis could comprise Russia, China or both of these nations. India could also support such an axis. In a free market world, vehement opposition of a rival could harm the commercial interests of a country. So, even a bipolar world would be a "market-sensible" system. There would be strategic preparations and plots but a World War would be avoided by both the axes. Proxy wars are likely to continue.

56. THE COMMONWEALTH

Commonwealth meet (CHOGM) organised from November 12-15, 1999—Pakistan censured and suspended at Commonwealth due to military rule—CMAG told to review the situation—HLG set up to review the role of the Commonwealth in the wake of challenges of the new millennium—Theme of 1999 was "Globalisation and People-centred Development"—India always played constructive roles at this forum—Poverty alleviation should be the major concern of the Commonwealth—Burma and Ireland have already withdrawn—Social, Cultural, and Sports programmes organised by the Commonwealth—The Commonwealth has a bright future.

During the meeting held in Durban (South Africa) from November 12-15, 1999, the fifteenth Commonwealth Heads of Governments Meeting (CHOGM) took an exceptional decision. It suspended the military regime of Pakistan from the council of Commonwealth, asking for the restoration of democracy in that trouble-torn State. The decision was taken by Commonwealth Ministerial Action Group (CMAG). The heads of the governments of Commonwealth nations have requested CMAG to keep the situation in Pakistan under review and be ready to recommend measures to be taken by the Commonwealth if restoration of democracy is not resorted to in Pakistan at a quick pace. Indian PM asked for the application of Millbrook Action Programme in the context of restoration of a democratic set up in Pakistan. The final statement of CHOGM read as follows, " Heads of governments condemn the unconstitutional overthrow of the democratically elected government of Pakistan on October 12, 1999." CHOGM also refused to recognise the military regime in Pakistan, which is being governed by General Pervez Musharraf. It called for the restoration of a civilian democratic rule in Pakistan at the earliest possible date.

This decision of the Commonwealth was quite expected. Pakistan was always uncomfortable at the meetings of the Commonwealth. The aforementioned decision is also related to India in an indirect manner because the suspension of Pakistan from the membership had emanated from the fact that Pakistan had become an autocratic State Pakistan has faced twenty-five years of military rule since her independence. And the military took over the nation because Pakistan had failed to satisfy the military, the mercenaries and the Kashmiri militants in the Kargil war. Therefore, some Pakistani diplomats might also trace the reason of suspension to the bitter relationships of their nation with India.

Further, a new High Level Group (HLG) was established by CHOGM (1999). Its objective is to review the role of Commonwealth organisation and advise it about the *modus operandi* for facing the challenges of the new millennium. HLG would be headed by Mr Thabo Mbeki who is also the President of South Africa. Mr Mbeki is also the Chairman of the Commonwealth. The British Queen is the ceremonial head of the Commonwealth. There are 10 members in HLG and include the heads of governments of Australia, Fiji, India, Malta, Singapore, Tanzania, Trinidad and Tobago, the UK and Zimbabwe. HLG would submit its report at the next CHOGM summit, which would be held in Canberra (Australia) in 2001 AD.

The theme of CHOGM (1999) was "Globalisation and People-centred Development." Issues related to economic development of the commonwealth nations were a part of the agenda for discussions. The Commonwealth has played constructive roles in the decolonisation processes in Zimbabwe, Namibia and South Africa. It has contributed towards the multi-party democratic system in South Africa. Poor member nations are given adequate financial support by the Commonwealth. The Colombo Plan and the Harare Declaration are the two vital landmarks in this context. Under the Colombo Plan, the underdeveloped countries can get assistance from the prosperous countries of the Commonwealth fold. Further, after the Harare summit of 1991, Britain and Canada announced that they would unilaterally write off one-third of the debts that were due to to them by the poorest nations. A Commonwealth Development Corporation has also been set up, which assists in the economic development of the developing nations by investing in those.

It is pleasing to note that India has always played constructive roles in all the Commonwealth meets. Further, Britain has also not imposed the dictates of the British monarchy on the member nations of the Commonwealth. In other words, the organisation has been treading a path that is virtuous, democratic and member-oriented. In another significant development in December, 1999, the masses of

Australia accepted the British Queen as the ceremonial head of that country. This would mean that the British monarchy enjoys a great following in the former British colonies. Till the time the Commonwealth operates as a truly democratic entity, there is no harm in supporting it.

The role of the UK in the Commonwealth is appreciable. As a former ruler of the member nations of the Commonwealth fold, Britain has never tried to impose her policies and directives. She has allowed the organisation to operate in a democratic manner. The Queen is only the ceremonial head of the organisation. Further, the strategic interests of Britain are being met by her close ties with the USA. She is an ally of the USA and represents Western dominance on the strategic and economic platforms of the world. There was a need to have friendly relationships with her former colonies like India, Zimbabwe, Australia, Singapore, Fiji *etc*. Hence, she did well to form an organisation—the Commonwealth—through which, she developed good relationships with these nations. This suits the British interests.

Most of the members of the Commonwealth are poor or developing nations. The organisation should assist in the removal of the poverty prevalent in these countries. The major issues faced by Commonwealth should therefore, have an economic tinge inherent in them. The poor nations could reap rich benefits from the Western nations through this important forum. There was no proposal of formation of a strategic alliance in Commonwealth. Perhaps, this is a good sign. If the organisation concentrates on the economic and social issues only, the member nations would be able to justify their alliance to the entire world.

Burma and Ireland withdrew from the Commonwealth. This proves that democracy thrives in this organisation. The membership in the Commonwealth is voluntary and any member could withdraw from the same at any point of time. The issue of withdrawal by Burma and Ireland and the issue of suspension of Pakistan should be viewed in a positive perspective by the Commonwealth. This is an organisation that has been created to promote harmony and economic development among its member nations. The objectives are pious. The actions and decisions are also in tune with the acceptable norms.

There is no harm in continuing an organisation that is able to protect the interests of its members.

The Commonwealth also promotes cultural and social programmes in various parts of the world. The Commonwealth Games are a regular fair and Australia dominates in almost all the sports events. Indian sports stars are also able to fetch some gold and silver medals at the Commonwealth Games. The sports spirit binds the member nations in an unique manner. Therefore, the member nations are able to satisfy their requirements on the economic, social, political and sports platforms of the organisation. These are healthy trends. In order to survive, any organisation needs the following inputs :—

(A) Financial resources.
(B) Political will.
(C) Ability to steer through grave crises.
(D) Harmony among member nations.
(E) Support of the global organisations like the UNO.

The commonwealth is adequately equipped in terms of these five inputs. Hence, the organisation is likely to survive in the new millennium as well. Its resilience has been proved beyond doubt. However, in order to make it stronger and more dominant at international fora, the economic prosperity of its member nations would have to be ensured. Economic prosperity of the members would lead to sustenance of the Commonwealth on a long term basis.

In the new century, the Commonwealth faces many challenges. Its member nations have to address the vital issues like the military rule in Pakistan, economic development of the poor member nations, economic reforms, liberal trade among the member nations, sports, the relationship of the organisation with the UNO, WTO, removal of poverty, health management *etc*. We hope that the organisation would be able to achieve its objectives in these vital areas.

A stable organisation at the global level would certainly ensure economic, political and social reforms. The member nations of the commonwealth are independent entities. While they enjoy their special status, they are also able to interact with other member nations for promoting mutual economic, social and political interests. Here is a forum that is sans cheap political ideologies and machinations. India is a proud member of the Commonwealth and ought to support its cause and functioning. The interests of all the members have to be protected. NAM has lost its relevance and many other organisations at the global level are also planning to call it a day in the wake of the liberal trading norms, political upheavals and strife. However, the Commonwealth continues to steer through the maze of problems and is likely to deliver concrete benefits for its member nations.

We wish a bright future for the Commonwealth movement and for its member nations. The major issue at Commonwealth summits should be economic development. Once the member nations become prosperous, they could add more issues in their agenda. India would continue to support the policies and actions of the Commonwealth.

57. FIFTY YEARS OF UN

UN was conceived and organised after Second World War—the UK, the USA, the USSR, China and France were the first few members—UN was born on October 24, 1945—Headquarters in New York—Completed fifty years in 1995—Faced many wars—Tried to solve the problems through peacekeeping missions, negotiations etc—Succeeded in putting off Third World War and in helping refugees around the world—Indo-Pak wars over Kashmir—UN could not do anything on the Kashmir issue—Kashmir issue bilateral and UN members support Indian stand on the issue of intrusion by Pakistan-backed mercenaries—Did great service to humanity through ILO, UNESCO, UNICEF, FAO etc—Facing severe economic crisis and the question of survival—Environment, nuclear debate, poverty are the main problems faced by UN.

The United Nations (UN) came into existence after the Second World War. It was the natural sequel to the long-term struggle of man for superiority over his brothers and sisters. It is believed that if the post-war world would not have created the UN, the nuclear weapons available at that time could have annihilated the mother earth. Hence, the UN came for the rescue of humanity at the right time.

When the world was witnessing bloodshed and gore, President Franklin D Roosevelt of the USA and Prime Minister Sir Winston Churchill of the UK, proposed a set of principles for international collaboration. These principles became the guiding spirit for maintaining peace and stability in the world. The document signed during their meeting was known as the "Atlantic Charter." A conglomerate of 26 countries, which was fighting the axis nations, supported the Atlantic Charter and signed the "Declaration of United Nations" on January 1, 1942.

The leaders from the USA, the UK, the USSR and China met in Moscow and later, in Teheran and decided to set up a world body for maintaining peace and security. The first blueprint of the UN was made at a conference held at a mansion called Dumberto Oaks in Washington, DC in 1944. The representatives of the USSR, the UK, the USA and China decided about the aims, structure and functioning of a global organisation. Later, President Roosevelt, Prime Minister Churchill and Mr Joseph Stalin met again on February 11, 1945 at Yalta. They declared their resolve for establishing a general international organisation for the maintenance of peace and security around the globe.

On April 25, 1945, the delegates from 50 countries met in San Francisco for attending the UN Conference on International Organisation. A 111-article charter was drafted and was accepted unanimously by 51 nations on June 25, 1945. The United Nations came into existence on October 24, 1945 when its charter was ratified by five permanent members of the security council as well as by other countries. The headquarters of the UN are in New York.

In 1995, the UN completed fifty years. By the end of 1997, 185 nations had become full-fledged members of the UN. The world has seen many technological, economic, social and political upheavals since the inception of the UN. The Internet age is at its peak. Satellites are used for communication, surveillance and warfare by all the major powers of the world. The nuclear club of five countries is no longer their forte but has been invaded by India and Pakistan due to their nuclear tests. Although the nuclear club denies the nuclear power status either to India or to Pakistan, yet the fact remains that nuclear capability is no longer the exclusive previlege of a few nations. There aremany other nations, which are working hard for riding the prestigious nuclear bandwagon. The USA and other affluent nations from the East and the West have imposed economic sanctions against India and Pakistan. But the UN is hardly able to stop the race for nuclear supremacy. The world has not forgotten the holocausts of

Hiroshima and Nagasaki in 1945. A nuclear arms race in Asia could trigger off a mini-war which could culminate in a full-fledged Third World War. The causes and effects would have to be studied deeply by the members of the general assembly and by the security council as well. If the UN does not attend to the serious issue of nuclear arms race, we could face extinction from the earth. On January 24, 1946, the General Assembly adopted its first resolution—peaceful uses of atomic energy and the elimination of atomic weapons and other weapons of mass destruction. The five nuclear powers have deadly nuclear arsenal in their possession and would be joined by many more in the years to come. Therefore, the resolution stands negated and defied by the member nations of the UN themselves.

Secondly, the world population has touched the 6 billion mark. The world population has grown at a tremendous pace. This has also multiplied the economic and social problems of the nations of the world. Poor countries like Bangladesh, India, Ethiopia, Nepal and other African nations are the chief victims of population explosion. The UN has tried to popularise birth control methods, maintain health of women in the poor countries and build an infrastructure for the population control through its organisations like UNESCO, UNHCR, UNICEF *etc*. However, despite the efforts of the UN, the population growth could not be checked. The nations, which deserved the lowest growth rates in population, have showed the highest growth rates. The resources of the earth are limited and cannot sustain the growing numer of human beings. It is very important to take extreme measures now as population explosion could lead to another World War, economic chaos and diseases.

Thirdly, the UN charter calls upon the member nations to settle disputes in a peaceful manner and through across-the-table negotiations. However, the world has faced many wars since the inception of the UN. The first achievement of the UN on war front is that the world has not faced any World War after 1945 due to consistent efforts of the UN. The cold war between the USA and the erstwhile USSR has ended. Both the nations are now staunch supporters of the world peace—a very vital objective of the UN charter. Further, the first UN observer mission was formed in 1948 in Palestine under the leadership of Dr Ralph Bundic and its objective was to ensure ceasefire between Israel and the Arab states. This is an example of successful UN mediation for world peace. In 1948, India approached the UN for third party mediation on Kashmir issue but the UN failed. In Arab-Israel war in 1967, the small Israeli nation defied the joint Arab military might and the UN watched as a silent spectator. The problem in Lebanon escalated during the sixties and seventies and the best efforts of the UN for maintaining peace in that region could not succeed.

Further, India fought six wars with her neighbours—in 1947, 1948, 1962, 1965, 1971 and 1999—and the UN was able to intervene only during a few occasions. India lost more than 90,000 square kms of territory to China and Pakistan. The Kashmir issue remains unsettled even today as a major part of the territory of Kashmir is under the control of Pakistan and China. Simla agreement was signed between India and Pakistan and both the nations decided to settle their issues through bilateral negotiations. The role of the UN was eliminated. India maintains till date that the Kashmir problem is the bilateral issue between India and Pakistan and the UN need not intervene in any manner. By attacking the strategic sectors in Jammu and Kashmir, Pakistan has tried to internationalise the Kashmir issue. But Indian statesmen are wise enough to see through her tricks.

The first UN Peacekeeping Force (known as the United Nations Emergency Force-UNEF) was sent to the middle-East. It was deployed in 1956 for the withdrawal of Anglo-French forces from Egypt under its supervision. It acted as a buffer between the Egyptian and the Israeli forces and patrolled the Egypt-Israeli demarcation line as well as the international frontier, South of Gaza strip. The Suez canal, which was blocked due to this conflict, was cleared due the efforts of the UN. The UNEF was withdrawn in May, 1967. This was the first UN peace-keeping mission that was quite successful in its efforts. Britain and France had to accede to the demands of the world and had to retreat. Similar peace-keeping forces, observers and fact-finding missions have been sent by the UN to the disturbed areas of the globe. Some examples as follows :—

(A) UN Inspection team for locating the chemical weapons arsenal in Iraq.
(B) UN Peacekeeping Forces in Korea, Afghanistan, Cambodia, Central America, Cypress, Iran, Somalia and Bosnia.

(C) UN Peacekeeping Force for Kashmir dispute between India and Pakistan.
(D) UN Peacekeeping Force in Sri Lanka.
(E) UN Peacekeeping Force in Ethiopia and other troubled African nations.
(F) UN Peacekeeping force in erstwhile Yugoslavia in which, Major General Satish Nambiar played a key role in a stand-off between Croats and Serbs.
(G) UN Peacekeeping force in Congo in which, Mr Rajeshwar Dayal played a vital role.
(H) Role of UN and its member nations in diffusing the Kosovo crisis and in effecting a peaceful accord in mid-1999.

Fourthly, the UN agencies like UNICEF, UNCTAD, UNHCR, WHO, ILO, FAO and UNESCO have contributed a lot towards the eradication of poverty, improvement in the health and education of children, agreement of terms of trade for bussinessmen of the world and for the improvement of the working conditions of labour around the world. India is a major beneficiary of the activities of these organisations. We are an essential building block of the UN and would continue to support it at all the major fora for global peace and prosperity.

Due to the global efforts of the UNICEF officials, 80 per cent of the children of the world have been provided immunity against polio, tetanus, measles, whooping cough, diphtheria and TB. On November 20, 1989, the General Assembly celebrated the thirtieth anniversary of the Declaration of Rights of the Child by adopting the UN convention on the Rights of the child. Further, December 10 is celebrated as Human Rights Day and aims at protecting the rights of all the individuals around the globe. UNHCR protects refugees (a total of 17 million around the world) through medicines, care, shelter and favourable legal battles in that country in which, they seek asylum. This humanitarian aspect of services of UNHCR has made it the premium organisation of the world. UNHCR was awarded Nobel Prize for Peace-in 1954 and in 1981-for humanitarian services rendered by it to the mankind.

The blue-green planet can survive only if the nations of the world look after the environment and the ecology and ensure a disaster-free future for the posterity. The first UN-sponsored conference on environment was held in June, 1972, in Stockholm. It appealed to the world community and the member nations for promoting economic and technological development without harming the environment and ecology of the earth. This conference created awareness by the media, the NGOs and the official UN agencies. Many issues face the world in the environmental context today. Usage of CFCs, greenhouse effect, creation of ozone hole, river pollution, growing urban pollution (involving food, water and air), ecological imbalances, global warming, extinction of plant and animal spices, marine pollution *etc* are some of the main issues facing us today. The UNCED (Earth Summit) held in Rio de Janeiro took up old and new issues in its agenda and pledged to make the earth more ecologically balanced and environmentally safe. All the nations of the world ought to contribute with enthusiasm in the efforts of the UN for a safer and cleaner environment as the future of our posterity depends upon it.

The discussion held so far truly describes the failure and achievements of UN over the last fifty three years. The UN has faced many problems—economic, social and political. But it has survived all the major and minor challenges and has become the chief international forum. The UN faces economic crisis as the member nations are not donating enough for its survival. It is a tool for political dialogues, economic negotiations and is an ideal platform for taking vital decisions on environmental issues. But the lack of resources is keeping the UN away from its desired objectives.

India is a member nation of the UN and has always contributed towards its growth since the time she joined the organisation. India had jointed the UN in 1949. Jawaharlal Nehru was a respected figure from Asia in the UN. He was treated as the messenger of peace by the UN body. Ms Vijay Laxmi Pandit was elected as the first women President of the UN General Assembly. Mr. VK Krishna Menon made great contributions as a trouble-shooter when he worked hard for liberation of several colonies and nations through the UN. Indian troops have been regularly accepted in UN peacekeeping missions. India is also a proud member of the UN and would contribute effectively and positively for its consolidation in the times to come.

58. PAKISTAN AFTER THE KARGIL WAR

Pakistan lost Kargil war—Lost nearly 700 men—India also lost 519 men and spent Rs 1,984 crore on the war—Pakistan under military rule—Ruled by military dictators for 25 years—Relationships with India at lowest ebb—Karachi is peaceful—Anti-India tirade of Pakistan continues—Owes US$ 38 billion to the world—Heading towards economic and political catastrophe.

On July 17, 1999, Pakistan beat a hasty retreat from the areas occupied by her troops, which were also supported by the Kashmiri militants and mercenaries. With this defeat, the political future of the trouble-torn nation on our North-Western borders has received a serious jolt. Today, in the new century, we wonder how Pakistan would survive the onslaught of time (and debts). She is a nation full of ethnic hatred, a peculiar aversion for India and an irrational passion for Kashmir. With these three inputs for her final destruction, this nation could not ask for more if she wanted to do away with herself and wipe out her entity from the global political map.

Let us recapitulate what happened during the year of the century goneby. In February, 1999 our Prime Minister Mr AB Vajpayee visited Lahore and tried to give a new impetus to the almost still mechanism of talks between the two neighbours. He thought that he had succeeded as he had assumed that Pakistani leadership was also equally warm and reciprocating while he had visited Lahore. But Mr Nawaz Sharif stabbed India in her back and while he and Mr Vajpayee exchanged sweet nothings in Lahore and Islamabad, trained mercenaries and Pakistani army regulars entered Indian territory in Kashmir. They occupied the key peaks in Drass, Kargil, Mushkoh Valley and Batalik sectors and prepared themselves for a war. The intrusion in Kargil was the culmination of the three-phase "Operation Topak," which was launched by Pakistan in 1988, apparently masterminded by General Zia-Ul-Haq. The three phases comprised indoctrination, intrusion and sabotage by the Pakistan-led forces. This operation was directly linked to planned cross-border terrorism, which is a regular feature of the strategic initiatives of Pakistani rulers.

When Indian troops went to the vital strategic peaks in order to make routine surveys and occupy the posts for the summer seasons (as was the normal practice), they were welcomed by bullets. Indian leaders and army commanders were taken aback. They had never expected this move from our neighbours. Later, while on a reconnaissance mission, one IAF plane was shot down near the LoC and its pilot was killed mercilessly. Another IAF pilot, Lieutenant Nachiketa, was also arrested in a similar incident when he was forced to eject out of his plane. Mr Nachiketa was handed over to Indian authorities later. By this time, Pakistani plans were evident; they had already made deep inroads into Indian territory in Kashmir, nearly 10 kms ahead of the actual LoC. Thus a mini-war was waged.

Indian army did rise to the occasion, albeit at a slow pace. The fire from the tops at Batalik, Drass and Kargil was fatal and our men lost their lives a bit too easily. It was difficult to fire upwards, notwithstanding the fact that we had the infamous Bofors guns for our assistance during such crucial phase of the war. India lost 519 men and officers who fought valiantly and recaptured the strategic areas like Tololing, Tiger Hills, Tiger Top, Point 4590, Jubbar Hills, Muntho Dhalo, Batalik, Shangruti and Drass. India deployed 20,000 army men and officers in the most painful and slow cleansing operation in her history. Pakistanis never expected to win the war; they knew that they were no match for Indian armed forces. They only wanted the world to know that the Kashmir issue was not in the dustbin; it was the major issue for discussion at the dining tables of all the Pakistani homes. India fought hard battles from May to July, 1999 and spent Rs 25 crore per day on the war. She spent Rs 1,984 crore for pushing the militants and Pakistani army regulars across the LoC. Pakistan lost nearly 700 army man, foreign mercenaries and terrorists owing their allegiance to various militant groups of Kashmir. On July 16, 1999, the government of Pakistan finally admitted that her forces did cross the LoC. By July 17, 1999, all the intruders vacted the occupied areas in Indian territory.

Mr Nawaz Sharif tried to get the help of Commonwealth but failed. He tried to gain the support of China but could not succeed. China urged India and Pakistan to negotiate among themselves to put an end to the clash. Mr Sharif also went to Washington but Mr Bill Clinton was tactful enough to see through the Pakistani trick and suggested that India and Pakistan take effective measures for ceasing hostilities and sorting out the Kashmir issue. This meeting took place on July, 4, 1999, which was the national day for the USA.

Therefore, Pakistan lost her fifth war with India with the culmination of "Operation Vijay," the official codename of the cleansing operation during the war. "Operation Vijay" would be conducted round the clock and would be designed to check intrusions from across the border. The failure of RAW, IB and the military intelligence agencies of India was highlighted by media during and after the war. We must also admit that there were flaws in data collection, deployment of troops for patrolling the border areas and proper actions after receipt of confirmed reports of an imminent attack by the Pakistani troops and *Mujahideen*. Pakistan tried to cash on the weaknesses of Indian intelligence agencies and slow movements of Indian army. They succeeded in putting Indian army at bay for nearly two and a half months. This is a matter of concern and shame for the Indian armed forces.

After the Kargil war, a subdued Nawaz Sharif could not sustain for a long time. He tried to kill General Parvez Mushrraf, the Pakistani army chief, through a well-planned machination. The DGCA of Pakistan, Mr Amannula Chaudhary instructed the airport authorities at Karachi airport not to allow the plane (carrying Mr Musharraf and others) to land. The plane landed on a narrow strip of land near Karachi. Mr Musharraf replied by overthrowing the PM and capturing power at Islamabad. Hence, the dark era for Pakistan began once again. Military rules are not new for Pakistanis. Earlier, General Yahya Khan and General Zia Ul Haq have given enough tantrums to that nation through their military rules. Pakistan remained under the military rule for twenty-five years since her independence. As on date, the chances of restoration of democracy in that nation are grim.

Pakistani economy is in doldrums. General Musharraf as the new CEO of the nation, is looking after the economic affairs as well. Pakistan owes US$ 38 billion to her international creditors. It would be difficult for General Musharraf to pay the interests on loans. Even if the Pakistani citizens work for twenty-four hours a day, they would not be able to repay the debts. In this precarious economic situation, Pakistan has not learned any lessons. Pakistanis have a craving for Kashmir and no sympathy for the national economic and sociopolitical milieu, which ought to be given the top priority. Further, Pakistan has lost her friends in the international arena in quick successions; the USA, China, Saudi Arabia, Iran, North Korea and other nations have either condemned the Pakistani intrusion in Kargil or are quiet over the issue. Further, the defeat of democracy in Pakistan has won her more enemies than friends. Nobody would like to talk to or negotiate with General Musharraf but everyone would love to interact with a democratically elected government in India.

The ethnic strife in the Pakistani city of Karachi has taken the toll of nearly 2,000 people so far. The city is calm as on date and that is because of the military rule. The Sunnis and the Shiites would be looking for occasions for reprisal against their rivals. How long could they stay at their homes ?

Further, Mr Nawaz Sharif was arrested and was chargesheeted for the attempt murder of General Parvez Musharraf. He could be hanged, according to the Pakistani laws, if the charge of an attempt of murder is proved to be true. General Musharraf would neither allow him to fight elections nor he would allow him to go scot free. This is the old Pakistani tradition and he shall follow the beaten track.

In January, 2000 AD, Mr AB Vajpayee urged the nations of the world to declare Pakistan a terrorist state and deal with her accordingly. Pakistani officials and leaders objected to the statements of Indian PM. Hence, a new type of verbal war has started in the South Asian region. This mudslinging emanates from the office of the Indian PM and also, from the External Affairs Department of Pakistani government. Further, General Musharraf has categorically stated that Kashmir remains the major cause of friction between the two neighbours. The USA has also declared Kashmir as the most disturbed area of the world. In the wake of these developments, Indian authorities have taken steps to carry out surveillance exercises along the LoC in Kashmir (under "Operation Vijay"). Satellite imagery, electronic intelligence, remotely piloted vehicles and surveillance radars would be used for round-the-clock vigil over the borders of Kashmir. This would create tantrums in the corridors of power of Pakistan. The intrusions of militants and army regulars would be cut down. Indians have already started feeling the effects of such measures. Recently, security forces were attached in Srinagar and in other incidents of sporadic violence, some civilians were also killed.

Pakistani terrorists, Kashmiri terrorists and many foreign militant groups have targeted civilians and security forces in Kashmir. Several lives have been lost and some property has also been reduced to ashes. This is the reply of Pakistani forces to the measures taken by our armed forces in terms of increased vigilance on our borders.

The new millennium has arrived. Pakistan could wage a full-fledged war against India by the year 2003 AD. General Musharraf is not controlling the nation for the sake of a military honour. He proposes to settle scores with India. Even if he could not, he would like to try. The beleaguered nation is a picture of gloom, despair and a subdued national spirit. It is difficult to imagine that these people were our brothers during the pre-independence era. Pakistan is heading towards economic and political catastrophe. However the Pakistani nation could leap into the decisive phase after the war of 1999. She could either embrace Mutually Assured Destruction (MAD), a concept closely linked to nuclear war, or she could rationalise her national priorities and demands, which could give her another chance to survive on the canvass of time. We have a premonition that the former option is likely to be chosen by Pakistan and the result of exercising the same is known to all of us.

59. THE GLOBAL GOVERNMENT CONCEPT

Earth is the only living planet—We have advanced in terms of technology and as a society—But we have also prepared ourselves for mutual destruction—Environmental pollution—Nuclear weapons threat—India-Pakistan row—Humanity wasting time over trifles—Many challenges for us ahead—UNO formed in 1945—Concept of world government beyond the UNO concept—A government of all the people of the world—No national bifurcations—Economic and financial issues to be handled by the governing council—Social issues could be tackled by the world government by taking local parties into confidence—All citizens to be treated equally—Economic and political barriers to be removed—Concerted efforts for eliminating deadly diseases—Some powers always to be vested in the individual nations—The concept remains a distant dream.

The mother earth is the only planet, which has humans, fauna and flora. To date, the scientists have not been able to locate another planet in the immediate vicinity of our solar system, which could support life. However, the war-torn nations, the nuclear threats from the global superpowers and the rising population levels are making our blue-green planet an unsafe place for living. As the responsible citizens of this planet, it is our duty to ponder over the most serious question of our lifetimes – shall we survive if we remain divided and strife-ridden ?

We have learned to fly. We have satellite communication systems, fast motor cars and jet aircraft, most modern medicine systems, high quality hardware and software for our entertainment and leisure and above all, a hope for the posterity. But we are more than 200 nations— divided amongst ourselves on various issues. We are prepared for Mutually Assured Destruction (MAD) through deadly nuclear arsenal. We are about to choke the environment with deadly chemicals and gases. We have already raised the noise levels to alarmingly high values. We have been fighting with other nations over trifles and would continue to do so in future as well. Our national egoes and the spirit of nationalistic fanaticism have led us to the ultimate brink of global annihilation. The cold war has ended but the new conflict between Yugoslavia and the NATO forces (led by the USA and the UK). has surfaced. It has taken a great toll of life and property. North Korea and South Korea have yet to reconcile the existence of each other's identity. There has always been tension between India and Pakistan over the Kashmir issue. The recently concluded war in Kargil, Batalik, Drass and Mushkoh Valley has proved that Pakistan would lead us to war in future. Pakistanis have not forgotten the debacle of the war in 1971 (as well as the earlier ones) and we have not forgotten the debacle of the war in 1962, which we sadly remember as Indo-China conflict. Further, the rich are getting richer and the poor are becomimg poorer. The Arab-Israeli accord has yet to take a solid shape in the wake of new Israeli constructions in Ghaza strip. The LTTE cadres in Sri Lanka have done more harm than good to their motherland during the past ten years. Osama Bin Laden has waged *Jihad* (holy war) against the USA.

These problems are only a tip of the iceberg. Let us think of the solutions, which need to be devised and implemented for a safe and prosperous mother earth. Bertrand Russel predicted that by the end of this century, the nations of the world would either unite under a world government or would perish. Russel was a visionary of his times. And we can predict that his prophecy might prove to be true one day. The elite of the world think on these lines. Why not the statesmen of the world think on the same lines for the sake of our children ?

The UNO was formed in 1945 as a world body. But it was not a world government. Rather, it was an organisation promoted by the nations of the world for their self-regulation. The concept of a world government goes beyond the concept of the UNO.

Let us understand the concept of world government. A world government should be an international body, which would draw representatives from all the nations of the world. There would be no gender, number, economic, social or caste bars. Every country would be an equal constituent. The economic and financial issues would be decided by the governing council of the world government. The social issues could be decided by the world government by taking into account the local conditions of the area under question. There would be logical distribution of the financial and natural resources among the nations of the world. Poverty would be eliminated completely from the face of the earth. Unemployment would also be completely eliminated Global resources like petroleum, forests, agricultural, industrial and manpower resources would be pooled. The underdeveloped areas would be allocated more resources so that they are made self-sufficient in a planned time-frame. The markets would be governed by the needs of the customer and not by the greed of the businessman. There would no socialism or capitalism anywhere. Researches would be done for exploring the space and distant stars for a possible settlement of human life there. Global efforts would be made for wiping out cancer, AIDS, Hepatitis B Virus, malaria, mental diorders and other deadly diseases. The population of humans would be planned and limited. No part of the world would dominate the other simply because it is rich, influential or powerful. Humans would plan and ensure bright and safe future for their posterity. There would be peace, prosperity, health and happiness around the globe.

Let us not conclude that we have almost built a Utopia. We are only propagating towards a global governance concept. If we do not even think on these lines, we would not be able to survive on the blue-green planet due to the troubles that our nations face. The world government concept is not only a distant reality, but also it is difficult to realise. The rich nations would try hard for retaining their supremacy. The poor nations would be skilfully sidelined. The developing nations, however, would certainly play a decisive role in this context. India leads the group of the developing nations. Indian policies have always supported humanity, environment, development and progress. Hence, an Indian initiative for such a noble task would be more than welcome. If we take the first step, many more are likely to join us in this mission. True, we would face opposition and the target is difficult to achieve. However, we should convince the heads of the nations that we must cut across the national barriers and must protect the mother earth through a world government. Initially, the powers of all the governments could be decentralised. Gradually, the governments should start thinking and planning on a common platform. The UNO could play a very constructive role in this context. Initially, let us govern issues, related to environment, child labour, ozone hole, space research, medicine, health disease management and poverty. These are the issues, which could be handled by the world government with complete cooperation from all the nations.

In the subsequent stages, more serious issues related to economy, employment, industrial development, technology transfers, biodiversity, petroleum products and other global resources could be governed. The nations would be benefitted from this pooling of global resources.

In the final stage, sensitive issues like elimination of international lines of control, defence, wars nuclear warheads, UNO and its role in the world governing body, ethnic conflicts, human rights in the global perspective, technology sharing and regionalism could be discussed. It should be noted that the structure of the world government should be federal in character. This would mean that some powers would always remain vested in the nations of the world and the world government could give advice in the context of regional and sub-regional problems. The local and regional issues could be handled at the appropriate levels within the region or within the nation. But the spirit of global governance should always be—"Live and Let Live."

The concept of world government remains a distant dream. However, our posterity may be able to see some form, of global unification, which could be more powerful and effective than the UNO. The objective is sacred and path towards the fulfilment of the same is no bed of roses. However, let us hope that man thinks beyond his personal, religious, materialistic and nationalistic reservations and tries to save the mother earth for the sake of future generations. ●

60. THE KASHMIR IMBROGLIO

Kashmir issue is vital for India and Pakistan—In 1947, Kashmiris decided to stay with India through a valid instrument of accession—Pakistan tried to annex Kashmir—Pakistan tried in 1947, 1948, 1965, 1971 and 1999—Pakistan has some part of Kashmir, called POK—India does not want a third party mediation and treats it as a bilateral issue—Western powers supporting India on war in Kargil, imposed upon India by Pakistan—Pakistan wants to annex Kashmir but Indian armed forces too strong for her—This would suit Pakistan due to her political end economic interests—Kashmir is now an international issue—Bilateral talks could sort out the issue—No solution in near future.

The recent developments on the political stage of South Asia have catapulted Kashmir issue to that of an international stature. Earlier, the Kashmir issue was treated as a bilateral issue between India and Pakistan. But there has been consistent interference (direct or indirect) from the Pakistani intelligence and troops since 1947. A few incidents of firing across the border were always noticed by India and skilfully ignored as well. However, the terrorism scenario in Kashmir took a dangerous turn when foreign mercenaries, supported by Pakistani army regulars entered Indian territory in Kashmiri in March, 1999.

Pakistan has always tried to rake up the Kashmir issue in the UNO. But the world leaders adopted a neutral stance and suggested that India and Pakistan should settle their issues after bilateral talks in the spirit of the Simla agreement. The recent nuclear explosions and the initiation of cold war in the region are no longer keeping the world leaders complacent about the recent developments. The USA has urged India and Pakistan to resort to bilateral negotations for the settlement of Kashmir issue. Indian Prime Minister AB Vajpayee has denied this interference categorically. The USA wants China as the third party whereas China is already in possession of 90,000 square kms of Indian territory. So, China is not eligible for a neutral position in the dispute. Kashmiris view themselves as the third party but they are most likely to take a decision, which could adversely affect the economic and political equations in this region.

When India and Pakistan attained freedom in 1947, the basic issue for Pakistan was–those areas, where Muslims have an absolute majority, should be treated as Pakistan. This directive led to the formation of East Pakistan, which is now known as Bangladesh. Pakistan had her eyes on Kashmir since 1947. The erstwhile ruler of Kashmir was Hari Singh who was a Hindu. The majority of the Kashmiri populace comprised Muslims. Pakistan attacked Kashmir in 1947 with the help of *Kabaili* mercenaries but did not declare the war directly. In the meantime, Hari Singh signed the document of accession and Prime Minister Mr JL Nehru sent armed forces to Kashmir in order to save it from the hands of marauders. Therefore, Indian stand was simple–Kashmir became a part of India through an instrument of accession, which is available for the world to see and judge. India took many princely states through peaceful negotiations with the erstwhile *Maharajas* and through the usage of force (as was done in the case of Goa where Indian armed forces took over that state). Pakistani view is tainted with religious sentiments. The terrorists and meicenaries claim that all those areas, in which, Muslim population thrives, ought to be liberated through *Jihad*. In the current international scenario, religion is going to play a very little role in the national, international, social, political and economic transactions. India has gained Kashmir on legal grounds. It was not an invasion but a bid to save her legally occupied territory in 1947 through armed intervention.

Pakistan continued to struggle for the Kashmir issue. She attacked India in 1965 and 1971. Armed mercenaries were sent to Kashmir and Punjab during the eighties in order to disturb peace in Kashmir and the entire North Indian region. Many precious lives were lost. There was a loss of property and business and the effects can be seen even today.

In 1971, Pakistani Prime Minister Bhutto and Indian Prime Minister—Mrs Gandhi—signed a historic agreement, known as the

Simla Agreement. According to this agreement, India and Pakistan are supposed to settle their disputes through bilateral negotiations and discussions. There is no scope for any third-party mediation. The USA wanted to mediate because Pakistan wanted her to intervene. But Indian Prime Minister tactfully refused for such a move.

The present scenario has put Kashmir on the agenda of the global powers. The USA is worried about the chain of events in South Asia. India and Pakistan are now nuclear powers. Indian stand is that this capability was developed in order to meet the Chinese threat and that Pakistan need not worry. Pakistan, on the other hand, assumes that Indian military might could be utilised against her in the times to come. The race for military superiority could take a serious toll of Kashmiri people and their economy, which is growing at a swift pace, thanks to heavy influx of tourist despite the war. The major issue is Kashmir and Pakistan, with military and economic aid from the Muslim world, could attack India again for annexing Kashmir.

It should be recalled that in 1948, India had raised the Kashmir issue in the UN Security Council. But she did not get a good response from the UN Security Council and only burned her fingers. Therefore, it is unlikely that India would seek the help of UN Security Council in future. On the other hand, Pakistan claims that India always uses talks as a ploy for diverting all eyes from Kashmir. The Pakistani leaders claim that Indian stand for bilateral talks is a trap. Thus this stalemate has put a big questionmark on the settlement process. India states that there is no need for a plebiscite either as the Kashmiris had already decided to join India in 1947.

The group of P-5, the most powerful group of G-8 and the UNO now realise that the real reason for the setback to peace and stability in South Asia lies in the unresolved Kashmir dispute. International defence experts also maintain that the Kashmir issue could also be responsible for a nuclear war.

It may be noted that the economic and military powers of the world are now not very keen for a third-party mediation on the Kashmir issue. If Kashmir is liberated, it would become weak on economic, political and military grounds. Therefore, either Pakistan or China could be able to annex her. China has already annexed Tibet and she could arrive at a 'convenient' settlement with Pakistan by sharing a part of Kashmir with Pakistan. If none of the nations occupies Kashmir (due to a strong international opinion), then Western nations would make it weak and economically dependant upon them. A weak Kashmir would provide good markets for arms, food, drugs and other products from the West. Therefore, Kashmir would become another Nepal and would become the poorest hill nation of the world.

The USA would persuade India and Pakistan so that they get down to talks. The new realities, under which both India and Pakistan have gatecrashed into the nuclear club, cannot be ignored by P-5, G-8, the UNO and even by India and Pakistan themselves. The policies of USA for South Asia have always boomeranged on her. Chinese diplomats are quiet and have a mischievous smile in their hearts. Russia has not interfered in this war. Our friends in the West have not openly supported us but would do so when the opportune moment arrives.

Kashmir is the most volatile region in the world today. Pakistan cannot live without it and Indian pride is nothing but Kashmir. The situation is tense and could deteriorate further. The global leaders and the UN are making honest efforts for settling the issue but some serious stumbling blocks remain. A well-defined settlement agreeable to all the parties involved in this dispute still eludes us. But the wisdom of our leaders and the maturity of the Pakistani leaders could bring concrete results after serious bilateral negotiations. All the issues could be resolved without any armed conflict. The only ingredient needed for solving a problem is the will to succeed. Terrorist activities and mini-wars (like the Kargil conflict) are not suitable for settlement of the Kashmir issue. Both sides must be willing to make compromises. If a stubborn attitude continues on the part of both the sides, the Kashmir issue could become a flashpoint for the Third World War. Let us pray that it never happens ! ●

61. HOW INDIA IS VIEWED BY THE WEST ?

India is a developing nation—Many problems—West is far ahead of us—Western society views India with respect—Our cultural heritage is respected abroad—Our freedom struggle—We taught the philosophy of Ahimsa—Materialistic society of the West learns that materialism is not everything—Our social and cultural values are supreme—Our music stirs the souls—Our masses are sensitive to the world around them—India has given and shown a lot to the world—The West views us with respect and seeks friendly cooperation.

India is a developing country with a population of more than 100 crore. She is a respected nation at all the international fora. Her steady economic progress, ancient civilisation, cultural diversity and zest for progress have been respected in the international circles. She is proud of being the birthplace of world's oldest civilisation and world's most liberal and oldest religion—Hinduism—which make our identity unique in the eyes of an international observer.

India is also facing many problems on her economic and social fronts. That is true for every developing nation. We have been fighting against poverty. We have built a sound industrial infrastructure but we have many miles to go. Our manpower, though the best in the world, is not able to procure resources and facilities for its healthy sustenance. Our politicians are corrupt and the crime graph is on the rise. Add to this, the problems of unemployment, social and economic backwardness and religious and caste conflicts. All these factors give a distinctive hue to the Indian fabric. The observer from abroad is impressed by our cultural diversity, impressed by our past heritage but is worried about our future.

Western society is far ahead of Indian society in many aspects. For example, the West has won all the wars over hunger, poverty, illiteracy and dogmas (except for only a few). Western society is logical, pragmatic and growth-oriented. The residents of the West have worked hard to learn how nature works. They have mastered the forces of nature for their economic and mental benefits. They have developed themselves through scientific methodologies. They have overcome myths, hackneyed ideas and religious systems. Western man has indeed, done very well. Most of the scientific discoveries and inventions were developed in the UK, Germany, the USA and other Western countries. Homoeopathy was started by Dr Samuel Hahnmann in Germany. During the modern times, with the exception of electronics technology, which as developed by Japan, most of the new production, processing, preservation and medical technologies were developed by the West. Hence, we should learn good lessons from the West and must grow on a scientific patternadioted by those nations.

Western society views India with respect. They respect our ancient cultural heritage. They also value our ideals of good family upbringing and social interactions. They shower economium on us when they discuss our heroic deeds during the wars and battles fought during the historic times. Whereas the Western warriors fought for land and money, Maharana Pratap fought for his principles. Guru Gobind Singh fought for the downtrodden and the weak. Guru Tegh Behadur laid his life for the sake of Hindus. Bhagat Singh, Rajguru and Sukhdev went to the gallows without any hesitation. There is no such example from the Western history. Further, the Westerners respect Mahatma Gandhi who won the battle for his motherland with the help of one stick, one lioncloth and *Ahimsa*.

Western society also learned family norms and moral values from us. They realise that the bonds of love are much stronger in India. So much so, many foreigners come to India and live here forever. They love this country so much that the sweltering heat and harsh weather conditions do not dissuade them from coming here and savouring our rich cultural heritage.

West has also learned the language of love from India. They flock in millions every year and visit the Tajmahal, which symbolises love and peace. Mosques, temples and churches spread across the country symbolise our unity in diversity and our belief in one Almighty. They are impressed by the *Ghats* of Banaras, the holy Ganges, the sacred Hindu shrines (*Char Dham*) and other religious places like Ajmer Sharif Mosque, Jama Masjid, Saint Thomas Cathedral etc. These landmarks symbolise the synthesis of Indian masses with the Almighty.

The materialistic society of the West learns from our culture that money is not everything in life. We believe in spiritual values and our relationship with God. We do not just say a prayer; rather, we bow before the majesty of the Almighty. Although the societal values are also changing in India, yet there are some intellectuals left in this country who are respected by the West for their spiritual values, selflessness and care for the masses. Examples can be cited of Baba Amte (the environmentalist), MF Hussain (the painter), MS Subbulaxmi (the singer), Hari Prasad Chaurasia (the flute player par excellence) and Pandit Shiv Kumar Sharma (the Santoor specialist). Indian music was the best and remains the best till date. Our singers, musicians and composers touch the souls of millions through an art, which is found only in India. Similarly, our painters, handicraft artists and craftsmen depict their souls on wood, stone, brass, iron, gold and diamonds. No doubt, the exports of brass handicrafts, textile products, handlooms, wooden handicrafts, false ivory items *etc* are soaring every year.

Western nations has also learned that we are non-aligned and believe in the policy of Llive and Let Live." We are the leaders of NAM movement and do not follow any 'ism' or 'block.' We are Indians and are proud to be so. We have a distinctive political identity. We are suffering on account of our economic backwardness but there is no other bliss comparable to independence. Most of the Western nations have to support their capitalist bosses–a feature missing in Indian context.

Western nations respect our commitment towards a free market economy, rational growth targets and overall development in all walks of life. They respect our engineers, software programmers, nurses, doctors and professional manpower. The British Prime Minister, Mr Tony Blair, recently nominated Professor Amartya Sen as the Master of Trinity College, which is an honour for India. Mr Sen received the Nobel Prize for economics, which was declared in October, 1998. However, Western experts feel that a lot needs to be done on economic and social fronts. They admit that we are hardworking, efficient and sincere workers. But they expect more output from us.

In sum, Western opinion of India is that of respect and friendly cooperation. Together, we form a great team. Our cooperation on all the fronts is likely to increase. We have good relationships with all the Western nations. We have good diplomatic and trade relationships with the UK, Italy, Germany, France and the USA. With the support of our friends in the Western block, we would be able to overcome all the hurdles faced by us *viz-a-viz* our relationships with the West. ●

62. THE AMERICAN DEFENCE POLICY

US defence policy basically based on military superiority and financial process—USA wants to have nuclear option for protecting her friends and allies—She wants to control aggression through nuclear capabilities—Greatest threat from developing and third world nations in terms of nuclear arsenal—Justified in protecting her interests but not willing to shoulder responsibilities for peace—Tests by India and Pakistan seen as threat to the US supremacy—Responsible role by the USA expected.

The United States, of America after the removal of the iron curtain of the Eastern block countries, is the only superpower left in the world. And she has started exploiting her newly earned status to her ful! advantage.

During the eighties, Grenada was attacked by the USA. This action was carried out by her to impose herself on that little island nation. The US marines are a part of peacekeeping forces in the Gulf, which are supervising the post-war tactics of Iraq. The peacekeepers in the Gulf are in fact, Americans. True, they are under the UN banner but all the terms are being dictated by Washington.

The Pentagon feels that the USA has the prerogative to use nuclear option in case of a conventional war. And Americans are the leading exponents of CTBT, which serves their interests in a most exquisite manner. The USA has the nuclear capabilities. And if others do not have it (by tests, experiments or even through borrowed technologies and equipment), the USA and four other nuclear states would have a great time on the nuclear canvass of the world.

The USA is in no mood to destroy the nuclear combat technology and the hardware (installed by her around the globe). A senior official, Mr Perssy, from the State Department of the US administration, states, "We need less deterrence and a smaller nuclear force." He however, insists that Washington must hedge against a possible reversal of political course in Moscow. He goes on to state that the nuclear arsenal could be reconstituted. Russia, who is a member at present, seems to pose a threat to the USA which, at the most, seems Utopian.

The second Strategic Arms Reduction Agreement (START-II) called for a ceiling on the American nuclear forces, which comprise around 3,500 warheads. Pentagon calls for an affordable hedge in which, the approved force structure could support weapon warheads greater than those called under START-II, if circumstances ask for the same.

The Pentagon goes on to state that maintaining US nuclear commitments with NATO and retaining the ability to deploy nuclear capabilities is a *modus operandi* for controlling aggression. It is also vital for protecting and promoting American interests, reassuring allies and friends and preventing proliferation. It adds that without the American nuclear umbrella, Germany and Japan could be tempted to acquire nuclear weapons of their own.

The Pentagon also states that third world countries have nuclear capabilities and arsenal and as such, maintenance of her large nuclear arsenal is justified. The Pentagon states, "The proliferation of nuclear weapons and other weapons of mass destruction, rather than the nuclear arsenal of a hostile superpower, pose the greatest security risk."

Her stand on NPT is clear but does not support the global interests. The Pentagon recommends that "extending the NPT will, therefore, do far more to improve individual nations' security than would a further decline in superpower weapon stocks."

The USA, as a superpower, is justified in protecting the interests of her allies. However, American statesmen must assume a greater responsibility for cleaning the mother earth from the nuclear arms. So far, she has not accepted that responsibility. Power and freedom bring more responsibilities. But American statesmen have not understood what should be the their role for promoting and ensuring world peace. For example, if India signs CTBT and stops going ahead with nuclear programmes, Pakistan could use a nuclear option and India would be left defenceless. The USA is fighting an imaginary enemy. There are no allies in the commercial world; there are only businessmen, who could only be friends if business were to be conducted.

American shadow over Asia has two-fold repercussions. China is a major ally of the USA. The commercial interests of American firms would be hurt if the USA does not accept China as a big brother in Asia. This is the sole reason why the USA does not give due credit to the achievements of Indian scientists, political institutions and democracy. Recently, the annoyed American administration denied visa to our renowned scientist, Dr APJ Abdul Kalaam. Sometime back prior to his being elected the President of India. The bias towards our nuclear programme was evident from this move.

USA does not want to ignore the vast Chinese markets. Further, China is a military and nuclear superpower. A toast of friendship between the two nations would certainly bring cheers across the globe. India stands to suffer in this vital diplomatic battle. True, American firms are also giving importance to Indian markets. Earlier, the US administration had not given much attention to the rising Indian military, economic and nuclear supremacy. The growing markets of Indian subcontinent the American policy makers. That is why, the US administration imposed economic sanctions immediately after the nuclear tests at Pokharan during May, 1998. Talks between Mr Jaswant Singh the then Foreign Minister and Mr Strobe Talbott could not yield concrete results for India. But Indo-US relationships have been given a positive impetus after declaration by Mr. Osama Bin Laden (that India and the USA are his staunch enemies. Further, the visit of President, Mr. Bill Clinton consolidated the relationships between two democracies.

Japan is an economic ally of the USA. The economic ties between the two nations are deep and defence arrangements are also sound. The USA has access to Japanese technology and in lieu of this facility, she has offered complete military security to Japan. Her military presence has been clearly felt in the Orient but the equations could change any time. The military bases in the Philippines were in news a few years ago. The removal of Russian bear from the international stage has left the USA and her allies pondering over a single thought—where is the enemy ? Therefore, the maintenance of existing bases or creation of new bases for military and defence vigilance would not be on the immediate agenda of Pentagon.

Taiwan, Vietnam and other former communist nations are now friendly towards the USA. The major issues before the nations of the world are social and economic. Politics and military superiority have taken a backseat. Hence, the American policy is soft towards most have proved that the international policies of the USA may not be accepted in ditto. The terrorist reperisals against innocent people of embassies should make American policy makers over table and think about the their rivals in an empathetic manner. If the USA adopts a tough posture, more innocent lives would be lost and this saga would continue.

Osama Bin Laden poses a great threat to the USA. In order to counter the same, she dropped two missiles in the training camps of Osama Bin Laden in Afghanistan. Laden has vowed to average the deaths and destenctio, though he himself suffers from a total kidney disease.

In the American subcontinent, the defence appetite of the USA has been more or less satiated. The military might of the world's only effective superpower is unquestionable. The Pentagon would no doubt, have smooth sailing till the resurrection of another competitor. Russia, China and India could form the second pole of the unipolar axis.

It must be noted that most of the wars between nations would be fought an economic fronts. We have developed enough of maturity after two World Wars that we would not fight direct wars in the new millennium. The USA and other powerful nations of the world are also likely to do the same during the next century.

Iraq is a typical case in the agenda of Pentagon despite international efforts. The attitude of the US and her allies could not be softened with respect to Iraq. This nation had already suffered on account of political and economic exile from all the global platforms. If the USA changes her attitude towards Iraq, the middle East (and Iraqi citizens in particular) would heave sigh of relief. Iraqi citizens have been living in conditions of starvation and malnutrition and they have not been able to meet the basic needs of food, clothing and medicine on account of economic sanctions imposed by the UN. The American attitude could change, which could lead to healthy relationships with Arab nations.

American defence analysts have been watching the recent incidents in Afghanistan with interest. Russia has declared that if Talibaan forces tried to cross the Russian borders, they would be paid back in the same coin. If a Indo-US joint task force is organised, then the militants could be eliminated from Afghanistan which task has been accomplished. A peaceful talk, however, must precede this extreme measure.

It is expected that the USA would play a more constructive role in the international military arena. The American top brass must realise her role for a secure world. Americans chose to remain neutral in the recently conducted Indo-Pak war in Kargil. However, NATO attacked Yuoslavia on the Kosovo Issue. This proves that the strategic priorities of Washington could change.

63. GIVE ME MY LAND

Pakistan and India fought five wars—No conclusions—Only losses—Pakistan annexed one-third of Kashmir and gave a part of it to China—Repeated attacks on Kashmir in the form of proxy wars—In Kargil war, India did not cross the LoC whereas it would—Legal and international opinions prove that Kashmir is our land—Why not take it back if across-the-table negotiations fail ?—Let Pakistan make a first hostile move—We must get back our land—Nuclear tests conducted by both nations—Pakistan is stronger in military terms—Taking help from Afghanistan which help now may not be available—Kashmir issue internationalised—We must work carefully towards our goal.

Pakistan and India were separated in 1947 on a bitter note. This bitterness continued for fifty years and is prevalent on both the sides of the border even today. The IXth SAARC summit, though ending on a positive note, has not generated positive ripples anywhere. The two nations of the region—India and Pakistan—agree to disagree on almost all the vital issues facing them.

India and Pakistan fought five wars — in 1947, 1948, 1965, 1971 and 1999—and the losses in terms of manpower, military hardware and money were tremendous on both the sides. Indian stand on Kashmir remains unruffled whereas Pakistan is hell-bent upon acquiring it by all means—fair or foul. The war, waged by Pakistan in Kargil, Drass, Batalik and Mushkoh Valley, indicated the never-ending affinity of Pakistan for Kashmir.

Pakistan has acquired approximately one-third of Kashmir through coercion. And she has declared that the territory under her control is "Azad Kashmir"—an irony, which cannot be chewed keeping in mind the political history of Pakistan.

And to give a boost to the blood-burning of her neighbours, Pakistan has virtually gifted more than 5,000 square kms of land to China who now has absolute control over that territory. This also land, belongs to India. The legal document signed by the erstwhile Maharaja of Kashmir, Hari Singh, amply proves this fact.

Pakistan's previous record of democratic experiences was very poor. A nation, dogged by revolts of the military junta, cannot control or manage her own provinces. How can she possibly manage a sensitive area like Kashmir ? There is no sign of prosperity in Azad Kashmir and Kashmiris are being exploited to the core in every inch of their land. In Pakistan, no effort has been made to uplift the economic and social standards of the masses. On the other hand, in Indian Kashmir, all the attempts for growth have been foiled by the ISI-trained Kashmiri militant groups. Hence, there is no growth in entire Kashmir. The state lacks funds for survival and development on a large scale.

Kashmir is a peace-loving state. Kashmiris are the best known people on the earth. They are prepared to lay down their lives for their motherland, their visitors and their ideals. They are being exploited through machinations from across the border. History has proved to be true and again that a state like Kashmir—full of hilly terrains, decent and sophisticated people and a history of enduring culture—wants no war or subversive activities on its soil. Then, why put scars of violence on the most beautiful part of the mother earth ?

Kashmir belongs to India. The history, the documents and the international community amply support this fact. Then why not take some hard decisions so that the ultimate results are soft to chew ? Why not demand the land that belongs to us? Indian approach has always been positive. We have been able to draw support from the East and the West without any hassles. We have made it clear that India and Pakistan must sort out the issue through bilateral negotiations.

Peaceful negotiations, however, cannot ignore the evil designs of ISI in the form of proxy wars and terrorist attacks on the innocent people of Kashmir. The capture of the holy Hazratbal Shrine, in not too distant past, was a glaring example. If guns continue to roar across the boarder, India must also retaliate with full vigour. After all, we would be trying to get back what belongs to us. Let us not wait for more time. Let us not play Prithviraj Chauhan at least this time. If negotiated settlement across the table solves the problem, we would welcome it. If, however, we are unable to reach a settlement, we must take strict measures to recapture our territory.

The nuclear tests conducted by India and Pakistan during May, 1998, proved that both the nations are preparing themselves for a military consolidation in lethal terms. These trends are bad and could trigger a war in the South Asian region. We would support bilateral negotiations though Pakistan has already raked up the Kashmir issue in the UN and has tried to make it an international issue. The intrusions of army regulars and extremists from Pakistan have violated the spirit of Lahore Agreement. Further, the indiscriminate and unprovoked firing from the Pakistani side, the incessant spate of violence in Jammu, Kashmir and Himachal Pradesh and an apathetic attitude on the part of the Pakistani leaders have amply demonstrated the theory that this issue is likely to take a violent turn at any time.

In the wake of a conflict, Pak Occupied Kashmir is likely to be annexed by India. Indian leaders were almost tempted to occupy POK during the Kargil war. However, it would be difficult to annex that part of Kashmir which is under Chinese control. As on date, 38,000 square kms of territory of Kashmir have been occupied by China. Further, Pakistan has gifted away 5,180 sq kms of Kashmir to China. A direct conflict with China would never be on the agenda of Indian leaders. For this purpose, bilateral talks with China should be initiated. We are very well aware that these talks had yielded no result earlier. However, China would have to change her attitude towards India in the wake of the nuclear tests conducted by the latter. They would have to treat us as equals.

If China supports Pakistan during the conflict, she would never enter the war directly. She had not supported Pakistan on the Kargil issue. Chinese diplomacy is very polished and it would never ignore the international protocols. In sum, China is not likely to repeat the history of 1962 war but Pakistan is likely to have a direct conflict. Even a nuclear initiative from Islamabad could not be ruled out. Pakistan has a consistent record of political and economic instabilities and their effects could spill into our territory as well.

Pakistan is not going to return our territory on a platter. We would have to struggle hard for it. The international community is also awestruck by the developments that took place in Kargil, Batalik, Drass and Mushkoh Valley. Pakistan lost 267 regular soldiers and her 204 soldiers were injured. Pakistani military officials admitted these losses on July 27, 1999. They admitted the evil fact that the were directly involved in the Kargil war during May-July, 1999. Third party intervention has been ruled out by India. Kashmiri people are with India. However, Pakistani propaganda has been able to antagonise them in their favour. India plans to launch a counter-attack through media blitzkreig by updating the hardware and software related to television transmission. A decision in this context was taken by the caretaker government in July, 1999.

If China factor could be effectively controlled through Russian influences, Indian forces could settle all the scores with Pakistan. Fifty years of independence and separation from Pakistan have given us bitter wars, destruction and lack of control over a territory, which truly belongs to us. The time is ripe to pronounce with full vigour—"give me my land." Be prepared to take whatever is yours; the costs do not matter for those issues, which are sacred and are concerned with the security and prosperity of the nation.

64. THE MAGNIFICENT INDIANS

India is a nuclear force—Sound industrial infrastructure—Military might acquired over a period of fifty years—We are a power to reckon with in South Asia—We want to play bigger role in international arena—Nuclear tests earned sanctions—Economic situation is better now—Military superiority cannot guarantee us a slot on the centre stage—We won the war against Pakistan in Kargil which proved our military might but exposed our weaknesses as well—Economic independence is a must—Economic development is painfully slow—Adopt dynamic and creative economic policies—Stock markets have showed signs of improvement—Strengthen the democratic institutions—Export more—Develop good relationships with neighbours India politiccally stable but no stable government in the centre—A stable government could take the nation out of political and economic chaos—National unity is essential

The recent incidents in the Indian subcontinent have been observed by the world with anxiety and awe. India conducted nuclear tests on May 11 and May 13, 1998. Indian military might is also a serious issue of debate among the international circles. Further, the change at the centre also led everyone in the West to believe that a change in foreign policy could be on the cards.

The BJP manifesto had promised to make efforts for India for becoming a permanent member of the UN Security Council. Further, our economic muscle, though not in a very good stead, has been acknowledged due to our sound industrial infrastructure and our highly skilled technical and managerial manpower bases. All these facts lead us to believe that we could be the "global strategic player" of the new millennium. Could we make such assertions in terms of our economic might, nuclear capabilities or military potential ? Could India alter the balance of power in Asia ? Could India assume the role of a "big brother" like the USA and China ? Let us analyse.

Let us analyse the repercussions of the nuclear tests first. The post-Pokharan II scenario has brought new questions in the minds of the world elite. The international community believes that India has tried to flex her nuclear muscle and that she proposes to increase her influence on the international stage. The world would always try to suppress an emerging power and everybody is doing so in the case of India as well. However, it is a glaring fact that we have nuclear and thermonuclear capabilities. We must, however, keep in mind that we cannot make our presence felt at the international fora merely on the basis of nuclear capabilities. Indian economy would also be coupled with nuclear capabilities. Indian economy has shown signs of improvement despite sluggish trends of economic growth around the world. Political instability in the centre gave India some setbacks to the economy but industrial production did pick up during the first half of 1999. Stock markets also did well during these time periods.

Acquiring nuclear capability was of utmost necessity. Our neighbours have already planned a possible direct or indirect war against us. This could be corroborated by infiltration of armed mercenaries and Pakistani army regulars in Kargil, Mushkoh Valley, Drass and Batalik on our Northern frontiers. The nuclear war is not in immediate sight but Pakistan threatened to use her nuclear missiles against India during the Kargil war. India is however, unlikely to use nuclear weapon as she has developed nuclear capability as a deterrent and not for offence. Due to the nuclear tests conducted by India, the international community (and the nuclear weapon States in particular) would be persuaded towards time-bound disarmament efforts. The complete elimination of nuclear weapons from the earth would be expedited if the attitude of the nuclear weapon States is positive.

India stands isolated an all the major international platforms and so is Pakistan. Our nuclear tests have invited the wrath of the world in terms of economic sanctions. Even some of the developing countries are apprehensive about our nuclear might, India's chances of becoming a permanent member of the UN are bleak now. The world would not like India to play a major role on the global platforms like the UN and therefore, would try to pressurise us for signing the CTBT. India would not be granted "nuclear weapon power" status. We must also note that our nuclear weapon abilities and technologies are still not sufficient. Once these have been fully developed, India could play vital role on the international stage.

The next issue is that of economic development. We must note that economic development and an improvement in the quality of life of the Indian masses are important factors that would enable India to earn an appropriate status in the international stage. We are not independent in economic terms and are far behind the G-8 group (the five nuclear weapon powers, Japan, Germany and Italy). We are way behind China in terms of GDP and economic growth.

In terms of quality of life, we are not anywhere near the standards of the developed nations. It is pity that we have not been able to provide adequate food, water, shelter, pure air, medicines, education and employment facilities to the residents of this vast nation. Fifty years have already gone by and we are more than 1,000 million in number. The population control measures have proved to be futile. Over 400 million Indians live below poverty line. The average rate of growth has been between 5.5 per cent per annum during the last decade—not a rosy figure by any norm. Our share in international trade is very low. Our literacy rates are the lowest in the world.

This situation would warrant the adoption of dynamic and creative economic policies and budgets. State expenditures would have to be pruned. Bureaucratic delays would have to be minimised and sick PSUs would have to be put in the dustbin. A major thrust would be required in exports, infrastructure development and productivity. But all this is easier said than done. Sick PSUs have not been discarded. Bureaucracy has not tried to meet the needs of the modern economy. The productivity levels remain painfully low. The stock markets had plummeted to new depths and Indian Rupee but recently, the NSE sensex crossed the prestigious mark of 5,000 points. The bull phase in the fa end of 1999.

We are self-reliant to a large extent. We can meet our food and development needs. Only 2 per cent of the resources required for development is coming from abroad. Our economy is multi-faceted. Our economic potential does not depend upon export performance alone. Restructuring, modernisation and liberalisation of our economy have increased our economic performance. We have to align and tune our economic agenda with the world economy because we cannot foresee an isolated economic growth in the wake of the advent of free market system around the world.

The military, economic and technological achievements (as well as the implementation of creative economic policies) would depend upon the political finesse and the manner in which the economy would behave in future. The intellectual, economic and political growth centres of the nation would have to unite irrespective of their diverse ideologies. Our national leaders, institutions and elite think tanks would have to devise concrete solutions so that the nation could catapult herself into the international arena with pride and dignity.

We propose the following measures for the achievement of the coveted goals :—

(A) Indian democracy has to be strengthened and the communal forces have to be defeated so that a strong and secular India emerges from the shadows of the black decade of the nineties. The new millennium should presentt secular India to the world.

(B) The political processes must be transparent, stable and growth-oriented. There should be no bias towards the political parties. If a political party commits a mistake that could have national repercussions, that party must be advised to mend its policies and *modus operandi*.

(C) A sense of national unity must be inculcated among the masses. The collective social discipline and moral code of conduct are absent from our national fabric. We cannot fight any war outside our home if we are bent upon destroying our culture, economy and values.

(D) Our foreign policy is not tuned with the current requirements of nations of the world. China, despite her nuclear tests, is enjoying the MFN status but we are facing the wrath of economic sanctions as a result of the nuclear tests. We should use tactful international diplomacy and must develop healthy as well as long-lasting relationships with the USA and her allies. There is no doubt about the fact that the Western block is the only force left in the international arena. If we want to be recognised internationally, we would have to mend our relationships with the West.

(E) We must also develop healthy relationships with our immediate neighbours. Our neighbours would certainly help us assume more important role on the international political and economic fora.

A position of dominance at the international level could be achieved when the world would conclude that we are a capable and responsible nation for contributing effectively towards the healthy growth of the world. If, however, we only claim that we are major players, we would not be able to achieve the coveted objectives. All the nations exercise influence in any international endeavour on respectful invitation and not through gate-crashing. Dignity is the key issue. Assimilation with the world order come later. Let us prepare ourselves politically and economically so that we could be offered a position of recognition with due respect to our capabilities. Time is yet not ripe for that stage. It would be a wise decision to prepare ourselves first and then, wait for positive developments from the international political, diplomatic and economic circles. We deserve the slot but we should not show any anxiety or hurry. Time would settle many an issue. ●

THE NUCLEAR DEBATE

65. INDIA IS A NUCLEAR POWER

India conducted five nuclear tests on May 11 and May 13, 1998 under Operation Shakti—Fission device, low yield device and thermo-nuclear device developed—India is a nuclear power now—Pakistan also carried out five tests, which have dubious characteristics—World imposed economic sanctions on India and Pakistan—We are now left alone as Russia has shown friendly gestures towards India—China and Pakistan would not sit pretty and would certainly react—World perceives a change in our foreign policy and misinterprets our preparations for self-defence—NPT CTBT must be signed after necessary alternations—Need for diplomatic finesse.

On May 11 and May 13, 1998, India successfully conducted five nuclear tests and thus became the sixth nuclear power in the world with a giant leap in the field of nuclear technology.

This was a proud moment for Indian masses and for our scientists who had worked hard for fifty long years in order to reach the pinnacle of glory. It should be recalled that India conducted a nuclear explosion on May 18, 1974 which was fission device. The three tests conducted by India on May 11, 1998 included a fission device (of 12 killoton capacity), a low yield device (of 0.2 killoton capacity) and a thermo-nuclear device (of 43 killotons capacity).

The Prime Minister, Mr Atal Bihari Vajpayee, was one of the first few persons to congratulate Mr R Chidambaram (Chairman of Department of Atomic Energy) and Dr APJ Abdul Kalaam (Chairman,—Defence Research and Development Organisation). These two scientists and their teams were responsible for the successful Operation "Shakti" in Pokharan against all odds. On May 13, 1998, India conducted two more explosions—a low yield device of 0.5 sub-kiloton capacity and another low yield device of 0.3 sub-kilotons capacity. Table I gives the chain of events, which culminated into the explosions.

TABLE-I : "Operation Shakti"

S No	Date	Steps of Operation Shakti
1.	20-03-98	Chidambaram meets PM.
2.	08-04-98	Chidambaram and Kalaam meet PM. Asked to conduct tests on 11-05-98.
3.	07-05-98	Abdul Kalaam and senior army officials storm the test site Pokharan. Brijesh Mishra is aware of events.
4.	10-05-98	Three chiefs of armed forces and foreign secretary informed. President informed about the preparations.
5.	11-05-98	Three tests conducted in Pokharan at 15:45 PM.
6.	13-05-98	Two more tests conducted.

Indian initiative on nuclear tests came quickly after the Indian government realised that Pakistan was bent upon promoting her nuclear programme. The Pakistani army had successfully tested Ghauri missile a few days before the test. This was a good reason for Indians to prove to the world that they would not remain silent spectators to the happenings across the border.

Immediately after declaration by Indian Prime Minister, the shocked world criticied India and took no time to react in terms of sanctions. The USA imposed economic sanctions and decided to oppose loans to be granted by international lending agencies and barred the US banks from granting loans to India under a 1994 law. The US Department of Defence imposed sanctions covering International Military Education and Training (IMET) Programme and other military exchanges. Japan suspended US$ 26 million annual grant aid. Japan further refused to host World Bank sponsored Aid India Meet which was scheduled in June, 1998. Germany froze fresh development aid worth 300 million Deutsche Marks. Sweden cut short a three-year aid programme with India worth US$ 118 million. Denmark freezed aid at the current loan of 190 million Crowns per annum instead of raising it to 300 million Crowns. France and Russia did not impose any economic sanction. China remained quite. However on May 18, 1998, Chinese news agency Xinhua urged India to stop the development of nuclear weapons. It also stated that India had occupied 90,000 square kms of Chinese territory. The cold and threatening remarks from Chinese statements could only prove one fact—India took the right step at the right time.

On May 28, 1998, Pakistan also carried out "five successful nuclear tests" and therefore, evened her 'account' with India. She also conducted one more test on May 30, 1998 and tried to copy Indian nuclear programme like a child who longs for the same lollypop as the one being enjoyed by another child.

Indian nuclear might has been demonstrated before the world. However, we must analyse the economic and political repercussions of these tests. We may have to pay for these tests in terms of economic sanctions. Pakistan is also facing economic sanctions. Pakistani economy is not resilient enough for withstanding the aftermath of economic sanctions. In the beginning of 1999. Indian economy might be able to withstand the sanctions it faces; at least our then Finance Minister Mr Yashwant Sinha said so.

Kargil war had almost led to the initiation of nuclear war between India and Pakistan. President Bill Clinton intervened at the right time and a nuclear disaster was averted.

Russia is a "good friend" of India not so much China and Pakistan. The USA and other Western have supported us on the Kargil issue. ASEAN meet, held during July, 1999, in Singapore, supported Indian stand on the dispute and favoured a solution through bilateral talks. The USA has lifted most of the sanctions against India and Pakistan. We would not be able to grow at an anticipated rate of 6-7 per cent per annum. Debt servicing and infrastructure growth were affected. We would have to generate our own resources, which is a herculean task. Therefore, we could have tough times ahead on economic front.

Some type of reprisal from China and Pakistan is inevitable; Pakistani nuclear tests have amply demonstrated this fact. Pakistan behaves like a child who has accidentally put his hands on a sharp knife with which, she is going to harm himself as well as those who are around him. We have faced aggression from Pakistan and China and bitter interactions are likely to take place in international fora. Battles with Pakistan have been going on for the past several years. A full-fledged war with either China or with Pakistan in near future could not be ruled out, but for the present there seems no possibility.

The world has perceived our nuclear tests as a serious deviation from our earlier foreign policy of peaceful cooperation. India is now known to be an aggressive nation, which is ready to go to any level in order to prove her might. It must be noted that our image of a peace-loving nation at all the international fora must be maintained even if we keep our nuclear options open. If China could maintain a comfortable and friendly posture towards all the nations (despite her poor record as a neighbour), why could we not maintain our peaceful image ? The government made some diplomatic mistakes, which were quickly rectified. The remarks about China and Pakistan were not expected, especially from the veteran leaders. The international community expects us to behave like a 5,000 year old civilisation and not like the Pakistani Prime Minister. The perseverance and honesty of Indian diplomats would automatically persuade the world leaders to help us. During the Kargil war, international opinion was in favour of India as our soldiers did not cross the LoC. If the world is with us, we would be able to get our rights; nuclear power does not matter. Nuclear option is only a deterrent. We need nuclear power for electricity generation and not for making bombs. Indian leaders must make this fact known to our wellwishers around the globe. The nuclear alternative is for self-defence and not for an attack.

Finally, the nuclear explosions have brought the issue of CTBT to limelight. India does not sign CTBT as she finds them biased in the favour of a few nations. India is prepared to sign CTBT if it is modified. Indian Prime Minister has already stated that India would not carry out any more tests. This self-imposed moratorium should please the nations of the world. Further, if CTBT is modified (so that it is not discriminatory), then India should lose no time in signing the same. After all, we have to live peacefully in this world and international cooperation is the key to political and economic success of any nation. Nuclear disarmament remains a distant dream. India, as the chief proponent of this concept, should pursue this goal with utmost sincerity. Signing of CTBT (only the modified versions according to Indian viewpoints) should be able to eliminate nuclear warheads from this planet in the long run.

We can conclude by stating that India has been facing tough economic and political situations as a result of the nuclear explosions. The economic fallout is inevitable. Political reprisals are also going to affect our economic and foreign policies in the times to come. India should exercise restraint in nuclear testing and should adopt diplomatic techniques for diffusing tension in the region and on the international platforms. We have done the right thing. However, communicating this fact carefully and effecting the cooperation from all the nations, the UNO and our opponents requires highest levels of diplomatic finesse.

66. CTBT : SHOULD INDIA BUDGE ?

> *Indian stand on CTBT very clear—We want transparency in nuclear power testing and usage—Western nations want us to sign CTBT so that they have an edge over us—We are committed but nuclear disarmament must be on a global scale—Nuclear powers must eliminate nuclear weapons through time-bound programmes.*

Nuclear energy is the most dependable energy source for the future. For a country like India, which has limited coal and petroleum reserves, this vital energy source can be regarded as a new source of power. Indian stand on testing of nuclear devices has been made clear—usage of nuclear energy is for the development of technology and for power generation. Nuclear tests are also necessary as we have to maintain balance of power with China and Pakistan.

In 1954, Indian Prime Minister Jawahar Lal Nehru called for cessation of nuclear tests. In 1963, Partial Test Ban treaty was signed, which banned nuclear weapon tests in the atmosphere, outer space and under water. However, nuclear tests continued and NPT conferences held in 1975, 1980, 1985 and 1990 did not yield results.

In 1995, however Nuclear Non Proliferation Treaty (NPT) was signed. The nuclear weapon states (the USA, Russia, China, Britain and France) promoted the Comprehensive Test Ban Treaty (CTBT). India has so far refused to sign the CTBT.

Indian leaders are under pressure. The Western nations opine that CTBT would sustain the NPT and would ultimately result in nuclear disarmament. India feels that the USA is using the CTBT in order to chop down our nuclear alternatives. So, Indian leaders have driven home the fact that she is ready to sign CTBT provided the five nuclear powers also head towards complete nuclear disarmament and cessation of nuclear testing under a time-bound programme.

Russia, China and the USA have used their status as global powers to carry out these tests. The glory and soul-chilling effects of nuclear technology are amazing. A nuclear fission device could be used for generating electrical power in a nuclear power plant; it could also be loaded on a missile to destroy another Hiroshima ! Once a test is carried out, there is no need for further tests. The existing data could be used to make nuclear bombs and missiles in a matter of hours. The nuclear powers would continue to develop nuclear weapons. However, if the non-nuclear states are not allowed to conduct these tests, they are unlikely to master the nuclear technology. Therefore, it is very convenient for the five countries to sign CTBT and divest other nations from the ability to get nuclear technology. This is knwon as nuclear apartheid.

During the visit of President, Mr. Bill Clinton, during March 21-25, 2000, the visiting official made it clear to our then Foreign Minister, Mr. Jaswant Singh that the remaining economic sanctions would go if India signed the CTBT. So, India cannot sit on the CTBT issue; she has to sign the treaty in order to align her nuclear policies with those of the world.

But India must not sign CTBT if nuclear weapon States are not disarmed. Pakistan, Iraq, Saudi Arabia, Korea and some African nations have their own nuclear programmes. Keeping in mind the experiences of the past, we should not have any doubts about the intentions of military-dominated administration of Pakistan. They could use nuclear bombs against India any time.

According to Mr Abdul Kalaam, "India must negotiate from the position of strength." Our stand is based on logic and moral grounds and many nations have supported us on the issue. The then Indian Ambassador, Arundhati Ghose, stated in Geneva (the venue of the last CTBT negotiation conference)—"India will not sign this treaty unless her concerns are taken on board. This is a position we hold and, which we are not likely to change."

Although the treaty was signed, yet Indian stand was absolutely right. Let us now analyse why India does not sign NPT and CTBT :—

(A) NPT was agreed upon in 1968 and prevents its signatories from assisting nations (not possessing nuclear explosives before 1968) in obtaining or producing them.

(B) This would lead to the conclusion that those nations, who possessed nuclear weapons by 1968—the USA, Russia, Britain, France and China—were not bound by the non-proliferation provisions of NPT.

(C) The globe has been divided into two parts—"nuclear haves" and "nuclear have nots." Horizontal proliferation was sought to be checked by preventing the addition of nuclear powers into the distinguished club. The vertical proliferation—the collection or development of more nuclear weapons by the big five—was considered to be legitimate. This was thought to be discriminatory. Hence, India did not sign NPT.

(D) The Comprehensive Test Ban Treaty (CTBT) enjoins upon all its members to stop nuclear explosions. However, it fails to define what constitutes an explosion. Hence, India has not signed the same.

(E) CTBT does not put a ban on the critical tests and tests conducted through computer simulation. The nuclear weapon States are always capable of improving the nuclear arsenal through most modern simulation techniques with the help of computers.

(F) CTBT, although agreed upon in 1996, has yet to enter into full force. That is because India and Pakistan have not signed the same. The treaty would have to be signed by India as well as by Pakistan in order for it to be effective. It may be noted that a total of 146 nations have signed the CTBT and 14 nations have ratified it. But implementation of CTBT is a distant dream. India and Pakistan are being persuaded to sign the CTBT.

India has repeatedly stated that she does not want a war with any nation. She is also in favour of negotiated settlement of all the issues through bilateral talks. She also values the importance of good relationships with China. However, she has conducted nuclear tests for the sake of her defence, which was necessary, keeping in mind the activities going on the other side of the border. Pakistani army rules the country and the head of State could declare war on India anytime if internal strife calls for such an eventuality. China has never been a good friend of India. Chinese missile systems have no other targets but Indian cities. One would never expect that China and Pakistan would develop high power and long range missiles warheads for usage against Russia as this imagination is anything but a Utopian dream. Therefore, our neighbours have fullscale preparations for mass scale destruction in which they would be destroyed to some extent but they would also destroy the Indian cities or industrial installations to a great extent. Indian answer to Pakistani and Chinese missiles was the need of the hour and hence, nuclear tests were justified. However, a war with Pakistan or China would certainly lead to death, destruction and economic chaos as this would lead the warring nations to the catastrophe of Mutually Assured Destruction (MAD).

The solution to this problem is the elimination of all the nuclear weapons from the mother earth, usage of nuclear warheads for electrical power generation, global strategy for disposal of nuclear wastes and finally, settlement of all the disputes through across-the-table negotiations.

India is a peaceful nation. She has no intention of being a military or a nuclear superpower. Nuclear tests were an absolute necessity and now, the government has imposed a moratorium on these tests. The world would understand our stand sooner or later. They would eventually understand why the nation, previously led by the Mahatma, is now forced to defend herself against the machinations of a handful of nations. We have only tried to prove that we are not an humble pie. ●

67. COULD INDIA AND PAKISTAN HAVE A NUCLEAR CONFLICT ?

Afghanistan was war-torn now of course at peace—Pakistan fully involved—The USA has attacked with Tomahawks—Situation grim—Osama Bin Laden wants to liberate Kashmir—Pakistan cannot win conventional war—The war in Kargil, Batalik, Drass and Mushkoh Valley proved that Pakistani military is no match for Indian military might—Nuclear war would destroy the most prosperous areas of both the nations—Ghauri and Shaheen missiles are lethal—Pakistan is now controlled indirectly by military—Nuclear option must be avoided by India and Pakistan.

The situation is quite complicated. Firstly, the Tomahawk missiles flew over the Pakistani territory before attacking the terrorist camps in Afghanistan. Secondly, Osama Bin Laden declared that only *Mujahideen* could liberate Kashmir. Thirdly, Pakistan has been facing internal political chaos as the Pakistani Army Chief had resigned in an unceremonious manner in the wake of differences with Mr Nawaz Sharif. Mr Sharif appointed General Parvez Musharraf as the new Army Chief. It has been alleged that he did not involve Mr Nawaz Sharif in the Kargil war. In a way, the Kargil war was initiated by Pakistani army only. History always teaches us to be vigilant in the wake of the unhealthy developments across our Western border. The heat of the fire across the border is always imposed on us and we suffer due to the immature democracies, which have not been able to settle down on our Northern and North-Western borders. Let us analyse.

The positive developments turned out to be a hoax. India and Pakistan had serious official talks when Mr K Raghunath visited Islamabad and met Mr Sartaj Aziz. The official level talks were held between the two nations on the issue of Tulmul, Siachen, New Delhi-Lahore bus service and grant of MFN status by Pakistan to India during November, 1998. But our neighbours played a different game when Mr Nawaz Sharif was hugging Mr AB Vajpayee in Lahore, General Musharraf was busy positioning his troops on the Indian side of the LoC.

Even if Pakistan is willing to talk, would the Pakistani military have a restraint ? The Afghan war now over could have been be converted into a global war (with the USA as the major player) and Pakistan could also be actually involved in it. President Bill Clinton wants to teach the terrorist group a lesson through his might. Pakistan would also like to settle her scores, which have not been in her favour since the wars of 1948, 1965, 1971 and 1999. So, Pakistan could try for a possible direct attack against India in 2003. General Pervez Musharraf is trying to grapple with economic problems. As and when he gets some financial support from is freiends, he is likely to engage India in another mini-war.

Pakistan cannot win a conventional war against India. She has been warned by her well-wishers that it is not possible to overcome Indian might, which is proud to be one of the best forces in the world. Then, the next step could be a nuclear interaction. Let us analyse what could Pakistan do if she failed to overcome India in conventional warfare.

Pakistan is also a nuclear State now. HATF, Shaheen and Ghauri missiles have already been developed by her and tests have been carried out to confirm their striking capabilities. Pakistan cannot develop a bomb on her own. Hence, it is clear that a 'friend' could have helped her (it could be North Korea or China). Now, that Pakistan has the bomb, she would use it against India but would fail to get deeper into Indian territory. But even if Indian defence efforts are estimated to be the best, we cannot ignore the fact that HATF, Shaheen and Ghauri missiles are quite lethal. So, on our North-Western borders, Amritsar, Tarantaran, Wagah and Runn of Kutch could be the prime targets. In the Northern side, Uri, Doda, Kaigil, Batalik and Poonch could face the nuclear wrath. We are very well aware that this attack would annihilate the target areas forever as was the case in Hiroshima and Nagasaki. Ferozepur is also on the border in Punjab and could be destroyed due to a single attack by nuclear missiles of Pakistan.

India has decided not to attack any nation in the first instance. We are a peace-loving nation. Our first defence initiative would be to destroy the nuclear missiles in the Pakistani territory. But if these missiles cross over into India, destruction and death are inevitable. Our view is that India should retaliate with limited attacks on the desert areas of the Pakistani territory. This would demonstrate our technology and nuclear superiority to our worthy 'friends.' We should not attack civil installations or factories. However, defence installations could be attacked, keeping in accordance with the international war protocols and rules declared in Geneva Accord.

This doomsday could only to be imagined. Let us pray that good sense prevails ! The reason is that neither India nor Pakistan can afford to have a nuclear conflict as this would hurt the global images of both the nations. It is a good measure to acquire power and show it. But when power is used (in this case, it would be misused), then it is likely to be reduced.

The next issue was that of Afghanistan. Afghan guerrillas and the Talibaan are hand-in-gloves with the Pakistani administration.

Osama Bin Laden has already stated that he would like to liberate Kashmir with the help of *Mujahideen*. Even in this state of crisis, Indian diplomats should not lose their cool. It is suggested that an indirect talk with Osama Bin Laden should be initiated and Indian stand on Kashmir should be explained to him. After all, Rajiv Gandhi also invited Vellupillai Prabhakaran of LTTE for talks. There is no harm in having an across-the-table discussions. If the talks fail, the final option is war. But war must be avoided at all costs. We should try to make friends and not foes. Pakistan should also understand this fact.

The political scenario in Pakistan could change for the worst in the wake of her ignonimous defeat in the Kargil war. Mr Nawaz Sharif has been sentenced to life imprisonment for his alleged involvement in an assassination bid against general Musharaaf. His counsel, Mr Laad, was also killed. Militant groups and Pakistani religious groups alleged that the agreement between Mr Sharif and Mr Clinton, to withdraw Pakistani forces from Indian territory was a sellout. Pakistani military could shift the attention of the masses by initiating war with India. However, a nuclear conflict is ruled out. Even if both the nations would try to have a nuclear conflict, they would destroy each other's territories and economies and would never be able to recover. Realities are much more harsh and need immediate and prudent actions, decisions and implementation.

68. NUCLEAR ENERGY : BOON OR BANE ?

New millennium belongs to nuclear energy—Population levels high—Energy needs soaring—Conventional sources depleting at a fast rate—Nuclear energy is a viable alternative—As an energy source, it is a boon—As a material for nuclear bombs and missiles, it is a bane—India, Pakistan, China have nuclear capabilities—India could face problems if Pakistan and China chose same line of action during the next war—The USA is supporting India on the international fora—A nuclear war could lead to MAD—Nuclear radiation harmful—Accidents like the one at Chernobyl dangerous—Over-exposure to nuclear radiation could lead to cancer—Use nuclear energy for the survival and growth of mankind.

The globe has already entered the new millennium and the scientists, politicians and elites of the world ponder over the future of the mankind and its environs. We have come a long way since the Stone Age. But now we are nearly 1 billion years old and are still growing in terms of number and aspirations. The population of the world, during September-October 1999, touched the dangerous figure of 6 billion. The population of India touched the 1,000 million mark during the latter half of 1999. We have been adding 17 million people to our population every year. If these trends continue, we would arrive at the figure of 162 crore by the year 2050 AD. The energy needs of the vast human populace of the globe-and those of the growing and developing nation like India-are colossal. We need coal, petroleum, wood, nuclear power and hydro-energy for meeting the survival and growth requirements of mankind. In India, the demand for electrical power has always been more than the actual production of the same.

In such a complicated situation, nuclear energy has arrived in order to solve our "energy riddles" and we have been wise enough to embrace this boon with finesse and careful planning. For India, nuclear energy would certainly be a blessing as we are a nation that has remained energy starved since her independence. The nations of the West have already exploited nuclear energy to the maximum extent and are quite self-sufficient in terms of generation and usage of nuclear power. India has to cross many more milestones, however, as we are still trying to grapple with the basic problems and issues related to the same.

At present, the installed nuclear power generation capacity of India is 2,225 MW and we propose to produce 20,000 MW of nuclear power by the year 2020 AD. The first nuclear research reactor of India was Apsara. Subsequently, more nuclear research reactors were installed and made critical. These reactors were Zerlina and Purnima. These research reactors spearhead our quest for supremacy in the fields of nuclear science and research.

Fossil fuels would not stay with us for a long period of time if we continue to exploit them at such a fast pace. Wood is not be an ideal fuel and hydro-electric power could be used for meeting the demands of base loads only. Hence, nuclear energy would have to be generated in India in order to meet the demands of the house holds, industry and the national populace. The State, through Department of Atomic Energy (DAE) and Nuclear Power Corporation (NPC), has taken proper steps for generating nuclear energy on a commercial scale. We have a well-defined programme for generating nuclear energy in India. At present, we are generating nuclear power at seven locations in the country.

We have used nuclear fission technology in all these plants. These plants utilise enriched Plutonium or Uranium-235 as fuels in their reactors. The plants for manufacturing Heavy Water are located at Thal, Hazira, Managuru, Trombay, Talchar, Tuticorin, Vadodara and Nangal. Further, Thorium is also used to make fuel for the nuclear reactors. Thorium is available in abundance in Kerala, Tamil Nadu, Andhra Pradesh, Karnataka and Bihar (the Ranchi belt). Beryllium rods are used to absorb the extra neutrons that are released in the nuclear fission reaction in the reactor. Beryllium is available from the mines of Bihar, Rajasthan and Madhya Pradesh. Further, Uranium ore is available from Jaduguda mines (Bihar), Himachal Pradesh and Madhya Pradesh. Our resources are limited but can import some vital components and fuels if we are able to support the Western policies on the CTBT issue.

If we keep the aforementioned discussion in view, we would be able to conclude that we are likely to produce nuclear power on a massive scale in the times to come. However, nuclear energy is not only a boon for us, but also it is a bane for the nation in the form of the deadly nuclear arsenal that has mushroomed in South Asia. India, China and Pakistan have nuclear capabilities and India could be a target in the near future for a nuclear catastrophe. China and Pakistan have been denied entry into the prestigious nuclear club that is owned by the five nuclear majors. Recently, the US Congress came down heavily on the proposals of the CTBT put forth by the American President, Mr. Bill Clinton. This event has given us more time to think whether we should sign CTBT or not. Our only contention is that CTBT would not be able to protect the interests in the missile-infested South Asian region. We view CTBT as a biased agreement that has been concocted by the West and would serve their interests, skillfully sidelining ours. Many nations are likely to suffer if they agree to the existing format and spirit of the CTBT.

We intend to utilise nuclear energy for peaceful purposes. But China and Pakistan are hell-bent upon making it a bane for us. And we should add here that if a nation uses the nuclear option during a conventional war, she would also face the threat of extinction as the conventional war could culminate into a deleterious nuclear conflict, according to the well-established gospel of Mutually Assured Destruction (MAD). It was this concept of MAD that persuaded the NATO nations and the erstwhile Eastern block nations to shed their egoes and put an end to the nuclear arms race during the late eighties.

There is a new military regime in Pakistan; it was quite expected that the defeat of the Pakistani army during the Kargil war would catapult the military to power. The 'able' leadership of General Parvez Musharraf may give many surprises to India and the world. Although the general ordered the reduction in the troops along the borders with India, the sporadic incidents of violence in Kashmir and firing across the LoC cannot be considered as the signs of warmth and peace. The intentions of Pakistani regime are not clear as on date. However, general Mushaarraf has categorically stated that Kashmir remains the major issue for discussions between India and Pakistan. Therefore, one thing should be clear to Indian leaders—Pakistan would not do away with her existing policies *viz-a-viz* Kashmir. We could have a full-fledged armed conflict with Pakistan during the fag end of 2003 AD. Pakistan has developed Shaheen, Ghouri and HATF missile systems and they are capable of carrying nuclear warheads. Many of these missiles have been targeted at Indian cities. At the same time, Indian defence establishment has also geared up for meeting any challenges from across our North-Western borders. We have developed Trishul, Nag, Akash, Prithvi and Agni missile systems and the same are also capable of carrying nuclear payloads. Further, the testing phase of Sagarika missile system has been suspended due to international pressures. We have designed these systems to counter any threat from our Northern or North-Western borders.

The aforementioned discussion would lead us to the conclusion that nuclear energy could prove to be a bane for three major players of Asia-China, Pakistan and India. If China and Pakistan choose to adopt the same line of action, India could face difficult situations during a war. The latest war was fought with Pakistan along the Northern border (in the cold hills of Kargil, Mushkoh Valley and Drass sectors) during July-September, 1999. This war cost India Rs 1,984 crore. China, in quite contrast with her behaviour during the past, chose to remain neutral during the recently concluded Indo-Pak war. Her political intentions were never clear but her strategic aims have been clearly defined; her nuclear arsenal is one of the most advanced and perhaps, most lethal after that of the USA. The Western nations chose to align their opinions with those of India and did not support the Pakistani attack on India during the recently concluded Kargil war. The American diplomacy gave a few surprises as the requests of Prime Minister, Mr Nawaz Sharif, fell on deaf ears when he visited the USA and called on Mr Clinton during the Kargil war. American President was wise enough to see through the situation and gave him a soothing advice to withdraw from the Indian side of the LoC. This incident proved to be a turning point in the Indo-American relationships and we have a friendly Uncle Sam who is likely to support us at many diplomatic fora. This is the most glorious time of the Indo-US relationships since the war between India and Pakistan in 1971. The credit squarely goes to the determination and grit of our PM, Mr AB Vajpayee, the visits and efforts of Mr Jaswant Singh and Mr Talbott and a friendly attitude of the then Foreign Minister Mr Bill Clinton. Finally, Americans have realised that Indian stand *viz-a-viz* Pakistan is not erratic or dumbfounded.

A nuclear war cannot be afforded by any nation. The problem is not of nuclear bane but of the political will for settlement of all the political and geographical disputes between India, China and Pakistan. Nuclear energy would certainly rule the roost during the present millennium. The conventional energy sources are depleting at a very fast rate and the long term dependence upon the same is an irrational proposition. India wants to utilise her nuclear resources for the benefit of her masses. Nuclear energy would not only help us generate electrical energy, but also it would be useful in nuclear research, medicine, scientific research and space exploration activities. Pakistan has not matured as a nation and this fact would certainly not impinge upon their minds that nuclear energy should be used as a boon only. The existing stockpile of nuclear weapons can also be used for generating nuclear power as the radioactive fuel could be used for these peaceful and constructive applications at any point of time. As already stated, the concept of nuclear energy a boon or as a bane could be given a decisive shape only by the leaders of the three nations-India, China and Pakistan. It is up to these leaders to decide whether they want their nations to grow through the next millennium or not. And above all, the citizens of these nations would have to be involved in this herculean effort. It is a question of their survival on this blue-green planet.

In other parts of the world, nuclear arms pose a great threat to mankind. The USA, France, Russia and the UK have nuclear arms and capabilities. Russia and the USA have the most dreadful nuclear weapons that must be destroyed so that the deadly radiation could be eliminated, thus protecting the citizens and the habitat of the mother earth. Although the process of destruction of nuclear arsenal had already started during the early nineties, yet the nuclear weapons must be completely annihilated in order to avoid accidental blasts or radiation hazards that are an essential part of these weapons. Even if the USA and Russia destroy their weapons, some of these would still be retained by them in order to have a strategic advantage over the other nation, in case they choose to be two poles of the global political axis; as on date, there is only one pole that is by the USA.

A mention must be made of the accidents that could wreak havoc in the nuclear power plants. We have not forgotten the incident of radiation leakage in Chernobyl plant in Russia. Such incidents could be repeated if the nuclear scientists did not take adequate precautionary measures for ensuring the safety of the plant personnel or the residents of the area in the immediate vicinity of a nuclear power plant. Therefore, the nuclear power plants and research facilities would have to be designed with the highest safety standards in mind else this could prove to be another bane for the nation that produces nuclear power. And finally, nuclear energy could also prove to be a bane for those who get themselves exposed to nuclear radiation for the sake of treatment of cancer. Nuclear radiation itself is carcinogenic. And even if the exposed patient does not have a cancer, he is likely to die due to other complications arising out of exposure to nuclear radiation. Doctors and nuclear physicists must devise safe methods for exposing only those parts of the human body that need treatment by the nuclear radiation.

Nuclear energy has a bright future as a source of power generation. India supports the usage of nuclear energy for peaceful purposes and she has also stated this categorically at various international fora, including the International Atomic Energy Agency (IAEA). Our nuclear capabilities have given us a power to negotiate and to survive despite harsh treatment from across the borders. However, India should not resort to nuclear war, as this would prove to be a bane for Indians as well. Let the rational minds of the world unite and decide the future of nuclear energy that is so useful for the mankind. A political solution to the problems faced by us would be the first step in this direction. When and how would that step is taken, has to be decided by the politicians and the CEOs of the nations. The ordinary citizens could only hope for a bright future for themselves that would not be fraught with the deliberate nuclear wars or accidental nuclear leakges, dumping exercises or plant failures. Nuclear technologies would have to be used for the survival and growth of the mankind.

69. NUCLEAR CONFLICT IN SOUTH ASIA

Nuclear conflict between India and Pakistan possible in near future—Hijack of IA plane—Kargil War—Pakistan threatened that it could use nuclear option—India only free South Asian nation—Some possibilities of nuclear conflict discussed—Some nations would support Pakistan—Others would support India—Pakistan can import nuclear arsenal but India cannot—Concept of MAD applicable—North Indian states would be affected—A non-conventional conflict inevitable—A remote possibility of nuclear war.

The nuclear ambitions of Pakistan would be the major cause of concern for India and the world in the new millennium. Pakistan has developed advanced missile systems like Ghauri and Shaheen. India has also developed 'Sagarika' missile system. However, international pressures forced Indian leaders to go ahead with testing the 'Sagarika' missile. We are in a precarious situation now. Pakistan can import nuclear arsenal at will from North Korea and China whereas. India, who is supposed to depend upon her internal resources, is not allowed to develop and test nuclear missiles. The nuclear equation in South Asia could therefore, become favourable for our neighbour on the North-Western borders.

A self-imposed ban by the Indian government would not allow it to protect the naton from a nuclear war. And if we are forced to sign the CTBT, our strategic status *viz-a-viz* Pakistan would be lowered. The wars of the future would essentially incorporate nuclear weapons. But once the CTBT has been signed, India would be forced to cease all tests in nuclear parlance. Pakistan need not carry out tests as she could procure the nuclear arsenal from other nations. Therefore, Indian leaders would face a complex situation in case of a nuclear conflict between India and Pakistan.

This situation could become even more complicated with the entry of the Talibaan in the Kashmir embroglio. The recent hijack of an aircraft of Indian Airlines and death of one passenger and one militant prove that Afghanistan was another hotbed of terrorism and violence in South Asia. The USA considers Kashmir as a flashpoint for a war.

On January 4, 2000, General Pervez Musharraf threatened India and warned that Pakistan might attack India with nuclear weapons. We know that he is capable of initiating a nuclear war. An unstable State like Pakistan can always trigger wars and cross-border conflicts. Therefore, Indian leaders should accept the statements of General Musharraf in letter and spirit. Further, the USA and the UK have refused to declare Pakistan as a terrorist State. This decision of the superpowers has gone in favour of Pakistan. India should not have demanded this declaration. A terrorist State like Pakistan need not be branded as one because her implied actions automatically reveal her true identity behind the veneer of a respectable country. Indian leaders are wasting time in trifles. By declaring Pakistan a terrorist State or by imposing some economic sanctions, the objectives of the military rulers and those of the Kashmiri militants cannot be ignored. India would have to defend herself without any external political or economic support. We have always stood the tests of time due to the power of our people. Like Pakistan, we need not import Dong Feng missiles or 'smuggle' nuclear fuel or machinery from abroad. We are a self-respecting State whose subjects wish to live with dignity. In the case of Pakistan, the subjects are guided by religion in the daily lives. Their orientations are quite different from Indian psyche. We are a secular nation to the core whereas Pakistan was created in the name of religion. History has proved that the nations, which depend upon religion in order to propagate their economic and political interests, are wiped out sooner or later. Even if they exist, their citizens lead lives of misery and poverty. With the exception of same Arab nations, who are prosperous despite being deeply religious, other nations have not been able to survive solely on the basis of religion only.

India is the only free South Asian nation. Other nations are only partly free. Democracy, liberty and free market systems thrive in India. In Pakistan, there has never been a long term rule of the democratically elected governments. In the entire history of 50 years of Pakistan, military rule was imposed for 25 years. The Western States should understand this fact that their support to India would strengthen democracy and free markets of the world. Pakistan does not have the basic ingredients for succeeding as a nation. As an example, the Supreme Court of Pakistan has directed the government, in January, 2000, that the concept of charging of interest is un-Islamic. Hence, this ought to be deleted from the gamut of Pakistani economy. The apex court has directed the government of Pakistan to establish an economic system in the country that should be sans interest payments.

Therefore, Pakistan would not be able to keep pace with the changing times. India would certainly do well on economic, political, social and international platforms. Her resilience and ability to handle crises has been established. This characteristic of Indian nation would win her many a friend in the case of a conflict.

Let us study the nuclear equations in case a war is declared, overtly or covertly, between India and Pakistan. If nuclear weapons are used, the USA and Russia would not be silent spectators. China is the dark horse of the Asian subcontinent. She is likely to support Pakistan if a nuclear conflict is witnessed in South Asia. If fact, the Pakistani nuclear programme had full support of China. Further, North Korea is also likely to support Pakistan. China and North Korea could also give nuclear technologies during the war. Other nations, which could support Pakistan during the conflict, are Iran, Saudi Arabia, United Arab Emirates, Kuwait etc. These nations would support Pakistan on the pretext that Pakistan is an Islamic nation and her interests must be protected.

The list of friends of Indian masses is also long. But our friends would not be able to give us strategic support (*ie,* nuclear weapons, fighter aircraft, defence technologies, manpower, right of way through their territories *etc*). India is self-sufficient and would be able to meet the challenges of the war without any external support. We would need advance versions of Mig 29B, Sukhoi fighters, ammunition for Bofors Guns and components for maintaining the war equipment. We have purchased the defence equipment by paying according to international norms. The major arms suppliers of the world would certainly support India. For example, during the Kargil war, France suspended the delivery of fighter aircraft to Pakistan. Therefore, the French government favoured India during the Kargil War.

During the hijack drama that was enacted during the dying days of the last millennium, the Talibaan seemed to have supported Indians. But this report of Indian media is only a semi-baked observation by our correspondents. The Talibaan organisation is an inseparable ally of Pakistan and Pakistan would form a formidable front against India in the event of a nuclear war. The Talibaan cannot be made neutral in the conflict. Further, Mr Osama Bin Laden would also support his hosts if a war breaks out in the region. There is no dearth of resources in the organisation of Mr Osama Bin Laden. Hence, he could give financial support to Pakistani nuclear programme, which is the need of the hour of Pakistani exchequer.

Without any support from her friends, India would have to go through the crucial chapter of history on her own. We are respected as an independent nation. Hence, we would have to prove our mettle at the hustings. A nuclear war may not necessarily lead to a World War; in fact, there is no reason for the superpowers to join the fray. All the nations would watch the happenings silently. India on one side and the combined front of Kashmiri militants, Pakistani army, the Talibaan, and the men of Osama Bin Laden on the other side would decide the future of South Asia. The concept of Mutually Assured Destruction (MAD) would be applicable in case of a nuclear war. India could witness destruction of parts of her bread basket—Punjab—as the nuclear missiles of Pakistan have been directed against Amritsar. Similarly, Lahore could be attacked by India. Karachi, Quetta, Islamabad and Hyderabad are also the potential targets in case of conventional war or nuclear conflict Pakistanis could send their IRBMs up to Mumbai, Surat, Calcutta, Guwahati, Imphal or Srinagar. However, they would not be able to strike the South Indian States like Kerala, Tamil Nadu, Andhra Pradesh and Karnataka. The North Indian States and Kashmir would have to face the wrath of Pakistani nuclear missiles.

We are against the war but unfortunately a decisive conflict between India and her adversaries is inevitable. This may lead to some solutions but permanent solutions would still elude the major players—India and Pakistan. Both the nations are firm on their respective stands. MAD would wreak havoc on their economies but they would not change their stands. Pakistan is likely to face economic problems after the war. India would be able to overcome the economic problems due to her resilient free market system.

We can predict that a conventional military conflict could be organised between India and Pakistan in the year 2003 AD. A nuclear conflict could take place in the same year. Alternatively, a nuclear conflict could be witnessed in 2005 AD. At least a conventional war is on the cards within a few years in South Asia.

INDIAN EDUCATIONAL SCENARIO

70. SCHOOL AND SOCIETY

School is a temple of learning—The society dominated by commercialism and violence—Improper schooling responsible for the decay of student—Schools are money-making shops—They develop a degraded society—Solution lies in proper schooling without commercialism—Respect for teachers—Hardworking students Gurukul system should be combined with technology-based educational aids—School children getting involved in crimes, sex and drugs—They must be persuaded to tread the right path—Teacher should recognise talented children for their complete growth—Rational system of education is needed—Schools are the nurseries of our civilisation—They must impart practical education, which should look after societal and other vital aspects.

A school is a temple of learning. The foundation of a child is laid in a school and it is strengthened in the college and the university. A good school background helps in building the career of the student. A well-groomed child is able to contribute more towards his family, employer and society.

The society is the collection of human beings. They are the products of schooling and hence, they affect the society through their own mindset and perceptions. If the school background is good, it has a direct and positive impact on society.

However, all is not well on the societal front in India. We find people involved in commercial activities but lacking in social interactions that form the foundations of our society. Violence, drugs, inter-personal friction and a longing for the pleasure-oriented life have indicated that there must be certain flaws in the schooling of the individuals. After all, the individuals (who are now a part of the adult society), were school-going children many years ago.

Let us trace our origins to the school. In a school, we were taught to read, write, behave and act property. This is being done today as well. But most of the schools are money-making shops.

Convent schools charge exorbitant fees and donations and train us in accordance with foreign cultures. The tender mind of the child learns about the distant and unknown civilisations and assimilates them in his mind. He also learns to be more aggressive, competitive and fast in life. Disruptive behaviour and psychological disorders are common in the children of big cities. And add to it, the big burden of studies, which must be carried on in order to make a career. The agonies of children are not understood by the teachers and the parents. Their confusions remain within themselves. They do not think creatively but according to the syllabi that are taught in their classes.

Now, this child becomes an adult and starts contributing towards the society. Naturally, his frustrations, ego, mental inhibitions and reservations (earned in the school) reflect upon his actions and behaviour. So, the child builds a society, which reflects his schooling and formative years.

The era of competition, technology and wooden relationships has taken its toll. The society has degraded due to commercialism, nepotism, high-tech culture and a passion for the pleasures. Improper or snobbish schooling is responsible for this decay. It is an irony that the students of a convent school learn to waste as much as they want and do not study purposely whereas the village school cannot afford even the basic educational facilities and books for its children. The children from both these areas are not studying or learning anything.

The solution is in the hands of the society. The schools should stop following the mad rush for commercialism. Schools should be the temples of learning. Further, they should prepare the students for practical vocations. They should not inject such inputs of knowledge in their minds, which enable them to get a useless degree without any benefit. Vocational training should start at the school level itself. The relationships between the student and the teacher must be full of faith, reverence and reasoning. Teachers must give complete knowledge and students must accept it with all humility. The *Gurukul* system of ancient India should be combined with modern educational techniques.

Society should be built on the foundations of a sound educational system and proper schooling of the child. This fact must be understood clearly and at the earliest so that damage done to the society due to improper and negligent schooling could be minimised.

Our teachers are directly responsible for building a healthy society so that the nation is eventually handed over to responsible and strong individuals. And it is the responsibility of teachers to develop their students. Teachers must identify the talented students in the schools. They must inform the senior staff and Principal about the abilities of these young children. Many children have exceptional abilities in painting, drawing, mathematics, engineering, sciences, sculpture making, fashion, music and computers. The keen eye of the teacher can identity the talent of the student. If the talented students are put on the right path from their early childhood years than they would develop themselves later on due to regular and professional training. They would also be able to contribute effectively towards the economy of the nation. Many of the young school students of the past are bright engineers, scientists and artists of the present era.

Further, good school and healthy educational environment do contribute a, lot towards the development of young minds. We would be able to develop good individuals for our society only if we can give them good schooling years. It should be noted that convent education is not bad. We would support the scientific system of learning. Our contention is that our culture should never be overshadowed due to the onslaught of Western culture. In the schools of major cities, the cultural invasion by the West is complete. Now, the school-going child learns to speak English or French first and his native language seems insipid for him. We do not want him to stop learning English, French or Mathematics. However, our own culture should also be assimilated within us and the same should guide us when the Western culture fails to solve the riddles of life.

A senseless craving for sex and pornographic material, a passion for entertainment and drugs and finally, petty politics (and even violence) have taken their own toll in terms of precious academic careers. Students smoke, drink and even go to the movie theatres during the school. They try to imitate the adults and therefore, fall in the dark pits of modern culture. There are some who are able to escape this darkness but many others continue to drag on till they finally arrive in the crime world. These children are not able to complete their schooling and hence, are confused about their future. If requisite parental support is not given, these children become criminals and hooligans. After all, every smuggler was a child during early years of his life. He could have been caught in the crime dragnet due to some mistakes committed by him during his early childhood. Similarly, reasons could be identified with respect to other criminals in our society.

The State has accepted the free market system as the guiding force in all the spheres. Therefore, education is no exception to the rules of the modern era. This has created more opportunities for the students in terms of jobs, careers and growth. But it has also created chaos and confusion in the young and tender minds; they are unable to choose careers in which, they would be efficient. Our society does not accept an individual without a degree. Hence, every student is working hard for getting an entry into a college. Further, our society respects engineers, doctors and professionals. Hence, all the students are working hard for professional courses. There is no career counselling and proper guidance for the students. They are on their own so far as their career-building exercise is concerned. Parents can supply only the funds and have an apathetic attitudes towards their children. They are busy in their offices, entertainment activities and household chores. They ignore their children who need their guidance on academic, extracurricular and moral fronts.

We must conclude by stating that schools and society are deeply related as the schools satisfy the complex objectives of the nations in terms of human resources. Societal decay has started due to the decay of the educational system in our country. Too much commercialism, satellite television and Westernisation have done more harm than good. The only solution is the adoption of the correct education policies, training of students about moral values and finally, the introduction of career-oriented curricula in the schools. Empathy and not coercion, could save our students. Schools are the nurseries of our civilisation. If the nurseries are healthy and morally upright, the final crops would be assets the society and for the nation.

71. INDIAN EDUCATION AT THE CROSSROADS

Every Individual needs education—Necessary for survival and growth—Knowledge can be divided into natural sciences, social sciences, technology and vocational studies—Indian education had a glorious past—At present, the scenario is grim—Syllabi are theoretical—Teachers not working hard on students—Lack of resources, infrastructure and facilities—First educational policy in 1968 and second policy in 1986—NPE (1986)—Revised in 1992—Privatisation, reservations lack of resources created problems for educational system—10 + 2 + 3 system of education adopted but not very effective—Must take serious steps.

Every individual has a basic right for education in all the societies. Knowledge is required for a better understanding of the world around us and for solving the problems related to our survival and growth. Further, we need a strong knowledge base so that we could earn a decent living either through employment or entrepreneurship. Finally, we need education for knowing the ultimate truth in life—why we are in this world and what God expects us to do during our lifetimes ?

During ancient times, man lived on the basis of day-and-night cycles, movement of wind and water, superstitions and agricultural produce. He used laws of nature but in a very crude manner. For example, a boat or a raft used to move across a river or a pond is nothing but the application of principle of science.

Further, as the human society migrated from villages to cities, social interactions and human problems came to the fore. This necessitated the need for social sciences. The natural sciences (chemistry, physics, botany, zoology, biology, astronomy, nuclear physics *etc*) formed the basis of human knowledge over a period of centuries. There were developments in social sciences also during the middle ages (history, political science *etc*). During the modern ages and especially after the middle of sixties of the last century, the application of sciences was in vogue and we call it technology now a days. The acquisition, correlation, transmission and further enhancement of natural sciences, social sciences and technology are considered to be the basic functions of education.

Keeping in mind the pace of growth of human society, we must also add 'vocation' to the existing set of knowledge streams. A vocation is a practical course of training in a particular field of technology that develops a human brain for performing a technical task at high speeds and with great precision. Thus the total number of streams of knowledge at the verge of the next millennium are four in number—natural sciences, social sciences, technology and vocational studies.

Education in any one of the afore-mentioned categories should develop a spirit of inquisitive thinking and technical or logical application of the knowledge base acquired.

It may he noted that a knowledge base, which fails to produce concrete and constructive results for the human society, ecology and the universe, must be discarded for good. For example, nuclear bombs were dropped over Hiroshima and Nagasaki and have proved beyond doubt that they are the weapons of death and destruction. Hence, nuclear weapons must be discarded by all the nations. However, we should always support peaceful applications of nuclear energy (for example, we need a nuclear power reactor). In sum, educational system must be tuned to the modern needs of the society and the mother earth. At the same time, it should teach basic moral values, integrity and sophisticated traits that human race is supposed to develop in order to distinguish itself from other living species of the planet.

In India, we had a glorious past in terms of academics. During the ancient times, Indian educational centres and universities were the temples of immense knowledge. Students used to study at Texila, Patliputra and Ujjaini. The popular subjects included sciences, medicine, spiritualism, astrology, philosophy, politics, economics *etc.* Even students from abroad used to study at these reputed institutions of learning. There were exchanges of students, knowledge and books. Indian educational system was respected around the world for its high quality syllabi and learned teachers. However, past did not project itself into the future. British, Mughals, Pathans, Afghans, Persians, Macedonians and Aryans attacked this country from time to time. Some settled here while others took away whatever they could. This disturbed our economy, educational system and polity. When we became independent, we had no infrastructure or financial resources left for education. Everything had to be started from scratch.

There was an humble beginning after independence and partition. Syllabi were theoretical in nature. Teaching methods were primitive. Examination system was based on the British educational pattern. We followed Lord McCaulay's system of education, which had no relevance in our social or cultural milieu. In fact, educational system of McCaulay tried to produce clerks who were required to support British administration in India. That system was supposed to perpetuate loyalty for British educational and political institutions. During the pre-Independence era, there were convent schools but they were meant only for the British diplomats, Indian royalties or those who could afford high fees and Christian culture for their children. Even after this era was gone, our students did not do well on the educational front. They were casual about their careers, irresponsible, directionless and above all, impractical about the application of the knowledge they had. An arts graduate should be an artist; at least, he should not work as a clerk. However, the graduates of today are mostly lower division clerks, typists or peons.

The first policy document on education was adopted in 1968. The National Education Policy (1968) had an aim of promoting national progress, developing a sense of common citizenship and building national integration. It emphasised upon greater attention to sciences, technology and moral values. It also called for a closer association between education and the life of people. But the draft (of 1968) of the educational policy failed to deliver concrete results. However, some of the achievements of NPE (1968) could be summarised as follows :—

(1) Common system of education in the entire country.
(2) Introduction of 10 + 2 + 3 system by most of the states.
(3) Inclusion of science and mathematics as compulsory subjects.
(4) Restructuring of the courses at the undergraduate levels for more understanding.
(5) Establishment of centres of advance studies for post-graduation and research.

The new National Policy on Education was approved by Parliament in May, 1986. The "Programme of Action" for implementing the new policy was adopted by the government in August 1986. This policy is based on a document known as "A Challenge of Education : A Perspective" and was presented by the then Education Minister in Parliament on August 20, 1985. The document stated that Indian education was at the crossroads. The catalytic role of education in the process of our national development had to be planned carefully and executed with precautions. It further stated that the future held great tensions and opportunities in store for us.

If the new generation wants to be benefited from the new and challenging environments, it must have the abilities to develop and implement new ideas consistently. The new generation must also have a strong commitment to human values and social justice. All this requires educational standards and practices of highest quality.

The new Education Policy had stated that all the students, irrespective of caste, creed, location or sex, should have an access to education of good standards. The system would have a basic or a common core of subjects. It would be supplemented with other flexible components that could be designed or chosen depending upon regional or local needs.

In higher education—and especially in technical educational streams—every Indian would get equal opportunities based only on his merit. The illiteracy of women would be removed and they would be given at least elementary education throughout the nation. Major thrust would be on their vocational, technical and professional education. Scheduled Castes and Scheduled Tribes would be given advantages *viz-a-viz* their previleged counterparts. The mentally handicapped children and adults would also be treated at par with their normal brothers and sisters. Adult education programme would be given emphasis. Continuing education would also be emphasised upon in rural and urban areas. The new policy also called for promotion of post-secondary educational institutions, books, radio, television, films, distance learning programmes and vocational training courses. The new policy put major emphasis on:

(a) universal enrolment and retention of children of the age of 14 years; and

(b) considerable improvement in the quality of education.

The National Policy on Education (NPE-1986) also planned to launch "Operation Blackboard" for imparting high-quality education in primary schools. It also planned to supply better equipment and facilties to the primary schools. It introduced a non-formal form of education for school dropouts, working children and those girls who could not attend whole day schools.

In 1985-86, *Navodaya Vidyalayas* were started—one in each district of the country. These were fully residential and co-educational schools upto 10 + 2 level and were affiliated to CBSE. There are 359 sanctioned *Vidyalayas* operating in 30 states and union territories.

NPE (1986) also put emphasis on vocational education after secondary stage. The NPE (1986) was revised in 1992. It set the target of achieving a diversion of 10 per cent of the students at 10 + 2 level to vocational courses by 1995 and diversion of 25 per cent by 2000 AD. A Joint Council of Vocational Education (JCVE) was set up in April, 1990, for policy formulation.

The other important features of NPE (1992) were as follows :—

(1) Good equipment and facilities would be provided for colleges and universities.

(2) Researches would be promoted in all the academic disciplines.

(3) The open university system would be started. Indira Gandhi National Open University would be promoted among the masses.

(4) Degrees would be delinked from jobs. For getting jobs, university education would not be made mandatory.

(5) Technical and management education would be made more cost effective and within the reach of common man.

(6) The computer literacy programme would begin from schools and would go up to the university level. This initiative was implemented in 1993-94 by making computer education compulsory in schools.

(7) The school children would be trained to develop sensitivity towards beauty, harmony and abstract things in life. They would also be exposed to the cultural heritage of India.

(8) Relationship would be developed between the university system and the institutions of higher learning in art, Oriental studies, archeology and related subjects.

(9) Books would be provided to the students for all courses and from all economic levels at reasonable rates.

(10) Teachers would be recruited and trained for the herculean task of countrywide educational programme. They would be selected strictly on merit.

(11) District Institutes of Education and Training (DIET) would be set up for the organisation of pre-service and in-service courses for elementary school teachers and for teachers involved in adult education.

The new educational policy asked for funds from the centre, state governments and donations from across the nation. It was also proposed that fees could be raised for some courses. The union government budgets, over a period of years, have shown rising outlays for education. The government also started Free Meal Scheme for primary school children throughout the nation. In all the government schools, education is free till class VIII. Even after this level, the fees are very reasonable and within the spending powers of the poor masses. The action plan of the government includes the following :—

(1) Better pay packages for and better accountability of teachers.
(2) Better services for students.
(3) Expectation of better behaviour from students.
(4) Provision of better facilties for the institutions.
(5) Development of an effective performance appraisal system for the institutions.

The new policy was accepted by the nation wholeheartedly as it had a noble cause. However, as we are aware, the concrete results on educational front have yet to be achieved. Some of the glaring disasters in the educational scene in India are :—

(1) Student unrest, violence and confusion have increased over the past few years. The youth is unable todifferentiate between good and bad aspects of our social, educational and economic systems. The educational system gives degrees, which are useless. Unemployment is on the rise. The curricula are not practice-oriented or career-oriented.
(2) Non-formal education can never compete with formal education as the educational base of the student remains incomplete in case of non-formal education.
(3) *Navodaya* schools have created disparities.
(4) The new policy promotes privatisation of education. Hence, commercialism has crept in. Educational institutions are minting money in the name of importing knowledge (which

is of poor standards) and degrees (which have no market value for getting a good job).

(5) States like Bihar continue to be the backwaters of our educational system. Copying, violence during examinations and total disregard for the teachers, syllabi and the educational norms have brought Bihar on the brink of total educational fiasco. The North-Eastern states also lack educational institutions, equipment and good teachers. As a result, the North-Eastern region is terror-prone, sans good opportunities for jobs or self-employment and is lagging in industrial and economic progress. All this is due to an absence of good educational facilities.

(6) The policy in vogue proposes to cut down on subsidies. That would mean that the students may have to bear (at least to some extent) their educational expenses. The rich can afford to spend more on their education but the poor cannot. Therefore, a vital niche of the population of students may miss opportunities for studies.

(7) The reservation policy is supposed to work for the academic and economic upliftment of the *Dalits*. However, the rich *Dalits* always bag the best seats in engineering, medical and other professional courses. In our view, reservation policy should be scrapped. The students should be admitted to all the courses on the basis on their past performances, written tests and interviews. They must be judged according to fixed norms, which should be common in all the states. We can give weightage to the students according the economic criteria during the selection process. But religion and caste must be eliminated from our educational system. This policy has done more harm than good. According to the economic criterion, the candidate, beside having sound eligibility and scores for a given curriculum, must submit an affidavit that he or she belongs to a poor family. The reservation should be done according to various income brackets and not according to the divisions of caste or religion.

(8) The trend, now a days, is for a stint of 2-4 years of education abroad. Our young students go to the USA, the UK, Australia

and New Zealand and never come back. The educational system abroad is pragmatic and builds careers of the youth. Our educational system is theoretical, hackneyed and needs serious revamping exercise. It must be made clear that 80 per cent of education has to be job-oriented. Only 20 per cent of the education has to be research oriented. Research scholars must be encouraged but only those researches should be undertaken by students (in India and abroad), which could contribute effectively towards technology, engineering, social sciences, nuclear science and space research.

(9) Our educational system is not linked with Indian industry and business. This lack of continuity between the two major engines of growth has proved to be harmful for our national economic and industrial growth. Education should be planned keeping the requirements of industry and business in mind. Similarly, industry must supply relevant inputs (money, training, equipment *etc*) so that educational system remains tuned to the needs of the industry and business.

The educational policy has yet to deliver a concrete output at the state and national levels.

72. PRIVATE COACHING INSTITUTES

Private Coaching institutions help school students, college students and students of competition examinations—The history of private coaching traced—Schools and colleges not adequate for competitions and regular syllabi—The private institutes charge heavy fees and many poor students leave there jobs and join these courses but later, disappointed—Our educational system has faults—No immediate solutions—A fresh educational policy and reforms are needed—Educational policy and reforms are needed—Education is a pious field—Do not let it decay—The State has to play a major role for reversing the decay process.

Education has got a new definition in the new millennium—get ready to earn. This rule has changed all the facets of education. Today, education is not imparted to the students for the sake of knowledge but for the sake of giving them brand names, which are so essential for their growth in their careers and lives. These brand names include a 10 + 2 course from a reputed (five-star) school, admission into a professional educational institution, a job in a multinational or educational stint abroad. Some affluent parents are able to settle their children abroad by helping them get lucrative jobs. And how does all this happen ? Simple ! They push their children or wards to the limits of academic excellence. And how do they effect it ? Another simple answer—they do it by getting them trained at the private coaching institutes.

Private coaching was confined only to the four major metropolises and fifty minor cities of the nation during the early sixties. Those times were not competitive. Now a days, man has to pay through his nose even to breathe. The educational standards in the government schools were good during the sixties but these fell sharply by the mid-seventies. Therefore, the students rushed towards "public schools." The public schools did well during the seventies as money was not the major consideration even for them (during those times). However, the seventies saw the rise of commercialism, materialism and individualism in the West. Indians are fond of copying the Western norms and so they did. Indian educational system became Westernised. Public schools came to be known as the temples of knowledge. Government schools lost their grandeur and it was lapped up by the public schools (our reader should not assume that public schools are government schools; in fact, public schools are those schools that are operated and maintained by private societies and there is always a hidden element of profit in their operations).

The number of admissions in public schools increased; government schools lost all the gloss. But as the public schools became overcrowded, the teachers lost interest in their teaching jobs. At the same time, the syllabi of the senior classes were upgraded. The students opted for private coaching and called teachers at their homes. The school teachers happily obliged.

But this trend did not stop here. A teacher cannot teach for more than 8 hours a day. So, demand for good teachers, spurred by requirements of competitive examinations and difficult subjects of science, mathematics, accounts and drawing, reached new heights. Therefore, in order to meet the rising demand, some senior teachers, started operating the coaching institutes for schools. This happened in the end of eighties. When schools education was forward to coaching centres, college education was also sent along the same route. The students were happy as they studied in groups and paid lesser than when they paid as individual students. The teachers were happy as they earned enough in one month, which was more than double of their salaries of 6 months. The schools and colleges were also relieved of the teaching assignments. "Please come to my residence in the evening !" was the popular sentence quoted by many a teacher. And the student would understand that the teacher would tell him the basics of mathematics or physics only if he joined his coaching classes in the evening.

Private coaching is going on full swing in all the four major metropolises and the 450 small and medium cities of this country. The teachers have earned millions through this "education wave." Many students have got the benefit of such type of coaching. There are toppers in various disciplines who ascertain that they could make it to the highest echelons of academic excellent because they had private coaching. There are nearly 25,000 private coaching institutes and professionals. The average teacher, in Delhi and its surrounding areas of the National Capital Region, earns Rs 6,000 to Rs 30,000 per month, besides his salary from the school, the college or the university. An average teacher charges Rs 80 for a student of class VIII, Rs 90 for a student of class IX and Rs 100 for a student of class XII, while he teaches for one hour. For higher classes, the rates vary from Rs 125 per hour per subject to Rs 300 per hour per subject. These incomes are never shown in the calculations of income tax. Hence, these are unaccounted for earnings of the coaches.

The late eighties saw an orientation of the students towards preparation of competitive examinations. The IITs, the IIMs, engineering colleges, medical colleges as well as the courses in management, architecture and fashion technology led to a growth in the field of coaching for competitive examinations. The late eighties saw the mushrooming of these specialised institutes in New Delhi, Mumbai, Calcutta and Chennai. Other cities followed suit and today, we have good and bad institutes in all the nooks and corners of the country that prepare the students for glorious careers. Further, many institutions also prepare the candidates for CA, ICWA, CS, GMAT, SAT, GRE and TOEFL tests and examinations. Many students have gained knowledge and qualifications. There are many successful candidates who are either studying abroad or have been placed abroad, after they were trained in these institutes. These institutes train the students for fees that range from Rs 3,000 per month to Rs 1,50,000 per annum. The actual amount of fee depends upon the type of course, the level of training and the duration for which, the candidate would like to study.

We do not censure these institutions. They have been able to deliver excellent results; the examples of school-going students as well as those of collegiates give ample evidence that these institutions do give high-quality training. Many professional trainers, managers, engineers and scientists have joined these institutions and their extremely high knowledge levels are a delight for those students who learn from them.

However, there are some limitations of these institutions. All the institutions do not offer high-quality education. Let us take the example of computer training. There are many institutions that offer 'excellent' training in computers and IT but no one offers enough of "computer laboratory time." They want to expose the students to computers and for practice, they expect the students to have their own computer systems. The poor students cannot buy computers. So, they lose money and do not get valuable and constructive computer time.

Further, some institutions offer courses that might help the students get jobs. But most of the students do not get jobs; they get nicely printed certificates and that is all.

Thirdly, some institutions charge exorbitant fees from their students. Many students are unable to afford. On the other hand, many students, who belong to the rich strata of the society, come only for gossiping or for making friends. They waste time of others. They do not seem to be interested in knowledge or careers. Others suffer while they relish the niceties of "mini campuses."

Finally, many students leave their jobs or academic curricula and join these courses in the hope of getting a (fake) degree or clearing a competitive examination. It they able to get through their efforts and inputs are worth appreciation. But many students are left behind. They spoil their careers and lose their jobs. They continue to struggle for the rest of their lives.

We would like to mention the case of students who go to the schools and later, in the evening, go to the coaching centres. The physical and mental demands on them are so high that they feel completely exhausted at the end of the day. Is this the real concept of education ? Is education meant for cramming and getting 'good' marks in the examination ? What about the knowledge levels and mental development of the students ? Could these be developed at the coaching centres ? The answer is an emphatic No !

There are no immediate solutions for this education mania, primarily spurred by the faulty educational system and perpetrated by the intelligentsia of this country who know more then their junior generations. Gone are the days when one used to respect his teacher due to his knowledge level. Today, teacher is 'paid' or 'pampered' because he either knows the contents of the next examination or can help the student get excellent marks in the entire set of examinations. Morality in education is a distant dream due to the fact that the element of immorality has been added by the wrong educational system and the corrupt educationists. This decay would continue unless the State takes concrete measures and effects strict educational reforms. The pious principles of education seem to be timid before the ever-rising wave of commercialism. Private educational institutions are having a great time now a days. And Indian education, as usual, is at its nadir. Who would reverse this trend ? ●

73. HIGHER EDUCATION IN INDIA

Higher education is a must—Colleges and universities throughout India impart higher education—University Education Commission set up in 1948—In 1976, education was a State subject—Even during the eighties, 80 per cent of higher education was financed by the state or central governments—Nineties saw privatisation and entry of foreign universities in India—Competence and competition are the keywords for success today—Privatisation could also deprive poor students education as they may not be able to afford it—Strong educational institutions would have a major role to play whereas poor ones would be sidelined—Privatisation would eliminate corruption and bureaucratic delays as well—Some suggestions appended.

Higher education for the elite mind, the professional and the intellectual is a must. A post-graduate or a doctoral qualification enables the individual to search for the unknown and makes him more useful in his profession. A graduate degree is not a proof of specialisation and in this competitive world, specialisation is the key to success in any field.

Take for example, the case of a doctor with MBBS degree. He is a respected figure in the society. He has taken a hypocratic oath to serve the humanity. He would do everything to save the life of a patient. However, nobody would like him to operate open his kith or kin if a doctor with MS degree is available (at higher price and from a far-off place) for treatment. Why ? Because MS is a specialisation nobody can ignore for the sake of his near and dear ones. This brings us to the main issue of higher education. We do not need higher education for the sake of degrees and glossy academic awards. We need higher education for solving the riddles of AIDS, surgery, engineering, architecture, sciences and other branches of knowledge. We need higher education so that our posterity could grapple with the problems that would face them tomarrow. We need the same for building a better society. We need more knowledge about this universe in order to solve our material and spiritual problems. Education is the only way for getting over the ocean of problems we are in.

Higher education in India is being imparted by many colleges and universities. The State understood the need for professional and higher education and has taken vital steps for imparting higher education of high quality. However, it is sad to note that all the regions and pockets of the country do not impart high quality education to Indian students and professionals. Therefore, the students are tempted to go abroad and study. Some even settle down in the country of learning. The real loss is for the country that spends a lot on these talented young people.

After independence, a need for quality education was felt by our national leaders. A University Education Commission was set up under the chairmanship of Dr Radha Krishnan in 1948. The commission observed that a central authority for allocating recurring and capital grants to the universities from the centre was necessary. On the recommendations of the Commission in 1953, University Grants Commission (UGC) was set up. UGC funds universities and colleges in the fields of arts, sciences and humanities. The states were also supposed to look after higher education.

However, the educational needs of a vast country like those of India are diverse as well as complex. Partnership and financial contribution of centre, states and private educational managements are inevitable. Until 1976, education was a State subject. However coordination, determination of standards of the institutions for higher education and research *etc* were under the purview of the central government. After 1976, the requirements of funds of educational entities connected to central government, state governments and the private players become more prominent.

Privatisation of higher education has always been an issue of serious debate. As on date, 80 per cent of all enrolments in the institutions are financed and governed by the state governments or by the centre. However, with the advent of professional training institutions in the early eighties and also, with the mushrooming of new private educational players from India and abroad, the trends are pointing towards the possible privatisation of higher education.

Let us discuss some of the benefits of this concept. Firstly, the educational system would become more competent and efficient. Only good students would be able to make it to professional post-graduate, doctoral and post-doctoral courses. Ph D theses would not be mere typed materials churned out for the sake of degrees. They would be research oriented. Doctors would be awarded degrees only if they are capable of saving the lives of patients. The entire educational set up would be sans bureaucratic delays. The best would come to the fore and the rest would be discarded. Secondly, private sector participation in educational sector would lead to more campus recruitments. Unemployment would be reduced. The corporate firms would be keen to take candidates from those institutions that they support. The candidates, groomed for professional jobs in the post-graduate educational curricula, would get better salaries and would have a bright future. Thirdly, if the students are offered good educational and career opportunities, they would not be tempted to go abroad. As a result, brain drain would be minimised. Finally, privatisation of education has already brought foreign universities on the educational scenario of India. An Indian student can get the best degrees and knowledge from these institutions. He has only to spend a year or two in a foreign country. Rest of the curriculum would be completed by the branch of the foreign educational institution in India. Money is also saved and latest concepts are also imparted to our students.

The negative points of privatisation of higher education would have far-reaching effects on our economy and society. Let us analyse this aspect in detail. The situation, as on date, is quite fluid. The states give grant-in-aid to private affiliated colleges. They also supply funds to many universities. So, a large number of students is able to get professional and higher education at low costs. Parents have to pay a minimal fee which is reasonable. The pay-scales of the teachers have also been hiked *wef* July, 1998, as was promised by Dr Murali Manohar Joshi, the Minister of Education in the centre. If the states withdraw these funds and subsidies, the students would have to pay more. Today, 85 per cent of the students are pursuing higher education in the country. Further 80 per cent of the affiliated colleges are private institutions. Thus the needy students would be deprived of higher education. Further, the privatisation of higher education would lead to dirty competition in the educational sector of India. The corporate players would pump funds into the reputed institutions, leaving the ordinary ones. That is because, they would seek benefits and favours (either in cash or in kind) from these institutions. The divide between the 'haves' and "have nots" would be widened. A financially strong educational institution would command better resources, get better teaching faculty and demand more fees from the students. A financially weak institution would not be able to command a good price in the market. The free market winds would ultimately take the poor and needy students for a ride.

Privatisation of higher educations would eliminate corruption, bureaucracy and red-tape, a phenomenon associated with the functioning of all the systems promoted and managed by the State. But this efficient system would be full of snobbery. Rich students would sneer at the poor ones. The gap between the rich and the poor students, which is not visible now, would be prominent. This could lead to large scale violence, riots, strikes and arson. The students would be actively involved in dirty politics, which would be supported and funded by the private sector and corrupt politicians.

In sum, the privatisation of higher education is inevitable. However, we would not recommend complete privatisation in the interest of the poor and the needy students. India is an illiterate nation and lacks resources for uplifting her masses from the lowest levels of poverty, economic backwardness and social chaos.

Privatisation of higher education should be done in such a manner as would ensure that poor but talented students do not suffer. On the other hand, private sector participation would generate more employment opportunities and participation with the industrial sector.

Some suggestions have been appended as follows :—

(1) Human resource is the most precious asset for a society or a nation. Higher education develops the human resource of a country. Indian educational scenario can get a big boost if private sector participates in the activities of funding, equipment, technology, training and manpower absorption. The private sector would naturally have its own axe to grind. However, the overall impact on our education (and on our economy) would be healthy.

(2) The private sector players could send generous donations through taxes and not directly.

(3) The rich students should be told to pay more fees. Secondly, they should not ask for scholarships or research grants. The funds saved due to this measure could be channelised for meeting the educational needs of the poor students.

(4) No new colleges or educational institutions should be set up. Only engineering colleges, medical colleges and vocational institutions for imparting technical education should be started wherever these are required.

(5) The educational institutions should be able to generate their own revenues through engineering consultancy, vocational jobs and management consultancy assignments. The students of the respective educational institutions should be allowed to work on such projects. The culture of "earn while you learn" should be made a part and parcel of our higher educational policy.

(6) International financial institutions could extend a helping hand on easy terms for educational reforms in India. There is no harm in accepting the educational norms of the world and there should be no problem in accepting their financial support for the sake of our educational upgradation. A well-trained student, graduating from a professional or higher educational institute, would contribute more effectively

towards Indian economy. He would either work in a firm or for a PSU or would set up an enterprise that would generate more jobs. The global financial community should be made aware of this fact.

We can conclude that the higher education scenario in India has changed for a better future for students of this country. However, the State and the educational institutes must join hands for a student-oriented system of higher education. Participation of the corporate sector, reputed educationists, NGOs and individuals is welcome as this step would support our commitment to a free market world. ●

74. EDUCATION IN OUR SCHOOLS

RGICS introduced the curriculum of economic reforms in some schools of Delhi—The student is already overburdened—Sans natural growth—The burdened minds cannot develop—Too many books, syllabi and procedures—Senior class students subjected to tortures—Studying useless subjects that would not lead to any knowledge in their disciplines—Accept five-day academic session—Upgrade the syllabi but keep them simple in language and understanding—Start structured education after Class VIII.

During July, 1998, a new educational concept was born. The Rajiv Gandhi Institute of Contemporary Studies (RGICS), under the aegis of Rajiv Gandhi Foundation, is seeking a total change in the curriculum of the vital subject of economics in schools. This experiment began in July, 1998, on a trial basis when RGICS wrote to 30 schools of Delhi and asked for changing the curriculum of economics. Out of those 30 schools, 20 schools showed interest in the project. The institute worked hard towards its coveted goal and decided to hold six sessions per school. The subjects included a host of topics related to economic reforms currently going on in India. A few examples included Rupee devaluation, disinvestments, PSUs and above all, economic reforms.

This example has been cited in order to depict the poor state of affairs of our educational system. We do not object to the upgradation of the syllabi according to the latest international norms. However, the young mind of the child can assimilate the complex principles only up to a limit. Already, our young citizen is over-burdened with books of mathematics, English, sciences and computers. Economics would be too heavy for him to digest. We cannot recommend the advanced economics curricula for the senior secondary classes as the students of arts and commerce are overloaded in these classes as well.

One-fifth of primary school children, in the developing nations, are out of schools. About one-fifth do not get enough of energy and proteins. Nearly 850 million people in the developing nations are illetrate. If their creative talents and abilities are nipped in the bud, then how would they manage such a vast nation when the baton is over to them handed ?

Our educational system is sans a rational and logical programme. We are churning out students and not learned minds who would be keen to learn more in the colleges or universities. The overburdened child refuses to study or play. He is under constant stress and reports quite often that he has headache or fatigue. He ignores social circles. He avoids social interactions. His poor marks are a bane for him and he never sits on the front-bench in his class. His young and innocent mind longs for freedom but the rotten system forces him to take classes and to appear in examinations. He could even get swayed by the wrong company and could take up smoking, drugs and liquor as his routine habits. The decay starts at an early age and the vices remain with him throughout his life. He is not understood at home; there are no empathisers. He is scolded for poor marks a lack of attention; the teacher is harsh on him everyday as he has no sympathy for the mentally weak students. So, the child longs for love and soothing company. Drugs, tobacco and liquor give him the 'solace' and an escape from his problems.

This society is not developing our children but is destroying their careers. Many young students who failed in their tests and examinations, could have become artists, sculptors and painters of repute. After all, Rabindra Nath Tagore had no formal education and he won the Nobel Prize for literature !

The solutions to this most critical problem must be devised and implemented quickly. Some of the solutions are as follows :—

(A) The educational institutions, especially the private schools, must stop charging exorbitant fees from the students. They should allow the poor students to be admitted in their schools so that talent could be identified from all the strata of the society. Recently, the administration has taken concrete steps under the aegis of which, the public schools in Delhi would not be able to charge fees beyond a ceiling.

(B) The academic sessions should be designed in such a manner as would ensure that there would be teaching for only five days in a week (some schools have already accepted a five-day norm). There should not be long holiday stints like the autumn break. It has been observed that the students waste their holidays. They are more confused and less organised as a result of long durations of absence from the schools.

(C) Senior students (*ie*, the students of classes X, XI and XII should attend their classes for six days a week. Their curricula are tough and very lengthy. These students must be allocated more time and attention by the teachers.

(D) The curricula must be upgraded as has been done by RGICS in the case of economics. But economic reforms and free market economics would be too heavy to digest even for a class XII student. The syllabi must be upgraded very carefully. If need be, the length of the courses should be reduced and chapters related to environment, sciences, ecology, civic life, mathematics and general knowledge should be added.

(E) The chief limitation of school education is that the students are forced to learn those subjects that they would never like to study in future. When the basic streams have already been decided in class XI, then there is no need to study those subjects that the student would never study. For example, a science student should study English, mathematics, physics, chemistry and any elective subject (to be selected by the candidate). There is no need to study any other subject because the attention of the student would be diverted from his main subjects. Basic information about those subjects (that are not being studied) should be provided in a nutshell up to Class X.

(F) The educational system is highly structured. We would suggest that the education upto class VII should not have structured curricula. It should be made structured from class

VIII onwards. The students upto class VII should be allowed to develop themselves on the basis or *Shantiniketan* pattern promoted by Rabindra Nath Tagore. The student of class VIII is mature enough to accept the academic responsibilities and hence, he should be offered highly structured and reasonably difficult syllabi.

The free and young minds of our school children have been chained to tough syllabi, procedures and stresses of the examinations. They want to come out of their academic shells and do not want to be mere bookworms. They should be groomed for life and not for degrees. Education should be pragmatic, slow and vocation oriented. Our policy-makers must resort to serious educational reforms in the interest of a better nation. Our children deserve a better academic treatment for their bright future.

75. VOCATION ORIENTED EDUCATIONAL SYSTEM

Our educational system based on Western sytem but we have many limitations—More opportunities for semi-skilled jobs—Students should be sent to vocational stream or research stream depending upon their aptitude and talents—Restructuring required—In rural areas, vocation oriented edcational system could eliminate rural unemployment and poverty—In urban centres, good opportunities for telecommunications, computers and Internet—Exports and Imports are also growth areas—Graduates from vocational institutes contribute towards to national economy—For globally oriented economy, vocational education is a must.

Our education system is based on the Western system of schooling. Our mentality and intelligence levels have been tuned according to the educational formats of the West. The Western system of education has advantages as well as disadvantages. However, there is an inherent disadvantage in our educational system. We tend to educate students for useless knowledge. Education imparted in our schools and colleges does not help the students in making their careers or earning a decent living. Now a days, there is a glut of arts graduates, doctors, engineers, chartered accountants and architects in India. Most of them are struggling for boarding a ship that they could call their own. Education has not given them directions; there is only darkness in store for them.

Further, the educational system in the West has also become vocation-based. That means that the students pass their basic schooling levels and then, they go on to complete a semi-skilled course of their choice—engineering, medicine, paramedical streams, arts, print media, nursing, computer operations *etc*—and then, they take up jobs in industry or business. There are students who take up serious studies and go on to clear competitions and even go abroad. Out of these students, the most studious ones take up Ph D or D Litt in the reputed universities. These students become reputed scientists, spacecraft engineers, doctors and professors in reputed Western universities. Thus the Western educational system caters to the needs of all types of students.

In India too, we must have vocation-oriented and research-oriented courses. Most of the students are interested in settling down in decent middle management jobs. For these students, vocation-based education should be made compulsory. For the senior level professionals, Indian colleges and universities have ample number of courses to offer. For higher studies like the Ph D, only a few students should be selected and they should be taught either in selected Indian universities or they should be sent abroad.

Our educational system needs serious re-structuring for eliminating unemployment, poor knowledge levels and economic imbalances in Indian society. The State, the educational institutions and the students from all the disciplines should understand the need of the hour and should change the present educational system into a pragmatic, job oriented and specialised knowledge-based system. This would help the family, the economy and finally, the nation.

We must plan our vocational education system on the basis of needs of Indian populace. Our economy is agriculture-based. Therefore, agricultural industries have bright future. Therefore, farm products processing, beverage manufacture, processing of horticulture products and other agro-based activities would be suitable in rural areas. The rural youth must be trained for occupational skills in rural and farm sectors. The rural institutes should train the youth for developing job-oriented skills in farming, agriculture, horticulture, natural fertilisers, natural pest control, bio-mass technologies, *Gobar-gas* plants, seeds development, agricultural machinery and other related fields. This would lead to more productivity in the rural and agricultural sectors, less unemployment and an overall improvement in the rural economy. Further, enterprising rural youth could be given loans by the state governments so that they could start small-scale agro-based industries. These industries could generate more employment and production if they are managed efficiently.

In urban areas, the most popular vocations are computer software, secretarial practice, refrigeration, automobile repair, denting and painting, electrical repairs, civil construction, electronic products repairs and servicing, transportation services, telecommunications engineering, marine engineering and international trade. These fields have tremendous potential for growth in India. Our economy is being tuned in accordance with the *modus operandi* of the major economies aof the world. We must learn new skills like computer programming, Internet operations, Internet webpage designing and programming, systems programming, SAP, telecommunication technologies, latest automobiles technologies etc.

Another area is environment. The vocational courses in this vital sector would be offered to the candidates in the near future. The trained environmental techniques would help maintain the human and animal habitats for the sake of a better life of the residents of the only living planet.

Vocational system should train the students in a specialised stream within a period of three years. The student can then, go to his respective industry and can learn the tricks of the trade through on-the-job training. There is no need to feed him with the useless theory and the knowledge base that he does not need in his occupation. This is the era of specialisation. The student must develop exptertise in one or two fields and should start earning after he has been exposed to the basic techniques of his profession.

The growth rates of the economy and productivity are directly governed by the toil and efficiency of the vocation-oriented workers in farming, agriculture, industry and services sectors. New technologies have opened new vistas for students as the number of vocations is much more and very interesting. Examples could be quoted of Internet, telecommunications, exports and imports, mechanical engineering, refrigeration engineering and consumer electronics.

The economic and social canvasses of our nation are being transformed due to the process of economic liberalisation, new technologies, changing value systems and addition of materialistic hues. During the first week of March, 2000, Indian economy looked up. Kargil war was over and Indian industries were heading for better productivity and profits. The stress is on productivity, efficiency and international orientation. Vocation-oriented educational system would be a sound proposition for eliminating unemployment, social unrest and rural poverty. Moreover, our economy would be able to match national and international challenges due to free market waves that are sweeping across the globe. Vocation-oriented education is therefore, the need of the order.

76. EDUCATIONAL SYSTEM OF THE FUTURE

Education must for every society—Indian education system not very beneficial for the masses—The aims of education are pious and ambitious—Kerala's literacy level is 100 per cent but their operational levels are compatible with low grade office jobs only—Only a few professionals in Kerala—There should be seven basic types—(a) Basic education upto 10 + 2 level—(b) Graduation level (arts)—(c) Post-graduation level (arts)—(d) Professional level (technical graduates)—(e) Professional level (technical post graduates)—(f) Vocational studies—(g) The illiterate masses programme—The future educational system should be pragmatic, vocation- oriented, economical for masses and merit based.

Education is the distinctive indenty of every society or nation. It is the most important task for human resource development of any country. India had a glorious educational past. However, the educational trends are now in favour of Western education. Indian masses are lagging behind in this vital field and even the developing countries are having on edge over us. The basic objective of education is to help the individual and adjust with his surroundings. The secondary objective is to earn enough for himself and for his family. The tertiary objective of education is to contribute something of worth to his society, nation and humanity. Our educational system has not been able to satisfy even the primary goals.

The aims of education, on pragmatic grounds, could be summed up as follows :—

(1) To think logically.

(2) To develop mental abilities for survival and for earning a livelihood.

(3) To work in a cooperative but highly competitive environment dominated by rapidly growing and changing technologies.

(4) To develop mental faculties so that man could contribute something of great value to the society.

(5) To manage the scarce resources in a prudent manner for maximum output in all spheres of life.

(6) To develop mental faculties that enable man to respect others and get the maximum out of their capabilities.

(7) To plan the tasks of the individual and carry out these plans in accordance with the norms laid down by the individual, family, society and nature.

When the objectives are so pious, it would be consequential to think that an educational system upto matriculation or arts graduation would not be able to develop an individual, a group, a nation or a society. Something more than basic education is required. For example, the literacy level in Kerala is 100 per cent. But have we ever tried to understand that the educational levels of most of the Keralites would not be able to match professional levels of today ? A mere graduation or a 10+2 course would not be able to build the career. Such Keralites join jobs of Rs. 1,500-2,000 per month in the metropolises and are at the lowest rung of the economic ladder. Keralite nurses are among the best in the world. Keralite doctors are still better. But how many Keralites are doctors and nurses ? The educational profiles of the masses remain questionable and prone to disasters. Therefore, we should plan for future education keeping in mind the requirements of the next millennium.

There are seven basic types of education :—

(1) **Basic Education upto 10 + 2 level**—The students would study for 12 years in their schools. Those students, who are unable to develop any distinctive faculty in life, would be left out of the educational race. They would learn some skills and crafts which would be highly manual. Brainpower would be used minimally. These children would grow as operators of looms, artisans, craftsman, peons, operative staff in factories and offices, packers and drivers. They

would be trained in their respective fields for at least two years and would be independent by the age of twenty years. They could be granted loans for running a shop or a small trading business, depending upon their abilities.

(2) **Graduation level (Arts)**—The students with fine arts in their blood would be segregated at the 10+2 level. They could become great painters, actors, theatre artists, literacy figures, sculptures and think-tanks. They would not take up agraduation course (BA) for the sake of a degree. They would be trained in the field of their interest; history, arts, painting, cinema, literature, sculpture, handicrafts, books-writing *etc* are some of the prominent areas. Their training would incorporate practical sessions, theory, history of the arts (each discipline would need separate course material) and even some visits to foreign countries for exposure to the centres of the art world. These individuals would be the pride of our nation. They would represent our cultural heritage and artistic finesse. They would either be Self Employed Professional (SEPs) or would be absorbed in reputed public sector firms or government departments at senior levels. They could also be absorbed by the private sector firms. Some could go ahead with professional or post-graduation studies.

(3) **Post Graduation Level (Arts)**—Those artists, who want to take up post-graduate studies in India or abroad, would be sent on scholarships. The prosperous candidates could go on their own or could be supported by the corporate sector.

(4) **Professional Level (Technical)**—The bright students in medicine, architecture, engineering, management, commerce, chartered accountancy, computers and other highly technical fields would be allowed to grow in their respective streams. They would pass competitive examinations and would be selected in prestigious technical and professional institutions in India or abroad. These professionals would build modern India through their contributions in industry, business, management, publishing, computer software, international politics, surgery and medicine. These would be our star performars who would bring honour to the nation as well as build a prosperous future for their motherland.

(5) **Professional Level (Technical-Post Graduates)**—These would form a part of our research and development pool in various

disciplines. They would take up post-graduation and doctoral (even post doctoral) courses in India or abroad. They would be our research engines in the areas of space research, electronics, AIDS research, information technology (software and hardware), defence applications, nuclear applications (peaceful uses), management and other high-technology applications. They would also help the corporate and public sector enterprises for the development of new products, processes and technologies for economic and social revolution of India.

(6) **Vocational Studies**—Those students, who are better than their counterparts 10+2 levels but are unable to compete in the tough world of competition, would be awarded diplomas in technical disciplines. The ITIs, engineering diplomas and vocational courses are the examples of this vital educational sector The graduates of these institutions would either work for the private sector for public sectors enterprises as junior engineers, paramedical staff or in similar capacities or they would start a small business on their own. The State could extend financial help to the deserving candidates.

(7) **The Illiterate Masses Programme**—These would include adult illiterates, children of the backward families, Scheduled Castes and Scheduled Tribes, *Aadivasis* and other rural masses who are not aware of educational reforms. They would be trained for basic education upto matriculation. They would also be trained for some lower level skills so that they could survive the vagaries of life. However, they would not be granted any certificates or degrees. They would be at the lowest level of our educational system. The State would be liberal with adequate financial help, loans, housing, medical facilities *etc* for these people.

The futuristic educational system should have the following characteristics :—

(1) It would be vocation-oriented.
(2) It would be able to screen out the candidates according to their capabilities. Only the deserving candidates would be admitted to the courses offered.
(3) It would be highly competitive.
(4) Basic education would be free. Graduation would require minor expenses on the part of the candidates.
(5) The postgraduate courses would need some funding on the part of the candidates. However, scholarships would be offered.

(6) Education would be sans political machinations and campus friction. Good teachers would be paid well. Poor teachers would be fired. Similarly, the students with dubious and anti-social backgrounds would be screened out from the educational institutions at all the levels. The campus environment would be kept healthy for a natural growth of the minds of Indian students.

(7) International scholars and professors as well as industry specialists would be asked to teach Indian students. They would be able to keep our students abreast with the latest knowledge developed around the world.

(8) The relationship between the student and the teacher would become intimate and friendly. The ancient norms of education would be followed which were based upon *Guru-Shishya* traditions.

(9) Informal discussions and brain storming techniques would be promoted for better understanding of students.

(10) The educational system would provide adequate technical facilities and equipment for the students in order to promote learning.

(11) Failure would not be treated as unfortunate. It would be assumed to be a stepping stone for success.

(12) The hackneyed educational system would be replaced by interactive learning approach. The teacher would discuss the problem with his students with an open mind. It is just possible that he could get a better solution from one of his students. Books would be allowed for consultation during the examinations.

(13) Understanding and applications of knowledge would be promoted.

(14) Individual attention would be given to all the students at all the levels. Knowledge is dynamic mechanism that carries the best of the past and responds uniquely to the future. Education in the future would shift from mass teaching to personalised instruction, from single learning to multiple learning, passive absorption to action oriented and participative learning, rigid daily teaching sessions to flexible

schedules, theoretical sweet nothings to technical and practical knowledge base, teacher orientation to student's initiative, isolated curriculum to technical and society-oriented syllabi, emphasis on textbooks to the usage of computers, interactive learning and Internet and finally, passive mastery of information to action-simulation of the brain.

If our educational system has to help our the nation succeed in the new millennium, far-reaching changes would have to be effected. If pragmatic, technology-oriented and vocation rich-dominated system is not adopted (which should favour global orientation for our international presence), we might be left behind in the race *viz-a-viz* other developed nations of the world in all the vital areas of economy, business and technology. The government must take concrete steps for revamping our educational system.

77. STUDYING ABROAD

Studying abroad is dream for many an Indian student—Good educational standards abroad—Parents have to spend a lot of money—Good scope for the students of undergraduate, graduate and postgraduate courses—Procedures for admission difficult—Admission tests—Academic records and references to be submitted—H1 visa issued—Expenses for the first year are normally borne by the students—Scholarships, study grants and teaching scholarships are available—Total expenses range from US$ 11,000 to US$ 17,000 per annum—Students gain practical knowledge and reputation—Good scope for jobs and business after studies—Problem of brain drain—Cost is another problem—Cultures are different and the students get into new moulds—Good for researchers—Ego problems in graduates from abroad—They do not value Indian traditions and family ties after their academic stints abroad.

Now a days, the trends for studying abroad have shown an upward surge. The rising population levels of the students and researchers in India have triggered this phenomenon. There is no serious debate about the difference in the educational norms in the West and those in India; the Western societies are much ahead of us in terms of quality education. The inquisitive students of India certainly do well after studying in the educational institutions abroad. The pragmatic and scientific approach of the educational institutions of the West gives the students an edge over those who get education in India. Further, research students also find that their efforts are very much productive (and respected) in the foreign countries and not in India. This unique feature of education in the alien lands has made our students queue up for admissions into the foreign universities.

However, the grass may not always be greener in the distant lands. There are some pitfalls and problems associated with the education in foreign countries. Let us analyse the pros and cons of education abroad. We would like to make a rational assessment of the whole scenario in the context of the current social, economic and political scenarios prevalent in India and the in the countries where the students like to go for studies.

The advanced nations like the USA, the UK, Canada, Australia and New Zealand are offering professional and non-professional courses in various streams of education. Some of the streams include major engineering disciplines, pure sciences, architecture, medicine, surgery, arts, English language, computer science and engineering, nursing, management, nuclear engineering, publishing, printing technology, plastics technology, fashion design, textile engineering, space research and food sciences. The courses are offered for undergraduate, graduate and post-graduate degrees. The academic sessions begin in the January (Winter Session), September (Autumn Session) and March (Spring Session), though some universities also offer four sessions for admission.

The students are required to appear in the tests that are specially conducted by the educational testing institutions abroad (like those conducted by the Educational Testing Service at Princeton, New Jersey). If the candidates clear the tests with good scores, they are eligible for admission to those universities that accept the results of such institutes. The students then apply for admission and send their marks sheets (of the entrance tests), records of academic qualifications, a note on their abilities and limitations in the context of the course applied for, their financial status, support of a relative abroad and some useful academic references. Their academic records are scrutinised thoroughly by the universities and colleges and the students are admitted if they fulfil the pre-specified criteria. The students are then informed about the admissions and they are supposed to get the students' visas (normally, H1 visa for admission to the universities in the USA). When the visas are issued, they are required to make preparations for enough of resources for their studies, boarding and lodging in the foreign country. The students join the university from the session that has already been decided. They are also required to pay the fees and for boarding and lodging in advance for the first academic year (which is normally of two semesters).

When a student gets admitted to a foreign university or college, he becomes thrilled and exhilarated. A bright future beckons him in a distant land and he gears up for the testing times that lie ahead. Some students are offered scholarships and study grants. The universities offer the scholarships depending upon the funds available for the same. The admissions committee decides the number of scholarships and the candidates who would get them after careful scrutiny. The past academic performances of the candidates as well as the marks obtained in the admission tests are the major criteria. The students of undergraduate courses are not offered any scholarships but exceptions are also there to this general rule. The students of graduate and post-graduate courses are eligible for scholarships if they fulfil the criteria mentioned earlier. Some students of graduate and post-graduate courses are also eligible for teaching assignments in the department in which, they study. For that purpose, they have to prove their teaching abilities and are required to possess the knowledge about the subject to be taught.

The total course fees for an undergraduate degree are in the range of US$ 4,000-7,000 per academic session comprising two semesters of six months each. The course fees for the graduate and post-graduate courses vary from US$ 7,000 to US$ 12,000 per academic session, depending upon the nature of the course. Visa expenses, travelling expenses, boarding and lodging expenses and the sundry expenses during the stay abroad are in addition to the course fees. As a rule of thumb, the student would be required to pay US$ 150-300 per month for the food, accommodation and other living expenses in a foreign university. Entertainment expenses are not included in this estimate. The total cost of study abroad on per annum basis would vary from US$ 11,000 to US$ 17,000 per annum.

The student has to slog for hours in order to get the degree or diploma he is pursuing for. This puts a great burden on his eyes, brain and physique. The student would also be required to participate in physical activities, games and other events that are vital for his personality development (like extempore contests, debates, quiz contests, music competitions, painting exhibitions, competitions and political debates). He would not remain a bookworm throughout his life. If he becomes a doctor after getting a degree from a professional medical college of repute, his lifestyle and working hours would be different from those of other professionals. He would be able to enjoy his life in the foreign country, though he would have little time for leisure. Similarly, an engineer would be exposed to the latest technologies in his discipline. When he is back to India after a short educational stint abroad, he is likely to get a job as a senior engineer in the very beginning of his career.

Normally, the undergraduate courses are for four or five years, graduate courses are for two years (additional six months are required for the submission of thesis) and the post-graduate courses have a duration ranging from three years to five years (that includes the time period for the preparation and submission of thesis). Research students can go back to their home countries after they have attended the academic sessions and have also conducted the research activities required for completion of their theses. There are admissions to the Doctorate of Science (D Sc) courses as well but the entrants are very senior professionals, engineers and scientists. They are required to put in at least twenty years of their useful lives in a particular field, normally related to engineering, sciences and medicine. The objective of conducting these rare courses is to develop the knowledge base in that particular discipline so that the human race could solve those riddles that remain mystry for it. There is no dearth of funding from the universities in the case of the students of D Sc courses.

After learning about the *modus operandi*, we would like to discuss some of the advantages and disadvantages of foreign education. The advantages are as follows : —

(A) The education is of better quality. The teachers are professionals and researchers and give the latest information and knowledge base to the students.

(B) Teaching is scientific and is based on interactive mode of learning. In India, a student can earn his MBA even through correspondence (how could he ?) but universities insist on the classroom teaching methods, participation of the students during academic sessions and laboratory sessions. They do not emphasise upon cramming of the books but try to give a knowledge base (or a skill) to the students.

(C) The students are prepared for life; there is no emphasis upon degrees but upon the practical knowledge that the students get from their educational curricula. This feature is missing in Indian education.

(D) The students have an exposure to distant lands, people and the diverse cultures from all the parts of the world. The foreign universities attract students from around the globe and the multiracial canvass of the university campuses gives the students an idea about the world they live in. New contacts are made, which assist the students in migration, further studies, employment and business. The possibilities are virtually endless.

(E) The graduates of a foreign university are respected in India. They get lucrative jobs in India and have bright carrers.

The disadvantages of foreign education are no less alarming. Some of them are as follows :—

(A) Most of the students do not come back after their education in the foreign universities. They get jobs or professional assignments abroad and therefore, they get lucrative salaries that are much higher than Indian pay packages. The problem of brain drain has cost India dearly and during the past thirty years, we have lost most of the productive manpower to the West. There is no end to this problem as the Western nations welcome the talented individuals from all the nations with open arms.

(B) The cost factor is very crucial. Most of the parents cannot afford to pay the fees and other costs of their children and wards. They have to borrow these funds from banks, private financiers or relatives. The problems of repayment of these loans remain a major headache as the children are not likely to pay back these loans. The rich and neo-rich families are able to afford the costs and therefore, are able to go abroad. Scholarships are limited as the foreign universities have also been facing funds shortages due to global recession.

(C) The demands of the graduates (who have got a foreign degree) are quite unreasonable. Only the foreign companies operating in India, multinationals and big corporate firms are in a position to afford them. The small-scale industries and medium scale industries are not in a position to offer them jobs. Moreover, after a brief stint in the industry, these professionals start small enterprises of their own. The firms suffer as they groom them for specific professional jobs after years of hard work and investments in terms of time and money.

(D) These professionals have a new cultural orientation after they come from abroad. They do come back but they go back to foreign lands because they are sans emotional affiliations with their families in India. Some of the professionals get married and settle down in the foreign countries of their choice. The families (especially, the parents) miss their children but they are not in a position to go to that foreign country and meet them. The families break up in this manner. Social security and the norms of the joint family are sidelined. What remains is the hunger for money and materialistic assets.

(E) Ego levels of these professionals reach new heights as they are *Creme de' la Creme* of the human race. They are superior, feel superior and are treated as superior. They generate many problems, duels and corporate wars in India and abroad. This could be a nuisance for those who have plaebian status or moderate abilities and are forced to work with these professionals. When these professionals face confrontation on a routine basis, they try to lead secluded lives and meet only those who have a status that is at par with theirs. They ignore the ordinary mortals and the society at large.

(F) Due to the human problems faced by them, these professionals develop serious health or psychological

problems that include heart ailments, asthma, bronchitis, respiratory diseases, hypertension and diabetes.
(G) Confidence levels of many a student remain at their lowest ebb despite educational stints abroad.

It must be noted that by the year 2005, the service oriented jobs would be nearly 30-40 per cent of the total jobs offered in the markets. Further, there would be a shift from white-collar jobs (which requires managerial abilities and humanistic approach for solving the problems) to computer-based and analytical jobs (which involves engineering talent and scientific knowledge bases). The most lucrative careers would be in Artificial Intelligence (AI), Information technology (IT), Bio Engineering, Computer Graphics and Multimedia, Electronics Engineering, Space Research, Nuclear Science and Engineering, Oceanographic Research and Applications and Surgery.

We do not dissuade the students from going abroad. However, we must point out that educational standards in India are also improving. One may not need to go abroad in order to earn a degree. There are many institutions in the foreign countries also that merely offer degrees and no knowledge is imparted by them. These educational institutions have mushroomed around the world because of the rise in demand for quality education by the Asians and the Africans. For example, a university located abroad would certainly give the degree in Computer Science but if the same degree is earned in India (and the young boy or the girl can go abroad for a training for one year or so after the graduation), then he would be saving a lot of his financial resources. Many universities are offering courses that allow the students to attend academic sessions in the foreign country for one year or so. The rest of the academic curricula are completed by the students in India as those universities have liaison offices or affiliated colleges in India. This is a good concept and should be appreciated

In sum, the students of the new millennium should work hard if they wish to earn a good degree from a foreign university. They have to keep their sights on their targets and have to burn the midnight oil for achieving their short term and long term academic objectives. Nothing is impossible if they are determined, committed and willing to slog. They must, however, avoid applying for admission to spurious universities that abound in the foreign countries. Indian education scenario is also changing and we also have professional courses and institutions in India as well. The idea is to build a career and not make a visit to a foreign country as many of the students think. ●

78. CAREER OPTIONS FOR THE NEW MILLENNIUM

Careers are available in management, administration, fashion, engineering, computers etc—Administration is a better career now a days—All major careers explained in brief—A career in administration offers diversity—More knowledge about the interiors of the nation—Functioning of our national administration is quite fascinating—Job satisfaction and security—Youth must accept this career for bright future.

Students and the youth are normally not aware of the career that they should adopt in order to help them survive and grow in financial, professional and moral terms. Some educationists contend that a career in administration (IAS, IFS, IPS *etc*) would be more lucrative *viz-a-viz* a career in management (MBA, CA, PGDBM). Let us analyse this interesting issue in detail as this has direct impact upon the careers of our students.

We have nine major streams to choose from. The first stream is that of engineering, semi-technical and technicians. Unfortunately, there has been a glut in the technical jobs market for the past ten years. The number of jobs is lesser than the number of engineers and other technical personnel churned out by the institutes. Therefore, this career option does not seem to be lucrative.

The second option is that of management. The manager opts for a bright career if he thinks that he is a good marketing or sales professional. The current economic trends now favour market surges. In such a condition, sales can be effected easily. Sales and marketing targets would be slightly difficult to achieve. True, the a degree in management can fetch good money but there is only limited money circulation in the market. Moreover, there is a glut of MBAs as well. So too many management graduates have been chasing too few jobs. And add to it the large number of PGDBM graduates who are equally competent. The graduates from IIMs, FMS, XLRI and Jamnalal Bajaj.

Institutes either start their own entrepreneurs or go abroad for jobs or for higher studies. Some prefer to stay back. However, everybody is not able to get admission to these management institutes. Indian economy is likely to grow at a faster face now as the trends of January-March, 2000 indicate. Stock markets are heading for the Bulls Phase, industrial production is higher than that during the beginning of 1999. So, management graduates can hope for good jobs and business transactions.

A part of the management stream is Chartered Accountancy. CAs are in great demand. But the courses are gruelling. The accountancy practice is difficult and the student has to pass many an acid test before coming out with flying colours. Further, there is a saturation in the accountancy market as well. Cost and Management accountants are also in demand but there are too many cost accountants in the market for too few jobs.

The next profession is that of medicine. A doctor can earn money and status in a short time span. But the urban areas are already full of doctors and surgeons. Although there are many patients, yet the competition is stiff. We would find doctors and clinics in all the big or small colonies of Indian metropolitan cities. The rural areas do not form lucrative market niches, though it is a good idea to practise medicine in a village from the viewpoint of social service. The real career for a doctor is in the village and most of the doctors do not prefer to migrate to villages. Surgery is a part of medical profession but it requires sophisticated equipment and training of highest order.

Another lucrative profession is that of textiles and fashion designing. IIFT is the leading institute in the country and is funded by the Ministry of Textiles. This is a good career and satisfies the creative as well as the financial needs of the students.

Further, careers in the army, the navy and the air force are still quite lucrative. These could also be opted for if the candidate has physical and mental capabilities for the same.

Law is another profession but is no longer lucrative on account of procedural delays in the courts. However, bright lawyers always shine.

Computers, I T and Internet are the most rapidly changing and advancing fields. There is a great career in computer software development. Internet would be the information superhighway of the future. Hence, their is a good career in Internet operations as well. Private educational institutes offer courses in Internet, web page design, programming in JAVA, C++ and HTML and multimedia. A degree of MCA however, would be more useful in the field of IT.

Finally, the administrative services offer the candidate a bright future. The candidate learns the administrative and management skills. He or she ought to be a bright student in his main stream (engineering, arts, science, commerce *etc*). He is posted in an Indian village or city and is moving at fixed intervals of 2-5 years. So, he learns more about India and is fascinated to learn how this vast nation is managed. He gets a home, a vehicle, staff and many facilities, which cannot be imagined in other professions. He falls in love with his country and countrymen. He realises the dream of Indians by living and working in close association with them. He has a truely thrilling and prosperous career. After his retirement, he is able to avail of pension and other benefits, which are not available in other professions. In sum, he is part of the administrative growth mechanism of the nation. He spearheads the economic and social development processes. He transforms the policies (framed by the leaders of the central and state governments) into action plans. He allocates resources for the action plans and gets them executed. He could be an IAS, IPS or IFS officer who would be able to contribute according to his basic qualifications calibre and training. He performs at the maximum level of his efficiency and is proud to be an administrative official.

This discussion amply proves the fact that Indian administrative services offer lucrative opportunities for growth and job satisfaction. Our students would certainly opt for a stable and prosperous career and would work hard for achieving their coveted goal—an illustrious carrer in administration for the service of the nation. The nation would be proud of him for his achievements and contributions. The nation beckons him for opening a glorious chapter of his life.

INDIAN DEFENCE

79. IAF

IAF born in 1950—It had old fighters and transportation aircraft—Did a good job in 1962 aggression—Operation Gibralter" conducted in 1965 Indo-Pak war—Modernisation was on-going process—Performed very well during 1971 war—Gnat fighter did marvellous job—Nirmaljeet Singh Sekhon won PVC—Now IAF has latest fleet of fighters and transportation aircraft—IAF lacks the power of F-16 and F-22—MIG-29 and Mirage-2000 could be the answers—AWACS and EW being developed—Developing LCA—We have IRBM capability—Modernisation requires money and will-power.

Indian Air Force (IAF) was born in 1950. Prior to its nationalisation, the air power of Indian armed forces was known as "The Royal Indian Air Force." The history of Indian Air Force started with World War-II. At that time, there were only 100 aviators and 4 Awanti aircraft. The RIAF was under the British administration and did a commendable job during the Second World War.

In 1950, RIAF was indegenised to form IAF. Immediately after its formation, the IAF faced challenge from Pakistan in Jammu and Kashmir. IAF had Dakotas, Tempests and Harvards, which were primitive machines by all norms. However, the men behind the machines did commendable jobs and transported ammunition, weapons and supplies. They also struck targets in Muzaffarabad and Kotli. They helped us maintain our supremacy over Punch and Skardu. However, these operations also exposed the weaknesses of our air force.

In 1962, China offended our territories. IAF could not understand the exact potential of Chinese air power. It remained on the defensive rather than going on an offensive strike. However, IAF supported the army in logistics, especially for lifting of 30 tonne AMX-13 tanks to Chushul (Ladakh).

In 1965, Pakistani SSK guerrillas stormed Jammu and Kashmir. IAF codenamed its action as "Operation Gibralter." It performed well despite the obsolete flying machines and lack of proper infrastructure. After the Indo-Pakistan war in 1965, IAF modernised itself for better air strike capabilities, efficient ground maintenance and extremely accurate striking capabilities in the territory of the enemy.

By 1971, the IAF had already been developed as a major air power in the region. It had 23 fighter squadrons, 3 maritime reconnaissance squadrons and a sound infrastructure for maintenance at the air force bases. During the Indo-Pakistan war in 1971, IAF had a commanding edge over the Pakistan Air Force (PAF) and our fighter planes pumped the enemy installations with shells with amazing finesse. Flying Officer Nirmal Jeet Singh Sekhon faced enemy fighters (Sabres) and diverted them from their main task. He gave up his life in the process. He was awarded Param Vir Chakra posthumously. The small indigenously built GNAT fighter plane wreaked havoc on the enemy installations and the superiority of man behind the machine was once again proved at the hustings.

After the war in 1971, IAF was divided among 5 commands. The four commands were located at Delhi, Allahabad, Jodhpur and Shillong while the fifth command (Training Command) was located at Bangalore. Today, IAF is proud to possess the most modern airborne machines available with man. These include MiG-29s, deep strike penetration Jaguars, Mirage-2000 Interceptors and MIG-27s. Strategic reconnaissance tasks are carried out by MIG-25s and old Canberras have been grounded. IAF has a sturdy fleet of transportation aircraft that includes AN-12s, AN-32s and IT-76s. The IT-76 is capable of airlifting more than 50,000 kgs. Further, the IAF has advanced helicopters like MI-17s, MI-26s and MI-35s. This fleet performed well against the LTTE in "Operation Pawan." The indigenously built Chetak helicopters are also serving the nation well and are compatible with their imported counterparts. The latest addition to the air force fleet is the massive Sukhoi aircraft, which is a marvel in the sky.

The IAF has the most deadly arsenal of missiles. We have mostly imported missiles. However, indigenously built missiles have also been added to the stocks. Defence technology grows at a very fast pace and hence, IAF has to import air-strike weapons and fighter planes in order to have a decisive edge over its rivals.

Operation "Desert Storm" proved the fact that IAF must continue to upgrade its fighter planes, ground maintenance techniques and manpower training. It also needs a Light Combat Aircraft (LCA) which must replace MIG-21s soon. Further, F-16s fighters aircraft are superior to MIG-29s and Mirage-2000s. Pakistan has acquired F-16s from the USA. The maximum weight of MiG-29 is 16,500 kgs while that of a F-16 fighter is 10,000 Kgs. The maximum speed of MIG-29 is 0.2 Mach, which is higher than that of F-16. But strike range of F-16 is 2,200 km as against the strike range of MIG-29 of 2,000 km. F-16 can carry more missiles than MIG-29. F-16 has an overall edge over MiG-29 and its technology as well as air strike capabilities are strikingly superior. The IAF has to take this fact into account and must procure an aircraft, which is at least at par with F-16. And the air defence shops now offer much more than the F-16 stealth bombers; Mirage 2000-5, MIG-29B, MIG-31 and MIG-35 are some examples of *avante garde'* war machines for air combat.

IAF proved its superiority during the Kargil war as well. Pakistani military regulars and hired intenders had occupied positions on the Indian side of LoC. IAF conducted connaisance operations during May-July, 1999. Ajay Ahuja was captured by Pakistani army and shot dead. Flight Lieutenant Nachiketa was captured as his Mig 27 was destroyed by Pakistani shells. He was released later. Our heroes maintained the traditions of IAF, during "Operation Vijay". The entire region (comprising Drass, Batalik, Tololing, Kargil, Kaksar, Tiger Hill and Mushkoh valley) was scanned. The IAF officers mapped the area first and planned to attack the intruders by aerial attacks. Army supported these sorties (nearly 40 per day were carried out with the help of Mig 21, Mig 23, Mig 27 and Mig 29B fighters). IAF was able to strike its targets with 100 percent accuracy. Over a short span of sixty years, IAF has developed a tradition of excellence. Our fighter pilots, ground technicians, aircraft maintenance engineers and support staff have built the organisations. The motto of the IAF is— *Ittehad Mein Shakti Hai* (strength lies in unity). All the divisions, departments and personnel of the IAF work in a wonderful coherence and are able to deliver outputs of highest quality during war and peace.

The IAF has been serving the nation duting peacetime operations for quite some time now. There is a visible tension on the Indo-Pak border on account of nuclear tests carried out by both the countries during May, 1998. Therefore, IAF has to be vigilant as our neighbours could initiate provocative combat exercise. Kargil war proved that these apprehensions were not false. The peacetime operations include air force logistics, army logistics, supply of food and medicines to the flood-hit areas and movement of defence personnel in the North-East and inhospitable terrains. China and Pakistan have acquired deadly air strike capabilities. Both of these nations have nuclear warheads as well. Both of them have had a war with us at least once. Therefore, we must continue to modernise IAF as latest technology in air defence system playies a vital role in success at the hustings.

During the sixties and the seventies, Electronic Warfare (EW) had assumed great significance. The Arab-Israeli conflict proved that EW could play a decisive role in air combat. China and Pakistan already have EW capabilities but IAF is not fully conversant with this technology. Further, we have not developed the equipment for and have yet to import the same.

The second issue in the context of modernisation is the development of a Light Combat Aircraft (LCA). India has developed a completely indigenous LCA, which is swift, carries light weaponry and is cheaper to build at home. Missiles Warfare (MW) has acquired great significance during the modern times. The missile capabilities of Iraq and the USA were evident from the US-Iraq conflict, witnessed during the early nineties. India has developed Trishul, Prithvi, Agni, Nag, Akash and Sagarika missiles carrier systems and these give ample evidence of our indigenous defence manufacturing potential. Missiles are no replacements of combat aircraft but they have good strike and destruction capabilities.

IAF has had a glorious past. However, in order to meet the challenges of the future, we need to take a serious look at the modernisation imperatives. The air defence equipment of today would be absolete within five or seven years. Therefore, modernisation has to be a regular routine at IAF.

The first step in the process of modernisation is the upgradation of the basic machinery and aircraft without changing the basic infrastructure. For the existing MIG-29 and Mirage-2000 aircraft, we need better firepower and payload. Most of the arsenal has to be procured from abroad as our in-house researches might take some time. New weapons and machinery for the existing aircraft and air defence systems do not cost us much and are easy to procure as these have to be procured from Russia, France or other friendly nations. It would be difficult to procure F-16 from the USA. Moreover, the USA could not deliver the due consignment to Pakistan against an advance already paid by that country. F-16s and their spares are out of bounds for us. We can however, procure F-16s and their ammunition from the international defence markets, which could be a costly affair.

Electronic Warfare (EW) is another vital element of our modernisation plans. The showdown in Bekka valley (in 1967) was totally based on EW. We should continue our research in EW and must procure the best EW equipment from the international defence markets.

India has been able to develop Light Combat Aircraft (LCA) on her own. However, we still need more time and upgradations as our competition at the hustings would be with most modern anti-aircraft guns and fighter planes. Although we have a LCA for meeting the requirements of IAF, yet we have to import sophisticated fighters from abroad. Russia and France have supplied war birds to India during the past and this trend is likely to continue in future as well.

Further, we have been spending nearly Rs 1,000 crore on the spares for the aircraft and ground equipment. CIS and Russia are the major spares suppliers. These spares must be indegenised gradually and the obsolete spares must be discarded. Alternatively, the aircraft or the ground machinery, which use these spaces, should be discarded in a phased manner. New machinery must be procured regularly from the international markets. It must be ensured that the spares for the new equipment can be arranged in abundance (especially during the time of war). Normally, agreements are signed with the suppliers for ensuring the supplies of spares for at least ten years.

Russia is an old friend of India. We have been getting SU-30, MIG-29B and other aircraft from her without any problems. However, the latest F-22, the B-2 Stealth Bomber and the latest Airborne Warning And Control System (AWACS), developed and manufactured by the USA, still elude us. Russia does not have a winning edge over the latest machinery and technology developed by the USA, France and the UK are able to supply us comparable technologies. However, the best always remains the best. Further, Russian politics may incite political upheavals and this could stop the supplies of fighter planes, air defence machinery or spares to us. Finally, we should not forget that Russia is now an ally of the West and equations of defence supply could be changed, which could leave us in a position of disadvantage. But recently India and Russia have developed more friendly relations.

A single F-22 fighter costs US$ 200 million. Even if we were offered a F-22 fighter plane, could we afford it ? The cost factor is vital one. Our army and navy also need modernisation. Budget allocations have to be prudent and favourable to all the three defence systems.

Many issues remain unresolved on the modernisation front. The main issue is the lack of resources. The private sector firms are likely to join their hands with the State in a bid to modernise IAF (in the air as well as on the groound). The public sector undertakings are already doing their best. An Air Marshal heads the indegenisation cell in IAF. Further, the free markets of the world have now allowed us to choose from a variety of latest equipment and techniques. This goes in the favour of IAF, which is always eager to adopt new technologies and assimilate latest equipment and and weapons. The security of the nation is the top priority.

80. INDIAN SPACE RESEARCH FEATS

India has done remarkably well in space research—PSLV-C2 has launched IRS-P4 in space. We are capable of launching 1,000 kg satellites—We are in the select group of nations that have this unique capability—We are the leaders in remote sensing technology, PSLV type launchers and small satellites upto 1,200 kg payloads—INSAT, PSLV, IRS technologies could be sold in international markets—GSLV prestigious project of future—We could send a payload of 2,500 kgs to space—ISRO deserves all praise for its impeccable record—Launched INSAT 2E and PSLV C-2 recently.

India is the only nation of the world where talented manpower from all the castes, creeds, religions and ideologies thrives and grows. We are a nation of more than 100 crore people and during the past fifty years, we have proved that we can achieve success in all the fields of human endeavour. Space research is one such feather in Indian cap. Indian space research programme has made us proud. The high rate of success has made us the leaders in this technology among the developing world and one of the first few in the group of developed nations.

On May 26, 1999, Indian Space Research Organisation did us proud by launching multiple satellites through the launch vehicle-PSLV-C2. These satellites, placed into their respective orbits through a single launch effort, sent the satellites of Germany (Tubsat), Korea (Kitsat-3) and India (IRS-P4). Further, India sent her next satellite, INSAT-3B, into space in March, 2000. This satellite was propelled into space by Ariane launcher from Kouru (Rench Guyana). The Satellite was finally placed in its geostationery orbit on March 27, 2000. The Scientist have been controlling its operations since then from the Master Control Facility at Hassan (Karnataka).

On April 3, 1999, India launched her multipurpose telecommunications satellite-INSAT 2E—from Kouru (French Guyana). A European Ariane 42 P rocket carried the satellite (weighing 2,250 kg) into space at 3:33 PM (IST) and transferred it into its geostatonery orbit, twenty-two minutes after its launch. Six minutes later, the Master Control Facility (MCF) at Hassan took over the control of the satellite. The satelite was finally put into its geostationary and circular orbit at a height of 36,000 km above the equator. Movement from the oval geo-syncheonous orbit to the final geostationary orbit was effected by an engine aboard the satellite itself. The satellite has been built at the cost of Rs 220 crore. It has 17 C-band transponders that can be used for TV broad casting, telecommunications and meterological services. For meteorological imaging, a very High Resolution Rediometer (VHRR) has been installed in the satellite. It also has a passive cooler for infrared imaging. It would operate in there spectral bands, one of which, is in the visible region, with a ground resolution of 2 kms. This satellite is the last of its series.

INSAT-2 series of satellites had an edge over the INSAT-1 series (which was built by the USA). In terms of higher capacities. But INSAT-2 series also faced serious problems; there were problems with Japanese electronic devices, the design of fuel tanks on INSAT-2A has some anomalies and finally, INSAT-2D was lost just four months after it was launched,. Now, we have only two fully operational INSAT-2 satellites and a total of 33 transponders.

The guiding spirit behind our successful space research programme is Indian Space Research Organization (ISRO). This prestigious technological functionary of the central government was established on August 15, 1969. Since then, our hardworking and dedicated space scientists have never looked back. We faced many failures. But each one of them nurtured a belief that India would succeed one day. And we did that as is evident from the list of successful missions carried out by ISRO. Table-I gives the brief account of Indian space research feats in a chronological order.

Table-I : Indian Space Research Feats

SNo	Year	Operation
1.	1962	Indian National Committee for space research formed. Work on equatorial rocket launching station at Thumba (TERLS) began.
2.	1963	First sounding rocket launched from TERLS on November 21.
3.	1965	Space Science and Technology Centre established in Thumba.
4.	1967	Satellite Communication Earth Station set up at Ahmedabad.
5.	1968	TERLS dedicated to the United Nations on February 2.
6.	1969	Indian Space Research Organisation (ISRO) formed on August 15.
7.	1972	Space Commission and Department of Space set up on June 1. Airborne remote-sensing experiments commenced.
8.	1975	First Indian satellite, Aryabhatta, placed in orbit on April 19 by Cosmos Rocket from Russian Cosmodrome at Baikanour. Satellite Instructional Television Experiment (SITE) begun.
9.	1977	Satellite Telecom Experiments Project (STEP) undertaken.
10.	1979	Experimental satellite for earth observations, Bhaskara-1, placed in orbit by Cosmos Rocket from Russian Cosmodrome on June 7. First experimental launch of SLV-3 from Sriharikota Range (SHAR) on August 10 partially failed.
11.	1980	Second experimental launch SLV-3 from SHAR on July 18 place Rohini satellite RS-D1 in orbit.
12.	1981	First developmental flight SLV-3 from SHAR placed IRS-D1 satellite in orbit on June 19. APPLE, an experimental geo-stationary communication satellite placed in orbit by Ariane rocket from Kourou in French Gayana on June 19. Bhaskara-2 placed in orbit by Cosmos Rocket from Russian Cosmodiome on November 20.

SNo	Year	Operation
13.	1982	Insat-1A placed in orbit by Delta rocket of the USA on April 10. Deactivated five months later.
14.	1983	Second developmental launch of SLV-3 from SHAR placed IRS-D2 satellite in orbit on April 17. INSAT-1B placed in orbit by US Space Shuttle on August 30. Active for the next ten years.
15.	1984	Indo-Soviet manned space mission in April.
16.	1987	First developmental launch of ASLV from SHAR on March 24 Flight unsuccessful.
17.	1988	First operational Indian remote sensing satellite, IRS-1A, placed by Vostok rocket from Russian Cosmodrome on March 17. INSAT-1C placed by Ariane rocket from Kourou on July 21 abandoned 15 months later. Second developmental launch of ASLV on July 13 unsuccessful.
18.	1990	Insat 1-D placed by American Delta rocket on June 12.
19.	1991	IRS-1B placed by Vostok rocket from Russian cosmodrome on August 29.
20.	1992	Third developmental flight of ASLV from SHAR on May 20 placed Sross-C Satellite in a low earth orbit. INSAT-2A, the first indigenously built second generation INSAT satellite, placed by Ariane rocket from Kourou on July 10.
21.	1993	INSAT-2B placed by Ariane rocket from Kourou on July 23. The first developmental flight of PSLV from on September 20proved to be unsuccessful.
22.	1994	The fourth developmental flight of ASLV placed Sross-C2 satellite in a low-earth orbit on May 4. PSLV-D2 launched successfully from SHAR for placing IRS-P2 in polar sunsynchronous orbit.
23.	1995	INSAT-2C satellite placed in orbit on December 28.
24.	1996	PSLV-D3 launched successfully from SHAR to place IRS-P3 satellite in intended orbit.
25.	1997	INSAT-2D placed in orbit by Ariane rocket from Kourou on June 4.
26.	1999	Insat-2E sent into space on April 3 by European Ariane 42 P rocket from Kourou.
27.	1999	PSLV-C2 launched three satellites on May 26-IRS-P4 (India), Kitsat-3 (Korea) and DLR Tubsat (Germany).
28.	2000	INSAT-3B launched by Ariane Rocket in March 22, 2000. Placed in its geostationary orbit on March 27, 2000.

ISRO can hope to reach new horizons as its previous record had a high rate of success. The launch of PSLV-C2 has drawn attention of international customers who wish to launch satellites of weights as low as 100 kg. While an IRS-Series satellite would be the main payload to be carried by PSLV vehicles, it would also be able to carry one or two 100-kg satellites. Such piggy-back launches would be at cheaper rates than the international rates (for example, the rates quoted to India by Russia for the launch of IRS-1C satellite). ISRO would also find huge markets of telecommunications companies want to launch their own communication satellites into space.

Further, we have already achieved high levels of accuracy in the design and production of INSAT series of satellites, IRS series of satellites and PSLV series of launch vehicles. These capabilities would yield concrete results as the low orbit satellites encircling the earth would need replacements. Satellite imagery is a vital growth area. It has commercial and non-commercial connotations. Internet and remote sensing are the new tools of information technology. Internet has finally arrived and would become the information superhighway in the next century. Satellite communication and satellite launches are essential for growth in information technology, surveillance of our borders (after learning some bitter lessons from the Kargil war), development of activities related to Electronic-Commerce (E-com) and for commercial launches of satellites for other nations. It has been estimated that during the next ten years, data to be made available by remote-sensing satellites would be of a value close to US$ 1 billion.

Indian technology is superior and our products are cheaper. We could sell the INSAT and IRS series to needy countries. PSLV range of vehicles could be used for launches. Indian equipment has been fitted on NASA—EOSAT's ground station at Norman, Oklahoma, USA. Other ground stations ground the globe have also ordered such equipment from ISRO. Further, India has won global contracts in land-sky communications and for earth observation studies. Indian space research programme has taken a healthy turn now. Now ISRO can endorse the PSLV configuration and could replace the six solid strap-on motors with four liquid strap-on motors for the indigenous design and manufacture of GSLV. GSLV is a prestigious project of ISRO. It would help us launch a satellite of payload of 2,500 kg at an altitude of 36,000 km above the earth. The success is not far away as the GSLV launch could be executed after a couple of PSLV launches. Research efforts are going on in this project.

In sum, we could state that Indian scientists have brought India the glory and self-fulfilment in the field of space research after long and arduous years of toil and research. Our scientists deserve all the credit and support from Indian public as well as from the State for this glorious saga of success.

81. INDIA'S DEFENCE PREPARATIONS

> *India's defence record glorious—India is a regional military superpower—Armed with latest weaponry—China and Pakistan are threats—So we have to be prepared despite our commitment to peace and non-alignment—Missiles developed—MBT (Arjun) is ready—We must develop our equipment at home—Bring technology from abroad—Now we are nuclear power—We need at least 50 nuclear warheads with missiles to carry them—Kargil war during May-July, 1999—We lost many lives—Our army was not ready—Must remain vigilant—Devise new methods of surveillance—Kargil war highlighted the role of army—We lost many lives—We were not vigilant.*

India is a nation of over 100 crore people. Ours is a developing nation that is facing many problems. The internal issues can be sorted out within the national framework. However, for the protection of our rights across the globe, we have to present ourselves as a strong nation.

Our borders in the North extend upto 3,000 kms, mostly passing through the Himalayas. Our coastline is 6,100 kms, which requires a collossal amount of money, manpower and time for its protection against the foreign invaders and smugglers. Our neighbour in the North is China and in North-West, Pakistan has been preparing to show her military prowess. We had major wars with both the nations. The relationships with all other neighbours are cordial. Keeping in mind the afore-mentioned facts, Indian armed forces must upgrade their potential and powers so as to meet challenges from across the borders in North and North-West.

Our leaders have been very wise in supporting the policy of non-alignment and at the same time, keeping India in the forefront of military technology. The State-owned and army-affiliated Defence

Research and Development Organisation (DRDO), under the aegis of Ministry of Defence, has been producing indigenous technologies and weaponry for Indian armed forces.

In future, the enemy would be located, tracked and targeted using the data links, computer assisted intelligence evaluation and automated fire control. The battlefield, now under manual surveillance, would be guarded round the clock using satellites, electronic surveillance equipment and radars. The USA would be able to attain that superiority within the next decade. Future warfare would be a deadly combination of electronic control equipment, supercomputers, satellite surverllance systems and the powerful human mind. The guarding principle in future would be—identify the target most qucikly and efficiently and destroy it if identified as hostile.

There is a great difference between the pace at which, we are developing our military technology and the swiftness with which, Western nations have developed their might in the battlefield. Our military hardware needs were being met by erst while Soviet Union and her allies. Then came the Indo-Pakistan in 1971 in which, a small fighter plane GNAT made the generals across the border shake their heads in disgust. In 1976, India conducted her first nuclear explosion in Pokharan in Rajasthan and thus, become a nuclear entity. Our relationships with France, the UK, Sweden and other Western nations were very good. Therefore, we could procure fighter aircraft and guns from these countries though they were the chief allies of the USA.

After the fall of the Soviet empire, we were left out in the open, without any mentor for defence preparations. However, India accepted the challenge and started developing her own tanks and missiles. Our missile projects like Agni, Agni-II, Trishul, Akash, Prithvi and Nag were highly successful. Sagarika—the latest submarine fired missile— was also tested and was successful. We are designing state-of-the-art laser systems for installation in the third generation missiles. Our multi-barrel rocket launching system has been christened 'Pinaca' and it can fire 44 rockets in a duration of 12 seconds. Main Battle Tank (MBT) Arjun was developed at home. Advanced Light Helicopter (ALH) was also designed and tested in India. Radar data processing and image processing are some of the projects, which are in the able hands of our defence experts and scientists.

Indian armed forces are one of the most efficient security forces on the earth. We have total 11,00,000 armed soldiers in Indian armed forces. The ratio of defence expenditure to GDP is 2.31 per cent. Per Capital defence expenditure is US$ 10.65. There are 1.11 soldiers to protest every 1,000 citizens of the country.

Technological upgradation is a result of years of research and agony in the defence laboratories as well as under adverse conditions in the battlefield. The lessons of Kargil war would be used to develop new techniques and equipment so that the next combination of man and machine is more effective than the previous one. Out of 2,30,000 scientists and engineers working throughout the world on research projects, 5,00,000 (*ie*, nearly 70 per cent) are busy developing new weapon systems, improving the present ones or developing connected support systems.

Indian defence preparedness is marred by low budgets in research. We are unable to procure sophisticated equipment for testing and latest materials and technologies for modern combat. India is a resource-starved nation and cannot afford to spend as much on the defence research and hardware manufacture as Western nations can. Further, international pressure is mounting on Indian statesmen and they are being pressurized to cut down defence expenditures. Western assumption is that India, already a military power, is likely to become a global military superpower. However, our contention is that we have to match our defence capabilities with our neighbours—China and Pakistan—who can create havoc with their indigenous and imported military hardware. India is likely to fight another war with Pakistan. Since the war of 1999, we connot leave our borders unprotected. The regional military power equation has to be balanced so that a "no-war" situation continues. The latest developments in microclectronics, new defence materials, efficient fuels, armour, artillary, better firing platforms and lighter but smaller combat weapons would help us achieve sound balance of power in Asia.

The war in Kargil proved that our intelligence agencies and personnel of BSF failed to monitor the tough terrians of Batalik, Drass, Turtuk, Kargil and Mushkoh Valley. This strategic area is marked by tough mountainous terrains and sub-zero temperatures. It is always under the firing range of Pakistani rangers. Pakistani forces had to retreat with disgrace in July, 1999. However, India lost her able soldiers and officers. Four Indians—Rifleman Sanjay kumar, Captain Vikram Batra, Lieutenant Majoj Kumar Pandey and Grenedier Yogendra Singh Yadav—were awarded the prestigious Param Vir Chakra. Pakistan had also threatened to exercise the nuclear option during the Kargil war. We do not propose to use the nuclear option. However, possession of the neculear weapons (in fully operational mode) would dissuade Pakistan from taking any irresponsible measure. It must be noted that our defence preparations would essentially include nuclear capabilities. This is the only way to inform our 'friends' that we have the nuclear deterrent option. A lion and a goat can never drink water from the same stream; two lions can.

We need new equipment and technology on a regular basis. The research efforts at home would take many years and the soldier at the border cannot wait for so long. Hence, new defence equipment would have to be imported. Unfortunately, the superior hardware and technologies developed by the USA and some of her allies are beyond our reach. Therefore, we would have to scan international markets for comparable equipment, which are is not easy to procure. Further, the Indian youth have shown more interest in getting enrolled in the armed services during the second half of 1999. The youth must be motivated to join armed forces. The salaries, perks and facilities of the armed forces must be raised with immediate effect. After all, man is more important than the machine.

We can conclude by stating that India would be able to retain her status as a regional superpower. Her role as an Asian and international military power is likely to be expanded soon. The Kargil war is another landmark in the history of Indian armed forces.

DISTINGUISHED PERSONALITIES

82. MOTHER TERESA : AN ANGEL OF LOVE

Mother was an angel of peace — A picture of compassion and love—Birth—Coming to India—Darjeeling Incident—Missionaries of Charity—Service to destitutes of Kolkatta—Awarded many prizes—Died after illness—Great daughter of the Almighty—Likely to be conferred Sainthood—Procededings initiated for conferring the title of 'Saint.'

Very few people in this world carry the legacy of the Almighty in a human form. Mother Teresa was one of them. An angel of love, an apostle of peace and a mother of all the tortured and deprived people, the mother was the last apostle of peace and self-less service who walked on the earth for the sake of its citizens.

Mother was born to Albanian parents in Skopje (earstwhile Yugoslavia) on August 29, 1910. She went to Ireland when she was 18. She took veil there and than entered the Congregation of Loreto. Six weeks later, she sailed to India for teaching in the schools of the Congregation. She also taught Geography at St Mary's High School in Kolkatta. For some years, she was its Principal as well. She took her first vows in Darjeeling on May 24, 1931 and her final vows on May 24, 1937 in the Loreto school. Her "inspiration day" was September 10, 1946 when, aboard a train to Darjeeling, she heard the "call of God" to bring peace, love and solace to the people whom the world shunned. She applied to the Pope for decloisteration, which was granted in 1948.

Then, began the saga of compassion, love and service. The mother started from a small room in Kolkatta and started attending to the poor, sick and destitutes lying in the slums and streets of the metropolis. She founded the Missionaries of Charity in 1950. With a few nuns, she opened her first home, "Nirmal Hriday" in 1955. She faced problems of religion and colour, which could not dissuade her from carrying out the noble task. At last, people understood that she was a true angel of peace and compassion and the whole world gave her a helping hand.

Over a period of years, Mother Teresa built up the Order and opened more than 160 centres in India. These include schools, charitable dispensaries, homes for leprosy patients, a TB clinic and homes for the dying destitutes. She maintained that the biggest evil was not the disease but the lack of love, compassion and above all, a feeling of being unwanted. Holy mother and her team picked up the destitutes from the streets, cleaned them, provided them with medical treatment and care and helped them re-build their lives.

Mother Teresa was awarded Magasaysay Award in 1962, Joseph Kennedy Jr Award (for services to the mentally retarded) in 1971, Nehru award for International Understanding in 1979, Nobel Peace Prize in 1979 and Bharat Ratna in 1980. She has received many other awards during her lifetime and has been respected throughout the globe.

She was untouched by fame and glory and was a selfless worker. She was the embodiment of compassion whose *Karmabhumi* was the City of Joy, which is better known as Kolkatta. After struggling for life in a hospital, the holy mother breathed her last in the month of October, 1997. According to her, death was like going home and the mortals should not be afraid of it. She also believed that fruit of silence is prayer; the fruit of prayer is faith; the fruit of faith is love; the fruit of love is service and the fruit of service is peace.

Mother Teresa was the great daughter of the Almighty who has contributed a lot to the cause of the human society. The future generations would always look for an angel of peace as they would find this world more ugly, materialistic, wooden and harsh for them. And only an angel from the heavens can repeat whatever mother has done for mankind during the past fifty years.

The life and selfless devotion of Mother Teresa teaches us the divine lesson of love for humanity and care for the needy destitutes. The poor, sick, mentally handicapped and physically disabled people deserve our attention, care, compassion and financial assistance. Mother Teresa did a lot for the destitutes. Why cannot we make a small contribution and keep her mission alive ? There are many social service organisations, public sector organisations, NGOs and institutions funded by the corporate sector and the UN that are serving the humanity through their financial, social and medical services. We should also try to help and serve the destitutes, poor children, lepers, mentally handicapped children and adults, spastics and other needy children and individuals. The selfless service to humanity is a divine experience. Whatever Mother Teresa did during her lifetime, was indeed highly commendable. She would be remembered along with the great souls of the world which include Holy Jesus Christ, Mahatma Gandhi, Lord Buddha and Lord Mahavira. All these great souls symbolised peace, compassion for humanity and righteousness. Mother Terasa was last of the apostles witnessed by the mortal world. Mankind would not see another great soul of her stature in many centuries to come. May God rest her soul in peace !

83. THE SAINT WARRIOR

Guru Gobind Singh was a great saint and warrior—Born in 1666 AD—Showed a new direction to the downtrodden Hindu and Sikh masses—Father martyred at Delhi—Elevated to the status of the Sikh Guru at the tender age of nine years—Learned man with a vision—Prepared for fighting the Mughal oppression—Fought three major wars—Lost four sons, mother and thousands of Sikh soldiers—Poet, scholar and a lover of music—Founded the Khalsa Panth on April 13, 1699 at Anandpur Sahib—Gave a new direction to the Sikh forces—Wrote Zafarnama that scolded the tyrant emperor, Aurangzeb—Trained Sikh forces and Banda Bahadur—Attacked by Pathans sent by Wazir Khan—Died in 1708 AD—A role model of the masses and messiah of the weak and the downtrodden—Rare personality that must be emulated by one and all.

Indian subcontinent has witnessed the wrath of time for several millennia. This part of the earth was responsible for the creation of most respectable tenets of human race. These tenets, albeit in some modified forms, still guide our lives. We owe our rich cultural and religious legacies to those great sages and men of courage who sacrificed their lives for the protection of the common masses and did not leave the path of righteousness and virtue despite all odds and adversities that they came across. India is a true harbinger of hope for the entire world in the context of the rising spate of evil forces and mad rush for commercialism. We are really proud of such a rich cultural heritage and the legends of the yore that paved the path of sincerity, morality and hope for all of us to tread. One of the great sages of India was the true *Khalsa* who protected the downtrodden masses of India and gave them a hope, the hope to live with dignity and self-respect. He was the great Guru of the Sikhs-the tenth succession-Shri Guru Gobind Singh Ji.

On April 13, 1999, the *Khalsa* tercentenary celebrations came to an end amidst the chanting of the holy hymns from the Sikh religious book, Shri Guru Granth Sahib, at Ananadpur Sahib (Punjab). Lakhs of devotees attended the ceremony (along with the members of the erstwhile government) and remembered the Guru and his contributions towards humanity. It was a show of the century, though the rift between the Sikh factions was also evident due to some incidents that occurred prior to the celebrations. But nobody could underscore the importance of the occasion-the homage to the great man of India who taught us to live with honour and simplicity and face the odds with unequalled courage. That great man was, indeed, the best among the saviours of mankind and we are deeply indebted to him for what he gave to the mankind during a short tenure of his life.

Guru Gobind Singh was born on December 26, 1666 AD, at Patna Sahib (Bihar). He was the son of Shri Guru Tegh Bahadur Ji. The wise and courageous Guru was a picture of simplicity and sacrifice and knew for sure that he would not be spared by the Mughal marauders who were after his life. Young Gobind understood that his father was going to be a martyr very soon. This stark reality had dawned upon him at a very tender age of nine years. When Guru Tegh Bahadur was summoned by the Mughal emperor, he went to his court. He refused to be converted into Islam and was therefore, ordered to be executed by the emperor. Guru Tegh Bahadur was tortured by the Mughal forces and finally, beheaded at Gurudwara Sisganj at Delhi. Grief-stricken Sikh masses and warriors could only bring his head to complete the cremation ceremonies; his body was cremated by one of his disciples secretively in a remote hut so that the Mughal soldiers might not be able to defile it. There was a deep gloom and stunned silence in the Sikh camp.

Amidst this melancholy and agony, Guru Gobind Singh took over as the tenth Guru of the Sikh masses at the age of nine years.

Historians confirm that he was the most extraordinary person of his times that were marked by the pinnacle of Mughal tyranny. The Hindu masses were totally under the control of the Mughal rulers and the only respite for them was the opposition provided by the Sikh warriors from Punjab. It must be noted that Guru Tegh Bahadur gave up his life for the Hindu cause and till the end of his tenure as a Guru, he and his disciples did not resort to counter-offensive measures as the Guru was a peaceful man. It was during the reign of Guru Gobind Singh that the Sikh forces united to form a formidable front in order to confront the Mughal oppression. Guru Gobind Singh realised that mere peaceful tactics would not save the Hindu race and that sword would be the only reply to the sword. Therefore, he declared, " When all the measures for getting justice fail, lifting of the sword is right and justified." Guru Ji was a great visionary even at a young age and he decided to organise the Hindu and Sikh masses for countering the tyranny of the Mughal rule.

The Mughal Empire was heading towards a decline. The Guru prepared himself first of all. He read the holy scriptures like *The Quran, The Geeta* and the ancient Hindu scriptures. He became an expert in Persian, Hindi and Sanskrit. He learned the art and science of warfare and trained Sikh soldiers who revered him as their saviour and guide. He had a spiritual bent of mind but he was also aware of the fact that Hindu and Sikh races were not safe till they learned to defend themselves through a valiant fight with the oppressors. This aspect of his personality of the Guru is quite remarkable as he is perhaps the only spiritual leader in the entire history of mankind who taught the masses to read the holy books as well as to keep their swords ready at the time of an attack by the marauders.

Guru Gobind Singh fought many wars during his early years as the Guru. He knew that he was not prepared to fight the mighty Mughal forces but he continued to train his soldiers in the techniques of warfare. He fought wars with Afghans, Rajput Kings and Hindu marauders. His trained soldiers did very well on the battlefront and he established himself as the saviour of the Hindu masses. The rising power of the Guru became a thorn in the eye of the Mughal emperor. The Hindu masses and Sikh soldiers were not organised. They had no guide or mentor to count on. The wise Guru organised them and made them a formidable force. And this fact was not acceptable to the Mughals. The Guru spent twenty years for preparing the soldiers.

In the meanwhile, Mughal emperor, Shajahan, was captured by the Mughal forces and his son, Aurangzeb Alamgir, succeeded him. Aurangzeb was a tyrant and had a typical anti-Hindu attitude. The rising Sikh power could be 'smelled' by him. He was, however, more interested in winning the vast territories in Southern India. He went to Deccan in order to satisfty his lust for more land and revenues by winning the vast geographical areas. However, in Maharashtra, Shivaji gave him tantrums. The Maratha warriors were as brave as the Sikh warriors and did not let the Mughal rulers have a single moment of relief.

The Guru got married and had four sons-Sahibzada Ajit Singh, Sahibzada Jujzar Singh, Sahibzada Fateh Singh and Sahibzada Zorawar Singh. His sons were as noble and brave as their father. They knew that they had to protected the interests of the Hindu masses as was being done by their great father. The wife and the mother of the Guru remained with him and inspired the Sikh warriors for a decisive war against the Mughal forces.

On April 13, 1699 AD, the Guru organised a congregation of the Sikh masses at Anandpur Sahib. He wielded his sword and asked five persons to sacrifice their lives. Five persons (a Kshatriya, a Jat, a water-bearer, a barber and a calico printer) offered themselves for the supreme sacrifice. He took them inside the tent one by one and a few seconds later, blood trickled out from the tent, indicating that they had been sacrificed. The stunned audience was unable to make out what was in the mind of the Guru. The Guru called upon the masses to unite themselves against the tyranny of the oppressors. He brought all the five devotees from the tent; instead of sacrificing them, he had sacrificed five goats whose blood had been mistaken by the audience to be the blood of the five men who were later called *Panj Piaras*. The Guru offered them a mixture of water, milk and Patashas, after mixing them with a double-edged sword. This mixture was likened to be as Amrit, the holy elixir. The Guru himself drank the Amrit and several thousands of devotees also drank it. Thereafter, he declared that the Sikh warriors would be known as the *Khalsas* and decided that the Khalsa Panth had been given a name and an identity. He named all the Sikh warriors as *Khalsas* and told them to protect the lives, property and dignity of the Hindu and Sikh masses. Thus the *Khalsa Panth* was born. The five symbols of the true *Khalsa-Kaccha* (the underwear), *Kara* (the metallic bangle), *Kirpan* (the sword), *Kesha* (the hair) and *Kangha* (the comb)-were adopted as the distinguishing marks of the Sikh warriors; these five items were always found on the person of a Sikh warrior. Further, Sikhs were forbidden from drinking, smoking, consuming tobacco, killing the cow or oppressing the weak and the downtrodden masses. This is a turning point in the Sikh history because the Sikhs had been sacrificing their lives on the altar of oppression; they had not protested against the tortures of the Mughal forces. But the Guru gave them a new direction. It is remarkable to note that the Guru was only thirty-three years of age at the time of this historical ceremony that changed the course of the Sikh history.

Guru Gobind Singh prepared the Sikh masses and soldiers for twenty years. Finally, he decided to take the plunge and challenge the Mughal emperor. He knew that Aurangzeb was busy in Deccan and would not be able to devote time to the Northern territories of India. There were small wars or fights between the Mughal forces and the Sikh soldiers but were not so significant. However, the Guru fought three major wars with the Mughal forces at Ananadpur Sahib, Chamkaur Sahib and Muktsar. All the battles that he fought with the Mughal forces could not prove to be decisive. The reason was that his army was not as powerful as that of the Mughals. He lost many of his brave soldiers during the conflicts. The Sikh soldiers were also able to diminish the Mughal supermacy to a great extent but they could not move beyond the State of Punjab, a known forte of the Sikhs. The Guru also lost four sons during the wars. Mughal Commander, Wazir Khan, was responsible for the death of the sons of the Guru. The two captured sons of the Guru-Sahibzada Fateh Singh and Sahibzada Zorawar Singh-were told to embrace Islam but they refused. They were embedded alive in the wall by Mughal officers. So, they laid down their lives, keeping the dignity of their faith and motherland as the most respected gospel of their lives. The other two sons-Sahibzada Ajit Singh and Sahibzada Jujhar Singh-laid down their lives during the war. The Sikh masses and the public at large were stunned by these tortures and gory incidents. Several thousand Sikh soldiers lost their lives during the wars with the Mughal forces. When the Guru was informed about the death of his sons, he replied, "I have lost four of my sons for the sake of my several other sons (the Sikh masses). If those four have died, so what ? There are several thousands more to take their places !"

The brave Sikh warriors suffered many casualties and losses as a result of wars but they did not give up their resolve to eliminate tyrannical rule of the Mughals from this country. Although it was a formidable task, yet they fought the oppressors valiantly. The struggle of the Guru spanned nearly twenty-five years. During his long struggle with the Mughal forces, Guru Gobind Singh met Bairagi Lakhman Dev. The Guru motivated him to fight the Mughal tyranny and trained him for the task. He re-christened him as Banda Bahadur. Banda Bahadur led the Sikh forces and inflicted heavy losses upon the Mughal State. He therefore, avenged the deaths of the four sons of the Guru and the several thousand warriors who had laid their lives for the cause of the Khalsa Panth. Banda Bahadur was captured in 1716 AD and was executed by orders from the emperor Farrukhsiar who ruled during those times.

A mention must be made of the great poetic abilities and the literary tastes of the Guru. He was a learned man with a vision of the future. He wrote several books including *Zafarama* that was addressed to the erstwhile tyrant Mughal ruler, Aurangzeb. In Zafarnama, the Guru condemned the oppression and the anti-Hindu stance of the emperor and gave him a clear warning that the Sikh warriors would fight a "do or die" battle with the Mughal forces. Therefore, the Guru did not come under any kind of pressure and wrote fluently, without any fear of the erstwhile State. He knew many languages but most of his works have been written either in Gurumukhi or in Hindi (the earlier version of Hindi used now). His lifestyle was simple. He was at peace with himself as he was basically a saint. He fought wars for the sake of the oppressed Hindus and the downtrodden. There is no other example of such a personality in the entire history of the mankind.

During his later years, he went to Maharashtra. He had gone down too deep into the territory of the enemy. This mistake proved to be fatal for him. At Nanded (Maharashtra), he was attacked by two mighty Pathans (sent by Wazir Khan). He suffered severe injuries at the stomach. The bleeding was profuse and the chances of his survival were dim. However, Alamgir II, the Mughal emperor of those times, was respectful towards the Guru. Upon hearing the news, he sent his own physician, Dr Kohl, for treating him. Dr Kohl was a British doctor and an efficient one. He operated upon the Guru and therefore, saved his life. But once, the Guru tried to repair the bow by putting the string across its diametrically opposite ends. In this process, the wounds on the stomach opened up and blood loss was severe. The Guru now knew that his end was near. He called the Sikh soldiers and told them that *Shri Guru Granth Sahib*, the holy book of the Sikhs compiled by Guru Arjun Dev, would be the only Guru of the Sikhs after him. He died in 1708 AD, at the age of forty-two years at Nanded. A Gurudwara (Sikh temple) has been constructed at that site and is known as Gurudwara Hazur Sahib. The Guru, therefore, showed the path of righteousness, simplicity and valour to millions of downtrodden Indian masses.

This period of Indian history could be termed as a turning point. Had the Sikhs not taken up swords, the Mughal rule would have continued over the entire subcontinent for many more centuries to come. The opposition from the Sikhs weakened the Mughal rulers. Later, the Sikhs became a major power to reckon with in Northern India. They ruled the territory from Peshawar to Ambala, including many parts of Jammu and Kashmir and Himachal Pradesh. The credit of rise of Sikh power and the decline of Mughal power squarely goes to Guru Gobind Singh.

As the students of history and morality, we ought to learn many lessons from the life story of the Guru. He was a committed soldier, a compassionate leader, a spiritual guide of the masses and an educator who enlightened those who came near him for the divine knowledge. His virtues cannot be described in a few words as he was a perfect man, a perfect saint and a perfect human being. His creativity, love for music, passion for good literature and a respect for his friends and foes are some of the qualities that we should try to inculcate in our personalities. Another virtue that he had was the tenacity of purpose and the courage to fight the evil forces with all his might. Ironically, only a few among us possess it and those who possess it, are losing it quickly in the wake of the rising commercialism and the unfazed wave of immorality. Today, we need the Guru more than we did three centuries ago. His guidance and sermons could be read and listened to in order to continue on the path that would lead us to the Lord.

"Those who killed by the sword shall be killed by the sword," was the slogan of Guru Gobind Singh. He meant that the result of one's deed shall be bestowed upon him sooner or later. Therefore, we should take a pledge to do the Satkarmas (good deeds) and avoid Kukarmas (bad deeds) as we cannot escape the wrath of our deeds or their very nature.

The Sikhs respect Guru Gobind Singh as the messiah and the guide of the Sikh nation. He stands out in the list of the ten Gurus who devoted three centuries to the cause of Sikhism. The basic tenet of Sikhism emanated from the simple fact that Hindu masses had to be protected from the oppressors. Today, Sikhism is a full-fledged religion and the credit for this goes to Guru Gobind Singh Ji.

The saint did not live long but he could have guided the destiny of this nation if he were given a chance to lead the right-minded forces on this subcontinent. And had Shivaji, a contemporary of Guru Gobind Singh, joined hands with him, the Indian nation would have come out of the dark ages much earlier. We owe a lot to his legacy and sacrifices. Persons of his calibre and patience are indeed, rare. In fact, the entire Sikh community is proud of him for whatever he has given to the entire humanity. He would always be remembered for his sacrifices and would continue to be a role model for all the times to come. He was a true angel of God and we rightly know him as the messiah and the saviour of the masses. Let us pay our respect and reverence for the great saint of India who was not merely a saint but was more than that-a saint warrior !

THE GLOBAL ECONOMY

84. AN OVERVIEW OF THE GLOBAL ECONOMY

World economy undergoing changes for good—World trade has increased—GDP figures of all the nations are on the rise—US$ and Yen have shown sharp falls during the past few months—Global raw material production is cost effective—Pure fluctuations affect international trade—Foreign exchange markets suffer due to regulation over the capital transactions—Globalisation has picked up in manufacturing and services—WTO is still a hotbed of international politics—Indian Rupee was able to float independently—Electronic commerce lalready initiated in India—New concept in international trade—internet operations would help—Financial crisis in Europe, Japan and Pakistan—MNCs would play vital role in international trade—Trade Protectionism must be stopped.

The global economy is the combined effect of international trade activities and the policies adopted by the nations of the world for a smooth flow of goods and services across the globe. The new world is dominated by trans-national economic activities. After the Second World War, the world economy was characterised by a rapid growth. During the past twenty years, the world economy surged ahead with clear growth signs in Latin America, Far East and the third world nations. The GDP of the global economy has more than quintupled since 1950 or by a factor of ten. There are three major aspects of the world economy\—international commodities, foreign exchange markets and the WTO. Let us discuss them in brief.

The commodity markets of the world deal in goods like raw materials and crude oil. There are no major differences in quality. Price is a factor for the developing economies. The US Dollar and Japanese Yen have shown sharp falls during recent months. This would mean that it is easier to import in Dollar terms. But exports would be hurt at the same time as the earnings of the exporters have

have diminished considerably. Indian Rupee is stable against the US Dollar.

Raw materials are the most briskly traded commodities of the world. The international markets have developed uniform prices for raw materials. This has balanced the global supply and demand for raw materials. The exchange currency is US Dollars and hence, the commodity markets have global operations now, a feature missing in the markets of other goods. Further, the commodity prices are fixed at the commodity exchanges. The commodity exchanges facilitate simultaneous price fixing around the world. The futures contracts facilitate trading along the time axes.

The globalisation of commodity markets has led to the distribution of worldwide investments in raw materials. Thus global raw material production is highly cost effective.

But there is a negative aspect of this phenomenon. The price fluctuations at the international level create uncertainties in the international commodity markets. That is because the developments in the international commodity markets provide inputs for the domestic economic policies and *vice-versa*. All the developing nations of Asia, Africa and America are dependant upon the fluctuations in price and demand of the raw materials that form a major part of their exports. The sharp variations in the price of crude oil have proved that even the industralised nations are also not immune to the disturbances resulting from the developments in the international commodity markets. Therefore, market globalisation would not only affect the world economy, but also it would cause imbalances in the individual national economies. This effect would ultimately reflect in the global economy in qualitative and quantitative terms.

The second major issue of the world economy is the foreign exchange markets. With the introduction of convertibility, deregulation of exchange rates and the removal of most of the limitations on the capital transactions, the foreign exchange markets have become global markets in the true sense of the word. Now international capital transactions and the efficient exchange of goods and services are possible. But the foreign exchange markets can also cause serious disturbances for the global economy when the market forces are suppressed by political pressures.

Globalisation is also being witnessed in the manufacturing sectors in the services sectors. The industrialised nations have done more business in these vital areas. The developing economies are also picking up on these fronts.

The third vital aspect of the world economy is the development of common international trading protocol through GATT and its transformation into World Trade Organisation (WTO). It is disappointing to note that some nations of the world are trying to dictate their terms for their benefit on this major international trade forum. However, India and other developing nations have completely opposed these moves by a handful of nations as their economies are likely to be adversely affected due to biased trade policies. The debates are still on and WTO is now a hotbed of international politics. It is likely to be a constructive platform for world economy in the times to come.

Let us discuss the development of the world economy. It has been stated earlier that the world economy picked up quickly after the second World War. This positive development was due mainly to the expansion of International trade. The UN support come through UNCTAD and WTO. World Food Organisation also contributed effectively in this sphere. Bilateral trade agreements and opening up of the communist economies led to more opportunities for exports and imports. The end of the cold war in the eighties led to reduction in demand for arms and tools for anihilation. However, there was a great demand for consumer products and telecommunication equipment. Demand for cars also rose, though the American economy faced crisis on this front.

There was an increase in the international division of labour. This resulted in increased productivity and efficiency. Therefore, real income jumped to new heights in the industrialised world. During the late fifties, the trade barriers either removed or lowered. A procedure for currency conversion was introduced. India joined the free market revolution during the late eighties and early nineties and allowed her Rupee to float freely. To the delight of Indian economists, the Indian Rupee was able to float independently *viz-a-viz* the major currencies like the US Dollar, Euro, Pound Sterling *etc*.

The domestic supplies to the nations of the world have increased. Consumer electronics, mobile communication products and computers have occupied the centre-stage in the domestic product markets. The foundation for the creation for such global markets were laid over several decades. This process started with removal of trade barriers and an end to the celings on capital transactions.

Another major aspect of the world economy is the rapid advancements made in all the fields of science and technology. Transportation, communication, computerisation, software development and electronics sectors saw far-reaching changes on the international front. The regional markets were networked and were converted into global markets. Business transactions are now possible through E-mail and E-com. Internet and web surfing are the latest terms. The rapid growth of information technology has opened up new vistas for the developed and the developing economies. In India, E-com has already been started. This would also allow the electronic money transfer across the globe. E-com is likely to revolutionise the *modus operandi* of Indian business firms and their orientation towards global markets.

The next vital component of the dynamic world economy is the convergence of the financial markets. The internationalisation of the financial markets has been quite rapid during the past few years. This was made possible due to the removal of restrictions on capital transactions, currency convertibility and the opening up of markets to foreign banks. Now a days, capital is circulated freely in almost all the major commercial centres of the world.

Another vital part of the world economy is the spread of the derivatives. Derivatives are financial tools (like futures, options and swaps) and have been derived from traditional financial tools like shares, bonds and currency. Their central economic function is the cost effective coverage of individual risk options. The growth of derivative markets was enhanced through the usage of latest techniques in information technology. The exchange rates were deregulated during the seventies and also, due to the debt crisis during the eighties. 1980s. Both these events needed a strong diversification of the risks involved in international financial transactions between the market players. The debt crisis in the world trade could not have been resolved in the absence of the derivatives.

The balance between savings and investments is settled on an international level and no longer on the level of a national economy.

Free trans-national capital transactions make the savings of one country available to all the citizens of another country who might need them urgently. Further, the seeker of capital is always looking for the most favourable conditions for borrowings and capital requirements. Today, we have a growing global savings pool for money and capital supply.

The final phase of discussion would focus on the emerging markets of the world economy. Those nations, which promoted dynamic investment climates and a good return on capital employed in international terms, got the maximum benefit from the developments in the past few years. The main reason was the capital flow into these economies.

For good quantum and healthy direction of capital flows, the differences in rates of return are vital in international marketing. But exchange rate forecasts and actual development of the exchange rates constitute a crucial factor for controlling the international capital flows into the international markets. This could result in temporary disturbances in the financial markets in which, there is a crisis of confidence in an individual currency or an economy.

The recessionary trends in Europe, Japan, Singapore and Pakistan continue. India economy is taking a U-turn and industrial production has improved. Overall growth rate of our economy is nearly 6 per cent.

During the fiscal year 1999-2000, the American stock markets operated in tune with the bulls phase. The Dow Jones jumped by a record number of points during March 12-19, 2000. By the end of March, 2000, Indian economy showed an upsurge and the inflation rate was contained well within limits. There is no crisis of pulses, vegetables and necessities in the markets. Money supply is slightly better but not adequate.

The globalisation of markets has led to the conclusion that the economies of Asia, Latin America and Eastern Europe have become more important in terms of their shares in global production and trade. The industrialised nations would have to accept the emergence of these nations as global players. Imports by as well exports from the developing nations of Asia, Latin America and Eastern Europe are likely to rise sharply in the years to come. These nations enjoy low labour cost advantage but as they progress, the labour cost advantage would be lost. The main reason would be rapid industrialisation and very high rates of inflation in these countries. These nations are also able to acquire modern technologies and therefore, would emerge as major competitors for all the product and service ranges *viz.-a-viz* the industrialised nations of the world.

The industrialised nations have their own advantages on international trading front. Capital goods and financial services would remain the major thrust areas for exports by these nations. In low-wage sector, they would face stiff competition from the developing countries. Therefore, we can conclude that consumer goods sector would be the exclusive playground of the developing nations.

Multinational Corporations (MNCs) have a vital role to play in the global economic scenario. The MNCs are aiming to exploit the maximum number of target market riches around the world. They would, therefore, contribute effectively towards the emergence of new international markets by supplying technologies and expertise to these markets. With intensified investment activities in the emerging markets, there is a surge in the demand for imported goods in these countries as a result of their operations. Therefore, the regional production structures are changing and MNCs are contributing towards this end in a unique manner.

On January 1, 1999, twelve European nations declared amalgamation of their currencies and introduced a new currency—the Euro—in their financial structures. Currency unification would help these nations tide over their recessions. The UK did not take part in the Euro fever. Eventually, all the twelve nations moved towards a single currency system in the new millennium. These nations also hope to overcome exchange rate fluctuations through a common currency.

Account-like balancing of exchange rate fluctuations is not possible on international front. Uncertainties related to future exchange rate movements certainly hinder international trading activities. So, they limit competition with its price-curbing and efficiency-increasing effects. Further, unexpected re-valuations and devaluations lead to misallocations of capital; only a small amount is invested in export-oriented industries but very small amount is invested in domestic. Re-valuation affects the investment climate and devaluation seriously hurts the confidence of the consumers in their respective countries. So, exchange rate fluctuations wipe out some of the benefits of market globalisation. The solution to this problem is the creation of large monetary area in a region.

On April 8, 1999, World Bank's Annual Global Development Finance Report (1999) was released in Washington. The report stated that India, China and Mexico would be able to withstand the continued steep fall in average growth rates. It stated that chronic fiscal deficits persisted in the economies of India, Turkey, Brazil and Russia. The Bank praised Ethiopia, Male, Uganda and India for adopting policies that facilitate growth while keeping nations out of a total of 113 developing called for greater financial assistance to them.

85. THE AMERICAN ECONOMY

The American economy is the growth engine of the world—Largest and most prosperous economy—MNCs generate most of export revenues—The USA also sells arms and defence equipment to other nations—Heading towards a service-based economy—All types of industries thriving—Unemployment is also prevalent—She is the leading exporter and importer of the world—Faced severe recession due to recessionary trends in Japan, Hongkong, Oriental nations and Europe—An end of boom period could lead to low consumer spending trends—The USA is the largest investor in India—Oriental economies coming out of recession and this would help the American economy.

The United States of America is the major growth engine of world economy. She is proud of having one of the most dynamic and versatile economic systems in the free market world that is synonymous with efficiency, growth and capitalistic supermacy. Our worthy readers can easily judge the economic prosperity levels of the citizens of that nation by understanding the simple fact that there is a car for every 2 persons in the USA but there is hardly any method of transport for every 200 persons in India. The American dream of prosperity emanated from the commitment of the British settlers to the tenets of liberty and toil. When British settlers went there nearly 500 years ago, they cleared the dense jungles through the rocky mountains in Utah and tamed the wild river Mississippi-Missouri. It took them nearly 100 years to control the native "American Red Indians" and build a nation that was unique in many aspects. Today, the USA spearheads the global economic growth and is a true mirror of the progress achieved by mankind in all its endeavours.

The American economy has faced many tantrums during the decade of the nineties of the past century. As the economy of a prosperous nation cannot grow in isolation, the impact of 'crash' in the major Asian economies affected the American economy as well; the retardation of these economies affected the US economy in a harsh manner. This had happened in 1997 when the economies of Japan, Malaysia, Singapore and Thailand had nose-dived and the American exporters were left, cringing with tear about the shape of worst things to come. However, that dark period is now over and American economy is on its way to a healthy recovery.

Before we discuss the major statistics of the American economy, let us analyse how the American economy works. There are some components of the US economy, which are as follows :—

(A) Exports generated by MNCs.

(B) Revenues generated by the large corporate players who operate in the North American subcontinent only.

(C) Small and medium entrepreneurs who are involved in the manufacture and marketing of products and services in the United States alone.

(D) The Department of Defence of the American administration that sells arms, ammunition, technologies (related to defence) and other war machines to the nations, rebels and individuals around the world.

Our readers would be surprised to note that unemployment and poverty are prevalent in the USA as well. However, the State takes adequate care of the unemployed persons (citizens). They are paid enough of allowances and financial security, which would enable them to lead their idle lives with dignity. Further, the entire operations of industries, banking, commerce, international trade, medicine, education and business firms are fully computerised. Every citizen has a Social Security Number that enables him to enjoy his or her rights and privileges. As the problem of unemployment has assumed alarming proportions, the qualified young professionals prefer to start their own firms. Hence, in the USA, there is a very large number of very small-sized firms. The leading firms and MNCs of the USA are Procter and Gamble, Sears Reabock and Co., General Motors, Colgate Palmolive, Ford Motors, Microsoft Corporation, Mcgraw Hill Group of Companies, 3 M and Du Pont. The economies of the USA, Japan and Europe constitute nearly half of the global economy. And the USA emerges as the leader in the group of most developed nations; her standards of living are next only to those in Canada, Singapore, Switzerland and Sweden. She is also the largest consumer of fossil fuels, electrical energy and other energy sources.

On February 8, 2000, Mr. Bill Clinton presented his last budget as President. The budget has a spending plan of US$ 1.84 trillion and had very poor chances of its approval by the Congress, which is led by opposition at present. It would yield a surplus of US$ 184 billion in the fiscal 2001, which would commence on October 1, 2000. The budget had proposed a surplus of US$ 2.519 trillion over the next decade. So, the US Administration would be able to pay off debt of US$ 3 trillion by 2013. Budget surplus in the current fiscal year is US$ 167 billion. The budget had special allocation of US$ 20 million for South Asia. Out of this amount, an amount of US$ 5 million had been earmarked for India for welfare activities in India, economic reforms of India and liberalisation programmes.

The American economy is service oriented. That would mean that the services sector plays a vital role in the growth of American firms. Further, the USA is proud of having many multinationals, perhaps the largest number in the entire world. These firms generate enough of revenues on a global basis. Despite her commitment to service-related industries, however, the USA had unemployed people as well; the unemployment rate in that country was 4.2 per cent.

The trade imbalance was not in favour of the USA. The nation was importing more than she is exporting. In July, 1999, imports increased by 1 per cent, to a value of US$ 104.2 billion. The rise in exports was to the tune of US $ 79 billion. In July 1999, whereas the exports during June, 1999 were to the tune of US $ 0.4 billion was too small for a large economy like that of the USA. Trade deficit with China in July, 1999, was US$ 6.31 billion and trade deficit with Japan was US$ 6.78 billion in July, 1999. In NAFTA, the American partners of accounted for one-third of the total deficit, which is likely to be US$ 250 billion during the fiscal year 1999-2000. The trade agreements of the USA with Mexico, Canada, and other partners of

Asia had led to higher revenues for those partners; the American economy could not reap the benefits of these agreements as it laid emphasis on imports.

If trade deficit increased, it would undercut the value of US Dollar as money would keep on flowing out of the USA in order to meet the obligations of import bills. The Dollar would become weaker and therefore, imports would be costly as it would be difficult for the importers of the USA to buy more from the foreign markets. This possibly led to inflation. The bank rate of interest would be stepped up. This would lead to the dampening of the present economic boom. And if this had happened, the global economy would have been affected.

The American economy had been growing and ought to slow down. This would be necessary in order to rectify the imbalance in trade. But the brighter side of the American economy was also having some dark spots. The slump in the Asian markets was over. The recovery of the economies of Japan, Malaysia, Singapore and Thailand is quite visible. The large capital outflows caused by the crisis of 1997 did not allow these nations to pay for imports and their economic growth rates were slashed. These nations reduced their imports but continued to export. Hence, there were trade surpluses in the Asian nations. The foreign exchange reserves increased.

This situation could be repeated at a later stage as well. There could be an end in the boom of the American economy. This could lead to a fall in consumer expenditures. The American economy would drag the economies of Europe and Japan, both these nations being heavily dependent upon the USA for their exports.

Further, the developing nations would also have an impact of the totally transparent and open American economic mechanisms. These nations do not export much and they do not have the financial leverages to get loans from the international markets. Therefore, the developing nations may be plagued with another financial crisis, the one that was witnessed by the major economies of the Asian subcontinent.

Most of the global capital is in the USA. The American stock markets account for more than half the value of the equity markets of the world. If the American economy were to lose its tempo and faces a serious slump in its domestic front, the tremor would be felt directly in Japan, Thailand, Singapore and China and indirectly in the developing nations.

Let us take a close look at the economic relationships between India and the USA. The political events are a harbinger of a healthy trend in the field of Indo-US relationships. India and the USA are close to each other now and share many views. However, Enron and Cognetrix have already burned their fingers and if red tape continued in India, American businessmen may refrain from investing here or operating their plants here. It must be noted that many American firms specialise in the fields of automobile engineering, car manufacture and power generation. And these are the fields in which, India has to concentrate. Power generation is the major area to be explored. The power generation companies of the USA are watching the course of events with interest. The ball is in Indian Court. Despite these problems, the USA continues to be biggest investor in India and this is a healthy sign. American Bill Clinton arrived in India on March 21, 2000 and signed trade agreements worth US$ 2 billion with Indian firms. It was hoped that his visit would open new chapters in Indo-US trade cooperation.

American economy is the major economic and industrial growth engine of the entire world. Experts feel that it could run out of steam. If the American economy is forced to commit suicide, many Asian economies would be forced to commit a *Sati*. However, American economy, as on date, is resilient enough to meet the challenges it now faces. We should pray that this engine may continue to move bravely on its path !

86. IS WTO BIASED TOWARDS THE WEST ?

The WTO agenda for liberal international trade has drawn criticism from the poor and developing nations—Bias towards the rich nations quite evident—UNCTAD conference held in 1964 for liberalisation of international trade and for removal of trade barriers—Subsequent UNCTAD conferences did not yield results—WTO is the natural outcome of UNCTAD—Ministerial Meeting of WTO held in Seattle during December, 1999—Anomalies exist in the areas of agriculture, textiles and intellectual property rights, labour, trade norms and environment—The USA and her allies want to push WTO in the direction of their choice—Rich nations want trade liberalisation in those areas in which they should be benefited—Some solutions suggested.

The agenda of WTO for conducting international trade on mutually agreeable terms had again attracted the attention of all the economic thinkers around the globe. All the nations support WTO and its policies but sincerely feel that these policies are biased in favour of the rich and industrial nations. Let us try to analyse this complex global phenomenon in the context of new economic equations that are being developed around the world.

WTO and its predecessors were the outcomes of UNCTAD conference. The first conference was held in 1964 in Geneva and one hundred nations participated in the conference. The main agenda was to improve the economy of the developing nations. In order to fill the gaps between the standards of the developed and the developing nations, UNCTAD took some remedial measures. The developing nations needed technology, goods and investments in terms of foreign capital. The exports of raw materials were declining whereas the prices of imported machinery and other goods were rising. In order to overcome this crisis, UNCTAD (1964) made the following suggestions :—

(A) The industrialised nations (the USA, Japan, Western European nations, Canada, Australia *etc*) should allocate cne per cent of their national incomes for the developing nations.

(B) An international Trade Organisation-comprising 77 developing nations of Asia, Africa and Latin America-was set up to review the problems of international trade. It was also proposed that international trade would be developed through this platform.

(C) The demand of the developing nations for preference in the industrialised nations and reduction of 50 per cent cut in duties on certain types of goods was rejected.

(D) The land-locked nations demanded the freedom of right of transit of their goods through the seas.

The subsequent UNCTAD meetings generated much furore but minimal results. The rich nations were not keen to liberalise the international trade norms in favour of the poor nations. WTO is the indirect outcome of UNCTAD conferences. WTO would guide and mould international trade policies and issues related to trade protectionism. It must be stated categorically here that WTO has not been able to achieve its coveted objectives as the international trade consensus could not be arrived at between the developed and the developing nations. The apathetic attitude of the industrialised nations had led to economic and political stalemates around the world.

On May 18, 1998, the former Indian Commerce Minister, Mr Ramakrishna Hegde, warned that unilateral trade actions by the developed countries would jeopardise to multilateral trading system governed by the WTO. Such measures, according to him, would slow down the impetus for economic reforms in the developing nations. Mr Hegde was giving the Indian opinion at the Second Ministerial Meeting of the WTO held in Geneva during the second week of May, 1998. He added that the Uruguay round of talks had brought forth some concrete and positive economic measures for liberal international trade. The provisions of the Uruguay Round Agreements could be jeopardised if the Western nations resorted to unilateral economic decisions.

Developing nations have to struggle against severe resource crunch and the WTO does not offer much support as the concerted efforts of the rich nations would not allow any decisions to be taken in the favour of the developing and the least developed countries.

Further, a series of anomalies exists in the pacts of WTO on agriculture, intellectual property protection and textiles. Promotion of trade as an instrument should be the major building block of the multilateral trading system whereas it is not so. The developing nations had been given a period of ten years to introduce product patents in pharmaceuticals and agro-chemicals. But the obligation to provide exclusive marketing rights neutralises this cushion, according to the former Indian Commerce Minister. He also stated that there was a visible imbalance (and bias) in the Agreement on Trade Related Intellectual Property Rights (TRIPS). He noted that there was a tendency to resort to anti-dumping measures so that nations like India may not have access to the markets, which they would like to explore. Such measures could create uncertainties and economic chaos in the domestic and international markets.

The concept of borderless commerce is fine and it is the chief objective of the WTO. However, the developed nations want to reap the maximum benefits of this system without giving any consideration to the needs of the poor nations. The Marrakesh Summit was held four years ago and no concrete headway was made between the haves and the have-nots. The Second Ministerial Meeting held in Geneva during May, 1998, again brought the authoritarian tendencies of the USA and other affluent nations to limelight. The USA and her rich allies want to push WTO in the direction of their choice but the developed nations have adopted a 'gradual' approach for accepting and assimilating the decisions of the organisation. The USA, however, has been able to promote her interests by forcing WTO to address issues which she likes to be discussed and resolved in the times to come.

The USA wants to have rapid trade liberalisation where she enjoys the advantage. These areas could include agriculture, services and electronic commerce. For example, the USA managed to push through an agreement in Geneva, which forced the nations not to improve tariffs on the transmission of digital information via Internet. It is the fastest developing field of information technology and would have to be studied deeply before a final commitment is made on paper by the developing nations. Other areas for agreement include investments, liberalisation of procurements by the governments and linkage between market access and environmental as well as labour standards. These areas are not linked directly to international trade. These are the disguised efforts of the multi-nationals for promoting their commercial interests at the expense of the interests of developing nations. Further, the developing nations could not get their major concerns addressed at Geneva. These included tariff and non-tariff barriers (which affect their exports) and TRIPS regime on patents. Both these issues have made the developing nations vulnerable to biopiracy. Indian traders would be seriously affected as a result of the deliberations concluded at Geneva.

There are 135 members of WTO. Its Director General is Mr Mike Moore who would have retired by now. The forum has not been able to provide adequate trade protection to all its members. Indian concern is justified as the Western block and rich nations of the world have their own axe to grind in the WTO meetings. The developing nations have been skilfuly sidelined.

On December 4, the latest WTO conference ended in a whimper at Seattle (Washington). Nearly 25,000 protestors marched through the streets of Seattle and opposed the discriminatory trade policies of the USA and the Western nations. These protestors included citizens of the USA and Canada. Some representatives of NGOs were also among them. President Clinton pacified them and stated that there demands would be given due consideration.

Further, issues like labour, environment and trade protection measures were discussed in Seattle but no decisions could be taken. The Cairnes Group, the European nation, the developing nation and the USA (along with Canada) are the four major power blocks at WTO. The poor nations do not have any identity or political clout. India is also a member of "Green Room," which comprises 23 nations. The meeting of "Green Room" was also held during the deliberations at Seattle. Indian policymakers are giving their support to Western nations and the USA, which indicates a drastic policy shift. European nations have refused to remove subsidies on agricultural products.

Some solutions have been suggested by the author in this regard and are as follows :—

(A) Our problems arise from our economic dependence. Hence, we must raise our productivity, quality of output and resource generation capabilities.

(B) We must also export more. This would help us earn valuable foreign exchange.

(C) The economic fora like WTO and UNCTAD would demand an immediate conformance with their norms and agreements. Our diplomats should make it clear that we cannot embrace free market system with a single hop; we should move towards a free market world slowly and carefully. It is true that we are heading towards the free market economic system (which is coupled with global economy) but we may not be able to accept all the features of free markets and capitalism. Our needs are entirely different.

(D) We have been opposing the West and the rich few on all the major fora. Instead of opposing them, we should start cooperating with them by signing some simple (and harmless) agreements at the international fora.

(E) The mutlilateral trade agreements should be signed keeping the requirements of all the parties in mind. WTO would certainly become a platform for the right-minded people in the times to time.

(F) We propose that the Asian nations should merge their currencies and form a single currency unit. This would eliminate bilateral trade hassles in the Asian region.

The next conference of WTO is due to be held in Geneva within a few months from now. Further, the UNCTAD conference was also held recently. The rich nations and poor ones were seen at loggerheads during this meeting. India should align her trading policies with those of the developing nations. Child labour and environmental control are critical issues and are likely to give tantrums to the developing nations and LOCs. The developing nations would have to rise to the occasion by uniting their political and economic powers on all the major international platforms. Let us begin with the next meeting of WTO.

OUR ENVIRONMENT

87. ENVIRONMENTAL CHALLENGES

Earth only living planet—Environmental degradation beyond repair—Depletion of forests—Ozone layer—Floods—Earthquakes—Man-made causes—Hazards due to nuclear explosions—Global Warming—Greenhouse Effect—We must check environmental degradation through afforestation, fuel economy, control of toxic wastes and regulation of nuclear plants.

The earth is the only living and breathing planet in our solar system. The life of fauna and flora as well the future of the human race would depend upon its health. However, rapid advancements in sciences, industry and nuclear armaments have led to considerable changes in the environment of this beautiful planet.

There are many contributing factors that lead to ecological imbalances and environmental degradation. The major causes have been appended as follows :—

(A) **Depletion of Forests**

The food chain depends upon the vegetation of the earth. Forests are an integral part of the vegetation. Man has cut down the vast forest reserves in the name of industrialisation and rapid urbanisation. Moreover, the rural masses depend upon wood from the forests to keep their kitchen fires alive.

The loss of forest cover has resulted in an unstable rainfall pattern. There is a reduction in annual rainfall in those areas where forest covers have been depleted. For example, poor or only moderate rain fall in Northern India and in the National Capital Region during June-September, 1999, amply demonstrated that our rainfall patterns are no longer normal as they were a decade ago. Imbalance of proper supply of oxygen has adversely affected all the living organisms. Air pollution has increased. Forest covers minimise soil erosion during floods and are also, a natural habitat for wild life. With the reduction in their size, the fertile land as well as wild life have been seriously affected. Several wild life species, like Dodo, have become extinct. The temperature in the forest covers has increased at an alarming rate. If afforestation measures are not taken around the globe, the posterity may have to pay heavily in terms of the costs of environmental degradation.

(B) Ozone layer

Ozone layer surrounds the atmosphere of the earth and protects us from harmful solar radiations. It also protects the earth from overheating. However, Chloro Flouro Carbons (CFCs), Carbon Monoxide and other gases rise up in the atmosphere and form compounds with Ozone gas. Thus density of Ozone gas is reduced above the surface of the earth in the upper atmosphere. This phenomenon is termed as Ozone Hole. This hole allows the harmful ultraviolet rays to pierce through the atmosphere and fall on to the surface of the earth. The earth gets heated up and the living beings are also exposed to these rays. If these unhealthy trends continued, then polar ice caps would melt which would eventually raise the ocean levels.

(C) Floods

Due to melting of the polar ice caps, the ocean levels would rise. So, low levels areas of the earth would be submerged. There would be small land left for us. For example, low lying areas like those of Bangladesh would be submerged first due to the melting of polar ice caps.

(D) Earthquakes

If the poles of the earth get heated up due to Ozone holes, the ice would melt and would flow into the oceans. This would result in dangerous imbalances. So, the axis of the earth would shift. This could result in earthquakes. This natural disaster has already affected many nations; India, Iran, Mexico, the USA and China are examples.

(E) Man-made Causes

Man is causing environmental degradation through pollution. He is polluting the mother earth by three methods.

Firstly, man is polluting the air by burning millions of tonnes of hydrocarbon fuels. The poisonous gases coming out of the vehicles, plants and factories, generators *etc* are making life a misery for our children. Delhi is as the fourth largest polluted city in the world. Environmental pollution has brought diseases like TB, lung cancer, eye defects, Asthma, infections, bronchitis *etc* for adults and children alike.

Secondly, man is polluting water (underground as well water of oceans) by mixing industrial and household waste materials and chemicals in it. Water drilled from beneath the earth is also polluted beyond repair; this phenomenon is more prominent in the industrial townships and big cities. We can always read about a few incidents of spillage of crude oil in the high seas, which pose a major threat to the environment on the high seas as well as their acquatic lives.

Finally, man is polluting the soil by mixing pesticides, fertilisers and toxic chemicals for agricultural production into the same. The soil is becoming toxic because of the lust of man for more money. Industrial wastes are being dumped in the rural areas (where the chemical industries are operating) and the crops produced in the immediate vicinity of the factories and processing units are harmful for human consumption.

(F) Hazards due to Nuclear Radiation

The dumping of nuclear wastes by the Western countries has raised a hue and cry in all the corners of the world. The pro-environment international organisation-Green Peace-has vehemently opposed such measures taken by the nuclear powers from time to time. The nuclear wastes would be dumped either in water (high seas) or in soil (deep inside the earth). Whatever may be the method of disposal, the harmful radiation and toxicity so generated could reach the living beings and this could create havoc for them.

Further, nuclear tests are being carried out frequently by the nuclear States as well as by other nations. This also affects the environment in an adverse manner. Nuclear weapons could wipe out the entire humanity several times over or could annihilate all the living forms or processes within a few minutes. Even if we use nuclear power for peaceful purposes, the results could be highly detrimental to the mankind and our example. Chernobyl disaster in Russia is the most glaring evidence in this context.

We must control this global disaster by resorting to afforestation, using eco-friendly vehicles, consuming lesser amounts of fuel than we are consuming today, avoiding the piling up of nuclear weapons and finally, taking utmost care in the operations of chemical and nuclear plants around the globe.

After the nuclear tests on May 11 and May 13, 1998, India has come under severe attack by the world. Indian leaders have been criticised on political grounds only. However, our responsible scientists and politicians have political as well as environmental implications in view. Our policy supports peaceful usage of nuclear power. We would not be interested in polluting our environment with nuclear bombs and wastes. Further, we are also keen to eliminate pollution, which is being caused by thermal power plants. This fact can be supported by the measures by the Ministry of Environment to stop clearances of fourteen power projects on environmental degradation grounds. Table I shows the list of ten thermal projects that await clearances from the ministry.

Table-I: Projects Awaiting Clearances From Ministry of Environment

S No	Name of Thermal Project	Capacity (MW)	State of Operation	Pending Since
1.	Gautami Power Ltd	330	Andhra Pradesh	November, 97
2.	Snehlata Power Ltd	220	Andhra Pradesh	December, 97
3.	Maithon Thermal Power Station (RB)	4×250	Bihar	June, 97
4.	Apollo Energy Co Ltd	300	Delhi	April, 97
5.	Mysore Power Gen Ltd	4×250	Karnataka	August, 97
6.	Pulakeshi Power Co	110	Karnataka	December, 97
7.	Tahir Bavi Power Co	170	Karnataka	April, 97
8.	Saran Rajasthan	650	Rajasthan	December, 97
9.	Pacific Electric Power	2×400	UP	September, 95
10.	NTPC	650	UP	January, 98

Some of the aforementioned projects are being cleared by the ministry subject to assurances that environmental degradation would not be effected due to execution of the same. Negotiations are on and pollution control measures are being taken by the concerned authorities for putting a check on pollution of all forms.

We must conclude by stating that environmental protection is the most serious issue to be addressed by the masses, the scientists and the politicians in the interest of the health of our planet. ●

88. ILL-EFFECTS OF URBAN POLLUTION

Pollution is a bane for the urban society—It has adversely affected the city dwellers—(a) Air pollution—(b) Water pollution—(c) Food pollution (d) Noise pollution—Many diseases are caused due to pollution—Some of the diseases are bronchial asthma, TB, headache, blood pressure, suffocation, cancer etc.—Get your vehicles checked or tuned regularly—Use lead-free petrol—Grow more trees—Shift industryiesoutside towns and cities—Industries must conform to pollution control norms —Euro-II pollution emission norms being followed for cars in New Delhi—Avoid using CFCs—Every individual must contribute towards pollution control.

Nearly 30 per cent of Indian population is in the major and minor cities of this subcontinent. There are 4 major cities, 28 minor cities and a total of 450 cities and towns across the length and breadth of this nation. Rapid urbanisation has forced the dwellers of our cities to lead a life full of shortages, diseases and poverty. However, as their economic conditions are better than their brothers and sisters in the rural homes, the immigrants to the cities always try tosettle down in the area of their choice. There are only a few exceptions to this rule.

The burgeoning population levels have taken their own toll. The impact on the urban canvass of India has been tremendous and rationally speaking, negative. We are living in the most crowded and populous cities of the world sans many vital facilities that are essential for human life. Water contamination, shortage of medicines, good food, traffic congestion and fast life are some of the features of today's urban India. However, the most prominent feature that deserves immediate attention of the urban populace, the environmentalists and the government is the problem of pollution.

Pollution could be defined as the excessively high levels of irritants or toxic substances in the elements of the biological habitat that are essential for human life and growth. There are four types of pollution on our planet today :—

(1) Air Pollution—Polluted air contains CO_2, CO, NO_2, Suspended Particulate Matter (SPM), oxides of lead, and SO_2. A dangerous rise in the levels of these gases or chemicals leads to nausea, suffocation, vomitting and even death. The deadly viruses and bacteria of Hepatitis B, Dengue, TB, lung and chest infections, polio, hay fever *etc.* are also the result of this pollution and have their origins in the chemical and biological sources. Air is polluted by vehicles, factories, generators and large scale industries like pharmaceutical industries and thermal plants.

(2) Water Pollution—Water is polluted in the urban strata by factories, sewage from houses and general garbage in the urban areas. Water is contaminated even if it goes below the surface of the earth. When it is extracted in the cities by means of pumps, it still remains contaminated. Until and unless it is purified, it remains poisonous. It also contains dangerous viruses and bacteria.

The contaminated water is supplied by the municipal corporations for households and factories. It is normally not purified, though, now a days, the urban trend is towards the purchase of modern ultra-violet filters. The urban residents are aware of the need of a good filter but many are unable to purchase the same.

(3) Food Pollution—Due to polluted air and water in urban centres, the food products, which are produced or cooked in the presence of water or air, are polluted. Most of the food items sold by roadside shops are unfit for human consumption. People are tempted to eat them because of the taste. Hence, they fall sick after consuming the efforts of the state and central governments for implementing healthy food norms, the sellers of sub-standard and contaminated food abound. The lust for money takes its toll everyday in terms of numerous cases of cholera, viral fever and typhoid in Indian hospitals.

(4) Noise Pollution—The urban centres are highly mechanised. The noise of vehicles, machinery, factories, generators and other urban utilities (which are increasing everyday) is unbearable. This results in loss of hearing, headache, mental tensions, partial mental imbalances and migraine. The urban noise levels are much higher than the safe levels stipulated by the administration.

The ill effects of air pollution have already been manifested in terms of dangerous diseases like TB, bronchial asthma, respiratory diseases, eye defects, skin problems and overall reduction in the agility of the bodies. The long term exposure to Lead Oxide could be dangerous as this chemical is carcinogenic and is a probable causative factor of lung cancer. Similarly, SO_2 is also a dangerous pollutant. It can get mixed with H_2 and O_2 in the atmosphere and can produce H_2SO_4, which could come down on earth as acid rain. Similarly NO_2, NO and CO are noxious gases and could induce sleep, nausea vomitting and even death.

Polluted water can bring bacteria and viruses into the body. It could also fill our bodies with dangerous factory chemicals (especially, Mercury salts, Lead salts, colour dyes and acids). Some of the chemicals are carcinogenic and could put the urban dwellers in serious troubles. Polluted water could also cause skin cancer and ulcers in the stomach. It is more effective for bringing the disease into the human body *viz-a-viz* other elements like food and air. Water is circulated in the body almost instantaneously whereas food requires 40-90 minutes for digestion in the stomach and the small intenstine. Air pollution starts affecting the lungs and the respiratory tract. Further, 4.4 billion people in the developing nations lack sanitation facilities. This fact leads to further deterioration in their health.

Food pollution is associated with water pollution. It is capable of bringing the victim to the state of complete disability (as is in the case of amaebiosis) or partial complications (as in the case of viral fever). Sometimes, polluted food could cause death also if medical help were given in time. Urban areas are prone to viral fevers, cholera, tuberculosis and hay fever, Hepatitis B infections, cirrhosis of liver, skin eczema, bronchitis, bronchial asthma and serious diseases of the brain.

Noise pollution could create mental problems, deafness, high blood pressure and brain haemorrhage. It is a growing menace in the urban centres, especially in the areas marked by extremely high traffics and industrial production.

We should devise concrete methods for fighting the urban pollution. Some of the logical steps should include :—

(1) Get your vehicles checked regularly. If needed, get the engines tuned after every two months.

(2) Avoid usage of petrol, which contains lead. Lead Oxide is a great killer of the modern times and is carcinogenic. In New Delhi, usage of petrol containing lead was banned recently. The absence of Lead leads to "engine knock" but it would have to be tolerated by the motorists.

(3) Avoid using two wheelers and three wheelers as they are basically two stroke engines. Two stroke engines consume mobil oil in the engine chamber. This leads to extra pollution. Four stroke engines do not create high pollution levels.

(4) Grow more trees and vegetation in the urban areas. This initiative should come from the urban masses. The State could extend a helping hand.

(5) The industrialists should try to shift the industry outside the urban centres. Basically, the urban centres are meant for human populace and trading. Manufacturing processes create pollution and hence, must be avoided in an urban context.

(6) If at all, the industries have to operate in urban areas, we should ensure that they conform to pollution norms set by the state and central regulatory authorities. We would recommend that only non-polluting industries (like electronics, packaging, furniture *etc*) should be allowed to operate in the cities and townships.

(7) The four major metropolises and twenty-eight minor cities of India must be divested of all types of industries. These industries should be shifted to rural areas or satellite townships of these cities.

(8) The usage of Chloro Flouro Carbons (CFCs) must be banned they deplete the Ozone layer in the upper atmosphere.

Every year, 15 million areas of dry land are added to already desetified 3.2 billion acres of dry land aroud the world. Further, the global availability of water has dropped.

By the year 2010, CO_2 emissions would increase by 30-40 per cent as compared to the present emission levels. During 1990-2030 period, lead emissions would be five times the emissions of present times. Over the last fifty years, the temperature of the world has increased by 1 degree Celsius due to global warming effect. Industrialisation has not been followed by efficient waste management and disposal of toxics at a matching pace around the globe. As a result, sweet water lakes of Sweden and Canada have been polluted due to flow of industrial wastes from their neighbouring nations through air or water.

The Earth Summit (at Rio De Janiro in 1992) prepared "Agenda-21" which was adopted by 178 countries of the world. One hundred nations agreed to roll back emissions to the levels of 1990 by the year 2000 AD. Although these summits cannot deliver concrete results in terms of environmental management, yet we would expect nations of the world to adopt at least those clauses of "Agenda-21," which are easy for them to adopt.

Urban areas are easy targets for pollution related problems. We have to take care of the urban centres by monitoring the pollution levels in all the vital ingredients—water, soil, food and air. Earth summits would continue their "Window-dressing actions." The urban dwellers have to devise cost effective and pragmatic solutions so that they could save themselves and their children from the ill-effects of rising urban pollution.

89. INDIAN ENVIRONMENT

The world continues to grow at an amazing pace—Environmental degradation process in its full swing—Environmental statistics about India cited—Pollution levels rising—Many plant and animal species under threat of extinction—Ozone layer depletion—Nuclear plant wastes very dangerous—Pollution of air, water and food prominent in urban centres—We keep our homes clean but forget about our habitat—No help from industrialised nations—We must use strict social and legal procedures for controlling degradation of our environment.

The world continues to grow at an amazing pace. But the price of growth is being paid by the natural resources of the mother earth, the habitat, the environment and our children who would eventually inherit this world from us. Environmental degradation has assumed alarming proportions. As we have to assess the complete situation in a correct perspective, we should discuss some vital environmental statistics in Indian context.

We must check the environmental degradation process. Pollution in air, food and water has reached dangerous levels. Add to it, the problem of noise pollution, garbage disposal, non-degradable waste disposal and nuclear waste disposal and are ready with the most evil instruments for the destruction of life on the green-blue planet. Reduction of forest areas, depletion of ozone layer, frequent floods and draughts, earthquakes (especially in the Himalayan region), displacement of villagers due to construction of dams and finally, nuclear radiation hazards have made this scenario even more awesome All these developments on the environmental front do not auger well for our planet and its residents; after all, it is the only living planet in this part of the universe.

The environmental statistics in relation to the Indian environment have been appended in Table I. India has a highly diverse, multi-weather and multi-terrain ecology. All the climates have been known to exist here. The figures shown in Table I are very vital from the viewpoint sof our environmental protection and management. The environmental X-ray of Indian subcontinent is necessary as every nation is keen on finding out what is wrong with her eco-system.

As is evident from Table I, our commitment to ecological balance, biodiversity and environmental maintenance is not very religious. After comparing the environmental statistics of India, the environmentalists were deeply shocked. To state an example, we have 40 threatened species of mammals, 71 species of birds and 1,256 threatened species of higher plants in India alone. CO_2 emissions are also increasing everyday. The forest covers are being reduced due to continuous expansion of human habitats, industrial townships and industrial activities like mining, manufacturing and processing. The living areas for the animals are shrinking every year and humans are occupying their habitat on the pretext of development of their race.

In India, the following chief symptoms have been noted in the degrading environment scenario :—

(A) The forest cover is being reduced steadily.

(B) Floods and draughts are more frequent.

(C) Ozone layer depletion, though not at a fast rate, would be clearly dangerous enough during the times to come. The West is already feeling the heat of Ozone layer depletion. The ice caps on the Himalayan mountain ranges are now melting at a much faster rate and we are not aware of the consequences of this dangerous development.

(D) The fertile top soil is being eroded due to the lack of **trees** and vegetation.

TABLE-I : India Under the Environmental X-ray

S. No.	Parameter	Year of Measurement	Unit	Value
1.	Population	2000	Million	1,000.0
2.	GDP Growth Rate	1999	Billion US $	456.16
3.	Per Capita Income	1998-99	Rs	14682.3
4.	Life Expectancy Upon Birth	2000	Years	61.0
5.	Child Malnutrition	1990-96	Percentage of Children Under 5 years	66.0
6.	Sanitation	1995	Percentage of Population With Access to Sanitation	29.0
7.	Safe water	1995	Percentage of Population With Access to Safe Water	81.0
8.	Crop Land	1995	Crop Land as Percentage of land area	57.0
9.	Forests	2000	lakh hectares	633.4
10.	Annual Deforestation	1990-95	sq kms	– 72.0
11.	Fresh Water Resources	1996	cubic meters per capita	1,957.0
12.	Emissions of Organic Water pollutants	1993	kgs per day	1,441,293
13.	Biodiversity	1994	Threatened Mammal Species (Number)	40.0
14.	Biodiversity	1994	Threatened Bird Species (Number)	71.0
15.	Biodiversity	1994	Threatened Higher Plant Species (Number)	1,256.0
16.	CO_2 Emissions	1995	Million Metric Tonnes	908.7

(E) The nuclear power plants and research facilities are spewing out dangerous chemicals, effluents and radiations that are likely to cripple or annihilate the mankind. There are no effective methods of nuclear waste management as the ill-effects of the nuclear research and experimentation are not visible today. However, this would be a major issue of concern for the environmentalists during the times to come..

(F) Pollution of air, water and food is very prominent in the urban centres. The irony is that we are ignoring it skilfully in India. And the final damage could be done by pollution in the rural areas as well.

(G) In the noise pollution levels have reached dangerous proportions and the resulting psychological illnesses have taken their toll in terms of reduced industrial and managerial outputs.

The state of environmental affairs of other developing naions is not different from that of the Indian scenario. The ecological doomsday near. The reasons are as follows :—

(A) We are lacking resources. Hence, we are unable to eliminate the effluents, wastages and pollutants from our environment. Environmental protection needs effluent treatment technologies, machinery and technical manpower. The processing technologies are new and complicated. Some firms have started manufacturing such equipment in India. We would require time and money for adopting new and cost-effective technologies related to environmental control.

(B) We are not organised either. The environmental management issues needs planning and resource allocation at the central, state and regional levels. And we have not decided our environmental management strategy though we have the basic infrastructure executing authorities.

(C) The population (and especially, rural population) is not aware of the hazards of ecological imbalances and environmental degradation.

(D) Urban people is very much aware but they lack time, money and attention for such vital issues. For example, all the fifteen year old vehicles in New Delhi were banned *wef* October, 1998. But there is a great hue and cry from the truck drivers, bus drivers and auto-rickshaw owners. They contend that they cannot replace the old machinery with the new one. And the State is bent upon executing the order, which was released by the Supreme Court. How can we pacify these "responsible citizens" and how could we ever persuade them to accept non-polluting vehicles in the interest of residents of the city ? They are keen on making money with minimum costs. Hence, the Supreme Court had to intervene in the interest of the environmental cause and for the better health of the residents of New Delhi. This is a clear example of imposition of environmental regulations upon the Indian citizens. There is no voluntary adoption of such vital measures. The Indian Capital would soon be invaded by electric auto-rikshaws that are totally eco-friendly and would not generate pollution.

(E) Financial help and technologies from the industrial world have not been forthcoming in this context. The pollution scenario is dominated by the rich and industrialised nations. These nations have also developed methodologies for controlling the same. These technologies and equipment, if adapted according to our conditions, could bring very favourable results for us. We have to ask for these technologies, equipment and manpower.

(F) We are very religious about the cleanliness of our homes and surroundings. We are not concerned about the area we live in. We are not responsible about our cities. The civic sense, very much alive in the West, is totally missing in India. For example, we would never throw garbage in our drawing room. But we would be pleased to put this garbage in a disposable bag and would throw it out of the car window when we move out of our homes. That garbage deserved a well defined dust bin but was thrown on the road. Little do we realise that these activities harm us ultimately (or, other citizens). The urban scene is full of such examples. Similarly, many urban areas do not have proper sanitation facilities. And the government is unable to provide these vital amenities due to the lack of money or due to a procedural bottleneck. The quality of life in urban India has been jointly degraded by her citizens and the government. And there seems to be no end to this urban disaster. Garbage lies scattered on the roads. Stray animals feed on that garbage. Diseases and epidemics spread through dirty water, sewage *Nullahs* and leaking drain-pipes. The government takes adequate measures but the unplanned growth in population offsets the impact of the measures taken.

It is a do-or-die situation in the Indian context. Our pollution levels are one of the highest in the world. The price is being paid by the urban and semi-urban of this continent in terms of money, health and psychological problems. If we do not rise to the occasion now, our posterity would face the doomsday sooner than we could probably imagine.

Solutions must be devised for this problem at the earliest. These solutions would demand the participation by the citizens, strict laws by the judiciary and finally, strict implementation by the government. Time is now ripe for protecting Indian habitat and environment from a serious environment disaster. Indian environment is vulnerable to serious decay and we should manage the same through concerted efforts of the masses, the State and the latest technologies at our disposal. We all know that there is no second mother earth to protect; we have only one mother for ensuring our survival.

90. INDIA'S ENVIRONMENTAL STRATEGY

Environment is the major issue in the new century—Fifth Round of negotiations on climate change held at Bonn in 1999—Developing and developed nations were at loggerheads—Developed nations to cut down greenhouse gas emissions by 5 percent by 2012 AD—Developing nations contend that rich nations would sell technologies and equipment but would not achieve the pre-decided emission norms—33 per cent of Indian land to have forest cover—Draft Biological Diversity Act proposed to be brought into force—JMS made an integral part of plantation projects—Preventive measures taken by the State for curbing pollution and protecting wildlife—India is conscious on this front.

Environment is the major issue at all the economic and political fora of the twenty-first century. The habitat now deserves an empathetic treatment, contend our environmentalists and ecologists. Stunned by the dangerous pollution levels in water, soil, air and food, our national and global priorities have been shifted towards a more pragmatic and eco-friendly approach towards the environment. Let us discuss some latest developments related to environmental management that were witnessed by India and the world.

The fifth round of negotiations on climatic change was concluded in Bonn in 1999. The differences between the developing and the developed nations were evident during the conference. The chief issue was the efforts to meet the targets (established in the Kyoto Protocol), which were supposed to cut down the emission of harmful gases. The conference led to a clash between the developing and the developed nations over this issue. The rich nations demanded the usage of equipment by the poor nations, which are based on the *avant gardé* technologies. The developing nations objected to these demands and feared that their development could adversely affected as a result. The commercial aspects of attaining the state of clean environment was also brought to prominence and focus.

It should be recalled that the Kyoto Protocol (1997) forces the developed nations to cut greenhouse gas emissions by at least 5 per cent on the average below the levels of 1990, by the year 2012 AD. The greenhouse gas emissions are produced due to the combustion of fossil fuels like coal and oils. But only 14 nations have ratified it and no other nation has decided to ratify the Kyoto Protocol unless the treaty permits the unrestricted usage of the market mechanisms and unless there is meaningful participation on the part of the developing nations in the treaty. The proposed treaty and its *modus operandi* require the developing nations to accept funds and technologies in return for the a strict over emissions. The developed nations have been persuaded to give credits to poor nations that would enable them to meet parts of their emission reduction commitments. The G-77 group and China gave fresh terms for participating in the pact. The character of the G-77 states that the nation opting for market mechanism would be the sole judge of whether the project in question is able to meet her national. sustainable development objectives and priorities. The funds to be supplied by the developed world would be supplementary to the nation in question for her efforts regarding the control of emissions. All the aspects of such projects would be kept transparent.

The developing nations contend that the rich nations would try to sell the equipment and technology for reducing emissions in the developing nations; they would not like to achieve the pre-decided emission norms at their ends. On this issue, the developing nations have shown solidarity of views. India has urged the developing nations to concentrate on safeguarding their own interests. Therefore, the summit at Bonn ended in a stalemate. The next meeting was slated to be organised in The Hague after one year. The developing nations would have to develop a concrete agenda for the same.

Environment has started dominating Indian polity, society and economy as well. On June 5, 1999, World Environment Day was observed. The railways announced a ban on sale and smoking of cigarettes on the railway platforms as well as in trains. The government of Delhi state announced a ban on usage of recycled plastic bags. The Union Minister for environment and forests, Mr S Prabhu, stated that the government would soon declare environmental audit compulsory to ensure civic discipline and self-compliance with and environmental protection norms.

Further, Mr AB Vajpayee proposed to bring 33 per cent of land of the nation under the forest cover according to a twenty-year plan. The Environment ministry was given a pat on the back for promoting the participation of rural women in revising forest nurseries through the Integrated Rural Development Programme (IRDP). The PM also appreciated the plan of addition of six new tiger reserves to the existing 23 reserves. He also praised the biodiversity legislation, which has been drafted recently.

Some major policy decisions taken by the central government, in respect to the environmental regulation and control, are as follows :—

(A) Plan to achieve 33 per cent forest cover in the nation.

(B) Coastal Zone Management Authorities to protect India's Coastline.

(C) A strategy for revitalising the education regarding environmental issues in schools.

(D) A draft Biological Diversity Act proposed for conservation, sustainable utilisation and equitable sharing of advantages of the biological resources.

(E) Identification of parameters for declaring eco-sensitive zone.

(F) A national environmental policy for the nation.

Other incentives included in the national environmental policy are as follows :—

(A) One hundred per cent centrally funded scheme, for reducing pollution loads in 22 major cities.

(B) Programmes for planting 50 trees in each village of the country already launched.

(C) Action plans for pollution control for the National Capital Region of Delhi and Mumbai Metropolitan areas.

(D) Creation of an Authority under the EPA for the conservation of the Taj Mahal.

(F) Institution of Amrita Devi Bishnoi National Award for the village communities to promote protection of wildlife.

(G) Establishment of Environment Surveillance Squad for controlling industrial pollution.

(H) A new tiger reserve created in each one of the states of Karnataka and Maharashtra.

(I) A comprehensive national level policy on biodiversity, including the macro-level action strategy for the same.

(J) An all-India coordinated project on taxonomy.

In the present century, the State would seek participation of people for ensuring strict environmental regulation. Some of the aspects in this context are as follows :—

(A) The status of all the clearances would be hosted on the official website of the Ministry of Environment.

(B) State of Environment Report for the entire nation would be prepared.

(C) Establishment of 40 Waste Minimisation Circles (WMCs) for the adoption of environmental-friendly and useful technologies in small industries.

(D) Networking done among 25 premier institutes to provide information under the ENVIS network.

(E) Joint Forest Management (JMS) programme made an integral part of the projects related to plantations.

(F) A new website, named http://sdn.delhi.nic.in launched for Sustainable Development Networking Programme (SDNP).

The preventive measures, for checking the environmental decay, are as follows :—

(A) Export of 29 endangered medicinal plants banned.
(B) Export of Deer Antlers banned.
(C) Conservation of Panchimashi Ecologically Sensitive Area Draft planned. Notification to this effect issued.
(D) Ban on the usage of recycled plastic bags for ready-to-eat food. Notification to this effect issued.
(E) The segregation of wastes, treatment and disposals in the hospitals regulated under Biomedical Wastes Rules, 1998.
(F) Ban on 2T mobil oil in the NCT of Delhi for two-stroke engines. Lead removed from petrol in the NCT of Delhi.

The government plans to achieve its major targets in terms of environmental conservation and protection of wildlife in the country. Some of the thrust areas of the future include the following :—

(A) Action plan to achieve 33 per cent forest cover in the country.
(B) National Environmental Action Plan for the Control of Pollution (NEAPCP) promoted.
(C) Economic decisions to incorporate environmental concerns and issues.
(D) Notification of Municipal Solid Wastes Management.
(E) Conservation of biodiversity of the Western Ghats and that of the North-East.
(F) Amendments in Indian Forest Act and Wildlife Protection for more effective Conservation.
(G) Setting up of National Environmental Fund (NEF).

The environmental policy of the State is an ambitious exercise but its implementation and pragmatic sustenance are the key issues for its successful adoption. Let the Indian masses support the government for building a nation that is green, environmentally clean and sans the poisons, which now dominate our lives at present. ●

91. AIR POLLUTION

Air required by everyone—Air pollution is wreaking havoc in rural, urban and suburban areas in India—WHO laid down guidelines in 1973—SO_x, NO_x, SPM and CO are the major pollutants—Pollution due to vehicles, factories, generators and due to human activities in urban and rural areas—Trace metals also found in the atmosphere—Sound pollution is also a matter of serious concern—All noises above 45 decibels are harmful—Discard old vehicles—Supreme Court ordered that Euro-II emission norms have to be followed in new cars—Maruti cars came out of trouble—Tune the vehicles for low pollution levels—Electricity driven vehicles would arrive soon—Devise corrective measures quickly—Our children would inherit this pollution.

All biological organisms require air for breathing. All the green plants need Carbon Dioxide for photosynthesis and hence, for making their food. The atmospheric air contains Nitrogen, Oxygen, Carbon Dioxide, Carbon Monoxide, Ozone and other gases. Oxygen is vital for human survival and also for animal life. Carbon Dioxide is required by plants. Air pollution is caused by industrialisation, urbanisation and excessive exploitation of resources. This polluted air is inhaled by humans and plants. The result is a complete catastrophe. We are falling prey to new diseases and epidemics. The plants are getting extinct for want of proper air supply. Carbon Dioxide-Oxygen cycle of nature has been disturbed by man himself. The impact of this imbalance has not been felt seriously. However, our environmentalists and the responsible citizens of urban India can feel the heat.

World Health Organisation (WHO) established some norms for air quality in 1973. The basic aim was the collection of data on air and effective control of air pollution so that the eco-system was not disturbed. WHO studies population distribution, industrial development, topography and climatology. The idea was to promote information exchange between the nations. The project studies a wide range of parameters such as percentages SO2, SPM, NO_2 and supplies vital data to 50 nations (1991 figures) for SO_2 and SPM levels. There were 175 locations in 75 cities till 1991 for the collection of this data.

Table-I clearly delineates the guidelines of WHO for major air pollutants.

TABLE-I : WHO Guidelines for Major Air Pollutants

Pollutant	WHO Norms	
	Annual Mean (Micrograms per m^3 of Air)	98 Percentile (Micrograms per m^3 of Air)
1. SO_2	40-60	100-150
2. Suspended Particulate Matter (SPM)		
(a) Black Smoke	40-60	100-150
(b) Total SPM	60-90	150-230
(c) Lead	0.5-1.0	0
3. NO_2		
(a) 1 Hour	400	—
(b) 24 Hours	0	150
4. CO (mg/M)		
(a) 15 Minutes	100	—
(b) 1 Hour	30	—
(c) 30 Minutes	—	60
(d) 8 Hours	—	10
5. Carboxhamoglobin (as percent)		2.5-3

    The air pollution scenario has taken the turn for the worse. For example, in urban India, industrial units are located in densely populated residential areas. The noxious gases like NO_2, SO_2, hydrocarbons, CO_2, CO and SPM easily find a place in the urban homes. Add to it, the emissions from the automobiles, industrial generators and generators installed at homes. Further, air pollution is also effected by H_2S, F^-, NH_3, trace metals (like Co, Cu, Cd, Ni, Pb *etc*) and othercompounds in different particle size ranges. These alarmingly high levels of pollution have destroyed the health of many a healthy city dweller. The oil resources of the world would last for another century. By the end of next decade, most of the urban centres of Indian subcontinent would be deemed to be misfit for human livings. And the situation would become more volatile as the small cities and townships are also becoming vulnerable to pollution, diseases and merciless exploitation of the natural habitat. This menace is already taking its toll in terms of the growing number of epidemics, money spent on medical treatments, increasing human agony and above all, inconvenience and irritation due to pollution.

The Supreme Court ruled recently that all fifteen year old commercial vehicles and three wheelers would have to be scrapped. The administration of NCT of Delhi also proposes to impose Euro-II norms on cars. In fact, the transport department has been instructed to issue registration certificates to only those cars that pass Euro-II norms for emissions. This has already raised a lot of hue and cry in the city capital. People are resistant to change and so are the city skylines due to the alarming levels of pollution. The number of vehicles in the metropolises has been rising steadily. Further, according to a the ruling of a court, the city capital started consuming lead-free petrol with effect from September 1, 1998. This would lead to the total elimination of PbO_2, which is the major culprit behind respiratory diseases and lung cancer. Two-stroke two wheelers are likely to be scrapped in NCT of Delhi within a time frame to be decided by the Supreme Court and four-stroke two wheelers would rule the roads in future.

The woes of the residents of the mother earth have not ended here. Noise pollution has also occupied the centre stage on the environmental scene today. Table-II gives the noise levels generated by various sources of sound. The normal threshold of hearing for humans is 25-45 decibels. However, our cities are full of noises above 100 decibels. Ironically, we can take only a few remedial measures; the control of noise pollution in the broader context is not feasible even if tough measures were taken by the administration.

Table II clearly demarcates the normal threshold of hearing. It should be noted that even noise level beyond 45 dB could wreak havoc on our ears. Noise generated in the industrial sheds affects the industrial workers. The most offending culprits in the industries are compressors, generators, grinders, forced draught fans andsteam-release valves installed in the steam boiler circuits. In industry, the noise level of 80-120 dB(A) is common and this is too high to be ignored.

The Environment Protection Act specifies that the industrial workers should be exposed to a noise level of 90 dB(A) at the most for an eight-hour shift. The time limit has to be halved for an increase of every 3dB(A). Exposure to continuous or intermittent noise should not exceed 115 dB(A). Further, exposure to impulse noise should never exceed 140 dB(A) of peak acoustic pressure.

TABLE-II : Impact of Noise Pollution

S. No.	Type of Noise	Sound pressure (Decibels)	Impact upon Humanbeings
1.	(a) Clock Chime (b) Rustling of Trees (c) Chirping of Birds (d) Discussions in a Low Tone	25-45	Comfortable
2.	(a) Office Jobs (b) Occupational Noises (c) Barking of Dogs (d) Speeches	45-60	Annoys the person; Disturbs the digestive system.
3.	(a) Water Pump Operation (b) Ringing of Telephone Bell (c) Operation of Mixie (d) Crackers Put on Fire	60-80	Nervous system is strained; violence observed in behaviour mental illnesses.
4.	(a) Train Movement (b) Bus/Lorry Movement (c) Aircraft Moving Ahead (d) Hammer Strike	80-120	Ear drums are seriously affected; person becomes deaf in the long run.

Air pollution has led to a new environmental catastrophe. Respiratory illnesses, anaemia, pulmonary disorders, deafness, severe psychological and psychosomatic diseases and hyperactivity are some of the after-effects of pollution.

Pollution has also started affecting our nervous and mental systems. We must take adequate measures today so that our future could remain healthy and hazard-free.

All the vehicles must be checked for pollution control norms. It is sad to note that people have to be not concerned about pollution control and hence, are forced to get their vehicles tuned. There is no voluntary adoption of pollution control norms. Further, the materials that absorb sound should be used in our everyday lives. The workers must be provided with ear-muffs. Children must not be over-exposed to the noise of television, radio and high pitch music. Silence zones should be created near hospitals, parks, educational institutes and courts. Electricity-driven vehicles should be promoted as has been done in Russia and other Eastern European nations. In Delhi, the experience of introducing battery-powered rickshaw has been successful. Full scale introduction of these vehicles is expected very soon. The elimination or reduction of petrol driven or diesel driven vehicles would certainly reduce the pollution menace to a great extent. But the metropolises like Delhi are awaiting the execution of the transportation network being built by Delhi Metro Rail Corporation. The construction of various sites is already under way.

Further, car pools should be promoted so that people could save fuel and money. The urban centres could also get immense benefit from this unique scheme, which is quite popular in cities like New Delhi, Mumbai, Calcutta, Chennai and other big cities.

Smokleess vehicles and electric cars would soon be a reality. However, efforts should be made to tame the industrial air pollution menace as well. The polluting industries must be taken away from the urban landscape. It is proposed that the heavily polluting industries must be told to shut down their operations else there would be repetition of another disaster on the pattern of the leakage (of MiC gas) in a factory in Bhopal.

Industrial pollution, if at all it has to be generated, must be controlled within the premises of that particular industry only. NTPC is using its fly ash wastes for making low-cost construction chemicals and bricks. This is a good example of ecological prudence as well as economic prudence. The other industrial units must follow suit else they should be given legal notices for shutting down their manufacturing plants.

Air pollution control equipment are being manufactured by several Indian and foreign forms. Some popular air pollution control devices include centrifugal blowers, electrostatic separators, load fans, mine ventilating fans, cyclones, guillotine dampers, butterfly dampers, bag fitters, wet scrubbers and dust collectors. The technology for the control of air pollution has already been developed and many firms have been using the techniques and equipment for ensuring a complete (or almost complete) control over air pollution.

We must conclude by stating that the will to succeed on the pollution front would emanate from the urban and rural masses. We have accepted the status of our polluted environment without any protest; in fact, we are also contributing towards air pollution and hence, remain silent. Mass campaigns for the control of air pollution would have impact only if the population of our country is made fully aware about the ill-effects of air pollution. The State is playing its constructive role through radio, television and print media. There is an awareness among the masses but concrete steps would be needed to be taken in this direction. Our health and the future of our children are at stake. We must address this issue on the national scale and must seek long term solutions for a better environmental hygiene.

The world is painfully aware of the ill-effects of pollution. Some strict measures have been taken in the West for the control of air pollution. In Britain, for example, electricity is being used for driving bicycles and small vehicles. Westerners also realise the need for control of pollution and are busy developing vehicles that would either work an electricity or on hydrogen fuel. India must join the world for controlling pollution. Some popular pollution control measures would include a ban on the usage of CFCs, more emphasis on car pool system, development of metro railways, plantation of more trees and finally, afforestation. The citizens of the nations must become fully alert to the menace of air pollution and must join hands with the government agencies for controlling it. If suitable measures were not taken, our blue-green planet would decay in environmental terms. Let us rise to the occasion and save it.

INDIA-POLITICAL

92. PHYSICAL FEATURES OF INDIA

India is a vast nation—Six major regions in Indian peninsula—Himalayan region comprises the Shivaliks, the middle Himalayas and the greater Himalayas—The Indo-Gangetic plain contains the Eastern plains and the Western plains—The Malwa-Deccan Plateau comprises the Malwa plateau and the Deccan plateau—Thar desert lies in the North-West and is very hot—The coastal plains are on the peninsular periphery of Southern India—A large cluster of Indian Islands in Bay of Bengal and in the Arabian Sea—Our geographic profile is impressive.

India is a vast nation. She has impressive physical features. She also has all types of geographic terrains, seasons and fauna and flora. Indian peninsula is a rich and versatile land and is proud to be the cradle of the oldest civilisation in the world.

The Republic of India is a peninsula. It has 25 states that make up her national identity. India has a coastline of 7516.6 kms (which includes the coast-line of her islands also) and a border of 2,933 kms from East to West. She has a total land frontier of 15,200 kms. Her neighbouring countries on the land are China, Pakistan, Myanmar, Bangladesh, Bhutan, Tibet and Nepal. The North-to-South extremes measure 3,214 kms. India lies in the tropical zone from latitude of 8°4′ North to 37°6′ North and from longitude 68°7′ East to 97°25′ East. She has a total land area of 32,87,263 square kms. She is the seventh largest nation in the world in terms of land area. She includes 247 islands of which, 204 lie in the Bay of Bengal. The remaining 47 are located in the Arabian Sea and the Gulf of Mannar. A total of 47 per cent of the land area has been cultivated.

India is a hot country with moderate to severe temperature ranges for almost the entire year. For only four months, the solar radiation is incident upon India at an angle and hence, winter sets in during that period. The remaining part of the year (8 months) is a hot season in almost all the parts of the country. Coastal areas and Southern states are mostly hot and humid. Temperatures could go up to as high as 45-50°C.

Let us divide the physical features into six major heads :—

(A) The Himalayan Region

On the Northern side, India has the greatest mountain ranges on the earth. These majestic mountains are in the shape of an arc in the Northern part of our country. In India, the Himalayas start from the river Indus in the West to the river Brahmaputra in the East. The largest mountain peak of the world is Mount Everest (Nepal) and it lies in the Himalayas. It has a height of 8,848 meters above mean sea level. Other prominent landmarks of this mountain range are **Pamir plateau** (Tibet), Baltora glacier, Karakoram highway, Khyber pass and Zanskar range of mountains in Jammu and Kashmir.

The total length of the Himalayan range in India is 2,500 kms. The average height of the Himalayas is 19,000 feet. The Himalayas prevent moisture-bearing winds of the South from going to other countries. They also prevent the coldest waves from the Northern frontiers from overtaking the Indo-Gangetic plains. These mountains comprise green valleys, river systems, ecological wonders and flora and fauna, which provide life, thrill and solace to the habitat and the residents of this vast peninsula in various forms. Important cities include Srinagar, Simla, Gangtok, Kulu, Kangra, Almora, Nainital, Manali and Mussourie. These cities and townships are highly attractive tourist spots. The higher reaches of the mountains yield a rich variety of apples, apricots, almonds, peers, plums, peaches and many varieties of dry fruits.

Near the plains and upto a height of 500 feet, the Himalayan region includes bamboo trees, palm trees and rice fields. Above this, deciduous and coniferous trees such as oak, beech, ash, fir, pine and Deodar are found. In the East, rice, tea and maize are grown. Tea is cultivated in the valley of Assam, Darjeeling, Dehradun and Kangra. Fruits and dry fruits are grown in higher reaches of the mountains.

The important passes in the Himalayas include the Khyber, the Bolan, Shipki La, Nathu La and Bomdi La. Poorvanchal mountains are located on the North-Eastern side. These comprise Patkai Bum Naga hills in the North, Mizo and Lushai hills in the South and the Garo, Khasi and Jaintia hills in the centre.

The Himalayas can be sub-divided into three broad mountain ranges :—

(1) The Shivaliks—The Shivalik range of mountains is the Southern-most range of the Himalayas. It has a height of 900 to 1,200 meters above Mean Sea Level (MSL). They are made up of soft rocks, are discontinuous and lie on the Northern border of the Indo-Gangetic plain. They extend towards the East to merge with the main Himalayas.

(2) The Middle Himalayas—They are also called the Lesser Himalayas. They have a height of 3,700 to 4,500 meters above MSL. These mountains contain green valleys, river systems, ecological wonders and fauna and flora. The beautiful and bewitching Kashmir valley, Kulu valley, Kangra valley and Kathmandu valley (Nepal) lie in this range. The popular hill stations include Simla, Mussourie, Nainital and Darjeeling.

(3) The Greater Himalayas—They are also called the Upper Himalayas. They lie on the edge of the Tibetan Plateau. The average height is 6,000 meters above MSL. Mount Everest (Nepal) lies in this range and has a height of 8,848 meters. In Indian territory, Kanchanjunga (8,597 meters), Nanga Parbat (8,125 meters) and Nanda Devi (7,816 meters) are the highest peaks. Mount K-2 is also located in this range and has a height of 8,610 meters.

The Himalayas have always been dominating the culture, economy and spiritual orientations of Indian masses for the past five thousand years. The Ganges, The Yamuna and The Brahmaputra rivers have their origins in these mountains. The ancient system of herbs and medicines originated from the Himalayan fauna and flora. The Himalayas have the most beautiful tourist attractions in the world. The tourists from the entire globe flock to these destinations for the sake of health and leisure.

(B) The Indo-Gangetic Plain

This is the most extensive and fertile plane in the world. It is made up of alluvial soil that was brought down by the rivers from the mountains in the form of fine silt over a period of thousands of years. This plain consists of Indus basin, the Ganges-Brahmaputra basin and their tributaries. A bulk of Indus basin is in Pakistan. However,

Punjab and Haryana have a share in the same. The Ganges-Brahmaputra basin is larger one. This plain stretches from Sulaiman mountains in the West to Garo and Lushai hills in the East. Its width is 100-500 miles.

There is no striking difference between the Indus basin and the Ganga-Brahmaputra basin. However, a water divide (of a height of not more than 300 meters) separates these plains from each other. This divide has been made by a narrow ridge of Aravali range that passes through Delhi and Ambala. The two plains have similar terrains and characteristics except for this water divide.

The Indo-Gangtic plain can be divided into two major parts :—

(1) **The Eastern plain**—This plane is made up of The Ganges, Brahmaputra and its tributaries. The Ganges emanates from the Himalayas and enters the plains at Haridwar. Then, it flows towards the South-East and makes a big delta where it enters the Bay of Bengal. From the North, Gomti, Ghaghra and Gandak rivers water this plain. From the South, this plain receives the Yamuna river. The three rivers—The Ganges, Yamuna and Saraswati — merge at Allahabad. Saraswati river existed during the ancient times but is no longer visible. The tributaries of Ganga include Gomti, Ghaghra, Gondak and Kosi. The tributaries of Yamuna are Chambal, Betwa and Ken.

(2) **The Western Plain**—Basically, this is the Indus basin that has been described earlier. This plain has been formed by Indus, Sutlej, Beas, Ravi and Chenab rivers. It originates in Tibet and flows throughout Pakistan. Jhelum and Chenab are its tributaries and flow through Pakistan. Ravi river is also its tributary and it flows through India for some distance. Another tributary of Indus and a trans-Himalayan-river-(Sutlej) flows through India for most of its mileage. Beas is another tributary of Indus and flows through India completely. The major part of the Western basin belongs to Pakistan and only a small part belongs to India.

The Ganges-Brahmaputra river system covers one fourth of the total land area of the country. Beyond Farakka, the river Ganges flows into Bangladesh and is known as river Padma. At a distance of 80 kms from the Bay of Bengal, Padma is joined by Brahmaputra.

The delta so formed is one of the most fertile regions of the world. It is also the largest delta in the world. The other stream of The Ganges, bifurcated at Farakka, runs Southwards into West Bengal and is called river Hoogly. It splits up into a number of small rivers before finishing its journey in the Bay of Bengal.

(C) The Malwa Deccan Plateau

This region lies to the South of the Indo-Gangetic plain. It is made up of hard metamorphic rocks. It is bounded on the North by the Vindhyas and Satpuras and on the West, it is flanked by Western Ghats. On the Eastern side, it is enclosed by Eastern Ghats. Western Ghats rise abruptly from the Western coast and run from North and South from the Gulf of Cambay to Cape Comorin. They receive heavy rainfall and are covered with forests. Eastern Ghats run parallel to the Eastern coast and are not continuous in nature. They are dry and lack vegetation. The Deccan Plateau can be sub-divided into two parts :—

(1) **The Malwa Plateau**—It comprises the Northern region of the Deccan Plateau. In the North-West, it is bounded by the Aravalis. From South, it is bounded by the Vindhyas. The third side of the Malwa Plateau slopes gradually towards the Gangetic plain and gets merged with it. The valley formed by river Narmada forms the Southern boundary of this plateau. Its extensions to the East form the Bundelkhand and Baghelkhand in Southern UP. Similarly, its extensions in Southern Bihar include Chotta Nagpur. Most of the rivers in this region flow Northwards into the river Yamuna. The Malwa Plateau—especially, the Chotta Nagpur plateau—is a rich source of mineral deposits.

(2) **The Deccan Plateau**—It is triangular in shape. It extends from Satpura hills in the North to Kanyakumari in the South. On the Western edge, Sahyadri, Nilgiris, Annamalai and Cardamom hills form the boundaries. These are called the Western Ghats. Their average height is 2,695 meters above MSL. These hills run along the Arabian sea and their height increases as we go Southwards. Anaimudi peak in Kerala (with a height of 2,695 meters above MSL) is the highest peak in peninsular India. In the Nilgiris, Ootaccamund is a well known hill station.

From Western ghats, the Deccan plateau gradually slopes away towards East to Bay of Bengal. Eastern Ghats have discontinuous and low hills called Mahendra Giri. The major rivers of Deccan Plateau (Mahanadi, Godavari, Krishna and Cauvery) flow from West to East. They pass through the low hills of the Eastern Ghats and merge in the Bay of Bengal. Only Narmada and Tapti rivers flow from East to West and fall into the Arabian sea.

The North-Western part of the plateau is made up of lava flows or the igneous rocks, called Basalt. This is also called the Deccan Trap. These rocks have a thickness of several hundreds of meters and are spread over Maharashtra as well as over parts of Gujarat and Madhya Pradesh. The result is a dark soil called black soil (or Regur soil) and is excellent for cotton cultivation.

Many parts of the Deccan plateau are rich in minerals. Examples can be cited of Kolar (gold fields), Tamil Nadu (Uranium), Bihar (mica and uranium), Madhya Pradesh (coal deposits) etc. Further, iron ore, copper ore, manganese ore *etc* are deposited in the North-Eastern region of this plateau in rich abundance.

(D) The Thar Desert
To the North-West of the Malwa Plateau, is the Thar Desert. It comprises sand and rocky hills as well as waterless valleys. It begins from the Aravali range of hills and extends deep into the Pakistani territory. The rivers in this region either merge with the lakes or disappear into the sands. Only Luni river drains off into the Runn of Kutch. The region is hot and lacks rainfall. It is inhospitable to human, plant and animal lives. The temperatures during summer go up to 50°C and the night temperatures could be as low as 20°C. The region is marked by sandstorms and low population settlements.

(E) The Coastal Plains
These are two narrow strips along the Eastern and Western ridges of the Indian peninsula in South. The Western coastal plain lies between Western Ghats and the Arabian sea. The Southern part of the Western coast is called the Malabar coast. It is narrow and uneven. It has been divided by fast flowing rivers and streams. It also has lagoons, backwaters and raised beaches. The Northern part of the Western coastal plains is called the Konkan coast and includes the plains of Gujarat.

The Eastern coastal plain lies between Eastern Ghats and the Bay of Bengal. It is wider than the Western coast. It comprises deltas created by Krishna, Cauvery, Godawari and Mahanadi rivers. It is a highly fertile region. The Southern part of the Eastern coast is called the Coromandel coast. Its Northern part is called the Northern Sircars.

(F) Indian Islands

There are two main groups of islands :—

(1) The Andaman and Nicobar Group—These islands are located in the Bay of Bengal. They are small and have sparse population. The Northern cluster is called the Andamans and is a group of 204 islands. The Southern cluster is called the Nicobar islands and contains 19 islands. Port Blair is the capital of Andaman and Nicobar. The islands are marked by temperate climate, average temperatures and rains.

(2) The Lakshadweep Group—They comprise a total of 27 coral islands. These islands are located in the Arabian sea and are 300 km away from the Kerala coast. They have horseshoe or ring shapes and are not very lengthy or wide. Approximately, 17 Islands are sans human population. Kavarati is the capital of the Union Territory of Lakshadweep. The climate and rainfall are almost similar to those in the Andaman and Nicobar Islands.

We should conclude by stating that Indian geographic features are fascinating and give a unique status to our nation. The ambience of Indian geographic characteristics reflects itself in its land, climate and people. India is truly a diverse geographic marvel. ●

93. THE UNFIT TO RULE ALWAYS RULE US

Indian politics fpolity characterised by immoral practices—Coalition governments are doing well now—Profiles of political parties poor because their workers and members lack abilities to deliver concrete results on political, social and moral platforms—Lust for money and power corrupts senior workers and officials—Businessman uses the political parties for his gains—Corrupt leaders gain power—They exploit the nation—Corrupt politicians thrive in all political parties—Solution in the hands of Indian public—Define eligibility criteria for election to parliament and state legislative assemblies—Separate politics from business.

Indian polity is characterised by immoral practices. Coalition governments at the centre have been able to deliver some economic and political results. Indian masses have always given convincing mandates to the regional and local political parties. However, everytime an election is announced, the *Lok Sabha* is likely to head for chaos an account of the absence of a clear mandate in favour of a single party. These are not good signs for our national progress and stability.

The crux of the problem lies in the profiles of the political parties and their cadres. Political parties comprise callous, dumb and greedy workers and senior cadres. They play the communal card to their advantage during the elections. They always fulfill their own base objectives during elections and during the periods of power. So, Indian electorate does not like to vote for such dubious personalities. However, every party has such elements. Moreover, monetary power and muscle power forces the poor masses to vote for such candidates. Hence, they manage to sneak into Indian Parliament through unfair means. The workers of all the political parties are not corrupt but some corrupt elements spoil the image of the parties. These workers have not been able to deliver political, economic or social outputs on behalf of their parties.

In our Parliament, the political parties show selfish and chaotic behaviours. Hence, coalition governments fail. The nation suffers on account of lack of direction and slowdown in economic growth.

Further, the politicians with dubious records are made Chairmen and Presidents of PSUs. They exploit the national resources and government machinery for their gains. They try to allocate quotas and favours to their nearest kith and kin. They receive kickbacks, *hawala* money and cash or goods in one form or the other. Even Indian Prime Ministers are also not aloof from dirty politics and manipulations.

The basic reason for this decay is the large scale poverty of the masses and the incapable political parties who rule various regions of the nation. Take for example, an ordinary party worker (*Karyakarta*). He has to take up a job for survival or he must do some business. If he has to attend or organise meetings for his party, he must be paid so that he could survive. So, he takes some money from the party funds. Who would pay this money ? Naturally, Indian businessman who wants to reap rich dividends when that party comes to power. So, funds are supplied by the businessmen during the election campaigns and during the time for which, the party is out of power. Whenever the political party gains power, the businessman encashes his goodwill in the form of quotas, LPG agencies, coal stocks, raw material supplies, tenders for government departments and above all, favours for his men in the bureaucratic hierarchies. This nexus between the politician and the bureaucrat has been going on for the past fifty years. This has sucked up all the vigour, resources and morality of our democratic and economic systems. Politics is also a business and business is done now a days by using the political connections.

The overall impact of this nexus manifests itself in the form of corrupt leaders coming to power; state governments are also formed in this manner. Therefore, the unfit to rule are ruling us. The politicians with criminal records become Members of Parliament. They misuse the powers granted to them and perpetuate hooliganism, anarchy and economic chaos. Governments may come and go but the corrupt politician from one political party is replaced by another when the latter comes to power. The Parliament is let down by these wicked manipulators. The rulers exploit the masses and the masses have no alternatives. The truthful and honest politicians are skilfully sidelined. Gone are the days of Nehru, Gandhi, Sardar Patel and Maulana Azad. Nobody bothers about the historic sacrifices of our martyrs. Every politician wants to fill his pockets. Later, even if he is removed from office, he does not regret because he has already taken his quota from the loot.

The solution certainly remains in the hands of the public. We must take the following steps in order to cleanse our political system :—

(1) We must not vote for a politician who has a criminal record. The Election Commission has defined some criteria for the eligibility of the candidates in elections. Some politicians with criminal backgrounds were barred from taking part in the elections for the thirteenth *Lok Sabha*.

(2) If the voters are threatened by muscle power during elections or election campaigns, the voters should unite to form anti-political fronts. These fronts should take the help of the

police machinery in order to meet the challenges of the hooligans.

(3) If the voters are told to vote for a particular party in lieu of liquour, money, food or other materialistic assets, they should oppose this gesture vehemently.

(4) All the political parties must cleanse their organisations by removing politicians of dubious distinctions. It is in their best interests. The politicians, who have criminal records or have cases pending against them in any court of the world, should be treated as suspended. If, however, the designated judicial authority exculpates them from the charges, levelled against them, then they are welcome to join their respective political parties once again. We should not deny justice to the innocent politicians.

(5) Constitution must be amended so that basic educational and political qualifications could be fixed for any person for entering active politics. In our view, a political worker must be at least a graduate and must have worked for a political party at the grassroot level (*ie*, at village, block, tehsil or district level) for at least two years. After his "probation of two years" is over, he should be inducted as "party worker." Similarly, a candidate for a seat in the state assembly should be at least a post-graduate. He must have thorough knowledge of politics, law, international relationships and mass communication techniques. He should have a fine record of five years of serving the people of his constituency (or from the constituency from which, he wants to be elected).

The prospective MLA must be a practical person with good family background and economic status. Our experience concludes that a hungry politician fills his belly first of all. When he has his fill, then he thinks about serving the masses. A well-to-do politician would avoid this action. However, a poor person should also be allowed to come to power. The State should eliminate his poverty (in terms of cash and kind) so that he does not misuse his powers, if he is elected.

(6) A candidate for the Parliament (*Lok Sabha*) must be at least a postgraduate. He must have thorough knowledge of Indian polity, economy and the national problems. He must have served a single political party for at least five years. He must have a neat and clean record as a party worker. He must be a very pragmatic person who should have leadership qualities and drive. He must talk in terms of figures. He should know about international politics and the status of India around the world.

(7) A candidate for the Parliament (*Rajya Sabha*) must be an artist or a man of letters. He should never be a politician but an elder man in his early sixties. He should be well read and internationally acclaimed in his field. He should have at least a doctorate with an overall experience of thirty five years. The *Rajya Sabha* comprises the elder elites of this nation. Their main task is to guide the national polity and to bless the democratic system that thrives in our country.

If we take these steps, we would be able to separate politics from business. Some steps have been taken by the Election Commission in order to keep corrupt and criminal-minded politicians out of elections. The nation would not be exploited by the inept politicians and would progress towards a healthy and prosperous future of her subjects. ●

94. THE FOURTH FRONT

There are many political parties—Major parties not in a position of strength—BJP, Congress and left front are the three major fronts—They cannot lead the nation as they are in minority—No ifs and buts if we join a political party—Small regional parties not able to deliver results—If they shed their egoes, some solutions could emerge—Let the like-minded parties form the fourth front—Let the good leaders of the existing fronts discuss the issue—regional parties and small parties have a chance to capture power—Fourth front could be viable by 2005 AD—An Alternative to three fronts must be found.

Our politicians have the habit of forming new political party after almost every six months. So, we have forty-one political parties operating at national, regional or sub-regional levels in India. History has proved that a nation with the least number of political parties has always done well in terms of the standards of living, industrial production, international trade, social reforms and political stability. Examples could be cited of the USA, the UK, Japan, Germany, Taiwan, South Africa and other nations. In China, where people have to be content with " one party rule," the standards of living are much better than those in India. The political chaos in India has emanated from the large number of political ideologies that govern only a small set of masses of this vast nation.

But who would bell the cat ? Who would tell an Indian politician to pay heed to the cries of the common man ? Our political parties do not emerge for the sake of a revolution or for the benefit of the voters they serve. They are created for serving the base interests of a handful of politicians who do not get tickets for elections for the *Lok Sabha* or the state assemblies. They too want to have political identities and this leads them to the belief that they are being sidelined by the leaders of their parties. So, they quit that party and form a new one. Some of these leaders are genuine and they deserve what they have not been given. They prove their point when they win elections as independents or as members of another (rival) party. But most of the dissidents have some selfish motives and this forces them to launch a new party immediately before elections.

When India gained freedom, we had four major political factions—Congress, Jan Sangh, the Muslim voters and "the Comrades." But today, we have an alarmingly high number of political parties, the number of independents being excluded from the number mentioned earlier. We shall never state that the regional and local parties should not be formed. They should be. But would these small players be able to play a useful role on the national political platform ? Cannot they join a single party that might be having at least one or two thoughts common with them ? Why create a new organisation that has only meagre following in only a small region of this vast country ?

The profile of twelfth *Lok Sabha* had indicated that the new *Lok Sabha* was also going to have a multifarious profile. The Exit Polls also indicated that no party would be able to muster complete majority in order to capture power in the centre. The general elections for the constitution of the thirteenthe Lok Sabha proved the accuracy of the Exit Polls. The BJP came in limelight when it formed the National Democratic Alliance, a concoction of 22 political parties. The government promoted by the NDA rules this nation. BJP and its allies form the first front, Congress is the second front and communists (leftists) constitute the third front. Janata Dal, RJD and other parties are too small or immature to be known as independent political entities. So, they would have to align themselves with any of these three fronts, depending upon the benefits (in terms of tickets in elections, berths in ministries or support in state assemblies) that could be obtained by them from the political parties that are chosen by them as their ships. However, if the tide is not in favour of the ship in which, they travel for some years (normally, one or two), they try to switch their loyalties and form alliances to another front. There could be dissatisfactions, grievances of differences or opinions. Sometimes, the small regional and sub-regional parties jump out of the alliance due to sheer lack of common sense. This is a crime but political parties (especially, the smaller ones) have become habitual to it. If a major political party refuses to take care of the interest of a supporting political party, then these changes or shifts do occur more frequently.

Our idea of the fourth front is slightly different from this routine that has been going on in Indian political polity for the past thirty years, Why don't the small political parties form a strong and stable political entity ? They could have across-the-table discussions in this context and match their needs and demands with those of others. If some agreement among the like-minded political groups could be chalked out, this integration would strengthen the individual political groups and they could become the components of the new front.

Let us examine the structure of National Democratic Alliance (NDA). There are twenty-two parties in NDA. This structure does not alter the political status and demands of the constituent factions. Why do they not form a single political party and name it NDA ? They do not. That is because their political interests are not common. Mr Geroge Farnandes continues to head his own party and so does Mr Bal Thackeray. The same could be said about all other factions of the NDA. And all these leaders would continue to support Mr Vajpai at all the political platforms. This is not fair. If we hold a hand, we hold it forever. Let us not keep any "ifs or buts" in an alliance. If the constituent factions approve of the ideologies of BJP, then they should become BJP. The question of issue-based support or differences over some issues should evaporate into thin air. The fourth front must not commit these mistakes. Mr Vajpayee should not have taken the support of Ms Jayalalitha in the beginning of his earlier coalition term. Her unfair demands proved to be disastrous for the coalition government in the centre. The fourth front should single out those parties that could give them trouble. The lessons learned during the past two years should teach them that only the right-minded, politically stable, nationalist and unselfish parties could work together for achieving the objectives that are more pious than the shortsighted interests of the constituent political parties.

We have already stated that a new front should eliminate all the characteristics of the parties that merge to form it. This would go a long way in building it as a national alternative to other three fronts. When we board a political train, we are all passengers for the same destination; jumping out of the train could prove to be suicidal for any passenger. There are examples of many leaders of India who remained committed to a single party throughout their lives. They reaped rich benefits and their political parties also prospered.

In our view, Mr Sharad Pawar, Ms Maneka Gandhi, Mr Farookh Abdullah, Mr Chandrababu Naidu, Mr GK Moopnar, Mr Bansi Lal, Mr TN Seshan, Mr Arun Nehru, Mr Arun Shourie, Mr Khairnar, Ms Sushma Swaraj, Mr Rajesh Pilot, Mr Sikander Bakht, Mr Sitaram Yechuri and other leading politicians of our nation could have a preliminary discussion for forming a brave fourth front with a purpose. This front should be created for complete democracy among its cadres (which, ironically, is missing in Congress party), for nil communal affiliations towards one particular sect (which was allegedly existing among the BJP cadres during not so recent past) and for a definite anti-poverty agenda (which was always missing in the actions and plans of the entire left front).

The new millennium is knocking at our doors. The new face of Indian polity could please the Indian voter. The general elections for the thirteenth *Lok Sabha*, held during September-October, 1999, proved that the voters are not interested in this costly and agonising exercise any more (and this dangerous trend of low voter turnout would certainly chill the spines of many a political party). Here, is an opportunity for those political groups that do not have an identity or those that have small voter bases in their regions. They could join hands in order to create one of their own.

Congress, BJP and Janata Dal have been struggling for making their presence felt at the national level. Small political groups cannot bring about political revolution or social transformation at the mass level. But if a fourth front is formed, it could take the advantage of the political hiatus created by the chaotic conditions in the centre. And once, the battle in the centre is won, the state assemblies would also be easy to win.

There cann be a better opportunity than this. Let the like-minded political groups come together and discuss the issue with open minds. Time is running out. Although the BJP-led and NDA-supported government is stable as on date, nothing could be predicted about the future; they are all Indian politicians, after all !

The nation does not belong to the scams, saffron or the sickle-hammer. It belongs to the masses. And those political parties, which are capable of delivering concrete economic, political and social benefits to the masses, would certainly be welcomed with open arms. The concept of the fourth front might take a concrete shape when our romance with coalition governance is over. That could be true by the end of year 2010 AD. If a plan is mooted today, than by the end of year 2007 AD, we could see the rise of a viable and stable national party with highest standards of political ethics. The glorious corridors of power beckon the fourth front !

95. IS DEMOCRACY A GAME OF NUMBERS ?

The democratic mechanism is a game of numbers—Mr Vajpayee lost the confidence motion by 1 vote (269 votes to 270 in the motion)—This is not democracy—Small parties have base objectives—national interests sidelined by regional parties—Small political players try to change their loyalties for the sake of power—If Exit Poll results favoured Mr Vajpayee, then he could have continued as the head of the new government—Costly election exercises—Small parties trying to move the nation towards chaos—Redefine democratic norms.

Sometimes, we wonder whether our nation is really operating on a democratic pattern in the centre as well as in the states of India. At least the events during the first half of the year 1999 do not indicate a healthy trend towards a mature democratic state. Let us take the example of the political debacle in the centre and the rise of NDA after the general elections in order to analyse the aforesaid statement.

On April 17, 1999, the coalition government led by Mr AB Vajpayee lost the confidence motion in the *Lok Sabha* and was voted out of power as it could not get the support of a single voter. Losing a confidence motion by a single vote seems to be slightly odd, though many political analysts view this exercise as a victory for democratic forces. We do not think that this was a victory for our democracy as the erstwhile government had fell prey to the machinations of the political *hoi polloi*. This exercise could be termed as a political assassination of a weak but right-minded government in the parlance of democratic norms.

The political parties, which voted against the confidence motion, were as follows (with the number of votes cast by them in the parenthesis against the name of each party) :—

(A) Congress — 139
(B) CPI (M) — 32
(C) SP — 20
(D) AIADMK — 17
(E) RJD — 16
(F) CPI — 8
(G) Janata Dal — 6
(H) RSP — 5
(I) BSP — 5
(J) TMC — 3
(K) Forward Block — 2
(L) IUML — 2
(M) Janata Party — 1
(N) Majlis (Owaisi) — 1
(O) ASDC — 1
(P) Arunanchal Congress (M) — 1
(Q) AICC (Ola) — 1
(R) NC (Soz) — 1

(S)	Kerala Congress	—	1
(T)	UM	—	1
(U)	Buta Singh	—	1
(V)	PWP	—	1

On the other hand, those political parties, which favoured the confidence motion, were as follows :—

(A)	BJP	—	182
(B)	Samata Party	—	12
(C)	Telugu Desam	—	11
(D)	BJD	—	9
(E)	Akali Dal	—	8
(F)	Trinamul Congress	—	7
(G)	DMK	—	6
(H)	Shiv Sena	—	6
(I)	PMK	—	4
(J)	INLD	—	4
(K)	MDMK	—	3
(L)	Lok Shakti	—	3
(M)	National Conference	—	2
(N)	Maneka Gandhi	—	1
(O)	TRC	—	1
(P)	RJP (Anand)	—	1
(Q)	Arunanchal Congress	—	1
(R)	HVP	—	1
(S)	SDF	—	1
(T)	Independents	—	3
	(Satnam Singh, Lallungmauna and Biswamuthiary)		
(U)	MSCP	—	1
(V)	Nominated	—	2

Mr R Muthiah (AIADMK) did not vote, Mr Kim Gangte (CPI) was absent and Ms Malti Devi (RJD) was also absent. BSP had decided to abstain from the voting process during the confidence motion but turned the tables on the BJP-led coalition government at the last moment by voting against the confidence motion. Mr Giridhar Gamang (Congress) voted; perhaps, his conscience allowed him to do so when the Speaker of the *Lok Sabha* told him to take a decision himself. The member of National Conference, Professor Saifuddin

Soz, defied the party whip and voted against the motion. The party president, Mr Farookh Abdullah, later expelled him from the party.

The BJP-led coalition lost the battle by 269 votes to 270 and Mr AB Vajpayee quit his office. The next phase of events proved to be quite grotesque for India as Pakistani army regulars and armed mercenaries entered Indian territory on our Northern borders; perhaps, they had already planned their operations in advance since February, 1999 as if visualising that the political instability in New Delhi would perpetuate political chaos, giving them an opportunity for a possible victory over a temporarily feeble democracy. However, they were proved wrong. Our soldiers fought bravely under the guidance of the caretaker government led by Mr Vajpayee. This mini-war cost the nation dearly. We lost 519 army personnel (and also, Captain Ajay Batra, the brave air force officer, who lost his life after he fell into the hands of the Pakistani armed forces). Pakistan lost nearly 650 - 700 men, which included hired mercenaries as well. Indian Army and Indian Air Force fought a mini war in order to flush out the infiltrators from Indian territory. Till the time of formation of a new government at the centre, Mr Vajpayee led a caretaker government. The tenure of this caretaker government is the longest in the history of Indian polity so far.

This saga does not prove our faith in a democratic process. This was a gruesome and shameless game of revenge. Morever, the rival parties do not wish that the other parties should remain in power. In the absence of an absolute majority, all the political parties have become pygmies and they have to resort to "numbers game" in order to topple those who have somehow managed to stick to the throne. The nation should not approve of such a state of political chaos that is prevalent in India. And this is only because of the game of numbers. Indian masses, businessman, industry, society and the other elite have now accepted the modified axiomatic law-"Heads I win, tails you lose." India always loses, no matter, which party wins at the hustings or during the confidence motions in the Parliament.

The costly and grueling exercise of general elections is over and the new government is in power. Had our political heroes acted wisely, this expenditure could have been avoided. Why could we not accept the results of the Exit Polls and let Mr Vajpayee and his men take over in the centre. If he was tipped for a comeback, then why was the costly exercise of general elections carried out ? Our Constitution must have provision for taking such a step. The funds spent on the general elections could have been spent to alleviate the poverty of million of Indian masses. The game of numbers has been taking its toll for the past fifty years. We consider that candidate as elected who gets the maximum number of votes. But what about the runner up ? He also obtained some votes ! He also had some plans and ideas for useful implementation in his constituency. The winner is the one who gets the maximum number (of votes) through coercion, liquor distribution, sweet canvassing, political pressures, money and social compulsions. This is the shameless new method of amassing power and wealth. Indian polity is now heading towards a show of strength only in terms of numbers; now, it is sans political grace, decorum and honest representation. In political rallies, respect for rival candidates, hard work in one's own constituency, honesty in financial management (of national resources) and an overall clean image of the politician are the fables of the distant past.

Political *Pundits* around the world ought to think again. This is not a democratic *modus operandi* but a mockery of democracy. We must know what is good for the nation and accordingly, we must define and implement an error-proof process of elections and political governance. Elections and number games have not yielded concrete benefits for Indian society and polity. Perhaps, a new and modified system of democratic governance would be better for India. If we continued to support the hackneyed procedures of democracy, we might end up with a total extinction of democratic thoughts in India. Numbers are not important, nation is !

96. THE DECAY OF INDIAN INSTITUTIONS

Our institutions comprise police, judiciary, PSUs, educational institutes, telecommunications facilties, municipal corporations etc.—Total decay due to materialism, inefficiency, red tape and bureaucracy—National interests sidelined—Justice denied to masses—Police exploits people—PSUs are white elephants—Some solutions suggested.

Indian economic and industrial progress has been hailed by all the global fora. Indian independence has seen fifty years of growth, democracy and struggle for economic and social liberation. Our record is truely impressive.

However, we have also failed in many spheres. We have been able to make progress but at the cost of some vital sacrifices that should not have been made.

Let us consider the decline of the institutions—police, judiciary, PSUs, education, telecommunications and other basic facilities provided by the state. These institutions, which were supposed to run national machinery in an efficient manner, are in shambles today. The police department is corrupt and so is bureaucracy. The politician-bureaucrat-criminal nexus has strengthened over a period of fifty years and has exploited the masses in the most ruthless manner. Judiciary is slow in taking decisions. Justice delayed is justice denied. People are waiting for justice, land, pension and assets for survival through courts but the courts work at a painfully slow pace. Moreover, there is corruption in the lower levels of the court, which does not allow file movement unless we grease the palm of the *Munshi* or *Nayab*.

Further, public sector enterprises, which are supposed to increase the pace of economic development, have been converted into storehouses of political rivalary, inefficiency and red tape. National Textiles Corporation (NTC) has been running into losses for over a decade. Air India reported losses of Rs 181 crore during 1997-98 fiscal. Further Shipping Corporation of India (SCI), Hotel Corporation of India and Power Grid Corporation of India have also shown losses during the fag end of the nineties. Only a few of the PSUs are delivering profits for the national exchequer. The efficient PSUs like BHEL are doing Indians proud. But their market niches are well defined in the area of infrastructure development. They cannot contribute more than they are contributing now. The loss making PSUs are a burden on the national exchequer and hence, on the common man. Although we may not count PSUs among the 'institutions,' yet they have an equally constructive role to play and hence, are also equally liable as the institutions are for their blunders.

The educational system is virtually on the verge of collapse. Children go to schools to miss their classes. Teachers bluntly order students to take home tuitions from them. The educational sector is confused about its role in Indian Economy. The concentration and attention of students have been reduced and cinema, cable TV, music and Internet rule their minds now.

This decay of the institutions has emanated from the economic necessities of the masses. Poor people want to get rich and neo-rich want to be richer than ever before. India is a rich country managed by poor people. Institutional decay has led to the loss of revenues and national image. We must use strict legislations for checking corruption, red-tapism, bureaucratic bottlenecks and inefficiency.

Institutional decay in the nineties has taken new dimensions. New technologies and methods have allowed the institutions to exploit the masses through novel ways. Business, industry and society are seriously affected by the on-slaught of technology. The institutions do not adopt themselves with the pace of this change. There is retardation in all the sectors of Indian economy. However, no concrete measures have been taken to push up the growth process.

Exports are less whereas imports are increasing. The procedures are difficult and cumbersome. The exporter wants to earn for the nation but finds that his own profits are also dwindling. So, he ignores the next order from his importer due to bureaucratic bottlenecks.

Police does not treat people with respect and does not listen adequately to their genuine grievances. Money makes the mare go and that is very much true for all the institutions of the modern times. When the assassination is over, the police arrives at the scene and arrests all those who are available at the spot of the crime. The real culprits go scot-free through their political references and money power.

The judiciary is wise but slow. A normal court cases takes several years to settle; issues like accident cases, property cases, pension and gratuity issues take long time periods. The lower levels in judiciary are prone to corruption and hence, the common man is exploited there.

The bureaucrats are the pride of India. They run the State through well-defined procedures. However, their efficiency is deeply burried under these long and painful procedures. Real and concrete output from the ministeries and PSUs is lacking. All the municipal corporations, health departments, water supply boards, electricity boards and other State-run organisations are nothing but big heaps of files. The future of India lies buried under these files and no industrial, business or social organisation has the courage to stand up against the rotten system through which, the affairs of this nation are managed.

The solutions for this institutional decay could be discussed in a nutshell as follows :—

(A) The bureaucracy must be trained for better efficiency, honest working and commitment to the respective organisation. The inter-departmental and intra-departmental transfers must be stopped and the bureaucrat must be allowed to concentrate on his job. His salary structure should be revised so that he is not tempted to earn more through illegal means.

(B) The police force must be trained by expert police trainers from abroad. Their salary packages should be improved so that they are not tempted to go for illegal earnings. This would also lead to cessation of exploitation of Indian masses.

(C) The inefficient PSUs must be sold off to the private sector. NTC is a glaring example of an inefficient and loss-making PSU. The sale of sick PSUs to the private sector would certainly give them a new lease of life.

(D) Indian masses must keep a vigil on the inefficient officials of the government machinery. If bribe is demanded or offered by officer, the responsible citizens of India should report this to the appropriate authority. They should also ensure that necessary action is taken against the concerned official. Illegal practices of these corrupt officials should be made public through articles in magazines and newspapers. Public should be made aware of the corrupt practices prevalent in the official machinery at all the levels.

(E) The institutions comprise people and people are human-beings like us. Therefore, they could also be having a reason for being corrupt, apathetic or inefficient. Regular psychological counselling would help. The corrupt officials should be given opportunities to improve and lead a life free from vices.

We can sum up by stating that institutional decay is hurting our national economy as well as our socio-cultural fabric. Our sanguine opinion is that Indian democracy would certainly overcome this major challenge in the years to come. ●

97. COALITION POLITICS : A CRITICAL REVIEW

The present trends of Coalition politics are shameful—Mr Vajpayee heads the NDA in the centre—Ms Sonia Gandhi unable to come out of her "family shell"—Major political parties have to get the support of small and regional parties—Difficult for political parties to share power—Coalition governments successful in Europe—We can save the nation through coalition governance.

It is only a matter of shame to learn that coalition politics has not come of age in India despite the fact that we Indians have been known to be fault-tolerant, accommodating and persevering. Mr Vajpayee tried to please Ms J Jayalalitha but could not. Ms J Jayalalitha tried to avoid a coalition with Ms Sonia Gandhi for 13 months but could not. The nation tried to avoid general elections but could not. And the common man tries his best to keep his body and soul together but would not. Coalition politics affects us all. It is not a game of the few; it is a bleeding wound of our polity. The agonies increase by the day and manipulations reach new horizons by the night.

The thirteenth *Lok Sabha* has been formed. There are no drastic changes in the contents of the new *Lok Sabha*. Then, why did we indulge in such a massive exercise ? Just because we are a democracy and ought to take away the last morsels of food from the mouths of the hungry children of India ? If elections do not yield a result, then why should we have elections ? Instead, a neutral government, on behalf of the President, could manage the country. In that event, the ill-effects of a coalition rule would be eliminated. When the politicians realise that they ought to learn to live together, the old democratic system could be restored by the President.

This calls for drastic changes in our system of governance and our Constitution. Changes are not to be brought at such a frequency as would baffle Indian masses. Moreover, Indian politicians would also be perplexed. We are Indians after all; how could we change so quickly ?

National Democratic Alliance (NDA) is the new name of the old concoction of the thirteen-party coalition headed by Mr AB Vajpayee. The name sounds good. We pray that nobody leaves NDA now. Congress (I) has lost most of her stalwarts like Sharad Pawar, GK Moopanar and others. Some have inclinations towards the local polity but they have lost their respective identities. Ms Sonia Gandhi has only one identity—that of a *Bahu* (the daughter-in law of the Nehru family). She has to open her account in terms of her political finesse. Toppling governments is easy but forming a government and disseminating the message of unity among the party cadres is a different game altogether. During her tenure as a President of Congress (I), most of the 'heavyweights' have left the party. What could be the reason ? Her influence on the senior leaders could be likened to the impact of Mrs Indira Gandhi on her 'soldiers' while she was at the helm of affairs. During the rule of Mrs Gandhi, the Congress Party was managed as if it were a "family affair." And Ms Sonia Gandhi is making the same mistake by perpetuating the family rule; she is creating problems for the century-old organisation that could have captured power in the centre with confidence. Congress (I) is a mature and non-communal party and her stalwarts are capable of handling the most difficult situations. Why does Ms Gandhi not understand this fact ? The only solution would be to manage the party on democratic lines and develop a sense of belonging to those who have left the party. Perhaps, they might be waiting for her call. If old horses return to the fold, the party would gallop along its way to power. But when would that happen ?

Let us now concentrate on the BJP. Mr Vajpayee, Mr Advani, and Dr MM Joshi are the leading figures of this party. Mr Vajpayee has proved during his tenure of thirteen months in office that he is not a spineless Prime Minister. He has the guts to manage the nation. But the party ought to take the minorities into confidence. Mr Sikander Bakht and other Muslim leaders of the party must be given their due status and importance. Saffron colour is harmful for the party because India is a secular nation. The religious issues must never be discussed at political fora; for settling those issues, judiciary must be given adequate powers and prominence so that the pending disputes could be sorted out in an amicable manner (and according to the wishes of all those concerned).

Janata Dal has been split once again. Mr Sharad Yadav heads one faction and Mr Laloo Prasad Yadav heads another. And there is a Biju Janata Dal (BJD) as well. If Janata Dals continued to increase in terms of number, *Janata* (the public) might give them a bashing during the next general elections. Must of the smaller political factions have now agreed in principle that Mr AB Vajpayee and his men are not very poor performers; the only poor performance that could be highlighted here is the lack of proper judgement on the part of Mr Vajpayee before the Kargil war.

Coalition governments have been operating successfully in Europe. In India, we would have to understand the basic fact that poor masses, *Dalits* and people of the lower-middle strata of society tend to align themselves with regional or local political parties. They have lost confidence in major parties as they could not deliver concrete results when they were in power. Hence, the local and regional parties would remain where they are—having a limited following and weilding no power to rule at the centre on their own.

The overall picture is grim. Indians are desperate for installing a government at the centre. All political manipulations are of useless unless the major political parties realise that they have to get the support of smaller parties in the Parliament as well as in the state assemblies. They do not enjoy support of the masses any longer and the election saga of 1984 is not going to be repeated for many more years to come.

For many political parties, it is difficult to share power. But they ought to share it if they want to rule. And if they form rational and fruitful alliances with some like-minded parties (as NDA has done already among its factions), they could capture power at the centre. Every Indian was crying 'foul' when he went for casting his vote during the general elections for the thirteenth *Lok Sabha*. But he could not change the course of events; most of the people remained indoors (the poor voter turnout shows this feeling of resentment). Many elite voters did not exercise their right of franchise.

If the democratic process is tempered with, the nation would lose her stability, economic tempo and glorious image as a resilient civilisation. Coalition politics has come to stay. The policy of "Live and Let Live" would have to be accepted else the reactionary forces would lead the nation to a bloody civil war. The resulting chaos would be difficult to handle as India is a nation of 1,000 million perceiving and ambitious individuals. We can save political future of the nation through coalition politics. It is a sad to note that everyone wants to be in power sans the coalition system of governance. ●

98. USSA

> South Asian nations have their typical features and resources—They can combine to form single nation—European Union is a reality—Germany has become single nation—Koreas could also unite—India can take positive steps so that the SAARC nations could negotiate for a union—This would help the citizens of the region—Pakistan attached India in March, 1999—Kargil war continued till mid-July, 1999—Pakistan preparing for another war with India—Chances of unification are remote—Efforts must be made by SAARC.

Asian region is the most fertile of all the major economic regions of the world. Indian wheat, rice, fruit and vegetables have no match in the world. Pakistan is rich in wheat, natural gas and minerals like rock salt. Sri Lanka is known for her spices and fruits whereas Bangladesh is the leader in jute production. Nepal is dream tourism spot of the world and a favourite halt for the Western travellers. It is a buyer's paradise as well. Similarly, Bhutan, Maldives, Mauritius and Seychelles are the famous tourist destinations of the world. These regions are environment friendly and rich in fauna and flora.

Asians (especially, South Asians) always fight for their rights—the right for land, the right for cultural supremacy, the right for military domination and above all, the right for economic benefits) over other neighbours. Indo-Pak conflicts are deeply embedded in the history of South Asia. The two brothers are always ready to tear each other apart; at least, the hints from across the border during recent times confirm this fact clearly. Our relationships with other neighbours, though cordial, are not very warm. Economic cooperation is minimal. SAARC summit delivers no worthwhile results. The differences remain over many vital issues. All the seven countries are at logger heads over various issues. NAM summit at Durban (South

Africa) also failed to lead the member nations towards unity. A trite remark by President Nelson Mandela spoiled the mood of the summit.

Let us now have a look at the European Union. The European currency, the Euro, was introduced on January 1, 1999. Eventually, the economic amalgamation would lead to a political amalgamation. The already fully developed nations of Europe would get a major headstart to become a single economic and military force on the earth. Even the USA is eyeing this union with awe and respect.

Can we learn our lessons ? Can there be a union of the South Asian nations on the pattern of the European Union ? This dream is far from reality. However, keeping in mind the requirements of the present era, we must give a serious thought to it.

If we sink our differences and shed our egoes, we could really convert this region into the most properous one. Political problems could vanish within a few months. Single currency could regulate the international trade in our favour and the military might of South Asia could reach the most glorious heights of all times. The theory of comparative advantage could reap rich benefits for the citizens of this region.

Naturally, India could take a lead for achieving this objective. This union could benefit all the parties and Indians could be the most benefitted people. This should be a voluntary union and not due to any coercion. Otherwise, the union could result in a disaster.

North Korea and South Korea have differences. However, there are lobbies in both the countries, which favour unity of the two nations at war. East Germany and West Germany have already united. European Union is on the anvil. Then, what are we waiting for?

There is a need for positive, careful and constructive dialogue between the SAARC nations. The world is has become a global village and the South Asian nations must realise this fact. The aspirations of the people of this regoin can be fully achieved with this step and peace as well as prosperity would dawn upon the region in a short timespan. And why not name the union today itself— United States of Southern Asia (USSA).

The recent developments do not auger well for the USSA. concept. India and Pakistan are nuclear powers now, thanks to a series of explosions carried out by these countries in May, 1998. Agni-II has been tested by India whereas Ghauri-II has been test-fired by Pakistan. There were heated arguments over Kashmir and boundary disputes from both the sides. The tempers were lost during the month of April 29, 1999 and gradually cooled in July 17, 1999. India and Pakistan fought bitter war in Kargil, Drass, Batalik and Mushkoh Valley during May-July, 1999. India was able to push back Pakistani intruders but Pakistan has warned that there would be more 'Kargils' in the near future.

Against this backdrop of tension and economic shortages, the concept of USSA would take a backseat. The other nations of Asia, which are very small in size and very poor in terms of economic resources, would welcome the unification concept. However, they could also view this step as a threat to their national interests. Their fears would have to be allayed skilfully. Bhutan, Nepal, Maladives, Sri Lanka, Mauritius and other neigbhours should give a positive signal if diplomatic efforts are initiated.

Pakistan is likely to pose major problems. They have not forgotten their early defeats during the wars of 1965 and 1971. Now, Pakistani Military is licking its wounds, inflicted upon her by Indian Army and Indian Air Force during the Kargil war. All the international propaganda, nuclear tests and missile development programmes of Pakistan are aimed at India. Their fear is India only and there is no other opponent. China supports Pakistan and may not like her to join hands with India for unification. Russia and CIS states would welcome the unification move. The USA and her allies may not like the idea either.

Further, all the SAARC nations have poor economies. After unification, our major problem would be the provision of food, clothing, shelter, medical facilities, employment and basic amenities to more than one-fourth of the population of this globe. The defence outlays would be more. Infrastructure development is minimal in Pakistan, Bangladesh and Nepal. Bhutan and Maldives also need sound industrial bases. Hence, our political leaders and corporate doyens could offer some solutions for developing the entire region.

Free market system has arrived in India. We may have to promote hard work, efficiency and commitment in other parts of the new united State. Law and order would be a problem. After German unification, the less developed East Germans migrated to resource-rich West Germany. Similar problems could be faced by the USSA from pockets of Nepal and Bangladesh where poverty is the only phenomenon alive.

The USSA is a distant dream but it is certainly not a Utopian concept. If all the major SAARC players could unite under one umbrella, this dream could be a reality in the distant future. ●

99. POLITICIANS OF THE NEW CENTURY

Many challenges for India in the new century—There was no politician during pre-independence era—Gandhi gave him an identity—Many leaders came to the fore during the struggle for independence—After independence, politicians were respected during the fifties and the sixties—During the seventies, Western cultural influenced our masses—politicians also affected by the materialistic wave—Decay began during mid-eighties—Many scandles unearthed in the beginning of the nineties—Politicians drawn from the masses—They long for luxuries of life—They are materialistic and aggressive—The common man continues to suffer due to their deeds.

In the new century, India is likely to face many a change in her political, economic and social canvasses. Change is the only sign of healthy nature of a mechanism. Our country would also do well to tune her activities and national economic mechanisms according to the demands of the new millennium.

But what about our politicians ? Are they going to change ? And if they are not, would India able to achieve the ambitious targets that have been defined by her own citizens as well as those delineated by the world ? Let us analyse these questions in the perspective of the changing personalities and roles played by Indian politicians.

During the pre-independence era, Indian politician was almost non-existent. He was given concrete identity and character by MK Gandhi. The social workers, supporters and people from all walks of life joined Gandhiji for opposing the British dominance over the Indian subcontinent. From these cadres, politicians of highest calibre emerged. The reason of their political abilities and respectable status among Indian masses was their association with the greatest legend of their era — Mahatma Gandhi. Moreover, those leaders were pious to the core, knave, hardworking and ardent practitioners of highest moralistic norms. The masses adored them and were prepared to sacrifice their lives, property and sanity for the sake of the achievement of the sacred objectives, which were defined by these true leaders of our nation. The leaders of the yore were the most respected people of the society, the saviours of the nation and role models for the plebeian masses whom they always tried to emulate.

Some of those leaders were J L Nehru, Maulana Abdul Kalam Azaad, Dada Bhai Navroji, Khan Abdul Ghaffar Khan, Sardar Vallabh Bhai Patel, Moti Lal Nehru, Jai Prakash Narain, Aruna Asaf Ali, LB Shastri and many others. The masses adored them and followed in their footsteps in order to dethrone the British monarchy in India. They were prepared to make any type of sacrifice at the behest of their leaders. They were the real leaders of India and our nation is respected due to the virtues and contributions of these men of honour in all the parts of the world. After the death of MK Gandhi, he was accorded the status of a saint and his name was included in the list of those great and noble angels who are revered around the globe for their contributions towards the moral and spiritual values.

After independence, many great leaders were still left. They rose to power and managed the affairs of the country. There were no scams or the cases of financial misappropriation. The nation had emerged out of the dark ages and was heading towards a glorious future, elitist at a very slow pace. The sixties also saw the maintenance of highest moral values in Indian polity. Our leaders, who had become politicians, were still respected. Their statements were rational and their policies were mass-oriented. This trend continued up to the end of sixties in the previous century.

But the Western influences started affecting our social and moral fabric in during the early seventies. Europe had come out of the black shadow of the Second World War. There was a new religion in the West—"Enjoy to your heart's content as you do not know what would come next." Money and an undeterred infatuation for pleasures, materialistic assets and sex became the inseparable components of the Western nations. The USA emerged as the economic and political leader of the world. She consolidated her position in all the major market niches of the West. When Indian politicians interacted with their Western counterparts, they realised that their own lifestyles and materialistic achievements were too timid to be given a special status. The hunger for money and political supremacy was deeply embedded in their minds. The states were no longer clean, though the Indian political system still tried to cling to the old and respected norms for which, it was respected.

Indian masses also witnessed a wave of transformation. The business grew and so did the ambitions. Our politicians are drawn from our masses. Therefore, the new wave of materialism affected them as well. Earlier, their goals were decided by their constituencies and needs of the masses. But the priorities changedand they fought elections for the sake of their base ends. They did not serve the interests of the nation but those that were closely related to their personal growth or the prosperity of their own kith and kin. There were some cases of financial misappropriation during the eighties but the masses did not take much notice of the same, believing that their leaders were not supposed to tread the path of moral decay. They still had the same image about them, which was portrayed by their elders.

However, our politicians had tasted the blood by the middle of the eighties. In order to become rich and powerful, they used politics as a platform. Their efforts yielded fruits. And by the beginning of the nineties, their changed faces became two ugly to be tolerated. India witnessed many scams, including Bofors Scam, Fodders Scam, Securities Scam, Urea Scam, Telecommunications Scam *etc*. The bewildered masses could not digest the fact that even the highest office of the land was also singled out as a part of the network, which promoted the channels for financial misappropriation. Mr PV Narasimha Rao, the former Prime Minister, was charge-sheeted in the Lakhubhai Pathak case in which, it was alleged that he had taken US$ 1,00,000 from Mr Pathak and had never returned. Further, the former Prime Minister, Mr Rajiv Gandhi, was charge-sheeted by CBI in 1999 for his alleged involvement in the Bofors case. The total amount of kickbodis paid by the firm to Indian middlemen is to the tune of Rs 64 crore. There are many more skeletons in the cupboards of Indian politicians and our worthy readers are aware of them.

During the early years of the eighties, muscle power emerged as a key factor for deciding the elections of candidates at the hustings. UP, Bihar and Bengal are the poorest states of India and could be termed as the backwaters of Indian polity. Hooliganism and coercive power originated from these states and later, engulfed all the states of the country. Today, elections are not fought and won; these are 'planned' in advance. The honest voter sits at home whereas someone else exercises his right of franchise at the polling both. If he dares oppose the system, he is shot in the head or beaten up mercilessly. Polling booths are 'bought' and 'operated' by the musclemen and 'tenders' are invited from the 'reputed' gangs for winning elections through the selected polling booths. A common voter is a helpless spectator as his rights are not more powerful and effective than the piece of paper on which, he exercises his right of franchise. And the elections are won by the politicians with ease and confidence, irrespective of the fact they do not deserve to the members of the *Lok Sabha* or the state assemblies due to their dubious records.

As already pointed out, our politicians have been drawn from our masses. They have also tasted the luxuries of the modern era, albeit in different forms or reduced contents. Hence, political decay has emanated from societal decay, which was the result of Western influences during the mid-seventies and early eighties. The social norms, moral values and typical Indian characteristics, for which, we were so famous. have faded into oblivion. This total disregard for the typical Indian values has set a gangrenous trend in our cultural canvass. It threatens to make us mere cogs in the machines and forces us to generate what is supposed to be the most important commodity on the earth-money.

Then, why blame our politicians ? They too demand good standards of living, travel to foreign countries, costly medical treatments, secure future for their children, bank balances in Switzerland, unlimited access to the financial resources and quotas. Why should they be deprived of the nice basic necessities of life, which are already essential components of the daily lives of the Western people? Gone are the days of the respected politician. The politician of the new century is aggressive, calculative, mean and materialistic to the core. He promises to deliver results but need not. He yearns for the luxuries of life and must have them. He ought to win elections and no power on the earth could stop him from doing so. He is the most powerful businessman of India. He could alter the election results. He could force the corporate world to stoop to the lowest depths. He is the mastermind behind all the financial and social upheavals. The new politician is different from the old one. He rules the nation with a sword but proclaims that the free market system has arrived in the country.

The American President, Mr Bill Clinton, had a lewd affair with Ms Monica Lewinsky. Such types of affairs could be witnessed in India as well; perhaps, this is the only scandal left to be identified in Indian polity. And if we carefully scrutinise the lifestyles of the modern-day politicians, we might find many a skeletons in our political cupboard.

In the meantime, the tale of woes of Indian masses continues. The economic and social status of Indian politician has changed, thanks to media campaigns. But the common man remains downtrodden and deprived. The evil nexus between the politician, the bureaucrat and the businessman suits all the three and is able to generate and sustain a massive parallel economy. The nation is in doldrums, though we witness progress at all the fronts. The political ants keep on eating into the basic moral and economic pillars of our nation, forgetting the fact that they are supposed to nurture these pillars for national development. This century is likely to be spent in creating an awareness among the masses about their machinations. A violent reprisal could be witnessed in India in the year 2060 AD and then, our political system might become nation-friendly.

The decay of institutions and the loss of moral values in Indian polity occurred simultaneously. Institutional decay was also promoted through an evil nexus between the politician, the bureaucrat and the corporate sector firms. After a violent reprisal, our political system would become trustworthy and result oriented. The second stage would be dominated by the rectification of the operations of the basic institutions. Economic prosperity for the masses would follow after the reversal of the institutional decay process.

We have predicted the violent change in the year 2060 AD. Could the Indian masses effect it earlier ? After all, it is for their benefit. And the transformation (or, the cleansing process) need not be a violent one. That would be the last resort because democracy still thrives in our nation.

Would Indian masses accept the challenge ?

100. STUDENTS AND POLITICS

Students involved in politics—Wastage of time, money and careers—Politics in college is a hotbed of regional and national political manipulations—Politicians use students for their selfish interests—College and university elections become the success tools of major political parties—Youth not being directed towards positive career building—Legislation needed—Only healthy political activities should be allowed to continue—Only serious students should join political activities.

The political stage of our country is fraught with many complicated issues. Corruption, bureaucracy, violence and lack of empathy with the masses at the grassroot levels are some of the prominent features. Floor-crossing and switching of loyalties have become the order of the day.

Add a new dimension to the game of politics—students—and we have a new concoction of a dangerous political era that could affect our political as well economic lives for long times to come.

Politics in the college has become a hotbed of regional and national level political manipulations. Elections in the students unions of the colleges and the universities are in fact, proxy wars of the major political parties. Money, hooliganism, violence and gaudy promotions of Candidates in the elections of Students' Councils are some of the prominent characteristics of elections held in colleges and universities. The educational schedules take a backseat and struggle for power takes ugly proportions in many cases. Why students take to politics ? For example, why should there be elections in an engineering college whose students are unlikely to join a political party ? The students of arts and politics are likely to be interested in this profession. But wastage of time and energy is an important issue. This wastage leads the students to ill-planned careers as they suffer on account of their poor performances on the academic front.

However, only some of the students join active politics later. The politicians milk them during their college days and leave them without any career when they join a political party. After all, a social worker of a political party remains a social worker. However, he has no support from his party for building his future or even for meeting his basic needs. He has to take up a profession or a vocation in order to survive.

When the student leaders are elected in the college and university elections, they take their commands from their political bigwigs. Boys and girls, who are not adept at getting a decent job, are made Vice President, President and Secretary of a student union. They do not know what they are saying to the students as their words are the cooked up words of the politician who guides them. Their actions are controlled by the instructions from the offices of the major political parties.

Political events in the educational institutions lead to voilence, destruction and colossal wastage of money. It is an irony that a student, who goes to his college by bus, is able to arrange enough of donations through his efforts for posters, loudspeekers, campaigns and other promotional gimmicks. Further, the leader of the students always have one difference or another. The lost party always tends to resort to leg-pulling and violence. Elections bring outsiders—especially criminals, hooligans and opportunists—on the centre stages of educational temples. The incidents of beating of candidates, murders, destruction of buses and private property and kidnapping of rival candidates are quite common.

Academic sessions are not held regularly. Even if the classes are held, the powerful student leaders force the students to close the college or the university for the sake of their petty demands ego. Those students who are interested in studies, suffer the most. They are not interested in political affiliations but are forced to vote and support a particular set of candidates. The academic and sports performances are also adversely affected.

The solution should be provided by the State in the form of a legislation. Active politics is not bad for the college-going students but it should only assume dangerous proportions. Only those students, who are interested in taking up politics as career, should participate in political activities. The rest must avoid politics. Adoption of violence, money power, threats (physical and mental) and external political influences must be banned. Then only, the campus life would be more productive for the students.

The political parties must refrain from interfering in the educational institutes. Adequate legislations must be passed for separating politics from educational institutions. If a political party interferes in the affairs of the educational institutes, it should be banned. Students should join political mainstream of the country only after their educational stints in the colleges and universities are over. Only serious students should take up political science as a subject. It has been observed that political science is studied by the students of arts for pursuing their graduation or post-graduation courses in the arts stream. However, all these students end up with jobs of clerks and peons and political affiliations are cut off in the interest of the survival. Then, why study political science if it is not going to develop the students as political trendsetters of the future ?

Political affiliations are always welcome. But this should happen only after the minds of the youth have become mature. The young minds must be able to think about their survival and later, about the political streams, which they are about to join. The final touches to this training should be given when the student joins a political party and has been able to achieve some landmarks during his academic life.

It must be noted that the psyche described earlier is not prevalent in all the strata of students (which includes the students of politics as well). Most the students are interested in joining the educational institutions, learn some useful skills, pass out after enjoying the college or university days and finally, settle down in a job or a business. Politics never fascinates Indian students and many surveys have proved this fact. So, there is no need for linking politics with educational institutes. This would help the State maintain healthy environment in the educational campuses.

We must conclude that politics and students must be separated in the interest of healthy political growth of the nation. The students of today are the torch bearers of the national progress in all spheres. Their tender minds must be trained carefully so that they are able to assimilate the political ideologies in the right perspective. Further, they must remain responsible to their parents and families during their educational stints and much more committed when they join active politics after completion of their education.

101. POLITICS AND RELIGION

Politics has been coupled with religion—Nineties had seen violence and deaths—Some parties have been benefited due to this alliance—The secular forces have received a setback — Constitutional provisions do not link religion to politics—We are basically a secular nation—Rise of Hindutva—Pakistan succeeded in attaining a Muslim State—The majority community used the cultural crisis of the middle class to its advantage—Effects visible in urban and rural areas—Social scientists and elite thinkers have also joined this bandwagon—Not healthy trends—Must delink politics from religion in the interest at the nation.

The decade—has seen large goneby scale communal violence and religious polarisation of the masses. The politician used the trump card of religion in order to reach the highest echelons of power. The marriage of politics and religion was most beneficial for some parties who had an orientation for religion. But those non-communal and secular forces, which defied the communal forces throughout their histories, found it hard to gulp down the realities arising out of communal machinations. They could not digest the emergence of new power equations in the centre.

During the reign of the British in pre-independence era, the politicisation of religion by Hindus, Muslims as well by Britishers led to the partition of Bengal and eventually, India had to be partitioned on communal lines. We cannot forget the gory saga of partition in 1947 when millions were displaced from their homes. The loss of lives and property could never be compensated on either side of the border.

The constitutional provisions asked for political procedings without the interference of religion. There was supposed to be no scope for communal forces in India. Further, Gandhi supported a political system in which, self-less and a less polarised essence of religion was emphasised upon. Both these factors had a soothing effect on the political and social settings of Indian milieu, which was in a nascent stage of formation. However, steady but slow politicisation of religion started despite the attempts by our political stalwarts to institutionalise secular and democratic politics.

The hold of religion over politics has increased. This has resulted in a major shift from a secular, democratic and tolerant culture to a religion-tainted and highly polarised culture. This culture would not manifest itself directly in our national operations as we are wise enough to hide our sentiments. However, at the appropriate platforms, the communal snakes hiss and take their toll. During the last ten years, the quantitatively dominant majority has replaced democratic forces. Consensus has been replaced by conflict. Political scenario has been degraded and violence has become its most vital organ (even the movies brand the politician, the Chief Minister or *Netaji* as the villain and the film directors take pride in getting the politicians hanged or executed by the hero during the fag end of such movies).

During the nineties, the minorities were gripped by a sense of insecurity (both mental and physical). The majority community became aggressive. The rise of *Hindutva* saw the clouds of terror hover over the Indian subcontinent. The destruction of Babri Masjid was the striking evidence of the highly aggressive behaviour of the majority community.

Pakistanis succeeded in getting a State for themselves by preparing the convenient concoction of religion and politics. British rulers could not help as Mr M A Jinnah was bent upon getting what he claimed was the right of the Muslim citizens of the subcontinent. Back home, the BJP-led forces could not succeed in their efforts to capture power. But the combination of religion and politics yielded rich dividends. The Shiv Sena government in Maharashtra took over the reigns of the state. The BJP is now ruling the centre and its future is bright though there are uncertainties due to the fact that the NDA-led government has too many crutches than it needs. It is a real 'crowd' of 22 political parties. The elite as well as the opportunists have also joined BJP and its supporters as they feel that its future is bright. Congress was the chief proponent of secular forces but was branded as corrupt. The United Front Government was given adequate number of chances but could not come up to the national political norms. The third major force was the BJP and it was desperate for reaching the corridors of power. Although Mr AB Vajpayee is an able and seasoned politician and is adequately supported by Mr LK Advani, Dr MM

Joshi, and other bigwigs of BJP, yet the overall image about the party was that of a communal force during its formative years.

Amazingly, the BJP stalwarts are now trying to change this image but it would take years to wash out the previous slate and create a new picture Mr Vajpayee is a leader of international stature and he has helped India win the war at Kargil. He is also a fine diplomat. But political parties need good leaders in the entire rank and file of its structures. Congress failed due to the failure of the top leaders but BJP could lose due to a lack of political leadership at state levels.

Hindu religious politics drew its sustenance and ideological support from the cultural crisis of the middle class. The middle class is a decisive social force in India today. It has its own political preferences and hence, it can influence the political future of the nation. Due to rapid globalisation and liberalisation, the cultural crisis of the middle class has deepened. Culture is an integral component of the Hindu identity. The members of the middle class find easy solutions for their problems. Their support, arising out of this perceptions, has placed a significant part of infrastructure of culture and communication at the command of the political engines. These engines have used the communal card adequately for enforcing—in the minds of the middle class—that the national integrity and security are in danger on account of a possible onslought from the minority communities and the West.

The social base of religious politics has spread to the urban and rural areas as well. The slums of Mumbai, Delhi, Aligarh, Ahmedabad and Hyderabad have always provided fodder for religious riots during the recent past. The minority communities and trained militants also have devised some counter-measures for any reprisal against the majority community. However, the police and paramilitary forces have been trying their best to contain the communal tensions. They do succeed at some places but at others, there is death and destruction. Communal carnage involving the death of 37 Sikhs near Anantnag is the most glaring example of communal riots during the recent times.

It is true that the majority community is playing the communal card in order to attain political power. However, there are logical demands and issues where the majority community is also right. The acquisition of Ram *Janam Bhumi* at Ayodhya by Babar and construction of a mosque at the site of the birth of Lord Rama are examples. The demand for a total isolation of a Hindu shrine is not illogical but the majority community is trying to gather political mileage out of the entire episode. This issue could have been resolved through peaceful negotiations across the table. Supreme Court has already been consulted and its decision has not been declared. It is sad to note that even social scientists and elite thinkers have not hesitated to group themselves under the religious umbrellas. A secular State is not likely to exist when its citizens have been divided on religious lines. The elite are not required to take sides and their religions should support the nationalist forces. Then, why this moral degradation among them ?

102. NEED FOR ELECTORAL REFORMS IN INDIA

Currently, we have electoral chaos in the nation—Poll rigging, booth capturing, illegal votes—Territories are divided by hooligans on monetary basis—We should initiate the electoral reforms process—Define age groups for voting—Eliminate hooligans from election process—Electronic voting machines introduced in elections at limited places—No entry of hooligans or criminals as political candidates—Governors must be elected—Political parties should fund themselves through party-owned enterprises—Powers to Governors and President must be enhanced.

India is the largest democracy in the world. The democratic form of governance dates back to centuries. The post-independence Indian democracy has also set an many themselves an example before the world. There are some loopholes in the democratic *modus-operandi*, which reflect in the form of electoral blindness. However, our country is a developing economy and political ethics would also take time to develop. We should not take a negative view of the electoral mismanagement in Indian context. We would analyse this situation and would put forward some rational solutions.

Nearly 48 per cent of Indian people are illiterate. The educated masses are also perplexed about the roles, which ought to be played for building a politically mature nation. They do not know about their powers as voters. Poll-rigging is common. Hooligans are able to capture polling booths in rural areas and violence leads even to the death of the citizens and the politicians during the elections. It has been observed that the antisocial elements get the polling done in favour of a particular politician with the help of money power. Even the territories are hired by them on professional basis. Money, manpower and coercion (direct or indirect) are the tools for achieving the results of the choice of a few politicians with vested interests. Ironically, the political parties of the old times did not resort to these tactics. Today, there is not a single political party, which never resorted to illegal and morally unfair means for winning elections. Although the minimum age for exercising the right of franchise has been specified by the law, yet a typical poll analysis would reveal that voters of lower age groups also vote in elections. At the state levels, the governors are able to mould the fate of the assemblies due to their political affiliations. The role of speaker (known to be a neutral member of the state assembly) has been found to be highly objectionable and biased in favour of a political party in many an incident.

We propose some solutions as follows :—

(1) A person, who is 24 years of age, is an Indian citizen, has passed his graduate examination and has no more than three living children, should be enrolled as a voter. This would eliminate students of lower classes, people with more children and people without any idea of the national politics.

(2) A person should be qualified to be elected for the legislative assembly of a state only if he is a citizen of India, has completed his post-graduate degree and has completed thirty years of age on the day of his filing the nomination. He should not have more than three living children and must keep his income tax returns up to date till the year of filing his nomination papers.

(3) The qualifications, age and other eligibility conditions for election to the *Lok Sabha* must be the same as have been specified for election to the state assemblies.

(4) Any citizen of India should be allowed to contest for a seat in the *Lok Sabha* from any parliamentary constituency in any state. This would eliminate the coercive and negative

influence of the local politicians and hooligans. A provision has already been made in our Constitution for achieving this aim.

(5) For contesting a seat in the *Rajya Sabha*, the individual should be a bonafide resident of an Indian state for at least 10 years before the date of filing his nomination. The policy of nomination of eminent persons from the fields of arts, sciences, culture, social service streams *etc* should be continued as such.

(6) Governors should be elected by the constituent state assembly and should not be nominated by the President. The powers of the governor (as a result of the constitutional powers of the President) should be enhanced so that the state does not feel crippled in the absence of a chief minister.

(7) No individual should be allowed to contest from two constituencies, as is the practice now a days.

(8) If a candidate dies due to natural causes (and who polled the maximum number of votes), then the next candidate (who polled the next highest number of votes), should be declared elected. If the winning candidate dies due to unnatural causes, then re-election schedule should be announced.

(9) Political parties should start their own economic enterprises for generating funds; export units, factories, trading houses and shops are some of the examples. This would help them fight elections with their own resources, thus eliminating the need for money and support from the underworld. The State cannot supply funds for meeting the election costs and parties must be made self-sufficient. If, however, a candidate wishes to file his nominations as an independent candidate and he is either a poor person or belongs to a backward caste, he should be given adequate funds and facilities (during the election campaigns) by the State.

(10) Floor-crossing and switching over loyalties at the time of election should be banned. If a candidate is found to be indulged in such anti-party activities, he should be barred from taking part in any election in the country.

(11) Electronic voting machines should be used for all the elections for avoiding poll-rigging and discrepancies during the counting process. The Election Commission of India used electronic voting machines at selected polling booths during the general elections held for the thirteenth *Lok Sabha* during September-October, 1999.

(12) Adequate police force should be deployed for conducting free and fair polls. It is not necessary to hold elections in all the nooks and corners of the country simultaneously. The police force and the CRPF can be deployed in one region (for elections) and then, in another in which, elections are to be held.

(13) Only a Member of the Parliament (*Lok Sabha* or *Rajya Sabha*) should be made the Prime Minister. A non-member should never be made the PM.

(14) There should be no by-elections for the state assemblies or the Parliament. The houses must complete their terms. This would save precious funds and time.

(15) In case the President or the Prime Minister vacate their seats, then their positions should be filled up by the Vice President and Deputy Prime Minister respectively. The newly elected Prime Minister or President should complete the number of years for which, their predecessors were supposed to be in power.

(16) The powers of the President and the Governor should be increased so that they could play more effective and constructive roles in the national or state politics.

(17) The weak governments—those which are unable to perform on the domestic, economic, societal or international fronts—should be made to quit by a simple no confidence motion. The time period for calling such a motion should be minimised. The performance criteria for such a motion must be quantified.

(18) There should be a check on the number of ministers in the central and state cabinets. The CM or the PM could resort to such measures merely to please the warring factions or those parties that support them from outside, as is evident

from the "Jumbo Ministries" of the NDA-led government in the centre.

(19) The new era indicates a multi-party system at the central and state levels. Hence, the concept of majority of a single party in a legislative assembly or in both the houses of the Parliament should be eliminated. Instead, the governments should be formed at the central and state levels in the same ratio in which, various political parties have won the elections in the Parliament or the state assemblies.

(20) If possible, a council should be formed under the aegis of the President, which should monitor the performance of the government. This council should not include a member of the *Lok Sabha, Rajya Sabha* or the state assemblies. Its members should be from the masses. This council should also recommend to the President whether a particular government at the central or state level should continue. The final decision must lie with the President and not with the constituent assemblies or the Parliament.

(21) The term of *Lok Sabha* should be reduced to four years while that of Rajya Sabha should be reduced to three years. -No individual should be allowed to serve twice as President, Prime Minister or Governor.

It is hoped that these suggestions would go a long way in improving the electoral process in India. The suggestions mentioned here need to be implemented in letter and spirit. This is a turning point for our democracy. We are learning to cope with changes in our society, polity and economy. If far reaching changes are effected in the electoral process, then we would be able to build a better nation in the times to come. ●

103. WOMEN'S RESERVATION BILL

Women's Reservation Bill tabled in the Lok Sabha on December 23, 1999—Unruly scenes and friction between the political parties observed—47 women MPs in the thirteenth Lok Sabha—SP, RJD, BSP, JD (U) and DMK opposed the Bill—JD(U) and DMK are a part of NDA but they also opposed the Bill—Earlier, introduced in 1996 and 1998—Mr Vajpayee determined to get it passed—33 per cent reservation too high to be digested—Other categories might suffer—Some problems related to the Bill discussed—Reduce the reservation percentage from 33 per cent to 20 per cent.

On December 23, 1999, the women's Reservation Bill was introduced in the *Lok Sabha* amidst furore and protests. The unruly scenes witnessed during that crucial hour would put many a man of dignity in the abyss of shame. Our democracy has now become a filthy can of a few evil-minded politicians, which could neither be disposed of (as it is a necessary evil) nor it could be cleaned (as the rank and file of every political party would fill the same stuff again in this can).

In a democracy, all the parties have a right to oppose the Bill or the motion, which is tabled by their opponents in the Parliament. But there is a proper method of registering such a protest. The shameful course of events has put a blot on the canvass of democracy of our nation, which already has many other stains to cry over.

The Women's Reservation Bill is supposed to bring the total reserved quota of women in the *Lok Sabha* and state assemblies to the tune of 33 per cent. Therefore, women would have more power, in political and social terms, for managing the vast nation like India. Earlier, the Women's Reservation Bill was put in a cold bag during the last tenure of the BJP-led government. The opposition was so severe that the government had decided not to open the Pandora's box. But Mr Vajpayee had the Bill on the back of his mind. And he did succeed in retaining power through the magnanimous comeback of his party. This time, the BJP was a part and parcel of the new NDA and the sailing was supposed to be smooth, at least in respect of the Women's Reservation Bill.

In the twelfth *Lok Sabha*, Congress had 51 women candidates, BJP had 25, BSP had 11, CPM had 5, CPI had 4, JD (S) had 4 whereas JD (U) had only three. In the thirteenth *Lok Sabha*, the total number of women is 47. The number of women, as ministers, is 8. Further, according to National Commission for Women, the chances of a female candidate for a victory are 16.96 per cent whereas the chances for a male candidate for a victory are 12.73 per cent. At present, women are only 8.5 per cent of the total members in the *Lok Sabha*. The government wants to take this value to 33 per cent and this task seems to be herculean.

The Bill was opposed, on December 23, 1999, by Samajwadi, Rashtriya Janata Dal, Bahujan Samaj Party, Janata Dal (U) and DMK. It must be noted that JD (U) and DMK are the constituent members of NDA and they also opposed the Bill. Mr Ram Jathmalani was able to introduce the Bill, known as the Eighty-fifth Constitution Amendment Bill, as soon as the Speaker called out his name. Mr Jethmalani had to be protected by the members of NDA. Congress played a positive role in the *Lok Sabha* and supported the Bill.

This Bill was introduced in 1996 and again, in 1998. But, as has already been stated, the ruling parties or the government could not garner enough support for the Bill and the government led by Mr Vajpayee had to defer it till the arrival of an opportune moment for presenting it. While the politicians of our nation struggle with one another in the well of the *Lok Sabha*, let us take the stock of the situation that would arise if the Bill is passed.

There are two consequences if the Bill is passed. The positive consequence would be increased power for the fairer sex in the national political platforms of India. The negative consequence would be reduction in the reservation quotas of other minorities in the *Lok Sabha* and state assemblies. The power of the women members would help the largely illiterate and backward women of India. But it would also raise protests from the SCs, STs and OBCs who might be deprived of representation at these fora. The government might face tough times while trying to pacify these groups.

Reservations in the *Lok Sabha* are likely to continue till January 10, 2010. Ironically, no party is 'against' the reservation for women in the *Lok Sabha*. There is, however, a difference over the percentage of reservation, rotation of the seats and the procedure to be adopted for reservation. The percentage (33 per cent) was fixed by Joint Select Committee. The vocal opponents of the Bill were Mr Mulayam Singh Yadav, Mr Shared Yadav and Mr Laloo Prasad Yadav. Mr Mulayam Singh Yadav is in favour of giving 10 percent of all the tickets, allotted for elections, to women. Some members of Congress had suggested that 100 constituencies could be made double member constituencies. But this suggestion was rejected by many members of Congress itself. SP, RJD and IUML opposed the Bill in its present form.

They also demanded the reservation of OBCs and minorities as a quota within the quota.

While these debates would continue, the women of India would remain starved, illiterate and backward. The *Nari* of the vedic times was respected and reversed. The middle ages also saw many a woman changing the course of Indian history. The pre-independence era would remind us of stories of brave women of India who left no stone unturned for helping their male counterparts in the freedom struggle. After independence, women did well; in fact, we believe that they did better than men. And today, woman is as free, liberal, ambitious and progressive as man could be. The Bill has been meeting stiff resistance on the issue of the percentage of reservation. We feel that if the reservation percentage is brought to 20 per cent than to 33 per cent, in the *Lok Sabha* as well as in the state assemblies, the resistance to the Bill would evaporate into thin air. In that event, all the parties would support the Bill and the government would be able to get it passed without any hassles in the next session of Parliament.

The democratic norms ought to be followed in a nation like India as a conglomeration of 100 crore individuals cannot afford to go berserk, as the incidents of December 23, 1999, in the *Lok Sabha* insinuate. The large the mass base, the peculiar would be the need for political coherence and amity in the corridors of power.

If the women's reservation Bill is passed by both the houses of Indian Parliament, how would the candidates be selected for elections (for the *Lok Sabha* or for the state assemblies ? This is a crucial question that needs to be answered by the law makers and elite of this country. If, for example, a woman is *Dalit*, would she be eligible for elections as a SC or as a woman ? Further, the segregation of categories is quite difficult if there were more women in a state. For example, if a state has more women, the women candidates would be more and they are likely to outnumber the male candidates, simply because there may not be enough male candidates in the state for fighting the elections.

There is another aspect of reservation. If more women enter the *Lok Sabha* and the state assemblies, would they be able to deliver the results in their respective constituencies ? Indian woman is identified because of her commitments to her family, children and the social circle in which, she lives. The political duties would not allow her to socialise at well. Moreover, her children would suffer in case she opts for an active political life. There could be young women in the centre and the states who might have to shoulder many vital responsibilities in their respective families. How would Indian women do justice to their home affairs and political duties at the same time? This is a practical problem and must be addressed by those women who vehemently support the Bill.

We hope that the Bill would sail through the ocean of crises, which are forcing it to become another titanic. The prestige of the NDA-led government is closely linked with this Bill. If Mr Vajpayee is able to get it passed, he might become the first hero of the new century.

104. CENTRE-STATE RELATIONSHIPS

India following Westminister system—Controversy over centre-state relationships—Arm-twisting by Ms J Jayalalitha and Mr PS Badal—Due to political stabbing of Ms Jayalalitha, the BJP-led coalition lost power in the centre—Governors dismiss the democratically elected state governments due to recommendations of the central government—Coalition governments have come to stay—Mr Romesh Bhandari used his power to dismiss the state government in UP—The Constitution provides three lists for centre-state interaction—The Union List—The State list—The Government list.

India is a vast nation, which is administered by the Westminister system of Parliamentary governance in the centre. Our Constitution has been framed keeping the British Constitution in view. The relationships between the union government and the state government have always been a matter of controversy. The political parties of different political ideologies have occupied the positions of power in many states. They may not necessarily conform to the dictatorial terms of the union government, which would naturally support its political party in that state. Therefore, this complex and sensitive situation could adversely affect centre-state relationships. The chain of events in UP had resulted in the ouster of the governor of that state. It was alleged that the governor was not in a mood to support or maintain the BJP government in the state. This precarious situation, which was developed as a result of bitter relationships between the state government and the central government, culminated in the resignation of the governor.

Further, the arm-twisting exercises by Ms J Jayalalitha (over the Cauvery issue) and by Mr Prakash Singh Badal (over the Udham Singh Nagar issue) brought the fragile relationships of the central government and states to the centre-stage of Indian polity. These relationship can head for a disaster in case the political parties in the centre and in the states are different. If rival political parties have a long history of discord with each other, then let us forget about an efficient administration in the states. The interference of the union government was evident when a delegation was sent to Bihar for reviewing the law and order situation in the wake of killings in that state. The central government in New Delhi was criticised on the plea that the law and order situation was the internal matter of Bihar. The union home ministry emphasised that it was a national issue and certainly called for the intervention of the centre. The tensions between New Delhi and Patna continued and finally, the union government recommedned the President to dismiss Bihar government through the usage of Article 356. The centre recommended that Bihar assembly should be kept in suspended animation.

In the meantime, Ms J Jayalalitha struck at the right time and joined hands with Ms Sonia Gandhi, the unsure but confident leader of "leftover Congress party." BJP-led Coaliation lost power by a margin of one vote and Parliamentary elections were held in India.

It is very obvious that the powerful centre would certainly manipulate the state level political equations so that the final results could be in its favour. This phenomenon is more prominent if the state government belongs to the opposition party. The union government could try for a dismissal of the state government (as was proposed by Ms J Jayalalitha for the government led by Mr Karunanidhi) under Article 356 of Indian Constitution or could jeopardise the operations of the state by holding back the financial grants. There could be several excuses for giving tantrums to the state administration. By misusing the clauses appended in the Constitution, the union government can try to dethrone those governments in the states that either belong to opposition parties or do not conform to the norms dictated by the centre. The ugly episode of bitter centre-state relationships has been repeated many times since independence.

The basic reason behind this tendency is the hunger for political power. No political party would allow its rivals to prosper. The democratically elected state government has all the rights to govern the state. If it does not perform, it should be held accountable in the state assembly. But it should not be dismissed on account of petty reasons. Our political system promotes institutions and procedures for the victimisation of the democratically elected representatives. For example, the governor would dismiss the state government on the simple plea that the law and order situation is not under control (as was evident in the case of Bihar during the middle of 1999).

We have entered the era of coalition governments. This creates several bizarre situations that are not easy to grapple with. A minority party would resort to horse-trading and other political manipulations in order to gain power or to exercise his discretion and allow the majority party to take over. But the Indian political scenario is fraught with uncertainties and chaos. The decisions taken by the governor are always prone to criticism. Till such time, the Supreme Court adjudicates on the matter of role of the governor, the extent of his powers remains unclear. Allahabad High Court decided to strike down the dismissal of the government led by Mr Kalyan Singh in UP (which was dismissed by Mr Romesh Bhandari, the then Governor of UP). The Supreme Court has clarified that the power of a governor cannot be questioned but Allahabad High Court has not expressed any views in this context. So, it is still not clear whether the governor has the discretionary power under Article 164 read in conjunction with Article 261. The Supreme Court has yet to give a final verdict on this issue.

Let us now examine the constitutional provisions that guide centre-state relationships. There are three lists—The Union list, The State list and The Concurrent list — that regulate the powers of the union government and the state governments in accordance with the Indian constitution. The first list, called the Union List, comprises 97 items. Some of the important items included in this list are defence, arms and ammunition, atomic energy, foreign affairs, diplomatic representation, war and peace, railways, extradition matters, posts and telegraph, currency, inter-state trade and commerce, mining, survey of India, union public services, income tax, organisation of Supreme Court, customs duties, export duties, excise duties *etc*. The Parliament has exclusive powers of legislation for these items and this list requires uniformity of legislation in the interest of the country.

The State List is the second list and comprises 66 items. The important items in this list are police, administration of justice, prisons, public health and sanitation, intoxicating liquours, water supply and irrigation, agriculture, animal husbandary, gas and gas works, land rights, money lending, salaries and allowances of all state officers) state public service commissions, taxes on agricultural incomes, taxes on land and buildings, estate duty, succession duty on agricultural land, excise duties on alcoholic liqours, opium *etc* produced within the state, electricity taxes, taxes on sale and purchase of goods (other than those on newspapers), taxes on goods and passengers carried by roads or through inland waterways, taxes on vehicles, animals, boats, professions, trades and callings, capitation taxes, taxes on luxuries etc. The state legislature has the exclusive power of legislation with regard to each one of the items included in the State List.

The third list is called the Concurrent List. It contains 47 items. These are the items with respect to which, the uniformity of legislation throughout the country is desirable but is not essential. The items in this list have been placed under the jurisdiction of both the union government and the state government. The list includes security of states, marriage and divorce, transfer of property other than agricultural land, contracts, bankruptcy and insolvency, trust and trustees, civil procedures, contempt of court, vagrancy, lunacy and mental deficiency, adulteration of foodstuffs, drugs and poisons, economic and social planning, commercial and industrial monopolies, trade unions, social security, labour welfare, education, trade and commerce in a number of items, price control, factories, electricity, newspapers, books and printing presses, stamp duties *etc*. Indian Parliament and the state legislatures have concurrent powers of legislation over these items. So long as the Parliament does not pass a law on any one of these items, the states may pass any law on the same. But if the Parliament enacts a law on any one of the items of the Concurrent List, the Parliamentary law shall prevail. There is one exception to this general rule; a later law of the state legislature on any item of the Concurrent List shall prevail over an earlier law of Parliament on the same subject provided the state law was reserved for the consideration of President and received his assent.

The legal position of the centre-state relationships is quite clear, logical and transparent. However, under the disguise of Constitutional powers and also in the name of democracy (which is claimed to be in danger by most of the political bigwigs of our country), the state governments are toppled due to manipulations by a powerful government in the centre. As already explained, this typical feature of Indian polity has become a debatable table issue in millions cf Indian homes. The big shark naturally eats up the small fish. Our Constitution provides good legal tools for protection of the state governments. However, implementation of the law is altogether a different affair. The social responsibilities and political maturity of our masses and state legislatures need improvement. Further, a powerful and democratically elected state government must be able to stand up for itself.

This discussion has focussed on three issues :—

(A) The legal provisions of Constitution *viz-a-viz* state-centre relationships (the three lists).

(B) The dominance of a powerful central government over a weak state government through its powers (in the form of a governor) or through a legal battle.

(C) The dominance of a powerful governor over a weak state government (at the behest of his powerful masters in centre or elsewhere).

The coalition-government culture is likely to democratise the relationships between the centre and the states. We hope that the weak and minority governments in the state would find legal opinion in their favour as was the case in the case of recent political turmoil in UP.

THE SPORTS SCENARIO

105. CAN WE PRODUCE OLYMPIC GOLD MEDALLISTS ?

Indian sportsmen could not get any gold medal in Olympics—Poor performance—Lack of infrastructure—Sports gear and facilities are not available—Leander Paes did us proud by winning an Olympic Bronze Medal in Atlanta Olympic Games—Hard training must—Single out the promising sportsmen and train them separately—The State must play its vital role—Private sector participation is also desirable.

Indian sportsman have never been able to collect a single gold medal at the modern Olympics. Gone are the days when Indian Hockey team collected gold medal for hockey even from 1928 onwards. That historic winning streak in hochey is also over. Now, we collect a rare bronze medal (picked up by Leander Paes in Tennis Singles competition in Atlanta Olympics in 1996). Athletics is not worth discussion as our team was not even able to qualify in the events at a number of occasions. Football is a tough game and we have never fared well in it either. Swimming, archery, shooting, wrestling and other events have also not drawn talent from the nooks and corners of the country. Even if we have talent, it does not match the Olympics standards.

On the other hand, Hungary, Romania, China, Japan, Malaysia, Spain and many developing countries have been able to win medals. We are a great nation but still very backward in terms of sports.

The reasons are clear. Indian sports activities are affected by bureaucracy, corruption and a lack of resources at the centre and state levels. Poor training facilities, lack of funds for foreign travel and inadequate tools and kits are also responsible for this fiasco.

We can overcome these problems if we have a sporting spirit. The youth of today are more interested in nine-to-five jobs than in going to the tennis court or the athletics turf for hard practice. The killer instinct of the players is missing, though talent is available. Regular training and hard work must be made a routine for the promising players. Promising players must be singled out and they must be trained by foreign coaches. The State must provide adequate funds for international training and travel abroad. The private sector can also play its role by providing sports gear, finance and training facilities. Tata Football Academy (TFA) is one such example.

We should never give up hope for a medal in the Olympics. After all, Rome was not built in a day. Let us start from bronze medals. Then silver medals should follow suit and finally, we could see the Indian tricolour flutter in the Olympic stadia someday, watching our sports stars receiving the gold medals. This is not a mere dream. It could certainly be turned into reality.

Let us devise long term solutions for this problem. Firstly, we must spot sporting talent in all the urban and rural centres of the country. The sportsmen should be allowed to practise without any fees or other encumberances. The abilities of sportsmen (physical and technical) must be judged by impartial experts. These young players should be taken to the major training centres managed by Sports Authority of India and other organisations like IHF, BCCI *etc* Further these sportsman should be given tension-free and healthy sports environments for their training. They should be allowed to play at block level, state level, national level and finally, in international level competitions. Ironically, all these procedures are present. Yet, the best of sporting talent is left behind and the physically unfit and weak players are sent in national and international competitions. Merit and not the reference power, should be the key criterion for selection.

Secondly, the State must provide adequate funds at the central and state levels for promoting sports in various parts of the country. We have always raised our defence budget but the sports budget receives only a minor boost. Our leaders must know that sports is also an arena of the fight for supremacy of a nation. The budget outlays should be such as to satisfy the survival needs of the sports persons and also, to ensure their proper training, travel and sustenance after their sports careers are over. In the field of cricket, commercialism has already benefited our players. Sachin Tendulkar is one of the highest paid batsmen in the history of cricket; at present, Sachin has been awarded the honour of top ranking batsman in the world. But funds for other sports are not forthcoming. Lack of finances could make some of the sports (or our participation in the international events) extinct in our country.

Thirdly, the State has not promoted national level competitions on a commercial scale. National Games are organised and the competition is also fierce. However, sports streams like hockey, football, swimming and gymnastics do not draw attention of the spectators, sponsors or the official machinery. On the other hand, the European Soccer Circuit is a great event for all the Europeans. The tickets in all the matches are sold in advance. The players perform beyond their capabilities and the spectators become hysterical in support of their sports stars. We have never witnessed such a scene in India except in the case of cricket. Hockey is our national game and yet, it receives a step-motherly treatment from the State, the sporting organisations, the corporate sector and the audiences. After winning the gold medal at Asian Games (held at Kualalumpur), Indian team could not face well in any one of the tournaments that followed. It suffered humiliating defeats at the hands of Pakistani team and South African team. The spectators as well as the private sponsors must also support our national game in whatever ways they could.

Finally, the new sporting skills could be developed only if we learnt the same from the experts. For example, Brazil, Argentina and Mexico are the global leaders in soccer. Indian government must invite the coaches from these countries for training our sportsmen and sportswomen. Similarly, we could invite Chinese trainers for marshal arts games, Japanese and Romanian coaches for gymnastics, swimming trainers from the USA and Russia, hockey coaches from The Netherlands and so on. Further, we could also invite the teams of these countries for friendly tournaments. Alternatively, our best sports talent could be sent abroad for deeper exposure in their respective games. This sporting exchange would go a long way towards the development of our sports talent. Indian hockey players have done very well during April, 2000, by beating Germany in a four-nation hockey tournaent in Perth. This would boost their confidence for playing with confidence at Sydney Olypics (2000).

Indian sports scenario is also fraught with financial problems. We can perform on all the national and international platforms. However, we lack the will power, the finances and tough training for achieving success in the Olympics. Let us start working for our coveted goals today. It is never too late to begin afresh.

106. INDIA IN CRICKET

Indian sports not in very good shape—Indian cricket in most efficient form—We are a cricket power—Bowling, batting and fielding performances excellent—Our competitors are Australia, Pakistan, South Africa and Sri Lanka—World Cup (2003)—Could not witness Indian Cricketing magic—We did not play with killer instinct—Play with major cricket powers to hone the skills—Do not exhaust yourself—We could have won World Cup (2003).

Indian sportsmen have yet to deliver concrete performances on the international front. We are a sporting nation and have teams in all the major sports disciplines; hockey, cricket, athletics, swimming, weightlifting, wrestling and cycling are some of the streams to be mentioned. However, our performance has been very dismal in almost all these fields except one—cricket.

There is no doubt that India is one of the most efficient and powerful teams in the cricket circuit today. The overall performance of the team in one-day international matches as well as in test matches has been superb. Our cricketing stars are shining above all of their international compatriots. Sachin Tendulkar, Rahul Dravid, Saurav Ganguly, Mohammed Kaif, Yuvraj Singh, Harbhajan Singh and Ajit Agarkar are some of the Indian cricketing heroes, worshipped by their fans around the world.

In the field of batting, Sachin Tendulkar has achieved the highest pinnacles of glory by scoring 34 centuries in one day internationals and over 12,000 runs. He is the first batsman with highest number of aggregate runs in all editions of World Cup (1732 runs). Master blaster Sachin won the Man of the Tournament award for his consistently brilliant performances throughout the World Cup 2003. (673 runs at an average of 61.18). His record as a captain has always been dismal. The Indian squad lost the test series and one-day series in Australia during 1999-2000 session. Further, we lost to South Africa in test match series by two matches to nil. We won the one day series by three matches to two. Other stars in Indian squad include Saurav Ganguly, Rahul Dravid, Yuvraj Singh, Mohammed Kaif, Zakir Khan, Harbhajan Singh, Anil Kumble.

During the eighties, West Indies ruled supreme. During the early nineties, Australia ruled the cricketing fields. Now a days, Australia is the world champion. Our team was not consistent during world cup matches but Australians played steady games.

One-day cricket is anybody's game. This fact has been amply demostrated in several one-day matches and in the World Cup matches played in South Africa in 2003. Cricketing fortunes could turn in the favour of any team. The man of the moment wins the match. Therefore, it is important to perform when stress is the maximum. Our team did not had consistency in bowling, batting and fielding during the tour to New Zealand just before World Cup 2003.

Further, Indians must prepare themselves so that they remain physically fit. They have mastered all the departments of the game. Indian team is a perfect combination of batting, bowling and fielding. They must keep it up and must perform at their peak for winning the matches in the ensuing cricket season. Sachin Tendulkar is fit as a fiddle and Saurav Ganguly has also been doing well as an aggressive captain. The strategies and tactics should be planned now so that the results are evident in the matches. Instead of a long series of test matches and one day internationals, Indian team should be sent abroad for a limited number of matches.

India's dream run in the ICC Cricket World Cup 2003 came to a disappointing end when the mighty Australia thrashed India, the World Cup 1983 champions, by 125 runs in the final played at the Wanderers, Johannesburg (South Africa) on March 23, 2003. Australia smashed their way to a massive 359 after they were asked to bat first by India and bundled the Indians for 234 runs to retain the cup.

Cricket is a phenomenon in India. It has made Indians proud of our achievements. India is a cricketing power to reckon with. We hope that the Indian team would be able to deliver results in the matches that follow. Our team would bring glory to the Indian nation once again, thus repeating the performances of the past.

107. INDIA IN HOCKEY

India was nowhere in the tenth World Cup organised in Kuala Lumpur in 2002—India won the hockey silver in Asiad (2002)—unfit players and lack of teamwork—Could not convert simple opportunities into goals—Our record from 1928 to 1960 was impeccable—Degradation began from 1975 onwards—very poor performance levels till last year—Remove bureaucratic delays—Supply funds—Get private sponsors—Better training and exposure required.

The last World Cup Hockey tournament saw Germany emerging as the new force in hockey. Germany defeated Australia by two goals to one and bagged the most coveted trophy in hockey. The German team consolidated its position by decimating all the opponents systematically. Their robust play and coordination on the field were indeed remarkable. Netherlands beat South Korea to take the third place in tournament.

Indian hockey squad could only win the silver medal in Asian Games held at Busan (South Korea) in 2002 as South Korea beat them 4-3 in final. Our boys did show good potential though they were unimaginative at crucial junctures.

Let us analyse our rendezvous hockey from the very inception. Indians have a glorious record as a hockey playing nation. We had achieved this status way back during the early twenties. The World Cup was started in 1971. However, hockey had been given an Olympic game status in 1908 itself. World Cup tournaments were initially held after a gap of two years. After 1974, International Hockey Federation (FIH) decided to organise it after every four years.

The world has witnessed nine tournaments so far. Pakistan has won this tournament four times, the Netherlands has won it thrice, India has once and Australia has won the tournaament only once.

During the early twenties, hockey was the most natural bastion of Indians. Dhyan Chand was the undisputed king of world hockey.

India won all the hockey titles at the Olympics held from 1928 to 1960. The old days remind us of the golden nostalgia, which was very pleasant and glorious for our hockey. In 1960, Pakistan took away Olympic hockey title from India. In Mexico Olympics (1968) the Australian team did not allow us to enter finals for the first time.

In 1971, Pakistan won the first World Cup at Barcelona. Spain was placed second and India was placed third. The decline of Indian hockey was still not evident. We won World Cup in Kuala Lumpur in 1975. But we could not win any other World Cup tournament. The deterioration started from 1975 onwards.

In Olympic games, we could not perform well due to the lack of practice, inadequate facilities and bureaucratic hassles in our administrative structure. An Indian player cannot afford to spend asequate money on his sportsgear, training, practice sessions and foreign tours. The cricket scenario is totally commercialised but hockey tournaments continue to be under the aegis of the State funding. Private sponsorships are not easy to get. They are merely players who represent their nation. They are not stars like their counterparts in the game of cricket.

The former Indian Chief Coach—V Bhaskaran—stated that India lacked mental toughness in the World Cup tournament. He pointed out that other teams possessed this trait in order to survive in the international competitions like the World Cup and Champions Trophy. He also blamed missed chances as a reason for our defeat.

The technicalities of failure should be studied and scrutinised by the sports specialists, government and media over a long period of time. Indian Hockey Federation (IHF), as the controlling and governing authority of the game in this country, deliver positive results. The present chief of IHF, Mr KPS Gill, has a good record as a police chief and he is trying hard to improve bureaucratic mismanagement lack of facilities for the players and above all, selection of tired and injured players for an important tournament affect the game and hence, the nation in an adverse manner. The nation was shocked by the fiasco of the 1998 World Cup.

The junior hockey team had reached the finals in the Junior World Cup held in Milton Keynes (UK). Indians had a glimmer of hope that our boys would do well at all the major tournaments of the world. However, the drubbing of the senior hockey team at Utrecht did not created a sense of confidence in the junior team.

Argentina is doing very well. Spain is now a major hockey power to reckon with. Similarly, England, China, Scotland, the USA, Poland and New Zealand are improving their games everyday.

It is a time for deep introspection. In the Sydney Olympic Games (2000 AD) we lost the semi-final berth by a whisker. India must regain her lost glory. We are proud of international celebrities like Dhanraj Pillai, Aslam Sher Khan, Dhyan Chand, Baljit Singh Saini, Ashok Kumar, KD Singh Babu and many more who have done India proud. But we must eliminate the problems that plague Indian hockey. Let us suggest a few solutions as follows :—

(A) The Indian Hockey Federation (IHF) should be made a resource rich and autonomous body. It should be given the resources for team development. Further, well-defined targets should be set and achieved within a time frame. If need be, IHF should be privatised or made completely autonomous.

(B) The State must allocate more resources for the training, maintenance and post-career lives of hockey players. Most of the former players complain that they won laurels for the country but the country did not do anything for them. The careers and the economic mechanisms after the active careers of the players should be planned in advance. They should be offered stable jobs in government undertakings. When they retire from the game, they should be accepted as coaches and team managers. Although a lot is being done in this direction, yet the efforts being made are not exhaustive. These efforts must assist all the hockey players playing at national and international levels.

(C) The states should initiate programmes for popularising hockey in all the Indian states. Local tournaments and foreign tours should also be organised.

(D) The private sponsors should invest in the hockey tournaments. Privatisation has helped Indian cricket, which is touching new heights. The same could happen in the case of Indian hockey also. Recently Sahara Group has come forward in a big way to sponsor Indian hockey.

(E) Political interference, bureaucratic delays and internal politics from the governing bodies (at state and central levels) must be eliminated.

If these steps are taken and also, if IHF plans a well chalked-out strategy for removing the problems of Indian hockey, we could regain the lost glory in this field. The targets are difficult to achieve and the road to success is fraught with many thorns. If Indian hockey is to be revived, proper funding, disciplined training schedules and swift planning on the turf as well as off the turf are necessary. Success in hockey requires tough training and body conditioning, resources for the survival and growth of the players and finally, a total elimination of bureaucratic procedures. IHF is doing its best to revitalize the Indian hockey.

Lately, Indian hockey is showing signs of golden touch after winning two tournaments in Australia and Germany against strong opposition. Dhanraj Pillay, Captain of Indian team is counted as the best player of modern hockey. Players like Gagan Ajit Singh, Jugraj Singh, Devesh Chauhan and Baljit Saini aare well-known in world hockey for their magical skills and Indian hockey at last seems to be on the right path. ●

108. WORLD SOCCER

Soccer is the game of people—Nearly 150 soccer playing nations—First cup in 1930 in Uruguay—World cups organised in 1934, 1938, 1950, 1954, 1958, 1962, 1966, 1970, 1974, 1978, 1982, 1986, 1990, 1994 and in 1998—World Cup (1994) won by Brazil—1998 World Cup won by France, 2002 World Cup win by Brazil—Other strong contenders are Argentina, Mexico, England, Germany and Holland—Rivaldo, Ronaldo, David Beckham, Michael Owen, Ronaldinho, Zinedine Zidane, Ivan Zomolno etc are the star players—Game adored and loved by people around the world—India does not figure in the list of top 100 nations.

Soccer is "people's game." It is the most loved sport around the world. The World Cup, which was kicked off on June 10, 1998, was treated as the last mega-event of the previous century. Next only to the Olympics, the World Cup is played by the most powerful football playing nations of the world. It is a thrill and excitement for the players, the organisers and the audiences around the world and cannot be described in a few words. Soccer is a passion around the globe and the prestige of many soccer playing nations is at stake.

Let us trace the history of world cup football in brief.

The World Cup is organised by International Football Federation (FIFA). It is also known as Jules Rimmet Cup as Mr Jules Rimmet was the President of FIFA during 1921-1954 period. He contributed immensely towards the initiation of World Cup tournament and the subsequent popularisation of the game. World Cup is organised after four years. Most of the World Cup finals were won either by European or by Latin American nations. France is the present champion as she won World Cup (1998). However, FIFA continues to give the highest rating to Brazil as this country and soccer are synonymous.

The first World Cup was organised in 1930 in Uruguay. Although talks were on for starting the World Cup in soccer from 1928, yet the first major World Cup event could be kicked off only by 1930. Thirteen nations participated in the first World Cup tournament. Yugoslavia, Romania, Belgium, France, Uruguay and Argentina were the few nations, which participated in the maiden World Cup tournament. Uruguay won the first World Cup after they defeated Argentina in the finals.

In 1934, the second World Cup was organised in Italy. Sixteen teams participated in the tournament and Italy won the cup after defeating Czechoslovakia in the finals. Angelo Skiview (Italy), Olad Ritchejedley (Czechoslovakia) and Edmund Conill (Germany) were the top scorers. The (1938) World Cup was organised by France. Italian team was in full form at that time. Italian coach-Vottorio Pozzo-was a popular figure in the international soccer circles. Italy and Hungary struggled in the finals and Italy won the cup once again. Leonidis Sylva (Brazil) was the top scorer in the tournament.

The 1942 and 1946 World Cups could not be organized due to two World Wars.

In 1950, Brazil was the host nation for the World Cup. The final match was played between Brazil and Uruguay. Uruguay won the finals and Admir (Brazil) emerged as the top scorer.

In 1954, the world cup was organised in Switzerland. The Hungarian star player-Puskam-was the hero of those times. The final match was played between Hungary and West Germany. West Germany scored the winning goal only six minutes before the final whistle. The top scorer of the tournament was Sandus Cocsys (Hungary).

In 1958, the World Cup was organised in Sweden. Pele reigned supreme during those years and was the most respected scoccer god in the soccer world. Brazil and Sweden reached the finals and Brazil won the cup. Frenchman-Jest Fontaine-was the top scorer who scored 13 goals—a record to date.

The 1962, World Cup was hosted by Chile. Although Pele was left out of the Brazilian squad due to severe injuries, yet Brazil defeated Czechoslovakia in the finals. Yugoslav star-Dragin Jerkovich-was the top scorer with 5 goals to his credit.

In 1966, World Cup was organised in England. Brazil could not make it even to the quarterfinal round. The final was played between West Germany and England. England won the cup by scoring 4-2 against Germany in extra time. Isibean (Portugal) was the top scorer of this tournament.

In 1970, Mexico hosted World Cup. The teams, which played in 1966 world cup, could not even qualify for the semifinals. The final match was played between Brazil and Italy. Brazil defeated Italy 4-1 and lifted the cup. Therefore, Brazil becomes the only nation in the world to have won the cup three times. World Cup was stolen during this time period. This was also the last world cup tournament in which, Pele had participated. The top scorer of the tournament was Gerard Mueller who scored 10 goals in the tournament.

The 1974 World Cup was won by Germany. Germany won the finals after defeating Holland. This proved the rising dominance of the German soccer in international and European circles. In 1978, World Cup was won by Argentina after defeating Holland in the finals. In 1982, World Cup was won by Italy after defeating Germany.

In 1986, World Cup was won by Argentina. Diego Armando Maradona was the star player of Argentina and was able to fetch many victories for all the clubs for which, he played. Maradona used to charge astronomical fees for displaying his rare soccer skills in the field. In 1986, Argentina and Germany entered the finals and Argentina won simply because of the "Maradona Magic." He also scored the maximum number of goals in the tournament—a total of five and two against England.

In 1990, "Maradona Magic" gripped the world soccer once again. The 1990 World Cup final (1990) was held in Italy. Germany and Argentina entered the finals. But the magic of Maradona could not help Argentina win the World Cup as the Germans proved to be much stronger. Germany lifted the cup.

In 1994, World Cup was won by Brazil who walked away with the top honours after defeating Italy in the finals. The star players of the tournament were Salvatore Schillachi, Roberto Baggio and Raud Gullit. Brazil became the undisputed world soccer champion by annexing the World Cup four times.

The 1998, World Cup was organised in France. Thirty-two teams participated in the tournament. The competition was very stiff as star players like Rivaldo, Ronaldo, Juergen Klinsmann, Zinedina Zidane, Ivan Zomorano, Robert Baggio *etc* played in this tournament. Indian football team is at its lowest ebb. We are not counted even among the first hundred soccer playing nations of the world. World Cup (1998) saw the fall of soccer majors like Argentina, Brazil and Germany. In the finals held in Paris on July 13, 1998, France defeated Brazil by three goals to nil and captured the top spot in the world soccer history. The hero of the finals was Zinedine Zidane who dominated the field and the hearts of the world soccer fans through his superb footwork and movements among the rival team.

Maintaining their superb performance of not conceding a single match, Brazil convincingly trounced three-time champion,

Germany (2-0) in the final of the 2002 FIFA World Cup played at Yokohama (Japan) on June 30, 2002. In the process, Brazil became the world cup champion forthe record fifth time (1958, 1962, 1970, 1994 and 2002. Ronaldo won the Golden Boot Award for the Best Player of the tournament. Being South Korea, cohosts of this world cup withJapan, mesmerised everyone with their dazzling display end becamethe first Asian team to reach the semi-final of world cup.

MANAGEMENT

109. MANAGEMENT : THE NEW RELIGION

Management is the new religion—Management defined—Basic concepts—Five basic components of the management process—Planning—Organising—Staffing—Directing—Controlling—All strata of society and business would adopt it—Only the efficient managers would survive—Participative and liberal techniques would be successful—Management would take mankind to new heights of glory.

The modern concept of management is not confined to books, seminars and sleep-inducing lectures. We perceive management as the thought process and the result-oriented behaviour of every individual who wishes to make a mark in his life. We would not like to get into the mad jungle of management that is full of theories and concepts. We would like to project it as the new panacea for the ills that have been afflicted upon the human race since its inception.

We would like to define management as the professional modus operandi for solving the problems faced by the mankind, its habitat and the society at large. Management pervades all the strata of society and industry. It is practised by all the classes of business, industry, commerce and polity. In sum, every person, firm, organisation, society or nation manages for yielding a concrete output in numeric or qualitative terms. Management ought not to be learned through the voluminous texts and theories. It should become the practical and result oriented skill of the mankind so that it becomes its tool of survival and growth in the newmillennium.

Any firm or organisation, irrespective of its structure or objectives, would face three distinct situations while managing its affairs. The conditions and the methodologies of management during each one of those conditions have been discussed as follows :—

    (A) Management is the key when the resources are scarce. Any person, firm or organisation could face the scarcity of resources. The demands on the resources are high whereas the resources (like capital, fixed assets, movable assets, human resources, references in the industry, political references, technological resources etc) have to be utilised for meeting the pre-specified objectives. In that event, a manager has to select the priority areas in which, these scarce resources ought to be invested or utilised. Austerity and prudent management would be the key words in such a situation and survival would be the major issue.

(B) Management is the key when the resources are equal to the demands on the same. In such a situation, there is no need for austerity measures. Expansion plans could be forwarded. Employees could be given additional responsibilities so that they could work harder for a better future of the firm. Financial analysis could also be done. There is no need to panic as the concerned or organisation would be able to swim through difficult times with perfect finesse. However, there are no chances for growth in such a situation because the resources, though adequate, are not enough for a major leap forward.

(C) Management is the key when the resources are much more than the demand on the same. These are the happier times for the firm. Cash and funds flow in. New projects are undertaken for execution. New plants are constructed or old plants of the competitors are purchased through acquisition bids. The expansion plans, some of which, were finalised or proposed during Stage B), could be implemented with full vigour. These are the times of the plenty. Funds could be saved for utilisation during the difficult times. Employees could be given financial incentives and bonus packages. The shareholders could also be given additional dividends. New product lines, concepts, ideologies or services could be planned and introduced in the markets. When the resources are in abundance, then everyone is enthusiastic about the firm he works for. If the resources are allocated for profitable projects, product lines or services and good financial planning is also done, then the organisation and the individuals attached to it could achieve unknown heights. This phenomenon is aptly applicable in business, commerce, international trade, environmental control, politics and social reforms.

It is quite unfortunate to note that managers find resources to be lesser than the demands on the same. This situation always arises in all the organisations and even if Stage A and Stage B appear, their tenures are temporary. The reason is that the markets around the world, which consume the products and services of a firm, keep on changing with passage of time. This market dynamism forces the firms to adopt new products, services, management techniques and manufacturing technologies. Further, the effects of the policies and directives of the government, political upheavals, industrial recession, wars and *force majeure'* are also able to lead the firms from the position of resource abundance to a precarious position of resource scarcity. This is true for all the organisations, firms, nations and societies.

If, however, we accept management as the proper and logical *modus operandi*, then we could meet many challenges that face us during Stages A and B. We would then, realise that the management process would lead us to a stable and prosperous state in which, all those involved would be happy-customers, vendors, the top brass, nations, societies and the habitat in which, these mechanisms thrive. But for achieving that objective, we would have to manage strictly on professional lines. And that would mean that we would have to accept the practical concepts of management as our new guidelines for living through the next millennium. Management becomes the new religion of the mankind, the new spiritual and moral preacher that would help us sail through the difficult times in all walks of our lives. We would become the disciples of the most pragmatic and paying philosophies of management propounded by the mankind so far.

And management has rightly been accepted as the new religion in the USA and other Western nations. Modern techniques of management (like MBO, JIT, TQM, Human Re-engineering, PPC, Johari Window, Participative Management *etc*) have been accepted and practised in Japan, the USA, Canada, the UK, Belgium, France, Sweden, Italy and the Netherlands. Indians are way behind in this context, though we are proud of many managers who have made it to the hall of fame in the field of management and have been recognised the world over.

When God created this universe, he gave the most relished gift to the mankind-the human brain. And all the theories of management have emanated from the human brain itself. The application of the human mind to the day-to-day problems resulted in the finest methodologies of management. We have come a long way since the Stone Age. But we have many more miles to go before we could be sure of securing a safe and prosperous future for our future generations on this planet. The world faces poverty, hunger, famines, wars, internal strife, violence, clashes of egoes, embargoes and many complex problems in the fields of psychology and inter-personal relationships. Human mind is not predictable whereas the human brain is. Man does not use his brain but he depends more upon his heart (hunch or habit) and his heart takes him away from rationale, logic and result oriented thinking. The problems faced by mankind could be solved only through the time-tested and pragmatic techniques of management

The operational methodology of management is simple. The management process comprises five basic steps and the same have been discussed as follows :—

(A) **Planning**—The objectives of the organisation are decided by the top management. The resources of the firm are also carefully measured and studied by the management and the experts who could be hired by the firm. The strengths, weaknesses, opportunities and threats are judged in advance through SWOT Analysis. Keeping in mind the resources at its command, the top management plans the working of the organisation. It has been said that plans are nothing but planning is everything. In other words, plans are the blueprints that have to be used for achieving the coveted objectives of an organisation. If plans are not implemented, they are of no use as they are unable to achieve the desired objectives.

(B) **Organising**—This step is followed after planning. The structure of the organisation is defined by the top brass. The job profiles, responsibilities, pay packages and privileges of all the cadres are decided in advance. An efficient and goal-oriented organisational structure is important for the success of any firm or business. The line and staff organisation structure, the flat structure and the tall structure are the three major variations of the organisational structure. However, modern organisations choose those structures that are defined by them and that suit their interests and operations. The organisational structure is supposed to deliver the results for the organisation. If it does not, it has to be modified or changed completely so that it could be effective. Some firms might have a Vice President (Marketing) who could be having four General Managers for four product lines of the firm. Some other firms might have a General Manager (Marketing) under whom, there could be four Marketing Executives could be looking after the four different markets of the firm. These decisions are taken depending upon the market requirements, types of products or services and the resources at command. The hierarchy of the organisational structure would vary and so would the authority levels and pay packages. In a government organisation, all these factors are defined in advance and are followed in letter and spirit. In the smaller private organisations, there are no rules and the proprietor makes all the rules. The big corporate firms, however, define their organisational structures carefully and define the responsibilities, benefits and authority levels of each one of the hierarchies defined. The organisational structure has to be sturdy and flexible enough to help the firm achieve its objectives with the resources at its command.

(C) **Staffing**—After the finalisation of the organisation staructure (*ie*, after having the clarity of the issues-who would do it ? And how would he do it ?), the personnel recruitment process is initiated for filling up the vacancies in the firm. The job profiles are matched with the personnel of the human resource markets. Interviews, written tests and psychological tests are conducted after screening the profiles of the candidates who are called for inducting them in the organisation. After these procedures, the finally selected candidates are appointed. They are given training and are conditioned according to the needs of their job profiles so that they could deliver results in accordance with the objectives of the firm. Every employee is trained to deliver an output of a specific type.

(D) **Directing**—The staffing function recruits and trains. But the managers ought to be given orders so that they could deliver the results. Now a days, nobody takes orders but works along with his boss. The concept of 'order' has become obsolete. Working along with the boss is a more positive concept. Every person is an era. Hence, his ego would have to be given due respect in his firm. The manager has to direct his subordinates in such a manner as could incite desired responses from the subordinates and at the same time, does not hurt them as juniors. Tact is the latest buzzword; orders and directives are the tenets of the past.

(E) **Controlling**—The manager has to control the operations through budgets, meetings, financial tools, policies and procedures. The goals have already been defined. The goals of each department are also clearly delineated, preferably in a written format. The manager has to measure the performance of his subordinates against the targets set by the top management. If the performance of an individual is not up to the mark, then coercion (or even a firing tactic) could be resorted to. If, however, performance is well above the average level, the employee is given incentives and his status is elevated in the organisational hierarchy. But the "carrot and stick policy" may not be effective in all the situations. MBO and participative management have proved to be more useful in many a firm. For negotiation, the U-matic Technique, propounded by A Kumar, is a good attempt for matching the conflicting interests of the negotiating factions. This technique is likely to be implemented in a more effective manner in the times to come.

A manager is a leader, a motivator and a go-getter. He achieves results. And the new millennium would rightly belong to a successful manager. A commitment towards objectives would be the key to success for all the managers. This new religion would guide the social, moral and commercial transactions of all the strata of societies of the new millennium. Every person would have to manage efficiently in order to survive in this world. A religion helps the individual in his spiritual, moral and aesthetic cleansing processes. And management would certainly become a successful religion for the modern man. It would also acquire the status of the universal religion. It would become a philosophy, guiding light and established norm for the business firms, society, political parties and human race in the next millennium. There is no competition from any other religion; they cannot match the adroitness of management ! ●

110. JIT

Resources are limited—Reduce inventory carrying costs through JIT—JIT evolved during eighties—Throughput time comprises VAT and NVAT—Reduce NVAT—Procure items only when needed—Tune production schedules accordingly—JIT would be a part of India's manufacturing plants—JIT has bright future.

The modern world operates on the basis of three basic tenets :—

(A) The resources are limited and have to be utilised in such a manner as would enable the maximum output to be generated from these resources.

(B) The profits have to be maximised through increased sales and hefty margins, with the establishment of brands in the target market niches.

(C) The raw materials, parts and services have to be procured in such a manner as would ensure that the organisation or business spends the least possible resources and earns the maximum. The materials management function should be a well-planned operation that should manifest its efficacy in terms of the profits earned and savings effected.

Whereas the second tenet mentioned above is devoted to the manipulations in the markets, the first and the third tenets have a marked affiliation with the *avant garde'* production and material control techniques. We have to produce the maximum from the resources available at our command. We have also to sell the products and services (or even concepts, ideas) at the maximum possible profits for the organisation, society and the mankind. However, the markets also have competitors and they are likely to restrict the margins of an organisation. So, we have to cut down our costs in such a manner as would ultimately enable us to earn a decent amount of profits. A Rupee saved is a Rupee earned; and the first and the third tenets guide us towards this objective while we operate in an organisational mechanism of any class, turnover or objective. In this text, we shall discuss a new philosophy of materials management that would help the modern manager save through the effective utilisation of resources available.

Before moving towards Just In Time Technique (JIT), let us define materials management first. "Materials management is the process and methodology of defining, procuring, storing, issuing and maintaining the materials required for production of goods and services of the organisation and include fixed assets, raw materials, work-in-process goods, finished goods, semi-finished parts and final products. We resort to professional materials management techniques for the sake of saving valuable resources of the organisation, the process ultimately reflecting its efficiency and reliability in terms of the corporate profits or the achievement of the goals of the organisation in question." JIT is the latest technique of materials management function. It is normally applicable in a manaufacturing organisation. The most essential tenet of JIT is the total elimination of wastage of precious resources. JIT is also fully compatible with quality management techniques in vogue today. It is also compatible with the ISO system of industrial standardisation that is a much discussed and followed norm in the corporate and industrial circles.

JIT was initiated in Japan during the early eighties of the century goneby. Japanese are hardworking and efficient people. They produce more and the goods are sold at lower prices by them in the global markets, which are termed by them as their own homes. However, while cutting down the prices, Japanese do not make any compromises with the quality aspects of the goods or services they produce. During the early eighties, the production of cars was far more than the demand in the markets. The extra number of cars-the glut of final products-was a nuisance for Japanese car manufacturers. There were huge inventories of cars (finished goods) and therefore, the inventory carrying costs were very high. The markets were agog with the rumours that Japanese cars did not sell and that is why, there were no buyers, thus leading to a glut of new cars. The problem was analysed by Japanese car manufacturers and it was concluded that an extra number of cars was produced in order to cut down the per unit cost of the finished product. However, the inventory carrying costs of finished products were too high and the Japanese car manufacturers thought of the alternative methods of saving the same.

They, decided to follow Just In Time (JIT) technique of inventory control. The gist of JIT is as follows. When a product is ordered for manufacture by the production department, it needs some time to be completed from the raw materials stage to the final usable form. This time period, during which, value is added to the raw materials and the semi-finished products, is known as the Value Added Time (VAT). However, there are formalities involved in the execution of the order. These formalities fall under the gamut of order processing time that begins from the date or time of order finalisation to the final delivery of the product at the site of the client. The components of order processing time are as follows :—

(A) Order finalisation.
(B) Issue of the Purchase Order (PO).
(C) Order confirmation.
(D) Advance payments.
(E) Procurement of raw materials.
(F) Inspection of raw materials.
(G) Receipt of raw materials by the manufacturing department or section.
(H) Value Added Time (processing, machining and assembly at the site of the manufacturer).
(I) Movement of the semi-finished product or component to next stage of production.
(J) Inspection and testing.
(K) Packing.
(L) Delivery.

The concept of Throughput Time has to be understood here. Throughput Time comprises two time periods that they are:

(a) the Value Added Time (VAT); and

(b) the Non-value Added Time.

The Non-value Added Time (NVAT) is that time period during which, value is not added to the product. The Value Added Time (VAT) is that time period during which, value is added to the product. It is clear from the aforementioned discussion that the NVAT includes all those heads except the VAT. According to the Japanese concept of JIT.

$$\text{Throughput Time} = \text{VAT} + \text{NVAT}$$

For the benefit of our worthy readers, we would divide the total time for order execution into the following components.

Order Execution Time
$$= \text{Order Processing Time} + \text{Throughput Time}$$
$$= \text{Order Processing Time} + (\text{VAT} + \text{NVAT})$$
$$= (\text{Heads A, B, C, D}) + (\text{Head H})$$
$$+ (\text{Heads E, F, G, I, J, K, L})$$

The heads have been described as mentioned above.

Throughput Time (TT) is the time interval between the first stage of production and the point at which, the finished product comes out of the production line. For the sake of convenience, we have deleted the marketing and selling time periods as the definition mentioned above does not accept them as the 'involved' time periods related to the manufacturing facilities only.

The gist of JIT is that NVAT has to be minimised. VAT would remain as such and could be reduced with modern technologies and carefully designed plant layouts. The managerial techniques of Work Study and Time and Motion Study could also be used for the reduction of VAT but there is a limit up to which, we could reduce VAT. Production Planning and Control Techniques (PPC) would also help the production manager for reducing the VAT.

Further, if NVAT is minimised, the throughput time would be minimised. The concept of JIT assumes that :

(a) quality has to be enhanced;
(b) set up time periods have to be reduced;
(c) factory layouts have to be so designed (and implemented) to ensure minimum VAT;
(d) timely deliveries from the vendors have to be ensured so that they are executed as and when they are required; and
(e) delivery has to be made to the customer within the stipulated time limits.

According to the JIT concept, inventory is a wastage of financial resources. The concept assumes nil inventory of raw materials, work-in-process goods and semi-finished products. This condition, however, has never been realised in most of the manufacturing plants around the world, though the major manufacturers have been able to keep their inventory levels at the lowest possible levels. In sum, JIT lays stress on minimum or nil inventory and the best quality of the final products manufactured. The emphasis, in this system of manufacturing and materials management, is on the reduction of NVAT to a minimum value. Japanese firms have adopted JIT and the results have been excellent. Many American and German firms have also embraced JIT and are tuning their production operations according to its spirit.

Closely related to the concept of JIT is JIT **procurement**. According to this concept, which is nothing but a **component of the** entire gamut of JIT, the goods to be procured for the manufacture of a product, would be procured at the time of the actual demand of the final product. Utopian though it may seem, the concept is catching up quickly in the modern production facilities around the globe. The supplier is taken into confidence and is asked to supply smaller quantities of the plant raw materials, components, work-in-process goods and spares as and when required by the factory. There are minimum inventory carrying costs for the manufacturer. And this is the key to a successful JIT implementation. The ordering quantity is constant and the concept of Economic Ordering Quantity (EOQ) is not applicable here. The factory space, godown space and inventory carrying costs are reduced substantially.

And finally, the JIT concept also encompasses JIT production that is also quite essential for a successful for implementation of JIT in a manufacturing organisation. According to this concept, within a production line, a component is manufactured only when it is needed at the next stage of the production process. The Throughput Time (TT) is minimised as a result. The production line or the part of the production line is allowed to stop operation if the parts (inputs to the same) are either not available or the quality of the parts received from the previous stage is inadequate. Only those activities are carried out that would lead to the production of a product or a component of best quality.

JIT is a new concept in India. Only a few corporate players have adopted it so far. In our country, we are chronically obsessed with producing more so that manufacturing and processing costs could be minimised. However, this concept has given way to JIT in other parts of the industrial world. Most of the firms in India cringe with tear when they encounter the thought of minimum or nil inventory levels. However, JIT would soon enter Indian production plants. JIT has been tuned with Total Quality Management (TQM). Its basic objective is to reduce the unproductive time during the course of production. The other objective is to improve the quality of the product being manufactured. And finally, the aim of JIT is to improve the productivity of the plant personnel. All these aims are the basic foundations of management. Hence, JIT would stay and shall prosper as a management philosophy during the present millennium.

111. GIGA MARKETING

Marketing is the creation of a standard of living—Earlier concepts emphasised upon Product, Product promotion and Physical Distribution—Kotler added Power and Political Influence—New Ps include Place and Persuasion—Sum total of all the Ps is Giga marketing—New millennium would belong to those managers who would keep tthese concepts in mind while trying to win their markets.

Marketing is the creation of a standard of living. It is a process in which, the goods and services are exchanged by the **sellers for** money or other non-monetary privileges in the local, national **and international** markets. Marketing is the most vital activity of **business; all** other activities are subordinate to this activity as it would **decide the** future course of a business.

As the students of administration and management, we would not like to view marketing in the context of a business enterprises only. We feel that every person needs marketing stills. Within the set of skills of marketing, a person has to learn the concept of "selling his idea, products or concepts" to another person, firm or the society. This 'selling' is the basis of the marketing effort, though it may not necessarily be done for the sake of earning money. The objectives of marketing and selling efforts could be a combination of either of the following :—

(A) Improvement in the standards of living of the humanity (*eg*, medical services and 'selling' of immunisation programmes for controlling HBV).

(B) Generation of revenues for a non-profit organisation that is committed to charity and selfless service (*eg*, collection of funds for Missionaries of Charity).

(C) Management and conservation of the ecology of the mother earth. (*eg*, Narmada Bachao Aandolan).

(D) Management of a nation and projection of her healthy and clean image at the appropriate international fora (*eg*, India at the UNO on the issue of insurgency in Kashmir).

We can visualise that these are the pious objectives that are related to all of us; money is not the motive here. Human values take a frontseat *viz-a-viz* the commercial cultural that is divesting humanity of grace, morality and mental sanity. So, we consider marketing as a tool of management not only to earn enough of revenues, but also to improve the moral, national and spiritual standards of the mankind.

Way back during the late seventies of the last century, Dr Philip Kotler (a renowned professor of marketing) propounded that marketing is a four-legged strategy; the four legs are the essential Ps of marketing—Product, Price, Promotion and Physical Distribution. Kotler described these Ps as essential building blocks of any marketing effort. He also stated that all the products are designed to deliver some services; the products do not have any usage or significance unless they deliver the services for which, they have been manufactured. Kotler delineated the *modus operandi* for defining the strategies and winning situations in the national (American) and international market places by defining these four Ps and making them more acceptable to the marketing firms. The research work of

Kotler remains the single most of its kind, though many other authors have also conducted research projects in marketing and have written volumes on this subject.

During the mid-eighties (in the year 1986), Philip Kotler introduced a new concept that enthralled the marketing *Pandits* of the globe. He wrote on article (in 1986) that was published in a leading magazine devoted to management. He coined a new term—megamarketing—and added two more Ps to the existing set of four Ps. He termed those new elements as Power and Political Influence. This new theory was welcomed by the corporate sector as well as by the management researchers. So, Kotler propounded that there were six Ps in all—Product, Price, Promotion, Physical Distribution, Power and Political Influence.

Kotler stated that Power also helped the modern firms to get concrete results from the dynamic market places of today. This power could be financial, coercive or expertise-oriented. Finally, Kotler added that political influence also helped the marketer gain vital market niches; this P is especially useful for global marketing strategies. For example, Saudi petroleum firms, in collaboration with British and American firms, have captured markets in the Gulf nations and Europe. Iraqi oil is not available for sale, thanks to the bitter war that escalated between the USA and her allies during the early nineties. Iraqi oil is not being sold anywhere due to the UN sanctions, most of them being sponsored by the USA. Therefore, political rivalry is costing Iraq dearly in terms of oil revenues.

Despite research efforts undertaken by the marketing professionals, the woes of the marketers and sales personnel do not come to a happy end. Why we are unable to 'sell' our products, thought and concepts ? And why the firms fail ? Many of them are rich conglomerates that could depose the governments of many a small nation ? But markets are cruel to them. Why ?

We shall try to answer this question. It is just possible that Dr Kotler and many more researchers might have missed some vital elements in their marketing game plan. With due respect to the researchers in the wonderful field of marketing, we would like to give two new Ps that might be fitted on its fascinating chess-board. They are as follows :—

(A) Place

We are aware that many researchers have propounded this P. And we would support them, stating vehemently, "This should have been the first P."

Place is a spot, a building or an office from where, the marketer carries out his activities. His production facilities would never fetch him on order but his marketing office would. Therefore, Place would refer to a site for marketing activities and not a site for production.

We have always ignored place as the basic P of marketing. Quite often, people state that they can sell their products and services by sitting at their homes. We agree with them. The modern high-technology era has certainly led to the most modern concept of Small Office Home Office (SOHO). But that would lead to a terrible decay of the established markets. For example, if all hardware dealers start selling from their homes, then those markets, which are known for their hardware products, would be erased. The customer would be in trouble and the hardware seller, operating from his residence, would not earn enough as the dissatisfied customers of one shop would not go to his home; rather they would buy from another shop that is in close vicinity of the previous shop.

We must understand the psyche of the customer when he enters the market place. He thinks that he would be able to "strike a deal" with some shopkeeper or the other. If the place is disintegrated (for example, all the hardware sellers operate from their homes), he would not be able to go from door to door; he could go from shop to shop and take a quick decision after looking at the product ranges displayed by all the shopkeepers in a 'Place.' That is why, the concept of hardware market, shoes market, garments market, electronic markets and similar other niches has become quite popular in the modern metropolises.

(B) Persuasion

Some researchers could call it negotiation but that is a later stage of this P. It involves convincing the customer through :

    (a) across-the-table negotiations;

    (b) product demonstrations; and

    (c) finalisation of the deals by 'clinching' the strong points of the same.

Our worthy readers would state that these gimmicks are a part of the sales process. But we plan to define this P as a part of the marketing effort and not as a part of the sales strategy. The end-result (*ie*, sales) should have a plan in the marketing blueprint itself. Most of the marketing managers state that if already is a part whereas we must vehemently deny it.

Further, persuation is not a one-day affair as most of us consider it to be; it is a long and painful process, especially, for the new marketing managers. But once this P starts 'acting,' sky is the limit.

In sum, the total number of Ps could be considered to be seven if the marketing activity has to be successful. These Ps could be planned according to the requirements of the target markets.

The sum total of these Ps is the new concept that could be termed as Giga Marketing. We sincerely feel that no new P is likely to be added to this chess-board in near future with which, the fates of most of the corporate heavyweights of the new millennium would be decided.

112. SPECIALISTS *VERSUS* GENERALISTS

Management is effective when it is done through organisations—Managers manage the staff through organisational structures and operations—Three types of organisation—line, staff and line and staff—Staff members are experts and hence, they are generalists—Line members are not experts—Top management executives are generalists—When we go towards the higher levels of management, we become generalists—Specialists and generalists are required in all the firms—Specialists have expert knowledge levels—Generalists are human oriented and they manage the firms—The modern world needs both of them.

Management is synonymous with for efficiency, productivity and result-oriented behaviour. All the firms and organisations of the new millennium, whether belonging to the business strata or to the non-business strata, recognise the fact that efficient management is the key to organisational growth. We have to perpetuate the life of human race on this planet and for achieving this noble objective, we need efficient and effective managerial techniques that are needed to help us achieve this coveted goal.

All the techniques of management are applicable to organisations. There is no management without the existence of an organisation. The examples of organisations include family, army, business firms, the Red Cross, the voluntary health care associations, various NGOs, nations and social service firms. These organisations may or may not operate for the sake of generating tangible and monetary profits; the goals of these organisations could vary.

All the organisations have some structures. Without a clear and well-defined structure, no organisation would be able to function. We have three most commonly used structures of the modern-day organisations that have been described briefly as follows :—

(A) **The line structure**—In this structure, the hierarchy of the organisation has been clearly defined in the form of various operational levels. The top level is occupied by the General Managers. The next level is that of managers (the middle management stratum). Then, follows the lower level of management, which comprises supervisors and coordinators. The last level is that of the operative staff or workers. In all the key areas of operation in an organisation, these levels are clearly delineated. The orders and instructions flow from top to bottom whereas reports about the results (of various departments) and suggestions (if any) flow from bottom to top. Such types of structures are found in all the organisations, though their depth and width, operational procedures could vary.

(B) **The staff structure**—In this structure, the top brass, *i e,* the directors and General Managers, are guided by a group of experts, who are known as staff personnel. These members assist the top management by virtue of their expertise in one field or another. They advise the management but do not direct the operatives of an the organisation or for that matter, those managers who are supposed to get work done from the operatives. In a staff organisation, the presence of operative staff is not necessary. But if we discuss this issue in the context of a manufacturing organisation, the recruitment of operative staff is mandatory. So, we conclude that the operative staff and the experts work in the same organisation, both reporting to the respective senior levels, under whom (or with whom) they work. A pure staff organisation is rare, though exceptions might be found in software development firms or service organisations. In that event, the tasks to be carried out by the operatives and supervisors are allocated to vendors who report to the managers of the firm. It must be noted that in a staff organisation, the suggestions and recommendations of the experts (staff personnel) may or may not be accepted.

(C) **Line and Staff Organisation**—As is clear from the aforementioned discussion, a purely staff organisation may not be feasible, though some exceptions might be there. Hence, the ideal condition, in the organisational parlance, would have the normal levels of management (4 or 5) and some experts to guide the top management. This would lead us to line and staff organisational structure and is the most common one to be found in the organisations of the century. The staff personnel are experts whereas the hierarchies of management carry out various operations as per the instructions of the levels that are immediately above their levels. The staff personnel (experts) advise and suggest, the top managers (and even middle level managers) adopt these suggestions according to the needs of the organisational goals. Then, they instruct the personnel to carry out the tasks. The tasks are performed in an efficient manner and the organisation achieves its goals.

The aforementioned discussion would lead us to the concept of the generalists and the specialists. The staff members are the specialists. Even a machine operator is also a specialist. The managers are generalists. They have information of every type flowing into their offices. They have to be more humane, kind and empathetic in their approaches. They have the characteristics of "Mr Know-all" who has to get the things done by managing people. They have no time for the technical details. The specialists, on the other hand, have expertise in one field or another. They can perform only some specialised tasks and are poor managers of people or their emotions. In a line organisation, most of the people are specialists except those at the top level. In a line and staff organisation, there are specialists as well as generalists and staff personnel (experts) are one of them. In a staff organisation the top brass is naturally composed of a generalists but the staff personnel (experts) belong to the specialist category.

Quite often, a question has been raised by management thinkers—Should one become a specialist or a generalist ? The answer is simple—time would tell the difference. When the individuals join the organisations, they are accepted as trainees. They are trained to perform special tasks. They develop their competencies in one or two areas of organisational endeavour. However, when they become well-versed with their areas of operation, they long for job-enrichment. So, they try to learn about other tasks that are somewhat related to their fields or specialisations. They are also ambitious and would like to become supervisors, senior accountants or assistant marketing managers. So, they try to learn more about their departments and their functions. This brings us to the concept of "human side of enterprise" in organisational operations.

The lust for money, power and growth in terms of status forces the individual to learn more. Later, they acquire knowledge levels and skills that may not be related to their specialised skills that were acquired by them nearly eight years ago. They, therefore, become generalists and are more involved in man management than in machine management or technology management.

So, the golden rule is—if an individual wants to rise to the top, let him be more people-oriented; in that event, he is likely to forget his basic expertise or specialisation. If, on the other hand, if he wants to be an expert in one field, then tell him to be an expert in a limited area of his operations; he could hone his skills in that area only and would not become a manager or a man from the top brass.

A specialists are in great demand as computer software programmes, machinists, truck drivers, lathe operators, hardware engineers, masons and other operative experts. They have to be trained in special engineering (or technical) schools. They would need experience of the industry, technology or the process in which, they might be interested.

Generalists are not in great demand because room at the top is not spacious. However, if the specialists want to become generalists, they could leave their organisations and become entrepreneurs. This would give them enough leeway to act as generalists. However, now a days, growth in specialised terms is sought by all the individuals and the specialists are being paid good salaries, perks and packages. We should vote in favour of the specialists if we examine the trends of industry and business around the world. Hail the specialist ! His era has arrived !   ●

113. MANAGEMENT OF MORALS

Moral values not adhered to by the private entrepreneur, the politician and the individual—There is moral decay and managers are also responsible for it—Mad rush for materialistic assets and money—Free market world has defined some rules—These rules against the moral values defined by our forefathers—This mad rush for materialism has forced our managers to be corrupt, cruel and calculative—No immediate solutions in sight—It can be alleged that the management concepts of today lead us to immoral values—This decay prevalent everywhere—Some solutions suggested—These solutions are not likely to be implemented in the near future.

Most of the human beings on the earth are always curious to learn about their fates after their demise. However, they refuse to learn about their lives, eco-systems, living standards and societal interests with which, they are always associated even if they try to eschew them. For example, an office-goer would always visit a temple on a Sunday along with his family and would pray to God for a better life and treatment after his present birth. The same executive would, however, try to earn the maximum, spend the minimum and squeeze the person (or firm) across the table out of life. He would save income tax, sell his products or services (or those of his firm) at the maximum profit or force a vendor to reduce the margins to a shameful nadir. And he would proudly state, "I am doing this for the sake of my family, firm, society or my profession ! What is wrong in this ?"

Dear readers, this text is related to management, its deeper understanding and its practice for the benefit of the individual, the organisation, the society and the human kind. One would then, wonder why this issue has been raised here ? There are reasons for this.

Management, as a subject, was devoted to the maximisation of profits of a business firm or the achievement of the goals of an organisation. The objectives have to be achieved, state the management experts and thinkers. The main emphasis is on the objectives and not on the *modus operandi*. Then, what about the morals ? Has anybody cared to ponder over the moral issues that make a mere mockery of the entire management process ?

Let us take another example. A businessman buys goods on a credit of 60 days but never pays to the vendor in time. He pays only after the stipulated date, sometimes after 120 days or even later. He promised to pay on the sixtieth day after receiving the goods at his site. Where is the element of moral in his purchase ?

Let us take another example. Our avid readers would search for jobs. It is up to the prospective employer to employ anyone of them, irrespective of the fact that most of them are competent to do the specific job for which, they would apply. But the employer would select only that candidate who he likes and not the one who is most competent for the job. Where are the morals in HRD ? The number of jobless candidates is rising everyday, thanks to the callous attitude of the firms and organisations. And everyone does not have a certificate of OBC or SC so that he could get a cushy job in a government office. What about those candidates who are neither from backward classes nor rich enough to start small business enterprises ?

Similar examples could be quoted from other fields of management—marketing, sales, corporate finance, exports and imports, firing policies, research and development, materials management, finance *etc*. An individual of the new millennium painfully realises that he is in a free-market world, which is quite harsh on him. There are a few rules to be followed in this new system and these are as follows :—

(A) **Survival of the fittest**—Only the best and the most competent managers and executives are likely to survive. This fact is applicable to all other strata of human operations. That would mean that a person, who is not a good manager, would be sidelined to die a slow but painful death. He would not be offered job, jobwork, career or even some basic survival package. He would suffer and so would his family. A management graduate from the USA would be eligible for the most lucrative assignment in India or abroad but those, who studied from the C-grade management schools, would have to put their hands on their cheeks and wait for some angel to take them out of the distress they are in.

(B) **The corporate sector is the fittest**—Naturally, a man, who pays the piper, would call the tune. The private businessman would become a king in the new millennium. His kingdom would comprise his clients, vendors, managers, government officials who are on the payrolls of his firm, NGOs, the police department, sales tax officials, petty clerks in the municipal authorities and meek employees. He would own and expand a little kingdom with an amazing finesse and his family would prosper at the cost of the survival of his 'courtiers.' As he would be rich and powerfully connected, he would have no competition except the resistance offered to him by his competitors in his market niches or product lines.

(C) **Coercive power is the fittest**—Apart from the monetary power, which is growing everyday in the corporate circles, the power of coercion is assuming its importance in the political strata of the globe. A politician would be able to grab the coveted seats in state assembles and Parliaments, thanks to the hooligans controlled by him overtly or covertly. And he has not become a minister to serve the poor masses. He has an axe to grind. He would convert this political leverage to financial Advantage. He would help himself (and his nearest kith and kin) get quotas of steel, coal, petroleum products as well as other lucrative assignments or assets in India or abroad. Hence, politics is a glorified method of carrying out or perpetuating business; the politician would get fortune as well as notoriety and more notorious he is, the better.

(D) **The selfish individual is the fittest**—A manager or an executive is also a human being. He too has a family. He too wants a bungalow, a car, the comforts of life and the luxuries that elude him during his pursuit for a career or livelihood. Therefore, he tries to emulate the economic stratum immediately above his own. He earns money through all possible means, fair or foul. He kills his conscience and moral values for the sake of a better future for himself and his family. He becomes crafty, manipulative and money-minded to the core. The materialistic norms of the "new world" force him to be corrupt and mean. And he cannot check this moral decay as he is a part of the mad materialistic world now, which he cannot shun. The stars of morality beckon him but he would rather be a part of the wicked system than starve.

We have mentioned earlier in this text that management would be the new religion of the mankind in the new millennium. It would be adored and practised by people of all the societies and nations. Therefore, if we take some vital and spine-chilling conclusions from the aforementioned discussion, do we conclude that the new world would be sans any morality ? And should we address a very specific issue in blunt terms—does management forbid us from practising and imbibing moral values ?

As on date, the answers to both these questions are in the affirmative. Without capital and assets, there is no management. Without resources, there cannot be any type of planning or execution of those plans that try to achieve well-defined goals of the society, the individual or the firm. Management is loosing sanity as it is guided by materialistic considerations. Moral values do not count in the industrial and commercial landscapes of the world. All the branches of human life are guided by the spirit of wooden parade to those goals, which are nothing but pinnacles of surrealism. It is unlikely that this craving for the materialistic goals would end in the next few centuries.

Solutions for this problem do exist but the issue is of implementation and not of manufacturing the set of keys that would unlock the vaults of political treason, corporate games, corruption and money-making tendencies. Let us give some solutions in brief, which are as follows :—

(A) The tussle for economic independence and growth has emanated from the war between the haves and have-nots. If the have-nots are also allocated some resources (as well as some opportunities to grow and excel), then the rich-poor divide would be eliminated. The have-nots would also become haves. In other words, all the citizens of the earth would have enough of resources for sustenance and growth. We do not intend to state that all the people should be given cars, cellular phones and bungalows. We would like them to be given enough of resources so that they could sustain their families. They should also be given sufficient number of commercial opportunities so that they could lead prosperous lives.

(B) Political cleansing is a long and a painful process. It would also be cumbersome and perhaps, prone to violent reprisals. But the irony is that the process of political cleansing has not even started in any part of the globe. The political parties—from the level of the ordinary party worker to the levels of the political stalwarts and the CEOs of the nations—have to refurbish their images and remove the 'stains' from their political robes. As on date, the system perpetuates their cause and hence, they are prospering in the shadow of immorality. But if the trends reverse, they would have to face violent upheavals in all the corners of the globe. In that event, revolutionary trends would wipe the corrupt factions and ideologies that are sans moral values.

(C) The corporate sector would have to adopt a liberal attitude towards the management of the enterprises. Exploitation of juniors, the fairer sex, vendors, customers and society at large has reached a pinnacle. The businessman can go to any negative limit (during the course of operation of his business) for the sake of his loaves and fishes. The human side of the enterprise is always given a cold shoulder as the emphasis is on earning maximum amount of money. Therefore, this tendency would have to be rationalised by altering the objectives of the firm and making them more society-oriented and humane. The concern for environment, ecology, human resources and the fauna and flora of the earth would have to be given at least some priority. As the corporate sector has become an entity to reckon with, it would have to assume and accept serious responsibilities.

(D) The individual makes the social milieu, the corporate world and the social texture for the human race. The ultimate responsibility for checking this moral decay. This suggestion seems to be a heterodox thought, keeping in mind the trends of commercialism, perfection and avarice that are gaining momentum around the world. But there is no harm in having a Utopian thought for a while that man would try to cleanse his soul first. This is a herculean task as nobody would like to hook himself on the cross of morality as Lord Jesus Christ did. And we should not forget that Lord Jesus gave the sacrifice for others. Here, the individual has to go through the fire of penance for his own sake. This ordeal is much less painful than was faced by Lord Jesus. Why should we not try it ?

(E) Poor management of resources leads to frustration. Further, allocation of resources to those who do not know how to nurture them and develop them further, causes frustration and agony in the minds of those who know how to. Every individual finds himself to be a square peg in round hole. He can and would like to do something but he is forced to do something else. This rift between his actions and thoughts takes its toll in terms of poor health, moral decay, wastage of time and drainage of precious resources. Every individual has to carry out an introspection exercise. When he has learned why he has come to this world and what his objectives are (or could be), he should strive to achieve those objectives with maximum possible finesse and dedication.

As on date, management and morality are poles apart. But management as well as morality was born out of the brain of man. Both have to learn to be compatible with each other. This marriage has to take place; time is the only factor that prohibits their union. Man is the most intelligent creation of the Almighty and has to survive the wrath of several millennia. Management would ultimately help him manage the morals that he needs in his life. If the Sun, the earth and other celestial objects follow the time-tested principles defined by God, why cannot he tame himself by imposing moral values upon himself ? Nobody tells the Sun to rise but it rises in the morning. Similarly, nobody should tell a man, who wants to be manager par excellence, to follow the norms of a moral world but he himself should create one for himself and learn to live in the that world forever. He has enough time to think about this noble proposition.

114. COMMUNICATION

Communication is the process of transfer of information from one person to another—Communication needs a sender, a receiver and a communication medium—Must for every business organisation—Leaders and managers are outstanding only if they communicate properly—Communication must be free and healthy in all the departments of an organisation—The objectives of communication comprise primary and secondary goals—The communication functions comprise Information, Command, Motivation and Integration Functions—Communication process starts from sender and ends at the sender himself when he receives the feedback from the receiver—Barriers to communication include semantic barriers, barriers arising from the corporate climate and technical barriers—Consistency and coherence required for removal of communication barriers.

Introduction

Communication is one of the most basic functions of management. In fact, a manager is always communicating while he is getting the jobs done. No communication would mean no management. It forms a basis for management by objectives, long range strategic goal setting, strategic planning, organisational development, organisational effectiveness, decision making and other allied managerial activities. Managers must be sure of what is being communicated to the subordinate and must control his activities to get the results.

Defining Communication

We define communication as a process of transfer of information from the sender to the receiver with the exchanged information being understood by both the sender and receiver.

The word 'Communication' has been derived from the word *communis*, has been which means common. It is essentially a bridge of meaning between people. Professor Das Gupta is of the view that to communicate is to inform, tell, show or spread information. It is a technique by which, the management gets the job done.

According to Allen, "Communication is the sum of all things that a person does when he wants to create an understanding in the mind of others. It is a bridge of meaning. It involves a systematic and continuous process of telling, listening and understanding."

According to another connoisseur of management, "Communication is the process of meaningful interaction among human beings. It is a process by which meanings are perceived and understandings are reached among human beings."

According to Luthar, "It is the transmission of commonly meaningful information. It is a personal process that involves the exchange of behaviours."

To Kelly, communication is "a field of knowledge dealing with the systematic application of symbols to acquire common information regarding an object event."

The Communication Function in an Administrative Organisation
In the organisational context, communication function is the means by which the administrative activities are unified. If an organisation to operate as an integrated unit, it is important that the top management should keep the lower level supervisors and employees well informed about the ultimate objectives of the organisation.

By exchanging information freely, the administration takes employees into its confidence, prepares them for changes, avoids misunderstandings and makes them knowledgeable about the problems and policies of the enterprise. We would like to discuss various aspects of communication in the organisational context as follows :—

(1) Communication of information is a basic necessity for management. It is a tool for policy formulation, direction, action monitoring and supervision.

(2) The leaders in the organisational context are managers and executives and they would be able to perform only if they were having the abilities to communicate ideas and information clearly to their juniors.

(3) Effective communication is important in relationships between an employer and his employees.. It may cement an

organisation or disrupt it. It is a mechanism through which the administration produces an output. Although communication is not visible, yet its impact and spirit are visible indirectly when the organisation acquires a reputation on account of good communication abilities.

(4) Communication seeks to unify, coordinate and combine all the participants in the corporate context.

(5) When a manager manages his people, his only tool is the transfer of information and his effectiveness depends upon his ability to communicate. He needs skills for informing the people. He also needs an the ability for finding out what other people are after.

(6) The effectiveness of an organisation depends upon the effectiveness of its communication patterns. An organisation may be viewed as an elaborate system of gathering, evaluating, recombining and disseminating information.

(7) Good communication is the foundation of sound administration. Through a well-defined system of communication, management succeeds in establishing links between different management functions like planning, organising, staffing, directing and controlling.

(8) Effective and speedy communication would ensure that there are no delays, bottlenecks, confusion and misunder-standings in relation to work reports, sales reports, suggestions, grievances, settlement of departmental goals, setting of productivity norms and other vital functions of an organisation.

(9) Good communication in upwards, sideways and downwards directions is essential at all the administrative levels for the interpretation and adoption of policies, knowledge-sharing and morale-building. The process of communication could involve one department, many departments, many divisions of a firm, vendors, customers and the society at large. Within an organisation, communication process could take place between peers or between a peer and a superior and a peer.

(10) Another objective of a business or an organisation is the generation of maximum production at the lowest cost by

maintaining good relationships in the company. An administrator should encourage suggestions and should implement them whenever it is feasible. This means that communication has to be exact, polite and relevant to the subject for optimum performance.

Efficient communication means an efficiently run organisation. Good communication creates a good image in the eyes of markets, vendors, shareholders and the public at large.

Now-a-days, the business is developed on the basis of personal rapport and the market image of the businessman. The products, the technologies and the markets are same everywhere because they could be acquired by anybody. The machines, techniques and procedures for developing them are also the same everywhere. They could be acquired at reasonable costs around the globe. But organisational success belongs to only those few who have good relationships with their markets. For this purpose, effective communication gives us an edge over our competitors. Effective and positive communication builds our image and a good image leads us to prosperity.

The Objectives of Communication in Business

The basic objective of communication in the organisations is to influence action towards goals. It is essentially on two levels.

Level 1 : Internal Operations of the Company

Communication is essential for the internal operations of the organisation because it integrates various activities of an organisation. The goals at this level are as follows :—

Primary Goals

(1) To establish and inform about the goals of an enterprise.
(2) To develop plans for the achievement of those goals.
(3) To organise human and other resources in the most effective and efficient manner.
(4) To lead, direct, motivate and create a climate in which, people would like to work and contribute.
(5) To monitor the performance parameters of the employees at all the levels.
(6) To control the working of the employees after monitoring their performances and then, taking corrective actions.

Secondary Goals
  (1) To discourage the spread of wrong information andgrapevine.
  (2) To develop an attitude necessary for motivation, cooperation and job satisfaction.
  (3) To prepare workers for technological and organisational changes that are likely to be implemented in the organisation and administration.
  (4) To encourage suggestions from subordinates for improvement in work conditions, reduction in costs, development of more profitable markets and management of the business or the organisation in a more efficient manner.
  (5) To improve labour-management relations by keeping both in cordial contact with each other.
  (6) To ensure that status and authority of every employee are accepted.
  (7) To satisfy the needs of the employee for recognition and sense of belonging.
  (8) To serve auxiliary functions such as entertainment and maintenance of social relations.
  (9) To ensure proper functioning of the business enterprise in routine matters.

Level 2 : The External Environment of the Company

The organisation should also be alert to the needs and aspirations of its customers, suppliers, shareholders, employees, press, regulations of the government and the concerns of the community. Keeping these factors in mind, the objectives at this level could be delineated as follows :—

  (1) To advertise its product and services for the knowledge of customers.
  (2) To inform the customers or masses connected to the administrative organisations about changes in the products or product lines.
  (3) To give a clean image of the organisation in the media so that shareholders maintain their faith in the company and new investors are persuaded to invest.

(4) To give a neat and clean image of the company to the government and bureaucracy so that financial and legal obstructions are minimum.

(5) To inform the society about the social work, charity programmes and environmental issues handled by the company so that a environment-friendly image is formed in the minds of the masses.

The principles of communication are the same everywhere. Communication has to be made effective in order to get work out of people. A senior administrator or a manager is experienced and knows how to put across his idea or concept to another person.

Functions of Communication

Thayer has divided the functions of communication into four specific categories :—

(1) **The Information Function**—It provides knowledge of the need of the individuals for guidance in their actions. It also fulfils desires of the workers for awareness for things that affect them.

(2) **The Command Functions**—These functions make the employee aware of his obligations to the formal organisation and provide him with additional guidance about the tactics and procedures for performing his duties efficiently.

(3) **The Motivation Function**—It encourages the individual to perform or exhibit a desired behaviour. Messages communicated are used to convince individuals that their actions can be beneficial in the context of the functioning of the organisation to which, they belong.

(4) **The Integrative Function**—It refers to the fact that the communication of message, and ideas (if properly handled) should help in corelating the activities of the workers so that their efforts compliment each other rather than oppose each other.

THE COMMUNICATION PROCESS

We have to understand how the communication process materialises. This step would build the foundations of effective communication in our minds.

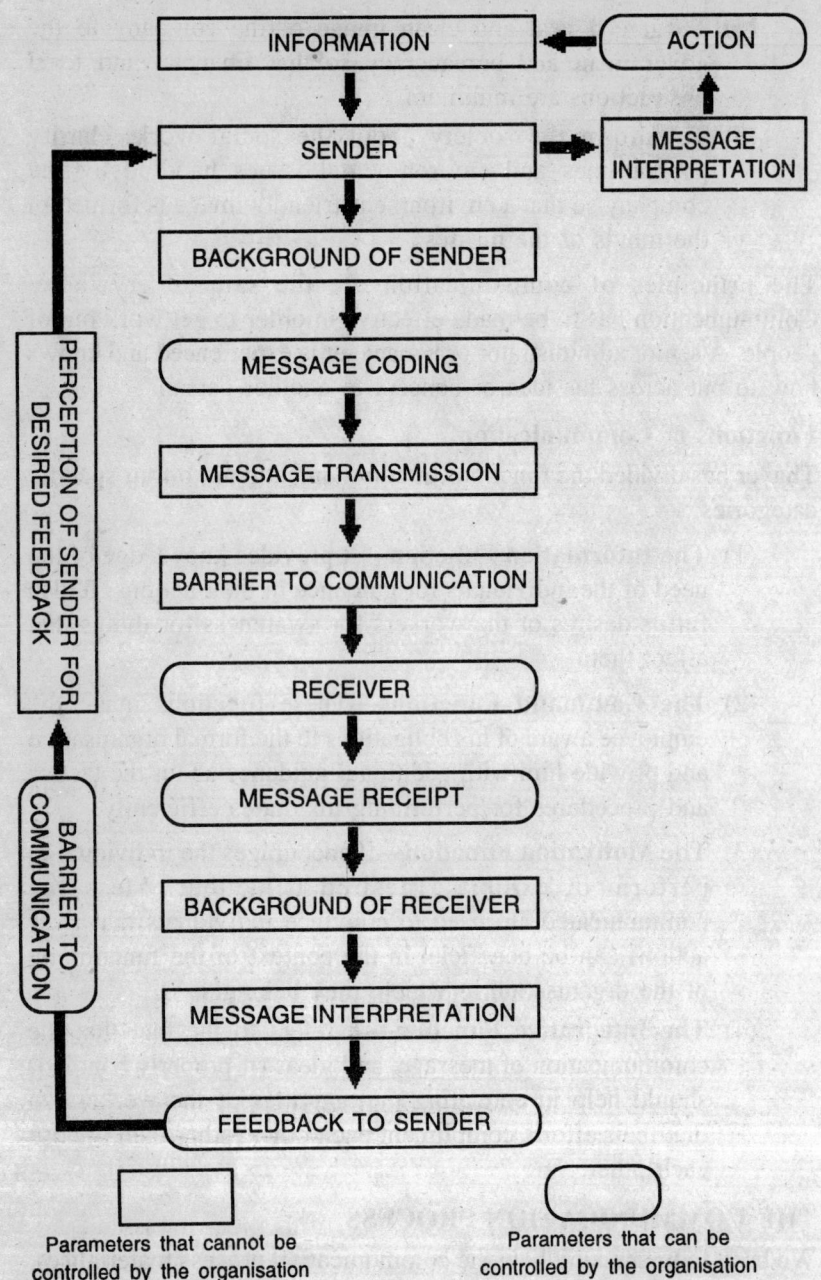

Fig 1 The communication process (latest updation by author over previous flow diagrams in vogue)

The communication process, as described in Fig 1, involves the sender who transmits a message through a selected channel to the receiver. Let us examine closely the process of communication with clear demarcation of parameters that can be influenced by the business and the organisation and those that cannot be influenced by them. The figure shows the straight line boxes, which are the parameters that cannot be controlled whereas the boxes with-rounded off corners are the ones that can be controlled.

Information That is of Utility for an Organisation

Every business or organisation transmits and receives some information. This information could be in the form of a business query, purchase order, IOM, promissory note, quotation, letter of credit, debit note, cheque or draft, legal notice *etc*. The information is useful for the business executive or the manager and is non-personal in nature. The information is in a raw form and is to be sorted out so that it could be put in a useful business form. Language and data are the main parts of the information. The information could be through fax, phone call, E-mail, Internet services or even a gesture by the manager to his junior.

Sender

A sender is a person who sends some information and wants to elicit a response from the receiver of the information. In the organisational context, the sender is a manager or a junior staff member. The information that is dealt with is relevant in the context of the organisation in question. We must remember that the effectiveness of the message depends upon the profile of the sender. A manager is able to put across his point well but a peon may not be able to communicate what he wants to say. Therefore, the level of information is decided by the managerial level, which is handling it. For example, a peon would be required to open up the mail, put the papers in a file and finally, present the file to the secretary of the Managing Director. The secretary would in turn, sort out the mail and would segregate the letters so that only vital letters reach her boss. The routine letters and messages would be sent by her to the junior staff who would be able to handle routine matters efficiently. The Managing Director would handle the most vital letters like orders, payments, important customers, board meetings and plant expansion plans *etc*.

Background of the Sender

Communication begins with the sender who has a thought or an idea. Some idea or information has to be created in his mind. This information transcended from his unconscious brain to the conscious brain. For this purpose, he should have some information, guidelines or motivational material that is of some interest to the receiver.

This brings us to a vital part of the communication process—the background of the sender. We have explained in the second step that the sender handles information that befits his or her level. We would now go a step further. The information that is processed and further sent by him depends upon his age, education, social and economic backgrounds and cultural factors that dominate his living style. He would like to generate and transmit information according to his mental setup, background, tensions and habits.

Information passes through his brain, which has been conditioned by his background. This information gets a colour or tinge of his background when it is finally ready to be taken to the next step of communication.

Message Coding by the Sender

The message or idea is to be put in a tangible form. That is in the format of logical and coded message-oral message, written, letter, fax, E-mail, Internet website, telegram, gestures, absence of gestures or even a frown of the eyes. As the sender prepares to encode the message, he considers the knowledge level of the receiver and his mental makeup, social background, financial capabilities (if it is a business message), the working and living conditions and other vital characteristics related to the receiver.

Message and its Transmission

The message is now ready. Now an appropriate method of communication has to be selected by the sender keeping the receiver in his mind. The message is directly affected by the code or group of symbols used for transfer, ring wrong meaning, the message content and the decisions made by the sender for the selection of transmission media. One may use fax, letter, telephonic conversation or telegram. He may use a language that he thinks would be understood by the receiver. If the language platform is not common, then communication is not feasible.

While selecting the appropriate medium, he has to keep in mind the requirements, background and the resources of the receiver. He can use a single picture, which is equivalent to one thousand words. He can use a blink of his eyes, which in some cases, is the most effective mode of communication.

Noise and Barriers in Communication

(1) The noise factor in communication—Unfortunately, communication is affected by 'noise,' which is an external element that hinders communication. A noisy or confined environment may hinder the transmission of a clear thought. Encoding could be faulty. Transmission may be interrupted by disturbance in the telephone lines. Inaccurate reception may be caused by the lack of attention. Decoding may be faulty or the receiver might be prejudiced against the sender. He may be having a headache.

We would define two types of noise :—

(A) **Physical noise**—It could be due to bad handwriting or due to a faulty telecommunication line.

(B) **Mental noise**—It could be due to a state of mental instability of the sender or the receiver due to any social, economic, personal or psychological reason.

(2) Barriers to communication—When communication is stopped or delayed, it becomes ineffective. The factors that delay or temper communication are known as barriers. There are five main types of barriers. Table I delineates them in a lucid manner.

(A) **Personal barriers**—Human beings differ from each other because of different geographical, economic, social, educational or occupational backgrounds. These are inherited by them due to their birth, family backgrounds, upbringings or social events that are unique to them. They include:

(*a*) personal emotions;
(*b*) biases;
(*c*) perceptual variations;
(*d*) competencies;
(*e*) fears;
(*f*) mental faculties;
(*g*) five senses of human beings; and
(*h*) psychological barriers.

TABLE I : Barriers to Communication

Type of Barrier	Example
(A) **Personal** — Personal emotions — Biases — Perceptual variations — Competencies — Mental faculties — Five senses of human being — Psychological barriers	— Anger — Racial Discrimination — Artistic background — Technical skill — Unstable mind — Impaired hearing — Hydrophobia
(B) **Semantic** — Word interpretations — Gestures — Language translations — Signs and symbols	— Hogg is a name but it means Pig. — Frown could mean disapproval or refusal — Language grammars are different — Signs or symbols differ in various cultures
(C) **Corporate Climate** (i) — Fears of being mis-interpreted — Distortion by grapevine — Exposing oneself to criticism — Being fired (ii) Poor supervision (iii) Lack of confidence	— Boss says, "Fire him." He meant only to pull up his subordinate. — Grapevine or dismissal of employee — Unnecessary arguments — Poor sales figures — Boss sleeps in the government office — An interest in repetitive tasks
(D) **Organisational Structure** — Lack of chain of command — Bureaucratic delays — Political manipulations — Class conflicts	— Boss by passes the subordinate — Delays in movement of files — Pressures from the minister — Bias against scheduled castes
(E) **Technical** — Geographical Limitations — Mechanical failures — Technological malfunctions — Improper timings — Language problems	— Too distant offices/factories — Mail van out of order — Bad telephone lines — Courier delivers at 1 PM in the night — Fax received in German language and we do not know German

(B) **Semantic barriers**—Semantics is the science of meanings. A word can carry as many as five hundred meanings, depending upon the situation. Semantic barriers arise due to the differences in meanings, which the people attach to the different words. The meanings of the words are not in the words; they are with us. A poor choice of symbols or their confused meanings could distort communication. They can be subdivided into:
- (a) word interpretations;
- (b) gestures (handshakes and frowns);
- (c) language translations;
- (d) signs and symbols; and
- (e) cue meanings.

(C) **Barriers Arising in the Corporate Climates**—These are the barriers which are created due to the problems in the culture of the organisation or due to the lack of proper directions from the owners or managers. They are as follows :—

(C1) *Fears*
- (C1.1) Fear of being misinterpreted
- (C1.2) Fear of distortion by grapevine
- (C1.3) Fear of exposing oneself to criticism
- (C1.4) Fear of reprisal

(C2) **Poor supervision**—The supervisor may block communication as he might think that he is being ignored or as if there is a conspiracy against him.

(C3) **Insincerity and lack of confidence**—Insincerity means that communication is superficial while lack of confidence means that the message or the communicator of the message are not trustworthing.

(C4) **Organisational structure barriers**—When the organisational structure is not clear, the responsibility and authority are not assigned and channels are unclear, then the communication would be ineffective and even harmful.

(D) **Technical Barriers**—These are the barriers arising due to the following factors :—
- (D1) Space or geographical distance.
- (D2) Mechanical failures and disturbances.
- (D3) Physical obstructions (too much emphasis on organisational structure.

(D4) Technological malfunctions (bad telephone lines, poor printouts from computer, bad typing *etc*)

(D5) Improper timings of communication.

The Receiver

The receiver is a person, obviously from an organisation, who is vital to the communication process. All the communication gimmicks are designed for him. He could be a customer also who is to be shown an advertisement on the television. He could be the Managing Director of a large multinational who is to be contacted for refurbishing his air conditioning plant.

Reception of the Message

The message has been transmitted. The receiver has to be prepared for the message so that it could be decoded into the relevant message. The receiver is the focal point of communication. The message has been framed keeping him in mind. The receiver is supposed to receive the message in the right context and at the right time.

Background of the Receiver

Just like the sender has a background, the receiver also has a background. It is a fact that no two persons in this world are alike. Here lies the crux of the issue. The receiver also has some thoughts, perceptions and mentality. These have been developed over the years due to influences of his education, age, social and family backgrounds, living standards, beliefs *etc*. He would try to grasp the message of the sender. If the sender is somehow able to send the message in tune with his mental ability, thinking and personality, then three-fourth of the job is done. This magic formula is called empathy. Most of the communications fail due to lack of this magic formula.

Interpretation of the Message by the Receiver

The burden of interpretation lies on the receiver. He takes the message and tries to discover its meaning by analysing the message and by looking into the message deeply. He also visualises the basic idea behind the message, keeping in mind the role of the sender as well as his knowledge, experience and authority. He translates the symbols and ideas into a form that could be understood by him. Accurate communication can take place only when the sender and the receiver attach the same meaning to the symbols that form the message.

Understanding is in the minds of the sender and the receiver. If the information is contrary to the socio-cultural background and value system of the receiver, the message would not be understood properly. The receiver should be careful in listening, reading and reasoning and the sender should be clear about the message, the personality and the current socio-cultural status of the receiver.

Feedback on the Message

The receiver now acts or reacts to the message. This reaction in itself is a communication. The communication may be ignored or the task may be performed or the message may be filed for future reference or action. The process of sending the feedback is similar to that described in the aforementioned steps.

A feedback determines whether understanding has been achieved. If a communication source decides the message that he encodes and if the message related to that is put back into his system, we have a feedback. Feedback is the measure of success of communication. Even no feedback is also a feedback. Silence could also be a form of a nod or protest. A mere blush on the cheeks, rewarding responses, smiles, nods, eye contact *etc* are called positive feedback messages whereas punishing responses like yawns, indifference, frowns *etc* are regarded as negative feedback messages. If feedback has been successful, the communication is successful else it is termed incomplete.

Barriers to Communication

The barriers and noise are the variables that alter communication and could deform the real message. These barriers could be present even when the receiver wanted to communicate his feedback or response to the sender. The barriers and noise mentioned earlier are applicable here also. The only difference is that the barriers or noise be different when the feedback is sent.

Perception of the Sender for Designed Feedback

The sender wanted an order for 1C,000 blankets but he got the order only for 5,000 blankets. The sender wanted the receiver to send him the status of the stock of raw material through a fax. But the sender sent the stock of finished goods instead. The sender wanted something to be done but something else was done and the purpose of communication was lost. The communication could not elicit the desired response from the receiver. This could lead to frustration in the mind of the sender.

Message Interpretation

The message is interpreted by the sender after he receives it from the receiver (which, in fact, is a feedback to his message. The sender has to compare the desired response with the actual response and then, he has to devise a suitable course of action so that the desired response is obtained from the receiver. If a response has been obtained, he can relax else he has to struggle. This struggle would force him to communicate again.

Action by the Sender

The action to be taken by the sender depends upon the response of the sender. He would again send the message if the communication is not completely effective. This would involve another or same piece of information. This information can be changed by the sender if he finds that response is not positive or it is not according to his wishes. The sender would do well if he empathises with the receiver and tunes his message with the requirements of the receiver.

How to Remove Communication Barriers ?

The following tips would enable us to remove communication barriers :—

(1) **Identify and analyse the barriers**—Identity the possible barriers that could hinder effective communication and try to remove them.

(2) **Convince the top brass**—Top management must remember that effective communication means good human relationship and good human relations mean good organisational operations and output.

(3) **Emphasise upon the written statement of policies**—There should be policy guidelines for communication in every business so that ambiguity is minimised.

(4) **Recognise that communication is a two way process**—We should encourage responses, questions and feedbacks so that confusion is removed.

(5) **Consistency and coherence are essential**—The communication should be in line with the goals of the organisation.

(6) **Remove the distance barriers**—Use telephone, telex, Internet fax or courier and cut down distances.

(7) **Communication is a continuous process**—Communication should be a never-ending process of listening, reading and understanding.

(8) **Empathetic speaking and hearing are essential**—The sender should know his audience and must design a message befitting their needs and feelings. Understanding the viewpoint of other person is known as empathy. Empathy wins friends and orders and develops a good image.

(9) **Optimum timing is important in communication**—Messages are most likely to be considered when they arrivce at his desk at the right time.

(10) **Use feedback tools**—It makes the communication process effective and the chances of transfer of wrong information are minimised.

(11) **Repetition of messages is useful**—A second or a third message may bring the desired result.

(12) **Check timings your messages**—The messages should be sent when they are needed.

In sum, communication is the lifeline of any organisation. Healthy and result-oriented communication is the key to success for the smooth functioning of social and administrative organisations of our country.

115. LEADERSHIP

Leadership is a motivating spirit for result oriented behaviour—No class, caste or gender bars—MK Gandhi, Churchill, Washington, Indira Gandhi, Martin Luther King, Nelson Mandela were great leaders—Leaders are made and not born—Leadership abilities can be developed—Leader is an expert, honest, good communicator, impartial and hardworking individual—Motivates his team-mates for results—Five types of power—coercive, financial, expert, reference, affirmative—A good leader has an expert power—A combination of the types could of power be used for becoming an effective leader—Six types of leadership—Political, corporate, spiritual, military, professional and social—India has produced the finest leaders—Management schools and administrative staff training institutes can help us develop leadership abilities.

Leadership can be defined as the ability of a person to motivate his team members for carrying out specific tasks so that he and his team members could achieve the coveted objectives. Leadership is a healthy and positive trait of human personality. Leadership transcends the boundaries of nations, castes, classes, gender or economic status. Leaders are made and not born. Some leadership abilities are, no doubt, present in all the human beings. However, these abilities are developed and honed by a set of circumstances and the toil of the individual.

The world is full of examples of great leaders. From the time of Lord Jesus Christ to the leaders of today, the list is worth taking the lessons. Mahatma Gandhi led the Indian masses during freedom struggle. George Washington won the battle of independence for the American nation in 1776. Abraham Lincoln is regarded as one of the most powerful leaders and orators of the world. Garibaldi was the most prominent leader of the Italian nation. Further, the USSR witnessed a glorious era during the leadership of VI Lenin who stood for the rights and agonies of the working class. The Bolshevik revolution in 1917 was initiated by him and it gave birth to the communist ideology throughout the globe, which is still alive in many parts of the world.

More examples could be cited of Sardar Patel, Dada Bhoi Nauroji, Indira Gandhi, Jaiprakash Narain, Martin Luther King, John F Kennedy, Nelson Mandela, Alexander The Great, Napoleon, Bonaparte *etc*. These were leaders with great a sense of belonging to their followers and missions. A leader is respected only if he is committed to his ideals. He is loved for his commitments and adored for his supreme sacrifices.

According to the psychologists and management connoisseurs, the leadership capabilities could be developed. They remain latent even in the case of ordinary people who do not display such abilities. Some basic ingredients of leadership must be inherently present in the leader-to-be. A leader has the following chief characteristics :—

(1) He is an expert in a field. This field could be management, engineering, business, commerce, industry, politics, arts *etc*. He is a specialises set of knowledge and commands respects

from his subordinates and colleagues on account of this knowledge base.

(2) He is polite and empathetic. He understands the needs of his followers and tries to solve their problems.

(3) He is democratic, naive, honest and simple.

(4) He has no qualms about the outcome of the happenings of the future. He leads his team through the present, though he also keeps a watchful eye on the future.

(5) A true leader is selfless. He devotes more time and resources to his followers and downtrodden masses than on himself. He is a role model for his followers.

(6) A good leader is meticulous and result oriented. The basic cause of leadership activity in today's parlance lies in the action for concrete and worthwhile output for group and for the society at large. The struggle of Mahatma Gandhi is one such example.

(7) A good leader communicates his thoughts most lucidly to his subordinates and team-members. He is an excellent orator.

(8) A leader keeps on amassing knowledge from his environment. He uses this knowledge for upgrading the knowledge levels of his subordinates. Therefore, he leads his team towards a glorious future.

As already stated, a leader has an expertise in one field. Therefore, he has a power because of which, he is respected and followed. There are five types of power :—

(A) **Coercive Power**—We could force a person to acquire his wealth, assets and could get work done from him.

(B) **Financial Power**—We could use our financial powers for results from our subordinates.

(C) **Expert Power**—We could command respect and desired behaviour from our subordinates by virtue of our knowledge or expertise.

(D) **Reference Power**—We could utilise our affiliations with people in the highest offices, with financial bigwigs or political stalwarts for getting a result-oriented behaviour.

(E) **Affirmative Power**—This is the power of humbleness. The subordinates respect to leader because of his purity and selflessness. They adore him for his simplicity and gentle attitude. Getting the work done from the followers is not difficult (as was the case of *Satyagraha* protests organised by Gandhi throughout the country during freedom struggle). Love, non-violence and peaceful cooperation are the main building blocks of this type of power.

Expert power is the most important type of power in the present context. We could never get work done from our team-members through coercion or money. On the other hand, we could get the impossible done through our team-members if we were able to gain expertise in one or two areas of our choice. Some combination of power types could be utilised for the best leadership effectiveness in business, society and political situations.

Leadership could be divided into three sub-groups, depending upon the current trends in economy, society and international polity :—

(A) **Political Leadership**— This leadership category mesmerises the masses for peaceful or violent political upheavals. This leadership is selfish, cunning and materialistic. The followers suffer while the leaders prosper in this type of leadership.

(B) **Corporate Leadership**—This leadership draws its power from financial and industrial muscles. The rich business classes rule the masses. They develop the economy but they charge a high price in terms of pollution, rural poverty and tax evasions. The followers prosper to some extent but the corporate leaders prosper to a much larger extent.

(C) **Spiritual Leadership**—The spiritual leaders are able to give solace to the burning hearts of millions of human beings. A spiritual leader has no materialistic goals but the followers get a spiritual relief. It is sad to note that now a days, there are no spiritual leaders left (of the starture of Maharishi Dayanand, Swami Vivekanand, Swami Ramakrishna Paramhans *etc*). Today, most of the spiritual leaders are money-makers who exploit the common man for their base interests.

(D) **Military Leadership**—It is a type of coercive power through which, the followers are forced to abide by the laws made by the mighty few.

(E) **Professional Leadership**—This is based on expert power and is closely linked to the professions and vocations of the dynamic world of the modern era. The professional is an expert in his field (*eg*, an engineer, a doctor, a CA, a MBA, an IAS officer, a lawyer *etc*). He ought to use the expertise for the benefit of mankind. However, he exploits his fellow human beings for money and materialistic assets. The followers are benefited but, at a cost to their families. The leader always prospers despite some initial hardships.

(F) **Social Leadership**—This is selfless leadership style, which emanates from the hearts of the true leaders. Social issues, dowry problem, environmental degradation, political cleansing *etc* are some of the issues raised by the social leaders. These leaders work for the development of the society and not for their selfish interests. These leaders do not prosper but the society at large is benefited through their actions. Examples include environmentalist Baba Amte and American civil rights leader Martin Luther King.

A good leader must be selfless, honest and hardworking person. He must inculcate participative management techniques in his *modus operandi*. He must not direct his team but should motivate his team members for a collective group output.

India has produced some of the finest leaders of the world. However, over the past fifty years, we have not seen leaders of international status. We must develop leadership calibre in our children and youth so that they could become the growth engines of the future. Coercion must be avoided. A strong policy of political, economic, religious and social issues must be adopted by our leaders for the healthy growth of our nation. Our progress in all the fields is painfully slow and this could be truly attributed to the lack of corporate, political and social leaderships. We must educate our masses so that new and selfless leaders could be developed from our rural and urban areas. Our political leadership has not made up proud during recent times. Corporate leaders are also busy minting money and giving a complete disregard to the needs of the poor, the society and the nation. At this juncture, social leaders and spiritual leaders should come to the fore and must develop good leaders for the benefit of the nation as well as that of the society. Management schools, professional teachers and consultants, foreign universities and our own ancient educational practices could be utilised for the development of true and selfless leaders. Only good leaders could build healthy, economies, societies or nations. We must realise this fact for timely development and perfection of our human resources. We must have good leaders for the sake of a better future of the mankind. ●

116. THE U-MATIC TECHNIQUE

Management and administration need negotiations—We have to get work done from subordinates and peers without coercion—MBO concept is valid today but not so effective—U-matic is a skill of getting work done without coercion. All people practise this technique but not aware of It—There must be at least two common points between the abilities of ttwo competing firms or individuals—View the problem from that common point (or points)—Two examples cited—U-matic has great future in the fields of negotiation and liaison.

Management has been recognised by the scholars, business firms and researchers as the new religion. Management of the business enterprise and administration of a vast nation like India are the most vital activities that demand serious attention by the Indian students and executives. India has diverse cultural, political and social backgrounds. She cannot be treated as one single unit but is to be taken as a blend of large number of strikingly different cultures and economies. As an administrator or a manager, the maintenance and growth of this vast sub-continent poses great challenges before the young Indians of today. We are going to discuss how the task of management could be simplified in the context of complex interpersonal relationships during the course of administration of this nation.

The author has experienced many a complex situation involving inter-personal relationships. The manager has to face some typical work situations in which, he has to mould the activities or the behaviour of the individual in favour of the procedures or the ultimate objectives of the organisation. He has to do this in order to achieve the goals of the organisation. The manager could use either of these techniques in order to effect a change in their behaviour :—

(A) He could use coercion (threat of firing or of demoting the individual) and therefore, could mould the behaviour of the individual.

(B) He could use the incentive scheme (a new cabin or an increment without turn) and could mould the behaviour of the individual in the favour of the organisation.

(C) He could simply pass the instructions to the individual who would be free to decide what he thinks about the manager or the organisation. The individual himself would have to mould his behaviour and he would also have to deliver the requisite output. However, no reward is offered. Similarly, no threat is given to the employee. He is simply told to mould his behaviour in the favour of the organisational goals. His personal preferences would not matter. If his output is not of the requisite standard, he would be coaxed by the manager (or would be told politely) to execute the task or to mould the behaviour. The carrot and stick policy would eventually lead to the desired behaviour. This would also lead to a strange behaviour on the part of the individual. He could leave the department or even the firm in protest against the decision that was imposed upon him by the manager. He would not feel happy even if he continues. His performance could plummet to an all-time low.

We are aware that the concept of Management By Objections (MBO) does not work through either of the procedures mentioned above. This is an era of participative management. In the MBO concept, the subordinate defines his goals in consultation with the superior. If he is unable to achieve the goals set by himself, he is responsible for achieving them. He ought to achieve the goals set earlier because he had set these goals himself. So, he is fully accountable for his activities to himself and to his superiors in a totally democratic manner.

However, we would draw the attention of the manager to the situations in which, the behaviour has to be modified in favour of the organisational goals but the subordinate must be convinced so that he excutes the task with a happy heart. How to get the output from the subordinate against his wishes but without letting him know that his behaviour has been moulded by his superior ? We have a solution.

A Kumar, after twelve years of research in the field and after interaction with practitioners of management, developed a technique that has been termed as the U-matic Technique. The basic tenet of this technique is that we have to persuade the individual by a logic so that he is fully convinced by the new action strategy that he is going to adopt. He would also be able to change his goals if the U-matic is tested upon him carefully.

Let us take an example. Suppose the sales executive in a company is trying to sell 400 items of a product per month. The firm wants him to sell 600 items per month. The concept of MBO states that the sales executive should set his own targets but after consultation with the superior. When the sales target was discussed, the sales executive wanted to sell only 300 items per month and the sales manager convinced him that could sell 400 and even more. The sales executive was capable but did not want to work harder in the market. He got approval of only 400 items per month as his sales target and was satisfied that he was achieving his targets. How do we raise his targets ?

The solution is simple if the U-matic is applied. It states that there must be at least two common points between the abilities of the individual and the abilities of the firm. After carefully negotiating with the junior on the basis of these two common points, the superior could persuade the subordinate to achieve greater output levels. In the case of the sales executive, we should try to analyse those abilities that are in tune with the abilities of the firm. Let us assume that the firm is capable of advertising in the local newspaper about the product in question. The sales executive is called by the sales manager and is offered a cup of coffee.

He is praised first for his pleasing mannerisms and other abilities. Then, he is praised by the boss for achieving the sales target (which is 400 units of product per month). The beaming sales executive sips his coffee and awaits a good news; what else could he expect—a pay raise or increased incentives ? The sales manager also smiles.

Now, the sales manager tells the sales executive that he is going to advertise in the local newspaper about the product in question. He asks him casually whether he would be able to increase the sales to 450 units per month. The salesman has been fully convinced (during the discussions) that he would be in for a great deal (he could get a pay raise from the first of next month as was hinted by the sales manager while he was sipping coffee). He immediately agrees to sell 600 units per month if advertisement compaign is executed. He is convinced that the compaign would yield the desired result. But then, the boss tells him to start achieving his targets even before the advertising compaign. The sales executive, happy with the idea of an immediate pay raise and additional incentives due to extra sales, gives his heart to his boss and tells him that the compaign could come later. He states that he would start earlier for achieving the sales target of 600 units per month from the very next day.

In this episode, the common points were :

(a) the promotion of the product through advertisements in the local newspaper; and

(b) the pay raise to be given by the firm to the sales executive.

Out of these two common points, the first common point was skilfully eliminated by the sales manager when the sales executive promised the sales of 600 units per month (even without the campaign). The other common point has to be adhered to; the sales manager has to consider the issue of pay raise and this has to be implemented from the date specified by the sales manager. This is an unique example of the U-matic.

The second example has been drawn from the field of administration. Let us assume that a District Collector wants his revenue officer to go to a remote village under his jurisdiction and collect the revenues. The revenue officer is very hardworking and obedient. The time is 4 PM and it has been raining for the past three hours. The village is in a far-flung area and the revenue officer would have to go by bus. He would have to stay overnight in the village as it would be too late to return.

When the District Collector called the revenue officer in the morning, he politely refused to go to that village on the plea that he was going to visit a holy shrine with his family the very next day. What would the District Collecter do ?

Let us apply the U-matic. The District Collector calls revenue officer in his office. It is 4.20 PM and rains continue to pour. The District Collector would then, let him sip his tea and snacks. He would also ask whether his family members are fine.

Now, comes the crucial issue. The boss has to locate at least two common points. With the help of these two points, he would be able to convince the revenue officer for executing the coveted task. For example, one common point between the abilities of the organisation (the revenue department) and the individual (the revenue officer) is the availability of a vehicle. The revenue officer, who would have gone on a bus or a cart to the remote village, would be allocated a jeep by the District Collector. The revenue officer is pleased but not convinced. He does not want to go to the remote village as it is in a far flung area. Moreover, incessant rains have made the roads very miserable. How could he go?

The District Collector knows about thoughts in his mind. He states that if the revenue officer could take the jeep, he would be able to reach earlier. If he reaches earlier, then he could complete his tasks earlier. So, he could come back on the same day. The very next day, he could have leave for one day as he was supposed to go to a religious shrine with his family. The boss has paved the way for his tour and now, the revenue officer is happy. Ultimately, he decides to go to the remote village. The sooner he goes, the earlier he would be back. And so the next day, he would be able to go to the holy shrine. He had been planning for this tour but was not able to find time. The boss has himself offered him a leave. What could be more soothing than this offer? He immediately rushes to the remote village in the jeep and the rain is on its full swing. It does not matter, duty is duty!

The U-matic is practised by all of us even in our daily lives. But we are not able to identify one or two common points so that the goals of the other person are skilfully mingled with our goals. A pleasant, positive and logical approach would make this technique really effective in business, national administration and societal context. It must be noted that we can get the work done through a "carrot and stick policy." But this policy does not elicit an output in the long run. Human relations demand pleasing mannerisms, logic delivered in the packaging of empathy and above all, careful handling of the situation. The U-matic technique has been propounded by A Kumar after careful research and interactions. It would be eventually developed as the leading negotiation tool in the times to come.

It must be noted that the U-matic is one step ahead of the MBO technique. In the latter, the goals are set by a mutual agreement between the superior and the subordinate. The subordinate could downsize his targets by giving an excuse. But in the U-matic, the subordinate is logically convinced to embrace the coveted goal.

Further, we can use the U-matic for changing the qualitative goals and conviction of any person in our office, home or neighbourhood. If at least two common points can be extracted from the abilities of the negotiator and those of the other party, then the other party could be persuaded to view the situation from these two common points. It is the duty of the negotiator to bring the other party from the common point towards his own goal or conviction. The concept of common points is vital for the success of the U-matic. Once one or two common points have been identified, the other party could be logically persuaded to follow the goals or behaviours desired by the negotiator.

The U-matic was propounded in 1997. It is likely to be refined by Mr Kumar in the times to come. ●

POPULAR QUOTES

117. PEACE HATH HER VICTORIES NO LESS RENOWNED THAN WAR

This world has seen many wars—Destruction of life and property—War is for land, resources and also due to ego—War also indicates a step towards peace—Then why fight?—Have across-the-table negotiation and settlement—Ashoka gave up war—Cold war ended due to negotiations—Avoid conflicts and sort out matters peacefully—India and Pakistan, fought a bitter war in Kargil, Batalik, Drass and Mushkoh Valley—This war not complete—Wars in Kosovo, Chechnya, Kargil, Israel and Iraq—All the nations should sort out disputes amicably.

This earth has seen many wars and bloodshed since the time the mankind was born. The loss of human lives, property and precious resources can never be compensated by the technological advancements of the posterity. Add to this, the agony of the families of the deceased and the terrible state of the defeated nations in the aftermath of war. The picture that appears in the mind is depressing and spine-chilling.

We know that war is bad for the mankind and could prove fatal for him. Yet, the nations fight each other. The US-Vietnam war, the Indo-China conflict, the Kargil War, the two World Wars and the Chechnya conflict point out to a fact that war is always fought either for land and resources or for the sake of ego satisfaction.

Ironically, even the aim of war is peace. In fact, the nations on the brink a of war always search for peace and harmony. So, why fight and kill people or destroy valuable property?. Why not sit across the table and decide the issues in a peaceful manner?

War wastes the national resources, kills people (whose kith and kin cry throughtout their lives), puts a brake on industrial development and above all, promotes cruelty and violence in the minds of the individual. For example, Pakistan has not been able to digest defeats in the wars of five 1947, 1948, 1965, 1971 and 1999 with India.

Hence, she always looks for an excuse for escalating tension along the border of Punjab or Jammu and Kashmir in order to avenage the defeats inflicted upon her during the past.

India and Pakistan fought brief war in Kargil, Drass, Batalik and Mushkoh Valley along the stretch of our Northern border that was 140 km in length. Both the nations lost men, money, ammunition and peace of mind in this war, which proved to be costly for both the nations.

Peace has no substitute. The elite minds of the world support peaceful negotiations and empathy for solving personal, national and international disputes. We must rise above hatred, jealousy, pride and ego so that our planet becomes a better place for living. Prosperity would automatically follow suit.

The USA bombed Yugoslavia as the Yugoslav forces had taken Kosovo by storm and had killed thousands of Kosovans. Iraq-US war in the distant past, did not space innocent children and women. Israel and Palestine have still not settled the disputes related to land and in the event of no settlement of the territory dispute, a war could escalate after a few years from now. Osama, Bin Laden has already declared a war (*Jihad*) on the USA and her allies. The rebels of Chechnya have been supported by the mighty Russian forces.

And there are glaring example of victories in the peace arena also. Emperor Ashoka gave up war and adopted Buddhism. Mahatma Gandhi won the war of Indian Independence with the help policy of non-violence. The cold war between the USSR and the USA ended due to peaceful negotiations at the summit level and due to the fact that the top leaders wanted the mother earth to escape the wrath of nuclear war. There are many such examples that would help us take a decision in the favour of peace and harmony.

In Asia, North Korea and South Korea are fighting a bitter war. The unification of both the nations remains a distant dream. Further, India and Pakistan have fought five wars and the Kashmir issue always dominates their negotiations. However, there are no solutions in sight. The proxy wars (earlier, through the terrorists from Punjab and now, through the terrorists from Kashmir and from abroad) have harmed Kashmiri economy as well as Indian economy. The Pakistani side has always tried to raise the Kashmir issue in the UN. In fact, Pakistan is taking all types of immoral steps under the guidance of her Chinese masters. Pakistani leaders are playing in the hands of Chinese leaders. The nuclear explosions carried out by both India and Pakistan should make them more responsible as nuclear bombs are not toys.

Iraq and the USA also have not settled the issues amicably. The USA and her allies, under the umbrella of the UN Inspection agencies, have put Iraqi economy on the brink of disaster. Millions of Iraqi citizens face starvation and malnutrition due to stringent economic sanctions. This issue should also be settled amicably and at an early date. The latest being that US has taken over Iraq after a bitter attack.

The Sri Lankan populace has been witnessing bloodbath for the last ten years due to the aggressive attitude of the LTTE. Why do the rival parties not meet at a common platform and sort out the differences so that peace could return to that island ? There would be a need for a compromise from both the sides and that is the only method for the peaceful settlement of complex situations like these.

During the month of April, 1998, the complex issue of Irish right for self-rule was settled with the intervention of the British Prime Minister, Mr Tony Blair. This settlement adequately proves that peaceful negotiations can achieve even those objectives that are seemingly very difficult to achieve.

Beside the international issues, there are many regional, social and interpersonal issues faced by all of us in our everyday lives. We must settle these issues by peaceful negotiations and by adopting an empathetic attitude towards the rivals. We must always vote in favour of peace. Physical violence, arguments, heated debates and proxy wars give rise to mental tension, loss of property and money and wastage of time. We loose sight of our objectives due to the conflicts and our energies are wasted. We must avoid physical and mental voilence to the maximum possible extent. If, however, a war is inevitable, then it should be fought keeping peace as the cherished goal. After all, peace hath her victories no less renowned than war.

●

118. SWEET ARE THE USES OF ADVERSITY

Adversity brings the best out of man—He gets polished—More mature and wiser—A rich person cannot face difficult problems—A poor man always on his toes—Sufferings can teach us a lot—During a crisis, the inner mind wakes up — Adversity tries friends and foes and develops healthy and longlasting relationships.

Adversity tests the potential of man and brings out the best of him. He becomes clearer about his objectives, is much more wiser than ever before and is able to meet the challenges of the future with more confidence.

A man brought up in riches and plenty would find himself ill-placed in the times of trouble. The basic aptitude of a poor man is survival oriented. When he learns how to survive, growth follows suit. If he faces difficult times at any stage in his life, his training in the institute of adversity helps him spring back.

Let us consider the Indian example. The struggle for Indian independence started in 1857 and continued till 1947. This ninety year old war was fought by the liberal *Satyagrahis* and the extremist *Krantikaris* against all odds. Our national leaders were arrested and tortured. Millions of young, old and women were killed during these protests. Martyrs like Bhagat Singh, Azad, Ashfaqulla Khan, Ram Prasad Bismil and many others fought this bitter war with one aim in heart—freedom. Similarly, MK Gandhi, JL Nehru, Dada Bhoi Nauroji, Maulana Azad, Bal Gangadhar Tilak and other leaders spent many years in jail. The adverse circumstances proved to be difficult for their families and colleagues. But they did not give up and continued to struggle towards their goal. And at last, we won our freedom.

History is replete with many such examples. The liberation of Bangladesh, German unity, formation of the UNO, the two World Wars and the natural calamities faced by mother earth from time to time proved that adverse circumstances faced by man eventually brought him honours, freedom and prosperity. Nothing could deter man from survival and growth on the earth—wars, famines, earthquakes, floods, riots, divisions and ego-clashes. Man faced them all and emerged triumphant in the end.

Sufferings can teach us a lot. After pains and agony, happiness and prosperity are bound to follow suit. We should never give up our struggle in the right direction. Today, life has become more complicated and competitive. Firing of the young executives, poor pay packages, losses in business, bereavement in the family, problems of handicapped children, agonies of inter-personal relationships *etc* generate a feeling of nothingness and pathos and sometimes, force the individual to give up. But we should never give up as there is only one string, which joins success and failure—consistency.

During the period of problems and shortages, the inner mind of man wakes up and tries to solve the problems. Man must follow the advise of the mind as it can perform at the maximum efficiency during troubled times. He can take suggestions and can even apply them for resolving the conflicts. But he himself is the best judge of the situation and above all, he must be determined to solve the crisis. He must make an action plan during the adverse circumstances. He must solve his problems one by one.

Adversity also tries friends and foes and proves who is really with the individual at the time of need. Everybody laughs with the man who laughs. However, when one cries, nobody cries with him. During the adverse circumstances, one can judge who can share his pains. Therefore, one can share his feelings with his nearest friends and relatives.

Adversity is a great teacher. It leads to a the rational analysis of the problems of the poor, the needy and the underprivileged. It also teaches us that we should support our friends and relatives at the time when they need us. This reciprocity leads to cordial relationships and the person feels a sense of belonging.

Nobody can become a hero without a fight. Without adversity, one cannot excel. Gandhi's assassination, Socrates' demise due to the poison sip, crucification of Holy Christ—all these point to the vital reality of our lives that greatness and success could only come through the painful gateway of adversity.

Adverse circumstances are faced by all the people. The student loses his rank in the class, misses admission by a few marks or even fails in the examination. The young sales executive fails to effect sales and thus faces the threat of being fired from his job. The industry loses its production on account of labour trouble or power shortage. The trader loses business due to closure of the markets or price fluctuations. The girl loses the boy she wanted to marry and the boy is unable to have his date. The housewife toils for day and night but finds no end to her problems. The child, already burdened with school books, is under severe pressures to get good marks in the class tests and examinations. The nations go through economic recession, war and trade sanctions. The corporate houses come under attack an account of income tax problems and social responsibilities of business. These examples describe our era and insinuate that all of us are living under adverse circumstances.

But there is always a silver lining in the dark clouds. All of these individuals are fighting. The fight of man against the adverse circumstances would continue. Even if a man dies, the struggle never ceases. That is because, the posterity takes over with renewed vigour and zeal and tries to attain what its parents or forefathers could not achieve. Every failure leads us to the ultimate success. We learn from our mistakes and ultimately, we reach our coveted goals.

We must realise that adverse circumstances and problems are the tools for honing our abilities. We must not be afraid of problems. We must fight the adverse conditions of life with perseverance, poise and patience. We must plan our moves for solving the problems. If our efforts fail, we must review our plans and must start afresh. We must continue to try till we succeed. There is no harm in getting valuable advice from parents, teachers, spouse, children or friends. Even the boss or the subordinate could extend a helping hand or could give a valuable suggestion. We must never lose our cool in the time of crisis. Carefully planned approach would achieve the desired results. We should attack the problem from the simple end first. Gradually, we should move on to the difficult aspects or the core of the problem. The resources must be carefully planned in the solution of the problem. Timing is also a crucial factor. Solutions devised without a time frame would not yield desired results or would not solve the problem.

We must conclude by stating that adverse circumstances would determine the strengths and weaknesses of man, differentiate the friends from the foes and develop man as a more mature and powerful individual. Sweet are the uses of Adversity !   ●

119. KNOWLEDGE IS POWER

Man surviving on this planet due to vast knowledge base— Advancements made in sciences, engineering streams, medicine, space research etc—Nuclear power can be used for destruction— Knowledge must be used for the development of mankind on the planet—Use knowledge for peace, prosperity and posterity—Use knowledge for eliminating poverty and illiteracy in rural areas of India—Use knowledge for devising solutions to problems faced by man.

The growth and survival of mankind depends upon the growth of the knowledge base he possesses. From the stone age till the modern era, man continued to struggle for knowing the unknown. He explored the seven seas, the water depths, the high skies, the space beyond our galaxy, the human body and most important of all—the human mind. He struggled to get knowledge about this universe and its constituents. Earlier, his tools were primitive. But now, he is busy in his endeavour of getting knowledge through the most sophisticated tools available— telecommunications and satellites, electronic devices, lasers, psychology, *Reiki, Vaastu., Yoga*, Transcedental Meditation, space sciences, Internet, medical technologies *etc.*

Man has made progress in all the fields; science, technology, medicine, law, psychiatry, surgery, computer science, software development, space research, ocean engineering, power generation are some of the areas explored by him.

However, there are some new vistas to be explored and conquered. AIDS, cancer and other deadly diseases take the toll of innocent women, men and children. There is no positive development so far in these fields. Success must be achieved in terms of economical power generation techniques as the conventional energy resources are depleting at a fast rate. There are no energy alternatives available to the mankind. Pollution on the planet has reached dangerous levels. Ozone hole and global warning, coupled with greenhouse effect, are making this world a living hell. The solutions are not in sight.

And there are negative repercussions of knowledge as well. The nuclear power states are bent upon promoting their political and economic interests by using the threat of nuclear superiority over others. Similarly, knowledge acquired in various fields does not get transferred to poor masses or nations. We have to pay a price for acquiring every sophisticated technology. Knowledge is power and those who possess it, exploit the underprivileged.

Mankind should surge forward towards global prosperity by shedding these taboos and misconceptions. Knowledge must be acquired and shared as a collective effort. The progress made in the fields of science, technology, spiritualism, psychology and medicine *etc* must be shared with all the humans. It must be used for the perpetuation of peace, prosperity and growth. The nations must use the vast knowledge base for their development and not for global annihilation or for domination of poor citizens of this planet.

Although new researches are necessary in all the fields, yet the knowledge base developed by man should have a pragmatic orientation. This would mean that all the knowledge base developed by man should seek solutions to the problems faced by mankind. Even the researches done in various fields should be translated into solutions. Then only, the human race would be able to grow in the most difficult circumstances of the next millennium. Our posterity would find that future would pose serious challenges for its survival and growth. Only a strong and solution-oriented knowledge base could help our posterity prosper on the living planet.

As stated earlier, knowledge should not be misused for destroying the mankind. Nuclear power must be used for peaceful purposes and not for development of deadly weapons. Similarly, the vast knowledge base in sciences, engineering, social sciences, computers, medicine and psychological sciences must be used for the benefit of mankind. Some nations use knowledge as a coercive power and try to dictate their terms. This should never happen.

Knowledge needs time and money for its acquisition. It is beyond the reach of the poor and those with limited resources or mental capacities. We should try to spread the knowledge base in all the fields in the masses. India is an important example in this context.. In Indian rural areas, the knowledge levels about family, school education, problems of women, child rearing and other social issues are very poor. Illiteracy and social backwardness combine to put the rural masses at the receiving end. Lack of knowledge leads to poverty and an absence of efficient methods and technologies of productivity and economic prosperity. This vicious cycle continues.

If knowledge is imparted to our rural children, youth, women and farmers, they can emerge as the major facilitators for our economic growth. But this is easier said than done. The State-sponsored programmes on education, efforts of social workers, curricula of of Colleges and Universities,, programmes of NGOs and finally, the efforts of the state governments could bring about a great change in the rural educational scenario. We are an agriculture-based nation. So, our knowledge levels must be very high in agriculture, agricultural engineering, farming, agricultural products exports, rural education, rural sanitation and rural health.

The urban scene must also be critically analysed. The knowledge base is stronger in the cities but technologies change quickly and therefore, warrant frequent revisions. Computer software and hardware technologies are the examples in this context.

In sum, we can state that latest knowledge must be acquired in all the areas. Researches must be translated into practical solutions. The vast knowledge base must be utilised for removal of poverty, and upliftment of the poor masses. And finally, knowledge must never be used for causing harm to the mankind and its environment.

120. SIX FEET OF EARTH MAKE ALL MEN EQUAL

Man is the best creation of God—Created a beautiful and sustainable habitat for himself—Exploits other humans Ego problems—Reasons for clashes enlisted—Sexual exploitation—Wars and ego clashes—This must stop—All men are born equal—Property and humans sacrificed on the altar of false ego—No difference between a Hindu and a Muslim—Religion must be studied and used for the betterment of mankind—To date, hymns and religious scriptures are only read and not practised—Be religious in the true sense of the word—Books can alleviate human sufferings and can show the path of righteousness—Remove the gap between the rich and the poor and many problems would be solved—No solution in sight but strive for the same—Individual must improve himself first, society would come later—Cut down the false ego—Ego necessary but it would be justified only if someone is an expert in a particular field—Try to reverse the process of moral decay of mankind.

Man was born on the earth with many advantages. He has the most versatile and resilient body among all the living organisms. His average age is 75 years. His sensory organs are one of the best among all the living creatures. His ability to recuperate after a disease is miraculous. And to top it all, man has the most advanced brain among all the animals that live on the earth. This creation of the Almighty is a wonder of sorts. Within a period of 10,000 years, man has been able to establish his supremacy over this part of the galaxy that is called The Milky Way. Whereas other animal species are going through the drudgery of life, man has been trying his best to extend the life of his posterity and that of his natural habitat (fauna, flora and atmosphere) beyond the normal time limits allotted to him. Even God is also proud of man. What a creation !

But every man is supposed to die and so would his ego. Man thinks that he is immortal and is proud of his money and materialistic assets. He is also proud of his achievements and capabilities that were acquired painfully by him after toil of centuries. He does not indulge in the human process of self-respect; rather, he takes pride by involving himself in the wily procedures that make him feel proud, arrogant and haughty. He underestimates his brothers, sisters, colleagues, juniors and neighbours. He boasts before those who do not have enough to survive. He always insults those who are powerless, meek and gentle. Little does he know that he was catapulted to the platforms of fame and prosperity by the acts of God ? His brothers and sisters may not be as capable as him but he ought not to be arrogant, apathetic, abusive and insolent towards them.

We must remember that God has the ultimate power to make and unmake. He sees everything and takes care of all. He controls every leaf and the galaxies with unequalled finesse. A proud and disdainful individual is easily singled out by Him for punishment. When the best creature of God tries to go to the lowest ebb, He just moves one string or two and his best creation bites dust. We have many such examples as would prove the fact that rich and high-handed people were made miserable men due to famines, wars, losses in business, family disputes, violence, actions by the State or the society. Nobody can escape the wrath of God and man must realise that he gets the punishment as he himself is responsible for the same. He tortures his friends, relatives and parents. He flaunts his money power or muscle power. He exploits men and women in the offices. He earns money through unfair means. He declares wars on other people, races and nations. He tries to remain supreme and does not accept and tolerate the talent of others. He remains arrogant and presumptuous despite the warnings. And he laughs. But little does he know that God has the last laugh.

We always hear and read-All Men Are Born Equal. But we do not see this in our daily lives. The poor are exploited by the rich and the weak are given a very shabby treatment (or even death) by the powerful few. The clash of egoes has been going on since the time man was born and started living in groups. The group behaviour essentially shows the ego clashes and the battles for supremacy are always fought. It must be noted that ego clashes and battles are also witnessed among all the animal species. But does that mean that we too are animals ? Shame on us !

Psychoanalysts around the world feel that the ego clashes and the battle for supremacy are quite natural. Poor nations are given poor treatment by the rich ones. Powerful mafia dons exploit the common masses. Antisocial elements use the power of the gun to earn money and territories. In fact, the clashes amongst men are always because of the following causes :—

(A) The opposite sex.
(B) Land and property.
(C) Valuables (like jewellry and gold).
(D) Money.
(E) Ego due to professional rivalries.
(F) Difference in ideologies (*eg*, communism *versus* capitalism).
(G) Psychological defects in the individuals.
(H) National egoes.
(I) Religion.

Due to these factors (whose variations are found in all the societies), there are bitter battles and even wars. Due to these wars, property worth trillions of Dollars has been destroyed and millions of men, women and children have lost their lives. All the dead one sleep in peace while their nearest kith and kin cry for them. Did the Almighty create us for this purpose ? It is true that we are also a species of animals. But do we not have some characteristics that make us superior to other animals. Even the animals have hearts and souls for their own species. But we do not have.

And now, the ultimate truth. We are supposed to change forms (death is the name of decay of human cells). If everyone is supposed to die one day or the other, then why cannot he make the world a better place to live in ? Why cannot we cut down our egoes and become empathetic towards all those who interact with us ? Why cannot we help our poor brothers and sisters; they too have right to live with dignity and comfort ? If each one of us would either be buried or cremated, then why a hue and cry over the mortal issues and objects of the world ?

Religion has been the single biggest killer of mankind since the birth of mankind. The author (A Kumar) is of the view that there is no difference between the Hindus and the Muslims. When asked, he pointed out that the only difference was that Muslims were buried in the grave where they lost their hair at the end of the process of consumption by the underground organisms (as hair do not have any nutritive value for those organisms). Hindus, on the other hand, lose their hair in the first instance when they are put on the funeral pyre; the flames of the funeral pyre eat up the hair first and their bodies are consumed later. How could this petty difference create rift between the two communities ? Our psyche is sick and our religious beliefs have not been able to cleanse our souls.

Many great apostles and saints arrived on the earth and taught this ultimate truth. But we never paid heed to them. We continued to be wily, sinful, boastful and supercilious. We ignored the warnings of the sages and the men of nobility. They came, prayed for us and then left us. We never improved. The number of bungalows, cars, money, business and our egoes reached new peaks and we thought that we are the undisputed masters of this universe. But He, who created us, watches each one of us carefully and takes appropriate actions at the right point of time. Let us give an example. A patient normally does not die of a heart attack due to poor eating habits. He normally dies due to stress that is the leading killer of the world. And how he gets stress is very easy to describe. He tries to amass fortune by exploiting those around him. In this process, he develops mental imbalance that manifests itself in the form of stress. This stress leads to a cardiac problem. More people die due to stress related ailments (like cardiac arrests, hypertension, kidney failure, brain haemorrhage *etc*) than due to illnesses related to poor habits related to diet. The *Manas* (the psyche) of the person becomes sick and he falls prey to those diseases that could have been cured through simple treatments.

A man entered into a bookshop in England and asked for some good books from the salesman at the counter. The salesman said, "Sir. I think that you should read the books of W Sommerset Maughm. He is a great author. Here are some of his masterpieces." And he put some books on the counter for him to choose from.

"How could he be a great author?" the visitor asked him, "I don't think that he is."

"No, sir. Please believe me. You would be able to judge this fact from his books." The salesman insisted.

"Why should I believe you?" the agitated visitor asked.

"Why should you not, sir?" asked the salesman.

"Because I myself am W Sommerset Maughm!" replied the visitor and started searching for a 'good' book.

This simple incident confirms that men of great calibre lose their egoes and become more gentle, humane and empathetic. They forget about themselves and their personal objectives are sidelined in favour of the more pious tasks that lie ahead of them. Their humility, toil and submission teach us a lot. We must learn some lessons from the lives of these great men and women of the yore who sacrificed their ego for the sake of a better human race.

Six feet of land or a funeral pyre make all men equal. Then why should we indulge in mudslinging (the political parties indulged in the same during the last general elections of this century in India) ? Why should we try to win over the land that rightly belongs to another nation (Pakistan entered Kargil and Batalik sectors during May-July, 1999 and was given a befitting reply) ? Why should we indulge in genocide (Kosovans were recently given a reprieve by a UN mandate and therefore, their massacre was stopped) ? Why should we build deadly arsenal that could annihilate this planet many times over (we have enough of nuclear devices in India, Pakistan and China that could wipe out the humanity in this part of the world) ? Why should we outrage the modesty of the fairer sex (the Supreme Court recently ruled that the female office employees shall be protected by the law so that they could not be exploited by males at their workplaces) ? There are many such problems that could be solved through a rationalisation of egoes of the individuals involved and by putting the animal instincts of man in the dustbin.

We do not wish to state that man should not have ego. Every individual must possess ego. But before possessing ego, one must be able and competent in one field. If he has no expertise in one field, he has no right to be called an expert. And ego is the ornament of the experts only. There has to be a solid reason for possessing ego. Many individuals have egoes without any reason (or due to very petty reasons). Hence, their shallow knowledge levels always land them in trouble. They not only create nuisance for themselves, but also they create problems for others who come in contact with them. It is our opinion that most of the troubles in this world originate due to ego clashes. And most of the ego clashes could be avoided as these have no solid bases; the underlying causes are not worth the tantrums they create.

This world is changing at a very fast pace. Commercialism and free market mechanism have created enormous wealth. And where wealth accumulates, men certainly decay. Further, the generation of wealth has not been in equal amounts in all the parts of the world. The poor remain poor whereas the rich are becoming richer. This gap between the rich and the poor has also led to clashes and wars. We feel that many problems of the world could be solved if the riches were distributed in all the citizens of this world. But practical implementation of this thought remains a Utopian dream. Why should the rich share their money and why should the poor accept it as dignity is also a key issue ?

All the problems of this world have solutions but this phenomenon does not seem to have a solution. The mentality of the individuals in a materialistic society has been corrupted beyond compare. We are ourselves to be blamed for this catastrophe. Only a serious introspection by us could save us. Religious books have taught us to be noble, helpful, pious and sans any vices. We do read these books but we do not practise the teachings incorporated in them. The next time we read a religious book, we ought to read it with our souls; cramming has been going on for centuries. The decay of man is complete now and only salvation is the self-cleansing process through books on religion and morality. We do not persuade our worthy readers to be religious but would like them to become truly pious after reading religious scriptures. Perhaps, religious books and good literature, for developing the moral values in the mankind, were written for this day only. Further, a man with a pious soul would read books for his self-development whereas a crafty gang leader would read it out to his followers so that they would remain intoxicated under the opium of religion. The ability to discern between this difference (becoming a religious person or following a religion) is possessed by all our readers. They know the difference between right and wrong. They just do not take the first step towards their moral surgery. Again, this is a free market world and the choice is of the individual; he can either be a man with morals or an animal of the category of lower species.

The era of *Kalyuga* is not over yet. The age of *Satyuga* would not come during our lifetimes. And there were crimes evem during the times of Ramayana. The moral decay of man would continue in the times to come. Many saints tried to rectify the vices of the mankind but were either crucified or were forced to drink hemlock. Our message is addressed to the individuals. Let the individuals cleanse themselves and do only those deeds that do not put a burden on their souls. Let them cut down (or at least tone down) their egoes for the sake of a better family, neighbourhood and society. This transformation at the micro level would certainly yield positive results at the macro levels. But time is a major factor for effecting this transformation.

In all the circumstances, we should be guided only by our conscience and the ultimate judgement would be of the Almighty. ●

121. FAILURES ARE THE PILLARS OF SUCCESS

Success most coveted commodity—Failures are stepping stones to success—Guidelines for future course of action—History of mankind full of stories in which failures preceded success—Failures should never disappoint us—Indian space research programme ultimately succeeded—We must have a fighting spirit—Failure train us for achieving ultimate success.

Success is the most coveted commodity in the world today. However, everybody does not succeed in achieving his goals. Failures are a part of our lives because man is imperfect. A string of failures leads us to disappointment, dejection and even physical or mental sickness. This phenomenon is quite natural with all the living beings and cannot be avoided.

However, every failure is a stepping stone towards success. The success of one minute pays for the failure of years. We should not be afraid of failures as these failures teach us a lot. They tell us about our weaknesses that must be overcome. They bluntly inform us about the problem areas in our working. They bring out the weaknesses of our planning and resource allocation. Our weaknesses give us a guideline for future course of action. Once we eliminate the weak points in our personalities, resources and *modus-operandi,* we would definitely succeed in our endeavour.

History is full of examples in which, failures led to the ultimate success. Robert Bruce faced failures many times but he became the king of Scotland ultimately. Indian Space Research Programme faced many hurdles. However, Indian scientists worked hard. They learned from each failure and today, India is in an enviable position in the space research field. Many students worked hard for administrative and engineering entrance examinations but failed. However, they did not give up. Ultimately, they succeeded. Similar examples could be cited in the context of other disciplines of life in which, failures led to ultimate success.

Life is full of struggle. Failures should never disappoint us. Failures teach us a lot. They make us wiser, careful and meticulons. They add to our experiences. They are a blessing in disguise. They open our eyes to the realities and make us more alert for the future. The goals are clear before us and resources, planning and operational skills can be re-defined after learning from each failure.

After facing a failure, we become wiser. We make our next move very carefully and are always more rational and pragmatic than before. Therefore, success can be attained easily as we are not groping in the dark. Now, we know about our action plans and limitations. Ultimately, we succeed in achieving our aims and objectives. This brings us to the point of ecstasy and mental satisfaction. Those are the glorious moments of our lives. We should always struggle keeping those glorious moments in mind. We should plan for next venture by taking into account the failures encountered in the previous one. And we must also not forget how thrilled we were when we tasted success during our previous endeavours.

Therefore, we should fight in our lives with a sportsman's spirit. A hockey player does not always score goals whenever he plays. However, when he fails a number of times, his will to score a goal builds up. He becomes technically capable to score a goal with each game played. Ultimately, he becomes the master hockey player and scores goals at his own will. He develops physical and mental abilities for achieving his objective. Everybody can do so and can succeed in life by learning from each failure encountered. Man is born to succeed ultimately. Failures, are in fact, small tests through which, nature puts him so that he could succeed with flying colours. Never give up.

The triumph of France over Brazil in the finals of World Cup (Football) on July 13, 1998 proved beyond doubt that consistency is the ultimate key to success. France defeated favourites Brazil by a margin of three goals. Their hard work, consistency and training proved their worth at the hustings. Brazil was a global soccer power and it was not possible to defeat this strong team. However, French players played such a marvellous game that Brazilian defence was stunned. Victory ultimately kissed the foreheads of the French players. We can cite many such examples of success in the fields of culture, engineering, politics, economics, music and social sciences. Man continued to struggle in these areas and despite initial failures, worked hard towards his ultimate goal. He succeeded finally and proved his supremacy in those fields.

The young minds of today are restless and expect, results quite earlier. They should remember that Rome was not built in a day. Failures are bound to follow suit once we start running towards our objectives. We should learn from the mistakes and should accept failures as the building blocks for achieving success in the desired field. We should not be violent, depressed or dejected as most of the young people are in case of a failure. It is the duty of every human being to continue his struggle despite the failures faced by him. Hard work, dedication and consistency pay dividends in the long run.

Success can be achieved in education, career development, family affairs, social interactions, politics, sports and other human activities by adopting this philosophy. Our educational system does not teach our students about this golden rule of success. Our teachers and guides in the educational institutions are busy in looking after their interests. The students are left unattended and there is no one to advise them during the adverse periods of their lives. The students are not trained for adverse conditions during their academic sessions. They work for the sake of degrees and not for the sake of life. The foundations of knowledge are not solid enough. This results in subsequent failures in the next phase of life. This ultimately leads to frustration, confusion and mental decay. Our young generation is not able to get career guidance or knowledge about the future challenges. The students are not trained for meeting challenges and hence, they are unable to rise once they fall. These are bad tendencies and must be checked. The State, the educational institutions and the parents could extend a helping hand. We have to prepare the youth of today for meeting the herculean challenges of tomorrow. The youth of today would take over the reins of the country in the near future. Hence, their moral, educational and physical training schedules should prepare them for the failures they are going to face in the future. They must accept each failure as a challenge so that success belongs to them ultimately. Consistency and perseverance would yield rich fruits for the youth of today in the long run. ●

122. EVERYTHING THAT GLITTERS IS NOT GOLD

We are surrounded by artificial people and false promotional gimmicks—Free market economy has taken its deadly toll—Relationships are artificial—Advertisements project incompetent people, ideas and products—Cheating of general public—Lust for money—Must stop this Westernisation—Adopt simple lifestyle—Use Consumer Protection Courts—Have a pure heart—Be good and do good—Try to remove artificial relationships from life—This would eliminate many complications—Monetary show-off is not good—Simple living and high thinking should be followed as the most natural lifestyle.

A boy meets a girl and likes her. He asks for her hand and marries her. To his utter dismay, he realises that the girl, who impressed her with her beauty, could not come up to his mark. The body did not represent the soul.

A corporate firm hires an executive at the rate of Rs 50,000 per month. The firm thinks that this executive (who has been working for the competitors) would be a great asset for them. But the new entrant is unable to make his mark in the new firm and bows out in shame.

We meet a politician who has been able to achieve great heights in his political career. We are impressed by the man and his political achievements. But the very next day, the same apple of our eyes is known to be involved in a scam of crores of Rupees. We are angry and annoyed by our sense of judgement and the evil ways of the world.

Satyuga was the best period seen by the mankind, so the sages pronounce. *Kalyuga*, which depicts the present state of affairs of the world, has seen the moral degradation of man beyond compare. This moral degradation has manifested itself in the form of of lies, selfishness and artificial relationships. The veneer of artificial show-off, vague actions and unnecessary emotions is displayed by every individual.

Consider any field—cinema, business, industry, book writing, publishing, engineering, international relationships, family relationships *etc*. We would find that the person on the other side of the table is trying to prove himself as a hero of our times. However, after careful scrutiny he would prove to be a villain. The relationship would come to an abrupt and poisonous culmination once we come to know about his true identity.

Life has made people more selfish and materialistic. That is why, there is reason they are more interested in presenting themselves in the best possible manner in order to get the maximum possible financial advantage. The complexity in relationships has eliminated the real joy of living. Ego has dominated our official and personal lives. The artificial and commercial relationships have taken their toll; cardiac arrests, paralysis, loss of business and personal relationships, decay of image in the mind of kith and kin, executive stress and even violence in some cases are the common maladies.

Whatever our grocery shopkeeper says to us regarding the quality of the wheat flour, turns out to be false when we open the bag and eat that wheat flour. The advertisement states that the refrigerator being advertised is the best in India. However, when we have purchased one, we realise how poor it is as a performer. We buy a two-wheeler, an imported car, a stereo, gold, garments, shoes or any other service or concept. And we realise that it was not worth the money spent.

Advertising, promotion and selling gimmicks have created this false notion about quality of the products and services. Behind the curtain, all are naked. Everybody wants to present himself as genuine, *numero uno* and best. But without packing these features into one's products, services and personality, how could one gain money, respect and repeated attention from one's markets, families and social circles ?

This glittering darkness of *Kalyuga* must be eliminated in every possible manner. Some solutions for overcoming this problem are as follows :—

(1) Adopt a lifestyle of simple living and high thinking.

(2) Avoid buying "foreign and imported" products. These are assembled in India and carry a high price tag. There is no assurance of quality.

(3) Enquire completely about the product, service, person or concept that you are going to buy or hire. This is true for intimate relationships as well. For example, you would never like your sister or daughter to be married to a person of dubious character. So, enquire about the boy or the girl before you say 'yes.'

(4) Use the services of Consumer Protection Courts if the need arises. Inform people about the firms, salesmen, servants, shopkeepers, businessman *etc* who have given you a bitter experience due to their poor products, services or even due to their rude behaviour.

(5) Have a pure heart. Rectify yourself first. You could be as artificial and money-minded as the other person whom you criticise. Cleanse yourself first and then point an accusing fingure at others.

(6) The NGOs, the State and other social organisations must work collectively to eliminate the Western influences (which are the cansative vital factors for rising commercialism, artificial promotion and false ego in inter-personal relationships) from Indian society.

Let only the truth prevail beyond the flash of visual images on the television beyond the alluring promises of the glossy advertisements, beyond the evasive statements made by mediamen in the news and promotional gimmicks and finally, beyond the manipulations of the sweet language and faulty reasoning.

The individual only can protect himself from the onslaught of Western culture, artificial relationships and the mad world of commercialism. He must be adequately educated and informed about the technology, environment and polity around him. He must also know that falsehood in a free market economy is the common success gimmick. He has to carefully tear out this veneer of falsehood and get down to the realities after careful analysis. Illiteracy and ignorance are the root canses of all the agonies.

Further, the State must pass legislations for the protection of common man from the evil clutches of promotion by the private sector firms. The consumer protection acts, MRTP and other relevant legislations are not used by people for getting justice. They should realise that these legislations have been designed for protecting them from the evils of a free market system.

Finally, interpersonal relationships have assumed dangerously artificial proportions because of the lust for money, power and self-esteem. We must not forget that we are human beings first and our prime duty as the most civilised creatures is to help each other in the hour of need. False ego would hurt the other person but would not take us anywhere. Materialistic assets are required for upgrading our living standards but not for showing off to our neighbours who do not own them. Helping neighbours, assisting them without expectation reciprocation and sharing their sorrows would give us spiritual solace. This would also motivate our neighbours to help us when we need them.

Life has become highly artificial, full of surrealism and complicated. Let us take concrete measures for making it simple and sans artificial veneers. Simple living and high thinking should be adopted as the universal motto by the mankind.

123. TIME IS A TYRANT

Time is said to be a tyrant—Only weak persons should give that statement—For example, we have won many battles against time in the field of medicine—Time is not a tyrant but our misuse of time could be fatal\—Time would never be a tyrant if we know our goals and work in a planned manner to achieve them—Even if time becomes a tyrant, we should be strong enough to face it—We must do well in good times and plan for the bad times.

Man has met many a challenge during the past. He is going to face many more in the times to come. Some people, however, state that it is time that takes over a particular incident or event. Time controls the destiny of man, according to some individuals. They state that time is a tyrant and is eager to demolish man whenever it wishes to do so.

However, this could be a Utopian nightmare of those men and women who do not believe in themselves. History is replete with examples in which, man fought for his supremacy over nature. One such area is medicine. We have been able to overcome almost all the major and minor diseases except AIDS, leukaemia, various cancers and a few other diseases whose treatments would be developed soon. We have been able to extend the average life of a healthy individual from 55 years to 72 years. Even the terminally ill patients do well with most modern medicines and medical facilities. We always race against time and win. Medical history of the mankind amply proves this fact.

We could state another example from the field of social sciences. We have been able to devise solutions for many complex psychological disturbances. A pessimist could easily turn them aside by saying that they are failures and could serve no useful purpose in this world. However, doctors, psychiatrists and neuro-surgeons have worked relentlessly and brought many patients back within the precincts of normalcy. This is another miracle of human mind. Perseverance and hard work have led to great discoveries, miracles and inventions. These have helped mankind prosper and define a path for the future. In fact, times have changed for good. Time is not a tyrant but a watchdog for our follies. It warns us before the deadline date arrives. After the deadline date, the time reallybecomes a tyrant and ought to be one.

And time was never a tyrant. People, who made effective usage of time at their disposal, got the best from time in the form of money, accolades, satisfaction, fame, material assets *etc*. But those, who forgot the value of time, found to their utter dismay that it was harsh on them later. So, next time a student is not able to pass his examinations, tell him he forgot to value time. And time turned tyrant for him and reflected itself in the poor results of the student.

And time would never be a tyrant if we know our goals, plan for those goals, work hard systematically and learn from our mistakes. Where there is a will, there is a way. We can overcome the problems of life if we manage and utilise our time properly. Mahatma Gandhi always had a watch with him. He valued time.

And let the time become a tyrant. Why be afraid ? Problems are faced by men of courage only. Life is not a bed of roses. If difficult times arrive, they would make us stronger. They would prepare us for a better life. We would be able to handle problems in future with more maturity, stability and courage. Hard times teach us a lot. They prepare us for those difficulties that would appear during the subsequent years of life. Man becomes prepared for difficult phases of the future. So, he can handle those phases with maturity and elan.

Time would never be a tyrant for a man who believes in himself, his God and his planning. Time is only a tool of success. It is a reflection of God's will. It is a testing technique of mother nature. We should work hard in a pre-planned manner so that we could overcome the ill-effects of time.

If times are good, they could be bad as well. It is an established fact that good and bad times come in a cyclical order in all the parts of the world and for every citizen of the earth. This is the nature in its most effective form. We must make the best usage of good times. We must make arrangements for the bad times during the good times. When the bad times are knocking at our doorsteps, we should face them bravely and with patience. That is how a rational and strong man is supposed to fight his battles of life. Ultimately, a seasoned and experienced human being would be able to master time with his resources, skills and careful planning. He is born to succeed and so shall he, against all the tyrannies of time, which is a great teacher and a friend.

Life is nothing but a painful transition in time. But men of courage and determination achieve their goals despite the hardships. And they win even if the times are bad. The world bows to their superiority and is full of enconium for these great sons and daughters of God. They remain in the hearts of the mankind and tyranny of time is overcome by their qualities, hard work, sincerity and humility. Dare to be one !

124. POWER CORRUPTS

White House scandal rocked the world—The US President under criticism because of alleged relationships with Monica Lewinsky—Power corrupts and people misuse their powers in order to meet their base objectives—Bolshevik revolution in the USSR in 1917—Soviet empire ruled for nearly 70 years—Liberalisation during mid-eighties—Today, Russia is an ally of the USA—The USA only power left—No challenger on in the international stage—USA attacked Iraq, Yugoslavia, Afghan Camps during recent past—No opposition—China, Russia and India could form another block—The USA wants China to play a pivotal role in Asia—Financial and political powers take time for development—Thackeray used his powers for his party and the Hindu cause.

The recent scandals that rocked the White House during July and August, 1998 depicted a sordid tale of misuse of power in the highest echelons of the political world. Ms Monica Lewinsky, a former White House intern, testified before the Grand Jury that she had sexual relationships with President Bill Clinton during her tenure in the White House. This scandal, also termed as Monica Gate, could have cost the US President his job. President Clinton also testified before the Grand Jury and apologised for his relationships with Ms Lewinsky. He had always denied these allegations. Mr Clinton escaped an impeachment move against him. Althogh he was firmly entrenched in White House, yet he could not escape from the wrath of the American masses.

Power corrupts and absolute power corrupts absolutely. This naked truth has become more glaring in the wake of the recent disclosures made by many female employees of the White House. People in power exploit the weak and the downtrodden.

This has been going on for centuries. The poor masses were always exploited by the kings and their courtesans. The exploitation of women, the complete decimation of the poor strata of society and finally, the misuse of power for fighting and winning wars were common practices during the past. The situation changed when the King of England was forced to sign Magna Carta and this laid the foundations of democracy in the world. In India, there was a rule of the kings but the *Panchayats* and democratic system of governance thrived. The king was supreme, however. In some cases, the exploitation of mankind was more severe and sordid in India than in other parts of the world.

The Bolshevik revolution of 1917 brought the problems of the workers to the fore. It also catapulted the masses to power. VI Lenin succeeded in deposing the Czar and thus provided a platform for the communist ideology, which still exists.

However, when the communists came to power, they were corrupted beyond compare. The USSR captured the centre-stage of power in the post-world-war scenario and was the major contender for supremacy in terms of political, economic and social upheavals. The USA, a totally capitalistic system, used nuclear weapon threats and economic prowess in order to counter the threats of the communist block. The cold war continued for fifty years and the each superpowers spent billions of Dollars in order to take a decisive strategic edge over the other one.

The policy of Glasnost and free market orientation by the USSR in the late eighties finally yielded fruit. The Eastern block and the communist nations were converted into pro-West allies and joined the free market economies for their own benefit. Now, the USA and her allies rule the economic and military world and Russia is a major ally of the USA. This absolute power has tilted the balance in the favour of the West. There is no deterrent force, which could counter the Western supremacy. The balance of power is not always for the sake of war; we need balance of power for the sake of peace also. Therefore, a replacement for the erstwhile USSR and her Eastern block should be made so that the USA and the Western block nations are aware of the neutraliser. The balance of power concept is for the benefit of the Western nations also. The other superpower could be the best friend of the West and yet, could act as the power-balancing authority in the world.

But who would bell the cat ? Who would come to the fore ? Russia could be one choice and India could be another option. However, the free market world has tilted all of these nations in favour of the Western ideologies. The USA, though a powerful nation, has been facing economic and political crises for the past few months; Monica Gate scandal could prove costly for the present administration.India, China and Russia could form another pole in this unipolar world. This is a great idea and could be implemented if all the three nations sorted out their mutual differences through across-the-table negotiations. If China returns Indian territory under her control, then this alliance could be formed by the year 2010.

The identification of deterrent superpower is difficult and long term process ; moreover, and should be in tune with Western ideologies. For example, the USA may never accept a communist nation as a superpower, although her relationships with China are excellent, yet she would like a free market nation to dominate the international political scenario. And it is a wise decision. The USA views China as a major superpower for Asia alone and wants China to play the role of an elder. If disputes between China, Pakistan, India, Tibet and other territorial disputes of the Asian nations are sorted out through negotiations, there is no harm in accepting China as a major regional power in Asia. Americans would also sponsor this decision. Asian nations could grow at an amazing pace if the differences are completely eliminated.

Let us shift our focus to India. The present government in Maharashtra is being guided by Vilas Rao Deshmukh. The Shiv Sena lost power in Maharashtra due to its commitment to religious extremism. Let us pose one question—If Mr Thackeray is so powerful, why then does he not save innocent Hindus in Kashmir who are being killed almost every week ? The nation would support him and his supoorters. The masses would be with him. Instead of organising crime against the minority community, the politicians in power should plan the reprisal moves against the terrorists who are bent upon disturbing the communal scene in the country. Mr Thackeray is a powerful man. Had he used his powers in a logical manner, he could have occupied the highest post in this country. But his commitment to nation took a backseat and his ideologies and partymen were more vital for him. Mr Thackeray can still rise to the occasion if he wishes.

The only measure against absolute power is the acquisition of a deterrent power. It is not easy to become powerful but struggle makes the man. Acquisition of power would take its own toll. Financial, political and other vital powers take years to develop. As individuals, we must struggle for acquiring power. However, as a human being, we must utilise our power for the benefit of the masses. We must protect the oppressed and the tortured masses with the help of the powers acquired by us or granted to us. However, this is easier said than done.

125. WHERE THERE IS A WILL THERE IS A WAY

Struggle is the essence of life—Do not let disappointments harm our plans for the future—Keep on striving towards the goal with determination and with an eye on the goal—Life has no meaning without a goal—Great men and women showed courage and determination—We must never give up—Have a clear definition of your goals—Plan for your goals—Work hard—Revise your strategies if need be—Have faith in God—Success could be achieved by anyone who wants to go for it.

The real essence of life is struggle. The men of courage set targets themselves, work hard and achieve those targets in order to achieve something during their lifetimes. Everybody wants fortune, fame and satisfaction but only a few are able to achieve their coveted goals. Those few are the men and women of courage who give up comforts of life and are determined to achieve their objectives. They work hard for the sake of their goals and eventually, they achieve them with flying colours. Their will is superior to those of all others who are in the fray. Therefore, determination is a vital key to success.

Let the disappointments not deviate us from our main objectives. Our objectives could be diverse—a career in administration, a degree from a foreign university, a career in engineering or management, a top-notch position in a reputed advertising agency or even entrepreneurship. Failures are a part of our lives. But these should not deter us from achieving our goals. The fierce determination of courageous men and women helped them emerge as triumphant through serious crises. Mahatma Gandhi, Mother Teresa, Nelson

Mandela, Martin Luther King, Isaac Newton and other popular statesmen, literateurs, poets, playwrights, politicians, educationists and social workers had strong will, helped which them achieve the extraordinary goals of their lives.

Fortunes also favour those who help themselves. We should not be daunted by the failures and must try to eliminate our weaknesses through a time-bound programme. It has been said, "Little strokes fell mighty oaks." Our patience, commitment to the objectives and perseverance would certainly yield rich dividends. A man with strong will always succeeds. His patience, courage and endeavour come under scrutiny during the testing moments of life.

Life has no meaning without an aim. Therefore, we must have well-defined aims and must strive hard for achieving them. Hugh Walpole once said, "It is not life that matters. It is the courage that you bring to it." There is no life without courage. There is nothing more glorious in this world than defeat but one should not give up the struggle. Low aim is crime but failure is not.

If our determination is weak, we would not be able to overcome the hurdles that would come our way. However, a fierce desire and a strong determination would eliminate the difficulties and would lead us to success. The incessant desire of man has led to the discovery of unknown lands, valleys, planets and depths of the oceans. Madam Curie discovered Radium and continued research on this radioactive element. Her body was engulfed by the radioactive rays emitted by the radioactive samples of Radium. She died due to the ill-effects of Radium but she gave the world complete knowledge about the precious element that would be utilised by mankind for centuries. Marie Curie laid down her life for the cause of knowledge and humanity as she had unfailing determination for exploring the unknown.

Similarly, urban landscapes, jet aircrafts, Internet and information technology revolution, amazing achievements in engineering and medicine and above all, the achievements in space could not have been possible, had a few men of courage not possessed the strong will to succeed. The achievements of mankind to date are the products of strong determination and willpower.

In order to know the truth and to choose the right path, a person must be the master of his plans, actions and moral values. His willpower and self-control would certainly take him to the new heights of success and glory.

History is replete with the stories of men and women of courage. Mrs. Indira Gandhi, Sir Winston Churchil, Bachendri Pal, PT Usha, Yukta Mookhey, Kalpana Chawla, Eleen Collins, Kiran Bedi, Satyajeet Ray, Leander Paes, V Anand, Shabana Azmi, Baba Amte and Medha Patkar are some of the few personalities who had courage and conviction and therefore, were able make a mark in their respective fields.

King Harish Chandra underwent numerous sufferings but ultimately, he came out as a winner. He did not make compromises and fought for truth. Abraham Lincoln was born to a poor family and he failed many times in his life. But due to his hard work and determination, Lincoln became the President of the USA. Plato, the great Greek Philosopher, paid for his travelling expenses by selling oil during his journey. Hilter sold hand-made pictures on the roadside and eventually, he became the most powerful figure in Germany. William Wordsworth sold stamps. Lord Beaconsfield arrived in the House of Commons in London. When he spoke, the entire house burst with laughter. He angrily exclaimed, "The time will come when you shall hear me." He struggled hard and became one of the most famous orators of England.

Kalidasa was strongly rebuked by wife due to his lust for sex and due to his illetracy. He studied Sanskrit for twenty years and wrote the epic *Ramayana,* which is the best known work in Sanskrit literature. Mahatma Gandhi failed many times during the struggle of Indian independence. But eventually, he succeeded in making India a free nation. Nelson Mandela fought against apartheid in South Africa and spent twenty-six years of his youth in jail. Lal Bahadur Shastri sed to cross a river on his way to school. He belonged to a very poor family but he finally arrived at the highest office of this land. He proved his abilities in administration and during the war against Pakistan in 1965.

These courageous men and women had a positive attitude in their minds. And this positive attitude was towards all those who came in direct or indirect contact with them. The positive attitude assists us in achieving our objectives and people help us in this process. This is a very crucial characteristic of the famous successful figures of past and present. A positive mental attitude must be a part of our living and thinking.

Further, we must have faith in God. We must make firm resolution that we would try to make our lives morally clean, prosperous and successful. Faith and willpower are the vital keys for success in this world that offers nothing but frustration and uncertainties. Whenever a difficulty arises, we should accept the challenge. We should meet the challenge with meticulous planning, hard work and sheer determination. There cannot be any progress without a will to achieve the coveted objective. The determination of courageous man has turned the rivers, constructed dams, sent satellites into the space, overcome serious diseases and has converted barren lands into fertile ones.

Success is not the sole companion of the successful few. It can be possessed by anyone who wishes to go for it. But the will of man must be strong enough to endure the most discouraging experiences. If we are motivated by a heroic determination and a strong willpower to strive for our objective, nothing could stop us. Where there is a will, there is a way !